Core Java

Volume I—Fundamentals

Thirteenth Edition

Cay S. Horstmann

Pearson

Hoboken, New Jersey

Cover image: Jon Chica/Shutterstock
Figure 1.1: Sourceforge
Figures 2.2, 3.2-3.5, 4.9, 5.4, 7.2, 10.5, 10.6, 11.1: Oracle Corporation
Figures 2.3-2.6, 12.2: Eclipse Foundation, Inc.
Figure 4.2: Violet UML Editor

ISBN-13: 978-0-13-532837-8
ISBN-10: 0-13-532837-3

3 2024

Table of Contents

Preface

To the Reader

In late 1995, the Java programming language burst onto the Internet scene and gained instant celebrity status. The promise of Java technology was that it would become the *universal glue* that connects users with information wherever it comes from—web servers, databases, information providers, or any other imaginable source. Indeed, Java is in a unique position to fulfill this promise. It is an extremely solidly engineered language that has gained wide acceptance. Its built-in security and safety features are reassuring both to programmers and to the users of Java programs. Java has built-in support for advanced programming tasks, such as network programming, database connectivity, and concurrency.

Since 1995, over twenty revisions of the Java Development Kit have been released. The Application Programming Interface (API) has grown from about a hundred to over 4,000 classes. The API now spans such diverse areas as concurrent programming, collections, user interface construction, database management, internationalization, security, and XML processing.

The book that you are reading right now is the first volume of the thirteenth edition of *Core Java*. Each edition closely followed a release of the Java Development Kit, and each time, I rewrote the book to take advantage of the newest Java features. This edition has been updated to reflect the features of Java 21.

As with the previous editions, *this book still targets serious programmers who want to put Java to work on real projects.* I think of you, the reader, as a programmer with a solid background in a programming language other than Java. I assume that you don't like books filled with toy examples (such as toasters, zoo animals, or "nervous text"). You won't find any of these in the book. My goal is to enable you to fully understand the Java language and library, not to give you an illusion of understanding.

In this book you will find lots of sample code demonstrating almost every language and library feature. The sample programs are purposefully simple to focus on the major points, but, for the most part, they aren't fake and they don't cut corners. They should make good starting points for your own code.

I assume you are willing, even eager, to learn about all the features that the Java language puts at your disposal. In this volume, you will find a detailed treatment of

- Object-oriented programming
- Reflection and proxies
- Interfaces and inner classes
- Exception handling
- Generic programming
- The collections framework
- Concurrency

- Annotations
- The Java platform module system

With the explosive growth of the Java class library, a one-volume treatment of all the features of Java that serious programmers need to know is simply not possible. Hence, the book is broken up into two volumes. This first volume concentrates on the fundamental concepts of the Java language. The second volume, *Core Java, Volume II: Advanced Features*, goes further into the most important libraries.

For twelve editions, user-interface programming was considered fundamental, but the time has come to recognize that it is no more, and to move it into the second volume. That volume includes detailed discussions of these topics:

- The Stream API
- File processing and regular expressions
- Databases
- XML processing
- Scripting and Compiling APIs
- Internationalization
- Network programming
- Graphical user interface design
- Graphics programming
- Native methods

When writing a book, errors and inaccuracies are inevitable. I'd very much like to know about them. But, of course, I'd prefer to learn about each of them only once. You will find a list of frequently asked questions and bug fixes at https://horstmann.com/corejava. Strategically placed at the end of the errata page (to encourage you to read through it first) is a form you can use to report bugs and suggest improvements. Please don't be disappointed if I don't answer every query or don't get back to you immediately. I do read all e-mail and appreciate your input to make future editions of this book clearer and more informative.

A Tour of This Book

Chapter 1 gives an overview of the capabilities of Java that set it apart from other programming languages. The chapter explains what the designers of the language set out to do and to what extent they succeeded. A short history of Java follows, detailing how Java came into being and how it has evolved.

In **Chapter 2**, you will see how to download and install the JDK and the program examples for this book. Then I'll guide you through compiling and running a console application and a graphical application. You will see how to use the plain JDK, a Java IDE, and the JShell tool.

Chapter 3 starts the discussion of the Java language. In this chapter, I cover the basics: variables, loops, and simple functions. If you are a C or C++ programmer, this is smooth sailing because the syntax for these language features is essentially the same as in C. If you come from a non-C background such as Visual Basic, you will want to read this chapter carefully.

Object-oriented programming (OOP) is now in the mainstream of programming practice, and Java is an object-oriented programming language. **Chapter 4** introduces encapsulation, the first of two fundamental building blocks of object orientation, and the Java language mechanism to implement it—that is, classes and methods. In addition to the rules of the Java language, you will also find advice on sound OOP design. Finally, I cover the marvelous javadoc tool that formats your code comments as a set of hyperlinked web pages. If you are familiar with C++, you can browse through this chapter quickly. Programmers coming from a non-object-oriented background should expect to spend some time mastering the OOP concepts before going further with Java.

Classes and encapsulation are only one part of the OOP story, and **Chapter 5** introduces the other—namely, *inheritance*. Inheritance lets you take an existing class and modify it according to your needs. This is a fundamental technique for programming in Java. The inheritance mechanism in Java is quite similar to that in C++. Once again, C++ programmers can focus on the differences between the languages.

Chapter 6 shows you how to use Java's notion of an *interface*. Interfaces let you go beyond the simple inheritance model of Chapter 5. Mastering interfaces allows you to have full access to the power of Java's completely object-oriented approach to programming. After covering interfaces, I move on to *lambda expressions*, a concise way for expressing a block of code that can be executed at a later point in time. I then explain a useful technical feature of Java called *inner classes*.

Chapter 7 discusses *exception handling*—Java's robust mechanism to deal with the fact that bad things can happen to good programs. Exceptions give you an efficient way of separating the normal processing code from the error handling. Of course, even after hardening your program by handling all exceptional conditions, it still might fail to work as expected. Then the chapter moves on to logging. In the final part of this chapter, I give you a number of useful debugging tips.

Chapter 8 gives an overview of generic programming. Generic programming makes your programs easier to read and safer. I show you how to use strong typing and remove unsightly and unsafe casts, and how to deal with the complexities that arise from the need to stay compatible with older versions of Java.

The topic of **Chapter 9** is the collections framework of the Java platform. Whenever you want to collect multiple objects and retrieve them later, you should use a collection that is best suited for your circumstances, instead of just tossing the elements into an array. This chapter shows you how to take advantage of the standard collections that are prebuilt for your use.

Chapter 10 covers concurrency, which enables you to program tasks to be done in parallel. This is an important and exciting application of Java technology in an era where processors have multiple cores that you want to keep busy.

In **Chapter 11**, you will learn about annotations, which allow you to add arbitrary information (sometimes called metadata) to a Java program. We show you how annotation processors can harvest these annotations at the source or class file level, and how annotations can be used to influence the behavior of classes at runtime. Annotations are only useful with tools, and we hope that our discussion will help you select useful annotation processing tools for your needs.

In **Chapter 12**, you will learn about the Java Platform Module System that facilitates an orderly evolution of the Java platform and core libraries. This module system provides encapsulation for packages and a mechanism for describing module requirements. You will learn the properties of modules so that you can decide whether to use them in your own applications. Even if you decide not to, you need to know the new rules so that you can interact with the Java platform and other modularized libraries.

The **Appendix** lists the reserved words of the Java language.

Conventions

As is common in many computer books, I use `monospace` type to represent computer code.

 Note: Notes are tagged with "note" icons that look like this.

 Tip: Tips are tagged with "tip" icons that look like this.

 Caution: When there is danger ahead, I warn you with a "caution" icon.

 Preview Note: Preview features that are slated to become a part of the language or API in the future are labeled with this icon.

 C++ Note: There are many C++ notes that explain the differences between Java and C++. You can skip over them if you don't have a background in C++ or if you consider your experience with that language a bad dream of which you'd rather not be reminded.

Java comes with a large programming library, or Application Programming Interface (API). When using an API call for the first time, I add a short summary description at the end of the section. These descriptions are a bit more informal but, hopefully, also a little more informative than those in the official online API documentation. The names of interfaces are in italics, just like in the official documentation. The number after a class, interface, or method name is the JDK version in which the feature was introduced, as shown in the following example:

Application Programming Interface 21

Programs whose source code is on the book's companion web site are presented as listings, for instance:

Listing 1.1 NotHelloWorld.java

```
1  void main()
2  {
3     System.out.println("We will not use 'Hello, World!'");
4  }
```

Sample Code

The web site for this book at https://horstmann.com/corejava contains all sample code from the book. See Chapter 2 for more information on installing the Java Development Kit and the sample code.

Acknowledgments

Writing a book is always a monumental effort, and rewriting it doesn't seem to be much easier, especially with the continuous change in Java technology. Making a book a reality takes many dedicated people, and it is my great pleasure to acknowledge the contributions of the entire *Core Java* team.

A large number of individuals at Pearson provided valuable assistance but managed to stay behind the scenes. I'd like them all to know how much I appreciate their efforts. As always, my warm thanks go to my editor, Greg Doench, for steering the book through the writing and production process, and for allowing me to be blissfully unaware of the existence of all those folks behind the scenes. I am very grateful to Julie Nahil for production support, to Dmitry Kirsanov and Alina Kirsanova for copyediting the manuscript, and to Clovis L. Tondo for reviewing the final content. I wrote the book using HTML and CSS, and Prince (https://princexml.com) turned it into PDF—a workflow that I highly recommend. My thanks also to my coauthor of earlier editions, Gary Cornell, who has since moved on to other ventures.

Thanks to the many readers of earlier editions who reported errors and made lots of thoughtful suggestions for improvement. I am particularly grateful to the excellent reviewing team who went over the manuscript with an amazing eye for detail and saved me from many embarrassing errors.

Reviewers of this and earlier editions include Chuck Allison (Utah Valley University), Lance Andersen (Oracle), Gail Anderson (Anderson Software Group), Paul Anderson (Anderson Software Group), Alec Beaton (IBM), Cliff Berg, Andrew Binstock (Oracle), Joshua Bloch, David Brown, Corky Cartwright, Frank Cohen (PushToTest), Chris Crane (devXsolution), Dr. Nicholas J. De Lillo (Manhattan College), Rakesh Dhoopar (Oracle), Ahmad R. Elkomey, Robert Evans (Senior Staff, The Johns Hopkins University Applied Physics Lab), David Geary (Clarity Training), Jim Gish (Oracle), Brian Goetz (Oracle), Angela Gordon, Dan Gordon (Electric Cloud), Rob Gordon, John Gray (University of Hartford), Cameron Gregory (olabs.com), Andrzej Grzesik, Marty Hall (coreservlets.com, Inc.), Vincent Hardy (Adobe Systems), Dan Harkey (San Jose State University), Steve Haines, William Higgins (IBM), Marc Hoffmann (mtrail), Vladimir Ivanovic (PointBase), Jerry Jackson (CA Technologies), Heinz Kabutz (Java Specialists), Stepan V. Kalinin (I-Teco/Servionica LTD), Tim Kimmet (Walmart), John Kostaras, Jerzy Krolak, Chris Laffra, Charlie Lai (Apple), Angelika Langer, Jeff Langr (Langr Software Solutions), Doug Langston, Hang Lau (McGill University), Mark Lawrence, Doug Lea (SUNY Oswego), Gregory Longshore, Bob Lynch (Lynch Associates), Philip Milne (consultant), Mark Morrissey (The Oregon Graduate Institute), Mahesh Neelakanta (Florida Atlantic University), José Paumard (Oracle), Hao Pham, Paul Philion, Blake Ragsdell, Ylber Ramadani (Ryerson University), Stuart Reges (University of Arizona), Simon Ritter (Azul Systems), Rich Rosen (Interactive Data Corporation), Peter Sanders (ESSI University, Nice, France), Dr. Paul Sanghera (San Jose State University and Brooks College), Paul Sevinc (Teamup AG), Devang Shah (Sun Microsystems), Yoshiki Shibata, Richard Slywczak (NASA/Glenn Research Center), Bradley A. Smith, Steven Stelting (Oracle), Christopher Taylor, Luke Taylor (Valtech), George Thiruvathukal, Kim Topley (StreamingEdge), Janet Traub, Paul Tyma (consultant), Christian Ullenboom, Peter van der

Linden, Joe Wang (Oracle), Sven Woltmann, Burt Walsh, Dan Xu (Oracle), and John Zavgren (Oracle).

Cay Horstmann
Düsseldorf, Germany
October 2023

CHAPTER 1

An Introduction to Java

The first release of Java in 1996 generated an incredible amount of excitement, not just in the computer press, but in mainstream media such as *The New York Times*, *The Washington Post*, and *BusinessWeek*. Java has the distinction of being the first and only programming language that had a ten-minute story on National Public Radio. A $100,000,000 venture capital fund was set up solely for products using a *specific* computer language. I hope you will enjoy a brief history of Java that you will find in this chapter.

1.1. Java as a Programming Platform

In the first edition of this book, my coauthor Gary Cornell and I had this to write about Java:

"As a computer language, Java's hype is overdone: Java is certainly a *good* programming language. There is no doubt that it is one of the better languages available to serious programmers. We think it could *potentially* have been a great programming language, but it is probably too late for that. Once a language is out in the field, the ugly reality of compatibility with existing code sets in."

Our editor got a lot of flack for this paragraph from someone very high up at Sun Microsystems, the company that originally developed Java. The Java language has a lot of nice features that we will examine in detail later in this chapter. It has its share of warts, and some of the newer additions to the language are not as elegant as the original features because of compatibility requirements.

But, as we already said in the first edition, Java was never just a language. There are lots of programming languages out there, but few of them make much of a splash. Java is a whole *platform*, with a huge library, containing lots of reusable code, and an execution environment that provides services such as security, portability across operating systems, and automatic garbage collection.

As a programmer, you will want a language with a pleasant syntax and comprehensible semantics (i.e., not C++). Java fits the bill, as do dozens of other fine languages. Some languages give you portability, garbage collection, and the like, but they don't have much of a library, forcing you to roll your own if you want fancy graphics or networking or database access. Well, Java has everything—a good language, a high-quality execution environment, and a vast library. That combination is what makes Java an irresistible proposition to so many programmers.

1.2. The Java "White Paper" Buzzwords

The authors of Java wrote an influential white paper that explains their design goals and accomplishments. They also published a shorter overview that is organized along the following 11 buzzwords:

1. Simple
2. Object-Oriented
3. Distributed
4. Robust
5. Secure
6. Architecture-Neutral
7. Portable
8. Interpreted
9. High-Performance
10. Multithreaded
11. Dynamic

In the following subsections, you will find a summary, with excerpts from the white paper, of what the Java designers say about each buzzword, together with a commentary based on my experiences with the current version of Java.

 Note: The white paper can be found at `https://www.oracle.com/technetwork/java/langenv-140151.html`. You can retrieve the overview with the 11 buzzwords at `https://horstmann.com/corejava/java-an-overview/7Gosling.pdf`.

1.2.1. Simple

We wanted to build a system that could be programmed easily without a lot of esoteric training and which leveraged today's standard practice. So even though we found that C++ was unsuitable, we designed Java as closely to C++ as possible in order to make the system more comprehensible. Java omits many rarely used, poorly understood, confusing features of C++ that, in our experience, bring more grief than benefit.

The syntax for Java is, indeed, a cleaned-up version of C++ syntax. There is no need for header files, pointer arithmetic (or even a pointer syntax), unions, operator overloading, virtual base classes, and so on. (See the C++ notes interspersed throughout the text for more on the differences between Java and C++.) The designers did not, however, attempt to fix all of the clumsy features of C++. For example, the syntax of the switch statement is unchanged in Java. If you know C++, you will find the transition to the Java syntax easy.

At the time Java was released, C++ was actually not the most commonly used programming language. Many developers used Visual Basic and its drag-and-drop programming environment. These developers did not find Java simple. It took several years for Java development environments to catch up. Nowadays, Java development environments are far ahead of those for most other programming languages.

Another aspect of being simple is being small. One of the goals of Java is to enable the construction of software that can run stand-alone on small machines. The size of the basic interpreter and class support is about 40K; the basic standard libraries and thread support (essentially a self-contained microkernel) add another 175K.

This was a great achievement at the time. Of course, the library has since grown to huge proportions. There are now separate editions with a smaller library, suitable for embedded devices and smart cards.

1.2.2. Object-Oriented

Simply stated, object-oriented design is a programming technique that focuses on the data—objects—and on the interfaces to those objects. To make an analogy with carpentry, an "object-oriented" carpenter would be mostly concerned with the chair he is building, and secondarily with the tools used to make it; a "non-object-oriented" carpenter would think primarily of his tools. The object-oriented facilities of Java are essentially those of C++.

Object orientation was pretty well established when Java was developed. The object-oriented features of Java are comparable to those of C++. The major difference between Java and C++ lies in multiple inheritance, which Java has replaced with a simpler concept of interfaces. Java has a richer capacity for runtime introspection (discussed in Chapter 5) than C++.

1.2.3. Distributed

Java has an extensive library of routines for coping with TCP/IP protocols like HTTP and FTP. Java applications can open and access objects across the Net via URLs with the same ease as when accessing a local file system.

Nowadays, one takes this for granted—but in 1995, connecting to a web server from a C++ or Visual Basic program was a major undertaking.

1.2.4. Robust

Java is intended for writing programs that must be reliable in a variety of ways. Java puts a lot of emphasis on early checking for possible problems, later dynamic (runtime) checking, and eliminating situations that are error-prone. . . . The single biggest difference between Java and C/C++ is that Java has a pointer model that eliminates the possibility of overwriting memory and corrupting data.

The Java compiler detects many problems that in other languages would show up only at runtime. As for the second point, anyone who has spent hours chasing memory corruption caused by a pointer bug will be very happy with this aspect of Java.

1.2.5. Secure

Java is intended to be used in networked/distributed environments. Toward that end, a lot of emphasis has been placed on security. Java enables the construction of virus-free, tamper-free systems.

From the beginning, Java was designed to make certain kinds of attacks impossible, among them:

- Overrunning the runtime stack—a common attack of worms and viruses
- Corrupting memory outside its own process space
- Reading or writing files without permission

Originally, the Java attitude towards downloaded code was "Bring it on!" Untrusted code was executed in a sandbox environment where it could not impact the host system. Users were assured that nothing bad could happen because Java code, no matter where it came from, could never escape from the sandbox.

However, the security model of Java is complex. Not long after the first version of the Java Development Kit was shipped, a group of security experts at Princeton University found subtle bugs that allowed untrusted code to attack the host system.

Initially, security bugs were fixed quickly. Unfortunately, over time, hackers got quite good at spotting subtle flaws in the implementation of the security architecture. Sun, and then Oracle, had a tough time keeping up with bug fixes.

After a number of high-profile attacks, browser vendors and Oracle became increasingly cautious. For a time, remote code had to be digitally signed. Nowadays, browsers no longer trust Java, and the secure delivery of Java applications is a distant memory.

 Note: Even though in hindsight, the Java security model was not as successful as originally envisioned, Java was well ahead of its time. A competing code delivery mechanism from Microsoft, called ActiveX, relied on digital signatures alone for security. Clearly this was not sufficient: As any user of Microsoft's own products can confirm, programs from well-known vendors do crash and create damage.

1.2.6. Architecture-Neutral

The compiler generates an architecture-neutral object file format. The compiled code is executable on many processors, given the presence of the Java runtime system. The Java compiler does this by generating bytecode instructions which have nothing to do with a particular computer architecture. Rather, they are designed to be both easy to interpret on any machine and easy to translate into native machine code on the fly.

Generating code for a "virtual machine" was not a new idea at the time. Programming languages such as Lisp, Smalltalk, and Pascal had employed this technique for many years.

Of course, interpreting virtual machine instructions is slower than running machine instructions at full speed. However, virtual machines have the option of translating the most frequently executed bytecode sequences into machine code—a process called just-in-time compilation.

Java's virtual machine has another advantage. It increases security because it can check the behavior of instruction sequences.

1.2.7. Portable

Unlike C and C++, there are no "implementation-dependent" aspects of the specification. The sizes of the primitive data types are specified, as is the behavior of arithmetic on them.

For example, an int in Java is always a 32-bit integer. In C/C++, int can mean a 16-bit integer, a 32-bit integer, or any other size that the compiler vendor likes. The only restriction is that the int type must have at least as many bytes as a short int and cannot have more bytes than a long int. Having a fixed size for number types eliminates a major porting headache. Binary data is stored and transmitted in a fixed format, eliminating confusion about byte ordering. Strings are saved in a standard Unicode format.

The libraries that are a part of the system define portable interfaces. For example, there is an abstract Window class and implementations of it for UNIX, Windows, and the Macintosh.

The example of a Window class was perhaps poorly chosen. As anyone who has ever tried knows, it is an effort of heroic proportions to implement a user interface that looks good on Windows, the Macintosh, and ten flavors of UNIX. Java 1.0 made the heroic effort, delivering a simple toolkit that provided common user interface elements on a number of platforms. Unfortunately, the result was a library that, with a lot of work, could give barely acceptable results on different systems. That initial user interface toolkit has since been replaced, and replaced again, and portability across platforms remains an issue.

However, for everything that isn't related to user interfaces, the Java libraries do a great job of letting you work in a platform-independent manner. You can work with files, regular expressions, XML, dates and times, databases, network connections, threads, and so on, without worrying about the underlying operating system. Not only are your programs portable, but the Java APIs are often of higher quality than the native ones.

1.2.8. Interpreted

The Java interpreter can execute Java bytecodes directly on any machine to which the interpreter has been ported. Since linking is a more incremental and lightweight process, the development process can be much more rapid and exploratory.

This was a real stretch. Anyone who has used Lisp, Smalltalk, Visual Basic, Python, R, or Scala knows what a "rapid and exploratory" development process is. You try out something, and you instantly see the result. For the first 20 years of Java's existence, development environments were not focused on that experience. It wasn't until Java 9 that the jshell tool supported rapid and exploratory programming.

1.2.9. High-Performance

While the performance of interpreted bytecodes is usually more than adequate, there are situations where higher performance is required. The bytecodes can be translated on the fly (at runtime) into machine code for the particular CPU the application is running on.

In the early years of Java, many users disagreed with the statement that the performance was "more than adequate." Today, however, the just-in-time compilers have become so good that they are competitive with traditional compilers and, in some cases, even outperform them because they have more information available. For example, a just-in-time compiler can monitor which code is executed frequently and optimize just that code for speed. A more sophisticated optimization is the elimination (or "inlining") of function calls. The just-in-time compiler knows which classes have been loaded. It can use inlining when, based upon the currently loaded collection of classes, a particular function is never overridden, and it can undo that optimization later if necessary.

1.2.10. Multithreaded

[The] benefits of multithreading are better interactive responsiveness and real-time behavior.

Nowadays, we care about concurrency because Moore's law has come to an end. Instead of faster processors, we just get more of them, and we have to keep them busy. Yet when you look at most programming languages, they show a shocking disregard for this problem.

Java was well ahead of its time. It was the first mainstream language to support concurrent programming. As you can see from the white paper, its motivation was a little different. At the time, multicore processors were exotic, but web programming had just started, and processors spent a lot of time waiting for a response from the server. Concurrent programming was needed to make sure the user interface didn't freeze.

Concurrent programming is never easy, but Java has done a very good job making it manageable.

1.2.11. Dynamic

In a number of ways, Java is a more dynamic language than C or C++. It was designed to adapt to an evolving environment. Libraries can freely add new methods and instance variables without any effect on their clients. In Java, finding out runtime type information is straightforward.

This is an important feature in situations where code needs to be added to a running program. A prime example is code that is downloaded from the Internet to run in a browser. In C or C++, this is indeed a major challenge, but the Java designers were well aware of dynamic languages that made it easy to evolve a running program. Their achievement was to bring this feature to a mainstream programming language.

 Note: Shortly after the initial success of Java, Microsoft released a product called J++ with a programming language and virtual machine that were almost identical to Java. This effort failed to gain traction, and Microsoft followed through with another language called C# that also has many similarities to Java but runs on a different virtual machine. This book does not cover J++ or C#.

1.3. Java Applets and the Internet

The idea here is simple: Users will download Java bytecodes from the Internet and run them on their own machines. Java programs that work on web pages are called *applets*. To use an applet, you only need a Java-enabled web browser, which will execute the bytecodes for you. You need not install any software. You get the latest version of the program whenever you visit the web page containing the applet. Most importantly, thanks to the security of the virtual machine, you never need to worry about attacks from hostile code.

Inserting an applet into a web page works much like embedding an image. The applet becomes a part of the page, and the text flows around the space used for the applet. The point is, this image is *alive*. It reacts to user commands, changes its appearance, and exchanges data between the computer presenting the applet and the computer serving it.

Figure 1.1 shows the Jmol applet that displays molecular structures. By using the mouse, you can rotate and zoom each molecule to better understand its structure. At the time that applets were invented, this kind of direct manipulation was not achievable with web pages—there was only rudimentary JavaScript and no HTML canvas.

When applets first appeared, they created a huge amount of excitement. Many people believe that the lure of applets was responsible for the astonishing popularity of Java. However, the initial excitement soon turned into frustration. Various versions of the

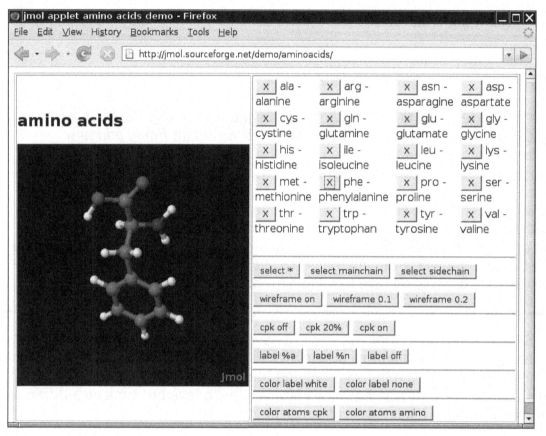

Figure 1.1: The Jmol applet

Netscape and Internet Explorer browsers ran different versions of Java, some of which were seriously outdated. This sorry situation made it increasingly difficult to develop applets that took advantage of the most current Java version. Instead, Adobe's Flash technology became popular for achieving dynamic effects in the browser. Later, when Java was dogged by serious security issues, browsers dropped applet support altogether. Of course, Flash fared no better.

1.4. A Short History of Java

This section gives a short history of Java's evolution. It is based on various published sources (most importantly an interview with Java's creators in the July 1995 issue of *SunWorld*'s online magazine).

Java goes back to 1991, when a group of Sun engineers, led by Patrick Naughton and James Gosling (a Sun Fellow and an all-around computer wizard), wanted to design a small computer language that could be used for consumer devices like cable TV switchboxes. Since these devices do not have a lot of power or memory, the language had to be small and generate very tight code. Also, as different manufacturers may choose different central processing units (CPUs), it was important that the language not be tied to any single architecture. The project was code-named "Green."

The requirements for small, tight, and platform-neutral code led the team to design a portable language that generated intermediate code for a virtual machine.

The Sun people came from a UNIX background, so they based their language on C++ rather than Lisp, Smalltalk, or Pascal. But, as Gosling says in the interview, "All along, the language was a tool, not the end." Gosling decided to call his language "Oak" (presumably because he liked the look of an oak tree that was right outside his window at Sun). The people at Sun later realized that Oak was the name of an existing computer language, so they changed the name to Java. This turned out to be an inspired choice.

In 1992, the Green project delivered its first product, called "*7." It was an extremely intelligent remote control. Unfortunately, no one was interested in producing this at Sun, and the Green people had to find other ways to market their technology. However, none of the standard consumer electronics companies were interested either. The group then bid on a project to design a cable TV box that could deal with emerging cable services such as video-on-demand. They did not get the contract. (Amusingly, the company that did was led by the same Jim Clark who started Netscape—a company that did much to make Java successful.)

The Green project (with a new name of "First Person, Inc.") spent all of 1993 and half of 1994 looking for people to buy its technology. No one was found. (Patrick Naughton, one of the founders of the group and the person who ended up doing most of the marketing, claims to have accumulated 300,000 air miles in trying to sell the technology.) First Person was dissolved in 1994.

While all of this was going on at Sun, the World Wide Web part of the Internet was growing bigger and bigger. The key to the World Wide Web was the browser translating hypertext pages to the screen. In 1994, most people were using Mosaic, a noncommercial web browser that came out of the supercomputing center at the University of Illinois in 1993. (Mosaic was partially written by Marc Andreessen as an undergraduate student on a work-study project, for $6.85 an hour. He moved on to fame and fortune as one of the cofounders and the chief of technology at Netscape.)

In the *SunWorld* interview, Gosling says that in mid-1994, the language developers realized that "We could build a real cool browser. It was one of the few things in the client/server mainstream that needed some of the weird things we'd done: architecture-neutral, real-time, reliable, secure—issues that weren't terribly important in the workstation world. So we built a browser."

The actual browser was built by Patrick Naughton and Jonathan Payne and evolved into the HotJava browser, which was designed to show off the power of Java. The browser was capable of executing Java code inside web pages. This "proof of technology" was shown at SunWorld '95 on May 23, 1995, and inspired the Java craze that continues today.

Sun released the first version of Java in early 1996. People quickly realized that Java 1.0 was not going to cut it for serious application development. Sure, you could use Java 1.0 to make a nervous text applet that moved text randomly around in a canvas. But you couldn't even *print* in Java 1.0. To be blunt, Java 1.0 was not ready for prime time. Its successor, version 1.1, filled in the most obvious gaps, greatly improved the reflection capability, and added a new event model for GUI programming. It was still rather limited, though.

The big news of the 1998 JavaOne conference was the upcoming release of Java 1.2, which replaced the early toylike GUI and graphics toolkits with sophisticated scalable versions. Three days (!) after its release in December 1998, Sun's marketing department changed the name to the catchy *Java 2 Standard Edition Software Development Kit Version 1.2*.

Besides the Standard Edition, two other editions were introduced: the Micro Edition for embedded devices such as cell phones, and the Enterprise Edition for server-side processing. This book focuses on the Standard Edition.

Versions 1.3 and 1.4 of the Standard Edition were incremental improvements over the initial Java 2 release, with an ever-growing standard library, increased performance, and, of course, quite a few bug fixes. During this time, much of the initial hype about Java applets and client-side applications abated, but Java became the platform of choice for server-side applications.

Version 5.0 was the first release since version 1.1 that updated the Java *language* in significant ways. (This version was originally numbered 1.5, but the version number jumped to 5.0 at the 2004 JavaOne conference.) After many years of research, generic types (roughly comparable to C++ templates) have been added—the challenge was to add this feature without requiring changes in the virtual machine. Several other useful language features were inspired by C#: a "for each" loop, autoboxing, and annotations.

Version 6 (without the .0 suffix) was released at the end of 2006. Again, there were no language changes but additional performance improvements and library enhancements.

As datacenters increasingly relied on commodity hardware instead of specialized servers, Sun Microsystems fell on hard times and was purchased by Oracle in 2009. Development of Java stalled for a long time. In 2011, Oracle released a new version, with simple enhancements, as Java 7.

In 2014, the release of Java 8 followed, with the most significant changes to the Java language in almost two decades. Java 8 embraces a "functional" style of programming that makes it easy to express computations that can be executed concurrently. All programming languages must evolve to stay relevant, and Java has shown a remarkable capacity to do so.

The main feature of Java 9 goes all the way back to 2008. At that time, Mark Reinhold, the chief engineer of the Java platform, started an effort to break up the huge, monolithic Java platform. This was to be achieved by introducing *modules*, self-contained units of code that provide a specific functionality. It took eleven years to design and implement a module system that is a good fit for the Java platform, and it remains to be seen whether it is also a good fit for Java applications and libraries.

Starting in 2018, Java versions are released every six months, to enable faster introduction of preview features. New features may go through several rounds of preview. For example, pattern matching for switch was previewed four times, starting in Java 17, before it was finalized in Java 21.

Ever so often, a version is designated by Oracle and other vendors to have long-term support (LTS), with bug fixes and security updates provided for several years. When using Java in production, it is common to stick to a LTS release and not use any preview features. So far, this has happened with Java 11, Java 17, and Java 21.

Table 1.1 shows the evolution of the Java language and library. As you can see, the size of the application programming interface (API) has grown tremendously.

Table 1.1: Evolution of the Java Language

Version	Year	New Language Features	Number of Classes and Interfaces
1.0	1996	The language itself	211
1.1	1997	Inner classes	477
1.2	1998	The strictfp modifier	1,524
1.3	2000	None	1,840
1.4	2002	Assertions	2,723
5.0	2004	Generic classes, "for each" loop, varargs, autoboxing, metadata, enumerations, static import	3,279
6	2006	None	3,793
7	2011	Switch with strings, diamond operator, binary literals, exception handling enhancements	4,024
8	2014	Lambda expressions, interfaces with default methods, stream and date/time libraries	4,240
9	2017	Modules, miscellaneous language and library enhancements	6,005

Version	Year	New Language Features	Number of Classes and Interfaces
11	2018	Local variable type inference (var), HTTP client, removal of Java FX, JNLP, Java EE overlap, and CORBA	4,410
17	2021	Switch expressions, text blocks, instanceof pattern matching, records, sealed classes	4,859
21	2023	Virtual threads, pattern matching	4,882

1.5. Common Misconceptions about Java

This chapter closes with a commented list of some common misconceptions about Java.

Java is an extension of HTML.

Java is a programming language; HTML is a way to describe the structure of a web page. They have nothing in common except that there once were HTML extensions for placing Java applets on a web page.

I use XML, so I don't need Java.

Java is a programming language; XML is a way to describe data. You can process XML data with any programming language, but the Java API contains excellent support for XML processing. In addition, many important XML tools are implemented in Java. See Volume II for more information.

Java is an easy programming language to learn.

No programming language as powerful as Java is easy. You always have to distinguish between how easy it is to write toy programs and how hard it is to do serious work. Also, consider that only seven chapters in this book discuss the Java language. The remaining chapters of both volumes show how to put the language to work, using the Java *libraries*. The Java libraries contain thousands of classes and interfaces and tens of thousands of functions. Luckily, you do not need to know every one of them, but you do need to know surprisingly many to use Java for anything realistic.

Java will become a universal programming language for all platforms.

This is possible in theory. But in practice, there are domains where other languages are entrenched. Objective C and its successor, Swift, are not going to be replaced on iOS devices. Anything that happens in a browser is controlled by JavaScript. Windows programs are written in C++ or C#. Java has the edge in server-side programming and in cross-platform client applications.

Java is just another programming language.

Java is a nice programming language; most programmers prefer it to C, C++, or C#. But there have been hundreds of nice programming languages that never gained widespread popularity, whereas languages with obvious flaws, such as C++ and Visual Basic, have been wildly successful.

Why? The success of a programming language is determined far more by the utility of the *support system* surrounding it than by the elegance of its syntax. Are there useful, convenient, and standard libraries for the features that you need to implement? Are there tool vendors that build great programming and debugging environments? Do the language and the toolset integrate with the rest of the computing infrastructure? Java is successful because its libraries let you easily do things such as networking, web applications, and concurrency. The fact that Java reduces pointer errors is a bonus, so programmers seem to be more productive with Java—but these factors are not the source of its success.

Java is proprietary, and should therefore be avoided.

When Java was first created, Sun Microsystems gave free licenses to distributors and end users. Although Sun had ultimate control over Java, they involved many other companies in the development of language revisions and the design of new libraries. Source code for the virtual machine and the libraries has always been freely available, but only for inspection, not for modification and redistribution. Java was "closed source, but playing nice."

This situation changed dramatically in 2007, when Sun announced that future versions of Java would be available under the General Public License (GPL), the same open source license that is used by Linux. Oracle has committed to keeping Java open source. There are now multiple providers of open Java implementations, with various levels of commitment and support.

Java is interpreted, so it is too slow for serious applications.

In the early days of Java, the language was interpreted. Nowadays, the Java virtual machine uses a just-in-time compiler. The "hot spots" of your code will run just as fast in Java as they would in C++, and in some cases even faster.

All Java programs run inside a web page.

There was a time when Java *applets* ran inside a web browser. Nowadays, Java programs are stand-alone applications that run outside of a web browser. In fact, most Java programs run on servers, producing code for web pages or computing business logic.

Java programs are a major security risk.

In the early days of Java, there were some well-publicized reports of failures in the Java security system. Researchers viewed it as a challenge to find chinks in the Java armor and to defy the strength and sophistication of the applet security model. The technical failures that they found had been quickly corrected. Later, there were more serious exploits, to which Sun, and later Oracle, responded slowly. Browser manufacturers discontinued support for Java applets. The security manager architecture that made applets possible is now deprecated. These days, Java applications are no less secure than other applications. Due to the protections of the virtual machine, they are far more secure than applications written in C or C++.

JavaScript is a simpler version of Java.

JavaScript, a scripting language that can be used inside web pages, was invented by Netscape and originally called LiveScript. JavaScript has a syntax that is reminiscent of Java, and the languages' names sound similar, but otherwise they are unrelated. In particularly, Java is *strongly typed*—the compiler catches many errors that arise from type misuse. In JavaScript, such errors are only found when the program runs, which makes their elimination far more laborious.

With Java, I can replace my desktop computer with a cheap "Internet appliance."

When Java was first released, some people bet big that this was going to happen. Companies produced prototypes of Java-powered network computers, but users were not ready to give up a powerful and convenient desktop for a limited machine with no local storage. Nowadays, of course, the world has changed, and for a large majority of end users, the platform that matters is a mobile phone or tablet. The majority of these devices are controlled by the Android platform which is based on Java. Learning Java programming will help you with Android programming as well.

CHAPTER 2

The Java Programming Environment

In this chapter, you will learn how to install the Java Development Kit (JDK) and how to compile and run Java programs. You can run the JDK tools by typing commands in a terminal window. However, many programmers prefer the comfort of an integrated development environment. You will learn how to use a freely available development environment to compile and run Java programs. Once you have mastered the techniques in this chapter and picked your development tools, you are ready to move on to Chapter 3, where you will begin exploring the Java programming language.

2.1. Installing the Java Development Kit

In days past, the most complete and up-to-date version of the Java Development Kit (JDK) was available from Oracle. Nowadays many different companies and organizations, including Amazon, Azul, Microsoft, and Red Hat, provide up-to-date OpenJDK builds. Each vendor has different licensing conditions and support offerings. The Eclipse Foundation provides free JDK builds for Linux, Mac OS, and Windows, which work well for learning Java.

2.1.1. Downloading the JDK

You can download the Java Development Kit from the Eclipse Foundation at `https://adoptium.net`, or from Oracle at `https://www.oracle.com/java/technologies/downloads`, or from many other providers.

Depending on the provider, the Java Development Kit may have a brand name, such as Temurin (Eclipse Foundation), Corretto (Amazon), or Zulu (Azul). The brand name is of no importance to Java programmers.

You should use the Java SE 21 (LTS) JDK. See Table 2.1 for a summary of the acronyms and jargon that you may encounter on the download site.

Table 2.1: Java Jargon

Name	Acronym	Explanation
Java Development Kit	JDK	The software for programmers who want to write Java programs.
Java Runtime Environment	JRE	The software for running Java programs, without development tools. Only supported until Java 8. You do not want that.
Standard Edition	SE	The Java platform for use on desktops and simple server applications. You want that.
Micro Edition	ME	The Java platform for use on small devices.
OpenJDK	—	A free and open source implementation of Java SE.
Hotspot	—	The "just in time" compiler developed by Oracle. If asked, choose this one.
OpenJ9	—	Another "just in time" compiler developed by IBM.
GraalVM	—	An "ahead of time" compiler for executables that start quickly, but don't support all Java features. You don't want it for this book.
Long Term Support	LTS	A release that is supported for multiple years, unlike the six-month releases that showcase new features. Choose the latest LTS release.
Eclipse	—	A foundation that distributes open-source software.
Temurin	—	The brand name for the OpenJDK version that the Eclipse foundation distributes.
Adoptium	—	The project within the Eclipse Foundation that provides an OpenJDK version and infrastructure support for its distribution.

2.1.2. Setting Up the JDK

After downloading the JDK, you need to install it and figure out where it was installed—you'll need that information later.

If you run Windows or have a Mac, simply launch the setup program and choose the default options.

On Linux, uncompress the .tar.gz file to a location of your choice, such as your home directory or /opt. Then set the PATH to the bin subdirectory of the directory into which the JDK was placed, such as /opt/jdk-21.0.4/bin. This is usually achieved by adding a line such as the following to the end of your ~/.bashrc or ~/.bash_profile file:

```
export PATH=/opt/jdk-21.0.4/bin:$PATH
```

Here is how you test whether you did it right. Start a terminal window. Type the line

```
javac --version
```

and press the Enter key. You should get a display such as this one:

```
javac 21.0.4
```

If instead you get a message such as "javac: command not found" or "The name specified is not recognized as an internal or external command, operable program or batch file," then you need to double-check your installation.

It is often useful to know where the JDK is installed on your system—see Table 2.2. In this book, the installation directory is denoted as *jdk*. For example, when referring to the *jdk*/bin directory, I mean the directory such as /opt/jdk-17.0.4/bin or C:\Program Files\Java\jdk-21\bin.

Table 2.2: The JDK Installation Directory

Platform	Sample Directory
Windows (Adoptium)	C:\Program Files\Eclipse Adoptium\jdk-21.0.4.11-hotspot
Windows (Oracle OpenJDK)	C:\Program Files\Java\jdk-21
Mac OS	/Library/Java/JavaVirtualMachines/jdk-21.0.4_11.jdk/Contents/Home
Linux	Where you uncompressed the .tar.gz file, such as /opt/jdk-21.0.4

 Note: On Windows, the Oracle JDK installer adds the directory C:\Program Files\Common Files\Oracle\Java\javapath to the PATH environment variable. That directory only contains the javac, javaw, java, and jshell executables. (You will see how to use javac, java, and jshell in this chapter. The javaw executable is a Windows-only feature for launching a program without a console window.) The other tools in the Java Development Kit can be found in the bin subdirectory of the JDK installation directory. When invoking those programs, either specify the complete path (such as C:\Program Files\Java\jdk-21\bin\javadoc for the javadoc tool), or add the bin subdirectory to the PATH environment variable. One way to achieve this is with the setx command:

```
setx PATH "%PATH%;c:\Program Files\Java\jdk-21\bin"
```

Open another terminal window for the change to take effect.

The https://adoptium.net installer does not have this issue. It adds all JDK tools to the PATH.

2.1.3. Installing Source Files and Documentation

The library source files are delivered in the JDK as a compressed file *jdk*/lib/src.zip. Unpack that file to get access to the source code. Simply do the following:

1. Make sure the JDK is installed and the *jdk*/bin directory is on the executable path.
2. Make a directory javasrc in your home directory. If you like, you can do this from a terminal window.

   ```
   mkdir javasrc
   ```

3. Inside the *jdk*/lib directory, locate the file src.zip.
4. Unzip the src.zip file into the javasrc directory. In a terminal window, you can execute the commands

   ```
   cd javasrc
   jar xvf jdk/lib/src.zip
   cd ..
   ```

 Tip: The src.zip file contains the source code for all public libraries. To obtain even more source (for the compiler, the virtual machine, the native methods, and the private helper classes), go to https://openjdk.org.

You can read the JDK documentation at https://docs.oracle.com/en/java/javase/21/docs/. If you prefer to have an offline version, follow these steps:

1. Download the documentation zip file from https://www.oracle.com/java/technologies/downloads. It is called jdk-21.0.x_doc-all.zip.
2. Unzip the file and rename the doc directory into something more descriptive, like jdk-21-docs. If you like, you can do this from the command line:

```
jar xvf Downloads/jdk-21.0.x_doc-all.zip
mv docs jdk-21-docs
```

3. In your browser, navigate to jdk-21-docs/index.html and add this page to your bookmarks.

You should also install the *Core Java* program examples. You can download them from https://horstmann.com/corejava. The programs are packaged into a zip file corejava.zip. Just unzip them into your home directory. They will be located in a directory corejava. If you like, you can do this from the command line:

```
jar xvf Downloads/corejava.zip
```

2.2. Using the Command-Line Tools

If your programming experience comes from a development environment such as Microsoft Visual Studio, you are accustomed to a system with a built-in text editor, menus to compile and launch a program, and a debugger. The JDK contains nothing even remotely similar. You do *everything* by typing in commands in a terminal window. This may sound cumbersome, but it is nevertheless an essential skill. When you first install Java, you will want to troubleshoot your installation before you install a development environment. Moreover, by executing the basic steps yourself, you gain a better understanding of what a development environment does behind your back.

However, after you have mastered the basic steps of compiling and running Java programs, you will want to use a professional development environment. You will see how to do that in the following section.

Let's get started the hard way: compiling and launching a Java program from the command line.

1. Open a terminal window.
2. Go to the *corejava*/v1ch02/Welcome directory. (The *corejava* directory is where you installed the source code for the book examples, as explained in Section 2.1.3.)
3. Enter the following commands:

```
javac Welcome.java
java Welcome
```

In the terminal window, you should see the output shown in Figure 2.1.

Congratulations! You have just compiled and run your first Java program.

What happened? The javac program is the Java compiler. It compiles the file Welcome.java into the file Welcome.class. The java program launches the Java virtual machine. It executes the bytecodes that the compiler placed in the class file.

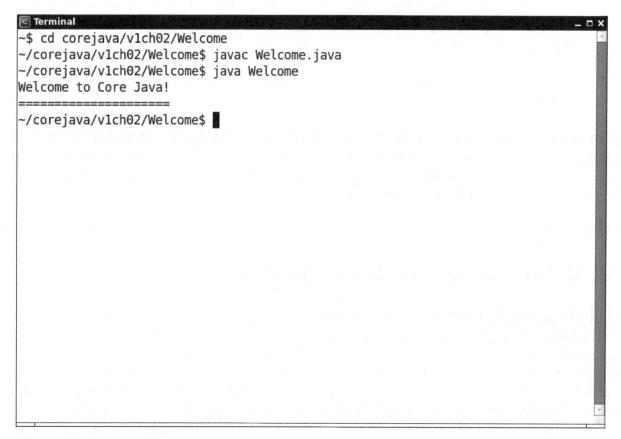

Figure 2.1: Compiling and running `Welcome.java`

The `Welcome` program is extremely simple. It merely prints a message to the terminal. You may enjoy looking inside the program, shown in Listing 2.1. You will see how it works in the next chapter.

Listing 2.1 `Welcome/Welcome.java`

```
1  /**
2   * This program displays a greeting for the reader.
3   * @version 1.30 2014-02-27
4   * @author Cay Horstmann
5   */
6  public class Welcome
7  {
8     public static void main(String[] args)
9     {
10        String greeting = "Welcome to Core Java!";
11        System.out.println(greeting);
12        for (int i = 0; i < greeting.length(); i++)
13           System.out.print("=");
```

```
14        System.out.println();
15     }
16 }
```

In the age of integrated development environments, many programmers are unfamiliar with running programs in a terminal window. Any number of things can go wrong, leading to frustrating results.

Pay attention to the following points:

1. If you type in the program by hand, make sure you correctly enter the uppercase and lowercase letters. In particular, the class name is Welcome and not welcome or WELCOME.

2. The compiler requires a *file name* (Welcome.java). When you run the program, you specify a *class name* (Welcome) without a .java or .class extension.

3. If you get a message such as "Bad command or file name" or "javac: command not found," go back and double-check your installation, in particular the executable path setting.

4. If javac reports that it cannot find the file Welcome.java, you should check whether that file is present in the directory.
    Under Linux, check that you used the correct capitalization for Welcome.java.
    Under Windows, use the dir command, *not* the graphical Explorer tool. Some text editors (in particular Notepad) insist on adding an extension .txt to every file's name. If you use Notepad to edit Welcome.java, it will actually save it as Welcome.java.txt. Under the default Windows settings, Explorer conspires with Notepad and hides the .txt extension because it belongs to a "known file type." In that case, you need to rename the file, or save it again placing quotes around the file name: "Welcome.java".

5. If you launch your program and get an error message complaining about a java.lang.NoClassDefFoundError, then carefully check the name of the offending class. If you get a complaint about welcome (with a lowercase w), then you should reissue the java Welcome command with an uppercase W. As always, case matters in Java. If you get a complaint about Welcome/java, it means you accidentally typed java Welcome.java. Reissue the command as java Welcome.

 Note: As of Java 11, you can skip the javac command if you have a single source file. This feature is intended for shell scripts (starting with a "shebang" line #!/path/to/java) and perhaps for simple student programs. Once your programs get more complex, you need to use javac.

The Welcome program was not terribly exciting. Next, try out a graphical application. This program is a simple image file viewer that loads and displays an image. As before, compile and run the program from the command line.

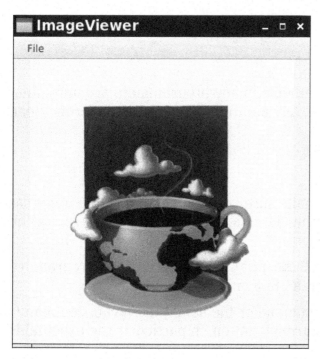

Figure 2.2: Running the ImageViewer application

1. Open a terminal window.
2. Change to the directory `corejava/v1ch02/ImageViewer`.
3. Enter the following:

```
javac ImageViewer.java
java ImageViewer
```

A new program window pops up with the ImageViewer application. Now, select File →
Open and look for an image file to open. (There are a couple of sample files in the same
directory.) The image is displayed (see Figure 2.2). To close the program, click on the Close
box in the title bar or select File → Exit from the menu.

Have a quick look at the source code (Listing 2.2). The program is substantially longer than
the first program, but it is not too complex if you consider how much code it would take in
C or C++ to write a similar application. Of course, nowadays it is not common to write
desktop applications with graphical user interfaces, but if you are interested, you can find
more details in Chapter 10 of Volume II.

Listing 2.2 ImageViewer/ImageViewer.java

```
1   import java.awt.*;
2   import java.io.*;
3   import javax.swing.*;
```

```java
  4
  5 /**
  6  * A program for viewing images.
  7  * @version 1.31 2018-04-10
  8  * @author Cay Horstmann
  9  */
 10 public class ImageViewer
 11 {
 12    public static void main(String[] args)
 13    {
 14       EventQueue.invokeLater(() ->
 15          {
 16             var frame = new ImageViewerFrame();
 17             frame.setTitle("ImageViewer");
 18             frame.setDefaultCloseOperation(JFrame.EXIT_ON_CLOSE);
 19             frame.setVisible(true);
 20          });
 21    }
 22 }
 23
 24 /**
 25  * A frame with a label to show an image.
 26  */
 27 class ImageViewerFrame extends JFrame
 28 {
 29    private static final int DEFAULT_WIDTH = 300;
 30    private static final int DEFAULT_HEIGHT = 400;
 31
 32    public ImageViewerFrame()
 33    {
 34       setSize(DEFAULT_WIDTH, DEFAULT_HEIGHT);
 35
 36       // use a label to display the images
 37       var label = new JLabel();
 38       add(label);
 39
 40       // set up the file chooser
 41       var chooser = new JFileChooser();
 42       chooser.setCurrentDirectory(new File("."));
 43
 44       // set up the menu bar
 45       var menuBar = new JMenuBar();
 46       setJMenuBar(menuBar);
 47
 48       var menu = new JMenu("File");
 49       menuBar.add(menu);
 50
 51       var openItem = new JMenuItem("Open");
 52       menu.add(openItem);
 53       openItem.addActionListener(event ->
 54          {
 55             // show file chooser dialog
```

```
56              int result = chooser.showOpenDialog(null);
57
58              // if file selected, set it as icon of the label
59              if (result == JFileChooser.APPROVE_OPTION)
60              {
61                 String name = chooser.getSelectedFile().getPath();
62                 label.setIcon(new ImageIcon(name));
63              }
64           });
65
66        var exitItem = new JMenuItem("Exit");
67        menu.add(exitItem);
68        exitItem.addActionListener(event -> System.exit(0));
69     }
70 }
```

2.3. Using an Integrated Development Environment

In the preceding section, you saw how to compile and run a Java program from the command line. That is a useful skill for troubleshooting, but for most day-to-day work, you should use an integrated development environment. These environments are so powerful and convenient that it simply doesn't make much sense to labor on without them. Excellent choices are the freely available Eclipse, IntelliJ IDEA, and NetBeans. In this chapter, you will learn how to get started with Eclipse. Of course, if you prefer a different development environment, you can certainly use it with this book.

Get started by downloading Eclipse from https://eclipse.org/downloads. Versions exist for Linux, Mac OS X, and Windows. Run the installation program and pick the installation set called "Eclipse IDE for Java Developers."

Here are the steps to write a program with Eclipse:

1. After starting Eclipse, select File → New → Project from the menu.
2. Select "Java Project" from the wizard dialog (see Figure 2.3).
3. Click the Next button. *Uncheck* the "Use default location" checkbox. Click on Browse and navigate to the corejava/v1ch02/Welcome directory (Figure 2.4).
4. Click the Finish button. The project is now created.
5. Click on the triangles in the left pane next to the project until you locate the file Welcome.java, and double-click on it. You should now see a pane with the program code (see Figure 2.5).
6. With the right mouse button, click on the project name (Welcome) in the left pane. Select Run → Run As → Java Application. The program output is displayed in the console pane.

Presumably, this program does not have typos or bugs. (It was only a few lines of code, after all.) Let us suppose, for the sake of argument, that your code occasionally contains a typo (perhaps even a syntax error). Try it out—ruin your file, for example, by changing the capitalization of String as follows:

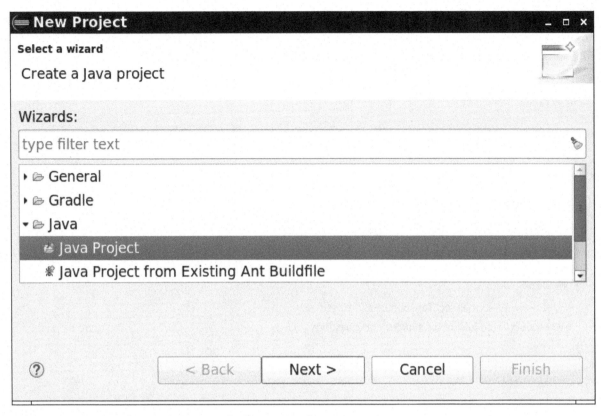

Figure 2.3: The New Project dialog in Eclipse

```
string greeting = "Welcome to Core Java!";
```

Note the wiggly line under `string`. In the tabs below the source code, click on Problems and expand the triangles until you see an error message that complains about an unknown `string` type (see Figure 2.6). Click on the error message. The cursor moves to the matching line in the edit pane, where you can correct your error. This allows you to fix your errors quickly.

 Tip: Often, an Eclipse error report is accompanied by a lightbulb icon. Click on the lightbulb to get a list of suggested fixes.

2.4. JShell

The JShell program provides a "read-evaluate-print loop," or REPL. You type a Java expression; JShell evaluates your input, prints the result, and waits for your next input. This is an excellent way to experiment—much faster than writing a complete program in an integrated development environment.

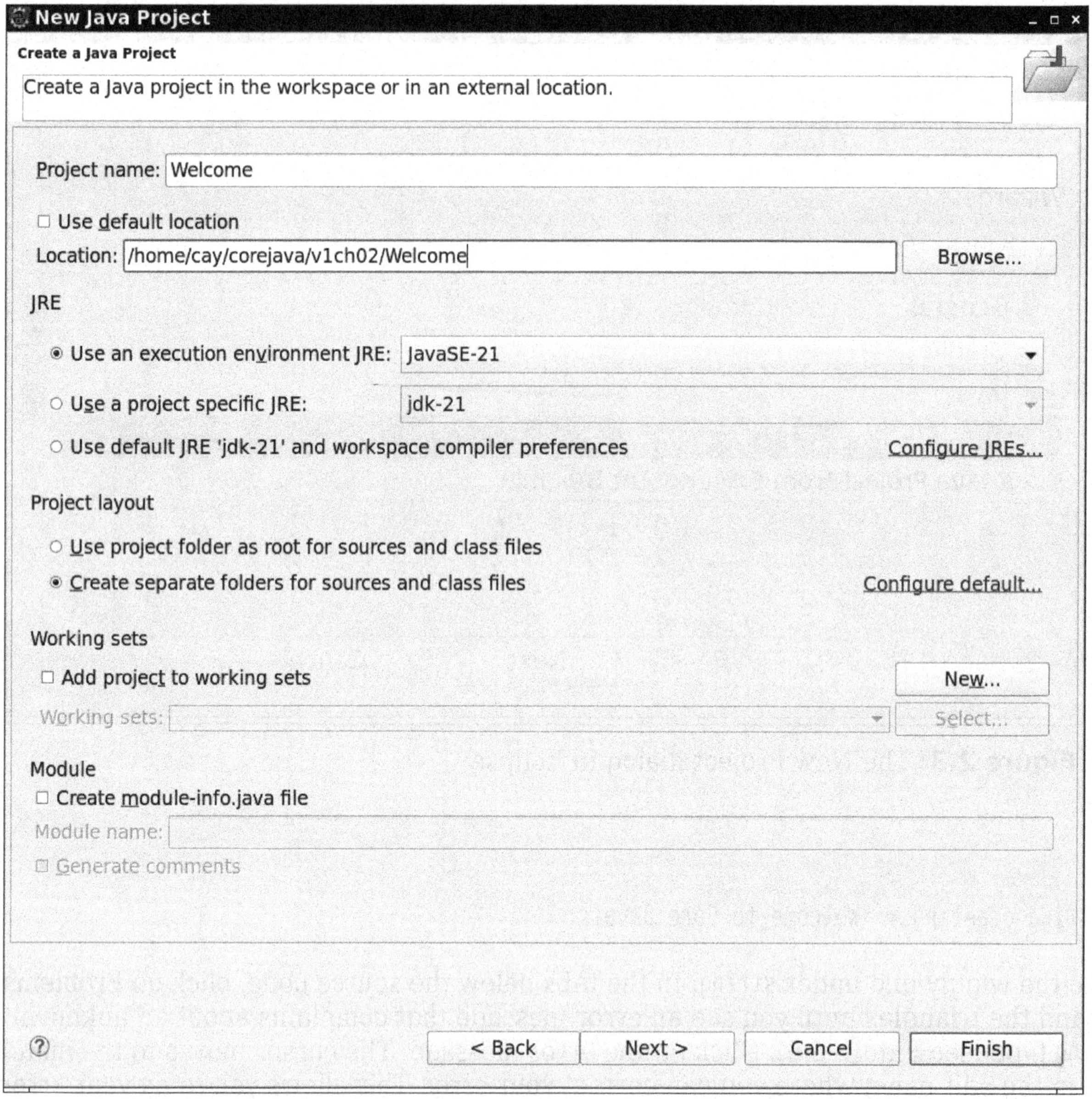

New Java Project   _ □ x

Create a Java Project

Create a Java project in the workspace or in an external location.

Project name: Welcome

☐ Use default location

Location: /home/cay/corejava/v1ch02/Welcome   Browse...

JRE

⦿ Use an execution environment JRE: JavaSE-21   ▾

○ Use a project specific JRE: jdk-21   ▾

○ Use default JRE 'jdk-21' and workspace compiler preferences   Configure JREs...

Project layout

○ Use project folder as root for sources and class files

⦿ Create separate folders for sources and class files   Configure default...

Working sets

☐ Add project to working sets   New...

Working sets: ▾   Select...

Module

☐ Create module-info.java file

Module name:

☐ Generate comments

⑦   < Back   Next >   Cancel   Finish

Figure 2.4: Configuring a project in Eclipse

To start JShell, simply type jshell in a terminal window (see Figure 2.7).

JShell starts with a greeting, followed by a prompt:

```
|  Welcome to JShell -- Version 21.0.4
|  For an introduction type: /help intro

jshell>
```

Now type an expression, such as

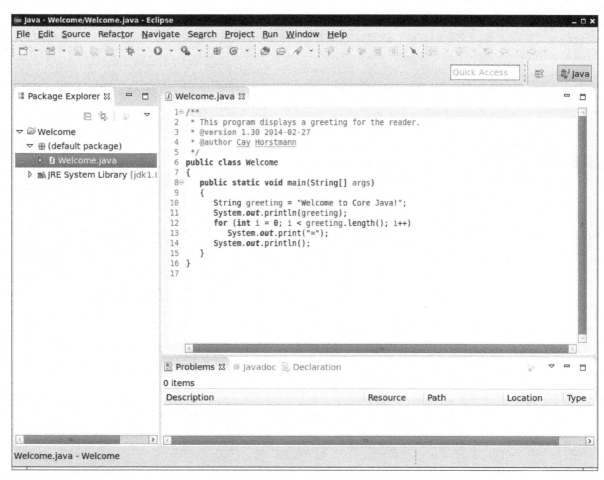

Figure 2.5: Editing a source file with Eclipse

```
"Core Java".length()
```

JShell responds with the result—in this case, the number of characters in the string "Core Java".

```
$1 ==> 9
```

Note that you do *not* type System.out.println. JShell automatically prints the value of every expression that you enter.

The $1 in the output indicates that the result is available in further calculations. For example, if you type

```
5 * $1 - 3
```

the response is

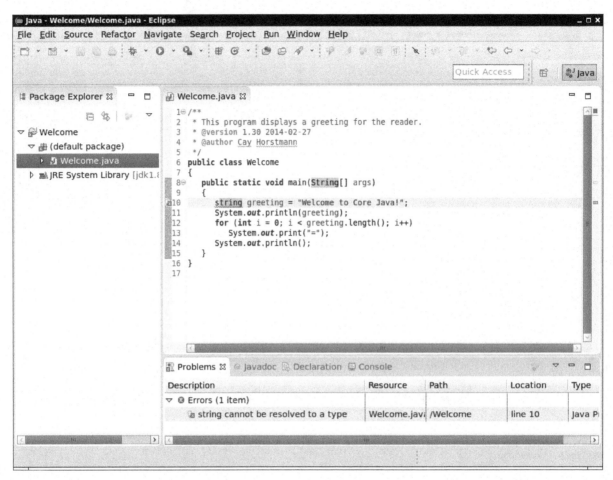

Figure 2.6: Error messages in Eclipse

```
$2 ==> 42
```

If you need a variable many times, you can give it a more memorable name. For example,

```
jshell> var answer = 6 * 7
answer ==> 42
```

Another useful feature is tab completion. Type

```
Math.
```

followed by the Tab key. Because there are so many completions, you are prompted to hit the Tab key again. You get a list of all methods that you can invoke with the Math class:

```
jshell> Math.
E                       IEEEremainder(          PI
TAU                     abs(                    absExact(
```

```
jshell                                                                    _ □ x
~$ jshell
|  Welcome to JShell -- Version 21.0.1
|  For an introduction type: /help intro

jshell> "Core Java".length()
$1 ==> 9

jshell> 5 * $1 - 3
$2 ==> 42

jshell> int answer = 6 * 7
answer ==> 42

jshell> Math.
<press tab again to see all possible completions; total possible completions: 103>
jshell> Math.
E                        IEEEremainder(           PI
TAU                      abs(                      absExact(
acos(                    addExact(                 asin(
atan(                    atan2(                    cbrt(
ceil(                    ceilDiv(                  ceilDivExact(
ceilMod(                 clamp(                    class
copySign(                cos(                      cosh(
decrementExact(          divideExact(              exp(
expm1(                   floor(                    floorDiv(
floorDivExact(           floorMod(                 fma(
getExponent(             hypot(                    incrementExact(
log(                     log10(                    log1p(
max(                     min(                      multiplyExact(
multiplyFull(            multiplyHigh(             negateExact(
nextAfter(               nextDown(                 nextUp(
pow(                     random()                  rint(
round(                   scalb(                    signum(
sin(                     sinh(                     sqrt(
subtractExact(           tan(                      tanh(
toDegrees(               toIntExact(               toRadians(
ulp(                     unsignedMultiplyHigh(
jshell> Math.
```

Figure 2.7: Running JShell

```
acos(                    addExact(                 asin(
atan(                    atan2(                    cbrt(
ceil(                    ceilDiv(                  ceilDivExact(
ceilMod(                 clamp(                    class
copySign(                cos(                      cosh(
decrementExact(          divideExact(              exp(
expm1(                   floor(                    floorDiv(
floorDivExact(           floorMod(                 fma(
getExponent(             hypot(                    incrementExact(
log(                     log10(                    log1p(
max(                     min(                      multiplyExact(
```

```
multiplyFull(          multiplyHigh(          negateExact(
nextAfter(             nextDown(              nextUp(
pow(                  random()              rint(
round(                scalb(                signum(
sin(                  sinh(                 sqrt(
subtractExact(        tan(                  tanh(
toDegrees(            toIntExact(           toRadians(
ulp(                  unsignedMultiplyHigh(
```

Now type l and hit the Tab key again. The method name is completed to log, and you get a shorter list:

```
jshell> Math.log
log(     log10(   log1p(
```

Now you can fill in the rest by hand:

```
jshell> Math.log10(0.001)
$4 ==> -3.0
```

To repeat a command, hit the ↑ key until you see the line that you want to reissue or edit. You can move the cursor in the line with the ← and → keys, and add or delete characters. Hit Enter when you are done. For example, hit the ↑ key and replace 0.001 with 1000, then hit Enter:

```
jshell> Math.log10(1000)
$5 ==> 3.0
```

You exit JShell with the command

```
/exit
```

JShell makes it easy and fun to learn the Java language and library without having to launch a heavy-duty development environment and without fussing with a program and a main method.

In this chapter, you learned about the mechanics of compiling and running Java programs. You are now ready to move on to Chapter 3 where you will start learning the Java language.

CHAPTER 3

Fundamental Programming Structures in Java

At this point, you should have successfully installed the JDK and executed the sample programs from Chapter 2. It's time to start programming. This chapter shows you how the basic programming concepts such as data types, branches, and loops are implemented in Java.

3.1. A Simple Java Program

Let's look more closely at one of the simplest Java programs you can have—one that merely prints a message to console:

```java
public class FirstSample
{
   public static void main(String[] args)
   {
      System.out.println("We will not use 'Hello, World!'");
   }
}
```

It is worth spending all the time you need to become comfortable with the framework of this sample; the pieces will recur in all applications. First and foremost, *Java is case sensitive*. If you made any mistakes in capitalization (such as typing Main instead of main), the program will not run.

Now let's look at this source code line by line. The keyword public is called an *access modifier*; these modifiers control the level of access other parts of a program have to this code. For more about access modifiers, see Chapter 4. The keyword class reminds you that everything in a Java program lives inside a class. You will learn a lot more about classes in the next chapter. For now, think of a class as a container for the program logic that defines the behavior of an application. Classes are the building blocks with which all Java applications are built. *Everything* in a Java program must be inside a class.

Following the keyword class is the name of the class. The rules for class names in Java are quite generous. Names must begin with a letter, and after that, they can have any combination of letters and digits. The length is essentially unlimited. You cannot use a Java reserved word (such as `public` or `class`) for a class name. (See the appendix for a list of reserved words.)

The standard naming convention (used in the name `FirstSample`) is that class names are nouns that start with an uppercase letter. If a name consists of multiple words, use an initial uppercase letter in each of the words. This use of uppercase letters in the middle of a name is sometimes called "camel case" or, self-referentially, "CamelCase."

You need to make the file name for the source code the same as the name of the public class, with the extension `.java` appended. Thus, you must store this code in a file called `FirstSample.java`. (Again, case is important—don't use `firstsample.java`.)

You compile the file with the command

```
javac FirstSample.java
```

If you have named the file correctly and not made any typos in the source code, you end up with a file containing the bytecodes for this class. The Java compiler names the bytecode file `FirstSample.class` and stores it in the same directory as the source file. Finally, launch the program by issuing the following command:

```
java FirstSample
```

(Remember to leave off the `.class` extension.) When the program executes, it simply displays the string `We will not use 'Hello, World!'` on the console.

When you use

```
java ClassName
```

to run a compiled program, the Java virtual machine always starts execution with the code in the `main` method in the class you indicate. (The term "method" is Java-speak for a function.) Thus, you *must* have a `main` method in the source of your class for your code to execute. You can, of course, add your own methods to a class and call them from the `main` method. (You will see in the next chapter how to write your own methods.)

Note: According to the Java Language Specification, the `main` method must be declared `public`. (The Java Language Specification is the official document that describes the Java language. You can view or download it from `https://docs.oracle.com/javase/specs`.)

However, several versions of the Java launcher were willing to execute Java programs even when the `main` method was not `public`. A programmer filed a bug report. To see it, visit `https://bugs.openjdk.org/browse/JDK-4252539`. In 1999, that bug was marked as "closed, will not be fixed." A Sun engineer added an explanation that the Java Virtual Machine Specification does not mandate that main is public and that "fixing it will cause potential troubles." Fortunately, sanity prevailed. The Java launcher in Java 1.4 and beyond enforces that the main method is public.

Of course, it is frustrating to have quality assurance engineers, who are often overworked and not always experts in the fine points of Java, make questionable decisions about bug reports. But it is remarkable that the bug reports and their resolutions have been available for anyone to scrutinize, long before Java was open source.

Notice the braces { } in the source code. In Java, as in C/C++, braces delineate the parts (usually called *blocks*) in your program. In Java, the code for any method must be started by an opening brace { and ended by a closing brace }.

Brace styles have inspired an inordinate amount of useless controversy. This book follows a style that lines up matching braces. As whitespace is irrelevant to the Java compiler, you can use whatever brace style you like.

For now, don't worry about the keywords static void—just think of them as part of what you need to get a Java program to compile. By the end of Chapter 4, you will understand this incantation completely. The point to remember for now is that every Java application must have a main method that is declared in the following way:

```
public class ClassName
{
   public static void main(String[] args)
   {
      program statements
   }
}
```

 Preview Note: The byzantine complexity of public static void main is about to give way to something simpler. Java 21 has a preview feature, described in Java Enhancement Proposal (JEP) 445, that allows you to write the main method like this:

```
class FirstSample
{
   void main()
   {
      System.out.println("We will not use 'Hello, World!'");
   }
}
```

That is nicer. No public, no static, no String[] args.

For now, you need to compile and run the program with a command-line flag:

```
javac --enable-preview --source 21 FirstSample.java
java --enable-preview FirstSample
```

Even simpler, since there is a single source file, you can skip the javac step:

```
java --enable-preview --source 21 FirstSample.java
```

In this book, we embrace classes and object-oriented programming. But for very simple programs, JEP 445 allows you to omit the class, provided, of course, there is only one. The file FirstSample.java can simply contain:

```
void main()
{
    System.out.println("We will not use 'Hello, World!'");
}
```

Since these features are still in preview, I won't use them in this edition, but in the future, the first sample program will be a bit simpler.

 C++ Note: As a C++ programmer, you know what a class is. Java classes are similar to C++ classes, but there are a few differences that can trap you. For example, in Java *all* functions are methods of some class. (The standard terminology refers to them as methods, not member functions.) Thus, in Java you must have a shell class for the main method. You may also be familiar with the idea of *static member functions* in C++. These are member functions defined inside a class that do not operate on objects. The main method in Java is always static. Finally, as in C/ C++, the void keyword indicates that this method does not return a value. Unlike C/ C++, the main method does not return an "exit code" to the operating system. If the main method exits normally, the Java program has the exit code 0, indicating successful completion. To terminate the program with a different exit code, call System.exit(code).

Now that you have seen the basic structure of all Java programs, turn your attention to the contents of the main method:

```
{
    System.out.println("We will not use 'Hello, World!'");
}
```

Braces mark the beginning and end of the *body* of the method. This method has only one statement in it. As with most programming languages, you can think of Java statements as sentences of the language. In Java, every statement must end with a semicolon. In particular, carriage returns do not mark the end of a statement, so statements can span multiple lines if need be.

The body of the main method contains a statement that outputs a single line of text to the console.

Here, we are using the System.out object and calling its println method. Notice the periods used to invoke a method. Java uses the general syntax

object.method(*arguments*)

as its equivalent of a function call.

In this case, the println method receives a string argument. The method displays the string argument on the console. It then terminates the output line, so that each call to println displays its output on a new line. Notice that Java, like C/C++, uses double quotes to delimit strings. (You can find more information about strings later in this chapter.)

Methods in Java, like functions in any programming language, can use zero, one, or more *arguments*. Even if a method has no arguments, you must still use empty parentheses. For example, a variant of the println method with no arguments just prints a blank line. You invoke it with the call

```
System.out.println();
```

Note: System.out also has a print method that doesn't add a newline character to the output. For example, System.out.print("Hello") prints Hello without a newline. The next output appears immediately after the letter o.

3.2. Comments

Comments in Java, as in most programming languages, do not show up in the executable program. Thus, you can add as many comments as needed without fear of bloating the code. Java has three ways of marking comments. The most common form is a //. Use this for a comment that runs from the // to the end of the line.

```
System.out.println("We will not use 'Hello, World!'"); // is this too cute?
```

When longer comments are needed, you can mark each line with a //, or you can use the /* and */ comment delimiters that let you block off a longer comment.

Finally, a third kind of comment is used to generate documentation automatically. This comment uses a /** to start and a */ to end. You can see this type of comment in Listing

3.1. For more on this type of comment and on automatic documentation generation, see Chapter 4.

Listing 3.1 FirstSample/FirstSample.java

```
 1  /**
 2   * This is the first sample program in Core Java Chapter 3
 3   * @version 1.01 1997-03-22
 4   * @author Gary Cornell
 5   */
 6  public class FirstSample
 7  {
 8     public static void main(String[] args)
 9     {
10        System.out.println("We will not use 'Hello, World!'");
11     }
12  }
```

 Caution: /* */ comments do not nest in Java. That is, you might not be able to deactivate code simply by surrounding it with /* and */ because the code you want to deactivate might itself contain a */ delimiter.

3.3. Data Types

Java is a *strongly typed language*. This means that every variable must have a declared type. There are eight *primitive types* in Java. Four of them are integer types; two are floating-point number types; one is the character type char, used for UTF-16 code units in the Unicode encoding scheme (see Section 3.3.3); and one is a boolean type for truth values.

 Note: Java has an arbitrary-precision arithmetic package. However, "big numbers," as they are called, are Java *objects* and not a primitive Java type. You will see how to use them later in this chapter.

3.3.1. Integer Types

The integer types are for numbers without fractional parts. Negative values are allowed. Java provides the four integer types shown in Table 3.1.

Table 3.1: Java Integer Types

Type	Storage Requirement	Range (Inclusive)
byte	1 byte	–128 to 127
short	2 bytes	–32,768 to 32,767
int	4 bytes	–2,147,483,648 to 2,147,483,647 (just over 2 billion)
long	8 bytes	–9,223,372,036,854,775,808 to 9,223,372,036,854,775,807

In most situations, the int type is the most practical. If you want to represent the number of inhabitants of our planet, you'll need to resort to a long. The byte and short types are mainly intended for specialized applications, such as low-level file handling, or for large arrays when storage space is at a premium.

Under Java, the ranges of the integer types do not depend on the machine on which you will be running the Java code. This alleviates a major pain for the programmer who wants to move software from one platform to another, or even between operating systems on the same platform. In contrast, C and C++ programs use the most efficient integer type for each processor. As a result, a C program that runs well on a 32-bit processor may exhibit integer overflow on a 16-bit system. Since Java programs must run with the same results on all machines, the ranges for the various types are fixed.

Long integer numbers have a suffix L or l (for example, 4000000000L). Hexadecimal numbers have a prefix 0x or 0X (for example, 0xCAFE). Octal numbers have a prefix 0 (for example, 010 is 8)—naturally, this can be confusing, and few programmers use octal constants.

You can write numbers in binary, with a prefix 0b or 0B. For example, 0b1001 is 9. You can add underscores to number literals, such as 1_000_000 (or 0b1111_0100_0010_0100_0000) to denote one million. The underscores are for human eyes only. The Java compiler simply removes them.

 C++ Note: In C and C++, the sizes of types such as int and long depend on the target platform. On a 16-bit processor such as the 8086, integers are 2 bytes, but on a 32-bit processor like a Pentium or SPARC they are 4-byte quantities. Similarly, long values are 4-byte on 32-bit processors and 8-byte on 64-bit processors. These differences make it challenging to write cross-platform programs. In Java, the sizes of all numeric types are platform-independent.

Note that Java does not have any unsigned versions of the int, long, short, or byte types.

 Note: If you work with integer values that can never be negative and you really need an additional bit, you can, with some care, interpret signed integer values as unsigned. For example, instead of having a byte value b represent the range from –128 to 127, you may want a range from 0 to 255. You can store it in a byte. Due to the nature of binary arithmetic, addition, subtraction, and multiplication will work provided they don't overflow. For other operations, call Byte.toUnsignedInt(b) to get an int value between 0 and 255, then process the integer value and cast back to byte. The Integer and Long classes have methods for unsigned division and remainder.

3.3.2. Floating-Point Types

The floating-point types denote numbers with fractional parts. The two floating-point types are shown in Table 3.2.

Table 3.2: Floating-Point Types

Type	Storage Requirement	Range
float	4 bytes	Approximately $\pm 3.40282347 \times 10^{38}$ (6–7 significant decimal digits)
double	8 bytes	Approximately $\pm 1.79769313486231570 \times 10^{308}$ (15 significant decimal digits)

The name double refers to the fact that these numbers have twice the precision of the float type. (Some people call these *double-precision* numbers.) The limited precision of float (6-7 significant digits) is simply not sufficient for many situations. Use float values only when you work with a library that requires them, or when you need to store a very large number of them.

Java 20 adds a couple of methods (Float.floatToFloat16 and Float.float16toFloat) for storing "half-precision" 16-bit floating-point numbers in short values. These are used for implementating neural networks.

Numbers of type float have a suffix F or f (for example, 3.14F). Floating-point numbers without an F suffix (such as 3.14) are always considered to be of type double. You can optionally supply the D or d suffix (for example, 3.14D).

An E or e denotes a decimal exponent. For example, 1.729E3 is the same as 1729.

Note: You can specify floating-point literals in hexadecimal. For example, $0.125 = 2^{-3}$ can be written as 0x1.0p-3. In hexadecimal notation, you use a p, not an e, to denote the exponent. (An e is a hexadecimal digit.) Note that the mantissa is written in hexadecimal and the exponent in decimal. The base of the exponent is 2, not 10.

All floating-point computations follow the IEEE 754 specification. In particular, there are three special floating-point values to denote overflows and errors:

- Positive infinity
- Negative infinity
- NaN (not a number)

For example, the result of dividing a positive floating-point number by 0 is positive infinity. Dividing 0.0 by 0 or the square root of a negative number yields NaN.

Note: The constants Double.POSITIVE_INFINITY, Double.NEGATIVE_INFINITY, and Double.NaN (as well as corresponding Float constants) represent these special values, but they are rarely used in practice. In particular, you cannot test

```
if (x == Double.NaN) // is never true
```

to check whether a particular result equals Double.NaN. All "not a number" values are considered distinct. However, you can use the Double.isNaN method:

```
if (Double.isNaN(x)) // check whether x is "not a number"
```

Caution: Floating-point numbers are *not* suitable for financial calculations in which roundoff errors cannot be tolerated. For example, the command System.out.println(2.0 - 1.1) prints 0.8999999999999999, not 0.9 as you would expect. Such roundoff errors are caused by the fact that floating-point numbers are represented in the binary number system. There is no precise binary representation of the fraction 1/10, just as there is no accurate representation of the fraction 1/3 in the decimal system. If you need precise numerical computations without roundoff errors, use the BigDecimal class, which is introduced later in this chapter.

3.3.3. The char Type

The char type was originally intended to describe individual characters. However, this is no longer the case. Nowadays, some Unicode characters can be described with one char value, and other Unicode characters require two char values. Read the next section for the gory details.

Literal values of type char are enclosed in single quotes. For example, 'A' is a character constant with value 65. It is different from "A", a string containing a single character. Values of type char can be expressed as hexadecimal values that run from \u0000 to \uFFFF.

Besides the \u escape sequences, there are several escape sequences for special characters, as shown in Table 3.3. You can use these escape sequences inside quoted character literals and strings, such as '\u005B' or "Hello\n". The \u escape sequence (but none of the other escape sequences) can even be used *outside* quoted character constants and strings. For example,

```
public static void main(String\u005B\u005D args)
```

is perfectly legal—\u005B and \u005D are the encodings for [and].

Table 3.3: Escape Sequences for Special Characters

Escape Sequence	Name	Unicode Value
\b	Backspace	\u0008
\t	Tab	\u0009
\n	Line feed	\u000a
\r	Carriage return	\u000d
\f	Form feed	\u000c
\"	Double quote	\u0022
\'	Single quote	\u0027
\\	Backslash	\u005c
\s	Space. Used in text blocks to retain trailing whitespace.	\u0020
\newline	In text blocks only: Join this line with the next	—

Caution: Unicode escape sequences are processed before the code is parsed. For example, "\u0022+\u0022" is *not* a string consisting of a plus sign surrounded by quotation marks (U+0022). Instead, the \u0022 are converted into " before parsing, yielding ""+"", or an empty string.

Even more insidiously, you must beware of \u inside comments. The comment

```
// \u000A is a newline
```

yields a syntax error since \u000A is replaced with a newline when the program is read. Similarly, a comment

```
// look inside c:\users
```

yields a syntax error because the \u is not followed by four hex digits.

Note: You can have any number of u in a Unicode escape sequence: \u00E9 and \uuu00E9 both denote the character é. There is a reason for this oddity. Consider a programmer happily coding in Unicode who is forced, for some archaic reason, to check in code as ASCII only. A conversion tool can turn any character > U+007F into a Unicode escape and add a u to every existing Unicode escape. That makes the conversion reversible. For example, \uD800 é is turned into \uuD800 \u00E9 and can be converted back to \uD800 é.

3.3.4. Unicode and the char Type

To fully understand the char type, you have to know about the Unicode encoding scheme. Before Unicode, there were many different character encoding standards: ASCII in the United States, ISO 8859-1 for Western European languages, KOI-8 for Russian, GB18030 and BIG-5 for Chinese, and so on. This caused two problems. First, a particular code value corresponds to different letters in the different encoding schemes. Second, the encodings for languages with large character sets have variable length: Some common characters are encoded as single bytes, others require two or more bytes.

Unicode was designed to solve both problems. When the unification effort started in the 1980s, a fixed 2-byte code was more than sufficient to encode all characters used in all languages in the world, with room to spare for future expansion—or so everyone thought at the time. In 1991, Unicode 1.0 was released, using slightly less than half of the available 65,536 code values. Java was designed from the ground up to use 16-bit Unicode characters, which was a major advance over other programming languages that used 8-bit characters.

Unfortunately, over time, the inevitable happened. Unicode grew beyond 65,536 characters, primarily due to the addition of a very large set of ideographs used for Chinese, Japanese, and Korean. Now, the 16-bit char type is insufficient to describe all Unicode characters.

We need a bit of terminology to explain how this problem is resolved in Java. A *code point* is an integer value associated with a character in an encoding scheme. In the Unicode standard, code points are written in hexadecimal and prefixed with U+, such as U+0041 for the code point of the Latin letter A. Unicode has code points that are grouped into 17 *code planes*, each holding 65536 characters. The first code plane, called the *basic multilingual plane*, consists of the "classic" Unicode characters with code points U+0000 to U+FFFF. Sixteen additional planes, with code points U+10000 to U+10FFFF, hold many more characters called *supplementary* characters.

How a Unicode code point (that is, an integer ranging from 0 to hexadecimal 10FFF) is represented in bits depends on the *character encoding*. You could encode each character as a sequence of 21 bits, but that is impractical for computer hardware. The UTF-32 encoding simply places each code point into 32 bits, where the top 11 bits are zero. That is rather wasteful. The most common encoding on the Internet is UTF-8, using between one and four bytes per character. See Chapter 2 of Volume II for details of that encoding.

Java strings use the UTF-16 encoding. It encodes all Unicode code points in a variable-length code of 16-bit units, called *code units*. The characters in the basic multilingual plane are encoded as a single code unit. All other characters are encoded as consecutive pairs of code units. Each of the code units in such an encoding pair falls into a range of 2048 unused values of the basic multilingual plane, called the *surrogates area* ('\uD800' to '\uDBFF' for the first code unit, '\uDC00' to '\uDFFF' for the second code unit). This is rather clever, because you can immediately tell whether a code unit encodes a single character or it is the first or second part of a supplementary character. For example, the beer mug emoji 🍺 has code point U+1F37A and is encoded by the two code units '\uD83C' and '\uDF7A'. (See https://tools.ietf.org/html/rfc2781 for a description of the encoding algorithm.) Each code unit is stored as a char value. The details are not important. All you need to know is that a single Unicode character may require one or two char values.

You cannot ignore characters with code units above U+FFFF. Your customers may well write in a language where these characters are needed, or they may be fond of putting emojis such as 🍺 into their messages.

Nowadays, Unicode has become so complex that even code points no longer correspond to what a human viewer would perceive as a single character or symbol. This happens with languages whose characters are made from smaller building blocks, with emojis that can have modifiers for gender and skin tone, and with an ever-growing number of other compositions.

Consider the Italian flag 🇮🇹. You perceive a single symbol: the flag. However, this symbol is composed of two Unicode code points: U+1F1EE (regional indicator symbol letter I) and U+1F1F9 (regional indicator symbol letter T). About 250 flags can be formed with these regional indicators. The pirate flag 🏴‍☠️, on the other hand, is composed of U+1F3F4 (waving black flag), U+200D (zero width joiner), U+2620 (skull and crossbones), and U+FE0F (variation selector-16). In Java, you need four char values to represent the first flag, five for the second.

In summary, a visible character or symbol is encoded as a sequence of some number of char values, and there is almost never a need to look at the individual values. Always work with strings (see Section 3.6) and don't worry about their representation as char sequences.

3.3.5. The boolean Type

The boolean type has two values, false and true. It is used for evaluating logical conditions. You cannot convert between integers and boolean values.

 C++ Note: In C++, numbers and even pointers can be used in place of boolean values. The value 0 is equivalent to the bool value false, and a nonzero value is equivalent to true. This is *not* the case in Java. Thus, Java programmers are shielded from accidents such as

```
if (x = 0) // oops... meant x == 0
```

In C++, this test compiles and runs, always evaluating to false. In Java, the test does not compile because the integer expression x = 0 cannot be converted to a boolean value.

3.4. Variables and Constants

As in every programming language, variables are used to store values. Constants are variables whose values don't change. In the following sections, you will learn how to declare variables and constants.

3.4.1. Declaring Variables

In Java, every variable has a *type*. You declare a variable by placing the type first, followed by the name of the variable. Here are some examples:

```
double salary;
int vacationDays;
long earthPopulation;
boolean done;
```

Notice the semicolon at the end of each declaration. The semicolon is necessary because a declaration is a complete Java statement, which must end in a semicolon.

The identifier for a variable name (as well as for other names) is made up of letters, digits, currency symbols, and "punctuation connectors." The first character cannot be a digit.

Symbols like '+' or '©' cannot be used inside variable names, nor can spaces. Letter case is significant: main and Main are distinct identifiers. The length of an identifier is essentially unlimited.

The terms "letter," "digit," and "currency symbol" are much broader in Java than in most languages. A letter is *any* Unicode character that denotes a letter in a language. For example, German users can use umlauts such as å in variable names; Greek speakers could use a π. Similarly, digits are 0–9 and *any* Unicode characters that denote a digit. Currency symbols are $, €, ¥, and so on. Punctuation connectors include the underscore character _, a "wavy low line" ﹏, and a few others. In practice, most programmers stick to A-Z, a-z, 0-9, and the underscore _.

 Tip: If you are really curious as to what Unicode characters can be used in identifiers, you can use the isJavaIdentifierStart and isJavaIdentifierPart methods in the Character class to check.

 Tip: Even though $ is a valid character in an identifier, you should not use it in your own code. It is intended for names that are generated by the Java compiler and other tools.

You also cannot use a Java keyword such as class as a variable name.

Underscores can be parts of identifiers. This is common for constant names, such as Double.POSITIVE_INFINITY. However, a single underscore _ is a reserved word.

 Preview Note: As of Java 21, a single underscore _ denotes a variable that is syntactically required but never used. You will see examples in Chapters 6 and 7.

You can declare multiple variables on a single line:

```
int i, j; // both are integers
```

I don't recommend this style. If you declare each variable separately, your programs are easier to read.

 Note: As you saw, names are case sensitive, for example, hireday and hireDay are two separate names. In general, you should not have two names that only differ in their letter case. However, sometimes it is difficult to come up with a good name for a variable. Many programmers then give the variable the same name as the type, for example

```
Box box; // "Box" is the type and "box" is the variable name
```

Other programmers prefer to use an "a" prefix for the variable:

```
Box aBox;
```

3.4.2. Initializing Variables

After you declare a variable, you must explicitly initialize it by means of an assignment statement—you can never use the value of an uninitialized variable. For example, the Java compiler flags the following sequence of statements as an error:

```
int vacationDays;
System.out.println(vacationDays); // ERROR--variable not initialized
```

You assign to a previously declared variable by using the variable name on the left, an equal sign (=), and then some Java expression with an appropriate value on the right.

```
int vacationDays;
vacationDays = 12;
```

You can both declare and initialize a variable on the same line. For example:

```
int vacationDays = 12;
```

Finally, in Java you can put declarations anywhere in your code. For example, the following is valid code in Java:

```
double salary = 65000.0;
System.out.println(salary);
int vacationDays = 12; // OK to declare a variable here
```

In Java, it is considered good style to declare variables as closely as possible to the point where they are first used.

 Note: You do not need to declare the types of local variables if they can be inferred from the initial value. Simply use the keyword var instead of the type:

```
var vacationDays = 12; // vacationDays is an int
var greeting = "Hello"; // greeting is a String
```

This is not too important for number and string types, but, as you will see in the next chapter, this feature can make the declaration of objects less verbose.

 C++ Note: C and C++ distinguish between the *declaration* and *definition* of a variable. For example,

```
int i = 10;
```

is a definition, whereas

```
extern int i;
```

is a declaration. In Java, no declarations are separate from definitions.

3.4.3. Constants

In Java, you use the keyword final to denote a constant. For example:

```
public class Constants
{
   public static void main(String[] args)
   {
      final double CM_PER_INCH = 2.54;
      double paperWidth = 8.5;
      double paperHeight = 11;
      System.out.println("Paper size in centimeters: "
         + paperWidth * CM_PER_INCH + " by " + paperHeight * CM_PER_INCH);
   }
}
```

The keyword final indicates that you can assign to the variable once, and then its value is set once and for all. It is customary to name constants in all uppercase.

It is probably more common in Java to create a constant so it's available to multiple methods inside a single class. These are usually called *class constants*. Set up a class constant with the keywords static final. Here is an example of using a class constant:

```
public class Constants2
{
   public static final double CM_PER_INCH = 2.54;

   public static void main(String[] args)
   {
      double paperWidth = 8.5;
```

```
        double paperHeight = 11;
        System.out.println("Paper size in centimeters: "
           + paperWidth * CM_PER_INCH + " by " + paperHeight * CM_PER_INCH);
    }
}
```

Note that the definition of the class constant appears *outside* the main method. Thus, the constant can also be used in other methods of the same class. Furthermore, if the constant is declared, as in this example, public, methods of other classes can also use it—in our example, as Constants2.CM_PER_INCH.

 Caution: Some coding style guides state that uppercase letters should only be used for static final variables. If you need to follow such a style guide, and you have a local constant, decide what is more important to you—the fact that it is local (and lowercase), or that it is visibly a constant (static and uppercase).

 C++ Note: const is a Java keyword, but it is not currently used for anything. You must use final for a constant.

3.4.4. Enumerated Types

Sometimes, a variable should only hold a restricted set of values. For example, you may sell clothes or pizza in four sizes: small, medium, large, and extra large. Of course, you could encode these sizes as integers 1, 2, 3, 4 or characters S, M, L, and X. But that is an error-prone setup. It is too easy for a variable to hold a wrong value (such as 0 or m).

You can define your own *enumerated type* whenever such a situation arises. An enumerated type has a finite number of named values. For example,

```
enum Size { SMALL, MEDIUM, LARGE, EXTRA_LARGE };
```

Now you can declare variables of this type:

```
Size s = Size.MEDIUM;
```

A variable of type Size can hold only one of the values listed in the type declaration, or the special value null that indicates that the variable is not set to any value at all. (See Chapter 4 for more information about null.)

Enumerated types are discussed in greater detail in Chapter 5.

3.5. Operators

Operators are used to combine values. As you will see in the following sections, Java has a rich set of arithmetic and logical operators and mathematical functions.

3.5.1. Arithmetic Operators

The usual arithmetic operators +, -, *, and / are used in Java for addition, subtraction, multiplication, and division.

The / operator denotes integer division if both operands are integers, and floating-point division otherwise. Integer division by 0 raises an exception, whereas floating-point division by 0 yields an infinite or NaN result.

Integer remainder (sometimes called *modulus*) is denoted by %. For example, 15 / 2 is 7, 15 % 2 is 1, and 15.0 / 2 is 7.5.

 Caution: When one of the operands of % is negative, so is the result. For example, n % 2 is 0 if n is even, 1 if n is odd and positive, and -1 if n is odd and negative. Why? When the first computers were built, someone had to make rules for how integer remainder should work for negative operands. Mathematicians had known the optimal (or "Euclidean") rule for a few hundred years: always leave the remainder ≥ 0. But, rather than open a math textbook, those pioneers came up with rules that seemed reasonable but are actually inconvenient.

Consider this problem. You compute the position of the hour hand of a clock. An adjustment is applied, and you want to normalize to a number between 0 and 11. That is easy: (position + adjustment) % 12. But what if the adjustment is negative? Then you might get a negative number. So you have to introduce a branch, or use ((position + adjustment) % 12 + 12) % 12. Either way, it is a hassle.

A better remedy is to use the floorMod method: Math.floorMod(position + adjustment, 12) always yields a value between 0 and 11. Unfortunately, floorMod still gives negative remainders for negative divisors, but that situation doesn't often occur in practice.

 Note: One of the stated goals of the Java programming language is portability. A computation should yield the same results no matter which virtual machine executes it. For arithmetic computations with floating-point numbers, it can be surprisingly difficult to achieve this portability. The double type uses 64 bits to store a numeric value, but some processors use 80-bit floating-point registers. These registers yield added precision in intermediate steps of a computation.

But the result may be *different* from a computation that uses 64 bits throughout. For perfect portability, the initial specification of the Java virtual machine mandated that all intermediate computations must be truncated to 64 bit. The numeric community hated it. The computations were *slower* because the truncation operations took time on popular processors. For that reason, the Java programming language was updated to recognize the conflicting demands for optimum performance and perfect reproducibility. Virtual machine designers were permitted to use extended precision for intermediate computations. However, methods tagged with the strictfp keyword had to use strict floating-point operations that yield reproducible results.

Processors have become more flexible, and they can now carry out 64-bit arithmetic efficiently. As of Java 17, the virtual machine is again required to carry out strict 64-bit arithmetic, and the strictfp keyword is now obsolete.

3.5.2. Mathematical Functions and Constants

The Math class contains an assortment of mathematical functions that you may occasionally need, depending on the kind of programming that you do.

To take the square root of a number, use the sqrt method:

```
double x = 4;
double y = Math.sqrt(x);
System.out.println(y); // prints 2.0
```

 Note: There is a subtle difference between the println method and the sqrt method. The println method operates on the System.out object. But the sqrt method in the Math class does not operate on any object. Such a method is called a *static* method. You can learn more about static methods in Chapter 4.

The Java programming language has no operator for raising a quantity to a power: You must use the pow method in the Math class. The statement

```
double y = Math.pow(x, a);
```

sets y to be x raised to the power a (x^a). The pow method's arguments are both of type double, and it returns a double as well.

The Math class supplies the usual trigonometric functions:

```
Math.sin
Math.cos
Math.tan
Math.atan
Math.atan2
```

and the exponential function with its inverse, the natural logarithm, as well as the decimal logarithm:

```
Math.exp
Math.log
Math.log10
```

Java 21 adds a method `Math.clamp` that forces a number to fit within given bounds. For example:

```
Math.clamp(-1, 0, 10) // too small, yields lower bound 0
Math.clamp(11, 0, 10) // too large, yields upper bound 10
Math.clamp(3, 0, 10) // within bounds, yields value 3
```

Finally, three constants denote the closest possible approximations to the mathematical constants π, $\tau = 2\pi$, and e:

```
Math.PI
Math.TAU
Math.E
```

Tip: You can avoid the `Math` prefix for the mathematical methods and constants by adding the following line to the top of your source file:

```
import static java.lang.Math.*;
```

For example:

```
System.out.println("The square root of π is " + sqrt(PI));
```

Static imports are covered in Chapter 4.

Note: The methods in the `Math` class use the routines in the computer's floating-point unit for fastest performance. If completely predictable results are more important than performance, use the `StrictMath` class instead. It implements the algorithms from the "Freely Distributable Math Library" (`https://www.netlib.org/fdlibm`), guaranteeing identical results on all platforms.

Note: The Math class provides several methods to make integer arithmetic safer. The mathematical operators quietly return wrong results when a computation overflows. For example, one billion times three (1000000000 * 3) evaluates to -1294967296 because the largest int value is just over two billion. If you call Math.multiplyExact(1000000000, 3) instead, an exception is generated. You can catch that exception or let the program terminate rather than quietly continue with a wrong result. There are also methods addExact, subtractExact, incrementExact, decrementExact, negateExact, and absExact, all with arguments of type int and long.

3.5.3. Conversions between Numeric Types

It is often necessary to convert from one numeric type to another. Figure 3.1 shows the legal conversions.

The six solid arrows in Figure 3.1 denote conversions without information loss. The three dotted arrows denote conversions that may lose precision. For example, a large integer such as 123456789 has more digits than the float type can represent. When the integer is converted to a float, the resulting value has the correct magnitude but loses some precision.

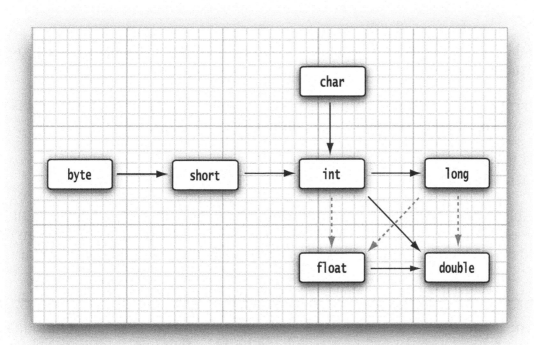

Figure 3.1: Legal conversions between numeric types

```
int n = 123456789;
float f = n; // f is 1.23456792E8
```

When two values are combined with a binary operator (such as n + f where n is an integer and f is a floating-point value), both operands are converted to a common type before the operation is carried out.

- If either of the operands is of type double, the other one will be converted to a double.
- Otherwise, if either of the operands is of type float, the other one will be converted to a float.
- Otherwise, if either of the operands is of type long, the other one will be converted to a long.
- Otherwise, both operands will be converted to an int.

3.5.4. Casts

In the preceding section, you saw that int values are automatically converted to double values when necessary. On the other hand, there are obviously times when you want to consider a double as an integer. Numeric conversions are possible in Java, but of course information may be lost. Conversions in which loss of information is possible are done by means of *casts*. The syntax for casting is to give the target type in parentheses, followed by the variable name. For example:

```
double x = 9.997;
int nx = (int) x;
```

Now, the variable nx has the value 9 because casting a floating-point value to an integer discards the fractional part.

If you want to *round* a floating-point number to the *nearest* integer (which in most cases is a more useful operation), use the Math.round method:

```
double x = 9.997;
int nx = (int) Math.round(x);
```

Now the variable nx has the value 10. You still need to use the cast (int) when you call round. The reason is that the return value of the round method is a long, and a long can only be assigned to an int with an explicit cast because there is the possibility of information loss.

 Caution: If you try to cast a number of one type to another that is out of range for the target type, the result will be a truncated number that has a different value. For example, (byte) 300 is actually 44.

C++ Note: You cannot cast between boolean values and any numeric type. This convention prevents common errors. In the rare case when you want to convert a boolean value to a number, you can use a conditional expression such as b ? 1 : 0.

3.5.5. Assignment

There is a convenient shortcut for using binary operators in an assignment. For example, the *compound assignment operator*

```
x += 4;
```

is equivalent to

```
x = x + 4;
```

(In general, place the operator to the left of the = sign, such as *= or %=.)

 Caution: If a compound assignment operator yields a value whose type is different from that of the left-hand side, then it is coerced to fit. For example, if x is an int, then the statement

```
x += 3.5;
```

is valid. It sets x to (int)(x + 3.5), that is, x + 3, with no warning!

As of Java 20, you get a warning if you compile with the -Xlint command line option.

Note that in Java, an assignment is an *expression*. That is, it has a value—namely, the value that is being assigned. You can use that value—for example, to assign it to another variable. Consider these statements:

```
int x = 1;
int y = x += 4;
```

The value of x += 4 is 5, since that's the value that is being assigned to x. Next, that value is assigned to y.

Many programmers find such nested assignments confusing and prefer to write them more clearly, like this:

```
int x = 1;
x += 4;
int y = x;
```

3.5.6. Increment and Decrement Operators

Programmers, of course, know that one of the most common operations with a numeric variable is to add or subtract 1. Java, following in the footsteps of C and C++, has both increment and decrement operators: n++ adds 1 to the current value of the variable n, and n-- subtracts 1 from it. For example, the code

```
int n = 12;
n++;
```

changes n to 13. Since these operators change the value of a variable, they cannot be applied to numbers themselves. For example, 4++ is not a legal statement.

There are two forms of these operators; you've just seen the postfix form of the operator that is placed after the operand. There is also a prefix form, ++n. Both change the value of the variable by 1. The difference between the two appears only when they are used inside expressions. The prefix form does the addition first; the postfix form evaluates to the old value of the variable.

```
int m = 7;
int n = 7;
int a = 2 * ++m; // now a is 16, m is 8
int b = 2 * n++; // now b is 14, n is 8
```

Many programmers find this behavior confusing. In Java, using ++ inside expressions is uncommon.

3.5.7. Relational and boolean Operators

Java has the full complement of relational operators. To test for equality, use a double equal sign, ==. For example, the value of

```
3 == 7
```

is false.

Use a != for inequality. For example, the value of

```
3 != 7
```

is true.

Finally, you have the usual < (less than), > (greater than), <= (less than or equal), and >= (greater than or equal) operators.

Java, following C++, uses && for the logical "and" operator and || for the logical "or" operator. As you can easily remember from the != operator, the exclamation point ! is the logical negation operator. The && and || operators are evaluated in "short circuit" fashion: The second operand is not evaluated if the first operand already determines the value. If you combine two expressions with the && operator,

*expression*₁ && *expression*₂

and the truth value of the first expression has been determined to be false, then it is impossible for the result to be true. Thus, the value for the second expression is *not* calculated. This behavior can be exploited to avoid errors. For example, in the expression

```
x != 0 && 1 / x > x + y // no division by 0
```

the second operand is never evaluated if x equals zero. Thus, 1 / x is not computed if x is zero, and no divide-by-zero error can occur.

Similarly, the value of *expression*₁ || *expression*₂ is automatically true if the first expression is true, without evaluating the second expression.

3.5.8. The Conditional Operator

Java provides the *conditional* ?: operator that selects a value, depending on a Boolean expression. The expression

condition ? *expression*₁ : *expression*₂

evaluates to the first expression if the condition is true, and to the second expression otherwise. For example,

```
x < y ? x : y
```

gives the smaller of x and y.

3.5.9. Switch Expressions

If you need to choose among more than two values, then you can use a switch expression, which was introduced in Java 14. It looks like this:

```
String seasonName = switch (seasonCode)
   {
      case 0 -> "Spring";
      case 1 -> "Summer";
      case 2 -> "Fall";
      case 3 -> "Winter";
      default -> "???";
   };
```

The expression following the switch keyword is called the *selector expression*, and its value is the *selector*. For now, we only consider selectors and case labels that are integral types (int, char, byte, or short), strings, or constants of an enumerated type. In Chapter 5, you will see how to use switch expressions with other types for *pattern matching*.

 Note: The switch expression, like every expression, has a value. Note the -> arrow preceding the value in each branch.

 Note: As of Java 14, there are four (!) forms of switch. This section focuses on the most useful one. See Section 3.8.5 for a thorough discussion of all forms of switch expressions and statements.

A case label must be a compile-time constant whose type matches the selector type. You can provide multiple labels for each case, separated by commas:

```
int numLetters = switch (seasonName)
   {
      case "Spring", "Summer", "Winter" -> 6;
      case "Fall" -> 4;
      default -> -1;
   };
```

When you use the switch expression with enumerated constants, you need not supply the name of the enumeration in each label—it is deduced from the switch value. For example:

```
enum Size { SMALL, MEDIUM, LARGE, EXTRA_LARGE };
. . .
Size itemSize = . . .;
String label = switch (itemSize)
   {
      case SMALL -> "S"; // no need to use Size.SMALL
      case MEDIUM -> "M";
      case LARGE -> "L";
      case EXTRA_LARGE -> "XL";
   };
```

In the example, it was legal to omit the default since there was a case for each possible value.

Caution: When the selector is an `enum`, and you don't have cases for all constants, you need a default. A `switch` expression with an integer or `String` selector must always have a default.

 Caution: If the selector is `null`, a `NullPointerException` is thrown. If you want to avoid this possibility, add a `case null`, like this:

```
String label = switch (itemSize)
   {
      . . .
      case null -> "???";
   };
```

This is a feature of Java 21. Note that `default` does *not* match `null`!

3.5.10. Bitwise Operators

For any of the integer types, you have operators that can work directly with the bits that make up the integers. This means that you can use masking techniques to get at individual bits in a number. The bitwise operators are

```
& ("and")   | ("or")   ^ ("xor")   ~ ("not")
```

These operators work on bit patterns. For example, if `n` is an integer variable, then

```
int fourthBitFromRight = (n & 0b1000) / 0b1000;
```

gives you a 1 if the fourth bit from the right in the binary representation of `n` is 1, and 0 otherwise. Using `&` with the appropriate power of 2 lets you mask out all but a single bit.

 Note: When applied to `boolean` values, the `&` and `|` operators yield a `boolean` value. These operators are similar to the `&&` and `||` operators, except that the `&` and `|` operators are not evaluated in "short circuit" fashion—that is, both operands are evaluated before the result is computed.

There are also `>>` and `<<` operators which shift a bit pattern right or left. These operators are convenient when you need to build up bit patterns to do bit masking:

```
int fourthBitFromRight = (n & (1 << 3)) >> 3;
```

Finally, a `>>>` operator fills the top bits with zero, unlike `>>` which extends the sign bit into the top bits. There is no `<<<` operator.

Caution: The right-hand operand of the shift operators is reduced modulo 32 (unless the left-hand operand is a long, in which case the right-hand operand is reduced modulo 64). For example, the value of 1 << 35 is the same as 1 << 3 or 8.

 C++ Note: In C/C++, there is no guarantee as to whether >> performs an arithmetic shift (extending the sign bit) or a logical shift (filling in with zeroes). Implementors are free to choose whichever is more efficient. That means the C/C++ >> operator may yield implementation-dependent results for negative numbers. Java removes that uncertainty.

 Note: The Integer class has a number of static methods for bit-level operations. For example, Integer.bitCount(n) yields the number of bits that are 1 in the binary representation of n, and Integer.reverse(n) yields the number obtained by reversing the bits of n. Not many programmers need bit-level operations, but if you do, have a look at the Integer class to see whether there is a method for the task that you need to accomplish.

3.5.11. Parentheses and Operator Hierarchy

Table 3.4 shows the precedence of operators. If no parentheses are used, operations are performed in the hierarchical order indicated. Operators on the same level are processed from left to right, except for those that are right-associative, as indicated in the table. For example, && has a higher precedence than ||, so the expression

    a && b || c

means

    (a && b) || c

Since += associates right to left, the expression

    a += b += c

means

    a += (b += c)

That is, the value of b += c (which is the value of b after the addition) is added to a.

Table 3.4: Operator Precedence

Operators	Associativity
[] . () (method call)	Left to right
! ~ ++ -- + (unary) - (unary) () (cast) new	Right to left
* / %	Left to right
+ -	Left to right
<< >> >>>	Left to right
< <= > >= instanceof	Left to right
== !=	Left to right
&	Left to right
^	Left to right
|	Left to right
&&	Left to right
||	Left to right
?:	Right to left
= += -= *= /= %= &= |= ^= <<= >>= >>>=	Right to left

C++ Note: Unlike C or C++, Java does not have a comma operator. However, you can use a *comma-separated list of expressions* in the first and third slot of a for statement (see Section 3.8.4).

3.6. Strings

Conceptually, Java strings are sequences of Unicode characters. As you have seen in Section 3.3.4, the concept of what exactly a character is has become complicated. And the encoding of the characters into char values has also become complicated.

However, most of the time, you don't care. You get strings from string literals or from methods, and you operate on them with methods of the String class. The following sections cover the details.

Note: You have already seen string *literals* such as "Hello, World!", which are instances of the String class.

To include "complicated" characters in string literals, be sure that you use the UTF-8 encoding for source files (which is the default for most IDEs). Then you can just paste them from web pages, and produce string literals such as "Ciao ".

In the past, programmers were more concerned that their collaborators might use a different file encoding, and instead provided escape sequences for the UTF-16 encoding: "Ciao \uD83C\uDDEE\uD83C\uDDF9".

3.6.1. Concatenation

Java, like most programming languages, allows you to use + to join (concatenate) two strings.

```
String expletive = "Expletive";
String PG13 = "deleted";
String message = expletive + PG13;
```

The preceding code sets the variable message to the string "Expletivedeleted". (Note the lack of a space between the words: The + operator joins two strings in the order received, *exactly* as they are given.)

When you concatenate a string with a value that is not a string, the latter is converted to a string. For example,

```
int age = 13;
String rating = "PG" + age;
```

sets rating to the string "PG13".

This feature is commonly used in output statements. For example,

```
System.out.println("The answer is " + answer);
```

is perfectly acceptable and prints what you would expect (and with correct spacing because of the space after the word is).

 Caution: Beware of string concatenations with expressions that have a + operator, such as:

```
int age = 42;
String output = "Next year, you'll be " + age + 1 + "."; // ERROR
```

Because the + operators are evaluated from left to right, the result is "Next year, you'll be 421.". The remedy is to use parentheses:

```
String output = "Next year, you'll be " + (age + 1) + "."; // OK
```

If you need to put multiple strings together, separated by a delimiter, use the static join method:

```
String all = String.join(" / ", "S", "M", "L", "XL");
    // all is the string "S / M / L / XL"
```

The repeat method produces a string that repeats a given string a number of times:

```
String repeated = "Java".repeat(3); // repeated is "JavaJavaJava"
```

3.6.2. Splitting Strings

The split method splits a string into parts along a given boundary. For example,

```
"Hello, World!".split(" ")
```

yields an array with two elements: the strings "Hello," and "World!". (Arrays are introduced in Section 3.10.)

The argument of the split method is a *regular expression*, describing where the splits should occur. See Chapter 2 of Volume II for a detailed discussion of regular expressions. Table 3.5 has some useful patterns.

Table 3.5: Splitting Patterns

Pattern	Description
"\\s+"	Whitespace
"\\s*,\\s*"	Comma with optional whitespace
"\\."	Period
\\PL+	Any non-letters
"\\R"	Line breaks
"\\b"	Word boundaries

| "\\b{g}" | Grapheme cluster boundaries (since Java 9) |

Splitting along *grapheme cluster* boundaries breaks a string into what humans perceive as the constituent characters:

```
"Ciao 🏳".split("\\b{g}")
    // An array with the six elements "C", "i", "a", "o", " ", "🏳"
```

3.6.3. Indexes and Substrings

Java strings are sequences of char values. As you saw in Section 3.3.4, the char data type is used for representing Unicode code points in the UTF-16 encoding. Some characters can be represented with a single char value, but many characters and symbols require more than one char value.

 Note: The virtual machine is not required to store strings as sequences of char values. For efficiency, strings that hold only single-byte code units store byte sequences, and all others char sequences. This is an implementation detail that has changed in the past and may again change in the future.

The length method yields the number of char values required for a given string. For example:

```
String greeting = "Ciao 🏳";
int n = greeting.length(); // is 9
```

The call s.charAt(n) returns the char value at position n, where n is between 0 and s.length() – 1. (Like C and C++, Java counts positions in a string starting with 0.) For example:

```
char first = greeting.charAt(0); // first is 67 or 'C'
char last = greeting.charAt(8); // last is 56825
```

However, these calls are not very useful. The last char value is just a part of the flag symbol, and you won't generally care what these values are.

Still, you sometimes need to know where a substring is located in a string. Use the indexOf method:

```
String sub = " ";
int start = greeting.indexOf(sub); // 4
```

As it happens, the position or *index* of the space is 4, but the exact value doesn't matter. It depends on the characters preceding the substring, and the number of char values needed to encode each of them. Always treat an index as an opaque number, not the count of perceived characters preceding it.

You can compute where the next character starts:

```
int nextStart = start + sub.length(); // 5
```

As it happens, the string " " has length 1, but do not hard-code the length of a string. Always use the length method instead.

You can extract a substring from a larger string with the substring method of the String class. For example,

```
String greeting = "Hello, World!";
int n = greeting.indexOf(",")
String s = greeting.substring(0, n);
```

creates a string consisting of the characters "Hello".

The second argument of substring is the first position that you *do not* want to copy. In our case, we copy everything from the beginning up to, but not including, the comma.

Note that the string s.substring(a, b) always has length $b - a$. For example, the substring "Hello" has length $5 - 0 = 5$.

3.6.4. Strings Are Immutable

The String class gives no methods that let you *change* a character in an existing string. If you want to turn greeting into "Help!", you cannot directly change the last positions of greeting into 'p' and '!'. If you are a C programmer, this can make you feel pretty helpless. How are we going to modify the string? In Java, it is quite easy: Concatenate the substring that you want to keep with the characters that you want to replace.

```
String greeting = "Hello";
int n = greeting.indexOf("lo");
greeting = greeting.substring(0, n) + "p!";
```

This declaration changes the current value of the greeting variable to "Help!".

Since you cannot change the individual characters in a Java string, the documentation refers to the objects of the String class as *immutable*. Just as the number 3 is always 3, the string "Hello" will always contain the code-unit sequence for the characters H, e, l, l, o. You cannot change these values. Yet you can, as you just saw, change the contents of the string *variable* greeting and make it refer to a different string, just as you can make a numeric variable currently holding the value 3 hold the value 4.

Isn't that a lot less efficient? It would seem simpler to change the characters than to build up a whole new string from scratch. Well, yes and no. Indeed, it is some amount of work to generate a new string that holds the concatenation of "Hel" and "p!". But immutable strings have one great advantage: The compiler can arrange that strings are *shared*.

To understand how this works, think of the various strings as sitting in a common pool. String variables then point to locations in the pool. If you copy a string variable, both the original and the copy share the same characters.

Overall, the designers of Java decided that the efficiency of sharing outweighs the inefficiency of string creation. Look at your own programs; most of the time, you probably don't change strings—you just compare them. (There is one common exception—assembling strings from individual characters or from shorter strings that come from the keyboard or a file. For these situations, Java provides a separate class—see Section 3.6.9.)

 C++ Note: C programmers are generally bewildered when they see Java strings for the first time because they think of strings as arrays of characters:

```
char greeting[] = "Hello";
```

That is a wrong analogy: A Java string is roughly analogous to a char* pointer,

```
char* greeting = "Hello";
```

When you replace greeting with another string, the Java code does roughly the following:

```
char* temp = malloc(6);
strncpy(temp, greeting, 3);
strncpy(temp + 3, "p!", 3);
greeting = temp;
```

Sure, now greeting points to the string "Help!". And even the most hardened C programmer must admit that the Java syntax is more pleasant than a sequence of strncpy calls. But what if we make another assignment to greeting?

```
greeting = "Howdy";
```

Don't we have a memory leak? After all, the original string was allocated on the heap. Fortunately, Java does automatic garbage collection. If a block of memory is no longer needed, it will eventually be recycled.

If you are a C++ programmer and use the string class defined by ANSI C++, you will be much more comfortable with the Java String type. C++ string objects also perform automatic allocation and deallocation of memory. The memory management is performed explicitly by constructors, assignment operators, and destructors. However, C++ strings are mutable—you can modify individual characters in a string.

3.6.5. Testing Strings for Equality

To test whether two strings are equal, use the equals method. The expression

```
s.equals(t)
```

returns true if the strings s and t are equal, false otherwise. Note that s and t can be string variables or string literals. For example, the expression

```
"Hello".equals(greeting)
```

is perfectly legal. To test whether two strings are identical except for the upper/lowercase letter distinction, use the equalsIgnoreCase method.

```
"Hello".equalsIgnoreCase("hello")
```

Do *not* use the == operator to test whether two strings are equal! It only determines whether or not the strings are stored in the same location. Sure, if strings are in the same location, they must be equal. But it is entirely possible to store multiple copies of identical strings in different places.

```
String greeting = "Hello"; // initialize greeting to a string
greeting == "Hello" // true
greeting.substring(0, greeting.indexOf("l")) == "He" // false
greeting.substring(0, greeting.indexOf("l")).equals("He") // true
```

If the virtual machine always arranges for equal strings to be shared, then you could use the == operator for testing equality. But only string *literals* are shared, not strings that are computed at runtime. Therefore, *never* use == to compare strings. Always use equals instead.

C++ Note: If you are used to the C++ string class, you have to be particularly careful about equality testing. The C++ string class overloads the == operator to test for equality of the string contents. In Java, strings appear at first glance to be similar to numbers. They have literal values and the + operator, but they are actually objects. As you will see in the next chapter, the == operator always checks whether two objects are identical.

C programmers know never to use == to compare char* strings but use strcmp instead. The Java method compareTo is the exact analog of strcmp. You can use

```
if (greeting.compareTo("Hello") == 0) . . .
```

but it seems clearer to use equals instead.

3.6.6. Empty and Null Strings

The empty string "" is a string of length 0. You can test whether a string is empty by calling

```
if (str.length() == 0)
```

or

```
if (str.equals(""))
```

or , for optimum efficiency

```
if (str.isEmpty())
```

An empty string is a Java object which holds the string length (namely, 0) and an empty contents. However, a String variable can also hold a special value, called null, that indicates that no object is currently associated with the variable. To test whether a string is null, use

```
if (str == null)
```

Sometimes, you need to test that a string is neither null nor empty. Then use

```
if (str != null && str.length() != 0)
```

You need to test that str is not null first. As you will see in Chapter 4, it is an error to invoke a method on a null value.

3.6.7. The String API

The String class in Java contains close to 100 methods. The following API note summarizes the most useful ones.

These API notes, found throughout the book, will help you understand the Java Application Programming Interface (API). Each API note starts with the name of a class, such as java.lang.String. (The significance of the so-called *package* name java.lang is explained in Chapter 4.) The class name is followed by the names, explanations, and parameter descriptions of one or more methods. A *parameter variable* of a method is the variable that receives a method argument. For example, as you will see in the first API note below, the charAt method has a parameter called index of type int. If you call the method, you supply an argument of that type, such as str.charAt(0).

The API notes do not list all methods of a particular class but present the most commonly used ones in a concise form. For a full listing, consult the online documentation (see Section 3.6.8).

The number following the class name is the JDK version number in which it was introduced. If a method has been added later, it has a separate version number.

---

java.lang.String 1.0

- char charAt(int index)
  returns the code unit at the specified location. You probably don't want to call this method unless you are interested in low-level code units.
- int length()
  returns the number of code units of the string.
- boolean equals(Object other)
  returns true if the string equals other.
- boolean equalsIgnoreCase(String other)
  returns true if the string equals other, except for upper/lowercase distinction.
- int compareTo(String other)
  returns a negative value if the string comes before other in dictionary order, a positive value if the string comes after other in dictionary order, or 0 if the strings are equal.
- boolean isEmpty() 6
  boolean isBlank() 11
  return true if the string is empty or consists of whitespace.
- boolean startsWith(String prefix)
- boolean endsWith(String suffix)
  return true if the string starts with prefix or ends with suffix.
- int indexOf(String str)
- int indexOf(String str, int fromIndex)
- int indexOf(String str, int fromIndex, int toIndex) 21
  return the start of the first substring equal to the string str, starting at index 0 or at fromIndex, and ending at the end of the string or at toIndex. Return -1 if str does not occur in this string or the specified substring.
- int lastIndexOf(String str)
- int lastIndexOf(String str, int fromIndex)
  return the start of the last substring equal to the string str, starting at the end of the string or at fromIndex, or -1 if str does not occur.
- String replace(CharSequence oldString, CharSequence newString)
  returns a new string that is obtained by replacing all substrings matching oldString in the string with the string newString. You can supply String or StringBuilder arguments for the CharSequence parameters.

- `String substring(int beginIndex)`
- `String substring(int beginIndex, int endIndex)`
  return a new string consisting of all code units from `beginIndex` until the end of the string or until `endIndex – 1`.
- `String toLowerCase()`
- `String toUpperCase()`
  return a new string containing all characters in the original string, with uppercase characters converted to lowercase, or lowercase characters converted to uppercase.
- `String strip()` **11**
  `String stripLeading()` **11**
  `String stripTrailing()` **11**

  return a new string by eliminating leading and trailing, or just leading or trailing whitespace in the original string. Use these methods instead of the archaic `trim` method that eliminates characters ≤ U+0020.
- `String join(CharSequence delimiter, CharSequence... elements)` **8**
  returns a new string joining all elements with the given delimiter.
- `String repeat(int count)` **11**
  returns a string that repeats this string `count` times.
- `String[] split(String regex)` **1.4**
  finds all matches of the regular expression and splits the string by removing them. Returns an array with the fragments, but not a trailing empty string.

 Note: In the API notes, there are a few parameters of type `CharSequence`. This is an *interface* type to which all strings belong. You will learn about interface types in Chapter 6. For now, you just need to know that you can pass arguments of type `String` whenever you see a `CharSequence` parameter.

3.6.8. Reading the Online API Documentation

As you just saw, the `String` class has lots of methods. Furthermore, there are thousands of classes in the standard libraries, with many more methods. It is plainly impossible to remember all useful classes and methods. Therefore, it is essential that you become familiar with the online API documentation that lets you look up all classes and methods in the standard library. You can download the API documentation from Oracle and save it locally, or you can point your browser to `https://docs.oracle.com/en/java/javase/21/docs/api`.

The API documentation has a search box (see Figure 3.2). Older versions have frames with lists of packages and classes. You can still get those lists by clicking on the Frames menu item. For example, to get more information on the methods of the `String` class, type "String" into the search box and select the type `java.lang.String`, or locate the link in the frame with class names and click it. You get the class description, as shown in Figure 3.3.

When you scroll down, you reach a summary of all methods, sorted in alphabetical order (see Figure 3.4). Click on any method name for a detailed description of that method (see

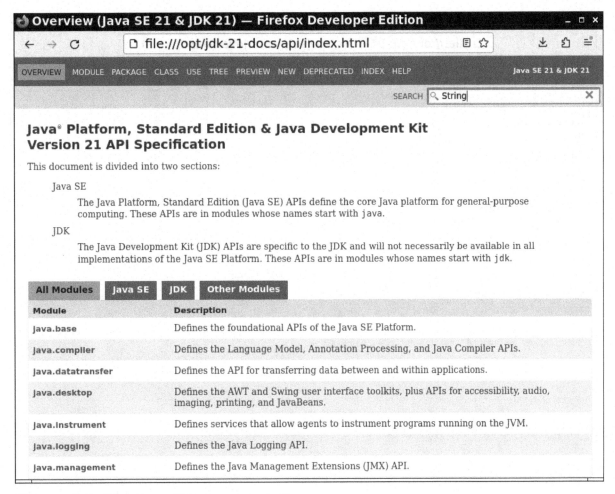

Figure 3.2: The Java API documentation

Figure 3.5). For example, if you click on the compareToIgnoreCase link, you'll get the description of the compareToIgnoreCase method.

 Tip: If you have not already done so, download the JDK documentation, as described in Chapter 2. Bookmark the index.html page of the documentation in your browser right now!

You can also add a new search engine to your browser with the query string

```
https://docs.oracle.com/en/java/javase/21/docs/api/search.html?q=%s
```

Figure 3.3: Class description for the String class

3.6.9. Building Strings

Occasionally, you need to build up strings from shorter strings, such as keystrokes or words from a file. It would be inefficient to use string concatenation for this purpose. Every time you concatenate strings, a new String object is constructed. This is time consuming and wastes memory. Using the StringBuilder class avoids this problem.

Follow these steps if you need to build a string from many small pieces. First, construct an empty string builder:

```
StringBuilder builder = new StringBuilder();
```

You can also provide initial content:

```
StringBuilder builder = new StringBuilder("INVOICE\n");
```

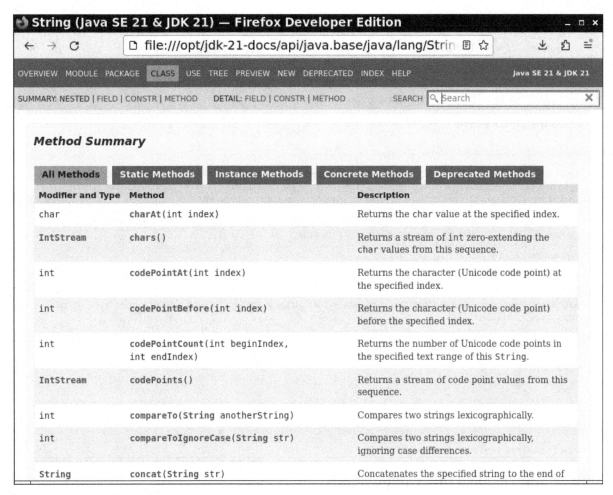

Figure 3.4: Method summary of the String class

Each time you need to add another part, call the append method.

```
builder.append(str); // appends a string
builder.appendCodePoint(cp); // appends a single code point
```

The latter method is occasionally useful when you need to compute a code point. Here is an example. Flag emojis are made up of two code points, each in the range between 127462 (regional indicator symbol letter A) to 127487 (regional indicator symbol letter Z). Now suppose you have a country string such as "IT". Then you can compute the code points as follows:

```
final int REGIONAL_INDICATOR_SYMBOL_LETTER_A = 127462;
String country = . . .;
builder.append(country.charAt(0) - 'A' + REGIONAL_INDICATOR_SYMBOL_LETTER_A);
builder.append(country.charAt(1) - 'A' + REGIONAL_INDICATOR_SYMBOL_LETTER_A);
```

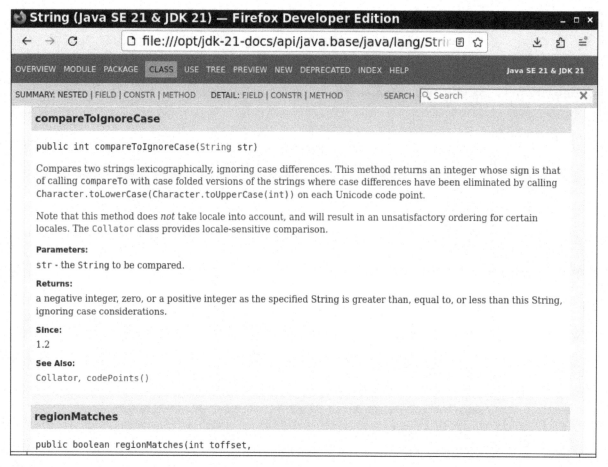

Figure 3.5: Detailed description of a String method

When you are done building the string, call the toString method. You will get a String object with the character sequence contained in the builder.

```
String completedString = builder.toString();
```

Cleverly, the StringBuilder methods return the builder object, so that you can chain multiple method calls:

```
String completedString = new StringBuilder()
    .append(str)
    .appendCodePoint(cp)
    .toString();
```

The String class doesn't have a method to reverse the Unicode characters of a string, but StringBuilder does. To reverse a string, use this code snippet:

```
String reversed = new StringBuilder(original).reverse().toString();
```

Caution: Reversing works correctly for characters that are encoded with two `char` values, but it does not take grapheme clusters into account.

 Note: The legacy `StringBuffer` class is less efficient than `StringBuilder`, but it allows multiple threads to add or remove characters. If all string editing happens in a single thread (which is usually the case), you should use `StringBuilder`. The APIs of both classes are identical.

The following API notes contain the most important methods for the `StringBuilder` class.

`java.lang.StringBuilder` 5.0

- `StringBuilder()`
- `StringBuilder(CharSequence seq)`
  constructs an empty string builder, or one with the given initial content.
- `int length()`
  returns the number of code units of the builder or buffer.
- `StringBuilder append(String str)`
  appends a string and returns the string builder.
- `StringBuilder appendCodePoint(int cp)`
  appends a code point, converting it into one or two code units, and returns this.
- `StringBuilder insert(int offset, String str)`
  inserts a string at position `offset` and returns the string builder.
- `StringBuilder delete(int startIndex, int endIndex)`
  deletes the code units with offsets `startIndex` to `endIndex - 1` and returns the string builder.
- `StringBuilder repeat(CharSequence cs, int count)` **21**
  Appends `count` copies of `cs` and returns the string builder.
- `StringBuilder reverse()`
  Reverses the code points in this string builder and returns the builder.
- `String toString()`
  returns a string with the same data as the builder or buffer contents.

3.6.10. Text Blocks

The text block feature, added in Java 15, makes it easy to provide string literals that span multiple lines. A text block starts with `"""`, followed by a line feed. The block ends with another `"""`:

```
String greeting = """
Hello
World
""";
```

A text block is easier to read and write than the equivalent string literal:

```
"Hello\nWorld\n"
```

This string contains two \n: one after Hello and one after World. The newline after the opening """ is not included in the string literal.

If you don't want a newline after the last line, put the closing """ immediately after the last character:

```
String prompt = """
Hello, my name is Hal.
Please enter your name:""";
```

Text blocks are particularly suited for including code in some other language, such as SQL or HTML. You can just paste it between the triple quotes:

```
String html = """
<div class="Warning">
   Beware of those who say "Hello" to the world
</div>
""";
```

Note that you don't have to escape the quotation marks. There are just two situations where you need to escape them:

- If the text block *ends* in a quotation mark
- If the text block contains a sequence of three or more quotation marks

Unfortunately, you still need to escape all backslashes.

All escape sequences from regular strings work the same way in text blocks.

There is one escape sequence that only works in text blocks. A \ directly before the end of a line joins this line and the next. For example,

```
"""
Hello, my name is Hal. \
Please enter your name:""";
```

is the same as

```
"Hello, my name is Hal. Please enter your name:"
```

Line endings are normalized by removing trailing whitespace and changing any Windows line endings (\r\n) to simple newlines (\n). If you need to preserve trailing spaces, turn the last one into a \s escape. In fact, that's what you probably want for prompt strings. The following string ends in a space:

```
"""
Hello, my name is Hal. \
Please enter your name:\s""";
```

The story is more complex for leading whitespace. Consider a typical variable declaration that is indented from the left margin. You can indent the text block as well:

```
        String html = """
            <div class="Warning">
                Beware of those who say "Hello" to the world
            </div>
            """;
```

The indentation that is common to all lines in the text block is subtracted. The actual string is

```
"<div class=\"Warning\">\n   Beware of those who say \"Hello\" to the world\n</div>\n"
```

Note that there are no indentations in the first and third line.

You can always avoid this indentation stripping by having no whitespace in the last line, before the closing """. But many programmers seem to find that it looks neater when text blocks are indented. Your IDE may cheerfully offer to indent all text blocks, using tabs or spaces.

Java wisely does not prescribe the width of a tab. The whitespace prefix has to match *exactly* for all lines in the text block.

Entirely blank lines are not considered when stripping common indentation. However, the whitespace before the closing """ is significant. Be sure to indent to the end of the whitespace that you want to have stripped.

 Caution: Be careful about mixed tabs and spaces in indentations. An overlooked space can easily yield a wrongly indented string.

Tip: If a text block contains code that isn't Java, you may actually prefer to place it at the left margin. It stands out from the Java code, and you have more room for long lines.

3.7. Input and Output

To make our example programs more interesting, we want to accept input and properly format the program output. Of course, modern programs use a GUI for collecting user input. However, programming such an interface requires more tools and techniques than we have at our disposal at this time. Our first order of business is to become more familiar with the Java programming language, so we use the humble console for input and output.

3.7.1. Reading Input

You saw that it is easy to print output to the "standard output stream" (that is, the console window) just by calling System.out.println. Reading from the "standard input stream" System.in isn't quite as simple. To read console input, you first construct a Scanner that is attached to System.in:

```
Scanner in = new Scanner(System.in);
```

(Constructors and the new operator are discussed in detail in Chapter 4.)

Now you can use the various methods of the Scanner class to read input. For example, the nextLine method reads a line of input.

```
System.out.print("What is your name? ");
String name = in.nextLine();
```

Here, we use the nextLine method because the input might contain spaces. To read a single word (delimited by whitespace), call

```
String firstName = in.next();
```

To read an integer, use the nextInt method.

```
System.out.print("How old are you? ");
int age = in.nextInt();
```

Similarly, the nextDouble method reads the next floating-point number.

The program in Listing 3.2 asks for the user's name and age and then prints a message like

```
Hello, Cay. Next year, you'll be 65.
```

Finally, note the line

```
import java.util.*;
```

at the beginning of the program. The Scanner class is defined in the java.util package. Whenever you use a class that is not defined in the basic java.lang package, you need to use an import directive. Packages and import directives are covered in more detail in Chapter 4.

 Caution: You may run into trouble if you run this program from a terminal (by calling java InputTest), and you use Windows, and your name contains characters other than the 26 Roman upper- and lowercase characters (such as Bérengère or Ὀδυσσεύς). By default, Windows terminals use an archaic character encoding for System.out, but not for the Scanner. The result is garbled output. To fix this, switch the terminal to the UTF-8 encoding, by issuing the following terminal command prior to running the program:

```
chcp 65001
```

Then, if you use Java 18 or above, all will be well. With older versions of Java, run the program as:

```
java -Dfile.encoding=utf-8 InputTest
```

If you use a development environment, you should not have to worry about this issue.

Listing 3.2 InputTest/InputTest.java

```java
 1  import java.util.*;
 2
 3  /**
 4   * This program demonstrates console input.
 5   * @version 1.11 2023-08-26
 6   * @author Cay Horstmann
 7   */
 8  public class InputTest
 9  {
10     public static void main(String[] args)
11     {
12        Scanner in = new Scanner(System.in);
13
14        // get first input
15        System.out.print("What is your name? ");
16        String name = in.nextLine();
```

```
17
18         // get second input
19         System.out.print("How old are you? ");
20         int age = in.nextInt();
21
22         // display output on console
23         System.out.println("Hello, " + name + ". Next year, you'll be " + (age + 1) + ".");
24     }
25 }
```

 Note: The Scanner class is not suitable for reading a password from a console since the input is plainly visible to anyone. Use the readPassword method of the Console class to read a password while hiding the user input:

```
Console cons = System.console();
String username = cons.readLine("User name: ");
char[] passwd = cons.readPassword("Password: ");
. . .
Arrays.fill(passwd, '*');
```

For security reasons, the password is returned in an array of characters rather than a string. After you are done processing the password, you should immediately overwrite the array elements with a filler value.

Input processing with a Console object is not as convenient as with a Scanner. You must read the input a line at a time. There are no methods for reading individual words or numbers.

---

java.util.Scanner 5.0

- Scanner(InputStream in)
  constructs a Scanner object from the given input stream.
- String nextLine()
  reads the next line of input.
- String next()
  reads the next word of input (delimited by whitespace).
- int nextInt()
- double nextDouble()
  read and convert the next character sequence that represents an integer or floating-point number.
- boolean hasNext()
  tests whether there is another word in the input.

- `boolean hasNextInt()`
- `boolean hasNextDouble()`
  test whether the next character sequence represents an integer or floating-point number.

---

java.lang.System `1.0`

- `static Console console()` **6**
  returns a `Console` object for interacting with the user through a console window if such interaction is possible, `null` otherwise. A `Console` object is available for any program that is launched in a console window. Otherwise, the availability is system-dependent.

---

java.io.Console **6**

- `char[] readPassword(String prompt, Object... args)`
- `String readLine(String prompt, Object... args)`
  display the prompt and read the user input until the end of the input line. The optional `args` parameters are used to supply formatting arguments, as described in the next section.

3.7.2. Formatting Output

You can print a number x to the console with the statement `System.out.print(x)`. That command will print x with the maximum number of nonzero digits for that type. For example,

```
double x = 10000.0 / 3.0;
System.out.print(x);
```

prints

```
3333.3333333333335
```

That is a problem if you want to display, for example, dollars and cents.

The remedy is the `printf` method, which follows the venerable conventions from the C library. For example, the call

```
System.out.printf("%8.2f", x);
```

prints x with a *field width* of 8 characters and a *precision* of 2 characters. That is, the printout contains a leading space and the seven characters

```
3333.33
```

You can supply multiple arguments to printf. For example:

```
System.out.printf("Hello, %s. Next year, you'll be %d.", name, age + 1);
```

Each of the *format specifiers* that start with a % character is replaced with the corresponding argument. The *conversion character* that ends a format specifier indicates the type of the value to be formatted: f is a floating-point number, s a string, and d a decimal integer. Table 3.6 shows all conversion characters.

The uppercase variants produce uppercase letters. For example, "%8.2E" formats 3333.33 as 3.33E+03, with an uppercase E.

Table 3.6: Conversions for printf

Conversion Character	Type	Example
d	Decimal integer	159
x or X	Hexadecimal integer. For more control over hexadecimal formatting, use the HexFormat class.	9f
o	Octal integer	237
f or F	Fixed-point floating-point	15.9
e or E	Exponential floating-point	1.59e+01
g or G	General floating-point (the shorter of e and f)	—
a or A	Hexadecimal floating-point	0x1.fccdp3
s or S	String	Hello
c or C	Character	H
b or B	boolean	true
h or H	Hash code	42628b2
tx or Tx	Legacy date and time formatting. Use the java.time classes instead—see Chapter 6 of Volume II.	—
%	The percent symbol	%
n	The platform-dependent line separator	—

Note: You can use the s conversion to format arbitrary objects. If an arbitrary object implements the Formattable interface, the object's formatTo method is invoked. Otherwise, the toString method is invoked to turn the object into a string. The toString method is discussed in Chapter 5 and interfaces in Chapter 6.

In addition, you can specify *flags* that control the appearance of the formatted output. Table 3.7 shows all flags. For example, the comma flag adds group separators. That is,

```
System.out.printf("%,.2f", 10000.0 / 3.0);
```

prints

```
3,333.33
```

You can use multiple flags, for example "%,(.2f" to use group separators and enclose negative numbers in parentheses.

Table 3.7: Flags for printf

Flag	Purpose	Example
+	Prints sign for positive and negative numbers.	+3333.33
space	Adds a space before positive numbers.	| 3333.33|
0	Adds leading zeroes.	003333.33
-	Left-justifies field.	|3333.33 |
(	Encloses negative numbers in parentheses.	(3333.33)
,	Adds group separators.	3,333.33
# (for f format)	Always includes a decimal point.	3,333.
# (for x or o format)	Adds 0x or 0 prefix.	0xcafe
$	Specifies the index of the argument to be formatted. For example, %1$d %1$x prints the first argument in decimal and hexadecimal.	159 9F

Flag	Purpose	Example
<	Formats the same value as the previous specification. For example, %d %<x prints the same number in decimal and hexadecimal.	159 9F

You can use the static `String.format` method to create a formatted string without printing it:

```
String message = String.format("Hello, %s. Next year, you'll be %d.", name, age + 1);
```

 Note: As of Java 15, you can use the `formatted` method instead, saving you five characters:

```
String message = "Hello, %s. Next year, you'll be %d.".formatted(name, age + 1);
```

You have now seen all features of the `printf` method. Figure 3.6 shows a syntax diagram for format specifiers.

 Note: Formatting is *locale-specific*. For example, in Germany, the group separator is a period, not a comma. On a computer with a German locale, the call

```
double x = 10000.0 / 3.0;
System.out.printf("%8.2f", x);
```

yields the output

```
3333,33
```

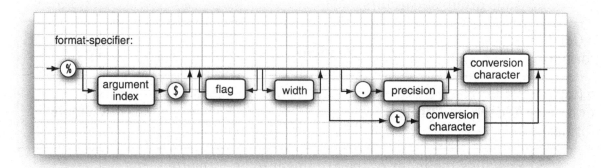

Figure 3.6: Format specifier syntax

This locale-specific behavior is normally what you want when you communicate with users. However, if you produce a file that is later consumed by a computer program, you may need to choose a fixed locale for the output. Specify the locale as the first argument to printf:

```
System.out.printf(Locale.US, "%8.2f", x);
```

3.7.3. File Input and Output

To read from a file, construct a Scanner object like this:

```
Scanner in = new Scanner(Path.of("myfile.txt"));
```

If the file name contains backslashes, remember to escape each of them with an additional backslash: "c:\\mydirectory\\myfile.txt".

Now you can read from the file, using any of the Scanner methods that you already encountered.

Note: Files store bytes, not Unicode characters. As you have seen in Section 3.3.4, there is more than one way of representing Unicode characters as bytes. By far the most commonly used character encoding is called UTF-8. In this book, all text files are assumed to use UTF-8. As of Java 18, this is the default encoding for all operations that read and write text. In older versions, the "default charset" of the computer running the Java program was used. That is not a good idea—the program might act differently depending on where it is run. If you use an older version of Java, always specify the character encoding:

```
Scanner in = new Scanner(Path.of("myfile.txt"), StandardCharsets.UTF_8);
```

Caution: You can construct a Scanner with a string argument, but the scanner interprets the string as data, not a file name. For example, if you call

```
Scanner in = new Scanner("myfile.txt"); // ERROR?
```

then the scanner will see ten characters of data: 'm', 'y', 'f', and so on. That is probably not what was intended in this case.

To write to a file, construct a PrintWriter object. In the constructor, supply the file name as a string:

```
PrintWriter out = new PrintWriter("myfile.txt");
```

If the file does not exist, it is created. You can use the print, println, and printf commands as you did when printing to System.out.

 Note: When you specify a relative file name, such as "myfile.txt", "mydirectory/myfile.txt", or "../myfile.txt", the file is located relative to the directory in which the Java virtual machine was started. If you launched your program from a command shell, by executing

```
java MyProg
```

then the starting directory is the current directory of the command shell. However, if you use an integrated development environment, it controls the starting directory. You can find the directory location with this call:

```
String dir = System.getProperty("user.dir");
```

If you run into grief with locating files, consider using absolute path names such as "c:\\mydirectory\\myfile.txt" or "/home/me/mydirectory/myfile.txt".

 Note: Prior to Java 18, you had to set the character encoding explicitly to UTF-8:

```
PrintWriter out = new PrintWriter("myfile.txt", StandardCharsets.UTF_8);
```

As you saw, you can access files just as easily as you can use System.in and System.out. There is just one catch: If you construct a Scanner with a file that does not exist or a PrintWriter with a file name that cannot be created, an exception occurs. The Java compiler considers these exceptions to be more serious than a "divide by zero" exception, for example. In Chapter 7, you will learn various ways of handling exceptions. For now, you should simply tell the compiler that you are aware of the possibility of an "input/output" exception. You do this by tagging the main method with a throws clause, like this:

```
public static void main(String[] args) throws IOException
{
    Scanner in = new Scanner(Path.of("myfile.txt"));
    . . .
}
```

You have now seen how to read and write files that contain textual data. For more advanced topics, such as dealing with different character encodings, processing binary data, reading directories, and writing zip files, turn to Chapter 2 of Volume II.

Note: If you dislike the exception declaration, read from System.in and write to System.out, as in the preceding sections. Then launch your program from a command shell, using the redirection syntax of your shell:

```
java MyProg < myfile.txt > output.txt
```

java.util.Scanner 5.0

- Scanner(Path p) **7**
- Scanner(Path p, Charset charset) **10**
  constructs a Scanner that reads data from the given path, using the default or given character encoding.
- Scanner(String data)
  constructs a Scanner that reads data from the given string.

java.io.PrintWriter 1.1

- PrintWriter(String fileName)
- PrintWriter(String fileName, Charset charset) **10**
  constructs a PrintWriter that writes data to the file with the given file name, using the default or given character encoding.

java.nio.file.Path 7

- static Path of(String pathname) **11**
  constructs a Path from the given path name.

3.8. Control Flow

Java, like any programming language, supports both conditional statements and loops to determine control flow. I will start with the conditional statements, then move on to loops, to end with a thorough discussion of the four forms of switch.

 C++ Note: The Java control flow constructs are identical to those in C and C++, with a few exceptions. There is no goto, but there is a "labeled" version of break that you can use to break out of a nested loop (where, in C, you perhaps would have used a goto). Finally, there is a variant of the for loop that is similar to the range-based for loop in C++ and the foreach loop in C#.

3.8.1. Block Scope

Before learning about control structures, you need to know more about *blocks*.

A block, or compound statement, consists of a number of Java statements, surrounded by a pair of braces. Blocks define the scope of your variables. A block can be *nested* inside another block. Here is a block that is nested inside the block of the main method:

```java
public static void main(String[] args)
{
   int n;
   . . .
   {
      int k;
      . . .
   } // k is only defined up to here
}
```

You may not declare identically named local variables in two nested blocks. For example, the following is an error and will not compile:

```java
public static void main(String[] args)
{
   int n;
   . . .
   {
      int k;
      int n; // ERROR--can't redeclare n in inner block
      . . .
   }
}
```

 C++ Note: In C++, it is possible to redefine a variable inside a nested block. The inner definition then shadows the outer one. This can be a source of programming errors; hence, Java does not allow it.

3.8.2. Conditional Statements

The conditional statement in Java has the form

   if (*condition*) *statement*

The condition must be surrounded by parentheses.

In Java, as in most programming languages, you will often want to execute multiple statements when a single condition is true. In this case, use a *block statement* that takes the form

```
{
    statement₁
    statement₂
    . . .
}
```

For example:

```
if (yourSales >= target)
{
    performance = "Satisfactory";
    bonus = 100;
}
```

In this code all the statements surrounded by the braces will be executed when yourSales is greater than or equal to target (see Figure 3.7).

 Note: A block (sometimes called a *compound statement*) enables you to have more than one (simple) statement in any Java programming structure that otherwise allows for a single (simple) statement.

The more general conditional in Java looks like this (see Figure 3.8):

```
if (condition) statement₁ else statement₂
```

For example:

```
if (yourSales >= target)
{
    performance = "Satisfactory";
    bonus = 100 + 0.01 * (yourSales - target);
}
else
{
    performance = "Unsatisfactory";
    bonus = 0;
}
```

The else part is always optional. An else groups with the closest if. Thus, in the statement

```
if (x <= 0) if (x == 0) sign = 0; else sign = -1;
```

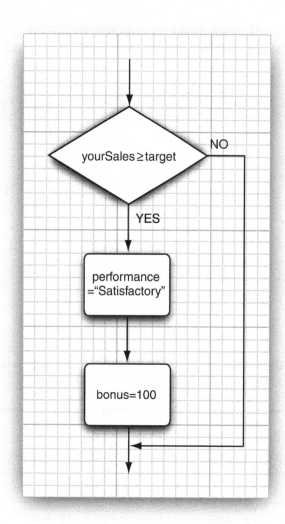

Figure 3.7: Flowchart for the if statement

the else belongs to the second if. Of course, it is a good idea to use braces to clarify this code:

```
if (x <= 0) { if (x == 0) sign = 0; else sign = -1; }
```

Repeated if . . . else if . . . alternatives are common (see Figure 3.9). For example:

```
if (yourSales >= 2 * target)
{
   performance = "Excellent";
   bonus = 1000;
}
else if (yourSales >= 1.5 * target)
{
   performance = "Fine";
```

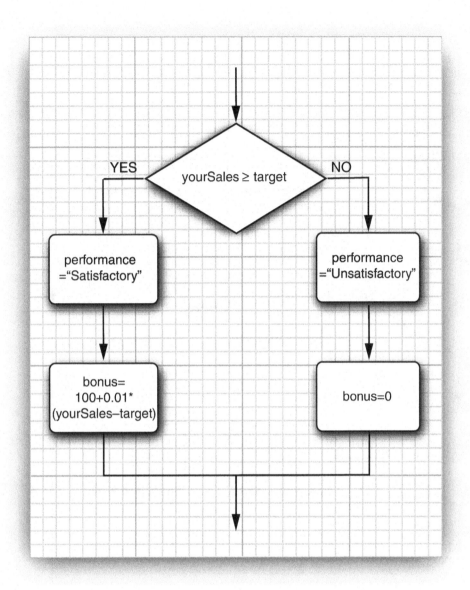

Figure 3.8: Flowchart for the if/else statement

```
    bonus = 500;
}
else if (yourSales >= target)
{
    performance = "Satisfactory";
    bonus = 100;
}
else
{
    System.out.println("You're fired");
}
```

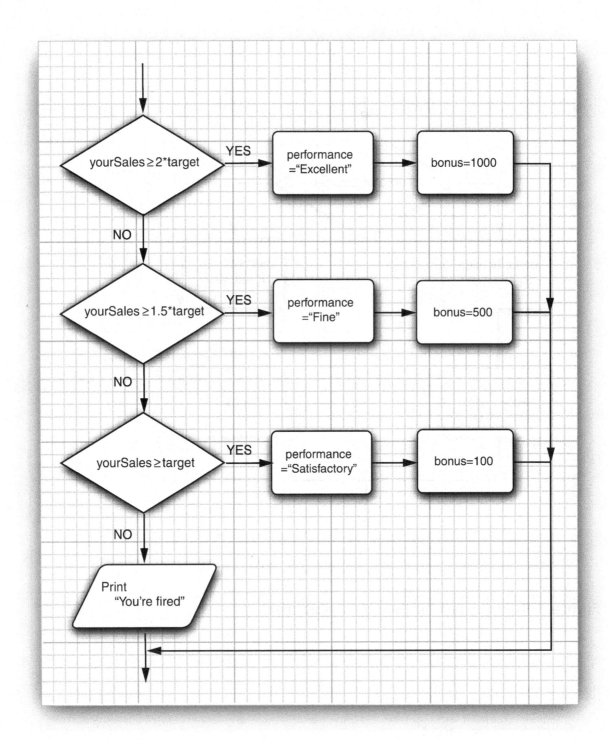

Figure 3.9: Flowchart for the if/else if (multiple branches)

3.8.3. Loops

The while loop executes a statement (which may be a block statement) while a condition is true. The general form is `while` (*condition*) *statement*

The `while` loop will never execute if the condition is `false` at the outset (see Figure 3.10).

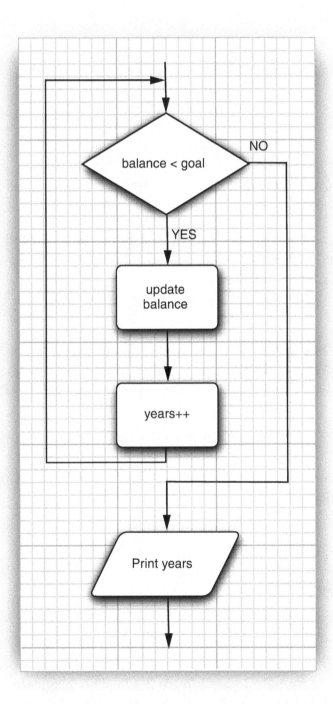

Figure 3.10: Flowchart for the `while` statement

The program in Listing 3.3 determines how long it will take to save a specific amount of money for your well-earned retirement, assuming you deposit the same amount of money per year and the money earns a specified interest rate.

In the example, we are incrementing a counter and updating the amount currently accumulated in the body of the loop until the total exceeds the targeted amount.

```java
while (balance < goal)
{
   balance += payment;
   double interest = balance * interestRate / 100;
   balance += interest;
   years++;
}
System.out.println(years + " years.");
```

(Don't rely on this program to plan for your retirement. It lacks a few niceties such as inflation and your life expectancy.)

A while loop tests at the top. Therefore, the code in the block might never be executed. If you want to make sure a block is executed at least once, you need to move the test to the bottom, using the do/while loop. Its syntax looks like this:

```java
do statement while (condition);
```

This loop executes the statement (which is typically a block) and only then tests the condition. If it's true, it repeats the statement and retests the condition, and so on. The code in Listing 3.4 computes the new balance in your retirement account and then asks if you are ready to retire:

```java
do
{
   balance += payment;
   double interest = balance * interestRate / 100;
   balance += interest;
   years++;
   // print current balance
   . . .
   // ask if ready to retire and get input
   . . .
}
while (input.equals("N"));
```

As long as the user answers "N", the loop is repeated (see Figure 3.11). This program is a good example of a loop that needs to be entered at least once, because the user needs to see the balance before deciding whether it is sufficient for retirement.

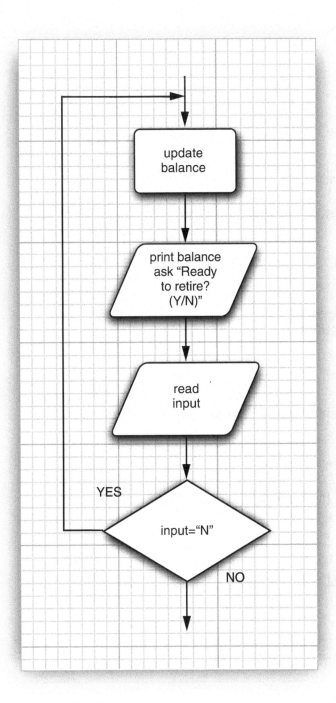

Figure 3.11: Flowchart for the do/while statement

Listing 3.3 Retirement/Retirement.java

```
1  import java.util.*;
2
3  /**
```

```java
 4     * This program demonstrates a <code>while</code> loop.
 5     * @version 1.20 2004-02-10
 6     * @author Cay Horstmann
 7     */
 8    public class Retirement
 9    {
10       public static void main(String[] args)
11       {
12          // read inputs
13          Scanner in = new Scanner(System.in);
14
15          System.out.print("How much money do you need to retire? ");
16          double goal = in.nextDouble();
17
18          System.out.print("How much money will you contribute every year? ");
19          double payment = in.nextDouble();
20
21          System.out.print("Interest rate in %: ");
22          double interestRate = in.nextDouble();
23
24          double balance = 0;
25          int years = 0;
26
27          // update account balance while goal isn't reached
28          while (balance < goal)
29          {
30             // add this year's payment and interest
31             balance += payment;
32             double interest = balance * interestRate / 100;
33             balance += interest;
34             years++;
35          }
36
37          System.out.println("You can retire in " + years + " years.");
38       }
39    }
```

Listing 3.4 Retirement2/Retirement2.java

```java
 1    import java.util.*;
 2
 3    /**
 4     * This program demonstrates a <code>do/while</code> loop.
 5     * @version 1.20 2004-02-10
 6     * @author Cay Horstmann
 7     */
 8    public class Retirement2
 9    {
10       public static void main(String[] args)
11       {
```

```
12          Scanner in = new Scanner(System.in);
13
14          System.out.print("How much money will you contribute every year? ");
15          double payment = in.nextDouble();
16
17          System.out.print("Interest rate in %: ");
18          double interestRate = in.nextDouble();
19
20          double balance = 0;
21          int year = 0;
22
23          String input;
24
25          // update account balance while user isn't ready to retire
26          do
27          {
28             // add this year's payment and interest
29             balance += payment;
30             double interest = balance * interestRate / 100;
31             balance += interest;
32
33             year++;
34
35             // print current balance
36             System.out.printf("After year %d, your balance is %,.2f%n", year, balance);
37
38             // ask if ready to retire and get input
39             System.out.print("Ready to retire? (Y/N) ");
40             input = in.next();
41          }
42          while (input.equals("N"));
43       }
44 }
```

3.8.4. Determinate Loops

The for loop is a general construct to support iteration controlled by a counter or similar variable that is updated after every iteration. As Figure 3.12 shows, the following loop prints the numbers from 1 to 10 on the screen:

```
for (int i = 1; i <= 10; i++)
   System.out.println(i);
```

The first slot of the for statement usually holds the counter initialization. The second slot gives the condition that will be tested before each new pass through the loop, and the third slot specifies how to update the counter.

Although Java, like C++, allows almost any expression in the various slots of a for loop, it is an unwritten rule of good taste that the three slots should only initialize, test, and update the same counter variable. One can write very obscure loops by disregarding this rule.

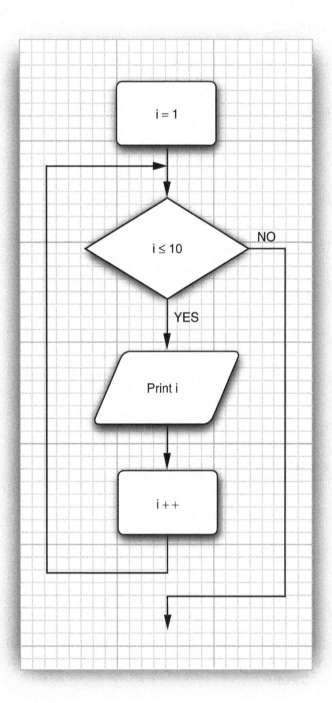

Figure 3.12: Flowchart for the for statement

Even within the bounds of good taste, much is possible. For example, you can have loops that count down:

```
for (int i = 10; i > 0; i--)
   System.out.println("Counting down . . . " + i);
System.out.println("Blastoff!");
```

 Caution: Be careful with testing for equality of floating-point numbers in loops. A for loop like this one

```
for (double x = 0; x != 10; x += 0.1) . . .
```

might never end. Because of roundoff errors, the final value might not be reached exactly. In this example, x jumps from 9.99999999999998 to 10.09999999999998 because there is no exact binary representation for 0.1.

When you declare a variable in the first slot of the for statement, the scope of that variable extends until the end of the body of the for loop.

```
for (int i = 1; i <= 10; i++)
{
   . . .
}
// i no longer defined here
```

In particular, if you define a variable inside a for statement, you cannot use its value outside the loop. Therefore, if you wish to use the final value of a loop counter outside the for loop, be sure to declare it outside the loop header.

```
int i;
for (i = 1; i <= 10; i++)
{
   . . .
}
// i is still defined here
```

On the other hand, you can define variables with the same name in separate for loops:

```
for (int i = 1; i <= 10; i++)
{
   . . .
}
. . .
for (int i = 11; i <= 20; i++) // OK to define another variable named i
{
   . . .
}
```

A for loop is merely a convenient shortcut for a while loop. For example,

```
for (i = 10; i > 0; i--)
    System.out.println("Counting down . . . " + i);
```

can be rewritten as follows:

```
i = 10;
while (i > 0)
{
    System.out.println("Counting down . . . " + i);
    i--;
}
```

The first slot of a for loop can declare multiple variables, provided they are of the same type. And the third slot can contain multiple comma-separated expressions:

```
for (int i = 1, j = 10; i <= 10; i++, j--) { ... }
```

While technically legal, this stretches the intuitive meaning of the for loop, and you should consider a while loop instead.

Listing 3.5 shows a typical example of a for loop.

The program computes the odds of winning a lottery. For example, if you must pick six numbers from the numbers 1 to 50 to win, then there are (50 × 49 × 48 × 47 × 46 × 45)/(1 × 2 × 3 × 4 × 5 × 6) possible outcomes, so your chance is 1 in 15,890,700. Good luck!

In general, if you pick *k* numbers out of *n*, there are

$$\frac{n \times (n - 1) \times (n - 2) \times \cdots \times (n - k + 1)}{1 \times 2 \times 3 \times 4 \times \cdots \times k}$$

possible outcomes. The following for loop computes this value:

```
int lotteryOdds = 1;
for (int i = 1; i <= k; i++)
    lotteryOdds = lotteryOdds * (n - i + 1) / i;
```

 Note: Section 3.10.3 describes the "generalized for loop" (also called "for each" loop) that makes it convenient to visit all elements of an array or collection.

Listing 3.5 LotteryOdds/LotteryOdds.java

```java
 1  import java.util.*;
 2
 3  /**
 4   * This program demonstrates a <code>for</code> loop.
 5   * @version 1.20 2004-02-10
 6   * @author Cay Horstmann
 7   */
 8  public class LotteryOdds
 9  {
10     public static void main(String[] args)
11     {
12        Scanner in = new Scanner(System.in);
13
14        System.out.print("How many numbers do you need to draw? ");
15        int k = in.nextInt();
16
17        System.out.print("What is the highest number you can draw? ");
18        int n = in.nextInt();
19
20        /*
21         * compute binomial coefficient n*(n-1)*(n-2)*...*(n-k+1)/(1*2*3*...*k)
22         */
23
24        int lotteryOdds = 1;
25        for (int i = 1; i <= k; i++)
26           lotteryOdds = lotteryOdds * (n - i + 1) / i;
27
28        System.out.println("Your odds are 1 in " + lotteryOdds + ". Good luck!");
29     }
30  }
```

3.8.5. Multiple Selections with switch

The if/else construct can be cumbersome when you have to deal with multiple alternatives for the same expression. The switch statement makes this easier, particularly with the form that has been introduced in Java 14.

For example, if you set up a menu system with four alternatives like that in Figure 3.13, you could use code that looks like this:

```java
Scanner in = new Scanner(System.in);
System.out.print("Select an option (1, 2, 3, 4) ");
int choice = in.nextInt();
switch (choice)
{
   case 1 ->
```

```
      . . .
   case 2 ->
      . . .
   case 3 ->
      . . .
   case 4 ->
      . . .
   default ->
      System.out.println("Bad input");
}
```

Note the similarity to the switch expressions that you saw in Section 3.5.9. Unlike a switch expression, a switch statement has no value. Each case carries out an action.

The "classic" form of the switch statement, which dates all the way back to the C language, has been supported since Java 1.0. It has the form:

```
int choice = . . .;
switch (choice)
{
   case 1:
      . . .
      break;
   case 2:
      . . .
      break;
   case 3:
      . . .
      break;
   case 4:
      . . .
      break;
   default:
      System.out.println("Bad input");
}
```

Execution starts at the case label that matches the value on which the selection is performed and continues until the next break or the end of the switch. If none of the case labels match, then the default clause is executed, if it is present.

 Caution: It is possible for multiple alternatives to be triggered. If you forget to add a break at the end of an alternative, execution falls through to the next alternative! This behavior is plainly dangerous and a common cause for errors.

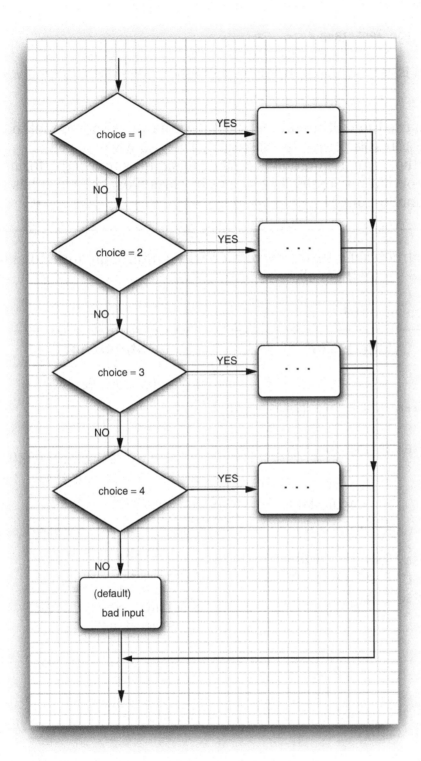

Figure 3.13: Flowchart for the switch statement

To detect such problems, compile your code with the -Xlint:fallthrough option, like this:

```
javac -Xlint:fallthrough Test.java
```

Then the compiler will issue a warning whenever an alternative does not end with a break statement.

If you actually want to use the fallthrough behavior, tag the surrounding method with the annotation @SuppressWarnings("fallthrough"). Then no warnings will be generated for that method. (An annotation is a mechanism for supplying information to the compiler or a tool that processes Java source or class files. Volume II has an in-depth coverage of annotations.)

For symmetry, Java 14 also introduced a switch expression with fallthrough, for a total of four forms of switch. Table 3.8 shows them all.

Table 3.8: The four forms of switch

	Expression	**Statement**
No Fallthrough	```int numLetters = switch (seasonName) { case "Spring" -> { System.out.println("spring time!"); yield 6; } case "Summer", "Winter" -> 6; case "Fall" -> 4; default -> -1; };```	```switch (seasonName) { case "Spring" -> { System.out.println("spring time!"); numLetters = 6; } case "Summer", "Winter" -> numLetters = 6; case "Fall" -> numLetters = 4; default -> numLetters = -1; }```

	Expression	Statement

Fallthrough	<pre>int numLetters = switch (seasonName)
	    {
	        case "Spring":
	            System.out.println(
	                "spring time!");
	        case "Summer", "Winter":
	            yield 6;
	        case "Fall":
	            yield 4;
	        default:
	            yield -1;
	    };</pre>
		<pre>switch (seasonName)
		{
		    case "Spring":
		        System.out.println(
		            "spring time!");
		    case "Summer", "Winter":
		        numLetters = 6;
		        break;
		    case "Fall":
		        numLetters = 4;
		        break;
		    default:
		        numLetters = -1;
		}</pre>

In the fallthrough variants, each case ends with a colon. If the cases end with arrows ->, then there is no fallthrough. You can't mix colons and arrows in a single switch statement.

Each branch of a switch *expression* must yield a value. Most commonly, each value follows an -> arrow:

```
case "Summer", "Winter" -> 6;
```

If that is not possible, use a yield statement. Like break, it terminates execution. Unlike break, it also yields a value—the value of the expression.

To use statements in a branch of a switch expression without fallthrough, you must use braces and yield:

```
case "Spring" ->
   {
      System.out.println("spring time!");
      yield 6;
   }
```

 Note: It is legal to throw an exception in a branch of a switch expression. For example:

```
default -> throw new IllegalArgumentException("Not a valid season");
```

Exceptions are covered in detail in Chapter 7.

Caution: The point of a `switch` expression is to produce a value (or to fail with an exception). You are not allowed to "jump out":

```
default -> { return -1; } // ERROR
```

Specifically, you cannot use `return`, `break`, or `continue` statements in a switch expression. (See Section 3.8.6 for the latter two.)

With so many variations of `switch`, which one should you choose?

1. Avoid the fallthrough forms. It is very uncommon to need fallthrough.
2. Prefer `switch` expressions over statements.

If each branch computes the value for a variable assignment or method call, yield the value with an expression, and then use it. For example,

```
numLetters = switch (seasonName)
   {
      case "Spring", "Summer", "Winter" -> 6
      case "Fall" -> 4
      default -> -1
   };
```

is better than

```
switch (seasonName)
{
   case "Spring", "Summer", "Winter" ->
      numLetters = 6;
   case "Fall" ->
      numLetters = 4;
   default ->
      numLetters = -1;
}
```

3.8.6. Statements That Break Control Flow

Although the designers of Java kept `goto` as a reserved word, they decided not to include it in the language. In general, `goto` statements are considered poor style. Some programmers feel the anti-goto forces have gone too far (see, for example, the famous article of Donald Knuth called "Structured Programming with goto statements"). They argue that unrestricted use of `goto` is error-prone but that an occasional jump *out of a loop* is beneficial. The Java designers agreed and even added a new statement, the labeled break, to support this programming style.

Let us first look at the unlabeled break statement. The same break statement that you use to exit a switch statement can also be used to break out of a loop. For example:

```
while (years <= 100)
{
   balance += payment;
   double interest = balance * interestRate / 100;
   balance += interest;
   if (balance >= goal) break;
   years++;
}
```

Now the loop is exited if either years > 100 occurs at the top of the loop or balance >= goal occurs in the middle of the loop. Of course, you could have computed the same value for years without a break, like this:

```
while (years <= 100 && balance < goal)
{
   balance += payment;
   double interest = balance * interestRate / 100;
   balance += interest;

   if (balance < goal)
      years++;
}
```

But note that the test balance < goal is repeated twice in this version. To avoid this repeated test, some programmers prefer the break statement.

The *labeled break* statement lets you break out of multiple nested loops. Occasionally something weird happens inside a deeply nested loop. In that case, you may want to break completely out of all the nested loops. It is inconvenient to program that simply by adding extra conditions to the various loop tests.

Here's an example that shows the labeled break statement at work. Notice that the label must precede the outermost loop out of which you want to break. It also must be followed by a colon.

```
Scanner in = new Scanner(System.in);
int n;
read_data:
while (. . .) // this loop statement is tagged with the label
{
   . . .
   for (. . .) // this inner loop is not labeled
   {
      System.out.print("Enter a number >= 0: ");
```

```
      n = in.nextInt();
      if (n < 0) // should never happen–can't go on
         break read_data;
         // break out of read_data loop
      . . .
   }
}
// this statement is executed immediately after the labeled break



if (n < 0) // check for bad situation
{
   // deal with bad situation
}
else
{
   // carry out normal processing
}
```

If there is a bad input, the labeled break moves past the end of the labeled block. As with any use of the break statement, you then need to test whether the loop exited normally or as a result of a break.

 Note: Curiously, you can apply a label to any statement, even an if statement or a block statement, like this:

```
   label:
   {
      . . .
      if (condition) break label; // exits block
      . . .
   }
   // jumps here when the break statement executes
```

Thus, if you are lusting after a goto and you can place a block that ends just before the place to which you want to jump, you can use a break statement! Naturally, I don't recommend this approach. Note, however, that you can only jump *out of* a block, never *into* a block.

Finally, there is a continue statement that, like the break statement, breaks the regular flow of control. The continue statement transfers control to the header of the innermost enclosing loop. Here is an example:

```
Scanner in = new Scanner(System.in);
while (sum < goal)
{
   System.out.print("Enter a number: ");
   n = in.nextInt();
   if (n < 0) continue;
   sum += n; // not executed if n < 0
}
```

If n < 0, then the continue statement jumps immediately to the loop header, skipping the remainder of the current iteration.

If the continue statement is used in a for loop, it jumps to the "update" part of the for loop. For example:

```
for (count = 1; count <= 100; count++)
{
   System.out.print("Enter a number, -1 to quit: ");
   n = in.nextInt();
   if (n < 0) continue;
   sum += n; // not executed if n < 0
}
```

If n < 0, then the continue statement jumps to the count++ statement.

There is also a labeled form of the continue statement that jumps to the header of the loop with the matching label.

 Tip: Many programmers find the break and continue statements confusing. These statements are entirely optional—you can always express the same logic without them. None of the programs in this book use break or continue.

3.9. Big Numbers

If the precision of the basic integer and floating-point types is not sufficient, you can turn to a couple of handy classes in the java.math package: BigInteger and BigDecimal. These are classes for manipulating numbers with an arbitrarily long sequence of digits. The BigInteger class implements arbitrary-precision integer arithmetic, and BigDecimal does the same for floating-point numbers.

Use the static valueOf method to turn an ordinary number into a big number:

```
BigInteger a = BigInteger.valueOf(100);
```

For longer numbers, use a constructor with a string argument:

```
BigInteger reallyBig
   = new BigInteger("222232244629420445529739893461909967206666939096499764990979600");
```

There are also constants `BigInteger.ZERO`, `BigInteger.ONE`, `BigInteger.TWO`, and `BigInteger.TEN`.

 Caution: With the `BigDecimal` class, you should always use the constructor with a string argument. There is a constructor `BigDecimal(double)` that is inherently prone to roundoff: `new BigDecimal(0.1)` has digits

0.1000000000000000055511151231257827021181583404541015625

Unfortunately, you cannot use the familiar mathematical operators such as + and * to combine big numbers. Instead, you must use methods such as `add` and `multiply` in the big number classes.

```
BigInteger c = a.add(b); // c = a + b
BigInteger d = c.multiply(b.add(BigInteger.valueOf(2))); // d = c * (b + 2)
```

 C++ Note: Unlike C++, Java has no programmable operator overloading. There was no way for the programmers of the `BigInteger` class to redefine the + and * operators to give the `add` and `multiply` operations of the `BigInteger` classes. The language designers did overload the + operator to denote concatenation of strings. They chose not to overload other operators, and they did not give Java programmers the opportunity to overload operators in their own classes.

 Note: In Java 19, the `BigInteger` class provides a `parallelMultiply` method that yields the same result as `multiply` but can potentially compute the result faster by using multiple processor cores. Use this method if you have to do a lot of multiplications and you know that your application does not need the CPU resources for other computations.

Listing 3.6 shows a modification of the lottery odds program of Listing 3.5, updated to work with big numbers. For example, if you are invited to participate in a lottery in which you need to pick 60 numbers out of a possible 490 numbers, you can use this program to tell you your odds of winning. They are 1 in 716395843461995557415116222540092933411717612789263493493351013459481104668848. Good luck!

The program in Listing 3.5 computed the statement

```
lotteryOdds = lotteryOdds * (n - i + 1) / i;
```

When big integers are used for lotteryOdds and n, the equivalent statement becomes

```
lotteryOdds = lotteryOdds
   .multiply(n.subtract(BigInteger.valueOf(i - 1)))
   .divide(BigInteger.valueOf(i));
```

Listing 3.6 `BigIntegerTest/BigIntegerTest.java`

```java
 1  import java.math.*;
 2  import java.util.*;
 3
 4  /**
 5   * This program uses big numbers to compute the odds of winning the grand prize in a lottery.
 6   * @version 1.21 2021-09-03
 7   * @author Cay Horstmann
 8   */
 9  public class BigIntegerTest
10  {
11     public static void main(String[] args)
12     {
13        Scanner in = new Scanner(System.in);
14
15        System.out.print("How many numbers do you need to draw? ");
16        int k = in.nextInt();
17
18        System.out.print("What is the highest number you can draw? ");
19        BigInteger n = in.nextBigInteger();
20
21        /*
22         * compute binomial coefficient n*(n-1)*(n-2)*...*(n-k+1)/(1*2*3*...*k)
23         */
24
25        BigInteger lotteryOdds = BigInteger.ONE;
26
27        for (int i = 1; i <= k; i++)
28           lotteryOdds = lotteryOdds
29              .multiply(n.subtract(BigInteger.valueOf(i - 1)))
30              .divide(BigInteger.valueOf(i));
31
32        System.out.printf("Your odds are 1 in %s. Good luck!%n", lotteryOdds);
33     }
34  }
```

---

java.math.BigInteger 1.1

- BigInteger add(BigInteger other)
- BigInteger subtract(BigInteger other)
- BigInteger multiply(BigInteger other)
- BigInteger divide(BigInteger other)
- BigInteger mod(BigInteger other)
- BigInteger pow(int exponent)

  return the sum, difference, product, quotient, remainder, and power of this big integer and other.
- BigInteger sqrt() `9

  yields the square root of this BigInteger.
- int compareTo(BigInteger other)

  returns 0 if this big integer equals other, a negative result if this big integer is less than other, and a positive result otherwise.
- static BigInteger valueOf(long x)

  returns a big integer whose value equals x.

---

java.math.BigDecimal 1.1

- BigDecimal(String digits)

  constructs a big decimal with the given digits.
- BigDecimal add(BigDecimal other)
- BigDecimal subtract(BigDecimal other)
- BigDecimal multiply(BigDecimal other)
- BigDecimal divide(BigDecimal other) **5.0**
- BigDecimal divide(BigDecimal other, RoundingMode mode) **5.0**

  return the sum, difference, product, or quotient of this big decimal and other. The first divide method throws an exception if the quotient does not have a finite decimal expansion. To obtain a rounded result, use the second method. The mode RoundingMode.HALF_UP is the rounding mode that you learned in school: round down the digits 0 to 4, round up the digits 5 to 9. It is appropriate for routine calculations. See the API documentation for other rounding modes.
- int compareTo(BigDecimal other)

  returns 0 if this big decimal equals other, a negative result if this big decimal is less than other, and a positive result otherwise.

3.10. Arrays

Arrays hold sequences of values of the same type. In the following sections, you will see how to work with arrays in Java.

3.10.1. Declaring Arrays

Declare an array variable by specifying the array type—which is the element type followed by [ ]—and the array variable name. For example, here is the declaration of an array a of integers:

```
int[] a;
```

However, this statement only declares the variable a. It does not yet initialize a with an actual array. Use the new operator to create the array.

```
int[] a = new int[100]; // or var a = new int[100];
```

This statement declares and initializes an array of 100 integers.

The array length need not be a constant: new int[n] creates an array of length n.

Once you create an array, you cannot change its length (although you can, of course, change an individual array element). If you frequently need to expand the length of arrays while your program is running, you should use *array lists*, which are covered in Chapter 5.

The type of an array variable does not include the length. For example, the variable a in the preceding example has type int[] and can be set to an int array of any length.

 Note: You can define an array variable either as

```
int[] a;
```

or as

```
int a[];
```

Most Java programmers prefer the former style because it neatly separates the type int[] (integer array) from the variable name.

Java has a shortcut for creating an array object and supplying initial values:

```
int[] smallPrimes = { 2, 3, 5, 7, 11, 13 };
```

Notice that you do not use new with this syntax, and you don't specify the length.

A comma after the last value is allowed, which can be convenient for an array to which you keep adding values over time:

```
String[] authors =
   {
      "James Gosling",
      "Bill Joy",
      "Guy Steele",
      // add more names here and put a comma after each name
   };
```

You can declare an *anonymous array*:

```
new int[] { 17, 19, 23, 29, 31, 37 }
```

This expression allocates a new array and fills it with the values inside the braces. It counts the number of initial values and sets the array length accordingly. You can use this syntax to reinitialize an array without creating a new variable. For example,

```
smallPrimes = new int[] { 17, 19, 23, 29, 31, 37 };
```

is shorthand for

```
int[] anonymous = { 17, 19, 23, 29, 31, 37 };
smallPrimes = anonymous;
```

Note: It is legal to have arrays of length 0. Such an array can be useful if you write a method that computes an array result and the result happens to be empty. Construct an array of length 0 as

> new *elementType*[0]

or

> new *elementType*[] {}

Note that an array of length 0 is not the same as null.

3.10.2. Accessing Array Elements

You access each individual element of an array through an integer *index*, using the bracket operator. For example, if a is an array of integers, then a[i] is the element with index i in the array.

The array elements are *numbered starting from 0*. The last valid index is one less than the length. In the example below, the index values range from 0 to 99. Once the array is created, you can fill the elements in an array, for example, by using a loop:

```
int[] a = new int[100];
for (int i = 0; i < 100; i++)
   a[i] = i; // fills the array with numbers 0 to 99
```

When you create an array of numbers, all elements are initialized with zero. Arrays of boolean are initialized with false. Arrays of objects are initialized with the special value null, which indicates that they do not (yet) hold any objects. This can be surprising for beginners. For example,

```
String[] names = new String[10];
```

creates an array of ten strings, all of which are null. If you want the array to hold empty strings, you must supply them:

```
for (int i = 0; i < 10; i++) names[i] = "";
```

 Caution: If you construct an array with 100 elements and then try to access the element a[100] (or any other index outside the range from 0 to 99), an "array index out of bounds" exception will occur.

To find the number of elements of an array, use *array*.length. For example:

```
for (int i = 0; i < a.length; i++)
   System.out.println(a[i]);
```

3.10.3. The "for each" Loop

Java has a powerful looping construct that allows you to loop through each element in an array (or any other collection of elements) without having to fuss with index values.

The *enhanced* for loop

```
for (variable : collection) statement
```

sets the given variable to each element of the collection and then executes the statement (which, of course, may be a block). The *collection* expression must be an array or an object of a class that implements the Iterable interface, such as ArrayList. Array lists are covered in Chapter 5 and the Iterable interface in Chapter 9.

For example,

```
for (int element : a)
   System.out.println(element);
```

prints each element of the array a on a separate line.

You should read this loop as "for each element in a." The designers of the Java language considered using keywords, such as foreach and in. But this loop was a late addition to the Java language, and in the end nobody wanted to break the old code that already contained methods or variables with these names (such as System.in).

Of course, you could achieve the same effect with a traditional for loop:

```
for (int i = 0; i < a.length; i++)
   System.out.println(a[i]);
```

However, the "for each" loop is more concise and less error-prone, as you don't have to worry about those pesky start and end index values.

Note: The loop variable of the "for each" loop traverses the *elements* of the array, not the index values.

The "for each" loop is a pleasant improvement over the traditional loop if you need to process all elements in a collection. However, there are still plenty of opportunities to use the traditional for loop. For example, you might not want to traverse the entire collection, or you may need the index value inside the loop.

Tip: There is an even easier way to print all values of an array, using the toString method of the Arrays class. The call Arrays.toString(a) returns a string containing the array elements, enclosed in brackets and separated by commas, such as "[2, 3, 5, 7, 11, 13]". To print the array, simply call

```
System.out.println(Arrays.toString(a));
```

3.10.4. Array Copying

You can copy one array variable into another, but then *both variables refer to the same array*:

```
int[] luckyNumbers = smallPrimes;
luckyNumbers[5] = 12; // now smallPrimes[5] is also 12
```

Figure 3.14 shows the result.

If you actually want to copy all values of one array into a new array, use the copyOf method in the Arrays class:

```
int[] copiedLuckyNumbers = Arrays.copyOf(luckyNumbers, luckyNumbers.length);
```

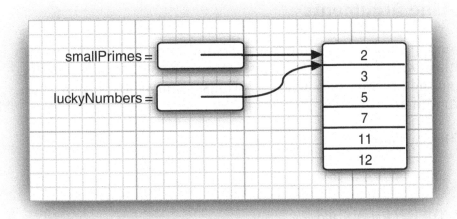

Figure 3.14: Copying an array variable

The second argument is the length of the new array. A common use of this method is to increase the length of an array:

```
luckyNumbers = Arrays.copyOf(luckyNumbers, 2 * luckyNumbers.length);
```

The additional elements are filled with 0 if the array contains numbers, `false` if the array contains `boolean` values. Conversely, if the length is less than the length of the original array, only the initial values are copied.

 C++ Note: A Java array is quite different from a C++ array on the stack. It is, however, essentially the same as a pointer to an array allocated on the *heap*. That is,

```
int[] a = new int[100]; // Java
```

is not the same as

```
int a[100]; // C++
```

but rather

```
int* a = new int[100]; // C++
```

In Java, the [] operator is predefined to perform *bounds checking*. Furthermore, there is no pointer arithmetic—you can't increment a to point to the next element in the array.

3.10.5. Command-Line Arguments

You have already seen one example of a Java array repeated quite a few times. Every Java program has a main method with a String[] args parameter variable. This parameter indicates that the main method receives an array of strings—namely, the arguments specified on the command line.

For example, consider this program:

```java
public class Message
{
   public static void main(String[] args)
   {
      if (args.length == 0 || args[0].equals("-h"))
         System.out.print("Hello,");
      else if (args[0].equals("-g"))
         System.out.print("Goodbye,");
      // print the other command-line arguments
      for (int i = 1; i < args.length; i++)
         System.out.print(" " + args[i]);
      System.out.println("!");
   }
}
```

If the program is called as

```
java Message -g cruel world
```

then the args array has the following contents:

```
args[0]: "-g"
args[1]: "cruel"
args[2]: "world"
```

The program prints the message

```
Goodbye, cruel world!
```

 C++ Note: Unlike in C++, the name of the program is not stored in the array of command-line arguments. For example, when you start up a program as

```
java Message -h world
```

from the command line, then args[0] will be "-h" and not "Message" or "java".

3.10.6. Array Sorting

To sort an array of numbers, you can use one of the sort methods in the Arrays class:

```
int[] a = new int[10000];
. . .
Arrays.sort(a)
```

This method uses a tuned version of the QuickSort algorithm that is claimed to be very efficient on most data sets. The Arrays class provides several other convenience methods for arrays that are included in the API notes at the end of this section.

The program in Listing 3.7 puts arrays to work. This program draws a random combination of numbers for a lottery game. For example, if you play a "choose 6 numbers from 49" lottery, the program might print this:

```
Bet the following combination. It'll make you rich!
4
7
8
19
30
44
```

To select such a random set of numbers, first fill an array numbers with the values 1, 2, . . ., n:

```
int[] numbers = new int[n];
for (int i = 0; i < numbers.length; i++)
   numbers[i] = i + 1;
```

A second array holds the numbers to be drawn:

```
int[] result = new int[k];
```

Now draw k numbers. The Math.random method returns a random floating-point number that is between 0 (inclusive) and 1 (exclusive). Multiplying the result with n yields a random number between 0 and n – 1.

```
int r = (int) (Math.random() * n);
```

Set the ith result to be the number at that index. Initially, that is just r + 1, but as you'll see presently, the contents of the numbers array are changed after each draw.

```
result[i] = numbers[r];
```

Now, you must be sure never to draw that number again—all lottery numbers must be distinct. Therefore, overwrite numbers[r] with the *last* number in the array and reduce n by 1.

```
numbers[r] = numbers[n - 1];
n--;
```

The point is that in each draw we pick an *index,* not the actual value. The index points into an array that contains the values that have not yet been drawn.

After drawing k lottery numbers, sort the result array for a more pleasing output:

```
Arrays.sort(result);
for (int r : result)
   System.out.println(r);
```

Listing 3.7 LotteryDrawing/LotteryDrawing.java

```
 1   import java.util.*;
 2
 3   /**
 4    * This program demonstrates array manipulation.
 5    * @version 1.20 2004-02-10
 6    * @author Cay Horstmann
 7    */
 8   public class LotteryDrawing
 9   {
10      public static void main(String[] args)
11      {
12         Scanner in = new Scanner(System.in);
13
14         System.out.print("How many numbers do you need to draw? ");
15         int k = in.nextInt();
16
17         System.out.print("What is the highest number you can draw? ");
18         int n = in.nextInt();
19
20         // fill an array with numbers 1 2 3 . . . n
21         int[] numbers = new int[n];
22         for (int i = 0; i < numbers.length; i++)
23            numbers[i] = i + 1;
24
25         // draw k numbers and put them into a second array
26         int[] result = new int[k];
27         for (int i = 0; i < result.length; i++)
28         {
29            // make a random index between 0 and n - 1
30            int r = (int) (Math.random() * n);
31
```

```
32              // pick the element at the random location
33              result[i] = numbers[r];
34
35              // move the last element into the random location
36              numbers[r] = numbers[n - 1];
37              n--;
38          }
39
40          // print the sorted array
41          Arrays.sort(result);
42          System.out.println("Bet the following combination. It'll make you rich!");
43          for (int r : result)
44              System.out.println(r);
45      }
46  }
```

---

java.util.Arrays **1.2**

- `static String toString(T[] a)` **5.0**
  returns a string with the elements of a, enclosed in brackets and delimited by commas. In this and the following methods, the component type *T* of the array can be int, long, short, char, byte, boolean, float, or double.
- `static T[] copyOf(T[] a, int end)` **6**
- `static T[] copyOfRange(T[] a, int start, int end)` **6**
  return an array of the same type as a, of length either end or end – start, filled with the values of a. If end is larger than a.length, the result is padded with 0 or false values.
- `static void sort(T[] a)`
  sorts the array, using a tuned QuickSort algorithm.
- `static void fill(T[] a, T v)`
  sets all elements of the array to v.
- `static boolean equals(T[] a, T[] b)`
  returns true if the arrays have the same length and if the elements at corresponding indexes match.

3.10.7. Multidimensional Arrays

Multidimensional arrays use more than one index to access array elements. They are used for tables and other more complex arrangements. You can safely skip this section until you have a need for this storage mechanism.

Suppose you want to make a table of numbers that shows how much an investment of $10,000 will grow under different interest rate scenarios in which interest is paid annually and reinvested.

```
        5%        6%        7%        8%        9%       10%
  10000.00  10000.00  10000.00  10000.00  10000.00  10000.00
  10500.00  10600.00  10700.00  10800.00  10900.00  11000.00
```

```
11025.00   11236.00   11449.00   11664.00   11881.00   12100.00
11576.25   11910.16   12250.43   12597.12   12950.29   13310.00
12155.06   12624.77   13107.96   13604.89   14115.82   14641.00
12762.82   13382.26   14025.52   14693.28   15386.24   16105.10
13400.96   14185.19   15007.30   15868.74   16771.00   17715.61
14071.00   15036.30   16057.81   17138.24   18280.39   19487.17
14774.55   15938.48   17181.86   18509.30   19925.63   21435.89
15513.28   16894.79   18384.59   19990.05   21718.93   23579.48
```

You can store this information in a two-dimensional array named balances.

Declaring a two-dimensional array in Java is simple enough. For example:

```
double[][] balances;
```

You cannot use the array until you initialize it. In this case, you can do the initialization as follows:

```
balances = new double[NYEARS][NRATES];
```

In other cases, if you know the array elements, you can use a shorthand notation for initializing a multidimensional array without a call to new. For example:

```
int[][] magicSquare =
   {
      {16, 3, 2, 13},
      {5, 10, 11, 8},
      {9, 6, 7, 12},
      {4, 15, 14, 1}
   };
```

Once the array is initialized, you can access individual elements by supplying two pairs of brackets—for example, balances[i][j].

The example program stores a one-dimensional array interest of interest rates and a two-dimensional array balances of account balances, one for each year and interest rate. Initialize the first row of the array with the initial balance:

```
for (int j = 0; j < balances[0].length; j++)
   balances[0][j] = 10000;
```

Then compute the other rows, as follows:

```
for (int i = 1; i < balances.length; i++)
{
   for (int j = 0; j < balances[i].length; j++)
   {
```

```
      double oldBalance = balances[i - 1][j];
      double interest = . . .;
      balances[i][j] = oldBalance + interest;
   }
}
```

Listing 3.8 shows the full program.

 Note: A "for each" loop does not automatically loop through all elements in a two-dimensional array. Instead, it loops through the rows, which are themselves one-dimensional arrays. To visit all elements of a two-dimensional array a, nest two loops, like this:

```
for (double[] row : a)
   for (double value : row)
      do something with value
```

 Tip: To print out a quick-and-dirty list of the elements of a two-dimensional array, call

```
System.out.println(Arrays.deepToString(a));
```

The output is formatted like this:

```
[[16, 3, 2, 13], [5, 10, 11, 8], [9, 6, 7, 12], [4, 15, 14, 1]]
```

Listing 3.8 CompoundInterest/CompoundInterest.java

```
 1  /**
 2   * This program shows how to store tabular data in a 2D array.
 3   * @version 1.41 2023-11-28
 4   * @author Cay Horstmann
 5   */
 6  public class CompoundInterest
 7  {
 8     public static void main(String[] args)
 9     {
10        final double STARTRATE = 5;
11        final int NRATES = 6;
12        final int NYEARS = 10;
13
14        // set interest rates to 5 . . . 10%
15        double[] interestRate = new double[NRATES];
16        for (int j = 0; j < interestRate.length; j++)
```

```
17              interestRate[j] = (STARTRATE + j) / 100.0;
18
19          double[][] balances = new double[NYEARS][NRATES];
20
21          // set initial balances to 10000
22          for (int j = 0; j < balances[0].length; j++)
23              balances[0][j] = 10000;
24
25          // compute interest for future years
26          for (int i = 1; i < balances.length; i++)
27          {
28              for (int j = 0; j < balances[i].length; j++)
29              {
30                  // get last year's balances from previous row
31                  double oldBalance = balances[i - 1][j];
32
33                  // compute interest
34                  double interest = oldBalance * interestRate[j];
35
36                  // compute this year's balances
37                  balances[i][j] = oldBalance + interest;
38              }
39          }
40
41          // print one row of interest rates
42          for (int j = 0; j < interestRate.length; j++)
43              System.out.printf("%9.0f%%", 100 * interestRate[j]);
44
45          System.out.println();
46
47          // print balance table
48          for (double[] row : balances)
49          {
50              // print table row
51              for (double b : row)
52                  System.out.printf("%10.2f", b);
53
54              System.out.println();
55          }
56      }
57 }
```

3.10.8. Ragged Arrays

So far, what you have seen is not too different from other programming languages. But there is actually something subtle going on behind the scenes that you can sometimes turn to your advantage: Java has *no* multidimensional arrays at all, only one-dimensional arrays. Multidimensional arrays are faked as "arrays of arrays."

For example, the balances array in the preceding example is actually an array that contains ten elements, each of which is an array of six floating-point numbers (Figure 3.15).

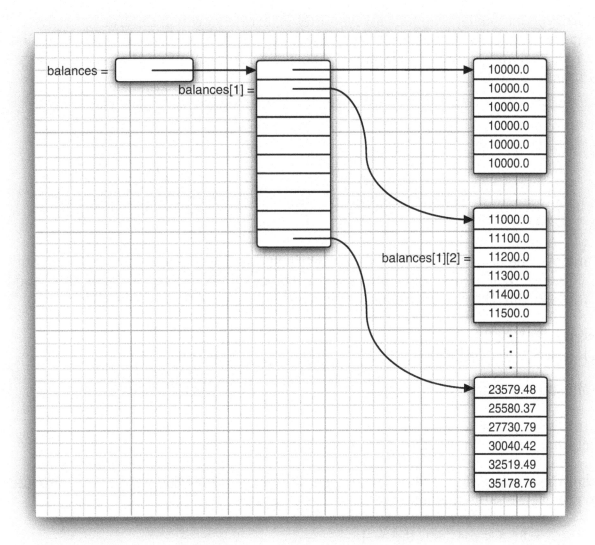

Figure 3.15: A two-dimensional array

The expression balances[i] refers to the ith subarray—that is, the ith row of the table. It is itself an array, and balances[i][j] refers to the jth element of that array.

Since rows of arrays are individually accessible, you can actually swap them!

```
double[] temp = balances[i];
balances[i] = balances[i + 1];
balances[i + 1] = temp;
```

Note that the number of rows and columns is not a part of the type of an array variable. The variable balances has type double[][]: an array of double arrays.

Therefore, you can make "ragged" arrays—that is, arrays in which different rows have different lengths. Here is the standard example. Let us make an array in which the element at row i and column j equals the number of possible outcomes of a "choose j numbers from i numbers" lottery.

```
1
1  1
1  2  1
1  3  3  1
1  4  6  4  1
1  5 10 10  5 1
1  6 15 20 15 6 1
```

As j can never be larger than i, the matrix is triangular. The ith row has i + 1 elements. (It is OK to choose 0 elements; there is one way to make such a choice.) To build this ragged array, first allocate the array holding the rows:

```
final int NMAX = 10;
int[][] odds = new int[NMAX + 1][];
```

Next, allocate the rows:

```
for (int n = 0; n <= NMAX; n++)
   odds[n] = new int[n + 1];
```

Now that the array is allocated, you can access the elements in the normal way, provided you do not overstep the bounds:

```
for (int n = 0; n < odds.length; n++)
   for (int k = 0; k < odds[n].length; k++)
   {
      // compute lotteryOdds
      . . .
      odds[n][k] = lotteryOdds;
   }
```

Listing 3.9 gives the complete program.

 Note: Just as with one-dimensional arrays, it is legal to construct multi-dimensional arrays where a dimension is zero. For example,

```
new int[3][0]
```

has three rows, each of which happen to have length zero. In contrast,

```
new int[0][3]
```

has no rows. The row length is immaterial, since no rows are actually allocated. In other words, new int[0][3], new int[0][4], and new int[0][] are all the same.

C++ Note: In C++, the Java declaration

```
double[][] balances = new double[10][6]; // Java
```

is not the same as

```
double balances[10][6]; // C++
```

or even

```
double (*balances)[6] = new double[10][6]; // C++
```

Instead, an array of ten pointers is allocated:

```
double** balances = new double*[10]; // C++
```

Then, each element in the pointer array is filled with an array of six numbers:

```
for (i = 0; i < 10; i++)
   balances[i] = new double[6];
```

Mercifully, this loop is automatic when you ask for a new double[10][6]. When you want ragged arrays, you allocate the row arrays separately.

Listing 3.9 `LotteryArray/LotteryArray.java`

```
 1  /**
 2   * This program demonstrates a triangular array.
 3   * @version 1.20 2004-02-10
 4   * @author Cay Horstmann
 5   */
 6  public class LotteryArray
 7  {
 8     public static void main(String[] args)
 9     {
10        final int NMAX = 10;
11
12        // allocate triangular array
13        int[][] odds = new int[NMAX + 1][];
14        for (int n = 0; n <= NMAX; n++)
```

```
15              odds[n] = new int[n + 1];
16
17          // fill triangular array
18          for (int n = 0; n < odds.length; n++)
19              for (int k = 0; k < odds[n].length; k++)
20              {
21                  /*
22                   * compute binomial coefficient n*(n-1)*(n-2)*...*(n-k+1)/(1*2*3*...*k)
23                   */
24                  int lotteryOdds = 1;
25                  for (int i = 1; i <= k; i++)
26                      lotteryOdds = lotteryOdds * (n - i + 1) / i;
27
28                  odds[n][k] = lotteryOdds;
29              }
30
31          // print triangular array
32          for (int[] row : odds)
33          {
34              for (int odd : row)
35                  System.out.printf("%4d", odd);
36              System.out.println();
37          }
38      }
39  }
```

You have now seen the fundamental programming structures of the Java language. The next chapter covers object-oriented programming in Java.

CHAPTER 4

Objects and Classes

In this chapter, I

- Introduce you to object-oriented programming;
- Show you how you can create objects that belong to classes from the standard Java library; and
- Show you how to write your own classes.

If you do not have a background in object-oriented programming, you will want to read this chapter carefully. Object-oriented programming requires a different way of thinking than procedural languages. The transition is not always easy, but you do need some familiarity with object concepts to go further with Java.

For experienced C++ programmers, this chapter, like the previous chapter, presents familiar information; however, there are enough differences between the two languages that you should read the later sections of this chapter carefully. You'll find the C++ notes helpful for making the transition.

4.1. Introduction to Object-Oriented Programming

Object-oriented programming, or OOP for short, is the dominant programming paradigm these days, having replaced the "structured" or procedural programming techniques that were developed in the 1970s. Since Java is object-oriented, you have to be familiar with OOP to become productive with Java.

An object-oriented program is made of objects. Each object has a specific functionality, exposed to its users, and a hidden implementation. Many objects in your programs will be taken "off-the-shelf" from a library; others will be custom-designed. Whether you build an object or use a pre-built one it might depend on your budget or time. But, basically, as long as an object satisfies your specifications, you don't care how the functionality is implemented.

Traditional structured programming consists of designing a set of procedures (or *algorithms*) to solve a problem. Once the procedures are determined, the traditional next step was to find appropriate ways to store the data. This is why the designer of the Pascal language, Niklaus Wirth, called his famous book on programming *Algorithms + Data Structures = Programs* (Prentice Hall, 1976). Notice that in Wirth's title, algorithms come first, and data structures second. This reflects the way programmers worked at that time.

First, they decided on the procedures for manipulating the data; then, they decided what structure to impose on the data to make the manipulations easier. OOP reverses the order: puts the data first, then looks at the algorithms to operate on the data.

For small problems, the breakdown into procedures works very well. But objects are more appropriate for larger problems. Consider a simple web browser. It might require 2,000 procedures for its implementation, all of which manipulate a set of global data. In the object-oriented style, there might be 100 classes with an average of 20 methods per class (see Figure 4.1). This structure is much easier for a programmer to grasp. It is also much easier to find bugs in. Suppose the data of a particular object is in an incorrect state. It is far easier to search for the culprit among the 20 methods that had access to that data item than among 2,000 procedures.

4.1.1. Classes

A *class* specifies how objects are made. Think of classes as cookie cutters; objects are the cookies themselves. When you *construct* an object from a class, you are said to have created an *instance* of the class.

As you have seen, all code that you write in Java is inside a class. The standard Java library supplies several thousand classes for such diverse purposes as user interface design, dates and calendars, and network programming. Nonetheless, in Java you still have to create your own classes to describe the objects of your application's problem domain.

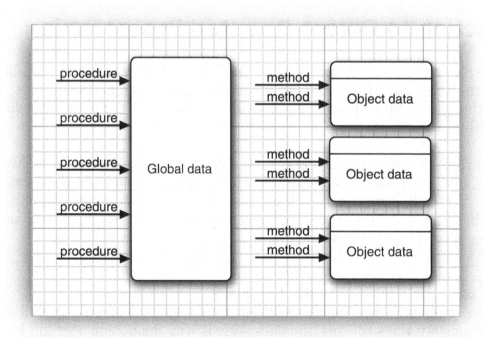

Figure 4.1: Procedural vs. OO programming

Encapsulation (sometimes called *information hiding*) is a key concept in working with objects. Formally, encapsulation is simply combining data and behavior in one package and hiding the implementation details from the users of the object. The bits of data in an object are called its *instance fields,* and the procedures that operate on the data are called its *methods.* A specific object that is an instance of a class will have specific values of its instance fields. The set of those values is the current *state* of the object. Whenever you invoke a method on an object, its state may change.

The key to making encapsulation work is to have methods *never* directly access instance fields in a class other than their own. Programs should interact with object data *only* through the object's methods. Encapsulation is the way to give an object its "black box" behavior, which is the key to reuse and reliability. This means a class may totally change how it stores its data, but as long as it continues to use the same methods to manipulate the data, no other object will know or care.

When you start writing your own classes in Java, another tenet of OOP will make this easier: Classes can be built by *extending* other classes. Java, in fact, comes with a "cosmic superclass" called Object. All other classes extend this class. You will learn more about the Object class in the next chapter.

When you extend an existing class, the new class has all the properties and methods of the class that you extend. You then supply new methods and instance fields that apply to your new class only. The concept of extending a class to obtain another class is called *inheritance.* See the next chapter for more on inheritance.

4.1.2. Objects

To work with OOP, you should be able to identify three key characteristics of objects:

- The object's *behavior*—what can you do with this object, or what methods can you apply to it?
- The object's *state*—how does the object react when you invoke those methods?
- The object's *identity*—how is the object distinguished from others that may have the same behavior and state?

All objects that are instances of the same class share a family resemblance by supporting the same *behavior.* The behavior of an object is defined by the methods that you can call.

Next, each object stores information about what it currently looks like. This is the object's *state.* An object's state may change over time, but not spontaneously. A change in the state of an object must be a consequence of method calls. (If an object's state changed without a method call on that object, someone broke encapsulation.)

However, the state of an object does not completely describe it, because each object has a distinct *identity.* For example, in an order processing system, two orders are distinct even if they request identical items. Notice that the individual objects that are instances of a class *always* differ in their identity and *usually* differ in their state.

These key characteristics can influence each other. For example, the state of an object can influence its behavior. (If an order is "shipped" or "paid," it may reject a method call that asks it to add or remove items. Conversely, if an order is "empty"—that is, no items have yet been ordered—it should not allow itself to be shipped.)

4.1.3. Identifying Classes

In a traditional procedural program, you start the process at the top, with the main function. When designing an object-oriented system, there is no "top," and newcomers to OOP often wonder where to begin. The answer is: Identify your classes and then add methods to each class.

A simple rule of thumb in identifying classes is to look for nouns in the problem analysis. Methods, on the other hand, correspond to verbs.

For example, in an order-processing system, some of the nouns are

- Item
- Order
- Shipping address
- Payment
- Account

These nouns may lead to the classes Item, Order, and so on.

Next, look for verbs. Items are *added* to orders. Orders are *shipped* or *canceled*. Payments are *applied* to orders. With each verb, such as "add," "ship," "cancel," or "apply," you identify the object that has the major responsibility for carrying it out. For example, when a new item is added to an order, the order object should be the one in charge because it knows how it stores and sorts items. That is, add should be a method of the Order class that has an Item object as a parameter.

Of course, the "noun and verb" is but a rule of thumb; only experience can help you decide which nouns and verbs are the important ones when building your classes.

4.1.4. Relationships between Classes

The most common relationships between classes are

- *Dependence* ("uses-a")
- *Aggregation* ("has-a")
- *Inheritance* ("is-a")

The *dependence*, or "uses-a" relationship, is the most obvious and also the most general. For example, the Order class uses the Account class because Order objects need to access Account objects to check for credit status. But the Item class does not depend on the Account class, because Item objects never need to worry about customer accounts. Thus, a class depends on another class if its methods use or manipulate objects of that class.

Try to minimize the number of classes that depend on each other. The point is, if a class A is unaware of the existence of a class B, it is also unconcerned about any changes to B. (And this means that changes to B do not introduce bugs into A.) In software engineering terminology, you want to minimize the *coupling* between classes.

The *aggregation*, or "has–a" relationship, is easy to understand because it is concrete; for example, an Order object contains Item objects. Containment means that objects of class A contain objects of class B.

 Note: Some methodologists view the concept of aggregation with disdain and prefer to use a more general "association" relationship. From the point of view of modeling, that is understandable. But for programmers, the "has–a" relationship makes a lot of sense. I like to use aggregation for another reason as well: The standard notation for associations is less clear. See Table 4.1.

The *inheritance*, or "is–a" relationship, expresses a relationship between a more special and a more general class. For example, a RushOrder class inherits from an Order class. The specialized RushOrder class has special methods for priority handling and a different method for computing shipping charges, but its other methods, such as adding items and billing, are inherited from the Order class. In general, if class D extends class C, class D inherits methods from class C but has more capabilities. (See the next chapter which discusses this important notion at some length.)

Many programmers use the UML (Unified Modeling Language) notation to draw *class diagrams* that describe the relationships between classes. You can see an example of such a diagram in Figure 4.2. You draw classes as rectangles, and relationships as arrows with various adornments. Table 4.1 shows the UML arrow styles that this book uses.

Table 4.1: UML Notation for Class Relationships

Relationship	UML Connector
Inheritance	——————————————▷
Interface implementation	– — — — — — — –▷
Dependency	– — — — — — — →
Aggregation	◇———————————

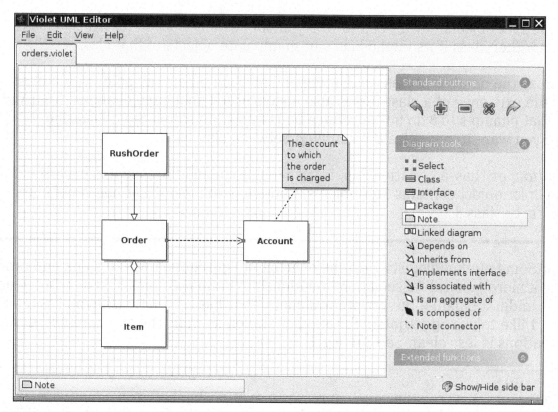

Figure 4.2: A class diagram

4.2. Using Predefined Classes

You can't do anything in Java without classes, and you have already seen several classes at work. However, not all of these show off the typical features of object orientation. Take, for example, the Math class. You have seen that you can use methods of the Math class, such as Math.random, without needing to know how they are implemented—all you need to know is the name and parameter types (if any). That's the point of encapsulation, and it will certainly be true of all classes. But the Math class *only* encapsulates functionality; it neither needs nor hides data. Since there is no data, you do not need to worry about making objects and initializing their instance fields—there aren't any!

In the next section, we will look at a more typical class, the Date class. You will see how to construct objects and call methods of this class.

4.2.1. Objects and Object Variables

To work with objects, you first construct them and specify their initial state. Then you apply methods to the objects.

In the Java programming language, you use *constructors* to construct new instances. A constructor is a special method whose purpose is to construct and initialize objects. Let us look at an example. The standard Java library contains a Date class. Its objects describe points in time, such as December 31, 1999, 23:59:59 GMT.

 Note: You may be wondering: Why use a class to represent dates rather than (as in some languages) a built-in type? For example, Visual Basic has a built-in date type, and programmers can specify dates in the format #12/31/1999#. On the surface, this sounds convenient—programmers can simply use the built-in date type without worrying about classes. But actually, how suitable is the Visual Basic design? In some locales, dates are specified as month/day/year, in others as day/month/year. Are the language designers really equipped to foresee these kinds of issues? If they do a poor job, the language becomes an unpleasant muddle, but unhappy programmers are powerless to do anything about it. With classes, the design task is offloaded to a library designer. If the class is not perfect, other programmers can easily write their own classes to enhance or replace the system classes. (To prove the point: The Java date library started out a bit muddled, and it has been redesigned twice.)

Constructors always have the same name as the class name. Thus, the constructor for the Date class is called Date. To construct a Date object, combine the constructor with the new operator, as follows:

```
new Date()
```

This expression constructs a new object. The object is initialized to the current date and time.

If you like, you can pass the object to a method:

```
System.out.println(new Date());
```

Alternatively, you can apply a method to the object that you just constructed. One of the methods of the Date class is the toString method. That method yields a string representation of the date. Here is how you would apply the toString method to a newly constructed Date object:

```
String s = new Date().toString();
```

In these two examples, the constructed object is used only once. Usually, you will want to hang on to the objects that you construct so that you can keep using them. Simply store the object in a variable:

```
Date rightNow = new Date();
```

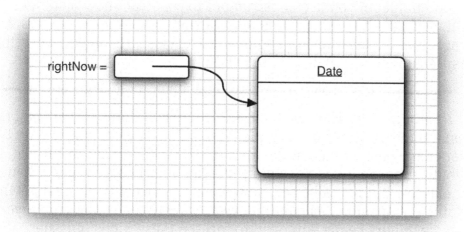

Figure 4.3: Creating a new object

Figure 4.3 shows the object variable rightNow that refers to the newly constructed object.

There is an important difference between objects and object variables. For example, the statement

```
Date startTime; // startTime doesn't refer to any object
```

defines an object variable, startTime, that can refer to objects of type Date. It is important to realize that the variable startTime *is not an object* and, in fact, does not even refer to an object yet. You cannot use any Date methods on this variable at this time. The statement

```
s = startTime.toString(); // not yet
```

would cause a compile-time error.

You must first initialize the startTime variable. You have two choices. Of course, you can initialize the variable so that it refers to a newly constructed object:

```
startTime = new Date();
```

Or you can set the variable to refer to an existing object:

```
startTime = rightNow;
```

Now both variables refer to the *same* object (see Figure 4.4).

It is important to realize that an object variable doesn't actually contain an object. It only *refers* to an object.

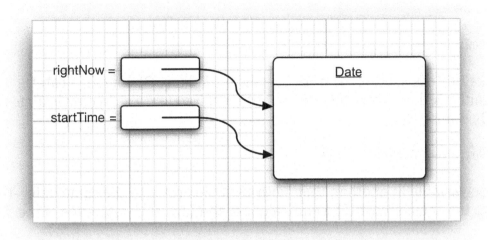

Figure 4.4: Object variables that refer to the same object

In Java, the value of any object variable is a reference to an object that is stored elsewhere. The return value of the new operator is also a reference. A statement such as

```
Date startTime = new Date();
```

has two parts. The expression new Date() makes an object of type Date, and its value is a reference to that newly created object. That reference is then stored in the startTime variable.

You can explicitly set an object variable to null to indicate that it currently refers to no object.

```
startTime = null;
. . .
if (startTime != null)
   System.out.println(startTime);
```

I discuss null in more detail in Section 4.3.6.

 C++ Note: Some people mistakenly believe that Java object variables behave like C++ references. But in C++ there are no null references, and references cannot be assigned. You should think of Java object variables as analogous to *object pointers* in C++. For example,

```
Date rightNow; // Java
```

is really the same as

```
Date* rightNow; // C++
```

Once you make this association, everything falls into place. Of course, a Date* pointer isn't initialized until you initialize it with a call to new. The syntax is almost the same in C++ and Java.

```
Date* rightNow = new Date(); // C++
```

If you copy one variable to another, then both variables refer to the same date—they are pointers to the same object. The equivalent of the Java null reference is the C++ NULL pointer.

All Java objects live on the heap. When an object contains another object variable, it contains just a pointer to yet another heap object.

In C++, pointers make you nervous because they are so error-prone. It is easy to create bad pointers or to mess up memory management. In Java, these problems simply go away. If you use an uninitialized pointer, the runtime system will reliably generate a runtime error instead of producing random results. You don't have to worry about memory management, because the garbage collector takes care of it.

C++ makes quite an effort, with its support for copy constructors and assignment operators, to allow the implementation of objects that copy themselves automatically. For example, a copy of a linked list is a new linked list with the same contents but with an independent set of links. This makes it possible to design classes with the same copy behavior as the built-in types. In Java, you must use the clone method to get a complete copy of an object.

4.2.2. The LocalDate Class of the Java Library

In the preceding examples, we used the Date class that is a part of the standard Java library. An instance of the Date class has a state—namely, *a particular point in time.*

Although you don't need to know this when you use the Date class, the time is represented by the number of milliseconds (positive or negative) from a fixed point, the so-called *epoch,* which is 00:00:00 UTC, January 1, 1970. UTC is the Coordinated Universal Time, the scientific time standard which is, for practical purposes, the same as the more familiar GMT, or Greenwich Mean Time.

But as it turns out, the Date class is not very useful for manipulating the kind of calendar information that humans use for dates, such as "December 31, 1999." This particular description of a day follows the Gregorian calendar, which is the calendar used in most countries of the world. The same point in time would be described quite differently in the

Chinese or Hebrew lunar calendars, not to mention the calendar used by your customers from Mars.

 Note: Throughout human history, civilizations grappled with the design of calendars to attach names to dates and bring order to the solar and lunar cycles. For a fascinating explanation of calendars around the world, from the French Revolutionary calendar to the Mayan long count, see *Calendrical Calculations* by Nachum Dershowitz and Edward M. Reingold (Cambridge University Press, 4th ed., 2018).

The library designers decided to separate the concerns of keeping time and attaching names to points in time. Therefore, the standard Java library contains two separate classes: the Date class, which represents a point in time, and the LocalDate class, which expresses days in the familiar calendar notation. Nowadays there is a much more robust set of classes for manipulating various aspects of date and time—see Chapter 6 of Volume II.

Separating time measurement from calendars is good object-oriented design. In general, it is a good idea to use different classes to express different concepts.

You do not use a constructor to construct objects of the LocalDate class. Instead, use static *factory methods* that call constructors on your behalf. The expression

```
LocalDate.now()
```

constructs a new object that represents the date at which the object was constructed.

You can construct an object for a specific date by supplying year, month, and day:

```
LocalDate.of(1999, 12, 31)
```

Of course, you will usually want to store the constructed object in an object variable:

```
LocalDate newYearsEve = LocalDate.of(1999, 12, 31);
```

Once you have a LocalDate object, you can find out the year, month, and day with the methods getYear, getMonthValue, and getDayOfMonth:

```
int year = newYearsEve.getYear(); // 1999
int month = newYearsEve.getMonthValue(); // 12
int day = newYearsEve.getDayOfMonth(); // 31
```

This may seem pointless because they are the very same values that you just used to construct the object. But sometimes, you have a date that has been computed, and then you will want to invoke those methods to find out more about it. For example, the plusDays method yields a new `LocalDate` that is a given number of days away from the object to which you apply it:

```
LocalDate aThousandDaysLater = newYearsEve.plusDays(1000);
year = aThousandDaysLater.getYear(); // 2002
month = aThousandDaysLater.getMonthValue(); // 09
day = aThousandDaysLater.getDayOfMonth(); // 26
```

The `LocalDate` class has encapsulated instance fields to maintain the date to which it is set. Without looking at the source code, it is impossible to know the representation that the class uses internally. But, of course, the point of encapsulation is that this doesn't matter. What matters are the methods that a class exposes.

Note: Actually, the `Date` class also has methods to get the day, month, and year, called `getDay`, `getMonth`, and `getYear`, but these methods are *deprecated*. A method is deprecated when a library designer realizes that the method should have never been introduced in the first place.

These methods were a part of the `Date` class before the library designers realized that it makes more sense to supply separate classes to deal with calendars. When an earlier set of calendar classes was introduced in Java 1.1, the `Date` methods were tagged as deprecated. You can still use them in your programs, but you will get unsightly compiler warnings if you do. It is a good idea to stay away from using deprecated methods because they may be removed in a future version of the library.

Tip: The JDK provides the `jdeprscan` tool for checking whether your code uses deprecated features of the Java API. See `https://docs.oracle.com/en/java/javase/21/docs/specs/man/jdeprscan.html` for instructions.

4.2.3. Mutator and Accessor Methods

Have another look at the `plusDays` method call that you saw in the preceding section:

```
LocalDate aThousandDaysLater = newYearsEve.plusDays(1000);
```

What happens to `newYearsEve` after the call? Has it been changed to be a thousand days later? As it turns out, it has not. The `plusDays` method yields a new `LocalDate` object, which is then assigned to the `aThousandDaysLater` variable. The original object remains unchanged. We say that the `plusDays` method does not *mutate* the object on which it is invoked. (This is similar to the `toUpperCase` method of the `String` class that you saw in Chapter 3. When you call `toUpperCase` on a string, that string stays the same, and a new string with uppercase characters is returned.)

An earlier version of the Java library had a different class for dealing with calendars, called GregorianCalendar. This code snippet adds a thousand days to a date represented by that class:

```
GregorianCalendar someDay = new GregorianCalendar(1999, 11, 31);
   // odd feature of that class: month numbers go from 0 to 11
someDay.add(Calendar.DAY_OF_MONTH, 1000);
```

Unlike the LocalDate.plusDays method, the GregorianCalendar.add method is a *mutator method*. After invoking it, the state of the someDay object has changed. Here is how you can find out the new state:

```
year = someDay.get(Calendar.YEAR); // 2002
month = someDay.get(Calendar.MONTH) + 1; // 09
day = someDay.get(Calendar.DAY_OF_MONTH); // 26
```

That's why the variable is called someDay and not newYearsEve—it no longer is new year's eve after calling the mutator method.

In contrast, methods that only access objects without modifying them are sometimes called *accessor methods*. For example, LocalDate.getYear and GregorianCalendar.get are accessor methods.

 C++ Note: In C++, the const suffix denotes accessor methods. A method that is not declared as const is assumed to be a mutator. However, in the Java programming language, no special syntax distinguishes accessors from mutators.

I finish this section with a program that puts the LocalDate class to work. The program displays a calendar for the current month, like this:

```
Mon Tue Wed Thu Fri Sat Sun
                          1
  2   3   4   5   6   7   8
  9  10  11  12  13  14  15
 16  17  18  19  20  21  22
 23  24  25  26* 27  28  29
 30
```

The current day is marked with an asterisk (*). As you can see, the program needs to know how to compute the length of a month and the weekday of a given day.

Let us go through the key steps of the program. First, we construct an object that is initialized with the current date.

```
LocalDate date = LocalDate.now();
```

We capture the current month and day.

```
int month = date.getMonthValue();
int today = date.getDayOfMonth();
```

Then we set date to the first of the month and get the weekday of that date.

```
date = date.minusDays(today - 1); // set to start of month
DayOfWeek weekday = date.getDayOfWeek();
int value = weekday.getValue(); // 1 = Monday, . . . , 7 = Sunday
```

The variable weekday is set to an object of type DayOfWeek. We call the getValue method of that object to get a numerical value for the weekday. This yields an integer that follows the international convention where the weekend comes at the end of the week, returning 1 for Monday, 2 for Tuesday, and so on. Sunday has value 7.

Note that the first line of the calendar is indented, so that the first day of the month falls on the appropriate weekday. Here is the code to print the header and the indentation for the first line:

```
System.out.println("Mon Tue Wed Thu Fri Sat Sun");
for (int i = 1; i < value; i++)
   System.out.print("    ");
```

Now, we are ready to print the body of the calendar. We enter a loop in which date traverses the days of the month.

In each iteration, we print the date value. If date is today, the date is marked with an *. Then, we advance date to the next day. When we reach the beginning of each new week, we print a new line:

```
while (date.getMonthValue() == month)
{
   System.out.printf("%3d", date.getDayOfMonth());
   if (date.getDayOfMonth() == today)
      System.out.print("*");
   else
      System.out.print(" ");
   date = date.plusDays(1);
   if (date.getDayOfWeek().getValue() == 1) System.out.println();
}
```

When do we stop? We don't know whether the month has 31, 30, 29, or 28 days. Instead, we keep iterating while date is still in the current month.

Listing 4.1 shows the complete program.

As you can see, the LocalDate class makes it possible to write a calendar program that takes care of complexities such as weekdays and the varying month lengths. You don't need to know *how* the LocalDate class computes months and weekdays. You just use the *interface* of the class—the methods such as plusDays and getDayOfWeek.

The point of this example program is to show you how you can use the interface of a class to carry out fairly sophisticated tasks without having to know the implementation details.

Listing 4.1 CalendarTest/CalendarTest.java

```java
1  import java.time.*;
2
3  /**
4   * @version 1.5 2015-05-08
5   * @author Cay Horstmann
6   */
7  public class CalendarTest
8  {
9     public static void main(String[] args)
10    {
11       LocalDate date = LocalDate.now();
12       int month = date.getMonthValue();
13       int today = date.getDayOfMonth();
14
15       date = date.minusDays(today - 1); // set to start of month
16       DayOfWeek weekday = date.getDayOfWeek();
17       int value = weekday.getValue(); // 1 = Monday, . . . , 7 = Sunday
18
19       System.out.println("Mon Tue Wed Thu Fri Sat Sun");
20       for (int i = 1; i < value; i++)
21          System.out.print("    ");
22       while (date.getMonthValue() == month)
23       {
24          System.out.printf("%3d", date.getDayOfMonth());
25          if (date.getDayOfMonth() == today)
26             System.out.print("*");
27          else
28             System.out.print(" ");
29          date = date.plusDays(1);
30          if (date.getDayOfWeek().getValue() == 1) System.out.println();
31       }
32       if (date.getDayOfWeek().getValue() != 1) System.out.println();
33    }
34 }
```

`java.time.LocalDate` 8

- `static LocalDate now()`
  constructs an object that represents the current date.
- `static LocalDate of(int year, int month, int day)`
  constructs an object that represents the given date.
- `int getYear()`
- `int getMonthValue()`
- `int getDayOfMonth()`
  get the year, month, and day of this date.
- `DayOfWeek getDayOfWeek()`
  gets the weekday of this date as an instance of the DayOfWeek class. Call `getValue` on the DayOfWeek instance to get a weekday between 1 (Monday) and 7 (Sunday).
- `LocalDate plusDays(int n)`
- `LocalDate minusDays(int n)`
  yield the date that is n days after or before this date.

4.3. Defining Your Own Classes

In Chapter 3, you started writing simple classes. However, all those classes had just a single `main` method. Now the time has come to show you how to write the kind of "workhorse classes" that are needed for more sophisticated applications. These classes typically do not have a `main` method. Instead, they have their own instance fields and methods. To build a complete program, you combine several classes, one of which has a `main` method.

4.3.1. An `Employee` Class

The simplest form for a class definition in Java is

```
class ClassName
{
    field1
    field2
    . . .
    constructor1
    constructor2
    . . .
    method1
    method2
    . . .
}
```

Consider the following, very simplified, version of an `Employee` class that might be used by a business in writing a payroll system:

```java
class Employee
{
    // instance fields
    private String name;
    private double salary;
    private LocalDate hireDay;

    // constructor
    public Employee(String n, double s, int year, int month, int day)
    {
        name = n;
        salary = s;
        hireDay = LocalDate.of(year, month, day);
    }

    // a method
    public String getName()
    {
        return name;
    }

    // more methods
    . . .
}
```

We break down the implementation of this class, in some detail, in the sections that follow. First, though, Listing 4.2 is a program that shows the Employee class in action.

In the program, we construct an Employee array and fill it with three Employee objects:

```java
Employee[] staff = new Employee[3];

staff[0] = new Employee("Carl Cracker", . . .);
staff[1] = new Employee("Harry Hacker", . . .);
staff[2] = new Employee("Tony Tester", . . .);
```

Next, we use the raiseSalary method of the Employee class to raise each employee's salary by 5%:

```java
for (Employee e : staff)
    e.raiseSalary(5);
```

Finally, we print out information about each employee, by calling the getName, getSalary, and getHireDay methods:

```
for (Employee e : staff)
   System.out.println("name=" + e.getName()
      + ",salary=" + e.getSalary()
      + ",hireDay=" + e.getHireDay());
```

Note that the example program consists of *two* classes: the Employee class and a class
EmployeeTest with the public access specifier. The main method with the instructions that we
just described is contained in the EmployeeTest class.

The name of the source file is EmployeeTest.java because the name of the file must match
the name of the public class. You can only have one public class in a source file, but you can
have any number of nonpublic classes.

Next, when you compile this source code, the compiler creates two class files in the
directory: EmployeeTest.class and Employee.class.

You then start the program by giving the bytecode interpreter the name of the class that
contains the main method of your program:

```
java EmployeeTest
```

The bytecode interpreter starts running the code in the main method in the EmployeeTest
class. This code in turn constructs three new Employee objects and shows you their state.

Listing 4.2 EmployeeTest/EmployeeTest.java

```
 1  import java.time.*;
 2
 3  /**
 4   * This program tests the Employee class.
 5   * @version 1.13 2018-04-10
 6   * @author Cay Horstmann
 7   */
 8  public class EmployeeTest
 9  {
10     public static void main(String[] args)
11     {
12        // fill the staff array with three Employee objects
13        Employee[] staff = new Employee[3];
14
15        staff[0] = new Employee("Carl Cracker", 75000, 1987, 12, 15);
16        staff[1] = new Employee("Harry Hacker", 50000, 1989, 10, 1);
17        staff[2] = new Employee("Tony Tester", 40000, 1990, 3, 15);
18
19        // raise everyone's salary by 5%
20        for (Employee e : staff)
21           e.raiseSalary(5);
22
```

```
23        // print out information about all Employee objects
24        for (Employee e : staff)
25           System.out.println("name=" + e.getName() + ",salary=" + e.getSalary() + ",hireDay="
26              + e.getHireDay());
27     }
28  }
29
30  class Employee
31  {
32     private String name;
33     private double salary;
34     private LocalDate hireDay;
35
36     public Employee(String n, double s, int year, int month, int day)
37     {
38        name = n;
39        salary = s;
40        hireDay = LocalDate.of(year, month, day);
41     }
42
43     public String getName()
44     {
45        return name;
46     }
47
48     public double getSalary()
49     {
50        return salary;
51     }
52
53     public LocalDate getHireDay()
54     {
55        return hireDay;
56     }
57
58     public void raiseSalary(double byPercent)
59     {
60        double raise = salary * byPercent / 100;
61        salary += raise;
62     }
63  }
```

4.3.2. Use of Multiple Source Files

The program in Listing 4.2 has two classes in a single source file. Many programmers prefer to put each class into its own source file. For example, you can place the Employee class into a file Employee.java and the EmployeeTest class into EmployeeTest.java.

If you like this arrangement, you have two choices for compiling the program. You can invoke the Java compiler with a wildcard:

```
javac Employee*.java
```

Then, all source files matching the wildcard will be compiled into class files. Or, you can simply type

```
javac EmployeeTest.java
```

You may find it surprising that the second choice works even though the Employee.java file is never explicitly compiled. However, when the Java compiler sees the Employee class being used inside EmployeeTest.java, it will look for a file named Employee.class. If it does not find that file, it automatically searches for Employee.java and compiles it. Moreover, if the timestamp of the version of Employee.java that it finds is newer than that of the existing Employee.class file, the Java compiler will *automatically* recompile the file.

 Note: If you are familiar with the make tool of UNIX (or one of its Windows cousins, such as nmake), you can think of the Java compiler as having the make functionality already built in.

4.3.3. Dissecting the Employee Class

In the sections that follow, we will dissect the Employee class. Let's start with the methods in this class. As you can see by examining the source code, this class has one constructor and four methods:

```
public Employee(String n, double s, int year, int month, int day)
public String getName()
public double getSalary()
public LocalDate getHireDay()
public void raiseSalary(double byPercent)
```

All methods of this class are tagged as public. The keyword public means that any method in any class can call the method. (The four possible access levels are covered in this and the next chapter.)

Next, notice the three instance fields that will hold the data manipulated inside an instance of the Employee class.

```
private String name;
private double salary;
private LocalDate hireDay;
```

The private keyword makes sure that the *only* methods that can access these instance fields are the methods of the Employee class itself. No outside method can read or write to these fields.

Note: You could use the public keyword with your instance fields, but it would be a very bad idea. Having public instance fields would allow any part of the program to read and modify the instance fields, completely ruining encapsulation. Any method of any class can modify public fields—and, in my experience, some code *will* take advantage of that access privilege when you least expect it. I strongly recommend to make all your instance fields private.

Finally, notice that two of the instance fields are themselves objects: The name and hireDay fields are references to String and LocalDate objects. This is quite usual: Classes will often contain instance fields of class type.

4.3.4. First Steps with Constructors

Let's look at the constructor listed in our Employee class.

```
public Employee(String n, double s, int year, int month, int day)
{
    name = n;
    salary = s;
    hireDay = LocalDate.of(year, month, day);
}
```

As you can see, the name of the constructor is the same as the name of the class. This constructor runs when you construct objects of the Employee class—giving the instance fields the initial state you want them to have.

For example, when you create an instance of the Employee class with code like this:

```
new Employee("James Bond", 100000, 1950, 1, 1)
```

you have set the instance fields as follows:

```
name = "James Bond";
salary = 100000;
hireDay = LocalDate.of(1950, 1, 1); // January 1, 1950
```

There is an important difference between constructors and other methods. A constructor can only be called in conjunction with the new operator. You can't apply a constructor to an existing object to reset the instance fields. For example,

```
james.Employee("James Bond", 250000, 1950, 1, 1) // ERROR
```

is a compile-time error.

We will have more to say about constructors later in this chapter. For now, keep the following in mind:

- A constructor has the same name as the class.
- A class can have more than one constructor.
- A constructor can have zero, one, or more parameters.
- A constructor has no return value.
- A constructor is always called with the new operator.

C++ Note: Constructors work the same way in Java as they do in C++. Keep in mind, however, that all Java objects are constructed on the heap and that a constructor must be combined with new. It is a common error of C++ programmers to forget the new operator:

```
Employee number007("James Bond", 100000, 1950, 1, 1); // C++, not Java
```

That works in C++ but not in Java.

Caution: Be careful not to introduce local variables with the same names as the instance fields. For example, the following constructor will not set the name or salary instance fields:

```
public Employee(String n, double s, . . .)
{
    String name = n; // ERROR
    double salary = s; // ERROR
    . . .
}
```

The constructor declares *local* variables name and salary. These variables are only accessible inside the constructor. They *shadow* the instance fields with the same name. Some programmers accidentally write this kind of code when they type faster than they think, because their fingers are used to adding the data type. This is a nasty error that can be hard to track down. You just have to be careful in all of your methods to not use variable names that equal the names of instance fields.

4.3.5. Declaring Local Variables with var

You can declare local variables with the var keyword instead of specifying their type, provided their type can be inferred from the initial value. For example, instead of declaring

```
Employee harry = new Employee("Harry Hacker", 50000, 1989, 10, 1);
```

you simply write

```
var harry = new Employee("Harry Hacker", 50000, 1989, 10, 1);
```

This is nice since it avoids the repetition of the type name `Employee`.

From now on, I will use the var notation in those cases where the type is obvious from the right-hand side without any knowledge of the Java API. But I won't use var with numeric types such as `int`, `long`, or `double` so that you don't have to look out for the difference between `0`, `0L`, and `0.0`. Once you are more experienced with the Java API, you may want to use the var keyword more frequently.

Note that the var keyword can only be used with *local* variables inside methods. You must always declare the types of parameters and fields.

 Note: Many programmers use the var keyword quite liberally, whenever they think that the the variable type is obvious or obviously uninteresting. A good set of guidelines is at `https://openjdk.org/projects/amber/guides/lvti-style-guide`.

4.3.6. Working with `null` References

In Section 4.2.1, you saw that an object variable holds a reference to an object, or the special value `null` to indicate the absence of an object.

This sounds like a convenient mechanism for dealing with special situations, such as an unknown name or hire date. But you need to be very careful with `null` values.

If you apply a method to a `null` value, a `NullPointerException` occurs.

```
LocalDate rightNow = null;
String s = rightNow.toString(); // NullPointerException
```

This is a serious error, similar to an "index out of bounds" exception. If your program does not "catch" an exception, it is terminated. Normally, programs don't catch these kinds of exceptions but rely on programmers not to cause them in the first place.

 Tip: When your program is terminated with a `NullPointerException`, the stack trace shows you in which line of your code the problem occurred. Since Java 14, the error message includes the name of the variable or method with the `null` value. For example, in a call

```
String s = e.getHireDay().toString();
```

the error message tells you whether e was null or getHireDay returned null.

When you define a class, it is a good idea to be clear about which fields can be null. In our example, we don't want the name or hireDay field to be null. (We don't have to worry about the salary field. It has primitive type and can never be null.)

The hireDay field is guaranteed to be non-null because it is initialized with a new LocalDate object. But name will be null if the constructor is called with a null argument for n.

There are two solutions. The "permissive" approach is to turn a null argument into an appropriate non-null value:

```
if (n == null) name = "unknown"; else name = n;
```

The Objects class has a convenience method for this purpose:

```
public Employee(String n, double s, int year, int month, int day)
{
   name = Objects.requireNonNullElse(n, "unknown");
   . . .
}
```

The "tough love" approach is to reject a null argument:

```
public Employee(String n, double s, int year, int month, int day)
{
   name = Objects.requireNonNull(n, "The name cannot be null");
   . . .
}
```

If someone constructs an Employee object with a null name, then a NullPointerException occurs. At first glance, that may not seem a useful remedy. But there are two advantages:

1. The exception report has a description of the problem.
2. The exception report pinpoints the location of the problem. Otherwise, a NullPointerException would have occurred elsewhere, with no easy way of tracing it back to the faulty constructor argument.

 Note: Whenever a parameter is an object reference, ask yourself whether you really intend to model values that can be present or absent. If not, the "tough love" approach of throwing an exception is preferred.

4.3.7. Implicit and Explicit Parameters

Methods operate on objects and access their instance fields. For example, the method

```
public void raiseSalary(double byPercent)
{
   double raise = salary * byPercent / 100;
   salary += raise;
}
```

sets a new value for the salary instance field in the object on which this method is invoked. Consider the call

```
number007.raiseSalary(5);
```

The effect is to increase the value of the number007.salary field by 5%. More specifically, the call executes the following instructions:

```
double raise = number007.salary * 5 / 100;
number007.salary += raise;
```

The raiseSalary method is called with two arguments. The first argument, called the *implicit* argument, is the object of type Employee that appears before the method name. The second argument, the number inside the parentheses after the method name, is an *explicit* argument. (Some people call the implicit argument the *target* or *receiver* of the method call.)

The method declaration has a parameter variable for the explicit argument, namely double byPercent. However, no parameter variable is declared for the implicit argument.

Every method has an *implicit parameter*, whose name is the keyword this, which is initialized with the implicit argument. If you like, you can write the raiseSalary method as follows:

```
public void raiseSalary(double byPercent)
{
   double raise = this.salary * byPercent / 100;
   this.salary += raise;
}
```

Some programmers prefer that style because it clearly distinguishes between instance fields and local variables.

 C++ Note: In C++, you generally define methods outside the class:

```
void Employee::raiseSalary(double byPercent) // C++, not Java
{
    . . .
}
```

If you define a method inside a class, then it is, automatically, an inline method.

```
class Employee
{
    . . .
    int getName() { return name; } // inline in C++
}
```

In Java, all methods are defined inside the class itself. This does not make them inline. Finding opportunities for inline replacement is the job of the Java virtual machine. The just-in-time compiler watches for calls to methods that are short and commonly called. If they are only one or two implementations, the code is inlined, avoiding the method call.

___

4.3.8. Benefits of Encapsulation

Finally, let's look more closely at the rather simple getName, getSalary, and getHireDay methods.

```
public String getName()
{
    return name;
}

public double getSalary()
{
    return salary;
}

public LocalDate getHireDay()
{
    return hireDay;
}
```

These are obvious examples of accessor methods. As they simply return the values of instance fields, they are sometimes called *field accessors*.

Wouldn't it be easier to make the name, salary, and hireDay fields public, instead of having separate accessor methods?

Using methods gives you more control and safety. Consider the salary field which is only changed by the raiseSalary method. Should the value ever turn out wrong, only that method needs to be debugged. Had the salary field been public, the culprit for messing up the value could have been anywhere.

Sometimes, it happens that you want to get and set the value of an instance field. Then you need to supply *three* items:

- A private instance field;
- A public field accessor method; and
- A public field mutator method.

This is a lot more tedious than supplying a single public instance field, but there are considerable benefits.

First, you can change the internal implementation without affecting any code other than the methods of the class. For example, if the storage of the name is changed to

```
String firstName;
String lastName;
```

then the getName method can be changed to return

```
firstName + " " + lastName
```

This change is completely invisible to the remainder of the program.

Of course, the accessor and mutator methods may need to do a lot of work to convert between the old and the new data representation. That leads us to our second benefit: Mutator methods can perform error checking, whereas code that simply assigns to a field may not go into the trouble. For example, a setSalary method might check that the salary is never less than 0.

 Caution: Be careful not to write accessor methods that return references to mutable objects. In a previous edition of this book, I violated that rule in the Employee class in which the getHireDay method returned an object of class Date:

```
class Employee
{
    private Date hireDay;
    . . .
    public Date getHireDay()
    {
        return hireDay; // BAD
```

```
        }
        . . .
    }
```

Unlike the LocalDate class, which has no mutator methods, the Date class has a mutator method, setTime, where you can set the number of milliseconds.

The fact that Date objects are mutable breaks encapsulation! Consider the following rogue code:

```
Employee harry = . . .;
Date d = harry.getHireDay();
double tenYearsInMilliseconds = 10 * 365.25 * 24 * 60 * 60 * 1000;
d.setTime(d.getTime() - (long) tenYearsInMilliseconds);
// let's give Harry ten years of added seniority
```

The reason is subtle. Both d and harry.hireDay refer to the same object (see Figure 4.5). Applying mutator methods to d automatically changes the private state of the Employee object!

You will see in Chapter 6 how to solve this problem by *cloning* the mutable object before returning it.

A better remedy is to use immutable objects when possible, such as LocalDate instead of the legacy Date class.

4.3.9. Class-Based Access Privileges

You know that a method can access the private data of the object on which it is invoked. What people often find surprising is that a method can access the private data of *all objects of its class*. For example, consider a method equals that compares two employees.

```
class Employee
{
    . . .
    public boolean equals(Employee other)
    {
        return name.equals(other.name);
    }
}
```

A typical call is

```
if (harry.equals(boss)) . . .
```

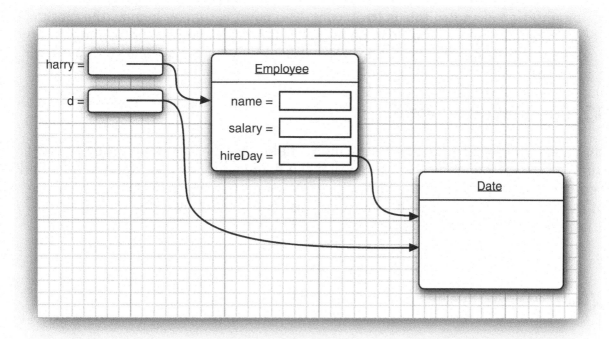

Figure 4.5: Returning a reference to a mutable instance field

This method accesses the private fields of harry, which is not surprising. It also accesses the private fields of boss. This is legal because boss is an object of type Employee, and a method of the Employee class is permitted to access the private fields of *any* object of type Employee.

 C++ Note: C++ has the same rule. A method can access the private features of any object of its class, not just of the implicit parameter.

4.3.10. Private Methods

When implementing a class, we make all instance fields private because public data are dangerous. But what about the methods? While most methods are public, private methods are useful in certain circumstances. Sometimes, you may wish to break up the code for a computation into separate helper methods. Typically, these helper methods should not be part of the public interface—they may be too close to the current implementation or require a special protocol or calling order. Such methods are best implemented as private.

To implement a private method in Java, simply change the public keyword to private.

By making a method private, you are under no obligation to keep it available if you change your implementation. The method may well be *harder* to implement or *unnecessary* if the data representation changes; this is irrelevant. The point is that as long as the method is private, the designers of the class can be assured that it is never used elsewhere, so they can simply drop it. If a method is public, you cannot simply drop it because other code might rely on it.

4.3.11. Final Instance Fields

You can define an instance field as final. Such a field must be initialized when the object is constructed. That is, you must guarantee that the field value has been set after the end of every constructor. Afterwards, the field may not be modified again. For example, the name field of the Employee class may be declared as final because it never changes after the object is constructed—there is no setName method.

```
class Employee
{
   private final String name;
   . . .
}
```

The final modifier is particularly useful for fields whose type is primitive or an *immutable class.* (A class is immutable if none of its methods ever mutate its objects. For example, the String class is immutable.)

For mutable classes, the final modifier can be confusing. For example, consider a field

```
private final StringBuilder evaluations;
```

that is initialized in the Employee constructor as

```
evaluations = new StringBuilder();
```

The final keyword merely means that the object reference stored in the evaluations variable will never again refer to a different StringBuilder object. But the object can be mutated:

```
public void giveGoldStar()
{
   evaluations.append(LocalDate.now() + ": Gold star!\n");
}
```

 Note: A final field can be null:

```
name = n != null && n.length() == 0 ? null : n;
```

Of course, it can then never be changed to a non-null value.

4.4. Static Fields and Methods

In all sample programs that you have seen, the main method is tagged with the static modifier. We are now ready to discuss the meaning of this modifier.

4.4.1. Static Fields

If you define a field as static, then the field is not present in the objects of the class. There is only a single copy of each static field. You can think of static fields as belonging to the class, not to the individual objects. For example, let's suppose we want to assign a unique identification number to each employee. We add an instance field id and a static field nextId to the Employee class:

```
class Employee
{
    private static int nextId = 1;

    private int id;
    . . .
}
```

Every Employee object now has its own id field, but there is only one nextId field that is shared among all instances of the class. Let's put it another way. If there are 1,000 objects of the Employee class, then there are 1,000 instance fields id, one for each object. But there is a single static field nextId. Even if there are no Employee objects, the static field nextId is present. It belongs to the class, not to any individual object.

 Note: In some object-oriented programming languages, static fields are called *class fields*. The term "static" is a meaningless holdover from C++.

In the constructor, we assign the next available ID to the new Employee object and then increment it:

```
id = nextId;
nextId++;
```

Suppose we construct the object harry. Then the id field of harry is set to the current value of the static field nextId, and the value of the static field is incremented:

```
harry.id = Employee.nextId;
Employee.nextId++;
```

Caution: If you accidentally declare what you want to be an instance field as static, the compiler won't help you find your mistake.

Conceptually, a static field (such as nextId in the preceding example) belongs to the class, not to any object. Nevertheless, in Java, you can refer to the field as Employee.nextId, or e.nextId, where e is any Employee object. And inside the methods of the Employee class, you can use nextId, this.nextId, or Employee.nextId.

Therefore, it is a good idea to pay attention to any static declarations in a class. Static variables are uncommon and deserve close scrutiny. Static constants, discussed in the following section, stand out because their names are typically in all caps.

4.4.2. Static Constants

Static variables are quite rare. However, static constants are more common. For example, the Math class defines a static constant:

```
public class Math
{
    . . .
    public static final double PI = 3.14159265358979323846;
    . . .
}
```

You can access this constant in your programs as Math.PI.

If the keyword static had been omitted, then PI would have been an instance field of the Math class. That is, you would need an object of this class to access PI, and every Math object would have its own copy of PI.

Another static constant that you have used many times is System.out. It is declared in the System class as follows:

```
public class System
{
    . . .
    public static final PrintStream out = . . .;
    . . .
}
```

As mentioned several times, it is never a good idea to have public fields, because everyone can modify them. However, public constants (that is, final fields) are fine. Since out has been declared as final, you cannot reassign another print stream to it:

```
System.out = new PrintStream(. . .); // ERROR--out is final
```

 Note: If you look at the System class, you will notice a method setOut that sets System.out to a different stream. You may wonder how that method can change the value of a final variable. However, the setOut method is a *native* method, not implemented in the Java programming language. Native methods can bypass the access control mechanisms of the Java language. This is a very unusual workaround that you should not emulate in your programs.

4.4.3. Static Methods

Static methods are methods that do not operate on objects. For example, the pow method of the Math class is a static method. The expression

```
Math.pow(x, a)
```

computes the power x^a. It does not use any Math object to carry out its task. In other words, it has no implicit parameter.

You can think of static methods as methods that don't have a this parameter. (In a nonstatic method, the this parameter refers to the implicit parameter of the method—see Section 4.3.7.)

A static method of the Employee class cannot access the id instance field because it does not operate on an object. However, a static method can access a static field. Here is an example of such a static method:

```
public static int advanceId()
{
    int r = nextId; // obtain next available id
    nextId++;
    return r;
}
```

To call this method, you supply the name of the class:

```
int n = Employee.advanceId();
```

Could you have omitted the keyword static for this method? Yes, but then you would need to have an object reference of type Employee to invoke the method.

Note: It is legal to use an object to call a static method. For example, if harry is an Employee object, then you can call harry.advanceId() instead of Employee.advanceId(). However, I find that notation confusing. The advanceId method doesn't look at harry at all to compute the result. I recommend that you use class names, not objects, to invoke static methods. (Your IDE will probably suggest a refactoring otherwise.)

Use static methods in two situations:

- When a method doesn't need to access the object state because all needed parameters are supplied as explicit parameters (example: Math.pow)
- When a method only needs to access static fields of the class (example: Employee.advanceId)

 C++ Note: Static fields and methods have the same functionality in Java and C++. However, the syntax is slightly different. In C++, you use the :: operator to access a static field or method outside its scope, such as Math::PI.

The term "static" has a curious history. At first, the keyword static was introduced in C to denote local variables that don't go away when a block is exited. In that context, the term "static" makes sense: The variable stays around and is still there when the block is entered again. Then static got a second meaning in C, to denote global variables and functions that cannot be accessed from other files. The keyword static was simply reused to avoid introducing a new keyword. Finally, C++ reused the keyword for a third, unrelated, interpretation—to denote variables and functions that belong to a class but not to any particular object of the class. That is the same meaning the keyword has in Java.

4.4.4. Factory Methods

Here is another common use for static methods. Classes such as LocalDate and NumberFormat use static *factory methods* that construct objects. You have already seen the factory methods LocalDate.now and LocalDate.of. Here is how to obtain formatter objects for various styles:

```
NumberFormat currencyFormatter = NumberFormat.getCurrencyInstance();
NumberFormat percentFormatter = NumberFormat.getPercentInstance();
double x = 0.1;
System.out.println(currencyFormatter.format(x)); // prints $0.10
System.out.println(percentFormatter.format(x)); // prints 10%
```

Why doesn't the NumberFormat class use a constructor instead? There are three reasons to prefer a factory method over a constructor:

- You can't give names to constructors. The constructor name is always the same as the class name. But we want two different names to get the currency instance and the percent instance.
- When you use a constructor, you can't vary the type of the constructed object. But the factory methods actually return objects of the class DecimalFormat, a more specialized class that inherits from NumberFormat. (See Chapter 5 for more on inheritance.)
- A constructor always constructs a new object. You may want to share instances. For example, the Integer.valueOf factory method yields the same instance when you call it twice with the same small argument.

4.4.5. The main Method

Note that you can call static methods without having any objects. For example, you never construct any objects of the Math class to call Math.pow.

For the same reason, the main method is a static method.

```
public class Application
{
    public static void main(String[] args)
    {
        // construct objects here
        . . .
    }
}
```

The main method does not operate on any objects. In fact, when a program starts, there aren't any objects yet. The static main method executes, and constructs the objects that the program needs.

 Tip: Every class can have a main method. That is a handy trick for adding demonstration code to a class. For example, you can add a main method to the Employee class:

```
class Employee
{
    public Employee(String n, double s, int year, int month, int day)
    {
        name = n;
        salary = s;
        hireDay = LocalDate.of(year, month, day);
    }
    . . .
    public static void main(String[] args) // unit test
```

```
   {
      var e = new Employee("Romeo", 50000, 2003, 3, 31);
      e.raiseSalary(10);
      System.out.println(e.getName() + " " + e.getSalary());
   }
   . . .
}
```

To see a demo of the Employee class, simply execute

```
java Employee
```

If the Employee class is a part of a larger application, you start the application with

```
java Application
```

and the main method of the Employee class is never executed.

 Preview Note: As a preview feature of Java 21, the main method no longer needs to be public or static, and it need not have a parameter of type String[] args. Here are the new rules:

- If there is more than one main method, static main methods are preferred over instance methods, and methods with a String[] parameter are preferred over those with no parameters.
- If main is not static, the class must have a no-argument constructor. Then the launcher constructs an instance of the class and invokes the main method.

If you want to try out this preview feature, remember to compile and run with the --enable-preview flag.

The program in Listing 4.3 contains a simple version of the Employee class with a static field nextId and a static method advanceId. We fill an array with three Employee objects and then print the employee information. Finally, we print the next available identification number, to demonstrate the static method.

Note that the Employee class also has a static main method that runs a simple demo. Try executing both:

```
java Employee
java StaticTest
```

Listing 4.3 StaticTest/StaticTest.java

```java
1  /**
2   * This program demonstrates static methods.
3   * @version 1.03 2021-09-03
4   * @author Cay Horstmann
5   */
6  public class StaticTest
7  {
8     public static void main(String[] args)
9     {
10        // fill the staff array with three Employee objects
11        var staff = new Employee[3];
12
13        staff[0] = new Employee("Tom", 40000);
14        staff[1] = new Employee("Dick", 60000);
15        staff[2] = new Employee("Harry", 65000);
16
17        // print out information about all Employee objects
18        for (Employee e : staff)
19        {
20           System.out.println("name=" + e.getName() + ",id=" + e.getId() + ",salary="
21              + e.getSalary());
22        }
23
24        int n = Employee.advanceId(); // calls static method
25        System.out.println("Next issued id=" + n);
26     }
27  }
28
29  class Employee
30  {
31     private static int nextId = 1;
32
33     private String name;
34     private double salary;
35     private int id;
36
37     public Employee(String n, double s)
38     {
39        name = n;
40        salary = s;
41        id = advanceId();
42     }
43
44     public String getName()
45     {
46        return name;
47     }
48
```

```
49   public double getSalary()
50   {
51      return salary;
52   }
53
54   public int getId()
55   {
56      return id;
57   }
58
59   public static int advanceId()
60   {
61      int r = nextId; // obtain next available id
62      nextId++;
63      return r;
64   }
65
66   public static void main(String[] args) // runs demo
67   {
68      var e = new Employee("Harry", 50000);
69      System.out.println(e.getName() + " " + e.getSalary());
70   }
71 }
```

---

java.util.Objects 7

- static <T> void requireNonNull(T obj)
- static <T> void requireNonNull(T obj, String message)
- static <T> void requireNonNull(T obj, Supplier<String> messageSupplier) **8**
  If obj is null, these methods throw a NullPointerException with no message or the given message. (Chapter 6 explains how to obtain a value lazily with a supplier. Chapter 8 explains the <T> syntax.)
- static <T> T requireNonNullElse(T obj, T defaultObj) **9**
- static <T> T requireNonNullElseGet(T obj, Supplier<T> defaultSupplier) **9**
  return obj if it is not null, or the default object if obj is null.

4.5. Method Parameters

Let us review the computer science terms that describe how parameters can be passed to a method (or a function) in a programming language. The term *call by value* means that the method gets just the value that the caller provides. In contrast, *call by reference* means that the method gets the *location* of the variable that the caller provides. Thus, a method can *modify* the value stored in a variable passed by reference but not in one passed by value. These "call by . . ." terms are standard computer science terminology describing the behavior of method parameters in various programming languages, not just Java. (There is also a *call by name* that is mainly of historical interest, being employed in the Algol programming language, one of the oldest high-level languages.)

The Java programming language *always* uses call by value. That means that the method gets a copy of all arguments. In particular, the method cannot modify the contents of any variables in the method call.

For example, consider the following call:

```
double percent = 10;
harry.raiseSalary(percent);
```

No matter how the method is implemented, we know that after the method call, the value of percent is still 10.

Let us look a little more closely at this situation. Suppose a method tried to triple the value of a method parameter:

```
public static void tripleValue(double x) // doesn't work
{
    x = 3 * x;
}
```

Let's call this method:

```
double percent = 10;
tripleValue(percent);
```

However, this does not work. After the method call, the value of percent is still 10. Here is what happens:

1. x is initialized with a copy of the value of percent (that is, 10).
2. x is tripled—it is now 30. But percent is still 10 (see Figure 4.6).
3. The method ends, and the parameter variable x is no longer in use.

There are, however, two kinds of method parameters:

- Primitive types (number types, char, boolean)
- Object references

You have seen that it is impossible for a method to change a primitive type parameter. The situation is different for object parameters. You can easily implement a method that triples the salary of an employee:

```
public static void tripleSalary(Employee x) // works
{
    x.raiseSalary(200);
}
```

When you call

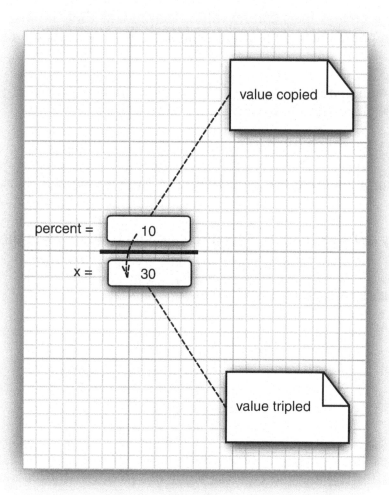

Figure 4.6: Modifying a parameter variable has no lasting effect.

```
harry = new Employee(. . .);
tripleSalary(harry);
```

then the following happens:

1. x is initialized with a copy of the value of harry—that is, an object reference.
2. The raiseSalary method is applied to that object reference. The Employee object to which both x and harry refer gets its salary raised by 200 percent.
3. The method ends, and the parameter variable x is no longer in use. Of course, the object variable harry continues to refer to the object whose salary was tripled (see Figure 4.7).

As you have seen, it is easily possible—and in fact very common—to implement methods that change the state of an object parameter. The reason is simple. The method gets a copy of the object reference, and both the original and the copy refer to the same object.

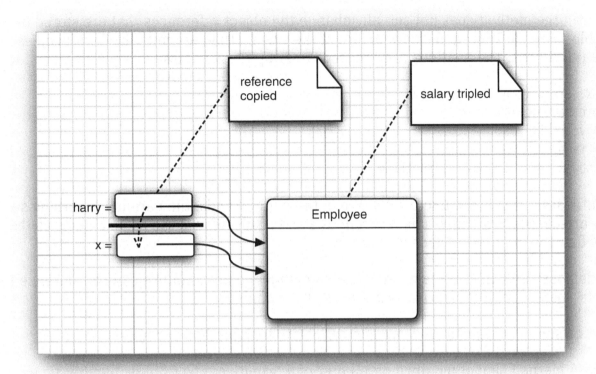

Figure 4.7: Modifying an object referenced by a parameter has a lasting effect.

Many programming languages (in particular, C++ and Pascal) have two mechanisms for parameter passing: call by value and call by reference. Some programmers (and unfortunately even some book authors) claim that Java uses call by reference for objects. That is false. As this is such a common misunderstanding, it is worth examining a counterexample in detail.

Let's try to write a method that swaps two Employee objects:

```
public static void swap(Employee x, Employee y) // doesn't work
{
   Employee temp = x;
   x = y;
   y = temp;
}
```

If Java used call by reference for objects, this method would work:

```
var a = new Employee("Alice", . . .);
var b = new Employee("Bob", . . .);
swap(a, b);
// does a now refer to Bob, b to Alice?
```

However, the method does not actually change the object references that are stored in the variables a and b. The x and y parameters of the swap method are initialized with *copies* of these references. The method then proceeds to swap these copies.

```
// x refers to Alice, y to Bob
Employee temp = x;
x = y;
y = temp;
// now x refers to Bob, y to Alice
```

But ultimately, this is a wasted effort. When the method ends, the parameter variables x and y are abandoned. The original variables a and b still refer to the same objects as they did before the method call (see Figure 4.8).

This demonstrates that the Java programming language does not use call by reference for objects. Instead, *object references are passed by value.*

Here is a summary of what you can and cannot do with method parameters in Java:

- A method cannot modify a parameter of a primitive type (that is, number types, char, or boolean).
- A method can change the *state* of an object parameter.

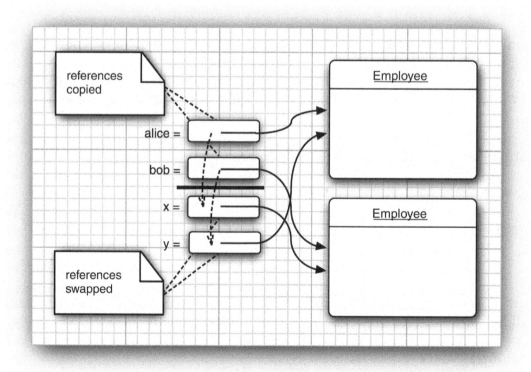

Figure 4.8: Swapping parameter variables has no lasting effect.

- A method cannot make an object parameter refer to a new object.

The program in Listing 4.4 demonstrates these facts. The program first tries to triple the value of a number parameter and does not succeed:

```
Testing tripleValue:
Before: percent=10.0
End of method: x=30.0
After: percent=10.0
```

It then successfully triples the salary of an employee:

```
Testing tripleSalary:
Before: salary=50000.0
End of method: salary=150000.0
After: salary=150000.0
```

After the method, the state of the object to which harry refers has changed. This is possible because the method modified the state through a copy of the object reference.

Finally, the program demonstrates the failure of the swap method:

```
Testing swap:
Before: a=Alice
Before: b=Bob
End of method: x=Bob
End of method: y=Alice
After: a=Alice
After: b=Bob
```

As you can see, the parameter variables x and y are swapped, but the variables a and b are not affected.

 C++ Note: C++ has both call by value and call by reference. You tag reference parameters with &. For example, you can easily implement methods void tripleValue(double& x) or void swap(Employee& x, Employee& y) that modify their reference parameters.

Listing 4.4 `ParamTest/ParamTest.java`

```
1  /**
2   * This program demonstrates parameter passing in Java.
3   * @version 1.01 2018-04-10
4   * @author Cay Horstmann
```

```
5    */
6    public class ParamTest
7    {
8       public static void main(String[] args)
9       {
10         /*
11          * Test 1: Methods can't modify numeric parameters
12          */
13         System.out.println("Testing tripleValue:");
14         double percent = 10;
15         System.out.println("Before: percent=" + percent);
16         tripleValue(percent);
17         System.out.println("After: percent=" + percent);
18
19         /*
20          * Test 2: Methods can change the state of object parameters
21          */
22         System.out.println("\nTesting tripleSalary:");
23         var harry = new Employee("Harry", 50000);
24         System.out.println("Before: salary=" + harry.getSalary());
25         tripleSalary(harry);
26         System.out.println("After: salary=" + harry.getSalary());
27
28         /*
29          * Test 3: Methods can't attach new objects to object parameters
30          */
31         System.out.println("\nTesting swap:");
32         var a = new Employee("Alice", 70000);
33         var b = new Employee("Bob", 60000);
34         System.out.println("Before: a=" + a.getName());
35         System.out.println("Before: b=" + b.getName());
36         swap(a, b);
37         System.out.println("After: a=" + a.getName());
38         System.out.println("After: b=" + b.getName());
39      }
40
41      public static void tripleValue(double x) // doesn't work
42      {
43         x = 3 * x;
44         System.out.println("End of method: x=" + x);
45      }
46
47      public static void tripleSalary(Employee x) // works
48      {
49         x.raiseSalary(200);
50         System.out.println("End of method: salary=" + x.getSalary());
51      }
52
53      public static void swap(Employee x, Employee y)
54      {
55         Employee temp = x;
56         x = y;
```

```
57          y = temp;
58          System.out.println("End of method: x=" + x.getName());
59          System.out.println("End of method: y=" + y.getName());
60       }
61    }
62
63    class Employee // simplified Employee class
64    {
65       private String name;
66       private double salary;
67
68       public Employee(String n, double s)
69       {
70          name = n;
71          salary = s;
72       }
73
74       public String getName()
75       {
76          return name;
77       }
78
79       public double getSalary()
80       {
81          return salary;
82       }
83
84       public void raiseSalary(double byPercent)
85       {
86          double raise = salary * byPercent / 100;
87          salary += raise;
88       }
89    }
```

4.6. Object Construction

You have seen how to write simple constructors that define the initial state of your objects. However, since object construction is so important, Java offers quite a variety of mechanisms for writing constructors. We go over these mechanisms in the sections that follow.

4.6.1. Overloading

Some classes have more than one constructor. For example, you can construct an empty StringBuilder object as

```
var messages = new StringBuilder();
```

Alternatively, you can specify an initial string:

```
var todoList = new StringBuilder("To do:\n");
```

This capability is called *overloading*. Overloading occurs if several methods have the same name (in this case, the StringBuilder constructor method) but different parameters. The compiler must sort out which method to call. It picks the correct method by matching the parameter types in the declarations of the various methods with the types of the arguments used in the specific method call. A compile-time error occurs if the compiler cannot match the parameters, either because there is no match at all or because there is not one that is better than all others. (The process of finding a match is called *overloading resolution*.)

Note: Java allows you to overload any method—not just constructor methods. Thus, to completely describe a method, you need to specify its name together with its parameter types. This is called the *signature* of the method. For example, the String class has four public methods called indexOf. They have signatures

```
indexOf(int)
indexOf(int, int)
indexOf(int, int, int)
indexOf(String)
indexOf(String, int)
indexOf(String, int, int)
```

The return type is not part of the method signature. That is, you cannot have two methods with the same names and parameter types but different return types.

Caution: The statement

```
StringBuilder builder = new StringBuilder('\n'); // ERROR
```

does *not* produce a StringBuilder containing a newline. There is a constructor with an int parameter, which yields a StringBuilder with a preallocated capacity. The char literal '\n' can be converted to an int but not to a String. The result is a builder with no contents and capacity 10, the integer value of '\n'.

In general, be careful with overloading when the argument types do not match the parameter types exactly.

4.6.2. Default Field Initialization

If you don't set a field explicitly in a constructor, it is automatically set to a default value: numbers to 0, boolean values to false, and object references to null. Some people consider it poor programming practice to rely on the defaults. Certainly, it makes it harder for someone to understand your code if fields are being initialized invisibly.

Note: This is an important difference between fields and local variables. You must always explicitly initialize local variables in a method. But in a class, if you don't initialize a field, it is automatically initialized to a default (0, false, or null).

For example, consider the Employee class. Suppose you don't specify how to initialize some of the fields in a constructor. By default, the salary field would be initialized with 0 and the name and hireDay fields would be initialized with null.

However, that would not be a good idea. If anyone called the getName or getHireDay method, they would get a null reference that they probably don't expect:

```
LocalDate h = harry.getHireDay();
int year = h.getYear(); // throws exception if h is null
```

4.6.3. The Constructor with No Arguments

Many classes contain a constructor with no arguments that creates an object whose state is set to an appropriate default. For example, here is a no-argument constructor for the Employee class:

```
public Employee()
{
    name = "";
    salary = 0;
    hireDay = LocalDate.now();
}
```

If you write a class with no constructors whatsoever, then a no-argument constructor is provided for you. This constructor sets *all* the instance fields to their default values. So, all numeric data contained in the instance fields would be 0, all boolean values would be false, and all object variables would be null.

If a class supplies at least one constructor but does not supply a no-argument constructor, it is illegal to construct objects without supplying arguments. For example, our original Employee class in Listing 4.2 provided a single constructor:

```
public Employee(String n, double s, int year, int month, int day)
```

With that class, it was not legal to construct default employees. That is, the call

```
e = new Employee();
```

would have been an error.

Caution: Please keep in mind that you get a free no-argument constructor *only* when your class has no other constructors. If you write your class with even a single constructor of your own and you want the users of your class to have the ability to create an instance by a call to

```
new ClassName()
```

then you must provide a no-argument constructor. Of course, if you are happy with the default values for all fields, you can simply supply

```
public ClassName()
{
}
```

 C++ Note: C++ has a special initializer list syntax for constructing fields, such as

```
Employee::Employee(String n, double s, int y, int m, int d) // C++
: name(n),
  salary(s),
  hireDay(y, m, d)
{
}
```

C++ uses this special syntax to avoid unnecessary invocations of no-argument constructors. In Java, there is no need for that because objects have no subobjects, only references to other objects.

4.6.4. Explicit Field Initialization

By overloading the constructor methods in a class, you can build many ways to set the initial state of the instance fields of your classes. It is always a good idea to make sure that, regardless of the constructor call, every instance field is set to something meaningful.

You can simply assign a value to any field in the class definition. For example:

```
class Employee
{
   private String name = "";
   . . .
}
```

This assignment is carried out before the constructor executes. This syntax is particularly useful if all constructors of a class need to set a particular instance field to the same value.

The initialization value doesn't have to be a constant value. Here is an example in which a field is initialized with a method call. Consider the `Employee` class where each employee has an id field. You can initialize it as follows:

```
class Employee
{
    private static int nextId;
    private int id = advanceId();
    . . .
    private static int advanceId()
    {
        int r = nextId;
        nextId++;
        return r;
    }
    . . .
}
```

4.6.5. Parameter Names

When you write very trivial constructors (and you'll write a lot of them), it can be somewhat frustrating to come up with parameter names.

We have generally opted for single-letter parameter names:

```
public Employee(String n, double s)
{
    name = n;
    salary = s;
}
```

However, the drawback is that you need to read the code to tell what the n and s parameters mean.

Some programmers prefix each parameter with an "a":

```
public Employee(String aName, double aSalary)
{
    name = aName;
    salary = aSalary;
}
```

That is better. Any reader can immediately figure out the meaning of the parameters.

Another commonly used trick relies on the fact that parameter variables *shadow* instance fields with the same name. For example, if you call a parameter salary, then salary refers to the parameter, not the instance field. But you can still access the instance field as this.salary. Recall that this denotes the implicit parameter—that is, the object being constructed. Here is an example:

```
public Employee(String name, double salary)
{
   this.name = name;
   this.salary = salary;
}
```

 C++ Note: In C++, it is common to prefix instance fields with an underscore or a fixed letter. (The letters m and x are common choices.) For example, the salary field might be called _salary, mSalary, or xSalary. Java programmers don't usually do that.

4.6.6. Calling Another Constructor

The keyword this refers to the implicit parameter of a method. However, this keyword has a second meaning.

If *the first statement of a constructor* has the form this(. . .), then the constructor calls another constructor of the same class. Here is a typical example:

```
public Employee(double s)
{
   // calls Employee(String, double)
   this("Employee #" + nextId, s);
   nextId++;
}
```

When you call new Employee(60000), the Employee(double) constructor calls the Employee(String, double) constructor.

Using the this keyword in this manner is useful—you only need to write common construction code once.

 C++ Note: The this reference in Java is identical to the this pointer in C++. However, in C++, you call another constructor in the member initialization list:

```
Employee(double s) : Employee("Employee #" + nextId, s) { nextId++; }
```

4.6.7. Initialization Blocks

You have already seen two ways to initialize an instance field:

- By setting a value in a constructor
- By assigning a value in the declaration

There is a third mechanism in Java, called an *initialization block*. Class declarations can contain arbitrary blocks of code. These blocks are executed whenever an object of that class is constructed. For example:

```java
class Employee
{
   private static int nextId;

   private int id;
   private String name;
   private double salary;

   // object initialization block
   {
      id = nextId;
      nextId++;
   }

   public Employee(String n, double s)
   {
      name = n;
      salary = s;
   }

   public Employee()
   {
      name = "";
      salary = 0;
   }
   . . .
}
```

In this example, the id field is initialized in the object initialization block, no matter which constructor is used to construct an object. The initialization block runs first, and then the body of the constructor is executed.

This mechanism is never necessary and is not common. It is usually more straightforward to place the initialization code inside a constructor.

 Note: It is legal to set fields in initialization blocks even if they are only defined later in the class. However, to avoid circular definitions, it is not legal to read from fields that are only initialized later. The exact rules are spelled out in Section 8.3.3 of the

Java Language Specification (https://docs.oracle.com/javase/specs). The rules are complex enough to baffle the compiler implementors—early versions of Java implemented them with subtle errors. Therefore, you should always place initialization blocks after the field definitions.

With so many ways of initializing instance fields, it can be quite confusing to give all possible pathways for the construction process. Here is what happens in detail when a constructor is called:

1. If the first statement of the constructor calls a second constructor, then the second constructor executes with the provided arguments.
2. Otherwise,
   - All instance fields are initialized to their default values (0, false, or null).
   - All field initializers and initialization blocks are executed, in the order in which they occur in the class declaration.
3. The body of the constructor is executed.

Naturally, it is always a good idea to organize your initialization code so that another programmer could easily understand it without having to be a language lawyer. For example, it would be quite strange and somewhat error-prone to have a class whose constructors depend on the order in which the instance fields are declared.

To initialize a static field, either supply an initial value or use a static initialization block. You have already seen the first mechanism:

```
private static int nextId = 1;
```

If the static fields of your class require complex initialization code, use a static initialization block.

Place the code inside a block and tag it with the keyword static. Here is an example. We want the employee ID numbers to start at a random integer less than 10,000.

```
private static RandomGenerator generator = RandomGenerator.getDefault();
// static initialization block
static
{
   nextId = generator.nextInt(10000);
}
```

Static initialization occurs when the class is first loaded. Like instance fields, static fields are 0, false, or null unless you explicitly set them to another value. All static field initializers and static initialization blocks are executed in the order in which they occur in the class declaration.

Note: Amazingly enough, up to Java 6, it was possible to write a "Hello, World" program in Java without ever writing a main method.

```
public class Hello
{
   static
   {
      System.out.println("Hello, World");
   }
}
```

When you invoked the class with java Hello, the class was loaded, the static initialization block printed "Hello, World", and only then was a message displayed that main is not defined. Since Java 7, the java program first checks that there is a main method.

This example uses a RandomGenerator instance for generating random numbers. Since JDK 17, the java.util.random package provides implementations of strong algorithms with various tradeoffs. There is a default that works well for most purposes, but if you are interested in alternatives, read through the API documentation of the java.util.random package for advice which algorithm to choose. You obtain a specific instance like this:

```
RandomGenerator generator = RandomGenerator.of("L64X128MixRandom");
```

Generate random numbers by calling generator.nextInt(n) or other RandomGenerator methods. (Technically, RandomGenerator is an *interface*, a concept introduced in Chapter 6. You don't need to worry about that when you invoke methods on a RandomGenerator instance.)

 Tip: The RandomGenerator interface improves upon the Random class from Java 1.0, which has a fairly short *period* of 2^{48}, after which the internal state repeats. As a rule of thumb, to generate n random numbers, the period should be at least n^2. By that rule, the classic Random generator is unsuitable if n exceeds 2^{24}, which is not that large—about 17 million. These days, much better algorithms are known, and it is a good idea to move away from the Random class.

If you want to use strong random number generators with legacy code that uses the Random class, use the static from method like this:

```
Random generator = Random.from(RandomGenerator.getDefault());
```

The program in Listing 4.5 shows many of the features discussed in this section:

■ Overloaded constructors

- A call to another constructor with this(. . .)
- A no-argument constructor
- An object initialization block
- A static initialization block
- An instance field initialization

Listing 4.5 ConstructorTest/ConstructorTest.java

```
 1  import java.util.random.*;
 2
 3  /**
 4   * This program demonstrates object construction.
 5   * @version 1.02 2018-04-10
 6   * @author Cay Horstmann
 7   */
 8  public class ConstructorTest
 9  {
10     public static void main(String[] args)
11     {
12        // fill the staff array with three Employee objects
13        var staff = new Employee[3];
14
15        staff[0] = new Employee("Harry", 40000);
16        staff[1] = new Employee(60000);
17        staff[2] = new Employee();
18
19        // print out information about all Employee objects
20        for (Employee e : staff)
21           System.out.println("name=" + e.getName() + ",id=" + e.getId() + ",salary="
22              + e.getSalary());
23     }
24  }
25
26  class Employee
27  {
28     private static int nextId;
29
30     private int id;
31     private String name = ""; // instance field initialization
32     private double salary;
33
34     private static RandomGenerator generator = RandomGenerator.getDefault();
35
36     // static initialization block
37     static
38     {
39        // set nextId to a random number between 0 and 9999
40        nextId = generator.nextInt(10000);
41     }
42
```

```
43       // object initialization block
44       {
45          id = nextId;
46          nextId++;
47       }
48
49       // three overloaded constructors
50       public Employee(String n, double s)
51       {
52          name = n;
53          salary = s;
54       }
55
56       public Employee(double s)
57       {
58          // calls the Employee(String, double) constructor
59          this("Employee #" + nextId, s);
60       }
61
62       // the default constructor
63       public Employee()
64       {
65          // name initialized to ""--see above
66          // salary not explicitly set--initialized to 0
67          // id initialized in initialization block
68       }
69
70       public String getName()
71       {
72          return name;
73       }
74
75       public double getSalary()
76       {
77          return salary;
78       }
79
80       public int getId()
81       {
82          return id;
83       }
84    }
```

java.util.random.RandomGenerator 17

- `int nextInt(int n)`
  returns a random integer between 0 and n − 1.
- `static RandomGenerator of(String name)`
  yields a random generator for the given algorithm name. The algorithm named "L64X128MixRandom" is suitable for most applications.

- `static RandomGenerator getDefault()`
  yields a strong random generator with 64 or more state bits.

---

java.util.Random 1.0

- `static from(RandomGenerator generator)` **19**
  returns a Random instance whose methods delegate to the given RandomGenerator. This is useful with legacy code.

4.6.8. Object Destruction and the `finalize` Method

Some object-oriented programming languages, notably C++, have explicit destructor methods for any cleanup code that may be needed when an object is no longer used. The most common activity in a destructor is reclaiming the memory set aside for objects. Since Java does automatic garbage collection, manual memory reclamation is not needed, so Java does not support destructors.

Of course, some objects utilize a resource other than memory, such as a file or a handle to another object that uses system resources. In this case, it is important that the resource be reclaimed and recycled when it is no longer needed.

If a resource needs to be closed as soon as you have finished using it, supply a `close` method that does the necessary cleanup. You can call the `close` method when you are done with the object. In Chapter 7, you will see how you can ensure that this method is called automatically.

If you can wait until the virtual machine exits, add a "shutdown hook" with the method `Runtime.addShutdownHook`. You can use the `Cleaner` class to register an action that is carried out when an object is no longer reachable (other than by the cleaner). These are uncommon situations in practice. See the API documentation for details on these two approaches.

 Caution: Do not use the `finalize` method for cleanup. That method was intended to be called before the garbage collector sweeps away an object. However, you simply cannot know when this method will be called, and it is now deprecated for removal.

4.7. Records

Sometimes, data is just data, and the data hiding that object-oriented programming provides gets in the way. Consider a class `Point` that describes a point in the plane, with x- and y-coordinates.

Sure, you can create a class:

```
class Point
{
    private final double x;
    private final double y;
    public Point(double x, double y) { this.x = x; this.y = y; }
    public getX() { return x; }
    public getY() { return y; }
    public String toString() { return "Point[x=%d, y=%d]".formatted(x, y); }
    // More methods . . .
}
```

But does it really buy us anything to hide x and y, and then make the values available through the getter methods?

Would we ever want to change the implementation of a Point? Sure, there are polar coordinates, but you would not use them with a graphics API. In practice, a point in the plane is completely described by its x- and y-coordinates.

To define such classes more concisely, JDK 14 introduced "records" as a preview feature. The final version was delivered in JDK 16.

4.7.1. The Record Concept

A record is a special form of a class whose state is immutable and readable by the public. To declare a record, provide the name and the instance variables that hold the object state. Here is how you define Point as a record:

```
record Point(double x, double y) { }
```

The result is a class with instance fields:

```
private final double x;
private final double y;
```

In the Java language specification, the instance fields of a record are called its *components*.

The class has a constructor

```
Point(double x, double y)
```

and accessor methods

```
public double x()
public double y()
```

Note that the accessors are called x and y, not getX and getY. (It is legal in Java to have an instance field and a method with the same name.)

```
var p = new Point(3, 4);
System.out.println(p.x() + " " + p.y());
```

 Note: Java doesn't follow the get convention because it is a bit messy. For boolean fields, it is common to use is instead of get. And the capitalization of the first letter can be problematic. What should happen if a class has fields x and X? Some programmers are unhappy because their legacy classes cannot trivially become records. But in practice, many of those legacy classes are mutable and therefore not candidates for conversion to records.

In addition to the field accessor methods, every record has three methods defined automatically: toString, equals, and hashCode. You will learn more about these methods in the next chapter.

You can add your own methods to a record:

```
record Point(double x, double y)
{
    public double distanceFromOrigin() { return Math.hypot(x, y); }
}
```

 Caution: You can define your own versions of the automatically provided methods, as long as they have the same parameter and return types. For example, this definition is legal:

```
record Point(double x, double y)
{
    public double x() { return 2 * x; } // BAD
}
```

But it is surely not a good idea.

You cannot add *instance* fields to a record.

```
record Point(double x, double y)
{
    private double r; // ERROR
    . . .
}
```

Caution: Instance fields of a record are automatically final. However, they may be references to mutable objects:

```
record PointInTime(double x, double y, Date when) { }
```

Then record instances are mutable:

```
var pt = new PointInTime(0, 0, new Date());
pt.when().setTime(0);
```

If you intend record instances to be immutable, don't use mutable types for fields.

A record, like any class, can have static fields and methods:

```
record Point(double x, double y)
{
    public static Point ORIGIN = new Point(0, 0);
    public static double distance(Point p, Point q)
    {
        return Math.hypot(p.x - q.x, p.y - q.y);
    }
    . . .
}
```

 Tip: Use a record instead of a class for immutable data that is completely represented by a set of variables. Use a class if the data is mutable, or if the representation may evolve over time. Records are easier to read, more efficient, and safer in concurrent programs.

4.7.2. Constructors: Canonical, Compact, and Custom

The automatically defined constructor that sets all instance fields is called the *canonical constructor*.

To validate or normalize the parameters for the canonical constructor, use a *compact* form. Don't specify the parameter list:

```
record Range(int from, int to)
{
    public Range // Compact form, validating parameters
    {
```

```
         if (from > to) throw new IllegalArgumentException();
      }
   }
```

or

```
   record Range(int from, int to)
   {
      public Range // Compact form, normalizing parameters
      {
         if (from > to) // Swap the bounds
         {
            int temp = from;
            from = to;
            to = temp;
         }
      }
   }
```

The body of the compact form is the "prelude" to the canonical constructor. It merely modifies the parameter variables from and to before they are assigned to the instance fields this.from and this.to. You cannot read or modify the instance fields in the body of the compact constructor.

You can define additional *custom constructors*. The first statement of such a constructor must call another constructor, so that ultimately the canonical constructor is invoked. Here is an example:

```
   record Point(double x, double y)
   {
      public Point() { this(0, 0); }
   }
```

This record has two constructors: the canonical constructor and a no-argument constructor yielding the origin.

If the canonical constructor needs to do additional work, you can provide your own implementation. But this is very uncommon. For example, the following implementation is valid, but, as you have seen, the same effect is easier to achieve with a compact constructor.

```
   record Range(int from, int to)
   {
      public Range(int from, int to) // legal, but more work than a compact constructor
      {
         if (from <= to)
         {
```

```
            this.from = from;
            this.to = to;
        }
        else
        {
            this.from = to;
            this.to = from;
        }
    }
}
```

Listing 4.6 RecordTest/RecordTest.java

```java
 1  import java.util.*;
 2
 3  /**
 4   * This program demonstrates records.
 5   * @version 1.0 2021-05-13
 6   * @author Cay Horstmann
 7   */
 8  public class RecordTest
 9  {
10      public static void main(String[] args)
11      {
12          var p = new Point(3, 4);
13          System.out.println("Coordinates of p: " + p.x() + " " + p.y());
14          System.out.println("Distance from origin: " + p.distanceFromOrigin());
15          // Same computation with static field and method
16          System.out.println("Distance from origin: " + Point.distance(Point.ORIGIN, p));
17
18          // A mutable record
19          var pt = new PointInTime(3, 4, new Date());
20          System.out.println("Before: " + pt);
21          pt.when().setTime(0);
22          System.out.println("After: " + pt);
23
24          // Invoking a compact constructor
25
26          var r = new Range(4, 3);
27          System.out.println("r: " + r);
28      }
29  }
30
31  record Point(double x, double y)
32  {
33      // A custom constructor
34      public Point() { this(0, 0); }
35      // A method
36      public double distanceFromOrigin()
```

```
37      {
38          return Math.hypot(x, y);
39      }
40      // A static field and method
41      public static Point ORIGIN = new Point();
42      public static double distance(Point p, Point q)
43      {
44          return Math.hypot(p.x - q.x, p.y - q.y);
45      }
46  }
47
48  record PointInTime(double x, double y, Date when) { }
49
50  record Range(int from, int to)
51  {
52      // A compact constructor
53      public Range
54      {
55          if (from > to) // Swap the bounds
56          {
57              int temp = from;
58              from = to;
59              to = temp;
60          }
61      }
62  }
```

4.8. Packages

Java allows you to group classes in a collection called a *package*. Packages are convenient for organizing your work and for separating your work from code libraries provided by others. In the following sections, you will learn how to use and create packages.

4.8.1. Package Names

The main reason for using packages is to guarantee the uniqueness of class names. Suppose two programmers come up with the bright idea of supplying an Employee class. As long as both of them place their class into different packages, there is no conflict. In fact, to absolutely guarantee a unique package name, use an Internet domain name (which is known to be unique) written in reverse. You then use subpackages for different projects. For example, consider the domain horstmann.com. When written in reverse order, it turns into the package name com.horstmann. You can then append a project name, such as com.horstmann.corejava. If you then place the Employee class into that package, the "fully qualified" name becomes com.horstmann.corejava.Employee.

Note: From the point of view of the compiler, there is absolutely no relationship between nested packages. For example, the packages java.util and java.util.jar have nothing to do with each other. Each is its own independent collection of classes.

4.8.2. Class Importation

A class can use all classes from its own package and all *public* classes from other packages.

You can access the public classes in another package in two ways. The first is simply to use the *fully qualified name*; that is, the package name followed by the class name. For example:

```
java.time.LocalDate today = java.time.LocalDate.now();
```

That is obviously tedious. A simpler, and more common, approach is to use the import statement. The point of the import statement is to give you a shorthand to refer to the classes in the package. Once you add an import, you no longer have to give the classes their full names.

You can import a specific class or the whole package. You place import statements at the top of your source files (but below any package statements). For example, you can import all classes in the java.time package with the statement

```
import java.time.*;
```

Then you can use

```
LocalDate today = LocalDate.now();
```

without a package prefix. You can also import a specific class inside a package:

```
import java.time.LocalDate;
```

The java.time.* syntax is less tedious. It has no negative effect on code size. However, if you import classes explicitly, the reader of your code knows exactly which classes you use.

However, note that you can only use the * notation to import a single package. You cannot use import java.* or import java.*.* to import all packages with the java prefix.

 Note: You never need to import classes from the java.lang package.

Tip: Integrated development environments have commands to organize imports. Package statements such as `import java.util.*;` are automatically expanded into a list of specific imports such as

```
import java.util.ArrayList;
import java.util.Date;
```

Unused import statements are removed. This is an extremely convenient feature, and it is a good idea to find out how to accomplish it with your IDE.

Most of the time, you just import the packages that you need, without worrying too much about them. The only time that you need to pay attention to packages is when you have a name conflict. For example, both the `java.util` and `java.sql` packages have a `Date` class. Suppose you write a program that imports both packages.

```
import java.util.*;
import java.sql.*;
```

If you now use the `Date` class, you get a compile-time error:

```
Date today; // ERROR--java.util.Date or java.sql.Date?
```

The compiler cannot figure out which `Date` class you want. You can solve this problem by adding a specific `import` statement:

```
import java.util.*;
import java.sql.*;
import java.util.Date;
```

What if you really need both `Date` classes? Then use the full package name with every class name:

```
var startTime = new java.util.Date();
var today = new java.sql.Date(. . .);
```

Locating classes in packages is an activity of the *compiler*. The bytecodes in class files always use full package names to refer to other classes.

 C++ Note: C++ programmers sometimes confuse `import` with `#include`. The two have nothing in common. In C++, you must use `#include` to include the declarations of external features because the C++ compiler does not look inside any files except the one that it is compiling and its explicitly included header files. The Java compiler will happily look inside other files provided you tell it where to look.

In Java, you can entirely avoid the import mechanism by explicitly naming all classes, such as java.util.Date. In C++, you cannot avoid the #include directives.

The only benefit of the import statement is convenience. You can refer to a class by a name shorter than the full package name. For example, after an import java.util.* (or import java.util.Date) statement, you can refer to the java.util.Date class simply as Date.

In C++, the construction analogous to the package mechanism is the namespace feature. Think of the package and import statements in Java as the analogs of the namespace and using directives in C++.

4.8.3. Static Imports

A form of the import statement permits the importing of static methods and fields, not just classes.

For example, if you add the directive

```
import static java.lang.System.*;
```

to the top of your source file, then you can use the static methods and fields of the System class without the class name prefix:

```
out.println("Goodbye, World!"); // i.e., System.out
exit(0); // i.e., System.exit
```

You can also import a specific method or field:

```
import static java.lang.System.out;
```

In practice, it seems doubtful that many programmers will want to abbreviate System.out or System.exit. The resulting code seems less clear. On the other hand,

```
sqrt(pow(x, 2) + pow(y, 2))
```

seems much clearer than

```
Math.sqrt(Math.pow(x, 2) + Math.pow(y, 2))
```

You can import enumerated constants:

```
import java.time.DayOfWeek;
import static java.time.DayOfWeek.*;
DayOfWeek w = FRIDAY; // Same as DayOfWeek.FRIDAY
```

Preview Note: The STR interpolator is a preview feature of Java 21. It is used to form strings with embedded expressions, such as:

```
STR."Hello, \{name}! Next year, you'll be \{age + 1}."
```

The identifier STR is always imported, as if there had been a statement:

```
import static java.lang.StringTemplate.STR;
```

4.8.4. Addition of a Class into a Package

To place classes inside a package, put the name of the package at the top of your source file, *before* the code that defines the classes in the package. For example, the file Employee.java in Listing 4.8 starts out like this:

```
package com.horstmann.corejava;

public class Employee
{
    . . .
}
```

If you don't put a package statement in the source file, then the classes in that source file belong to the *unnamed package*. The unnamed package has no package name. Up to now, all our example classes were located in the unnamed package.

Place source files into a subdirectory that matches the full package name. For example, all source files in the com.horstmann.corejava package should be in a subdirectory com/horstmann/corejava (com\horstmann\corejava on Windows). The compiler places the class files into the same directory structure.

Here is a sample program that is distributed over two packages: The PackageTest class belongs to the unnamed package—see Listing 4.7. The Employee class, shown in Listing 4.8, belongs to the com.horstmann.corejava package. Therefore, the Employee.java file must be in a subdirectory com/horstmann/corejava. In other words, the directory structure is as follows:

```
. (base directory)
├─ PackageTest.java
├─ PackageTest.class
└─ com/
   └─ horstmann/
      └─ corejava/
         ├─ Employee.java
         └─ Employee.class
```

To compile this program, simply change to the base directory and run the command

```
javac PackageTest.java
```

The compiler automatically finds the file com/horstmann/corejava/Employee.java and compiles it.

 Note: When you use an IDE or a build tool, the class files are typically placed in a separate directory tree.

Let's look at a more realistic example, in which we don't use the unnamed package but have classes distributed over several packages (com.horstmann.corejava and com.mycompany).

```
. (base directory)
└ com/
   ├ horstmann/
   │  └ corejava/
   │     ├ Employee.java
   │     └ Employee.class
   └ mycompany/
      ├ PayrollApp.java
      └ PayrollApp.class
```

In this situation, you still must compile and run classes from the *base* directory—that is, the directory containing the com directory:

```
javac com/mycompany/PayrollApp.java
java com.mycompany.PayrollApp
```

Note again that the compiler operates on *files* (with file separators and an extension .java), whereas the Java interpreter loads a *class* (with dot separators).

 Tip: Starting with the next chapter, we will use packages for the source code. That way, you can make an IDE project for each chapter instead of each section.

 Caution: The compiler does *not* check the directory structure when it compiles source files. For example, suppose you have a source file that starts with the directive

```
package com.mycompany;
```

You can compile the file even if it is not contained in a subdirectory com/mycompany. The source file will compile without errors *if it doesn't depend on other packages*. However, the resulting program will not run unless you first move all class files to the right place. The *virtual machine* won't find the classes if the packages don't match the directories.

Listing 4.7 PackageTest/PackageTest.java

```
1   import com.horstmann.corejava.*;
2   // the Employee class is defined in that package
3
4   import static java.lang.System.*;
5
6   /**
7    * This program demonstrates the use of packages.
8    * @version 1.11 2004-02-19
9    * @author Cay Horstmann
10   */
11  public class PackageTest
12  {
13     public static void main(String[] args)
14     {
15        // because of the import statement, we don't have to use
16        // com.horstmann.corejava.Employee here
17        var harry = new Employee("Harry Hacker", 50000, 1989, 10, 1);
18
19        harry.raiseSalary(5);
20
21        // because of the static import statement, we don't have to use System.out here
22        out.println("name=" + harry.getName() + ",salary=" + harry.getSalary());
23     }
24  }
```

Listing 4.8 PackageTest/com/horstmann/corejava/Employee.java

```
1   package com.horstmann.corejava;
2
3   // the classes in this file are part of this package
4
5   import java.time.*;
6
7   // import statements come after the package statement
8
9   /**
10   * @version 1.11 2015-05-08
11   * @author Cay Horstmann
12   */
```

```
13   public class Employee
14   {
15      private String name;
16      private double salary;
17      private LocalDate hireDay;
18
19      public Employee(String name, double salary, int year, int month, int day)
20      {
21         this.name = name;
22         this.salary = salary;
23         hireDay = LocalDate.of(year, month, day);
24      }
25
26      public String getName()
27      {
28         return name;
29      }
30
31      public double getSalary()
32      {
33         return salary;
34      }
35
36      public LocalDate getHireDay()
37      {
38         return hireDay;
39      }
40
41      public void raiseSalary(double byPercent)
42      {
43         double raise = salary * byPercent / 100;
44         salary += raise;
45      }
46   }
```

4.8.5. Package Access

You have already encountered the access modifiers public and private. Features tagged as public can be used by any class. Private features can be used only by the class that defines them. If you don't specify either public or private, the feature (that is, the class, method, or variable) can be accessed by all methods in the same *package*.

Consider the program in Listing 4.2. The Employee class was not defined as a public class. Therefore, only the other classes (such as EmployeeTest) in the same package—the unnamed package in this case—can access it. For classes, this is a reasonable default. However, for variables, this was an unfortunate choice. Variables must explicitly be marked private, or they will default to having package access. This, of course, breaks encapsulation. The problem is that it is awfully easy to forget to type the private keyword. Here is an example from the Window class in the java.awt package, which is part of the source code supplied with the JDK:

```
public class Window extends Container
{
    String warningString;
    . . .
}
```

Note that the warningString variable is not private! That means the methods of all classes in the java.awt package can access this variable and set it to whatever they like (such as "Trust me!"). Actually, the only methods that access this variable are in the Window class, so it would have been entirely appropriate to make the variable private. Perhaps the programmer typed the code in a hurry and simply forgot the private modifier? Perhaps nobody cared? After more than twenty years, that variable is still not private. Not only that—new fields have been added to the class over time, and about half of them aren't private either.

This can be a problem. By default, packages are not closed entities. That is, anyone can add more classes to a package. Of course, hostile or clueless programmers can then add code that modifies variables with package access. For example, in early versions of Java, it was an easy matter to smuggle another class into the java.awt package. Simply start out the class with

```
package java.awt;
```

Then, place the resulting class file inside a subdirectory java/awt somewhere on the class path, and you have gained access to the internals of the java.awt package. Through this subterfuge, it was possible to modify warning strings (see Figure 4.9).

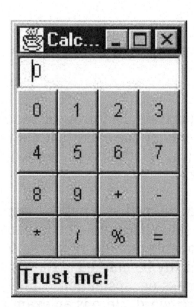

Figure 4.9: Changing the warning string in an applet window

Starting with version 1.2, the JDK implementors rigged the class loader to explicitly disallow loading of user-defined classes whose package name starts with "java.". Of course, your own classes don't benefit from that protection. Another mechanism, now obsolete, lets a JAR file declare packages as *sealed*, preventing third parties from augmenting them. Nowadays, you should use modules to encapsulate packages. Modules are discussed in detail in Chapter 12.

4.8.6. The Class Path

As you have seen, classes are stored in subdirectories of the file system. The path to the class must match the package name.

Class files can also be stored in a JAR (Java archive) file. A JAR file contains multiple class files and subdirectories in a compressed format, saving space and improving performance. When you use a third-party library in your programs, you will usually be given one or more JAR files to include. You will see in Section 4.9.1 how to create your own JAR files.

 Tip: JAR files use the ZIP format to organize files and subdirectories. You can use any ZIP utility to peek inside JAR files.

To share classes among programs, you need to do the following:

1. Place your class files inside a directory—for example, /home/user/classdir. Note that this directory is the *base* directory for the package tree. If you add the class com.horstmann.corejava.Employee, then the Employee.class file must be located in the subdirectory /home/user/classdir/com/horstmann/corejava.
2. Place any JAR files inside a directory—for example, /home/user/archives.
3. Set the *class path*. The class path is the collection of all locations that can contain class files.

In UNIX, the elements on the class path are separated by colons:

```
/home/user/classdir:.:/home/user/archives/archive.jar
```

In Windows, they are separated by semicolons:

```
c:\classdir;.;c:\archives\archive.jar
```

In both cases, the period denotes the current directory.

This class path contains

- The base directory /home/user/classdir or c:\classdir;
- The current directory (.); and
- The JAR file /home/user/archives/archive.jar or c:\archives\archive.jar.

You can specify a wildcard for a JAR file directory, like this:

```
/home/user/classdir:.:/home/user/archives/'*'
```

or

```
c:\classdir;.;c:\archives\*
```

In UNIX, the * must be escaped to prevent shell expansion.

All JAR files (but not .class files) in the archives directory are included in this class path.

The Java API is always searched for classes; don't include it explicitly in the class path.

 Caution: The javac compiler always looks for files in the current directory, but the java virtual machine launcher only looks into the current directory if the "." directory is on the class path. If you have no class path set, it's not a problem—the default class path consists of the "." directory. But if you have set the class path and forgot to include the "." directory, your programs will compile without error, but they won't run.

The class path lists all directories and archive files that are *starting points* for locating classes. Let's consider our sample class path:

```
/home/user/classdir:.:/home/user/archives/archive.jar
```

Suppose the virtual machine searches for the class file of the com.horstmann.corejava.Employee class. It first looks in the Java API classes. It won't find the class file there, so it turns to the class path. It then looks for the following files:

- /home/user/classdir/com/horstmann/corejava/Employee.class
- com/horstmann/corejava/Employee.class starting from the current directory
- com/horstmann/corejava/Employee.class inside /home/user/archives/archive.jar

The compiler has a harder time locating files than does the virtual machine. If you refer to a class without specifying its package, the compiler first needs to find out the package that contains the class. It consults all import directives as possible sources for the class. For example, suppose the source file contains directives

```
import java.util.*;
import com.horstmann.corejava.*;
```

and the source code refers to a class Employee. The compiler then tries to find java.lang.Employee (because the java.lang package is always imported by default), java.util.Employee, com.horstmann.corejava.Employee, and Employee in the current package. It searches for *each* of these classes in all of the locations of the class path. It is a compile-time error if more than one class is found. (Fully qualified class names must be unique, so the order of the import statements doesn't matter.)

The compiler goes one step further. It looks at the *source files* to see if the source is newer than the class file. If so, the source file is recompiled automatically. Recall that you can import only public classes from other packages. A source file can only contain one public class, and the names of the file and the public class must match. Therefore, the compiler can easily locate source files for public classes. However, you can import nonpublic classes from the current package. These classes may be defined in source files with different names. If you import a class from the current package, the compiler searches *all* source files of the current package to see which one defines the class.

4.8.7. Setting the Class Path

IDEs and build tools have their own mechanisms for managing the class path. But it is a good idea to know how to set it by hand so you can troubleshoot any configuration issues.

It is best to specify the class path with the option -classpath (or -cp or the more modern variant, --class-path):

```
java -classpath /home/user/classdir:.:/home/user/archives/archive.jar MyProg
```

or

```
java -classpath c:\classdir;.;c:\archives\archive.jar MyProg
```

The entire command must be typed onto a single line. It is a good idea to place such a long command line into a shell script or a batch file.

Using the -classpath option is the preferred approach for setting the class path. An alternate approach is the CLASSPATH environment variable. The details depend on your shell. With the Bourne Again shell (bash), use the command

```
export CLASSPATH=/home/user/classdir:.:/home/user/archives/archive.jar
```

With the Windows shell, use

```
set CLASSPATH=c:\classdir;.;c:\archives\archive.jar
```

The class path is set until the shell exits.

 Caution: Some people recommend to set the CLASSPATH environment variable permanently. This is generally a bad idea. People forget the global setting, and are surprised when their classes are not loaded properly. A particularly reprehensible

example was Apple's QuickTime installer in Windows. For several years, it globally set CLASSPATH to point to a JAR file it needed, but did not include the current directory in the classpath. As a result, countless Java programmers were driven to distraction when their programs compiled but failed to run.

 Caution: In the past, some people recommended to bypass the class path altogether, by dropping all JAR files into the jre/lib/ext directory. That mechanism is obsolete with Java 9, but it was always bad advice. It was easy to get confused when long-forgotten classes were loaded from the extension directory.

 Note: Classes can also be loaded from the *module path*. Modules and the module path are discussed in Chapter 12.

4.9. JAR Files

When you package your application, you want to give your users a single file, not a directory structure filled with class files. Java Archive (JAR) files were designed for this purpose. A JAR file can contain both class files and other file types such as image and sound files. Moreover, JAR files are compressed, using the familiar ZIP compression format.

4.9.1. Creating JAR files

Use the jar tool to make JAR files. (In the default JDK installation, it's in the *jdk*/bin directory.) The most common command to make a new JAR file uses the following syntax:

    jar cvf *jarFileName file1 file2* . . .

For example:

    jar cvf CalculatorClasses.jar *.class icon.png

In general, the jar command has the following format:

    jar *options file1 file2* . . .

Table 4.2 lists all the options for the jar program. They are similar to the options of the UNIX tar command.

Table 4.2: jar Program Options

Option	Description
c	Creates a new or empty archive and adds files to it. If any of the specified file names are directories, the jar program processes them recursively.
C	Temporarily changes the directory. For example, jar cvf jarFileName.jar -C classes *.class changes to the classes subdirectory to add class files.
e	Creates an entry point in the manifest (see Section 4.9.3).
f	Specifies the JAR file name as the second command-line argument. If this argument is missing, jar will write the result to standard output (when creating a JAR file) or read it from standard input (when extracting or tabulating a JAR file).
i	Creates an index file (for speeding up lookups in a large archive).
m	Adds a *manifest* to the JAR file. A manifest is a description of the archive contents and origin. Every archive has a default manifest, but you can supply your own if you want to authenticate the contents of the archive.
M	Does not create a manifest file for the entries.
t	Displays the table of contents.
u	Updates an existing JAR file.
v	Generates verbose output.
x	Extracts files. If you supply one or more file names, only those files are extracted. Otherwise, all files are extracted.
0	Stores without ZIP compression.

You can package application programs and code libraries into JAR files. For example, if you want to send mail in a Java program, you use a library that is packaged in a file javax.mail.jar.

4.9.2. The Manifest

In addition to class files, images, and other resources, each JAR file contains a *manifest* file that describes special features of the archive.

The manifest file is called `MANIFEST.MF` and is located in a special `META-INF` subdirectory of the JAR file. The minimum legal manifest is quite boring—just

```
Manifest-Version: 1.0
```

Complex manifests can have many more entries. The manifest entries are grouped into sections. The first section in the manifest is called the *main section*. It applies to the whole JAR file. Subsequent entries can specify properties of named entities such as individual files, packages, or URLs. Those entries must begin with a `Name` entry. Sections are separated by blank lines. For example:

```
Manifest-Version: 1.0
lines describing this archive

Name: Woozle.class
lines describing this file
Name: com/mycompany/mypkg/
lines describing this package
```

To edit the manifest, place the lines that you want to add to the manifest into a text file. Then run

```
jar cfm jarFileName manifestFileName . . .
```

For example, to make a new JAR file with a manifest, run

```
jar cfm MyArchive.jar manifest.mf com/mycompany/mypkg/*.class
```

To update the manifest of an existing JAR file, place the additions into a text file and use a command such as

```
jar ufm MyArchive.jar manifest-additions.mf
```

 Note: See `https://docs.oracle.com/en/java/javase/21/docs/specs/jar/jar.html` for more information on the JAR and manifest file formats.

4.9.3. Executable JAR Files

You can use the e option of the `jar` command to specify the *entry point* of your program—the class that you would normally specify when invoking the `java` program launcher:

```
jar cvfe MyProgram.jar com.mycompany.mypkg.MainAppClass files to add
```

Alternatively, you can specify the *main class* of your program in the manifest, including a statement of the form

```
Main-Class: com.mycompany.mypkg.MainAppClass
```

Do not add a .class extension to the main class name.

 Caution: The last line in the manifest must end with a newline character. Otherwise, the manifest will not be read correctly. It is a common error to produce a text file containing just the Main-Class line without a line terminator.

With either method, users can simply start the program as

```
java -jar MyProgram.jar
```

Depending on the operating system configuration, users may even be able to launch the application by double-clicking the JAR file icon. Here are behaviors for various operating systems:

- On Windows, the Java runtime installer creates a file association for the ".jar" extension that launches the file with the javaw -jar command. (Unlike the java command, the javaw command doesn't open a shell window.)
- On Mac OS X, the operating system recognizes the ".jar" file extension and executes the Java program when you double-click a JAR file.

However, a Java program in a JAR file does not have the same feel as a native application. On Windows, you can use third-party wrapper utilities that turn JAR files into Windows executables. A wrapper is a Windows program with the familiar .exe extension that locates and launches the Java virtual machine (JVM) or tells the user what to do when no JVM is found. There are a number of commercial and open source products, such as Launch4J (https://launch4j.sourceforge.net) and IzPack (https://github.com/izpack/izpack).

4.9.4. Multi-Release JAR Files

With the introduction of modules and strong encapsulation of packages, some previously accessible internal APIs are no longer available. This may require library providers to distribute different code for different Java versions. *Multi-release JARs* take care of this use case.

For backward compatibility, version-specific class files are placed in the META-INF/versions directory:

```
Application.class
BuildingBlocks.class
Util.class
```

```
META-INF
  ├ MANIFEST.MF (with line Multi-Release: true)
  └ versions
      ├ 9
      │   ├ Application.class
      │   └ BuildingBlocks.class
      └ 10
          └ BuildingBlocks.class
```

Suppose the Application class makes use of the CssParser class. Then the legacy Application.class file can be compiled to use com.sun.javafx.css.CssParser, while the Java 9 version uses javafx.css.CssParser.

Java 8 knows nothing about the META-INF/versions directory and will simply load the legacy classes. When the JAR file is read by Java 9, the new version is used instead.

To add versioned class files, use the --release flag:

```
jar uf MyProgram.jar --release 9 Application.class
```

To build a multi-release JAR file from scratch, use the -C option and switch to a different class file directory for each version:

```
jar cf MyProgram.jar -C bin/8 . --release 9 -C bin/9 Application.class
```

When compiling for different releases, use the --release flag and the -d flag to specify the output directory:

```
javac -d bin/8 --release 8 . . .
```

The -d option creates the directory if it doesn't exist.

The JDK ships with symbol files for two prior versions of the API. In Java 21, you can compile with --release set to 21, 20, or 19.

Multi-release JARs are not intended for different versions of a program or library. The public API of all classes should be the same for both releases. The sole purpose of multi-release JARs is to enable a particular version of your program or library to work with multiple JDK releases. If you add functionality or change an API, you should provide a new version of the JAR instead.

 Note: Tools such as javap are not retrofitted to handle multi-release JAR files. If you call

```
javap -classpath MyProgram.jar Application.class
```

you get the base version of the class (which, after all, is supposed to have the same public API as the newer version). If you must look at the newer version, call

```
javap -classpath MyProgram.jar\!/META-INF/versions/9/Application.class
```

4.9.5. A Note about Command-Line Options

The options of commands in the Java Development Kit have traditionally used single dashes followed by multiletter option names, such as

```
java -jar . . .
javac -Xlint:unchecked -classpath . . .
```

The exception was the jar command, which followed the classic option format of the tar command without dashes:

```
jar cvf . . .
```

JEP 293 (https://openjdk.org/jeps/293) provides guidelines for moving towards a more common option format, starting with Java 9. With most Linux tools, multiletter option names are preceded by double dashes, with single-letter shortcuts for common options. For example, the Linux ls command can be called with a "human-readable" option as

```
ls --human-readable
```

or

```
ls -h
```

With javac and java, you can now use --version instead of -version and --class-path instead of -classpath. As you will see in Chapter 12, the --module-path option has a shortcut -p.

Arguments of options with -- and multiple letters are separated by whitespace or an = sign:

```
java --class-path /home/user/classdir . . .
```

or

```
java --class-path=/home/user/classdir . . .
```

The = form is useful when an option needs to be passed through to another tool, where the passthrough mechanism cannot handle white space.

Tip: You can use the JDK_JAVA_OPTIONS environment variable to pass command-line options to the java launcher:

```
export JDK_JAVA_OPTIONS='--class-path /home/user/classdir -enableassertions'
```

 Caution: According to JEP 293, single-letter options without arguments can be grouped together:

```
jar -c -v -f myapp.jar -m MANIFEST.MF *.class
```

can be simplified to

```
jar -cv -f myapp.jar -m MANIFEST.MF *.class
```

But that does not currently work. Strangely,

```
jar -cvfm myapp.jar MANIFEST.MF *.class
```

works even though it should not. Until this is sorted out, it seems best to stick with the classic tar-style options for the jar command.

 Caution: According to JEP 293, arguments of single-letter options can be separated by whitespace or directly follow the option:

```
javac -d outputdir . . .
```

or

```
javac -doutputdir . . .
```

The latter doesn't currently work. It also seems like a bad idea since it would invite conflicts with legacy options. For example, what should happen if the output directory happens to be named eprecation?

4.10. Documentation Comments

The JDK contains a very useful tool, called javadoc, that generates HTML documentation from your source files. In fact, the online API documentation described in Chapter 3 is simply the result of running javadoc on the source code of the standard Java library.

If you add comments that start with the special delimiter /** to your source code, you too can easily produce professional-looking documentation. This is a very nice approach because it lets you keep your code and documentation in one place. If you put your documentation into a separate file, then, as you probably know, the code and comments tend to diverge over time. When documentation comments are in the same file as the source code, it is an easy matter to update both and run javadoc again.

4.10.1. Comment Insertion

The javadoc utility extracts information for the following items:

- Modules
- Packages
- Public classes and interfaces
- Public and protected fields
- Public and protected constructors and methods

Protected members are introduced in Chapter 5, interfaces in Chapter 6, and modules in Chapter 12.

You can (and should) supply a comment for each of these members. Each comment is placed immediately *above* the member it describes. A comment starts with a /** and ends with a */.

Each /** . . . */ documentation comment contains *free-form text* followed by *tags*. A tag starts with an @, such as @since or @param.

The *first sentence* of the free-form text should be a *summary statement*. The javadoc utility automatically generates summary pages that extract these sentences.

The most common javadoc tags are *block tags*. They must appear at the beginning of a line and start with @, optionally preceded by whitespace, the comment delimiter /**, or leading * which are often used for multi-line comments. In contrast, *inline tags* are enclosed in braces: {@tagname contents}. The contents may contain braces, but they must be balanced. Examples are the @code and @link tags.

4.10.2. Class Comments

The class comment must be placed *after* any import statements, directly before the class definition.

Here is an example of a class comment:

```
/**
 * A {@code Card} object represents a playing card, such
 * as "Queen of Hearts". A card has a suit (Diamond, Heart,
 * Spade or Club) and a value (1 = Ace, 2 . . . 10, 11 = Jack,
 * 12 = Queen, 13 = King).
 */
```

```
public class Card
{
    . . .
}
```

 Note: There is no need to add an * in front of every line. For example, the following comment is equally valid:

```
/**
    A <code>Card</code> object represents a playing card, such
    as "Queen of Hearts". A card has a suit (Diamond, Heart,
    Spade or Club) and a value (1 = Ace, 2 . . . 10, 11 = Jack,
    12 = Queen, 13 = King).
*/
```

However, most IDEs supply the asterisks automatically and rearrange them when the line breaks change.

4.10.3. Method Comments

Each method comment must immediately precede the method that it describes. In addition to the general-purpose tags, you can use the following tags:

- @param *variable description*
  This tag adds an entry to the "parameters" section of the current method. The description can span multiple lines and can use HTML tags. All @param tags for one method must be kept together.
- @return *description*
  This tag adds a "returns" section to the current method. The description can span multiple lines and can use HTML tags.
- @throws *class description*
  This tag adds a note that this method may throw an exception. Exceptions are the topic of Chapter 7.

Here is an example of a method comment:

```
/**
 * Raises the salary of an employee.
 * @param  byPercent the percentage by which to raise the salary (e.g., 10 means 10%)
 * @return  the amount of the raise
 */
public double raiseSalary(double byPercent)
{
    double raise = salary * byPercent / 100;
```

```
    salary += raise;
    return raise;
}
```

 Tip: It can be tedious to write comments for methods whose description and return value are identical, such as:

```
/**
 * Returns the name of the employee.
 * @return  the name of the employee
 */
```

In such cases, consider the the inline form of @return introduced in Java 16:

```
/**
 * {@return the name of the employee}
 */
```

The description section becomes "Returns the name of the employee.", and a "Returns" section with the same contents is added.

4.10.4. Field Comments

You only need to document public fields—generally that means static constants. For example:

```
/**
 * The "Hearts" card suit
 */
public static final int HEARTS = 1;
```

4.10.5. Package Comments

Place the class, method, and variable comments directly into the Java source files, delimited by /** . . . */ documentation comments. However, to generate *package* comments, you need to add a separate file in each package directory. You have two choices:

1. Supply a Java file named package-info.java. The file must contain an initial documentation comment, delimited with /** and */, followed by a package statement. It should contain no further code or comments.
2. Supply an HTML file named package.html. All text between the tags <body>. . .</body> is extracted.

4.10.6. HTML Markup

In the free-form text, you can use HTML modifiers such as `<em>`. . .`</em>` for emphasis, `<strong>`. . .`</strong>` for strong emphasis, `<ul>`/`<li>` for bulleted lists, and `<img . . ./>` to include an image.

To type monospaced code, use `{@code . . . }` instead of `<code>`. . .`</code>`—then you don't have to worry about escaping < and & characters inside the code. If you want to write unescaped < or & in the plain font, use the `@literal{ . . .}` tag.

For multi-line code displays in an HTML `pre` tag, you can use:

```
/**
 * ...
 * <pre>{@code
 *    ...
 *    ...
 * }</pre>
 */
```

or, since Java 18:

```
/**
 * ...
 * {@snippet :
 *    ...
 *    ...
 * }
 */
```

Either way, you don't have to escape < or & characters in the code. However, braces have to match, and you cannot have /* ... */ comments.

4.10.7. Links

You can use hyperlinks to other relevant parts of the javadoc documentation, or to external documents, with the `@see` and `@link` tags.

The tag `@see` *reference* adds a hyperlink in the "see also" section. It can be used with both classes and methods. Here, *reference* can be one of the following:

```
package.class#member label
<a href=". . .">label</a>
"text"
```

The first case is the most useful. You supply the name of a class, method, or variable, and javadoc inserts a hyperlink to the documentation. For example,

```
@see com.horstmann.corejava.Employee#raiseSalary(double)
```

makes a link to the `raiseSalary(double)` method in the `com.horstmann.corejava.Employee` class. You can omit the name of the package, or both the package and class names. Then, the member will be located in the current package or class.

Note that you must use a #, not a period, to separate the class from the method or variable name. The Java compiler itself is highly skilled in determining the various meanings of the period character as separator between packages, subpackages, classes, inner classes, and methods and variables. But the `javadoc` utility isn't quite as clever, so you have to help it along.

Constructors have the special name <init>, not the name of the class, such as

```
@see com.horstmann.corejava.Employee#<init>()
```

You can specify an optional *label* after the member that will appear as the link anchor. If you omit the label, the user will see the member name.

If the `@see` tag is followed by a < character, then you need to specify a hyperlink. You can link to any URL you like. For example:

```
@see <a href="horstmann.com/corejava.html">The Core Java home page</a>
```

If the `@see` tag is followed by a " character, then the text is displayed in the "see also" section. For example:

```
@see "Core Java Volume 2"
```

You can add multiple `@see` tags for one member, but you must keep them all together.

If you like, you can place hyperlinks to other classes or methods anywhere in any of your documentation comments. Insert a tag of the form

```
{@link package.class#member}
```

anywhere in a comment. The member reference follows the same rules as for the `@see` tag.

Since Java 20, ids are automatically generated for level 2 and level 3 headings. For example,

```
<h2>General Principles</h2>
```

gets an id `general-principles-heading`, which you can refer from `@see` and `@link` tags. You need two # symbols to link to an id:

```
{@link com.horstmann.corejava.Employee##general-principles-heading}
```

Use @linkplain instead of @link if a link should be displayed in the plain font instead of the code font.

 Note: If your comments contain links to other files, such as images (for example, diagrams or images of user interface components), place those files into a subdirectory, named doc-files, of the directory containing the source file. The javadoc utility will copy the doc-files directories and their contents from the source directory to the documentation directory. You need to use the doc-files directory in your link, for example <img src="doc-files/uml.png" alt="UML diagram"/>.

4.10.8. General Comments

The tag @since *text* makes a "since" entry. The *text* can be any description of the version that introduced this feature. For example, @since 1.7.1.

The following tags can be used in class documentation comments:

- @author *name*
  This tag makes an "author" entry. You can have multiple @author tags, one for each author. Don't feel compelled to use this tag—your version control system does a more thorough job tracking authorship.
- @version *text*
  This tag makes a "version" entry. The text can be any description of the current version.

The {@value *optionalFormat constantFieldReference*} inline tag inserts the value of a constant field, with an optional printf-style formatter since Java 20. For example, {@value %X Integer#MAX_VALUE} yields 7FFFFFFF.

The @deprecated tag is used together with the @Deprecated annotation. It is followed by text that tells the user when and why the deprecation occurred, and to describe alternatives.

Finally, you can use the {@index *entry*} tag to add an entry to the generated index.

4.10.9. Code Snippets

The purpose of this feature is to allow you to import (presumably well-tested and up-to-date) code from external files. This minimizes the risk of incorrect or stale documentation. Code snippets were introduced in Java 18.

You can import an entire file with these tags:

```
{@snippet file=EmployeeTest.java}
{@snippet class=com.horstmann.corejava.EmployeeTest.java}
```

Files should be placed in the snippet-files subdirectory of the current package.

More commonly, you want to copy a *region* from a file. In the source file, you specify the name and extent of a region as follows:

```
public class EmployeeTest
{
    . . .
    // @start region=default-employee
    var e = new Employee();
    String name = e.getName(); // name is null
    // @end
    . . .
}
```

To highlight a part of the snippet, use a comment:

```
var e = new Employee(); // @hightlight substring=new
String name = e.getName(); // @highlight regex=get[A-Z][a-z]+
```

Inside a region, you can replace a part with another string, for example to make the documentation more general:

```
var e = new Employee("Fred", 100000); // @replace regex=([^)]+) replacement="(..., ...)"
```

Then the documentation contains:

```
var e = new Employee(..., ...);
```

To add a link, use:

```
var c = new Card(); // @link substring=Card target=com.horstmann.games#Card.<init>()
```

These decorations and transformations are specified as comments, so that your source file compiles and runs.

4.10.10. Comment Extraction

Here, *docDirectory* is the name of the directory where you want the HTML files to go. Follow these steps:

1. Change to the directory that contains the source files you want to document. If you have nested packages to document, such as com.horstmann.corejava, you must be working in the directory that contains the subdirectory com. (This is the directory that contains the overview.html file, if you supplied one.)
2. Run the command

```
javadoc -d docDirectory nameOfPackage
```

for a single package. Or, run

```
javadoc -d docDirectory nameOfPackage1 nameOfPackage2. . .
```

to document multiple packages. If your files are in the unnamed package, run instead

```
javadoc -d docDirectory *.java
```

If you omit the `-d` *docDirectory* option, the HTML files are extracted to the current directory. That can get messy, and I don't recommend it.

The `javadoc` program can be fine-tuned by numerous command-line options. For example, you can use the `-author` and `-version` options to include the `@author` and `@version` tags in the documentation. (By default, they are omitted.) Another useful option is `-link`, to include hyperlinks to standard classes. For example, if you use the command

```
javadoc -link https://docs.oracle.com/en/java/javase/21/docs/api *.java
```

all standard library classes are automatically linked to the documentation on the Oracle web site.

If you use the `-linksource` option, each source file is converted to HTML (without color coding, but with line numbers), and each class and method name turns into a hyperlink to the source.

You can also supply an overview comment for all source files. Place it in a file such as `overview.html` and run the `javadoc` tool with the command line option `-overview` *filename*. All text between the tags `<body>. . .</body>` is extracted. The content is displayed when the user selects "Overview" from the navigation bar.

For additional options, refer to the online documentation of the `javadoc` utility at `https://docs.oracle.com/en/java/javase/21/javadoc/index.html`.

4.11. Class Design Hints

Without trying to be comprehensive or tedious, I want to end this chapter with some hints that will make your classes more acceptable in well-mannered OOP circles.

1. *Always keep data private.*
   This is first and foremost; doing anything else violates encapsulation. You may need to write an accessor or mutator method occasionally, but you are still better off keeping the instance fields private. Bitter experience shows that the data representation may change, but how this data are used will change much less

frequently. When data are kept private, changes in their representation will not affect the users of the class, and bugs are easier to detect.

2. *Always initialize data.*
Java won't initialize local variables for you, but it will initialize instance fields of objects. Don't rely on the defaults, but initialize all variables explicitly, either by supplying a default or by setting defaults in all constructors.

3. *Don't use too many basic types in a class.*
The idea is to replace multiple *related* uses of basic types with other classes. This keeps your classes easier to understand and to change. For example, replace the following instance fields in a Customer class:

```
private String street;
private String city;
private String state;
private int zip;
```

with a new class called Address. This way, you can easily cope with changes to addresses, such as the need to deal with international addresses.

4. *Not all fields need individual field accessors and mutators.*
You may need to get and set an employee's salary. You certainly won't need to change the hiring date once the object is constructed. And, quite often, objects have instance fields that you don't want others to get or set, such as an array of state abbreviations in an Address class.

5. *Break up classes that have too many responsibilities.*
This hint is, of course, vague: "too many" is obviously in the eye of the beholder. However, if there is an obvious way to break one complicated class into two classes that are conceptually simpler, seize the opportunity. (On the other hand, don't go overboard; ten classes, each with only one method, are usually an overkill.)
Here is an example of a bad design:

```
public class CardDeck // bad design
{
    private int[] value;
    private int[] suit;

    public CardDeck() { . . . }
    public void shuffle() { . . . }
    public int getTopValue() { . . . }
    public int getTopSuit() { . . . }
    public void draw() { . . . }
}
```

This class really implements two separate concepts: a *deck of cards*, with its shuffle and draw methods, and a *card*, with the methods to inspect its value and suit. It makes sense to introduce a Card class that represents an individual card. Now you have two classes, each with its own responsibilities. Since the Card class is so simple, it can be implemented as a record. Also, instead of using integer values for the suits, an enumeration is a better choice:

```
public class CardDeck
{
   private Card[] cards;

   public CardDeck() { . . . }
   public void shuffle() { . . . }
   public Card getTop() { . . . }
   public void draw() { . . . }
}

public enum Suit { DIAMONDS, HEARTS, SPADES, CLUBS }

public record Card(int value, Suit suit) {}
```

6. *Make the names of your classes and methods reflect their responsibilities.*
   Just as variables should have meaningful names that reflect what they represent, so should classes. (The standard library certainly contains some dubious examples, such as the Date class that describes time.)
   A good convention is that a class name should be a noun (Order), or a noun preceded by an adjective (RushOrder) or a gerund (an "-ing" word, as in BillingAddress). As for methods, follow the standard convention that accessor methods begin with a lowercase get (getSalary) and mutator methods use a lowercase set (setSalary).

7. *Prefer immutable classes.*
   The LocalDate class, and other classes from the java.time package, are immutable—no method can modify the state of an object. Instead of mutating objects, methods such as plusDays return new objects with the modified state.
   The problem with mutation is that it can happen concurrently when multiple threads try to update an object at the same time. The results are unpredictable. When classes are immutable, it is safe to share their objects among multiple threads.
   Therefore, it is a good idea to make classes immutable when you can. This is particularly easy with classes that represent values, such as a string or a point in time. Computations can simply yield new values instead of updating existing ones. Of course, not all classes should be immutable. It would be strange to have the raiseSalary method return a new Employee object when an employee gets a raise.

In this chapter, we covered the fundamentals of objects and classes that make Java an "object-based" language. In order to be truly object-oriented, a programming language must also support inheritance and polymorphism. The Java support for these features is the topic of the next chapter.

CHAPTER 5

Inheritance

Chapter 4 introduced you to classes and objects. In this chapter, you will learn about *inheritance,* another fundamental concept of object-oriented programming. The idea behind inheritance is that you can create new classes that are built on existing classes. When you inherit from an existing class, you reuse (or inherit) its methods, and you can add new methods and fields to adapt your new class to new situations. This technique is essential in Java programming.

This chapter also covers *reflection,* the ability to find out more about classes and their properties in a running program. Reflection is a powerful feature, but it is undeniably complex. Since reflection is of greater interest to tool builders than to application programmers, you can probably glance over that part of the chapter upon first reading and come back to it later.

5.1. Classes, Superclasses, and Subclasses

Let's return to the Employee class discussed in the previous chapter. Suppose (alas) you work for a company where managers are treated differently from other employees. Managers are, of course, just like employees in many respects. Both employees and managers are paid a salary. However, while employees are expected to complete their assigned tasks in return for receiving their salary, managers get *bonuses* if they actually achieve what they are supposed to do. This is the kind of situation that cries out for inheritance. Why? Well, you need to define a new class, Manager, and add functionality. But you can retain some of what you have already programmed in the Employee class, and *all* the fields of the original class can be preserved. More abstractly, there is an obvious "is-a" relationship between Manager and Employee. Every manager *is an* employee: This "is-a" relationship is the hallmark of inheritance.

 Note: In this chapter, I use the classic example of employees and managers, but I must ask you to take this example with a grain of salt. In the real world, an employee can become a manager, so you would want to model being a manager as a role of an employee, not a subclass. In my example, however, I assume the corporate world is populated by two kinds of people: those who are forever employees, and those who have always been managers.

5.1.1. Defining Subclasses

Here is how you define a Manager class that inherits from the Employee class. Use the Java keyword extends to denote inheritance.

```
public class Manager extends Employee
{
    added methods and fields
}
```

 C++ Note: Inheritance is similar in Java and C++. Java uses the extends keyword instead of the : token. All inheritance in Java is public inheritance; there is no analog to the C++ features of private and protected inheritance.

The keyword extends indicates that you are making a new class that derives from an existing class. The existing class is called the *superclass*, *base class*, or *parent class*. The new class is called the *subclass*, *derived class*, or *child class*. The terms superclass and subclass are those most commonly used by Java programmers, although some programmers prefer the parent/child analogy, which also ties in nicely with the "inheritance" theme.

The Employee class is a superclass, but not because it is superior to its subclass or contains more functionality. *In fact, the opposite is true:* Subclasses have *more* functionality than their superclasses. For example, as you will see when we go over the rest of the Manager class code, the Manager class encapsulates more data and has more functionality than its superclass Employee.

 Note: The prefixes *super* and *sub* come from the language of sets used in theoretical computer science and mathematics. The set of all employees contains the set of all managers, and thus is said to be a *superset* of the set of managers. Or, to put it another way, the set of all managers is a *subset* of the set of all employees.

Our Manager class has a new field to store the bonus, and a new method to set it:

```
public class Manager extends Employee
{
    private double bonus;
    . . .
    public void setBonus(double bonus)
    {
        this.bonus = bonus;
    }
}
```

There is nothing special about these methods and fields. If you have a Manager object, you can simply apply the setBonus method.

```
Manager boss = . . .;
boss.setBonus(5000);
```

Of course, if you have an Employee object, you cannot apply the setBonus method—it is not among the methods defined in the Employee class.

However, you *can* use methods such as getName and getHireDay with Manager objects. Even though these methods are not explicitly defined in the Manager class, they are automatically inherited from the Employee superclass.

Every Manager object has four fields: name, salary, hireDay, and bonus. The fields name, salary, and hireDay are taken from the superclass.

 Note: The Java language specification states: "Members of a class that are declared private are not inherited by subclasses of that class." This has confused my readers over the years. The specification uses the word "inherits" narrowly. It considers the private fields non-inherited because the Manager class cannot access them directly. Thus, every Manager object has three fields from the superclass, but the Manager class does not "inherit" them.

When defining a subclass by extending its superclass, you only need to indicate the *differences* between the subclass and the superclass. When designing classes, you place the most general methods in the superclass and more specialized methods in its subclasses. Factoring out common functionality by moving it to a superclass is routine in object-oriented programming.

 Note: In Chapter 4, you learned about *records*: classes whose state is entirely defined by the constructor parameters. You cannot extend a record, and a record cannot extend another class.

5.1.2. Overriding Methods

Some of the superclass methods are not appropriate for the Manager subclass. In particular, the getSalary method should return the sum of the base salary and the bonus. You need to supply a new method to *override* the superclass method:

```
public class Manager extends Employee
{
   . . .
   public double getSalary()
```

```
   {
      . . .
   }
   . . .
}
```

How can you implement this method? At first glance, it appears to be simple—just return the sum of the salary and bonus fields:

```
public double getSalary()
{
   return salary + bonus; // won't work
}
```

However, that won't work. Recall that only the Employee methods have direct access to the private fields of the Employee class. This means that the getSalary method of the Manager class cannot directly access the salary field. If the Manager methods want to access those private fields, they have to do what every other method does—use the public interface, in this case the public getSalary method of the Employee class.

So, let's try again. You need to call getSalary instead of simply accessing the salary field:

```
public double getSalary()
{
   double baseSalary = getSalary(); // still won't work
   return baseSalary + bonus;
}
```

Now, the problem is that the call to getSalary simply calls *itself,* because the Manager class has a getSalary method (namely, the method we are trying to implement). The consequence is an infinite chain of calls to the same method, leading to a program crash.

We need to indicate that we want to call the getSalary method of the Employee superclass, not the current class. Use the special keyword super for this purpose. The call

```
super.getSalary()
```

calls the getSalary method of the Employee class. Here is the correct version of the getSalary method for the Manager class:

```
public double getSalary()
{
   double baseSalary = super.getSalary();
   return baseSalary + bonus;
}
```

Note: Some people think of super as being analogous to the this reference. However, that analogy is not quite accurate: super is not a reference to an object. For example, you cannot assign the value super to another object variable. Instead, super is a special keyword that directs the compiler to invoke the superclass method.

As you saw, a subclass can *add* fields, and it can *add* methods or *override* the methods of the superclass. However, inheritance can never take away any fields or methods.

C++ Note: Java uses the keyword super to call a superclass method. In C++, you would use the name of the superclass with the :: operator instead. For example, the getSalary method of the Manager class would call Employee::getSalary instead of super.getSalary.

5.1.3. Subclass Constructors

To complete our example, let us supply a constructor.

```
public Manager(String name, double salary, int year, int month, int day)
{
    super(name, salary, year, month, day);
    bonus = 0;
}
```

Here, the keyword super has a different meaning. The instruction

```
super(name, salary, year, month, day);
```

is shorthand for "call the constructor of the Employee superclass with name, salary, year, month, and day as arguments."

Since the Manager constructor cannot access the private fields of the Employee class, it must initialize them through a constructor. The constructor is invoked with the special super syntax. The call using super must be the first statement in the constructor for the subclass.

When a subclass object is constructed without an explicit invocation of a superclass constructor, the superclass must have a no-argument constructor. That constructor is invoked prior to the subclass construction.

Note: Recall that the this keyword has two meanings: to denote a reference to the implicit parameter and to call another constructor of the same class. Likewise, the super keyword has two meanings: to invoke a superclass method and to invoke a superclass constructor. When used to invoke constructors, the this and super keywords are closely related. The constructor calls can only occur as the first statement in another constructor. The constructor parameters are either passed to another constructor of the same class (this) or a constructor of the superclass (super).

 C++ Note: In a C++ constructor, you do not call super, but you use the initializer list syntax to construct the superclass. The Manager constructor would look like this in C++:

```
// C++
Manager::Manager(String name, double salary, int year, int month, int day)
: Employee(name, salary, year, month, day)
{
    bonus = 0;
}
```

After you redefine the getSalary method for Manager objects, managers will *automatically* have the bonus added to their salaries.

Here's an example of this at work. We make a new manager and set the manager's bonus:

```
Manager boss = new Manager("Carl Cracker", 80000, 1987, 12, 15);
boss.setBonus(5000);
```

We make an array of three employees:

```
var staff = new Employee[3];
```

We populate the array with a mix of managers and employees:

```
staff[0] = boss;
staff[1] = new Employee("Harry Hacker", 50000, 1989, 10, 1);
staff[2] = new Employee("Tony Tester", 40000, 1990, 3, 15);
```

We print out everyone's salary:

```
for (Employee e : staff)
   System.out.println(e.getName() + " " + e.getSalary());
```

This loop prints the following data:

```
Carl Cracker 85000.0
Harry Hacker 50000.0
Tommy Tester 40000.0
```

Now staff[1] and staff[2] each print their base salary because they are Employee objects. However, staff[0] is a Manager object whose getSalary method adds the bonus to the base salary.

What is remarkable is that the call

    e.getSalary()

picks out the *correct* getSalary method. Note that the *declared* type of e is Employee, but the *actual* type of the object to which e refers can be either Employee or Manager.

When e refers to an Employee object, the call e.getSalary() calls the getSalary method of the Employee class. However, when e refers to a Manager object, then the getSalary method of the Manager class is called instead. The virtual machine knows about the actual type of the object to which e refers, and therefore can invoke the correct method.

The fact that an object variable (such as the variable e) can refer to multiple actual types is called *polymorphism.* Automatically selecting the appropriate method at runtime is called *dynamic binding.* I discuss both topics in more detail in this chapter.

 C++ Note: In C++, you need to declare a member function as virtual if you want dynamic binding. In Java, dynamic binding is the default behavior; if you do *not* want a method to be virtual, you tag it as final. (I discuss the final keyword later in this chapter.)

Listing 5.1 contains a program that shows how the salary computation differs for Employee (Listing 5.2) and Manager (Listing 5.3) objects.

Listing 5.1 inheritance/ManagerTest.java

```
 1  package inheritance;
 2
 3  /**
 4   * This program demonstrates inheritance.
 5   * @version 1.21 2004-02-21
 6   * @author Cay Horstmann
 7   */
 8  public class ManagerTest
 9  {
10     public static void main(String[] args)
11     {
12        // construct a Manager object
13        var boss = new Manager("Carl Cracker", 80000, 1987, 12, 15);
14        boss.setBonus(5000);
15
```

```
16        var staff = new Employee[3];
17
18        // fill the staff array with Manager and Employee objects
19
20        staff[0] = boss;
21        staff[1] = new Employee("Harry Hacker", 50000, 1989, 10, 1);
22        staff[2] = new Employee("Tommy Tester", 40000, 1990, 3, 15);
23
24        // print out information about all Employee objects
25        for (Employee e : staff)
26           System.out.println("name=" + e.getName() + ",salary=" + e.getSalary());
27     }
28  }
```

Listing 5.2 inheritance/Employee.java

```
1   package inheritance;
2
3   import java.time.*;
4
5   public class Employee
6   {
7      private String name;
8      private double salary;
9      private LocalDate hireDay;
10
11     public Employee(String name, double salary, int year, int month, int day)
12     {
13        this.name = name;
14        this.salary = salary;
15        hireDay = LocalDate.of(year, month, day);
16     }
17
18     public String getName()
19     {
20        return name;
21     }
22
23     public double getSalary()
24     {
25        return salary;
26     }
27
28     public LocalDate getHireDay()
29     {
30        return hireDay;
31     }
32
33     public void raiseSalary(double byPercent)
34     {
```

```
35        double raise = salary * byPercent / 100;
36        salary += raise;
37     }
38  }
```

Listing 5.3 `inheritance/Manager.java`

```
 1  package inheritance;
 2
 3  public class Manager extends Employee
 4  {
 5     private double bonus;
 6
 7     /**
 8      * @param name the employee's name
 9      * @param salary the salary
10      * @param year the hire year
11      * @param month the hire month
12      * @param day the hire day
13      */
14     public Manager(String name, double salary, int year, int month, int day)
15     {
16        super(name, salary, year, month, day);
17        bonus = 0;
18     }
19
20     public double getSalary()
21     {
22        double baseSalary = super.getSalary();
23        return baseSalary + bonus;
24     }
25
26     public void setBonus(double b)
27     {
28        bonus = b;
29     }
30  }
```

5.1.4. Inheritance Hierarchies

Inheritance need not stop at deriving one layer of classes. We could have an Executive class that extends Manager, for example. The collection of all classes extending a common superclass is called an *inheritance hierarchy,* as shown in Figure 5.1. The path from a particular class to its ancestors in the inheritance hierarchy is its *inheritance chain.*

There is usually more than one chain of descent from a distant ancestor class. You could form subclasses Programmer or Secretary that extend Employee, and they would have nothing to do with the Manager class (or with each other). This process can continue as long as is necessary.

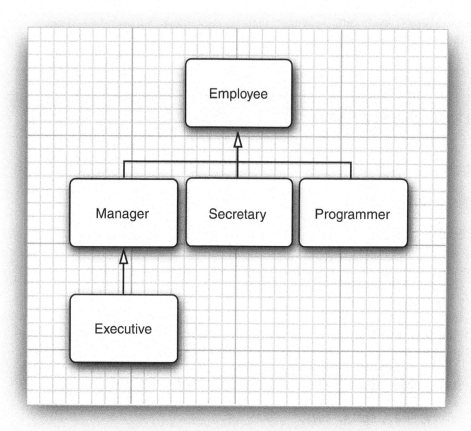

Figure 5.1: Employee inheritance hierarchy

 C++ Note: In C++, a class can have multiple superclasses. Java does not support multiple inheritance. For ways to recover much of the functionality of multiple inheritance, see Chapter 6.

5.1.5. Polymorphism

A simple rule can help you decide whether or not inheritance is the right design for your data. The "is-a" rule states that every object of the subclass is an object of the superclass. For example, every manager is an employee. Thus, it makes sense for the Manager class to be a subclass of the Employee class. Naturally, the opposite is not true—not every employee is a manager.

Another way of formulating the "is-a" rule is the *substitution principle.* That principle states that you can use a subclass object whenever the program expects a superclass object.

For example, you can assign a subclass object to a superclass variable.

```
Employee e;
e = new Employee(. . .); // Employee object expected
e = new Manager(. . .); // OK, Manager can be used as well
```

In the Java programming language, object variables are *polymorphic.* A variable of type Employee can refer to an object of type Employee or to an object of any subclass of the Employee class (such as Manager, Executive, Secretary, and so on).

We took advantage of this principle in Listing 5.1:

```
Manager boss = new Manager(. . .);
Employee[] staff = new Employee[3];
staff[0] = boss;
```

In this case, the variables staff[0] and boss refer to the same object. However, staff[0] is considered to be only an Employee object by the compiler.

That means you can call

```
boss.setBonus(5000); // OK
```

but you can't call

```
staff[0].setBonus(5000); // ERROR
```

The declared type of staff[0] is Employee, and the setBonus method is not a method of the Employee class.

However, you cannot assign a superclass reference to a subclass variable. For example, it is not legal to make the assignment

```
Manager m = staff[i]; // ERROR
```

The reason is clear: Not all employees are managers. If this assignment were to succeed and m were to refer to an Employee object that is not a manager, then it would later be possible to call m.setBonus(. . .) and a runtime error would occur.

 Caution: In Java, arrays of subclass references can be converted to arrays of superclass references without a cast. For example, consider this array of managers:

```
Manager[] managers = new Manager[10];
```

It is legal to convert this array to an Employee[] array:

```
Employee[] staff = managers; // OK
```

Sure, why not, you may think. After all, if `managers[i]` is a `Manager`, it is also an `Employee`. But actually, something surprising is going on. Keep in mind that `managers` and `staff` are references to the same array. Now consider the statement

```
staff[0] = new Employee("Harry Hacker", . . .);
```

The compiler will cheerfully allow this assignment. But `staff[0]` and `managers[0]` are the same reference, so it looks as if we managed to smuggle a mere employee into the management ranks. That would be very bad—calling `managers[0].setBonus(1000)` would try to access a nonexistent instance field and would corrupt neighboring memory.

To make sure no such corruption can occur, all arrays remember the element type with which they were created, and they monitor that only compatible references are stored into them. For example, the array created as `new Manager[10]` remembers that it is an array of managers. Attempting to store an `Employee` reference causes an `ArrayStoreException`.

5.1.6. Understanding Method Calls

It is important to understand exactly how a method call is applied to an object. Let's say we call `x.f(args)`, and the implicit argument `x` is declared to be an object of class `C`. Here is what happens:

1. The compiler looks at the declared type of the object and the method name. Note that there may be multiple methods, all with the same name, `f`, but with different parameter types. For example, there may be a method `f(int)` and a method `f(String)`. The compiler enumerates all methods called `f` in the class `C` and all accessible methods called `f` in the superclasses of `C`. (Private methods of the superclass are not accessible.)
   Now the compiler knows all possible candidates for the method to be called.

2. Next, the compiler determines the types of the arguments supplied in the method call. If among all the methods called `f` there is a unique method whose parameter types are a best match for the supplied arguments, that method is chosen to be called. This process is called *overloading resolution*. For example, in a call `x.f("Hello")`, the compiler picks `f(String)` and not `f(int)`. The situation can get complex because of type conversions (`int` to `double`, `Manager` to `Employee`, and so on). If the compiler cannot find any method with matching parameter types or if multiple methods all match after applying conversions, the compiler reports an error.
   Now the compiler knows the name and parameter types of the method that needs to be called.

Note: Recall that the name and parameter type list for a method are called the method's *signature*. For example, f(int) and f(String) are two methods with the same name but different signatures. If you define a method in a subclass that has the same signature as a superclass method, you override the superclass method.

The return type is not part of the signature. However, when you override a method, you need to keep the return type compatible. A subclass may change the return type to a subtype of the original type. For example, suppose the Employee class has a method

```
public Employee getBuddy() { . . . }
```

A manager would never want to have a lowly employee as a buddy. To reflect that fact, the Manager subclass can override this method as

```
public Manager getBuddy() { . . . } // OK to change return type
```

We say that the two getBuddy methods have *covariant* return types.

3. If the method is private, static, final, or a constructor, then the compiler knows exactly which method to call. (The final modifier is explained in the next section.) This is called *static binding*. Otherwise, the method to be called depends on the actual type of the implicit argument, and dynamic binding must be used at runtime. In our example, the compiler would generate an instruction to call f(String) with dynamic binding.

4. When the program runs and uses dynamic binding to call a method, the virtual machine must call the version of the method that is appropriate for the *actual* type of the object to which x refers. Let's say the actual type is D, a subclass of C. If the class D defines a method f(String), that method is called. If not, D's superclass is searched for a method f(String), and so on.
It would be time-consuming to carry out this search every time a method is called. Instead, the virtual machine precomputes a *method table* for each class. The method table lists all method signatures and the actual methods to be called. The virtual machine can build the method table after loading a class, by combining the methods that it finds in the class file with the method table of the superclass. When a method is actually called, the virtual machine simply makes a table lookup. In our example, the virtual machine consults the method table for the class D and looks up the method to call for f(String). That method may be D.f(String) or X.f(String), where X is some superclass of D. There is one twist to this scenario. If the call is super.f(param), then the virtual machine consults the method table of the superclass.

Let's look at this process in detail in the call e.getSalary() in Listing 5.1. The declared type of e is Employee. The Employee class has a single method, called getSalary, with no method parameters. Therefore, in this case, we don't worry about overloading resolution.

The getSalary method is not private, static, or final, so it is dynamically bound. The virtual machine produces method tables for the Employee and Manager classes. The Employee table shows that all methods are defined in the Employee class itself:

```
Employee:
    getName() -> Employee.getName()
    getSalary() -> Employee.getSalary()
    getHireDay() -> Employee.getHireDay()
    raiseSalary(double) -> Employee.raiseSalary(double)
```

Actually, that isn't the whole story—as you will see later in this chapter, the Employee class has a superclass Object from which it inherits a number of methods. I ignore the Object methods for now.

The Manager method table is slightly different. Three methods are inherited, one method is redefined, and one method is added.

```
Manager:
    getName() -> Employee.getName()
    getSalary() -> Manager.getSalary()
    getHireDay() -> Employee.getHireDay()
    raiseSalary(double) -> Employee.raiseSalary(double)
    setBonus(double) -> Manager.setBonus(double)
```

At runtime, the call e.getSalary() is resolved as follows:

1. First, the virtual machine fetches the method table for the actual type of e. That may be the table for Employee, Manager, or another subclass of Employee.
2. Then, the virtual machine looks up the defining class for the getSalary() signature. Now it knows which method to call.
3. Finally, the virtual machine calls the method.

Dynamic binding has a very important property: It makes programs *extensible* without the need for modifying existing code. Suppose a new class Executive is added and there is the possibility that the variable e refers to an object of that class. The code containing the call e.getSalary() need not be recompiled. The Executive.getSalary() method is called automatically if e happens to refer to an object of type Executive.

Caution: When you override a method, the subclass method must be *at least as visible* as the superclass method. In particular, if the superclass method is public, the subclass method must also be declared public. It is a common error to accidentally omit the public specifier for the subclass method. The compiler then complains that you try to supply a more restrictive access privilege.

5.1.7. Preventing Inheritance: Final Classes and Methods

Occasionally, you want to prevent someone from forming a subclass of one of your classes. Classes that cannot be extended are called *final* classes, and you use the final modifier in the definition of the class to indicate this. For example, suppose we want to prevent others from subclassing the Executive class. Simply declare the class using the final modifier, as follows:

```
public final class Executive extends Manager
{
   . . .
}
```

You can also make a specific method in a class final. If you do this, then no subclass can override that method. (All methods in a final class are automatically final.) For example:

```
public class Employee
{
   . . .
   public final String getName()
   {
      return name;
   }
   . . .
}
```

Note: Recall that fields can also be declared as final. A final field cannot be changed after the object has been constructed. However, if a class is declared final, only the methods, not the fields, are automatically final.

There is only one good reason to make a method or class final: to make sure its semantics cannot be changed in a subclass. For example, the getTime and setTime methods of the Calendar class are final. This indicates that the designers of the Calendar class have taken over responsibility for the conversion between the Date class and the calendar state. No subclass should be allowed to mess up this arrangement. Similarly, the String class is a final class. That means nobody can define a subclass of String. In other words, if you have a String reference, you know it refers to a String and nothing but a String.

If you call a method in a constructor, you should declare it as final. Otherwise, it can be overridden in a subclass, and it can access a partially constructed subclass instance. Here is an example. For debugging purposes, the Employee constructor displays a description of the constructed object.

```java
public class Employee
{
   public Employee(String name, double salary, int year, int month, int day)
   {
      this.name = name;
      this.salary = salary;
      hireDay = LocalDate.of(year, month, day);
      System.out.println("Constructed " + description());
   }

   public String description()
   {
      return "An employee with a salary of " + salary;
   }

   . . .

}
```

Now a new class is added to the hierarchy of employee classes—executives with titles:

```java
public class Executive
{
   private String title;

   public Executive(String name, String title, double salary,
      int year, int month, int day)
   {
      super(name, salary, year, month, day);
      this.title = title;;
   }

   public String getTitle()
   {
      return title;
   }

   public String description()
   {
      if (title.length() >= 30)
         return "An executive with an impressive title";
      else
         return "An executive with a title of " + title;
   }
}
```

When an Executive is constructed, its constructor first calls the Manager constructor, which calls the Employee constructor, which calls the description method. Because of polymorphism, that is the description method in the Executive class! Unfortunately, the Executive constructor hasn't finished yet. The title instance variable is still null, causing a NullPointerException.

Calling a method in a constructor is inherently dangerous. The constructor must have done enough work for the method to succeed. If the method can be overridden, this becomes very difficult to ensure. Therefore, it is best to call only final or private methods in a constructor.

Tip: Since Java 21, if you compile with the -Xlint or -Xlint:this-escape flag, the compiler issues a warning when the constructor of a public class calls a method that is not final or private.

The name of the flag is a bit unfortunate since there are other situations where the this reference can "escape" from a constructor that the compiler does not currently detect.

C++ Note: In C++, method calls in a constructor are not polymorphic. For example, if you call getDescription in an Employee constructor, it always invokes Employee::getDescription.

Some programmers believe that you should declare all methods as final unless you have a good reason to want polymorphism. In fact, in C++ and C#, methods do not use polymorphism unless you specifically request it. That may be a bit extreme, but I agree that it is a good idea to think carefully about final methods and classes when you design a class hierarchy.

In the early days of Java, some programmers used the final keyword hoping to avoid the overhead of dynamic binding. If a method is not overridden, and it is short, then a compiler can optimize the method call away—a process called *inlining*. For example, inlining the call e.getName() replaces it with the field access e.name. This is a worthwhile improvement—CPUs hate branching because it interferes with their strategy of prefetching instructions while processing the current one. However, if getName can be overridden in another class, then the compiler cannot inline it because it has no way of knowing what the overriding code may do.

Fortunately, the just-in-time compiler in the virtual machine can do a better job than a traditional compiler. It knows exactly which classes extend a given class, and it can check whether any class actually overrides a given method. If a method is short, frequently called, and not actually overridden, the just-in-time compiler can inline it. What happens if the virtual machine loads another subclass that overrides an inlined method? Then the optimizer must undo the inlining. That takes time, but it happens rarely.

Note: Enumerations and records are always final—you cannot extend them.

5.1.8. Casting

Recall from Chapter 3 that the process of forcing a conversion from one type to another is called casting. The Java programming language has a special notation for casts. For example,

```
double x = 3.405;
int nx = (int) x;
```

converts the value of the expression x into an integer, discarding the fractional part.

Just as you occasionally need to convert a floating-point number to an integer, you may need to convert an object reference from one class to another. Let's again use the example of an array containing a mix of Employee and Manager objects:

```
var staff = new Employee[3];
staff[0] = new Manager("Carl Cracker", 80000, 1987, 12, 15);
staff[1] = new Employee("Harry Hacker", 50000, 1989, 10, 1);
staff[2] = new Employee("Tony Tester", 40000, 1990, 3, 15);
```

To actually make a cast of an object reference, use a syntax similar to what you use for casting numeric expressions. Surround the target class name with parentheses and place it before the object reference you want to cast. For example:

```
Manager boss = (Manager) staff[0];
```

There is only one reason why you would want to make a cast—to use an object in its full capacity after its actual type has been temporarily forgotten. For example, in the ManagerTest class, the staff array had to be an array of Employee objects because *some* of its elements were regular employees. We would need to cast the managerial elements of the array back to Manager to access any of its new variables. (Note that in the sample code for the first section, I made a special effort to avoid the cast. I initialized the boss variable with a Manager object before storing it in the array. I needed the correct type to set the bonus of the manager.)

As you know, in Java every variable has a type. The type describes the kind of object the variable refers to and what it can do. For example, staff[i] refers to an Employee object (so it can also refer to a Manager object).

The compiler checks that you do not promise too much when you store a value in a variable. If you assign a subclass reference to a superclass variable, you are promising less, and the compiler will simply let you do it. If you assign a superclass reference to a subclass variable, you are promising more. Then you must use a cast so that your promise can be checked at runtime.

What happens if you try to cast down an inheritance chain and are "lying" about what an object contains?

```
Manager boss = (Manager) staff[1]; // ERROR
```

When the program runs, the Java runtime system notices the broken promise and generates a ClassCastException. If you do not catch the exception, your program terminates. Thus, it is good programming practice to find out whether a cast will succeed before attempting it. Simply use the instanceof operator. For example:

```
if (staff[i] instanceof Manager)
{
   boss = (Manager) staff[i];
   . . .
}
```

Finally, the compiler will not let you make a cast if there is no chance for the cast to succeed. For example, the cast

```
String c = (String) staff[i];
```

is a compile-time error because String is not a subclass of Employee.

To sum up:

- You can cast only within an inheritance hierarchy.
- Use instanceof to check before casting from a superclass to a subclass.

 Note: The test

```
   x instanceof C
```

does not generate an exception if x is null. It simply returns false. That makes sense: null refers to no object, so it certainly doesn't refer to an object of type C.

Actually, converting the type of an object by a cast is not usually a good idea. In our example, you do not need to cast an Employee object to a Manager object for most purposes. The getSalary method will work correctly on both objects of both classes. The dynamic binding that makes polymorphism work locates the correct method automatically.

The only reason to make the cast is to use a method that is unique to managers, such as setBonus. If for some reason you find yourself wanting to call setBonus on Employee objects, ask yourself whether this is an indication of a design flaw in the superclass. It may make sense to redesign the superclass and add a setBonus method. Remember, it takes only one uncaught ClassCastException to terminate your program. In general, it is best to minimize the use of casts and the instanceof operator.

 C++ Note: Java uses the cast syntax from the "bad old days" of C, but it works like the safe dynamic_cast operation of C++. For example,

```
Employee[] staff = ...;
Manager boss = (Manager) staff[i]; // Java
```

is equivalent to

```
Employee* staff[] = ...;
Manager* boss = dynamic_cast<Manager*>(staff[i]); // C++
```

There is one important difference. If the dynamic_cast fails, it yields a null pointer instead of throwing an exception.

5.1.9. Pattern Matching for instanceof

The code

```
if (staff[i] instanceof Manager)
{
   Manager boss = (Manager) staff[i];
   boss.setBonus(5000);
}
```

is rather verbose. Do we really need to mention the subclass Manager three times?

As of Java 16, there is an easier way. You can declare the subclass variable right in the instanceof test:

```
if (staff[i] instanceof Manager boss)
{
   boss.setBonus(5000);
}
```

If staff[i] is an instance of the Manager class, then the variable boss is set to staff[i], and you can use it *as a* Manager. You skip the cast.

If staff[i] doesn't refer to a Manager, boss is not set, and the instanceof operator yields the value false. The body of the if statement is skipped.

Tip: In most situations in which you use instanceof, you need to apply a subclass method. Then use this "pattern-matching" form of instanceof instead of a cast.

A useless instanceof pattern is a compile-time error:

```
Manager boss = . . .;
if (boss instanceof Employee e) . . . // ERROR: Of course it's an Employee
```

 Note: The equally useless

```
    if (boss instanceof Employee) . . .
```

is allowed, for backward compatibility with Java 1.0.

When an instanceof pattern introduces a variable, you can use it right away, in the same expression:

```
Employee e;
if (e instanceof Executive exec && exec.getTitle().getLength() >= 20) . . .
```

This works because the right-hand side of an && expression is only evaluated if the left-hand side is true. If the right-hand side is evaluated, exec must have been bound to an Executive instance.

However, the following is a compile-time error:

```
if (e instanceof Manager exec || exec.getTitle.getLength() >= 20) . . . // ERROR
```

The right-hand side of || is executed when the left-hand side is false, and then nothing is bound to the variable exec.

Here is another example with the conditional operator:

```
String title = e instanceof Executive exec ? exec.getTitle() : "";
```

The variable exec is defined in the subexpression after the ?, but not in the subexpression after the :.

 Note: The variable-declaring instanceof forms are called "pattern-matching" because they are similar to type patterns in switch, which are covered in detail in Section 5.9.

Caution: As any local variable, the local variable defined by a pattern can shadow a field. For example:

```
class Value
{
   private double v;
   public boolean equals(Object other)
   {
      if (other instanceof LabeledValue v)
         // v is the same as other
      else
         // v denotes the field
   }
   . . .
}
```

The preceding example showed a *type pattern*. If the type matches, the object is bound to a variable of that type. When the type is a record, you can, as of Java 21, do better and declare variables that are bound to the components. This is called a *record pattern*:

```
record Point(double x, double y) {}
Point p = . . .;
if (p instanceof Point(var a, var b)) distance = Math.hypot(a, b);
```

Now a and b are bound to the x and y components of p. Of course, you could also invoke p.x() and p.y(), but a record pattern can be more concise.

For added clarity, you can also specify explicit types for the introduced variables:

```
if (p instanceof Point(double a, double b)) . . .;
```

Record patterns can be nested:

```
record Circle(Point center, double radius) {}
Circle c = . . .;
if (c instanceof Circle(Point(var a, var b), var r)) . . .;
```

 Preview Note: JEP 443 introduces *unnamed variables* as a preview feature. If you don't need one of the variables in a record pattern, you can denote it with an underscore:

```
if (p instanceof Point(var a, _)) distance = Math.abs(a);
```

Until this feature becomes available, you can use var __ with two underscores, since a single underscore is a keyword since Java 9.

5.1.10. Protected Access

As you know, fields in a class are best tagged as private, and methods are usually tagged as public. Any features declared private won't be accessible in other classes. As explained at the beginning of this chapter, this is also true for subclasses: A subclass cannot access the private fields of its superclass.

There are times, however, when you want to restrict a method to subclasses only or, less commonly, to allow subclass methods to access a superclass field. In that case, you declare a class feature as protected. For example, if the superclass Employee declares the hireDay field as protected instead of private, then the Manager methods can access it directly.

In Java, a protected field is accessible by any class in the same package. Now consider an Administrator subclass in a different package. The methods of the Administrator class can peek inside the hireDay field of Administrator objects only, not of other Employee objects. This restriction is made so that you can't abuse the protected mechanism by forming subclasses just to gain access to the protected fields.

In practice, use protected fields with caution. Suppose your class is used by other programmers and you designed it with protected fields. Unknown to you, other programmers may inherit classes from your class and start accessing your protected fields. In this case, you can no longer change the implementation of your class without upsetting those programmers. That is against the spirit of OOP, which encourages data encapsulation.

Protected methods make more sense. A class may declare a method as protected if it is tricky to use. This indicates that the subclasses (which, presumably, know their ancestor well) can be trusted to use the method correctly, but other classes cannot.

A good example of this kind of method is the clone method of the Object class—see Chapter 6 for more details.

 C++ Note: As already mentioned, protected features in Java are accessible to all subclasses as well as to all other classes in the same package. This is slightly different from the C++ meaning of protected, and it makes the notion of protected in Java even less safe than in C++.

Here is a summary of the four access control modifiers in Java:

1. Accessible in the class only (private).
2. Accessible by the world (public).

3. Accessible in the package and all subclasses (protected).
4. Accessible in the package—the (unfortunate) default. No modifiers are needed.

5.2. Object: The Cosmic Superclass

The Object class is the ultimate ancestor—every class in Java extends Object. However, you never have to write

```
public class Employee extends Object
```

The ultimate superclass Object is taken for granted if no superclass is explicitly mentioned. Since *every* class in Java extends Object, it is important to be familiar with the services provided by the Object class. I go over the basic ones in this chapter; consult the later chapters or view the online documentation for what is not covered here. (Several methods of Object come up only when dealing with concurrency—see Chapter 10.)

5.2.1. Variables of Type Object

You can use a variable of type Object to refer to objects of any type:

```
Object obj = new Employee("Harry Hacker", 35000);
```

Of course, a variable of type Object is only useful as a generic holder for arbitrary values. To do anything specific with the value, you need to have some knowledge about the original type and apply a cast:

```
Employee e = (Employee) obj;
```

In Java, only the values of *primitive types* (numbers, characters, and boolean values) are not objects.

All array types, no matter whether they are arrays of objects or arrays of primitive types, are class types that extend the Object class.

```
Employee[] staff = new Employee[10];
obj = staff; // OK
obj = new int[10]; // OK
```

 C++ Note: In C++, there is no cosmic root class. However, every pointer can be converted to a void* pointer.

5.2.2. The equals Method

The equals method in the Object class tests whether one object is considered equal to another. The equals method, as implemented in the Object class, determines whether two object references are identical. This is a pretty reasonable default—if two objects are identical, they should certainly be equal. For quite a few classes, nothing else is required. For example, it makes little sense to compare two PrintStream objects for equality. However, you will often want to implement state-based equality testing, in which two objects are considered equal when they have the same state.

For example, let us consider two employees equal if they have the same name, salary, and hire date. (In an actual employee database, it would be more sensible to compare IDs instead. I use this example to demonstrate the mechanics of implementing the equals method.)

```java
public class Employee
{
    . . .
    public boolean equals(Object otherObject)
    {
        // a quick test to see if the objects are identical
        if (this == otherObject) return true;

        // must return false if the explicit parameter is null
        if (otherObject == null) return false;

        // if the classes don't match, they can't be equal
        if (getClass() != otherObject.getClass())
            return false;

        // now we know otherObject is a non-null Employee
        Employee other = (Employee) otherObject;

        // test whether the fields have identical values
        return name.equals(other.name)
            && salary == other.salary
            && hireDay.equals(other.hireDay);
    }
}
```

The getClass method returns the class of an object—we discuss this method in detail later in this chapter. In our test, two objects can only be equal when they belong to the same class.

Tip: To guard against the possibility that name or hireDay are null, use the Objects.equals method. The value of Objects.equals(a, b) is true if both arguments are null, false if only one is null, and a.equals(b) otherwise. With that method, the last statement of the Employee.equals method becomes

```
return Objects.equals(name, other.name)
   && salary == other.salary
   && Objects.equals(hireDay, other.hireDay);
```

When you define the equals method for a subclass, first call equals on the superclass. If that test doesn't pass, then the objects can't be equal. If the superclass fields are equal, you are ready to compare the instance fields of the subclass.

```
public class Manager extends Employee
{
   . . .
   public boolean equals(Object otherObject)
   {
      if (!super.equals(otherObject)) return false;
      // super.equals checked that this and otherObject belong to the same class
      Manager other = (Manager) otherObject;
      return bonus == other.bonus;
   }
}
```

 Note: Recall from Chapter 4 that a record is a special form of an immutable class whose state is entirely defined by the fields set in a "canonical" constructor. Records automatically define an equals method that compares the fields. Two record instances are equal when the corresponding field values are equal.

5.2.3. Equality Testing and Inheritance

How should the equals method behave if the implicit and explicit parameters don't belong to the same class? This has been an area of some controversy. In the preceding example, the equals method returns false if the classes don't match exactly. But many programmers use an instanceof test instead:

```
if (!(otherObject instanceof Employee)) return false;
```

This leaves open the possibility that otherObject can belong to a subclass. However, this approach can get you into trouble. Here is why. The Java Language Specification requires that the equals method has the following properties:

1. It is *reflexive*: For any non-null reference x, x.equals(x) should return true.
2. It is *symmetric*: For any references x and y, x.equals(y) should return true if and only if y.equals(x) returns true.
3. It is *transitive*: For any references x, y, and z, if x.equals(y) returns true and y.equals(z) returns true, then x.equals(z) should return true.
4. It is *consistent*: If the objects to which x and y refer haven't changed, then repeated calls to x.equals(y) return the same value.
5. For any non-null reference x, x.equals(null) should return false.

These rules are certainly reasonable. You wouldn't want a library implementor to ponder whether to call x.equals(y) or y.equals(x) when locating an element in a data structure.

However, the symmetry rule has subtle consequences when the parameters belong to different classes. Consider a call

```
e.equals(m)
```

where e is an Employee object and m is a Manager object, both of which happen to have the same name, salary, and hire date. If Employee.equals uses an instanceof test, the call returns true. But that means that the reverse call

```
m.equals(e)
```

also needs to return true—the symmetry rule does not allow it to return false or to throw an exception.

That leaves the Manager class in a bind. Its equals method must be willing to compare itself to any Employee, without taking manager-specific information into account! All of a sudden, the instanceof test looks less attractive.

Some authors have gone on record that the getClass test is wrong because it violates the substitution principle. A commonly cited example is the equals method in the AbstractSet class that tests whether two sets have the same elements. The AbstractSet class has two concrete subclasses, TreeSet and HashSet, that use different algorithms for locating set elements. You really want to be able to compare any two sets, no matter how they are implemented.

However, the set example is rather specialized. It would make sense to declare AbstractSet.equals as final, because nobody should redefine the semantics of set equality. (The method is not actually final. This allows a subclass to implement a more efficient algorithm for the equality test.)

The way I see it, there are two distinct scenarios:

■ If subclasses can have their own notion of equality, then the symmetry requirement forces you to use the getClass test.

■ If the notion of equality is fixed in the superclass, then you can use the instanceof test and allow objects of different subclasses to be equal to one another.

In the example with employees and managers, we consider two objects to be equal when they have matching fields. If we have two Manager objects with the same name, salary, and hire date, but with different bonuses, we want them to be different. Therefore, we use the getClass test.

But suppose we used an employee ID for equality testing. This notion of equality makes sense for all subclasses. Then we could use the instanceof test, and we should have declared Employee.equals as final.

 Note: The standard Java library contains over 150 implementations of equals methods, with a mishmash of using instanceof, calling getClass, catching a ClassCastException, or doing nothing at all. Check out the API documentation of the java.sql.Timestamp class, where the implementors note with some embarrassment that they have painted themselves in a corner. The Timestamp class inherits from java.util.Date, whose equals method uses an instanceof test, and it is impossible to override equals to be both symmetric and accurate.

 Caution: The commonly cited example of set equality is a cautionary tale, showing just how difficult it is to provide symmetric equality across subclasses.

Consider these two sets:

```
Set<String> x = new HashSet<>();
x.add("Hello");
x.add("World");
Set<String> y = new TreeSet<>(String.CASE_INSENSITIVE_ORDER);
y.add("Hello");
y.add("WORLD");
```

With these sets, equals is not symmetric:

```
x.equals(y) // false
y.equals(x) // true
```

TreeSet uses the sort order, and not equals, to compare elements. With case-insensitive order, the strings "World" and "WORLD" are deemed equal.

Here is a recipe for writing the perfect equals method:

1. Name the explicit parameter otherObject—later, you will need to cast it to another variable that you should call other.
2. Test whether this happens to be identical to otherObject:

   ```
   if (this == otherObject) return true;
   ```

   This statement is just an optimization. In practice, this is a common case. It is much cheaper to check for identity than to compare the fields.
3. Test whether otherObject is null and return false if it is. This test is required.

   ```
   if (otherObject == null) return false;
   ```

4. Compare the classes of this and otherObject. If the semantics of equals can change in subclasses, use the getClass test:

   ```
   if (getClass() != otherObject.getClass()) return false;
   ClassName other = (ClassName) otherObject;
   ```

   If the same semantics holds for *all* subclasses, you can use an instanceof test:

   ```
   if (!(otherObject instanceof ClassName other)) return false;
   ```

   Note that the instanceof test sets other to otherObject if it succeeds. No cast is necessary.
5. Now compare the fields, as required by your notion of equality. Use == for primitive type fields, Objects.equals for object fields. Return true if all fields match, false otherwise.

   ```
   return field1 == other.field1
       && Objects.equals(field2, other.field2)
       && . . .;
   ```

   If you redefine equals in a subclass, include a call to super.equals(other).

 Tip: If you have fields of array type, you can use the static Arrays.equals method to check that the corresponding array elements are equal. Use the Arrays.deepEquals method for multidimensional arrays.

 Caution: Here is a common mistake when implementing the equals method. Can you spot the problem?

```
public class Employee
{
    public boolean equals(Employee other)
```

```
    {
        return other != null
            && getClass() == other.getClass()
            && Objects.equals(name, other.name)
            && salary == other.salary
            && Objects.equals(hireDay, other.hireDay);
    }
    . . .
}
```

This method declares the explicit parameter type as Employee. As a result, it does not override the equals method of the Object class but defines a completely unrelated method.

You can protect yourself against this type of error by tagging methods that are intended to override superclass methods with @Override:

```
@Override public boolean equals(Object other)
```

If you made a mistake and are defining a new method, the compiler reports an error. For example, suppose you add the following declaration to the Employee class:

```
@Override public boolean equals(Employee other)
```

An error is reported because this method doesn't override any method from the Object superclass.

---

java.util.Arrays 1.2

■ static boolean equals(*xxx*[] a, *xxx*[] b) **5.0**
  returns true if the arrays have equal lengths and equal elements in corresponding positions. The component type *xxx* of the array can be Object, int, long, short, char, byte, boolean, float, or double.

---

java.util.Objects 7

■ static boolean equals(Object a, Object b)
  returns true if a and b are both null, false if exactly one of them is null, and a.equals(b) otherwise.

5.2.4. The hashCode Method

A hash code is an integer that is derived from an object. Hash codes should be scrambled—if x and y are two distinct objects, there should be a high probability that x.hashCode() and y.hashCode() are different. Table 5.1 lists a few examples of hash codes that result from the hashCode method of the String class.

Table 5.1: Hash Codes Resulting from the hashCode Method

String	Hash Code
Hello	69609650
Harry	69496448
Hacker	-2141031506

The String class uses the following algorithm to compute the hash code:

```
int hash = 0;
for (int i = 0; i < length(); i++)
   hash = 31 * hash + charAt(i);
```

The hashCode method is defined in the Object class. Therefore, every object has a default hash code. That hash code is derived from the object's memory address. Consider this example:

```
var s = "Ok";
var sb = new StringBuilder(s);
System.out.println(s.hashCode() + " " + sb.hashCode());
var t = new String("Ok");
var tb = new StringBuilder(t);
System.out.println(t.hashCode() + " " + tb.hashCode());
```

Table 5.2 shows the result.

Table 5.2: Hash Codes of Strings and String Builders

Object	Hash Code	Object	Hash Code
s	2556	t	2556
sb	20526976	tb	20527144

Note that the strings s and t have the same hash code because, for strings, the hash codes are derived from their *contents.* The string builders sb and tb have different hash codes because no hashCode method has been defined for the StringBuilder class and the default hashCode method in the Object class derives the hash code from the object's memory address.

If you redefine the equals method, you will also need to redefine the hashCode method for objects that users might insert into a hash table. (I discuss hash tables in Chapter 9.)

The hashCode method should return an integer (which can be negative). Just combine the hash codes of the instance fields so that the hash codes for different objects are likely to be widely scattered.

For example, here is a hashCode method for the Employee class:

```
public class Employee
{
   public int hashCode()
   {
      return 7 * name.hashCode()
         + 11 * Double.valueOf(salary).hashCode()
         + 13 * hireDay.hashCode();
   }
   . . .
}
```

However, you can do better. First, use the null-safe method Objects.hashCode. It returns 0 if its argument is null and the result of calling hashCode on the argument otherwise. Also, use the static Double.hashCode method to avoid creating a Double object:

```
public int hashCode()
{
   return 7 * Objects.hashCode(name)
      + 11 * Double.hashCode(salary)
      + 13 * Objects.hashCode(hireDay);
}
```

 Caution: If the instance variables have small ranges of possible values, you need to achieve as many distinct hash codes as possible. Consider hashing calendar dates. Computing 7 * year + 11 * month + 13 * day yields many collisions. In contrast, 31 * 12 * year + 31 * month + day is a "perfect hash function." Assuming a reasonable year range, no two dates have the same hash code. (The actual hashCode method of the LocalDate class, which supports a range of ±999,999,999 years, is a bit more complex.)

Combining multiple hash values can be tedious. In many cases, you can simply call Objects.hash with all fields. It will combine the hash codes of its arguments. Then the Employee.hashCode method is simply

```
public int hashCode()
{
    return Objects.hash(name, salary, hireDay);
}
```

However, you need to be careful with fields that are arrays. The hash code of an array is computed with Object.hashCode and does *not*depend on its elements. Instead, use the static Arrays.hashCode method which combines the hash codes of the array elements. There are overloads for primitive type arrays and arrays of objects. For multi-dimensional arrays, use Arrays.deepHashCode.

 Note: The Arrays.hashCode(Object[]) method works almost like String.hashCode, using the "multiply with 31 and add" operation to combine element hash codes. But there is a twist. A zero-length array has hash code 1, to distinguish it from null. Here is the implementation:

```
public static int hashCode(Object[] a)
{
    if (a == null) return 0;

    int result = 1; // Starting at 1, not 0

    for (Object element : a)
        result = 31 * result + (element == null ? 0 : element.hashCode());

    return result;
}
```

The Objects.hash method calls Arrays.hashCode. As a consequence, Objects.hash(x) equals 31 + x.hashCode().

A record type automatically provides a hashCode method that derives a hash code from the hash codes of the component values. Its exact behavior is left open in the Java Language Specification. In OpenJDK 21, the component hashes are simply combined with the "multiply with 31 and add" operation, starting with zero.

Your definitions of equals and hashCode must be compatible: If x.equals(y) is true, then x.hashCode() must return the same value as y.hashCode(). For example, if you define Employee.equals to compare employee IDs, then the hashCode method needs to hash the IDs, not employee names or memory addresses.

---

java.lang.Object 1.0

- `int hashCode()`
  returns a hash code for this object. A hash code can be any integer, positive or negative. Equal objects need to return identical hash codes.

---

java.util.Objects 7

- `static int hash(Object... objects)`
  returns a hash code that is combined from the hash codes of all supplied objects.
- `static int hashCode(Object a)`
  returns 0 if a is null or a.hashCode() otherwise.

---

java.lang.(Integer|Long|Short|Byte|Double|Float|Character|Boolean) 1.0

- `static int hashCode(xxx value)` **8**
  returns the hash code of the given value. Here *xxx* is the primitive type corresponding to the given wrapper type.

---

java.util.Arrays 1.2

- `static int hashCode(xxx[] a)` **5.0**
  computes the hash code of the array a. The component type *xxx* of the array can be Object, int, long, short, char, byte, boolean, float, or double.

5.2.5. The `toString` Method

Another important method in `Object` is the `toString` method that returns a string representing the value of this object. Here is a typical example. The `toString` method of the Point class returns a string like this:

```
java.awt.Point[x=10,y=20]
```

Most (but not all) `toString` methods follow this format: the name of the class, then the field values enclosed in square brackets. Here is an implementation of the `toString` method for the Employee class:

```
public String toString()
{
   return "Employee[name=" + name
      + ",salary=" + salary
```

```
    + ",hireDay=" + hireDay
    + "]";
}
```

Actually, you can do a little better. Instead of hardwiring the class name into the `toString` method, call `getClass().getName()` to obtain a string with the class name.

```
public String toString()
{
    return getClass().getName()
        + "[name=" + name
        + ",salary=" + salary
        + ",hireDay=" + hireDay
        + "]";
}
```

Such `toString` method will also work for subclasses.

Of course, the subclass programmer should define its own `toString` method and add the subclass fields. If the superclass uses `getClass().getName()`, then the subclass can simply call `super.toString()`. For example, here is a `toString` method for the `Manager` class:

```
public class Manager extends Employee
{
    . . .
    public String toString()
    {
        return super.toString()
            + "[bonus=" + bonus
            + "]";
    }
}
```

Now a `Manager` object is printed as

```
Manager[name=. . .,salary=. . .,hireDay=. . .][bonus=. . .]
```

The `toString` method is ubiquitous for an important reason: Whenever an object is concatenated with a string by the "+" operator, the Java compiler automatically invokes the `toString` method to obtain a string representation of the object. For example:

```
var p = new Point(10, 20);
String message = "The current position is " + p;
    // automatically invokes p.toString()
```

Tip: Instead of writing x.toString(), you can write "" + x. This statement concatenates the empty string with the string representation of x that is exactly x.toString(). Unlike toString, this statement even works if x is of primitive type.

If x is any object and you call

```
System.out.println(x);
```

then the println method simply calls x.toString() and prints the resulting string.

The Object class defines the toString method to print the class name and the hash code of the object. For example, the call

```
System.out.println(System.out)
```

produces an output that looks like this:

```
java.io.PrintStream@2f6684
```

The reason is that the implementor of the PrintStream class didn't bother to override the toString method.

 Caution: Annoyingly, arrays inherit the toString method from Object, with the added twist that the array type is printed in an archaic format. For example,

```
int[] luckyNumbers = { 2, 3, 5, 7, 11, 13 };
String s = "" + luckyNumbers;
```

yields the string "[I@1a46e30". (The prefix [I denotes an array of integers.) The remedy is to call the static Arrays.toString method instead. The code

```
String s = Arrays.toString(luckyNumbers);
```

yields the string "[2, 3, 5, 7, 11, 13]".

To correctly print multidimensional arrays (that is, arrays of arrays), use Arrays.deepToString.

The toString method is a great tool for logging. Many classes in the standard class library define the toString method so that you can get useful information about the state of an object. This is particularly useful in logging messages like this:

```
System.out.println("Current position = " + position);
```

As explained in Chapter 7, an even better solution is to use a logger object and call

```
logger.log(INFO, "Current position = " + position);
```

 Tip: I strongly recommend that you add a toString method to each class that you write. You, as well as other programmers who use your classes, will be grateful for the logging support.

However, for record types, a toString method is already provided. It simply lists the class name and the names and stringified values of the fields.

 Note: In the preceding sections, you learned how to override the equals, hashCode, and toString methods. In the perhaps unlikely case that you need access to the unmodified behavior, do this:

- Compare with == instead of equals
- Call System.indentityHashCode(obj) or Objects.identityToString(obj) to get what would have been returned if you had not overriden hashCode or toString

The program in Listing 5.4 tests the equals, hashCode, and toString methods for the classes Employee (Listing 5.5) and Manager (Listing 5.6).

Listing 5.4 equals/EqualsTest.java

```
1  package equals;
2
3  /**
4   * This program demonstrates the equals method.
5   * @version 1.12 2012-01-26
6   * @author Cay Horstmann
7   */
8  public class EqualsTest
9  {
10     public static void main(String[] args)
11     {
12        var alice1 = new Employee("Alice Adams", 75000, 1987, 12, 15);
13        var alice2 = alice1;
14        var alice3 = new Employee("Alice Adams", 75000, 1987, 12, 15);
15        var bob = new Employee("Bob Brandson", 50000, 1989, 10, 1);
16
17        System.out.println("alice1 == alice2: " + (alice1 == alice2));
18
19        System.out.println("alice1 == alice3: " + (alice1 == alice3));
20
```

```
21        System.out.println("alice1.equals(alice3): " + alice1.equals(alice3));
22
23        System.out.println("alice1.equals(bob): " + alice1.equals(bob));
24
25        System.out.println("bob.toString(): " + bob);
26
27        var carl = new Manager("Carl Cracker", 80000, 1987, 12, 15);
28        var boss = new Manager("Carl Cracker", 80000, 1987, 12, 15);
29        boss.setBonus(5000);
30        System.out.println("boss.toString(): " + boss);
31        System.out.println("carl.equals(boss): " + carl.equals(boss));
32        System.out.println("alice1.hashCode(): " + alice1.hashCode());
33        System.out.println("alice3.hashCode(): " + alice3.hashCode());
34        System.out.println("bob.hashCode(): " + bob.hashCode());
35        System.out.println("carl.hashCode(): " + carl.hashCode());
36     }
37  }
```

Listing 5.5 equals/Employee.java

```
1   package equals;
2
3   import java.time.*;
4   import java.util.Objects;
5
6   public class Employee
7   {
8      private String name;
9      private double salary;
10     private LocalDate hireDay;
11
12     public Employee(String name, double salary, int year, int month, int day)
13     {
14        this.name = name;
15        this.salary = salary;
16        hireDay = LocalDate.of(year, month, day);
17     }
18
19     public String getName()
20     {
21        return name;
22     }
23
24     public double getSalary()
25     {
26        return salary;
27     }
28
29     public LocalDate getHireDay()
30     {
```

```
31        return hireDay;
32     }
33
34     public void raiseSalary(double byPercent)
35     {
36        double raise = salary * byPercent / 100;
37        salary += raise;
38     }
39
40     public boolean equals(Object otherObject)
41     {
42        // a quick test to see if the objects are identical
43        if (this == otherObject) return true;
44
45        // must return false if the explicit parameter is null
46        if (otherObject == null) return false;
47
48        // if the classes don't match, they can't be equal
49        if (getClass() != otherObject.getClass()) return false;
50
51        // now we know otherObject is a non-null Employee
52        var other = (Employee) otherObject;
53
54        // test whether the fields have identical values
55        return Objects.equals(name, other.name)
56           && salary == other.salary && Objects.equals(hireDay, other.hireDay);
57     }
58
59     public int hashCode()
60     {
61        return Objects.hash(name, salary, hireDay);
62     }
63
64     public String toString()
65     {
66        return getClass().getName() + "[name=" + name + ",salary=" + salary + ",hireDay="
67           + hireDay + "]";
68     }
69 }
```

Listing 5.6 equals/Manager.java

```
1 package equals;
2
3 public class Manager extends Employee
4 {
5    private double bonus;
6
7    public Manager(String name, double salary, int year, int month, int day)
8    {
```

```
 9          super(name, salary, year, month, day);
10          bonus = 0;
11      }
12
13      public double getSalary()
14      {
15          double baseSalary = super.getSalary();
16          return baseSalary + bonus;
17      }
18
19      public void setBonus(double bonus)
20      {
21          this.bonus = bonus;
22      }
23
24      public boolean equals(Object otherObject)
25      {
26          if (!super.equals(otherObject)) return false;
27          var other = (Manager) otherObject;
28          // super.equals checked that this and other belong to the same class
29          return bonus == other.bonus;
30      }
31
32      public int hashCode()
33      {
34          return java.util.Objects.hash(super.hashCode(), bonus);
35      }
36
37      public String toString()
38      {
39          return super.toString() + "[bonus=" + bonus + "]";
40      }
41  }
```

---

java.lang.Object 1.0

- Class getClass()
  returns a class object that contains information about the object. As you will see later in this chapter, Java has a runtime representation for classes that is encapsulated in the Class class.
- boolean equals(Object otherObject)
  compares two objects for equality; returns true if the objects point to the same area of memory, and false otherwise. You should override this method in your own classes.
- String toString()
  returns a string that represents the value of this object. You should override this method in your own classes.

---

java.lang.Class 1.0

- `String getName()`
  returns the name of this class.
- `Class getSuperclass()`
  returns the superclass of this class as a `Class` object.

---

java.lang.System 1.0

- `static int identityHashCode(Object x)  1.1`
  returns the hash code that `Object.hashCode` would return for x if not overridden, or 0 if x is null.

---

java.util.Objects 7

- `static String identityToString(Object o)  19`
  returns the string that `Object.toString` would return for o if not overridden. Throws a `NullPointerException` if o is null.

5.3. Generic Array Lists

In some programming languages—in particular, in C and C++—you have to fix the sizes of all arrays at compile time. Programmers hate this because it forces them into uncomfortable tradeoffs. How many employees will be in a department? Surely no more than 100. What if there is a humongous department with 150 employees? Do we want to waste 90 entries for every department with just 10 employees?

In Java, the situation is somewhat better. You can set the size of an array at runtime.

```
int actualSize = . . .;
var staff = new Employee[actualSize];
```

Of course, this code does not completely solve the problem of dynamically modifying arrays at runtime. Once you set the array size, you cannot change it easily. Instead, in Java you can deal with this common situation by using another Java class, called `ArrayList`. The `ArrayList` class is similar to an array, but it automatically adjusts its capacity as you add and remove elements, without any additional code.

`ArrayList` is a *generic class* with a *type parameter*. To specify the type of the element objects that the array list holds, you append a class name enclosed in angle brackets, such as `ArrayList<Employee>`. You will see in Chapter 8 how to define your own generic class, but you don't need to know any of those technicalities to use the `ArrayList` type.

The following sections show you how to work with array lists.

5.3.1. Declaring Array Lists

Here is how to declare and construct an array list that holds `Employee` objects:

```
ArrayList<Employee> staff = new ArrayList<Employee>();
```

It is a good idea to use the var keyword to avoid duplicating the class name:

```
var staff = new ArrayList<Employee>();
```

It you don't use the var keyword, you can omit the type argument on the right-hand side:

```
ArrayList<Employee> staff = new ArrayList<>();
```

This is called the "diamond" syntax because the empty brackets <> resemble a diamond. Use the diamond syntax together with the new operator. The compiler checks what happens to the new value. If it is assigned to a variable, passed into a method, or returned from a method, then the compiler checks the generic type of the variable, parameter, or method. It then places that type into the <>. In our example, the new ArrayList<>() is assigned to a variable of type ArrayList<Employee>. Therefore, the generic type is Employee.

 Caution: If you declare an ArrayList with var, do *not* use the diamond syntax. The declaration

```
var elements = new ArrayList<>();
```

yields an ArrayList<Object>.

 Note: Before Java 5, there were no generic classes. Instead, there was a single ArrayList class, a one-size-fits-all collection holding elements of type Object. You can still use ArrayList without a <. . .> suffix. It is considered a "raw" type, with the type parameter erased.

 Note: In even older versions of Java, programmers used the Vector class for dynamic arrays. However, the ArrayList class is more efficient, and there is no longer any good reason to use the Vector class.

Use the add method to add new elements to an array list. For example, here is how you populate an array list with Employee objects:

```
staff.add(new Employee("Harry Hacker", . . .));
staff.add(new Employee("Tony Tester", . . .));
```

The array list manages an internal array of object references. Eventually, that array will run out of space. This is where array lists work their magic: If you call add and the internal array is full, the array list automatically creates a bigger array and copies all the objects from the smaller to the bigger array.

If you already know, or have a good guess, how many elements you want to store, call the ensureCapacity method before filling the array list:

```
staff.ensureCapacity(100);
```

That call allocates an internal array of 100 objects. Then, the first 100 calls to add will not involve any costly reallocation.

You can also pass an initial capacity to the ArrayList constructor:

```
ArrayList<Employee> staff = new ArrayList<>(100);
```

 Caution: Allocating an array list as

```
new ArrayList<>(100) // capacity is 100
```

is *not* the same as allocating a new array as

```
new Employee[100] // size is 100
```

There is an important distinction between the capacity of an array list and the size of an array. If you allocate an array with 100 entries, then the array has 100 slots, ready for use. An array list with a capacity of 100 elements has the *potential* of holding 100 elements (and, in fact, more than 100, at the cost of additional reallocations)—but at the beginning, even after its initial construction, an array list holds no elements at all.

The size method returns the actual number of elements in the array list. For example,

```
staff.size()
```

returns the current number of elements in the staff array list. This is the equivalent of

```
a.length
```

for an array a.

Once you are reasonably sure that the array list is at its permanent size, you can call the trimToSize method. This method adjusts the size of the memory block to use exactly as much storage space as is required to hold the current number of elements. The garbage collector will reclaim any excess memory.

Once you trim the size of an array list, adding new elements will move the block again, which takes time. You should only use trimToSize when you are sure you won't add any more elements to the array list.

 C++ Note: The ArrayList class is similar to the C++ vector template. Both ArrayList and vector are generic types. But the C++ vector template overloads the [] operator for convenient element access. Java does not have operator overloading, so it must use explicit method calls instead. Moreover, C++ vectors are copied by value. If a and b are two vectors, then the assignment a = b makes a into a new vector with the same length as b, and all elements are copied from b to a. The same assignment in Java makes both a and b refer to the same array list.

---

java.util.ArrayList<E> 1.2

- ArrayList<E>()
  constructs an empty array list.
- ArrayList<E>(int initialCapacity)
  constructs an empty array list with the specified capacity.
- boolean add(E obj)
  appends obj at the end of the array list. Always returns true.
- int size()
  returns the number of elements currently stored in the array list. (Of course, this is never larger than the array list's capacity.)
- void ensureCapacity(int capacity)
  ensures that the array list has the capacity to store the given number of elements without reallocating its internal storage array.
- void trimToSize()
  reduces the storage capacity of the array list to its current size.

5.3.2. Accessing Array List Elements

Unfortunately, nothing comes for free. The automatic growth convenience of array lists requires a more complicated syntax for accessing the elements. The reason is that the ArrayList class is not a part of the Java programming language; it is just a utility class programmed by someone and supplied in the standard library.

Instead of the pleasant [] syntax to access or change the element of an array, you use the get and set methods.

For example, to set the ith element, use

```
staff.set(i, harry);
```

This is equivalent to

```
a[i] = harry;
```

for an array a. (As with arrays, the index values are zero-based.)

 Caution: Do not call list.set(i, x) until the *size* of the array list is larger than i. For example, the following code is wrong:

```
var list = new ArrayList<Employee>(100); // capacity 100, size 0
list.set(0, x); // no element 0 yet
```

Use the add method instead of set to fill up an array, and use set only to replace a previously added element.

To get an array list element, use

```
Employee e = staff.get(i);
```

This is equivalent to

```
Employee e = a[i];
```

 Note: When there were no generic classes, the get method of the raw ArrayList class had no choice but to return an Object. Consequently, callers of get had to cast the returned value to the desired type:

```
Employee e = (Employee) staff.get(i);
```

The raw ArrayList is also a bit dangerous. Its add and set methods accept objects of any type. A call

```
staff.set(i, "Harry Hacker");
```

compiles without so much as a warning, and you run into grief only when you retrieve the object and try to cast it. If you use an ArrayList<Employee> instead, the compiler will detect this error.

You can sometimes get the best of both worlds—flexible growth and convenient element access—with the following trick. First, make an array list and add all the elements:

```
var list = new ArrayList<X>();
while (. . .)
{
    x = . . .;
    list.add(x);
}
```

When you are done, use the toArray method to copy the elements into an array:

```
var a = new X[list.size()];
list.toArray(a);
```

Sometimes, you need to add elements in the middle of an array list. Use the add method with an index argument:

```
int n = staff.size() / 2;
staff.add(n, e);
```

The elements at locations n and above are shifted up to make room for the new entry. If the new size of the array list after the insertion exceeds the capacity, the array list reallocates its storage array.

Similarly, you can remove an element from the middle of an array list:

```
Employee e = staff.remove(n);
```

The elements located above it are copied down, and the size of the array is reduced by one.

Inserting and removing elements is not terribly efficient. It is probably not worth worrying about for small array lists. But if you store many elements and frequently insert and remove in the middle of a collection, consider using a linked list instead. I explain how to program with linked lists in Chapter 9.

You can use the "for each" loop to traverse the contents of an array list:

```
for (Employee e : staff)
    do something with e
```

This loop has the same effect as

```
for (int i = 0; i < staff.size(); i++)
{
   Employee e = staff.get(i);
   do something with e
}
```

Listing 5.7 is a modification of the EmployeeTest program of Chapter 4. The Employee[] array is replaced by an ArrayList<Employee>. Note the following changes:

- You don't have to specify the array size.
- You use add to add as many elements as you like.
- You use size() instead of length to count the number of elements.
- You use a.get(i) instead of a[i] to access an element.

Listing 5.7 arrayList/ArrayListTest.java

```java
 1   package arrayList;
 2
 3   import java.util.*;
 4
 5   /**
 6    * This program demonstrates the ArrayList class.
 7    * @version 1.11 2012-01-26
 8    * @author Cay Horstmann
 9    */
10   public class ArrayListTest
11   {
12      public static void main(String[] args)
13      {
14         // fill the staff array list with three Employee objects
15         var staff = new ArrayList<Employee>();
16
17         staff.add(new Employee("Carl Cracker", 75000, 1987, 12, 15));
18         staff.add(new Employee("Harry Hacker", 50000, 1989, 10, 1));
19         staff.add(new Employee("Tony Tester", 40000, 1990, 3, 15));
20
21         // raise everyone's salary by 5%
22         for (Employee e : staff)
23            e.raiseSalary(5);
24
25         // print out information about all Employee objects
26         for (Employee e : staff)
27            System.out.println("name=" + e.getName() + ",salary=" + e.getSalary() + ",hireDay="
28               + e.getHireDay());
29      }
30   }
```

---

java.util.ArrayList<E> 1.2

- E set(int index, E obj)

  puts the value obj in the array list at the specified index, returning the previous contents.
- E get(int index)

  gets the value stored at a specified index.
- void add(int index, E obj)

  shifts up elements to insert obj at the specified index.
- E remove(int index)

  removes the element at the given index and shifts down all elements above it. The removed element is returned.

5.3.3. Compatibility between Typed and Raw Array Lists

In your own code, you will always want to use type parameters for added safety. In this section, you will see how to interoperate with legacy code that does not use type parameters.

Suppose you have the following legacy class:

```
public class EmployeeDB
{
    public void update(ArrayList list) { . . . }
    public ArrayList find(String query) { . . . }
}
```

You can pass a typed array list to the update method without any casts.

```
ArrayList<Employee> staff = . . .;
employeeDB.update(staff);
```

The staff object is simply passed to the update method.

 Caution: Even though you get no error or warning from the compiler, this call is not completely safe. The update method might add elements into the array list that are not of type Employee. When these elements are retrieved, an exception occurs. This sounds scary, but if you think about it, the behavior is simply as it was before generics were added to Java. The integrity of the virtual machine is never jeopardized. In this situation, you do not lose security, but you also do not benefit from the compile-time checks.

Conversely, when you assign a raw ArrayList to a typed one, you get a warning.

```
ArrayList<Employee> result = employeeDB.find(query); // yields warning
```

 Note: To see the text of the warning, compile with the option -Xlint:unchecked.

Using a cast does not make the warning go away.

```
ArrayList<Employee> result = (ArrayList<Employee>) employeeDB.find(query);
    // yields another warning
```

Instead, you get a different warning, telling you that the cast is misleading.

This is the consequence of a somewhat unfortunate limitation of generic types in Java. For compatibility, the compiler translates all typed array lists into raw ArrayList objects after checking that the type rules were not violated. In a running program, all array lists are the same—there are no type parameters in the virtual machine. Thus, the casts (ArrayList) and (ArrayList<Employee>) carry out identical runtime checks.

There isn't much you can do about that situation. When you interact with legacy code, study the compiler warnings and satisfy yourself that the warnings are not serious.

Once you are satisfied, you can tag the variable that receives the cast with the @SuppressWarnings("unchecked") annotation, like this:

```
@SuppressWarnings("unchecked") ArrayList<Employee> result
    = (ArrayList<Employee>) employeeDB.find(query); // yields another warning
```

5.4. Object Wrappers and Autoboxing

Occasionally, you need to convert a primitive type like int to an object. All primitive types have class counterparts. For example, a class Integer corresponds to the primitive type int. These kinds of classes are usually called *wrappers*. The wrapper classes have obvious names: Integer, Long, Float, Double, Short, Byte, Character, and Boolean. (The first six inherit from the common superclass Number.) The wrapper classes are immutable—you cannot change a wrapped value after the wrapper has been constructed. They are also final, so you cannot subclass them.

Suppose we want an array list of integers. Unfortunately, the type argument inside the angle brackets cannot be a primitive type. It is not possible to form an ArrayList<int>. Here, the Integer wrapper class comes in. It is OK to declare an array list of Integer objects.

```
var list = new ArrayList<Integer>();
```

Caution: An ArrayList<Integer> is far less efficient than an int[] array because each value is separately wrapped inside an object. You would only want to use this construct for small collections when programmer convenience is more important than efficiency.

Fortunately, there is a useful feature that makes it easy to add an element of type int to an ArrayList<Integer>. The call

```
list.add(3);
```

is automatically translated to

```
list.add(Integer.valueOf(3));
```

This conversion is called *autoboxing*.

 Note: You might think that *autowrapping* would be more consistent, but the "boxing" metaphor was taken from C#.

Conversely, when you assign an Integer object to an int value, it is automatically unboxed. That is, the compiler translates

```
int n = list.get(i);
```

into

```
int n = list.get(i).intValue();
```

Automatic boxing and unboxing even works with arithmetic expressions. For example, you can apply the increment operator to a wrapper reference:

```
Integer n = 3;
n++;
```

The compiler automatically inserts instructions to unbox the object, increment the resulting value, and box it back.

In most cases, you get the illusion that the primitive types and their wrappers are one and the same. There is just one point in which they differ considerably: identity. As you know, the == operator, applied to wrapper objects, only tests whether the objects have identical memory locations. The following comparison would therefore probably fail:

```
Integer a = 1000;
Integer b = 1000;
if (a == b) . . .
```

However, a Java implementation *may*, if it chooses, wrap commonly occurring values into identical objects, and thus the comparison might succeed. This ambiguity is not what you want. The remedy is to call the equals method when comparing wrapper objects.

Note: The autoboxing specification requires that boolean, byte, char <= 127, short, and int between -128 and 127 are wrapped into fixed objects. For example, if a and b had been initialized with 100 in the preceding example, then the comparison would have had to succeed.

Tip: Never rely on the identity of wrapper objects. Don't compare them with == and don't use them as locks (see Chapter 10).

Don't use the wrapper class constructors. They are deprecated and scheduled for removal. For example, use Integer.valueOf(1000), never new Integer(1000). Or, simply rely on autoboxing: Integer a = 1000.

There are a couple of other subtleties about autoboxing. First off, since wrapper class references can be null, it is possible for autounboxing to throw a NullPointerException:

```
Integer n = null;
System.out.println(2 * n); // throws NullPointerException
```

Also, if you mix Integer and Double types in a conditional expression, then the Integer value is unboxed, promoted to double, and boxed into a Double:

```
Integer n = 1;
Double x = 2.0;
System.out.println(true ? n : x); // prints 1.0
```

Finally, let us emphasize that boxing and unboxing is a courtesy of the *compiler*, not the virtual machine. The compiler inserts the necessary calls when it generates the bytecodes of a class. The virtual machine simply executes those bytecodes.

Preview Note: A future version of Java will allow *value types*, user-defined types that are like primitive types—with values that are not stored inside objects. For example, a value of a primitive type Point with double fields x and y is simply a

16-byte block in memory, with two adjacent `double` values. You can copy it, but you can't have a reference to it.

It is planned that at some point, the primitive wrapper classes will become value classes.

You will often see the number wrappers for another reason. The designers of Java found the wrappers a convenient place to put certain basic methods, such as those for converting strings of digits to numbers.

To convert a string to an integer, use the following statement:

```
int x = Integer.parseInt(s);
```

This has nothing to do with `Integer` objects—`parseInt` is a static method. But the `Integer` class was a good place to put it.

 Caution: The `parseInt` method and its analog `parseDouble` are not intended for parsing user input. They support a specific format, described in the Java API, that is similar to the format of decimal Java literals, but without embedded underscores. To parse human input, use a `Scanner`. Its `nextInt` and `nextDouble` methods use the current locale, or a locale that you specify, so that users to can enter the digits and separators to which they are accustomed.

The API notes show some of the more important methods of the `Integer` class. The other number classes implement corresponding methods.

The wrapper classes also define constants. For all integral wrapper types, `MIN_VALUE` and `MAX_VALUE` are the smallest and largest value of the type. For example, `Integer.MIN_VALUE` is -2147483648, and `Integer.MAX_VALUE` is 2147483647. Here is a typical example:

```
int largest = Integer.MIN_VALUE; // Replaced with first input
while (in.hasNextInt()) largest = Math.max(largest, in.nextInt());
```

 Caution: The `MIN_VALUE` constant of the `Double` and `Float` classes is the smallest *positive* value. If you want to compute the largest floating-point number and there may be negative inputs, you need to use:

```
int largest = -Double.MAX_VALUE; // Do NOT use Double.MIN_VALUE
while (in.hasNextDouble()) largest = Math.max(largest, in.nextDouble());
```

Caution: Some people think that the wrapper classes can be used to implement methods that can modify numeric parameters. However, that is not correct. Recall from Chapter 4 that it is impossible to write a Java method that increments an integer parameter because parameters to Java methods are always passed by value.

```
public static void triple(int x) // won't work
{
    x = 3 * x; // modifies local variable
}
```

Could we overcome this by using an Integer instead of an int?

```
public static void triple(Integer x) // won't work
{
    . . .
}
```

The problem is that Integer objects are *immutable*: The information contained inside the wrapper can't change. You cannot use these wrapper classes to create a method that modifies numeric parameters.

---

java.lang.Integer 1.0

- `int intValue()`
  returns the value of this Integer object as an int (overrides the intValue method in the Number class).
- `static String toString(int i)`
  returns a new String object representing the number i in base 10.
- `static String toString(int i, int radix)`
  lets you return a representation of the number i in the base specified by the radix parameter.
- `static int parseInt(String s)`
- `static int parseInt(String s, int radix)`
  return the integer whose digits are contained in the string s. The string must represent an integer in base 10 (for the first method) or in the base given by the radix parameter (for the second method).
- `static Integer valueOf(String s)`
- `static Integer valueOf(String s, int radix)`
  return a new Integer object initialized to the integer whose digits are contained in the string s. The string must represent an integer in base 10 (for the first method) or in the base given by the radix parameter (for the second method).

`java.text.NumberFormat` `1.1`

■ Number parse(String s)
   returns the numeric value, assuming the specified `String` represents a number.

5.5. Methods with a Variable Number of Arguments

It is possible to provide methods that can be called with a variable number of arguments. These are sometimes called "varargs" methods.

You have already seen such a method: printf. For example, the calls

```
System.out.printf("%d", n);
```

and

```
System.out.printf("%d %s", n, "widgets");
```

both call the same method, even though one call has two arguments and the other has three.

The printf method is defined like this:

```
public class PrintStream
{
   public PrintStream printf(String fmt, Object... args)
   {
      return format(fmt, args);
   }
}
```

Here, the ellipsis ... is part of the Java code. It denotes that the method can receive an arbitrary number of objects (in addition to the fmt parameter).

The printf method actually receives two parameters: the format string and an `Object[]` array that holds all other arguments. (If the caller supplies integers or other primitive type values, autoboxing turns them into objects.) It now faces the unenviable task of scanning the fmt string and matching up the ith format specifier with the value args[i].

In other words, for the implementor of printf, the `Object...` parameter type is exactly the same as `Object[]`.

The compiler needs to transform each call to printf, bundling the arguments into an array and autoboxing as necessary:

```
System.out.printf("%d %s", new Object[] { Integer.valueOf(n), "widgets" } );
```

You can define your own methods with variable arguments, and you can specify any type for the arguments, even a primitive type. Here is a simple example: a function that computes the maximum of a variable number of values.

```
public static double max(double... values)
{
    double largest = Double.NEGATIVE_INFINITY;
    for (double v : values) if (v > largest) largest = v;
    return largest;
}
```

Simply call the function like this:

```
double m = max(3.1, 40.4, -5);
```

The compiler passes a new double[] { 3.1, 40.4, -5 } to the max function.

 Note: It is legal to pass an array of the variable argument type instead of the variable arguments. For example:

```
System.out.printf("%d %s", new Object[] { Integer.valueOf(1), "widgets" } );
```

Therefore, you can redefine an existing function whose last argument is an array to a method with variable arguments, without breaking any existing code. For example, MessageFormat.format was enhanced in this way in Java 5. If you like, you can even declare the main method as

```
public static void main(String... args)
```

5.6. Abstract Classes

As you move up the inheritance hierarchy, classes become more general and probably more abstract. At some point, the ancestor class becomes *so* general that you think of it more as a basis for other classes than as a class with specific instances you want to use. Consider, for example, an extension of our Employee class hierarchy. An employee is a person, and so is a student. Let us extend our class hierarchy to include classes Person and Student. Figure 5.2 shows the inheritance relationships between these classes.

Why bother with so high a level of abstraction? There are some attributes that make sense for every person, such as a name. Both students and employees have names, and introducing a common superclass lets us factor out the getName method to a higher level in the inheritance hierarchy.

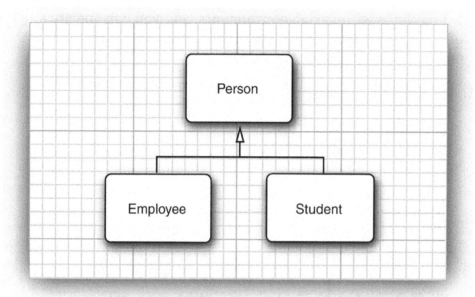

Figure 5.2: Inheritance diagram for Person and its subclasses

Now let's add another method, getDescription, whose purpose is to return a brief description of the person, such as

```
an employee with a salary of $50,000.00
a student majoring in computer science
```

It is easy to implement this method for the Employee and Student classes. But what information can you provide in the Person class? The Person class knows nothing about the person except the name. Of course, you could implement Person.getDescription() to return an empty string. But there is a better way. If you use the abstract keyword, you do not need to implement the method at all.

```
public abstract String getDescription();
   // no implementation required
```

For added clarity, a class with one or more abstract methods must itself be declared abstract.

```
public abstract class Person
{
   . . .
   public abstract String getDescription();
}
```

In addition to abstract methods, abstract classes can have fields and concrete methods. For example, the Person class stores the name of the person and has a concrete method that returns it.

```
public abstract class Person
{
   private String name;

   public Person(String name)
   {
      this.name = name;
   }

   public abstract String getDescription();

   public String getName()
   {
      return name;
   }
}
```

 Tip: Some programmers don't realize that abstract classes can have concrete methods. You should always move common fields and methods (whether abstract or not) to the superclass (whether abstract or not).

Abstract methods act as placeholders for methods that are implemented in the subclasses. When you extend an abstract class, you have two choices. You can leave some or all of the abstract methods undefined; then, you must tag the subclass as abstract as well. Or, you can define all methods, and the subclass is no longer abstract.

For example, we will define a Student class that extends the abstract Person class and implements the getDescription method. None of the methods of the Student class are abstract, so it does not need to be declared as an abstract class.

A class can even be declared as abstract though it has no abstract methods.

Abstract classes cannot be instantiated. That is, if a class is declared as abstract, no objects of that class can be created. For example, the expression

```
new Person("Vince Vu")
```

is an error. However, you can create objects of concrete subclasses.

Note that you can still create *object variables* of an abstract class, but such a variable must refer to an object of a nonabstract subclass. For example:

```
Person p = new Student("Vince Vu", "Economics");
```

Here p is a variable of the abstract type Person that refers to an instance of the nonabstract subclass Student.

 C++ Note: In C++, an abstract method is called a *pure virtual function* and is tagged with a trailing = 0, such as in

```
class Person // C++
{
public:
    virtual string getDescription() = 0;
    . . .
};
```

A C++ class is abstract if it has at least one pure virtual function. In C++, there is no special keyword to denote abstract classes.

Let us define a concrete subclass Student that extends the abstract class Person:

```
public class Student extends Person
{
    private String major;

    public Student(String name, String major)
    {
        super(name);
        this.major = major;
    }

    public String getDescription()
    {
        return "a student majoring in " + major;
    }
}
```

The Student class defines the getDescription method. Therefore, all methods in the Student class are concrete, and the class is no longer an abstract class.

The program shown in Listing 5.8 defines the abstract superclass Person (Listing 5.9) and two concrete subclasses, Employee (Listing 5.10) and Student (Listing 5.11). We fill an array of Person references with employee and student objects:

```
var people = new Person[2];
people[0] = new Employee(. . .);
people[1] = new Student(. . .);
```

We then print the names and descriptions of these objects:

```
for (Person p : people)
   System.out.println(p.getName() + ", " + p.getDescription());
```

Some people are baffled by the call

```
p.getDescription()
```

Isn't this a call to an undefined method? Keep in mind that the variable p never refers to a Person object because it is impossible to construct an object of the abstract Person class. The variable p always refers to an object of a concrete subclass such as Employee or Student. For these objects, the getDescription method is defined.

Could you have omitted the abstract method altogether from the Person superclass, simply defining the getDescription methods in the Employee and Student subclasses? If you did that, you wouldn't have been able to invoke the getDescription method on the variable p. The compiler ensures that you invoke only methods that are declared in the class.

Abstract methods are an important concept in the Java programming language. You will encounter them most commonly inside *interfaces*. For more information about interfaces, turn to Chapter 6.

Listing 5.8 abstractClasses/PersonTest.java

```
1   package abstractClasses;
2
3   /**
4    * This program demonstrates abstract classes.
5    * @version 1.01 2004-02-21
6    * @author Cay Horstmann
7    */
8   public class PersonTest
9   {
10     public static void main(String[] args)
11     {
12        var people = new Person[2];
13
14        // fill the people array with Student and Employee objects
15        people[0] = new Employee("Harry Hacker", 50000, 1989, 10, 1);
16        people[1] = new Student("Maria Morris", "computer science");
17
18        // print out names and descriptions of all Person objects
```

```
19         for (Person p : people)
20            System.out.println(p.getName() + ", " + p.getDescription());
21      }
22 }
```

Listing 5.9 abstractClasses/Person.java

```
1  package abstractClasses;
2
3  public abstract class Person
4  {
5     public abstract String getDescription();
6     private String name;
7
8     public Person(String name)
9     {
10        this.name = name;
11     }
12
13     public String getName()
14     {
15        return name;
16     }
17 }
```

Listing 5.10 abstractClasses/Employee.java

```
1  package abstractClasses;
2
3  import java.time.*;
4
5  public class Employee extends Person
6  {
7     private double salary;
8     private LocalDate hireDay;
9
10     public Employee(String name, double salary, int year, int month, int day)
11     {
12        super(name);
13        this.salary = salary;
14        hireDay = LocalDate.of(year, month, day);
15     }
16
17     public double getSalary()
18     {
19        return salary;
20     }
21
22     public LocalDate getHireDay()
```

```
23      {
24          return hireDay;
25      }
26
27      public String getDescription()
28      {
29          return "an employee with a salary of $%.2f".formatted(salary);
30      }
31
32      public void raiseSalary(double byPercent)
33      {
34          double raise = salary * byPercent / 100;
35          salary += raise;
36      }
37  }
```

Listing 5.11 `abstractClasses/Student.java`

```
1  package abstractClasses;
2
3  public class Student extends Person
4  {
5      private String major;
6
7      /**
8       * @param name the student's name
9       * @param major the student's major
10      */
11     public Student(String name, String major)
12     {
13         // pass name to superclass constructor
14         super(name);
15         this.major = major;
16     }
17
18     public String getDescription()
19     {
20         return "a student majoring in " + major;
21     }
22 }
```

5.7. Enumeration Classes

You saw in Chapter 3 how to define enumerated types. Here is a typical example:

```
public enum Size { SMALL, MEDIUM, LARGE, EXTRA_LARGE }
```

When you refer to these constants, qualify them with the class name, such as `Size.SMALL`. You can use the unqualified name in three situations:

1. As you will see shortly, enumerations can have methods. Inside the methods of an enumeration, you can use the unqualified name.
2. In a `case` of a `switch` whose selector has an enumerated type, you don't need the qualification:

```
Size s = . . .;
String abbrev = switch (s)
   {
       case SMALL -> "S";
       . . .
   };
```

3. You can statically import all constants of an enumeration:

```
import com.horstmann.util.Size;
import static com.horstmann.util.Size.*;
. . .
Size s = SMALL;
```

Caution: You cannot statically import constants from an enumeration in the default package. For example, if Size is in the default package, you cannot use

```
import static Size.*;
```

The type defined by an enum declaration is actually a class. The class has exactly four instances—it is not possible to construct new objects.

Therefore, you never need to use equals for values of enumerated types. Simply use == to compare them.

Note: You are allowed to put a comma after the last value. Trailing commas can be useful if you expect the number of values to grow.

```
public enum Size
{
   SMALL,
   MEDIUM,
   LARGE,
   EXTRA_LARGE,
   XXL,
   // add more values here and put a comma after each
}
```

All enumerated types are subclasses of the abstract class Enum. They inherit a number of methods from that class. The most useful one is name, which returns the name of the enumerated constant. For example, Size.SMALL.toString() returns the string "SMALL".

By default, the toString method returns name. However, you can override toString, whereas name is final.

The converse of name is the static valueOf method. For example, the statement

```
Size s = Enum.valueOf(Size.class, "SMALL");
```

sets s to Size.SMALL.

Each enumerated type has a static values method that returns an array of all values of the enumeration. For example, the call

```
Size[] values = Size.values();
```

returns the array with elements Size.SMALL, Size.MEDIUM, Size.LARGE, and Size.EXTRA_LARGE.

The ordinal method yields the position of an enumerated constant in the enum declaration, counting from zero. For example, Size.MEDIUM.ordinal() returns 1.

You can, if you like, add constructors, methods, and fields to an enumerated type. Of course, the constructors are only invoked when the instances are constructed. Here is an example:

```
public enum Size
{
    SMALL("S"), MEDIUM("M"), LARGE("L"), EXTRA_LARGE("XL");

    private final String abbreviation;

    Size(String abbreviation) { this.abbreviation = abbreviation; }
        // automatically private

    public String getAbbreviation() { return abbreviation; }
}
```

 Note: When an enum has fields or methods, you must terminate the list of constants with a semicolon, as in the example above.

It is legal to have a trailing comma and then a semicolon.

You can even override methods in each instance:

```
public enum Size
{
   SMALL,
   MEDIUM,
   LARGE,
   EXTRA_LARGE
   {
      public String toString() { return "XL"; }
   };
}
```

However, this is not common. In the preceding example, EXTRA_LARGE is an instance of a subclass of Size. Apart from this, you cannot form subclasses of an enumeration.

The constructor of an enumeration is always private. You can omit the private modifier, as in the preceding example. It is a syntax error to declare an enum constructor as public or protected.

 Caution: The constructor of an enumeration class cannot invoke a switch on the instance that is being constructed:

```
public enum Size
{
   SMALL, MEDIUM, LARGE, EXTRA_LARGE;
   private final boolean largish;
   Size()
   {
      largish = switch (this) // ERROR
         {
            case LARGE, EXTRA_LARGE -> true;
            default -> false;
         };
   }
}
```

This curious limitation is caused by the implementation strategy for switch on enum. Each switch consults an array that maps the ordinal values of the enum constants, as currently defined, to the ordinal values of the time when the switch was compiled. These arrays can only be built after the enum instances are constructed.

In a method, such a switch works fine.

The short program in Listing 5.12 demonstrates how to work with enumerated types.

Note: The Enum class has a type parameter that I have ignored for simplicity. For example, the enumerated type Size actually extends Enum<Size>. The type parameter is used in the compareTo method. (I discuss the compareTo method in Chapter 6 and type parameters in Chapter 8.)

Listing 5.12 enums/EnumTest.java

```java
1  package enums;
2
3  import java.util.*;
4
5  /**
6   * This program demonstrates enumerated types.
7   * @version 1.0 2004-05-24
8   * @author Cay Horstmann
9   */
10 public class EnumTest
11 {
12    public static void main(String[] args)
13    {
14       var in = new Scanner(System.in);
15       System.out.print("Enter a size: (SMALL, MEDIUM, LARGE, EXTRA_LARGE) ");
16       String input = in.next().toUpperCase();
17       Size size = Enum.valueOf(Size.class, input);
18       System.out.println("size=" + size);
19       System.out.println("abbreviation=" + size.getAbbreviation());
20       if (size == Size.EXTRA_LARGE)
21          System.out.println("Good job--you paid attention to the _.");
22    }
23 }
24
25 enum Size
26 {
27    SMALL("S"), MEDIUM("M"), LARGE("L"), EXTRA_LARGE("XL");
28
29    private Size(String abbreviation) { this.abbreviation = abbreviation; }
30    public String getAbbreviation() { return abbreviation; }
31
32    private String abbreviation;
33 }
```

java.lang.Enum<E> 5.0

■ static Enum valueOf(Class enumClass, String name)
returns the enumerated constant of the given class with the given name.

- `String name()`
  returns the name of this enumerated constant.
- `int ordinal()`
  returns the zero-based position of this enumerated constant in the enum declaration.
- `int compareTo(E other)`
  returns a negative integer if this enumerated constant comes before `other`, zero if `this` == `other`, and a positive integer otherwise. The ordering of the constants is given by the enum declaration.

5.8. Sealed Classes

Unless a class is declared final, anyone can form a subclass of it. What if you want to have more control? For example, suppose you need to write your own JSON library because none of the existing ones does exactly what you need.

The JSON standard says that a JSON value is an array, number, string, Boolean value, object, or null. An obvious approach is to model this with classes `JSONArray`, `JSONNumber`, and so on that extend an abstract class `JSONValue`:

```
public abstract class JSONValue
{
    // Methods that apply to all JSON values
}

public final class JSONArray extends JSONValue
{
    . . .
}

public final class JSONNumber extends JSONValue
{
    . . .
}
```

By declaring the classes `JSONArray`, `JSONNumber`, and so on as `final`, we can ensure that nobody forms a subclass. But we cannot stop anyone from forming another subclass of `JSONValue`.

Why might we want that control? Consider this code:

```
JSONValue v = . . .;
if (v instanceof JSONArray a) . . .
else if (v instanceof JSONNumber n) . . .
else if (v instanceof JSONString s) . . .
```

```
else if (v instanceof JSOBoolean b) . . .
else if (v instanceof JSONObject o) . . .
else . . . // Must be JSONNull
```

Here, the control flow implies that we know all direct subclasses of JSONValue. This is not an open-ended hierarchy. The JSON standard won't change; if it does, we as the library implementors will add a seventh subclass. We don't want anyone else out there mess with the class hierarchy.

In Java, a *sealed* class controls which classes may inherit from it. Sealed classes were added as a preview feature in Java 15 and finalized in Java 17.

Here is how to declare the JSONValue class as sealed:

```
public abstract sealed class JSONValue
        permits JSONArray, JSONNumber, JSONString, JSONBoolean, JSONObject, JSONNull
{
    . . .
}
```

It is an error to define a nonpermitted subclass:

```
public class JSONComment extends JSONValue { . . . } // Error
```

That's just as well, since JSON doesn't allow for comments. Sealed classes thus allow for accurate modeling of domain constraints.

The permitted subclasses of a sealed class must be accessible. They cannot be private classes that are nested in another class, or package-visible classes from another package.

For permitted subclasses that are public, the rules are more stringent. They must be in the same package as the sealed class. However, if you use modules (see Chapter 12), then they must only be in the same module.

 Note: A sealed class can be declared without a permits clause. Then all of its direct subclasses must be declared in the same file. Programmers without access to that file cannot form subclasses.

A file can have at most one public class, so this arrangement appears to be only useful if the subclasses are not for use by the public.

However, as you will see in the next chapter, you can use inner classes as public subclasses.

An important motivation for sealed classes is compile-time checking. Consider this method of the JSONValue class, which uses a switch expression with pattern matching (see Section 5.9):

```
public String type()
{
   return switch (this)
      {
         case JSONArray __ -> "array";
         case JSONNumber __ -> "number";
         case JSONString __ -> "string";
         case JSONBoolean __ -> "boolean";
         case JSONObject __ -> "object";
         case JSONNull __ -> "null";
         // No default needed here
      };
}
```

The compiler can check that no default clause is needed since all direct subclasses of JSONValue occur as cases.

Note: The preceding type method doesn't look very object-oriented. It would be in the spirit of OOP to have each of the six classes provide its own type method, relying on polymorphism instead of a switch. For an open-ended hierarchy, that is a good approach. But when there is a fixed set of classes, it is often more convenient to have all alternatives in one method.

At first glance, it appears as if a subclass of a sealed class must be final. But for exhaustiveness testing, we only need to know all direct subclasses. It is not a problem if those classes have further subclasses. For example, we can reorganize our JSON hierarchy as shown in Figure 5.3.

In this hierarchy, JSONValue permits three subclasses:

```
public abstract sealed class JSONValue permits JSONObject, JSONArray, JSONPrimitive
{
   . . .
}
```

The JSONPrimitive class is sealed as well:

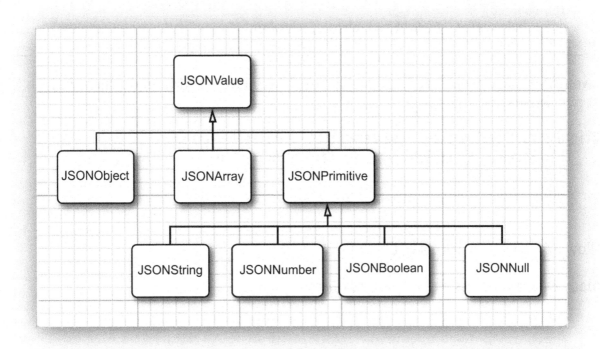

Figure 5.3: The complete hierarchy of classes for representing JSON values

```
public abstract sealed class JSONPrimitive extends JSONValue
      permits JSONString, JSONNumber, JSONBoolean, JSONNull
{
   . . .
}
```

A subclass of a sealed class must specify whether it is sealed, final, or open for subclassing. In the latter case, it must be declared as non-sealed.

 Note: The non-sealed keyword is the first Java keyword with a hyphen. This may well be a future trend. Adding keywords to the language always comes with a risk. Existing code may no longer compile. For that reason, sealed is a "contextual" keyword. You can still declare variables or methods named sealed:

```
int sealed = 1; // OK to use contextual keyword as identifier
```

With a hyphenated keyword, one doesn't have to worry about this. The only ambiguity is with subtraction:

```
int non = 0;
non = non-sealed; // Subtraction, not keyword
```

Why would you ever want a `non-sealed` subclass? Consider an XML node class with six direct subclasses:

```
public abstract sealed class Node permits Element, Text, Comment,
    CDATASection, EntityReference, ProcessingInstruction
{
   . . .
}
```

We allow arbitrary subclasses of `Element`:

```
public non-sealed class Element extends Node
{
   . . .
}

public class HTMLDivElement extends Element
{
   . . .
}
```

In this section, you learned about sealed *classes*. In the next chapter, you will learn about *interfaces*, a generalization of abstract classes. Java interfaces can also have subtypes. Sealed interfaces work exactly the same as sealed classes, controlling the direct subtypes.

The following sample program fleshes out the JSON hierarchy. The implementation of `JSONObject` uses a `HashMap`, which will be covered in Chapter 9. In the example, we use interfaces instead of abstract classes so that `JSONNumber` and `JSONString` can be records and the `JSONBoolean` and `JSONNull` classes can be enumerations. Records and enumerations can implement interfaces, but they cannot extend classes.

Listing 5.13 sealed/SealedTest.java

```
 1  package sealed;
 2
 3  import java.util.*;
 4
 5  sealed interface JSONValue permits JSONArray, JSONObject, JSONPrimitive
 6  {
 7     public default String type()
 8     {
 9        if (this instanceof JSONArray) return "array";
10        else if (this instanceof JSONObject) return "object";
```

```
11          else if (this instanceof JSONNumber) return "number";
12          else if (this instanceof JSONString) return "string";
13          else if (this instanceof JSONBoolean) return "boolean";
14          else return "null";
15      }
16 }
17
18 final class JSONArray extends ArrayList<JSONValue> implements JSONValue {}
19
20 final class JSONObject extends HashMap<String, JSONValue> implements JSONValue
21 {
22     public String toString()
23     {
24         StringBuilder result = new StringBuilder();
25         result.append("{");
26         for (Map.Entry<String, JSONValue> entry : entrySet())
27         {
28             if (result.length() > 1) result.append(",");
29             result.append(" \"");
30             result.append(entry.getKey());
31             result.append("\": ");
32             result.append(entry.getValue());
33         }
34         result.append(" }");
35         return result.toString();
36     }
37 }
38
39 sealed interface JSONPrimitive extends JSONValue
40         permits JSONNumber, JSONString, JSONBoolean, JSONNull
41 {
42 }
43
44 final record JSONNumber(double value) implements JSONPrimitive
45 {
46     public String toString() { return "" + value; }
47 }
48
49 final record JSONString(String value) implements JSONPrimitive
50 {
51     public String toString() { return "\"" + value.translateEscapes() + "\""; }
52 }
53
54 enum JSONBoolean implements JSONPrimitive
55 {
56     FALSE, TRUE;
57     public String toString() { return super.toString().toLowerCase(); }
58 }
59
60 enum JSONNull implements JSONPrimitive
61 {
62     INSTANCE;
```

```
63        public String toString() { return "null"; }
64    }
65
66    public class SealedTest
67    {
68        public static void main(String[] args)
69        {
70            JSONObject obj = new JSONObject();
71            obj.put("name", new JSONString("Harry"));
72            obj.put("salary", new JSONNumber(90000));
73            obj.put("married", JSONBoolean.FALSE);
74            JSONArray arr = new JSONArray();
75            arr.add(new JSONNumber(13));
76            arr.add(JSONNull.INSTANCE);
77
78            obj.put("luckyNumbers", arr);
79            System.out.println(obj);
80            System.out.println(obj.type());
81        }
82    }
```

5.9. Pattern Matching

You have already seen how to use the instanceof operator to check whether an object has a particular type. The most convenient form of instanceof declares a variable of the matching type:

```
Employee e = . . .;
String description;
if (e instanceof Executive exec)
   description = "An executive with a title of " + exec.getTitle();
else if (e instanceof Manager m)
   description = "A manager who deserves a bonus";
else
   description = "A lowly employee with a salary of " + e.getSalary();
```

The pattern-matching form of switch simplifies this type analysis:

```
Employee e = . . .;
String description = switch (e)
   {
      case Executive exec -> "An executive with a title of " + exec.getTitle();
      case Manager m -> "A manager who deserves a bonus";
      default -> "A lowly employee with a salary of " + e.getSalary();
   };
```

Note that, as with instanceof patterns, each case declares a variable of the matched type. You use those variables to access subclass methods (such as getTitle in our example).

Using the expression form of switch is simpler than a chain of if statements. The switch expression yields a value that is assigned to the description variable. In contrast, when using instanceof, each branch of the conditional statements must set the description value separately.

It is possible to use the statement and fallthrough forms of switch with type patterns. But the expression form without fallthrough is usually the most natural choice.

As you have just seen, the basic structure of pattern matching is straightforward. The following subsections go into technical details, some of which are a bit gnarly for compatibility reasons.

 Preview Note: Java 21 introduces *unnamed variables* as a preview feature. If you don't need the variable in a type pattern, use an underscore:

```
case Employee _ -> "A lowly employee"
```

Until this feature becomes generally available, you can use two underscores:

```
case Employee __ -> "A lowly employee"
```

5.9.1. Null Handling

The classic switch statement is null-hostile. If the selector expression is null, the switch throws a NullPointerException. You can avoid this by adding a case null:

```
String description = switch (e)
   {
      case Executive exec -> "An executive with a title of " + exec.getTitle();
      case Manager m -> "A manager who deserves a bonus";
      case null -> "No employee";
      default -> "A lowly employee with a salary of " + e.getSalary();
   };
```

You can combine case null with default, but not with any other case:

```
case null, default -> "No free parking";
```

 Note: You cannot use case _ to express a default case. That was done on purpose, so that you don't have to remember whether such a case covers null or not.

5.9.2. Guards

You can add a condition to a pattern called a *guard*, using the restricted when keyword.

```
case Executive exec when exec.getTitle().getLength() >= 20 ->
   "An executive with an impressive title";
```

In the guard expression, you can use the variable that the pattern introduces.

If the guard expression is not fulfilled, the case is not selected and the next case is tested.

If an exception occurs in the when clause, the switch throws that exception.

Guards are particularly useful in record patterns:

```
Point p = . . .;
String description = switch (p)
   {
      case Point(var x, var y) when x == 0 && y == 0 -> "origin";
      case Point(var x, var __) when x == 0 -> "on x-axis";
      case Point(var __, var y) when y == 0 -> "on y-axis";
      default -> "not on either axis";
   };
```

 Caution: A record pattern invokes the component accessors. In the unlikely case that one of them throws an exception, the switch throws a MatchException. This can only happen for custom accessors.

5.9.3. Exhaustiveness

Any switch *expression* must be *exhaustive*: there must be a case for each possible selector value. This is an obvious requirement since the expression must always yield a value.

There are several ways for a switch to be exhaustive:

- Cases for every instance of an enum
- Unguarded type patterns that cover every subtype of a sealed type
- An unguarded type pattern of the selector type
- A default clause

Guarded patterns cannot be used for exhaustiveness checks since the compiler cannot evaluate them. For example,

```
case Executive exec when exec.getTitle().getLength() >= 20 -> . . .
case Executive exec when exec.getTitle().getLength() < 20 -> . . .
```

is not exhaustive. You need to rewrite the second clause as

```
case Executive exec -> . . .
```

or

```
default -> . . .
```

 Note: When a sealed type hierarchy or an enumeration class is modified, then a previously exhaustive `switch` might become non-exhaustive. If no cases match, the `switch` throws a `MatchException`.

A classic `switch` *statement* need not be exhaustive. If no cases match, then no action takes place. But for greater clarity, all *enhanced* `switch` statements must be exhaustive. A `switch` statement is enhanced if it has a pattern, `case null`, or a selector type other than a primitive type, primitive type wrapper, `String`, or `enum`.

If you don't want to do anything when there is no match, add

```
default -> {} // No fallthrough
```

or

```
default: break; // Fallthrough
```

 Caution: Testing whether the selector value is `null` is not required for exhaustiveness. You can have an exhaustive `switch` without `case null`. It throws a `NullPointerException` when invoked with a `null` selector.

 Caution: The absence of `null` checking for exhaustiveness is problematic for nested records. Consider

```
record Box<T>(T contents) { }

Box<Box<String>> doubleBoxed = ...;
String unboxed = switch (doubleBoxed) {
    case Box(Box(String s)) -> s;
};
```

If `doubleBoxed` is null, the `switch` throws a `NullPointerException`. Conversely, if `doubleBoxed` is new `Box<>(new Box<>(null))`, the result of the expression is null.

However, if doubleBoxed is initialized with new Box<>(null), then a MatchException occurs. There should have been a case such as

```
case Box(b) where b == null
```

but the exhaustiveness checker ignores null.

5.9.4. Dominance

In a classic switch with only constant cases, it is illegal to have the same constant in two cases. Therefore, the branches are disjoint and their order does not matter. However, when the cases are patterns, then the order matters. The cases are checked in order, and the first matching case is followed.

When the compiler finds that a case can never match because of a preceding one, a compile-time error occurs. Here is an example:

```
Employee e = . . .;
String description = switch (e)
  {
      case Employee __ -> "A lowly employee with a salary of " + e.getSalary();
      case Manager m -> "A manager who deserves a bonus"; // ERROR
  };
```

Since every Manager is an Employee, the second case will never match. The first case *dominates* it.

This dominance checking is useful for finding programming errors, but it is not perfect. Here are the fine points that you need to worry about:

- Guarded patterns are not used for dominance checking. There is no way for for the compiler to reason about the guards. For example, the compiler cannot tell that

  ```
  case Executive exec when exec.getTitle().getLength() >= 20 -> . . .
  ```

  dominates

  ```
  case Executive exec when exec.getTitle().getLength() >= 30 -> . . .
  ```

- default does not dominate constant cases.
- default dominates case null, even though it does not cover it.

 Tip: While it is possible to place default before constant cases, it is a poor idea. Always put it last.

5.9.5. Patterns and Constants

You cannot match against constants inside record patterns. For example,

```
case Point(0, y) // ERROR
```

is wrong. Use a guard:

```
case Point(x, y) when x == 0 // Ok
```

Numeric constant patterns are only allowed when the *selector* type is int, short, char, or byte, or their wrapper types. String constant patterns are only allowed for a selector of type String. For example, the following is not legal:

```
Object obj = . . .;
String description = switch (obj)
   {
      case 0 -> "zero"; // ERROR
      case "" -> "empty string"; // ERROR
      case null -> "null";
      default -> obj.toString();
   };
```

Since the selector type is Object, the switch cannot have numeric or string constant patterns. The remedy is:

```
case Integer i when i == 0
case String s when s.equals("null")
```

The rules are different for enum constants. The selector type must merely be a supertype of the enumerated type; that is, Object, Enum, or an interface (see Chapter 6):

```
Object obj = . . .;
String description = switch (obj)
   {
      case DayOfWeek.FRIDAY -> "TGIF"; // Ok
      . . .
   };
```

5.9.6. Variable Scope and Fallthrough

This section covers subtle points about variables when execution falls through from one case to the next. If you never use fallthrough, just move on to the next section.

When a type or record pattern introduces a variable, its scope extends to the end of the case, even if execution falls through the next case. For example, consider the variable s in the following code snippet:

```
Object obj = . . .;
switch (obj)
{
   case String s when s.length() == 0:
      System.out.println("empty string"); // Scope ends here
   default:
      System.out.println(obj.toString());
}
```

You can use s in the guard clause and the statements following the :, but not in the next case. This makes sense since execution can start in that case when obj is not a String.

You cannot fall into a type pattern:

```
switch (obj)
{
   case String s when s.length() > 0:
      System.out.println(s.codePointAt(0)); // Fallthrough
   case Integer n:
      System.out.println(n); // ERROR
   . . .
}
```

If execution fell from the first case to the body of the second case, n could not be bound.

 Preview Note: You *can* fall into a type pattern with an unnamed variable (a preview feature of Java 21):

```
switch (obj)
{
   case String s when s.length() == 0:
      System.out.print("empty "); // Fallthrough
   case String _:
      System.out.println("string"); break; // Ok
   . . .
}
```

 Caution: Ever since Java 1.0, it has been legal to declare a variable in the body of a case. The scope of that variable extends to the end of the switch. This scope has never been useful since it leads to an error if you access the variable outside the case:

```
switch (obj) {
   case String s:
      String t = s; // OK
   default:
      System.out.println(t); // ERROR—t may not have been initialized
}
```

The programs in Listing 5.14 and Listing 5.15 demonstrate pattern matching with type and record patterns.

Listing 5.14 patternMatching/TypePatternTest.java

```java
 1  package patternMatching;
 2
 3  public class TypePatternTest
 4  {
 5     public static void main(String[] args)
 6     {
 7        int r = (int)(4 * Math.random());
 8        Employee e = switch (r)
 9           {
10              case 0 -> new Employee("Harry Hacker", 50000, 1989, 10, 1);
11              case 1 -> new Manager("Carl Cracker", 80000, 1987, 12, 15);
12              case 2 -> new Executive("Sue Striver",
13                    "Senior Associate Vice President", 200000, 1995, 1, 20);
14              default -> null;
15           };
16        String description = switch (e)
17           {
18              case Executive exec when exec.getTitle().length() >= 20 ->
19                 "An executive with an impressive title";
20              case Executive exec ->
21                 "An executive with a title of " + exec.getTitle();
22              case Manager m ->
23                 {
24                    m.setBonus(10000);
25                    yield "A manager who just got a bonus";
26                 }
27              case null -> "No employee";
28              default -> "A lowly employee with a salary of " + e.getSalary();
29           };
30        System.out.println(description);
31     }
32  }
```

Listing 5.15 patternMatching/RecordPatternTest.java

```
 1  package patternMatching;
 2
 3  record Point(double x, double y) {}
 4
 5  public class RecordPatternTest
 6  {
 7     public static void main(String[] args)
 8     {
 9        int r = (int)(4 * Math.random());
10        Point p = switch (r)
11           {
12              case 0 -> new Point(0, 0);
13              case 1 -> new Point(1, 0);
14              case 2 -> new Point(0, 1);
15              default -> new Point(1, 1);
16           };
17        String description = switch (p)
18           {
19              case Point(var x, var y) when x == 0 && y == 0 -> "origin";
20              case Point(var x, var __) when x == 0 -> "on x-axis";
21              case Point(var __, var y) when y == 0 -> "on y-axis";
22              default -> "not on either axis";
23           };
24        System.out.printf("%s %s%n", p, description);
25     }
26  }
```

5.10. Reflection

The *reflection library* gives you a very rich and elaborate toolset to write programs that manipulate Java code dynamically. Using reflection, Java can support user interface builders, object-relational mappers, and many other development tools that dynamically inquire about the capabilities of classes.

A program that can analyze the capabilities of classes is called *reflective*. The reflection mechanism is extremely powerful. As the next sections show, you can use it to

- Analyze the capabilities of classes at runtime
- Inspect objects at runtime—for example, to write a single toString method that works for *all* classes
- Implement generic array manipulation code
- Take advantage of Method objects that work just like function pointers in languages such as C++

Reflection is a powerful and complex mechanism; however, it is of interest mainly to tool builders, not application programmers. If you are interested in programming applications rather than tools for other Java programmers, you can safely skip the remainder of this chapter and return to it later.

5.10.1. The Class Class

While your program is running, the Java runtime system always maintains what is called *runtime type identification* on all objects. This information keeps track of the class to which each object belongs. Runtime type information is used by the virtual machine to select the correct methods to execute.

However, you can also access this information by working with a special Java class. The class that holds this information is called, somewhat confusingly, Class. The getClass() method in the Object class returns an instance of Class type.

```
Employee e;
. . .
Class cl = e.getClass();
```

Just like an Employee object describes the properties of a particular employee, a Class object describes the properties of a particular class. Probably the most commonly used method of Class is getName. This returns the name of the class. For example, the statement

```
System.out.println(e.getClass().getName() + " " + e.getName());
```

prints

```
Employee Harry Hacker
```

if e is an employee, or

```
Manager Harry Hacker
```

if e is a manager.

If the class is in a package, the package name is part of the class name:

```
var in = new Scanner(System.in);
Class cl = in.getClass();
String className = cl.getName(); // name is set to "java.util.Scanner"
```

You can obtain a Class object corresponding to a class name by using the static forName method.

```
String className = "java.util.Scanner";
Class cl = Class.forName(className);
```

Use this method if the class name is stored in a string that varies at runtime. This works if `className` is the name of a class or interface. Otherwise, the `forName` method throws a *checked exception*. See Section 5.10.2 for how to supply an *exception handler* whenever you use this method.

A third method for obtaining an object of type `Class` is a convenient shorthand. If `T` is any Java type (or the `void` keyword), then `T.class` is the matching class object. For example:

```
Class cl1 = Scanner.class; // if you import java.util.*;
Class cl2 = int.class;
Class cl3 = Double[].class;
```

Note that a `Class` object really describes a *type*, which may or may not be a class. For example, `int` is not a class, but `int.class` is nevertheless an object of type `Class`.

Note: The `Class` class is actually a generic class. For example, `Employee.class` is of type `Class<Employee>`. In this chapter, I'm not dwelling on this issue because it would further complicate an already abstract concept. For most practical purposes, you can ignore the type parameter and work with the raw `Class` type. See Chapter 8 for more information on the type parameter of `Class`.

Caution: For historical reasons, the `getName` method returns somewhat strange names for array types:

- `Double[].class.getName()` returns `"[Ljava.lang.Double;"`.
- `int[].class.getName()` returns `"[I"`.

The virtual machine manages a unique `Class` object for each type. Therefore, you can use the `==` operator to compare class objects. For example:

```
if (e.getClass() == Employee.class) . . .
```

This test passes if `e` is an instance of `Employee`. Unlike the condition `e instanceof Employee`, this test fails if `e` is an instance of a subclass such as `Manager`.

Caution: You would expect the instances in an enumeration to have as their class the enumeration class. Generally, this is true:

```
public enum Size { SMALL, MEDIUM, LARGE, EXTRA_LARGE; }
Size.SMALL.getClass() == Size.class // true
```

However, if you override a method in an instance, then it belongs to a different class:

```
public enum Size
{
   SMALL,
   MEDIUM,
   LARGE,
   EXTRA_LARGE
   {
      public String toString() { return "XL"; }
   };
}

Size.EXTRA_LARGE.getClass() == Size.class // false
```

If you have an object of type Class, you can use it to construct instances of the class. Call the getConstructor method to get an object of type Constructor, then use the newInstance method to construct an instance. For example:

```
var className = "java.util.Date";
   // or any other name of a class with a no-arg constructor
Class cl = Class.forName(className);
Object obj = cl.getConstructor().newInstance();
```

If the class doesn't have a constructor without arguments, the getConstructor method throws an exception. You will see in Section 5.10.7 how to invoke other constructors.

Note: There is a Class.newInstance method that also constructs an instance with the no-argument constructor. However, it is deprecated for a subtle reason. Any exception thrown in the constructor is rethrown as is. For checked exceptions, this violates the compile-time checking. In contrast, Constructor.newInstance wraps any constructor exception into an InvocationTargetException.

C++ Note: The newInstance method corresponds to the idiom of a *virtual constructor* in C++. However, virtual constructors in C++ are not a language feature but just an idiom that needs to be supported by a specialized library. The Class class is similar to the type_info class in C++, and the getClass method is equivalent to the typeid operator. The Java Class is quite a bit more versatile than type_info, though. The C++ type_info can only reveal a string with the name of the type, not create new objects of that type.

---

java.lang.Class 1.0

- `static Class forName(String className)`
  returns the `Class` object representing the class with name `className`.
- `Constructor getConstructor(Class... parameterTypes)` **1.1**
  yields an object describing the constructor with the given parameter types. See Section 5.10.7 for more information on how to supply parameter types.

---

java.lang.reflect.Constructor 1.1

- `Object newInstance(Object... initargs)`
  constructs a new instance of the constructor's declaring class, passing `initargs` to the constructor. See Section 5.10.7 for more information on how to supply arguments.

---

java.lang.Throwable 1.0

- `void printStackTrace()`
  prints the `Throwable` object and the stack trace to the standard error stream.

5.10.2. A Primer on Declaring Exceptions

I cover exception handling fully in Chapter 7, but in the meantime you will occasionally encounter methods that threaten to throw exceptions.

When an error occurs at runtime, a program can "throw an exception." Throwing an exception is more flexible than terminating the program because you can provide a *handler* that "catches" the exception and deals with it.

If you don't provide a handler, the program terminates and prints a message to the console, giving the type of the exception. You may have already seen exception reports when you accidentally used a `null` reference or overstepped the bounds of an array.

There are two kinds of exceptions: *unchecked* exceptions and *checked* exceptions. With checked exceptions, the compiler checks that you, the programmer, are aware of the exception and are prepared to deal with the consequences. However, many common exceptions, such as bounds errors, or accessing a `null` reference, are unchecked. The compiler does not expect that you provide a handler—after all, you should spend your mental energy on avoiding these mistakes rather than coding handlers for them.

But not all errors are avoidable. If an exception can occur despite your best efforts, then most Java APIs will throw a checked exception. One example is the `Class.forName` method. There is no way for you to ensure that a class with the given name exists. In Chapter 7, you will see several strategies for exception handling. For now, I just show you the simplest strategy.

Whenever a method contains a statement that might throw a checked exception, add a throws clause to the method name.

```
public static void doSomethingWithClass(String name)
      throws ReflectiveOperationException
{
   Class cl = Class.forName(name); // might throw exception
   do something with cl
}
```

Any method that calls this method also needs a throws declaration. This includes the main method. If an exception actually occurs, the main method terminates with a stack trace. (You will learn in Chapter 7 how to catch exceptions instead of having them terminate your programs.)

You only need to supply a throws clause for checked exceptions. It is easy to find out which methods throw checked exceptions—the compiler will complain whenever you call a method that threatens to throw a checked exception and you don't supply a handler.

5.10.3. Resources

Classes often have associated data files, such as:

- Image and sound files
- Text files with message strings and button labels

In Java, such an associated file is called a *resource*.

For example, consider a dialog box that displays a message such as the one in Figure 5.4.

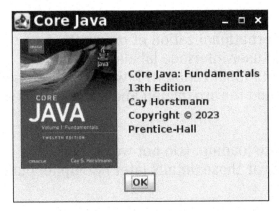

Figure 5.4: Displaying image and text resources

Of course, the book title and copyright year in the panel will change for the next edition of the book. To make it easy to track this change, we will put the text inside a file and not hardcode it as a string.

But where should you put a file such as about.txt? Of course, it would be convenient to simply place it with the rest of the program files inside a JAR file.

The Class class provides a useful service for locating resource files. Here are the necessary steps:

1. Get the Class object of the class that has a resource—for example, ResourceTest.class.
2. Some methods, such as the getImage method of the ImageIcon class, accept URLs that describe resource locations. Then you call

   ```
   URL url = cl.getResource("about.png");
   ```

3. Otherwise, use the getResourceAsStream method to obtain an input stream for reading the data in the file.

The point is that the Java virtual machine knows how to locate a class, so it can then search for the associated resource *in the same location*. For example, suppose the ResourceTest class is in a package resources. Then the ResourceTest.class file is located in a resources directory, and you place an icon file into the same directory.

Instead of placing a resource file inside the same directory as the class file, you can provide a relative or absolute path such as

```
data/about.txt
/corejava/title.txt
```

Automating the loading of files is all the resource loading feature does. There are no standard methods for interpreting the contents of resource files. Each program must have its own way of interpreting its resource files.

Another common application of resources is the internationalization of programs. Language-dependent strings, such as messages and user interface labels, are stored in resource files, with one file per language. The *internationalization API*, which is discussed in Chapter 7 of Volume II, supports a standard method for organizing and accessing these localization files.

Listing 5.16 is a program that demonstrates resource loading. (Do not worry about the code for reading text and displaying dialogs—we cover those details later.) Compile, build a JAR file, and execute it:

```
javac resources/ResourceTest.java
jar cvfe ResourceTest.jar resources.ResourceTest \
    resources/*.class resources/*.gif resources/data/*.txt corejava/*.txt
java -jar ResourceTest.jar
```

Move the JAR file to a different directory and run it again to check that the program reads the resource files from the JAR file, not from the current directory.

Listing 5.16 resources/ResourceTest.java

```
 1  package resources;
 2
 3  import java.io.*;
 4  import java.net.*;
 5  import javax.swing.*;
 6
 7  /**
 8   * @version 1.51 2023-08-16
 9   * @author Cay Horstmann
10   */
11  public class ResourceTest
12  {
13      public static void main(String[] args) throws IOException
14      {
15          Class cl = ResourceTest.class;
16          URL aboutURL = cl.getResource("about.gif");
17          var icon = new ImageIcon(aboutURL);
18
19          InputStream stream = cl.getResourceAsStream("data/about.txt");
20          var about = new String(stream.readAllBytes());
21
22          InputStream stream2 = cl.getResourceAsStream("/corejava/title.txt");
23          var title = new String(stream2.readAllBytes()).strip();
24
25          JOptionPane.showMessageDialog(null, about, title, JOptionPane.INFORMATION_MESSAGE, icon);
26      }
27  }
```

---

java.lang.Class 1.0

- URL getResource(String name) **1.1**
- InputStream getResourceAsStream(String name) **1.1**
  find the resource in the same place as the class and then return a URL or input stream that you can use for loading the resource. Return null if the resource isn't found, so do not throw an exception for an I/O error.

5.10.4. Using Reflection to Analyze the Capabilities of Classes

Here is a brief overview of the most important parts of the reflection mechanism for letting you examine the structure of a class.

The three classes Field, Method, and Constructor in the java.lang.reflect package describe the fields, methods, and constructors of a class, respectively. All three classes have a method called getName that returns the name of the item. The Field class has a method getType that returns an object, again of type Class, that describes the field type. The Method and Constructor classes have methods to report the types of the parameters, and the Method class also reports the return type.

All three of these classes also have a method called getModifiers that returns an integer, with various bits turned on and off, that describes the modifiers used, such as public and static. You can then use the static methods in the Modifier class in the java.lang.reflect package to analyze the integer that getModifiers returns. Use methods like isPublic, isPrivate, or isFinal in the Modifier class to tell whether a method or constructor was public, private, or final. All you have to do is have the appropriate method in the Modifier class work on the integer that getModifiers returns. You can also use the Modifier.toString method to print the modifiers.

Alternatively, the accessFlags method returns a set of values of the AccessFlag enumeration. For example, here is how you can test whether a method is static:

```
if (Modifiers.isStatic(m.getModifiers())) . . .
if (m.accessFlags().contains(AccessFlag.STATIC)) . . .
```

The getFields, getMethods, and getConstructors methods of the Class class return arrays of the *public* fields, methods, and constructors that the class supports. This includes public members of superclasses. The getDeclaredFields, getDeclaredMethods, and getDeclaredConstructors methods of the Class class return arrays consisting of all fields, methods, and constructors that are declared in the class. This includes private, package, and protected members, as well as members with package access, but not members of superclasses.

Listing 5.17 shows you how to print out all information about a class. The program prompts you for the name of a class and writes out the signatures of all methods and constructors as well as the names of all instance fields of a class. For example, if you enter

```
java.lang.Double
```

the program prints

```
public final class java.lang.Double extends java.lang.Number
{
    public java.lang.Double(double);
    public java.lang.Double(java.lang.String);
```

```
public boolean equals(java.lang.Object);
public static java.lang.String toString(double);
public java.lang.String toString();
public static int hashCode(double);
public int hashCode();
public static double min(double, double);
public static double max(double, double);
public static native long doubleToRawLongBits(double);
public static long doubleToLongBits(double);
public static native double longBitsToDouble(long);
public int compareTo(java.lang.Double);
public volatile int compareTo(java.lang.Object);
public static int compare(double, double);
public byte byteValue();
public short shortValue();
public int intValue();
public long longValue();
public float floatValue();
public double doubleValue();
public static java.lang.Double valueOf(java.lang.String);
public static java.lang.Double valueOf(double);
public static java.lang.String toHexString(double);
public volatile java.lang.Object resolveConstantDesc(
    java.lang.invoke.MethodHandles$Lookup);
public java.lang.Double resolveConstantDesc(java.lang.invoke.MethodHandles$Lookup);
public java.util.Optional describeConstable();
public boolean isNaN();
public static boolean isNaN(double);
public static double sum(double, double);
public boolean isInfinite();
public static boolean isInfinite(double);
public static boolean isFinite(double);
public static double parseDouble(java.lang.String);

public static final double POSITIVE_INFINITY;
public static final double NEGATIVE_INFINITY;
public static final double NaN;
public static final double MAX_VALUE;
public static final double MIN_NORMAL;
public static final double MIN_VALUE;
public static final int MAX_EXPONENT;
public static final int MIN_EXPONENT;
public static final int SIZE;
public static final int BYTES;
public static final java.lang.Class TYPE;
```

```
    private final double value;
    private static final long serialVersionUID;
}
```

What is remarkable about this program is that it can analyze any class that the Java interpreter can load, not just the classes that were available when the program was compiled. We will use this program in the next chapter to peek inside the inner classes that the Java compiler generates automatically.

Listing 5.17 reflection/ReflectionTest.java

```java
 1  package reflection;
 2
 3  import java.util.*;
 4  import java.lang.reflect.*;
 5  /**
 6   * This program uses reflection to print all features of a class.
 7   * @version 1.12 2021-06-15
 8   * @author Cay Horstmann
 9   */
10  public class ReflectionTest
11  {
12     public static void main(String[] args)
13           throws ReflectiveOperationException
14     {
15        // read class name from command line args or user input
16        String name;
17        if (args.length > 0) name = args[0];
18        else
19        {
20           var in = new Scanner(System.in);
21           System.out.println("Enter class name (e.g. java.util.Date): ");
22           name = in.next();
23        }
24
25        // print class modifiers, name, and superclass name (if != Object)
26        Class cl = Class.forName(name);
27        String modifiers = Modifier.toString(cl.getModifiers());
28        if (modifiers.length() > 0) System.out.print(modifiers + " ");
29        if (cl.isSealed())
30           System.out.print("sealed ");
31        if (cl.isEnum())
32           System.out.print("enum " + name);
33        else if (cl.isRecord())
34           System.out.print("record " + name);
35        else if (cl.isInterface())
36           System.out.print("interface " + name);
37        else
38           System.out.print("class " + name);
```

```
39          Class supercl = cl.getSuperclass();
40          if (supercl != null && supercl != Object.class) System.out.print(" extends "
41                  + supercl.getName());
42
43          printInterfaces(cl);
44          printPermittedSubclasses(cl);
45
46          System.out.print("\n{\n");
47          printConstructors(cl);
48          System.out.println();
49          printMethods(cl);
50          System.out.println();
51          printFields(cl);
52          System.out.println("}");
53      }
54
55      /**
56       * Prints all constructors of a class
57       * @param cl a class
58       */
59      public static void printConstructors(Class cl)
60      {
61          Constructor[] constructors = cl.getDeclaredConstructors();
62
63          for (Constructor c : constructors)
64          {
65              String name = c.getName();
66              System.out.print("    ");
67              String modifiers = Modifier.toString(c.getModifiers());
68              if (modifiers.length() > 0) System.out.print(modifiers + " ");
69              System.out.print(name + "(");
70
71              // print parameter types
72              Class[] paramTypes = c.getParameterTypes();
73              for (int j = 0; j < paramTypes.length; j++)
74              {
75                  if (j > 0) System.out.print(", ");
76                  System.out.print(paramTypes[j].getName());
77              }
78              System.out.println(");");
79          }
80      }
81
82      /**
83       * Prints all methods of a class
84       * @param cl a class
85       */
86      public static void printMethods(Class cl)
87      {
88          Method[] methods = cl.getDeclaredMethods();
89
90          for (Method m : methods)
```

```
91            {
92               Class retType = m.getReturnType();
93               String name = m.getName();
94
95               System.out.print("   ");
96               // print modifiers, return type and method name
97               String modifiers = Modifier.toString(m.getModifiers());
98               if (modifiers.length() > 0) System.out.print(modifiers + " ");
99               System.out.print(retType.getName() + " " + name + "(");
100
101              // print parameter types
102              Class[] paramTypes = m.getParameterTypes();
103              for (int j = 0; j < paramTypes.length; j++)
104              {
105                 if (j > 0) System.out.print(", ");
106                 System.out.print(paramTypes[j].getName());
107              }
108              System.out.println(");");
109           }
110        }
111
112        /**
113         * Prints all fields of a class
114         * @param cl a class
115         */
116        public static void printFields(Class cl)
117        {
118           Field[] fields = cl.getDeclaredFields();
119
120           for (Field f : fields)
121           {
122              Class type = f.getType();
123              String name = f.getName();
124              System.out.print("   ");
125              String modifiers = Modifier.toString(f.getModifiers());
126              if (modifiers.length() > 0) System.out.print(modifiers + " ");
127              System.out.println(type.getName() + " " + name + ";");
128           }
129        }
130
131        /**
132         * Prints all permitted subtypes of a sealed class
133         * @param cl a class
134         */
135        public static void printPermittedSubclasses(Class cl)
136        {
137           if (cl.isSealed())
138           {
139              Class<?>[] permittedSubclasses = cl.getPermittedSubclasses();
140              for (int i = 0; i < permittedSubclasses.length; i++)
141              {
142                 if (i == 0)
```

```
143                  System.out.print(" permits ");
144              else
145                  System.out.print(", ");
146              System.out.print(permittedSubclasses[i].getName());
147          }
148      }
149   }
150
151   /**
152    * Prints all directly implemented interfaces of a class
153    * @param cl a class
154    */
155   public static void printInterfaces(Class cl)
156   {
157      Class<?>[] interfaces = cl.getInterfaces();
158      for (int i = 0; i < interfaces.length; i++)
159      {
160         if (i == 0)
161            System.out.print(cl.isInterface() ? " extends " : " implements ");
162         else
163            System.out.print(", ");
164         System.out.print(interfaces[i].getName());
165      }
166   }
167 }
```

---

java.lang.Class 1.0

- `Field[] getFields()` **1.1**
- `Field[] getDeclaredFields()` **1.1**

  getFields returns an array containing Field objects for the public fields of this class or its superclasses; getDeclaredFields returns an array of Field objects for all fields of this class. The methods return an array of length 0 if there are no such fields or if the Class object represents a primitive or array type.

- `Method[] getMethods()` **1.1**
- `Method[] getDeclaredMethods()` **1.1**

  return an array containing Method objects: getMethods returns public methods and includes inherited methods; getDeclaredMethods returns all methods of this class or interface but does not include inherited methods.

- `Constructor[] getConstructors()` **1.1**
- `Constructor[] getDeclaredConstructors()` **1.1**

  return an array containing Constructor objects that give you all the public constructors (for getConstructors) or all constructors (for getDeclaredConstructors) of the class represented by this Class object.

- `isInterface()`

  returns true if this Class object describes an interface. (See Chapter 6 for interfaces.)

- `isEnum()` **1.5**

  returns true if this Class object describes an enum.

- isRecord() **16**
  returns true if this Class object describes a record.
- RecordComponent[] getRecordComponents() **16**
  returns an array of RecordComponent objects that describe the record fields, or null if this class is not a record.
- String getPackageName() **9**
  gets the name of the package containing this type, or the package of the element type if this type is an array type, or "java.lang" if this type is a primitive type.

---

java.lang.reflect.Field 1.1

---

java.lang.reflect.Method 1.1

---

java.lang.reflect.Constructor 1.1

- Class getDeclaringClass()
  returns the Class object for the class that defines this constructor, method, or field.
- Class[] getExceptionTypes() (in Constructor and Method classes)
  returns an array of Class objects that represent the types of the exceptions thrown by the method.
- int getModifiers()
  returns an integer that describes the modifiers of this constructor, method, or field. Use the methods in the Modifier class to analyze the return value.
- Set<AccessFlag> accessFlags() **20**
  returns a set of values in the AccessFlag enumeration that describe the access modifiers of this constructor, method, or field.
- String getName()
  returns a string that is the name of the constructor, method, or field.
- Class[] getParameterTypes() (in Constructor and Method classes)
  returns an array of Class objects that represent the types of the parameters.
- Class getReturnType() (in Method class)
  returns a Class object that represents the return type.

---

java.lang.reflect.RecordComponent 16

- String getName()
- Class getType()
  get the name and type of this record component.
- Method getAccessor()
  returns the Method object for accessing this record component.

---

java.lang.reflect.Modifier 1.1

- static String toString(int modifiers)

  returns a string with the modifiers that correspond to the bits set in modifiers.
- static boolean isAbstract(int modifiers)
- static boolean isFinal(int modifiers)
- static boolean isInterface(int modifiers)
- static boolean isNative(int modifiers)
- static boolean isPrivate(int modifiers)
- static boolean isProtected(int modifiers)
- static boolean isPublic(int modifiers)
- static boolean isStatic(int modifiers)
- static boolean isStrict(int modifiers)
- static boolean isSynchronized(int modifiers)
- static boolean isVolatile(int modifiers)

  test the bit in the modifiers value that corresponds to the modifier in the method name.

5.10.5. Using Reflection to Analyze Objects at Runtime

In the preceding section, we saw how we can find out the *names* and *types* of the instance fields of any object:

- Get the corresponding Class object.
- Call getDeclaredFields on the Class object.

In this section, we will go one step further and actually look at the *contents* of the fields. Of course, it is easy to look at the contents of a specific field of an object whose name and type are known when you write a program. But reflection lets you look at fields of objects that were not known at compile time.

The key method to achieve this is the get method in the Field class. If f is an object of type Field (for example, one obtained from getDeclaredFields) and obj is an object of the class of which f is a field, then f.get(obj) returns an object whose value is the current value of the field of obj. This is all a bit abstract, so let's run through an example.

```
var harry = new Employee("Harry Hacker", 50000, 10, 1, 1989);
Class cl = harry.getClass();
   // the class object representing Employee
Field f = cl.getDeclaredField("name");
   // the name field of the Employee class
Object v = f.get(harry);
   // the value of the name field of the harry object, i.e.,
   // the String object "Harry Hacker"
```

Of course, you can also set the values that you can get. The call f.set(obj, value) sets the field represented by f of the object obj to the new value.

Actually, there is a problem with this code. Since the name field is a private field, the get and set methods will throw an IllegalAccessException. You can only use get and set with accessible fields. The security mechanism of Java lets you find out what fields an object has, but it won't let you read and write the values of those fields unless you have permission.

The default behavior of the reflection mechanism is to respect Java access control. However, you can override access control by invoking the setAccessible method on a Field, Method, or Constructor object. For example:

```
f.setAccessible(true); // now OK to call f.get(harry)
```

The setAccessible method is a method of the AccessibleObject class, the common superclass of the Field, Method, and Constructor classes. This feature is provided for debuggers, persistent storage, and similar mechanisms. We will use it for a generic toString method later in this section.

The call to setAccessible throws an exception if the access is not granted. The access can be denied by the module system (Chapter 12) or a security manager (Chapter 9 of Volume II). The use of security managers is not common, and they are deprecated since Java 17.

For example, the sample program at the end of this section looks into the internals of ArrayList and Integer objects. When you run it with Java 9 to Java 16, the following ominous message appears:

```
WARNING: An illegal reflective access operation has occurred
WARNING: Illegal reflective access by objectAnalyzer.ObjectAnalyzer (file:/home/cay
    /books/cj11/code/v1ch05/bin/) to field java.util.ArrayList.serialVersionUID
WARNING: Please consider reporting this to the maintainers of
    objectAnalyzer.ObjectAnalyzer
WARNING: Use --illegal-access=warn to enable warnings of further illegal
    reflective access operations
WARNING: All illegal access operations will be denied in a future release
```

When you run the program with Java 17, an InaccessibleObjectException exception occurs.

To keep the program running, "open" the java.util and java.lang packages in the java.base module to the "unnamed module." The details are in Chapter 12. Here is the syntax:

```
java --add-opens java.base/java.util=ALL-UNNAMED \
    --add-opens java.base/java.lang=ALL-UNNAMED \
    objectAnalyzer.ObjectAnalyzerTest
```

Note: It is possible that future libraries will use *variable handles* instead of reflection for reading and writing fields. A VarHandle is similar to a Field. You can use it to read or write a specific field of any instance of a specific class. However, to obtain a VarHandle, the library code needs a Lookup object:

```
public Object getFieldValue(Object obj, String fieldName, Lookup lookup)
      throws NoSuchFieldException, IllegalAccessException
{
   Class cl = obj.getClass();
   Field field = cl.getDeclaredField(fieldName);
   VarHandle handle = MethodHandles.privateLookupIn(cl, lookup)
      .unreflectVarHandle(field);
   return handle.get(obj);
}
```

This works provided the Lookup object is generated in the module that has the permission to access the field. Some method in the module simply calls MethodHandles.lookup(), which yields an object encapsulating the access rights of the caller. In this way, one module can give permission for accessing private members to another module. The practical issue is how those permissions can be given with a minimum of hassle.

While we can still do so, let us look at a generic toString method that works for *any* class (see Listing 5.18). The generic toString method uses getDeclaredFields to obtain all instance fields and the setAccessible convenience method to make all fields accessible. For each field, it obtains the name and the value. Each value is turned into a string by recursively invoking toString.

The generic toString method needs to address a couple of complexities. Cycles of references could cause an infinite recursion. Therefore, the ObjectAnalyzer keeps track of objects that were already visited. Also, to peek inside arrays, you need a different approach. You'll learn about the details in the next section.

You can use this toString method to peek inside any object. For example, the call

```
var squares = new ArrayList<Integer>();
for (int i = 1; i <= 5; i++) squares.add(i * i);
System.out.println(new ObjectAnalyzer().toString(squares));
```

yields the printout

```
java.util.ArrayList[elementData=class java.lang.Object[]{java.lang.Integer[value=1][][],
java.lang.Integer[value=4][][],java.lang.Integer[value=9][][],
   java.lang.Integer[value=16][][],
java.lang.Integer[value=25][][],null,null,null,null,null},size=5][modCount=5][][]
```

You can use this generic `toString` method to implement the `toString` methods of your own classes, like this:

```java
public String toString()
{
    return new ObjectAnalyzer().toString(this);
}
```

This is a hassle-free and undoubtedly useful method for supplying a universal `toString` method. However, before you get too excited about never having to implement `toString` again, remember that the days of uncontrolled access to internals are numbered.

Listing 5.18 `objectAnalyzer/ObjectAnalyzerTest.java`

```java
 1  package objectAnalyzer;
 2
 3  import java.util.*;
 4
 5  /**
 6   * This program uses reflection to spy on objects.
 7   * @version 1.13 2018-03-16
 8   * @author Cay Horstmann
 9   */
10  public class ObjectAnalyzerTest
11  {
12     public static void main(String[] args)
13          throws ReflectiveOperationException
14     {
15        var squares = new ArrayList<Integer>();
16        for (int i = 1; i <= 5; i++)
17           squares.add(i * i);
18        System.out.println(new ObjectAnalyzer().toString(squares));
19     }
20  }
```

Listing 5.19 `objectAnalyzer/ObjectAnalyzer.java`

```java
 1  package objectAnalyzer;
 2
 3  import java.lang.reflect.AccessibleObject;
 4  import java.lang.reflect.Array;
 5  import java.lang.reflect.Field;
 6  import java.lang.reflect.Modifier;
 7  import java.util.ArrayList;
 8
 9  public class ObjectAnalyzer
10  {
```

```
11    private ArrayList<Object> visited = new ArrayList<>();
12
13    /**
14     * Converts an object to a string representation that lists all fields.
15     * @param obj an object
16     * @return a string with the object's class name and all field names and values
17     */
18    public String toString(Object obj)
19          throws ReflectiveOperationException
20    {
21       if (obj == null) return "null";
22       if (visited.contains(obj)) return "...";
23       visited.add(obj);
24       Class cl = obj.getClass();
25       if (cl == String.class) return (String) obj;
26       if (cl.isArray())
27       {
28          String r = cl.getComponentType() + "[]{";
29          for (int i = 0; i < Array.getLength(obj); i++)
30          {
31             if (i > 0) r += ",";
32             Object val = Array.get(obj, i);
33             if (cl.getComponentType().isPrimitive()) r += val;
34             else r += toString(val);
35          }
36          return r + "}";
37       }
38
39       String r = cl.getName();
40       // inspect the fields of this class and all superclasses
41       do
42       {
43          r += "[";
44          Field[] fields = cl.getDeclaredFields();
45          AccessibleObject.setAccessible(fields, true);
46          // get the names and values of all fields
47          for (Field f : fields)
48          {
49             if (!Modifier.isStatic(f.getModifiers()))
50             {
51                if (!r.endsWith("[")) r += ",";
52                r += f.getName() + "=";
53                Class t = f.getType();
54                Object val = f.get(obj);
55                if (t.isPrimitive()) r += val;
56                else r += toString(val);
57             }
58          }
59          r += "]";
60          cl = cl.getSuperclass();
61       }
62       while (cl != null);
```

```
63
64        return r;
65     }
66 }
```

---

java.lang.reflect.AccessibleObject 1.2

■ void setAccessible(boolean flag)
   sets or clears the accessibility flag for this accessible object, or throws an
   IllegalAccessException if the access is denied.
■ boolean trySetAccessible() **9**
   sets the accessibility flag for this accessible object, or returns false if the access is
   denied.
■ boolean canAccess(Object obj) **9**
   checks if the caller can access obj through this field, method, or constructor object.
   Pass null for a static field or method, or for a constructor.
■ static void setAccessible(AccessibleObject[] array, boolean flag)
   is a convenience method to set the accessibility flag for an array of objects.

---

java.lang.Class 1.1

■ Field getField(String name)
■ Field[] getFields()
   get the public field with the given name, or an array of all fields.
■ Field getDeclaredField(String name)
■ Field[] getDeclaredFields()
   get the field that is declared in this class with the given name, or an array of all fields.

---

java.lang.reflect.Field 1.1

■ Object get(Object obj)
   gets the value of the field described by this Field object in the object obj.
■ void set(Object obj, Object newValue)
   sets the field described by this Field object in the object obj to a new value.

5.10.6. Using Reflection to Write Generic Array Code

The Array class in the java.lang.reflect package allows you to create arrays dynamically.
This is used, for example, in the implementation of the copyOf method in the Arrays class.
Recall how this method can be used to grow an array that has become full.

```
var a = new Employee[100];
. . .
// array is full
a = Arrays.copyOf(a, 2 * a.length);
```

How can one write such a generic method? It helps that an Employee[] array can be converted to an Object[] array. That sounds promising. Here is a first attempt:

```
public static Object[] badCopyOf(Object[] a, int newLength) // not useful
{
    var newArray = new Object[newLength];
    System.arraycopy(a, 0, newArray, 0, Math.min(a.length, newLength));
    return newArray;
}
```

However, there is a problem with actually *using* the resulting array. The type of array that this code returns is an array of *objects* (Object[]) because we created the array using the line of code

```
new Object[newLength]
```

An array of objects *cannot* be cast to an array of employees (Employee[]). The virtual machine would generate a ClassCastException at runtime. The point is that, as mentioned earlier, a Java array remembers the type of its entries—that is, the element type used in the new expression that created it. It is legal to cast an Employee[] temporarily to an Object[] array and then cast it back, but an array that started its life as an Object[] array can never be cast into an Employee[] array. To write this kind of generic array code, we need to be able to make a new array of the *same* type as the original array. For this, we need the methods of the Array class in the java.lang.reflect package. The key is the static newInstance method of the Array class that constructs a new array. You must supply the type for the entries and the desired length as arguments to this method.

```
Object newArray = Array.newInstance(componentType, newLength);
```

To actually carry this out, we need to get the length and the component type of the new array.

We obtain the length by calling Array.getLength(a). The static getLength method of the Array class returns the length of an array. To get the component type of the new array:

1. First, get the class object of a.
2. Confirm that it is indeed an array.
3. Use the getComponentType method of the Class class (which is defined only for class objects that represent arrays) to find the right type for the array.
4. Conversely, for any Class object representing a class *C*, the arrayType method yields the Class object representing *C*[].

Why is getLength a method of Array but getComponentType a method of Class? I don't know—the distribution of the reflection methods seems a bit ad hoc at times.

Here's the code:

```
public static Object goodCopyOf(Object a, int newLength)
{
   Class cl = a.getClass();
   if (!cl.isArray()) return null;
   Class componentType = cl.getComponentType();
   int length = Array.getLength(a);
   Object newArray = Array.newInstance(componentType, newLength);
   System.arraycopy(a, 0, newArray, 0, Math.min(length, newLength));
   return newArray;
}
```

Note that this copyOf method can be used to grow arrays of any type, not just arrays of objects.

```
int[] a = { 1, 2, 3, 4, 5 };
a = (int[]) goodCopyOf(a, 10);
```

To make this possible, the parameter of goodCopyOf is declared to be of type Object, *not an array of objects* (Object[]). The integer array type int[] can be converted to an Object, but not to an array of objects!

Listing 5.20 shows both methods in action. Note that the cast of the return value of badCopyOf will throw an exception.

Listing 5.20 arrays/CopyOfTest.java

```
 1  package arrays;
 2
 3  import java.lang.reflect.*;
 4  import java.util.*;
 5
 6  /**
 7   * This program demonstrates the use of reflection for manipulating arrays.
 8   * @version 1.2 2012-05-04
 9   * @author Cay Horstmann
10   */
11  public class CopyOfTest
12  {
13     public static void main(String[] args)
14     {
15        int[] a = { 1, 2, 3 };
16        a = (int[]) goodCopyOf(a, 10);
```

```
17          System.out.println(Arrays.toString(a));
18
19          String[] b = { "Tom", "Dick", "Harry" };
20          b = (String[]) goodCopyOf(b, 10);
21          System.out.println(Arrays.toString(b));
22
23          System.out.println("The following call will generate an exception.");
24          b = (String[]) badCopyOf(b, 10);
25      }
26
27      /**
28       * This method attempts to grow an array by allocating a new array and
29       * copying all elements.
30       * @param a the array to grow
31       * @param newLength the new length
32       * @return a larger array that contains all elements of a. However, the returned
33       * array has type Object[], not the same type as a
34       */
35      public static Object[] badCopyOf(Object[] a, int newLength) // not useful
36      {
37          var newArray = new Object[newLength];
38          System.arraycopy(a, 0, newArray, 0, Math.min(a.length, newLength));
39          return newArray;
40      }
41
42      /**
43       * This method grows an array by allocating a new array of the same type and
44       * copying all elements.
45       * @param a the array to grow. This can be an object array or a primitive
46       * type array
47       * @return a larger array that contains all elements of a
48       */
49      public static Object goodCopyOf(Object a, int newLength)
50      {
51          Class cl = a.getClass();
52          if (!cl.isArray()) return null;
53          Class componentType = cl.getComponentType();
54          int length = Array.getLength(a);
55          Object newArray = Array.newInstance(componentType, newLength);
56          System.arraycopy(a, 0, newArray, 0, Math.min(length, newLength));
57          return newArray;
58      }
59 }
```

---

java.lang.Class 1.1

- boolean isArray()
  returns true if this object represents an array type.
- Class getComponentType()
  Class componentType() 12

return the `Class` describing the component type if this object represents an array type, or `null` otherwise.
- `Class arrayType()` **12**
  returns the `Class` describing the array type whose component type is represented by this object.

`java.lang.reflect.Array` **1.1**

- `static Object get(Object array, int index)`
- `static xxx getXxx(Object array, int index)`
  (*xxx* is one of the primitive types boolean, byte, char, double, float, int, long, or short.)
  These methods return the value of the given array that is stored at the given index.
- `static void set(Object array, int index, Object newValue)`
- `static setXxx(Object array, int index, xxx newValue)`
  (*xxx* is one of the primitive types boolean, byte, char, double, float, int, long, or short.)
  These methods store a new value into the given array at the given index.
- `static int getLength(Object array)`
  returns the length of the given array.
- `static Object newInstance(Class componentType, int length)`
- `static Object newInstance(Class componentType, int[] lengths)`
  return a new array of the given component type with the given dimensions.

5.10.7. Invoking Arbitrary Methods and Constructors

In C and C++, you can execute an arbitrary function through a function pointer. On the surface, Java does not have method pointers—that is, ways of giving the location of a method to another method, so that the second method can invoke it later. In fact, the designers of Java have said that method pointers are dangerous and error-prone, and that Java interfaces and lambda expressions (discussed in the next chapter) are a superior solution. However, the reflection mechanism allows you to call arbitrary methods.

Recall that you can inspect a field of an object with the get method of the `Field` class. Similarly, the `Method` class has an `invoke` method that lets you call the method that is wrapped in the current `Method` object. The signature for the `invoke` method is

```
Object invoke(Object obj, Object... args)
```

The first parameter is the implicit argument, and the remaining objects provide the explicit arguments.

For a static method, the first argument is ignored—you can set it to `null`.

For example, if `m1` represents the `getName` method of the `Employee` class, the following code shows how you can call it:

```
String n = (String) m1.invoke(harry);
```

If the return type is a primitive type, the invoke method will return the wrapper type instead. For example, suppose that m2 represents the getSalary method of the Employee class. Then, the returned object is actually a Double, and you must cast it accordingly. Use automatic unboxing to turn it into a double:

```
double s = (Double) m2.invoke(harry);
```

How do you obtain a Method object? You can, of course, call getDeclaredMethods and search through the returned array of Method objects until you find the method you want. Or, you can call the getMethod method of the Class class. This is similar to the getField method that takes a string with the field name and returns a Field object. However, there may be several methods with the same name, so you need to be careful that you get the right one. For that reason, you must also supply the parameter types of the desired method. The signature of getMethod is

```
Method getMethod(String name, Class... parameterTypes)
```

For example, here is how you can get method pointers to the getName and raiseSalary methods of the Employee class:

```
Method m1 = Employee.class.getMethod("getName");
Method m2 = Employee.class.getMethod("raiseSalary", double.class);
```

Use a similar approach for invoking arbitrary constructors. Supply the constructor's parameter types to the Class.getConstructor method, and supply the argument values to the Constructor.newInstance method:

```
Class cl = Scanner.class;
   // or any other class with a constructor that has a String parameter
Constructor cons = cl.getConstructor(String.class);
Object obj = cons.newInstance("Mary had a little lamb");
```

 Note: The Method and Constructor classes extend the Executable class. As of Java 17, the Executable class is sealed, permitting only Method and Constructor as subclasses.

Now that you have seen the rules for using Method objects, let's put them to work. Listing 5.21 is a program that prints a table of values for a mathematical function such as Math.sqrt or Math.sin. The printout looks like this:

```
public static native double java.lang.Math.sqrt(double)
      1.0000 |      1.0000
      2.0000 |      1.4142
      3.0000 |      1.7321
```

```
 4.0000 |     2.0000
 5.0000 |     2.2361
 6.0000 |     2.4495
 7.0000 |     2.6458
 8.0000 |     2.8284
 9.0000 |     3.0000
10.0000 |     3.1623
```

The code for printing a table is, of course, independent of the actual function that is being tabulated.

```
double dx = (to - from) / (n - 1);
for (double x = from; x <= to; x += dx)
{
   double y = (Double) f.invoke(null, x);
   System.out.printf("%10.4f | %10.4f%n", x, y);
}
```

Here, f is an object of type Method. The first argument of invoke is null because we are calling a static method.

To tabulate the Math.sqrt function, we set f to

```
Math.class.getMethod("sqrt", double.class)
```

That is the method of the Math class that has the name sqrt and a single parameter of type double.

Listing 5.21 shows the complete code of the generic tabulator and a couple of test runs.

Listing 5.21 methods/MethodTableTest.java

```
 1  package methods;
 2
 3  import java.lang.reflect.*;
 4
 5  /**
 6   * This program shows how to invoke methods through reflection.
 7   * @version 1.2 2012-05-04
 8   * @author Cay Horstmann
 9   */
10  public class MethodTableTest
11  {
12     public static void main(String[] args)
13           throws ReflectiveOperationException
14     {
15        // get method pointers to the square and sqrt methods
```

```
16          Method square = MethodTableTest.class.getMethod("square", double.class);
17          Method sqrt = Math.class.getMethod("sqrt", double.class);
18
19          // print tables of x- and y-values
20          printTable(1, 10, 10, square);
21          printTable(1, 10, 10, sqrt);
22       }
23
24       /**
25        * Returns the square of a number
26        * @param x a number
27        * @return x squared
28        */
29       public static double square(double x)
30       {
31          return x * x;
32       }
33
34       /**
35        * Prints a table with x- and y-values for a method
36        * @param from the lower bound for the x-values
37        * @param to the upper bound for the x-values
38        * @param n the number of rows in the table
39        * @param f a method with a double parameter and double return value
40        */
41       public static void printTable(double from, double to, int n, Method f)
42             throws ReflectiveOperationException
43       {
44          // print out the method as table header
45          System.out.println(f);
46
47          double dx = (to - from) / (n - 1);
48
49          for (double x = from; x <= to; x += dx)
50          {
51             double y = (Double) f.invoke(null, x);
52             System.out.printf("%10.4f | %10.4f%n", x, y);
53          }
54       }
55    }
```

As this example clearly shows, you can do anything with Method objects that you can do with function pointers in C (or delegates in C#). Just as in C, this style of programming is usually quite inconvenient, and always error-prone. What happens if you invoke a method with the wrong arguments? The invoke method throws an exception.

Also, the parameters and return values of invoke are necessarily of type Object. That means you must cast back and forth a lot. As a result, the compiler is deprived of the chance to check your code, so errors surface only during testing, when they are more tedious to find and fix. Moreover, code that uses reflection to get at method pointers is significantly slower than code that simply calls methods directly.

For that reason, I suggest that you use `Method` objects in your own programs only when absolutely necessary. Using interfaces and lambda expressions (the subject of the next chapter) is almost always a better idea.

`java.lang.reflect.Method 1.1`

■ `public Object invoke(Object obj, Object[] args)`
invokes the method described by this object, passing the given arguments and returning the value that the method returns. For static methods, pass `null` as the implicit argument. Pass primitive type values by using wrappers. Primitive type return values must be unwrapped.

5.11. Design Hints for Inheritance

I want to end this chapter with some hints that I have found useful when using inheritance.

1. *Place common operations and fields in the superclass.*
   This is why we put the name field into the `Person` class instead of replicating it in the `Employee` and `Student` classes.

2. *Don't use protected fields.*
   Some programmers think it is a good idea to define most instance fields as `protected`, "just in case," so that subclasses can access these fields if they need to. However, the `protected` mechanism doesn't give much protection, for two reasons. First, the set of subclasses is unbounded—anyone can form a subclass of your classes and then write code that directly accesses `protected` instance fields, thereby breaking encapsulation. And second, in Java, all classes in the same package have access to `protected` fields, whether or not they are subclasses.
   However, `protected` methods can be useful to indicate methods that are not ready for general use and should be redefined in subclasses.

3. *Use inheritance to model the "is-a" relationship.*
   Inheritance is a handy code-saver, but sometimes people overuse it. For example, suppose we need a `Contractor` class. Contractors have names and hire dates, but they do not have salaries. Instead, they are paid by the hour, and they do not stay around long enough to get a raise. There is the temptation to form a subclass `Contractor` from `Employee` and add an `hourlyWage` field.

   ```
   public class Contractor extends Employee
   {
      private double hourlyWage;
      . . .
   }
   ```

   This is *not* a good idea, however, because now each contractor object has both a salary and hourly wage field. It will cause you no end of grief when you implement methods for printing paychecks or tax forms. You will end up writing more code than you would have written by not inheriting in the first place.

The contractor-employee relationship fails the "is-a" test. A contractor is not a special case of an employee.

4. *Don't use inheritance unless all inherited methods make sense.*

   Suppose we want to write a Holiday class. Surely every holiday is a day, and days can be expressed as instances of the GregorianCalendar class, so we can use inheritance.

   ```
   class Holiday extends GregorianCalendar { . . . }
   ```

   Unfortunately, the set of holidays is not *closed* under the inherited operations. One of the public methods of GregorianCalendar is add. And add can turn holidays into nonholidays:

   ```
   Holiday christmas;
   christmas.add(Calendar.DAY_OF_MONTH, 12);
   ```

   Therefore, inheritance is not appropriate in this example.

   Note that this problem does not arise if you extend an immutable class. Suppose you have an immutable date class, similar to LocalDate but not final. If you form a Holiday subclass, there is no method that can turn a holiday into a nonholiday.

5. *Don't change the expected behavior when you override a method.*

   The substitution principle applies not just to syntax but, more importantly, to behavior. When you override a method, you should not unreasonably change its behavior. The compiler can't help you—it cannot check whether your redefinitions make sense. For example, you can "fix" the issue of the add method in the Holiday class by redefining add, perhaps to do nothing, or to throw an exception, or to move on to the next holiday.

   However, such a fix violates the substitution principle. The sequence of statements

   ```
   int d1 = x.get(Calendar.DAY_OF_MONTH);
   x.add(Calendar.DAY_OF_MONTH, 1);
   int d2 = x.get(Calendar.DAY_OF_MONTH);
   System.out.println(d2 - d1);
   ```

   should have the *expected behavior*, no matter whether x is of type GregorianCalendar or Holiday.

   Of course, therein lies the rub. Reasonable and unreasonable people can argue at length about what the expected behavior is. For example, some authors argue that the substitution principle requires Manager.equals to ignore the bonus field because Employee.equals ignores it. These discussions are pointless if they occur in a vacuum. Ultimately, what matters is that you do not circumvent the intent of the original design when you override methods in subclasses.

6. *Use polymorphism, not type information.*

Whenever you find code of the form

```
if (x is of type 1)
    action₁(x);
else if (x is of type 2)
    action₂(x);
```

think polymorphism.

Do *action1* and *action2* represent a common concept? If so, make the concept a method of a common superclass or interface of both types. Then, you can simply call

```
x.action();
```

and have the dynamic dispatch mechanism inherent in polymorphism launch the correct action.

Code that uses polymorphic methods or interface implementations is much easier to maintain and extend than code using multiple type tests.

7. *Don't overuse reflection.*
   The reflection mechanism lets you write programs with amazing generality, by detecting fields and methods at runtime. This capability can be extremely useful for systems programming, but it is usually not appropriate in applications. Reflection is fragile—with it, the compiler cannot help you find programming errors. Any errors are found at runtime and result in exceptions.

You have now seen how Java supports the fundamentals of object-oriented programming: classes, inheritance, and polymorphism. In the next chapter, I will tackle two advanced topics that are very important for using Java effectively: interfaces and lambda expressions.

CHAPTER 6

Interfaces, Lambda Expressions, and Inner Classes

You have now learned about classes and inheritance, the key concepts of object-oriented programming in Java. This chapter shows you several advanced techniques that are commonly used. Despite their less obvious nature, you will need to master them to complete your Java tool chest.

The first technique, called *interfaces*, is a way of describing *what* classes should do, without specifying *how* they should do it. A class can *implement* one or more interfaces. You can then use objects of these implementing classes whenever conformance to the interface is required. After discussing interfaces, we move on to *lambda expressions*, a concise way to create blocks of code that can be executed at a later point in time. Using lambda expressions, you can express code that uses callbacks or variable behavior in an elegant and concise fashion.

We then discuss the mechanism of *inner classes*. Inner classes are technically somewhat complex—they are defined inside other classes, and their methods can access the fields of the surrounding class. Inner classes are useful when you design collections of cooperating classes.

This chapter concludes with a discussion of *proxies*, objects that implement arbitrary interfaces. A proxy is a very specialized construct that is useful for building system-level tools. You can safely skip that section on first reading.

6.1. Interfaces

In the following sections, you will learn what Java interfaces are and how to use them. You will also find out how interfaces have been made more powerful in recent versions of Java.

6.1.1. The Interface Concept

In the Java programming language, an interface is not a class but a set of *requirements* for the classes that want to conform to the interface.

Typically, the supplier of some service states: "If your class conforms to a particular interface, then I'll perform the service." Let's look at a concrete example. The sort method of the Arrays class promises to sort an array of objects, but under one condition: The objects must belong to classes that *implement* the Comparable interface.

Here is what the Comparable interface looks like:

```
public interface Comparable
{
    int compareTo(Object other);
}
```

In the interface, the compareTo method is *abstract*—it has no implementation. A class that implements the Comparable interface needs to have a compareTo method, and the method must have an Object parameter and return an integer. Otherwise, the class is also abstract—that is, you cannot construct any objects.

 Note: As of Java 5, the Comparable interface has been enhanced to be a generic type.

```
public interface Comparable<T>
{
    int compareTo(T other); // parameter has type T
}
```

For example, a class that implements Comparable<Employee> must supply a method

```
int compareTo(Employee other)
```

You can still use the "raw" Comparable type without a type parameter. Then the compareTo method has a parameter of type Object, and you have to manually cast that parameter of the compareTo method to the desired type. I will do just that for a little while so that you don't have to worry about two new concepts at the same time.

All methods of an interface are automatically public. For that reason, it is not necessary to supply the keyword public when declaring a method in an interface.

Of course, there is an additional requirement that the interface syntax cannot express: When calling x.compareTo(y), the compareTo method must *compare* the two objects and return an indication whether x or y is larger. The method is supposed to return a negative number if x is smaller than y, zero if they are equal, and a positive number otherwise.

This particular interface has a single method. Some interfaces have multiple methods. As you will see later, interfaces can also define constants. What is more important, however, is what interfaces *cannot* supply. Interfaces never have instance fields. Before Java 8, all methods in an interface were abstract. As you will see in Section 6.1.4 and Section 6.1.5, it is now possible to have other methods in interfaces. Of course, those methods cannot refer to instance fields—interfaces don't have any.

Now, suppose we want to use the sort method of the Arrays class to sort an array of Employee objects. Then the Employee class must *implement* the Comparable interface.

To make a class implement an interface, you carry out two steps:

1. You declare that your class intends to implement the given interface.
2. You supply definitions for all methods in the interface.

To declare that a class implements an interface, use the implements keyword:

```
class Employee implements Comparable
```

Of course, now the Employee class needs to supply the compareTo method. Let's suppose that we want to compare employees by their salary. Here is an implementation of the compareTo method:

```
public int compareTo(Object otherObject)
{
    Employee other = (Employee) otherObject;
    return Double.compare(salary, other.salary);
}
```

Here, we use the static Double.compare method that returns a negative if the first argument is less than the second argument, 0 if they are equal, and a positive value otherwise.

 Caution: In the interface declaration, the compareTo method was not declared public because all methods in an *interface* are automatically public. However, when implementing the interface, you must declare the method as public. Otherwise, the compiler assumes that the method has package access—the default for a *class*. The compiler then complains that you're trying to supply a more restrictive access privilege.

We can do a little better by supplying a type parameter for the generic Comparable interface:

```
class Employee implements Comparable<Employee>
{
    public int compareTo(Employee other)
    {
        return Double.compare(salary, other.salary);
    }
    . . .
}
```

Note that the unsightly cast of the Object parameter has gone away.

Tip: The compareTo method of the Comparable interface returns an integer. If the objects are not equal, it does not matter what negative or positive value you return. This flexibility can be useful when you are comparing integer fields. For example, suppose each employee has a unique integer id and you want to sort by the employee ID number. Then you can simply return id - other.id. That value will be some negative value if the first ID number is less than the other, 0 if they are the same ID, and some positive value otherwise. However, there is one caveat: The range of the integers must be small enough so that the subtraction does not overflow. If you know that the IDs are not negative or that their absolute value is at most (Integer.MAX_VALUE - 1) / 2, you are safe. Otherwise, call the static Integer.compare method.

Of course, the subtraction trick doesn't work for floating-point numbers. The difference salary - other.salary can round to 0 if the salaries are close together but not identical. The call Double.compare(x, y) simply returns -1 if x < y or 1 if x > y.

Note: The documentation of the Comparable interface suggests that the compareTo method should be compatible with the equals method. That is, x.compareTo(y) should be zero exactly when x.equals(y). Most classes in the Java API that implement Comparable follow this advice.

A notable exception is BigDecimal. Consider x = new BigDecimal("1.0") and y = new BigDecimal("1.00"). Then x.equals(y) is false because the numbers differ in precision. But x.compareTo(y) is zero. Ideally, it shouldn't be, but there is no obvious way of deciding which one should come first.

Another exception is StringBuilder, which implements Comparable but does not override equals:

```
StringBuilder x = new StringBuilder("Hello");
StringBuilder y = new StringBuilder("Hello");
x.equals(y) // false
x.compareTo(y) // 0
```

Caution: There are minor differences between comparison operators with double operand and the corresponding methods of the Double class.

The first issue is negative zero, or -0.0. When compared with a relational operator such as == or <, it is indistinguishable from 0.0:

```
-0.0 == 0.0 // true
-0.0 < 0.0 // false
```

However, wrapped into Double instances, they are different:

```
Double.valueOf(-0.0).equals(Double.valueOf(0.0)) // false
Double.valueOf(-0.0).compareTo(Double.valueOf(0.0)) // -1
```

The other issue is Double.NaN. Any comparison with a relational operator where an operand is NaN returns false:

```
Double.NaN == Double.NaN // false
Double.NaN < Double.NaN // false
```

However, wrapped into a Double value, it behaves differently:

```
Double.valueOf(Double.NaN).equals(Double.valueOf(Double.NaN)) // true
Double.valueOf(Double.NaN).compareTo(Double.valueOf(Double.NaN)) // 0
```

The static Double.compare method follows the logic of the wrapper class:

```
Double.compare(-0.0, 0.0) // -1
```

Remarkably, Double.NaN is deemed larger than Double.POSITIVE_INFINITY:

```
Double.compare(Double.POSITIVE_INFINITY, Double.NaN) // -1
```

Note that the equals method of a record with double components uses Double.compare.

Now you saw what a class must do to avail itself of the sorting service—it must implement a compareTo method. That's eminently reasonable. There needs to be some way for the sort method to compare objects. But why can't the Employee class simply provide a compareTo method without implementing the Comparable interface?

The reason for interfaces is that the Java programming language is *strongly typed*. When making a method call, the compiler needs to be able to check that the method actually exists. Somewhere in the sort method will be statements like this:

```
if (a[i].compareTo(a[j]) > 0)
{
    // rearrange a[i] and a[j]
    . . .
}
```

The compiler must know that a[i] actually has a compareTo method. If a is an array of Comparable objects, then the existence of the method is assured because every class that implements the Comparable interface must supply the method.

Note: You would expect that the sort method in the Arrays class is defined to accept a Comparable[] array so that the compiler can complain if anyone ever calls sort with an array whose element type doesn't implement the Comparable interface. Sadly, that is not the case. Instead, the sort method accepts an Object[] array and uses a clumsy cast:

```java
// approach used in the standard library--not recommended
if ((((Comparable) a[i]).compareTo(a[j]) > 0)
{
   // rearrange a[i] and a[j]
   . . .
}
```

If a[i] does not belong to a class that implements the Comparable interface, the virtual machine throws an exception.

Listing 6.1 presents the full code for sorting an array of instances of the class Employee (Listing 6.2).

Listing 6.1 interfaces/EmployeeSortTest.java

```java
1  package interfaces;
2
3  import java.util.*;
4
5  /**
6   * This program demonstrates the use of the Comparable interface.
7   * @version 1.30 2004-02-27
8   * @author Cay Horstmann
9   */
10 public class EmployeeSortTest
11 {
12    public static void main(String[] args)
13    {
14       var staff = new Employee[3];
15
16       staff[0] = new Employee("Harry Hacker", 35000);
17       staff[1] = new Employee("Carl Cracker", 75000);
18       staff[2] = new Employee("Tony Tester", 38000);
19
20       Arrays.sort(staff);
21
22       // print out information about all Employee objects
23       for (Employee e : staff)
24          System.out.println("name=" + e.getName() + ",salary=" + e.getSalary());
25    }
26 }
```

Listing 6.2 `interfaces/Employee.java`

```java
1   package interfaces;
2
3   public class Employee implements Comparable<Employee>
4   {
5      private String name;
6      private double salary;
7
8      public Employee(String name, double salary)
9      {
10         this.name = name;
11         this.salary = salary;
12      }
13
14      public String getName()
15      {
16         return name;
17      }
18
19      public double getSalary()
20      {
21         return salary;
22      }
23
24      public void raiseSalary(double byPercent)
25      {
26         double raise = salary * byPercent / 100;
27         salary += raise;
28      }
29
30      /**
31       * Compares employees by salary.
32       * @param other another Employee object
33       * @return a negative value if this employee has a lower salary than
34       * other, 0 if the salaries are the same, a positive value otherwise
35       */
36      public int compareTo(Employee other)
37      {
38         return Double.compare(salary, other.salary);
39      }
40   }
```

java.lang.Comparable<T> 1.0

- int compareTo(T other)
  compares this object with other and returns a negative integer if this object is less than other, zero if they are equal, and a positive integer otherwise.

---

java.util.Arrays 1.2

- `static void sort(Object[] a)`
  sorts the elements in the array a. All elements in the array must belong to classes that implement the Comparable interface, and they must all be comparable to each other.

---

java.lang.Integer 1.0

- `static int compare(int x, int y)` 7
  returns a negative integer if x < y, zero if x and y are equal, and a positive integer otherwise.

---

java.lang.Double 1.0

- `static int compare(double x, double y)` 1.4
  returns a negative integer if x < y, zero if x and y are equal, and a positive integer otherwise.

 Note: According to the language standard: "The implementor must ensure sgn(x.compareTo(y)) = -sgn(y.compareTo(x)) for all x and y. (This implies that x.compareTo(y) must throw an exception if y.compareTo(x) throws an exception.)" Here, sgn is the *sign* of a number: sgn(n) is –1 if n is negative, 0 if n equals 0, and 1 if n is positive. In plain English, if you flip the arguments of compareTo, the sign (but not necessarily the actual value) of the result must also flip.

As with the equals method, problems can arise when inheritance comes into play.

Since Manager extends Employee, it implements Comparable<Employee> and not Comparable<Manager>. If Manager chooses to override compareTo, it must be prepared to compare managers to employees. It can't simply cast an employee to a manager:

```
class Manager extends Employee
{
   public int compareTo(Employee other)
   {
      Manager otherManager = (Manager) other; // NO
      . . .
   }
   . . .
}
```

That violates the "antisymmetry" rule. If x is an Employee and y is a Manager, then the call x.compareTo(y) doesn't throw an exception—it simply compares x and y as employees. But the reverse, y.compareTo(x), throws a ClassCastException.

This is the same situation as with the equals method discussed in Chapter 5, and the remedy is the same. There are two distinct scenarios.

If subclasses have different notions of comparison, then you should outlaw comparison of objects that belong to different classes. Each compareTo method should start out with the test

```
if (getClass() != other.getClass()) throw new ClassCastException();
```

If there is a common algorithm for comparing subclass objects, simply provide a single compareTo method in the superclass and declare it as final.

For example, suppose you want managers to be better than regular employees, regardless of salary. What about other subclasses such as Executive and Secretary? If you need to establish a pecking order, supply a method such as rank in the Employee class. Have each subclass override rank, and implement a single compareTo method that takes the rank values into account.

6.1.2. Properties of Interfaces

Interfaces are not classes. In particular, you can never use the new operator to instantiate an interface:

```
x = new Comparable(. . .); // ERROR
```

However, even though you can't construct interface objects, you can still declare interface variables.

```
Comparable x; // OK
```

An interface variable must refer to an object of a class that implements the interface:

```
x = new Employee(. . .); // OK provided Employee implements Comparable
```

Next, just as you use instanceof to check whether an object is of a specific class, you can use instanceof to check whether an object implements an interface:

```
if (anObject instanceof Comparable) { . . . }
```

Just as you can build hierarchies of classes, you can extend interfaces. This allows for multiple chains of interfaces that go from a greater degree of generality to a greater degree of specialization. For example, suppose you had an interface called Moveable.

```
public interface Moveable
{
   void move(double x, double y);
}
```

Then, you could imagine an interface called Powered that extends it:

```
public interface Powered extends Moveable
{
   double milesPerGallon();
}
```

Although you cannot put instance fields in an interface, you can supply constants in them. For example:

```
public interface Powered extends Moveable
{
   double milesPerGallon();
   double SPEED_LIMIT = 95; // a public static final constant
}
```

Just as methods in an interface are automatically public, fields are always public static final.

 Note: It is legal to tag interface methods as public, and fields as public static final. Some programmers do that, either out of habit or for greater clarity. However, the Java Language Specification recommends that the redundant keywords not be supplied, and I follow that recommendation.

While each class can have only one superclass, classes can implement *multiple* interfaces. This gives you the maximum amount of flexibility in defining a class's behavior. For example, the Java programming language has an important interface built into it, called Cloneable. (This interface is discussed in detail in Section 6.1.9.) If your class implements Cloneable, the clone method in the Object class will make an exact copy of your class's objects. If you want both cloneability and comparability, simply implement both interfaces. Use commas to separate the interfaces that you want to implement:

```
class Employee implements Cloneable, Comparable
```

 Note: Records and enumeration classes cannot extend other classes (since they implicitly extend the Record and Enum class). However, they can implement interfaces.

Note: Interfaces can be sealed. As with sealed classes, the direct subtypes (which can be classes or interfaces) must be declared in a permits clause or be located in the same source file.

6.1.3. Interfaces and Abstract Classes

If you read the section about abstract classes in Chapter 5, you may wonder why the designers of the Java programming language bothered with introducing the concept of interfaces. Why can't Comparable simply be an abstract class:

```
abstract class Comparable // why not?
{
    public abstract int compareTo(Object other);
}
```

The Employee class would then simply extend this abstract class and supply the compareTo method:

```
class Employee extends Comparable // why not?
{
    public int compareTo(Object other) { . . . }
}
```

There is, unfortunately, a major problem with using an abstract base class to express a generic property. A class can only extend a single class. Suppose the Employee class already extends a different class, say, Person. Then it can't extend a second class.

```
class Employee extends Person, Comparable // ERROR
```

But each class can implement as many interfaces as it likes:

```
class Employee extends Person implements Comparable // OK
```

Other programming languages, in particular C++, allow a class to have more than one superclass. This feature is called *multiple inheritance*. The designers of Java chose not to support multiple inheritance, because it makes the language either very complex (as in C++) or less efficient (as in Eiffel).

Instead, interfaces afford most of the benefits of multiple inheritance while avoiding the complexities and inefficiencies.

C++ Note: C++ has multiple inheritance and all the complications that come with it, such as virtual base classes, dominance rules, and transverse pointer casts. Few

C++ programmers use multiple inheritance, and some say it should never be used. Other programmers recommend using multiple inheritance only for the "mix-in" style of inheritance. In the mix-in style, a primary base class describes the parent object, and additional base classes (the so-called mix-ins) may supply auxiliary characteristics. That style is similar to a Java class with a single superclass and additional interfaces.

Tip: You have seen the CharSequence interface in Chapter 3. Both String and StringBuilder (as well as a few more esoteric string-like classes) implement this interface. The interface contains methods that are common to all classes that manage sequences of characters. A common interface encourages programmers to write methods that use the CharSequence interface. Those methods work with instances of String, StringBuilder, and the other string-like classes.

Sadly, the CharSequence interface is rather paltry. You can get the length, iterate over the code points or code units, extract subsequences, and lexicographically compare two sequences. Java 17 adds an isEmpty method.

If you process strings, and those operations suffice for your tasks, accept CharSequence instances instead of strings.

6.1.4. Static and Private Methods

As of Java 8, you are allowed to add static methods to interfaces. There was never a technical reason why this should be outlawed. It simply seemed to be against the spirit of interfaces as abstract specifications.

Previously, it had been common to place static methods in companion classes. In the standard library, you'll find pairs of interfaces and utility classes such as Collection/Collections.

As an example, you can construct a path to a file or directory from a URI, or from a sequence of strings, using static methods in the Path interface:

```
public interface Path
{
    public static Path of(URI uri) { . . . . }
    public static Path of(String first, String... more) { . . . }
    . . .
}
```

In previous versions of Java, there was a separate Paths class to hold these methods. Nowadays, there is no longer a reason to provide a separate companion class for utility methods.

Methods in an interface can be private. A private method can be static or an instance method. Since private methods can only be used in the methods of the interface itself, their use is limited to being helper methods for the other methods of the interface.

6.1.5. Default Methods

You can supply a *default* implementation for any interface method. You must tag such a method with the default modifier.

```
public interface Comparable<T>
{
    default int compareTo(T other) { return 0; }
        // by default, all elements are the same
}
```

Of course, that is not very useful since every realistic implementation of Comparable would override this method. But there are other situations where default methods can be useful. For example, in Chapter 9 you will see an Iterator interface for visiting elements in a data structure. It declares a remove method as follows:

```
public interface Iterator<E>
{
    boolean hasNext();
    E next();
    default void remove() { throw new UnsupportedOperationException("remove"); }
    . . .
}
```

If you implement an iterator, you need to provide the hasNext and next methods. There are no defaults for these methods—they depend on the data structure that you are traversing. But if your iterator is read-only, you don't have to worry about the remove method.

A default method can call other methods. For example, a Collection interface can define a convenience method

```
public interface Collection
{
    int size(); // an abstract method
    default boolean isEmpty() { return size() == 0; }
    . . .
}
```

Then a programmer implementing Collection doesn't have to worry about implementing an isEmpty method.

Note: The Collection interface in the Java API does not actually do this. Instead, there is a class AbstractCollection that implements Collection and defines isEmpty in terms of size. Implementors of a collection are advised to extend AbstractCollection. That technique is obsolete. Just implement the methods in the interface.

An important use for default methods is *interface evolution*. Consider, for example, the Collection interface that has been a part of Java for many years. Suppose that a long time ago, you provided a class

```
public class Bag implements Collection
```

Later, in Java 8, a stream method was added to the interface.

Suppose the stream method was not a default method. Then the Bag class would no longer compile since it doesn't implement the new method. Adding a nondefault method to an interface is not *source-compatible*.

But suppose you don't recompile the class and simply use an old JAR file containing it. The class will still load, even with the missing method. Programs can still construct Bag instances, and nothing bad will happen. (Adding a method to an interface is *binary compatible*.) However, if a program calls the stream method on a Bag instance, an AbstractMethodError occurs.

Making the method a default method solves both problems. The Bag class will again compile. And if the class is loaded without being recompiled and the stream method is invoked on a Bag instance, the Collection.stream method is called.

6.1.6. Resolving Default Method Conflicts

What happens if the exact same method is defined as a default method in one interface and then again as a method of a superclass or another interface? Languages such as Scala and C++ have complex rules for resolving such ambiguities. Fortunately, the rules in Java are much simpler. Here they are:

1. Superclasses win. If a superclass provides a concrete method, default methods with the same name and parameter types are simply ignored.
2. Interfaces clash. If an interface provides a default method, and another interface contains a method with the same name and parameter types (default or not), then you must resolve the conflict by overriding that method.

Let's look at the second rule. Consider two interfaces with a getName method:

```
interface Person
{
    default String getName() { return ""; }
```

```
}

interface Named
{
    default String getName() { return getClass().getName() + "_" + hashCode(); }
}
```

What happens if you form a class that implements both of them?

```
class Student implements Person, Named { . . . }
```

The class inherits two inconsistent getName methods provided by the Person and Named interfaces. Instead of choosing one over the other, the Java compiler reports an error and leaves it up to the programmer to resolve the ambiguity. Simply provide a getName method in the Student class. In that method, you can choose one of the two conflicting methods, like this:

```
class Student implements Person, Named
{
    public String getName() { return Person.super.getName(); }
    . . .
}
```

Now assume that the Named interface does not provide a default implementation for getName:

```
interface Named
{
    String getName();
}
```

Can the Student class inherit the default method from the Person interface? This might be reasonable, but the Java designers decided in favor of uniformity. It doesn't matter how two interfaces conflict. If at least one interface provides an implementation, the compiler reports an error, and the programmer must resolve the ambiguity.

If neither interface provides a default for a shared method, then there is no conflict. An implementing class has two choices: implement the method, or leave it unimplemented. In the latter case, the class is itself abstract.

We just discussed name clashes between two interfaces. Now consider a class that extends a superclass and implements an interface, inheriting the same method from both. For example, suppose that Person is a class and Student is defined as

```
class Student extends Person implements Named { . . . }
```

In that case, only the superclass method matters, and any default method from the interface is simply ignored. In our example, Student inherits the getName method from Person, and it doesn't make any difference whether the Named interface provides a default for getName or not. This is the "class wins" rule.

The "class wins" rule ensures compatibility with old versions of Java. If you add default methods to an interface, it has no effect on code that worked before there were default methods.

 Caution: You can never make a default method that redefines one of the methods in the Object class. For example, you can't define a default method for toString or equals, even though that might be attractive for interfaces such as List. As a consequence of the "class wins" rule, such a method could never win against Object.toString or Object.equals.

6.1.7. Interfaces and Callbacks

A common pattern in programming is the *callback* pattern. In this pattern, you specify the action that should occur whenever a particular event happens. For example, you may want a particular action to occur when a button is clicked or a menu item is selected. However, as you have not yet seen how to implement user interfaces, we will consider a similar but simpler situation.

The javax.swing package contains a Timer class that is useful if you want to be notified whenever a time interval has elapsed. For example, if a part of your program contains a clock, you can ask to be notified every second so that you can update the clock face.

When you construct a timer, you set the time interval and tell it what it should do whenever the time interval has elapsed.

How do you tell the timer what it should do? In many programming languages, you supply the name of a function that the timer should call periodically. However, the classes in the Java standard library take an object-oriented approach. You pass an object of some class. The timer then calls one of the methods on that object. Passing an object is more flexible than passing a function because the object can carry additional information.

Of course, the timer needs to know what method to call. The timer requires that you specify an object of a class that implements the ActionListener interface of the java.awt.event package. Here is that interface:

```
public interface ActionListener
{
    void actionPerformed(ActionEvent event);
}
```

The timer calls the actionPerformed method when the time interval has expired.

Suppose you want to print a message "At the tone, the time is . . .", followed by a beep, once every second. You would define a class that implements the `ActionListener` interface. You would then place whatever statements you want to have executed inside the `actionPerformed` method.

```
class TimePrinter implements ActionListener
{
   public void actionPerformed(ActionEvent event)
   {
      System.out.println("At the tone, the time is "
         + Instant.ofEpochMilli(event.getWhen()));
      Toolkit.getDefaultToolkit().beep();
   }
}
```

Note the `ActionEvent` parameter of the `actionPerformed` method. This parameter gives information about the event, such as the time when the event happened. The call `event.getWhen()` returns the event time, measured in milliseconds since the "epoch" (January 1, 1970). By passing it to the static `Instant.ofEpochMilli` method, we get a more readable description.

Next, construct an object of this class and pass it to the `Timer` constructor.

```
var listener = new TimePrinter();
Timer t = new Timer(1000, listener);
```

The first argument of the `Timer` constructor is the time interval that must elapse between notifications, measured in milliseconds. We want to be notified every second. The second argument is the listener object.

Finally, start the timer.

```
t.start();
```

Every second, a message like

```
At the tone, the time is 2017-12-16T05:01:49.550Z
```

is displayed, followed by a beep.

 Caution: Be sure to import `javax.swing.Timer`. There is also a `java.util.Timer` class that is slightly different.

Listing 6.3 puts the timer and its action listener to work. After the timer is started, the program puts up a message dialog and waits for the user to click the OK button to stop.

While the program waits for the user, the current time is displayed every second. (If you omit the dialog, the program would terminate as soon as the main method exits.)

Listing 6.3 `timer/TimerTest.java`

```java
1  package timer;
2
3  /**
4     @version 1.02 2017-12-14
5     @author Cay Horstmann
6  */
7
8  import java.awt.*;
9  import java.awt.event.*;
10 import java.time.*;
11 import javax.swing.*;
12
13 public class TimerTest
14 {
15    public static void main(String[] args)
16    {
17       var listener = new TimePrinter();
18
19       // construct a timer that calls the listener once every second
20       var timer = new Timer(1000, listener);
21       timer.start();
22
23       // keep program running until the user selects "OK"
24       JOptionPane.showMessageDialog(null, "Quit program?");
25       System.exit(0);
26    }
27 }
28
29 class TimePrinter implements ActionListener
30 {
31    public void actionPerformed(ActionEvent event)
32    {
33       System.out.println("At the tone, the time is " + Instant.ofEpochMilli(event.getWhen()));
34       Toolkit.getDefaultToolkit().beep();
35    }
36 }
```

javax.swing.JOptionPane 1.2

- `static void showMessageDialog(Component parent, Object message)`
  displays a dialog box with a message prompt and an OK button. The dialog is centered over the parent component. If parent is null, the dialog is centered on the screen.

---

javax.swing.Timer `1.2`

- `Timer(int interval, ActionListener listener)`
  constructs a timer that notifies `listener` whenever interval milliseconds have elapsed.
- `void start()`
  starts the timer. Once started, the timer calls `actionPerformed` on its listeners.
- `void stop()`
  stops the timer. Once stopped, the timer no longer calls `actionPerformed` on its listeners.

---

java.awt.Toolkit `1.0`

- `static Toolkit getDefaultToolkit()`
  gets the default toolkit. A toolkit contains information about the GUI environment.
- `void beep()`
  emits a beep sound.

6.1.8. The `Comparator` Interface

In Section 6.1.1, you have seen how you can sort an array of objects, provided they are instances of classes that implement the `Comparable` interface. For example, you can sort an array of strings since the `String` class implements `Comparable<String>`, and the `String.compareTo` method compares strings in dictionary order.

Now suppose we want to sort strings by increasing length, not in dictionary order. We can't have the `String` class implement the `compareTo` method in two ways—and at any rate, the `String` class isn't ours to modify.

To deal with this situation, there is a second version of the `Arrays.sort` method whose parameters are an array and a *comparator*—an instance of a class that implements the `Comparator` interface.

```java
public interface Comparator<T>
{
    int compare(T first, T second);
}
```

To compare strings by length, define a class that implements `Comparator<String>`:

```java
class LengthComparator implements Comparator<String>
{
    public int compare(String first, String second)
    {
```

```
        return first.length() - second.length();
    }
}
```

To actually do the comparison, you need to make an instance:

```
var comp = new LengthComparator();
if (comp.compare(words[i], words[j]) > 0) . . .
```

Contrast this call with words[i].compareTo(words[j]). The compare method is called on the comparator object, not the string itself.

Note: Even though the LengthComparator object has no state, you still need to make an instance of it. You need the instance to call the compare method—it is not a static method.

To sort an array, pass a LengthComparator object to the Arrays.sort method:

```
String[] friends = { "Peter", "Paul", "Mary" };
Arrays.sort(friends, new LengthComparator());
```

Now the array is either ["Paul", "Mary", "Peter"] or ["Mary", "Paul", "Peter"].

You will see in Section 6.2 how to use a Comparator much more easily with a lambda expression.

Note: The String class provides a Comparator for case-insensitive comparison. Here is how you can use it:

```
Arrays.sort(friends, String.CASE_INSENSITIVE_ORDER);
```

Caution: Do not try to shuffle an array by sorting it with a comparator that randomly returns positive or negative integers.

There are three rules that a comparator needs to fulfill:

1. Reflexivity: When x and y are equal, the comparator yields 0.
2. Antisymmetry: When swapping the arguments of the comparator, the sign of the result is swapped.
3. Transitivity: When x comes before y and y comes before z, then x must come before z.

The algorithm that Arrays.sort uses (called "Timsort") doesn't check these rules for all elements, but it can sometimes detect a rule violation at a trivial cost. Then it throws an exception with the message "Comparison method violates its general contract!". With an array of 1,000 elements, the chance of this occurring with a random comparator is over 10%.

The Collections.shuffle method randomly shuffles a list. To shuffle an array, first turn it into a list and then shuffle that.

6.1.9. Object Cloning

In this section, we discuss the Cloneable interface that indicates that a class has provided a safe clone method. Since cloning is not all that common, and the details are quite technical, you may just want to glance at this material until you need it.

To understand what cloning means, recall what happens when you make a copy of a variable holding an object reference. The original and the copy are references to the same object (see Figure 6.1). This means a change to either variable also affects the other.

```
var original = new Employee("John Public", 50000);
Employee copy = original;
copy.raiseSalary(10); // oops--also changed original
```

If you would like copy to be a new object that begins its life being identical to original but whose state can diverge over time, use the clone method.

```
Employee copy = original.clone();
copy.raiseSalary(10); // OK--original unchanged
```

But it isn't quite so simple. The clone method is a protected method of Object, which means that your code cannot simply call it. Only the Employee class can clone Employee objects. There is a reason for this restriction. Think about the way in which the Object class can implement clone. It knows nothing about the object at all, so it can make only a field-by-field copy. If all instance fields in the object are numbers or other basic types, copying the fields is just fine. But if the object contains references to subobjects, then copying the field gives you another reference to the same subobject, so the original and the cloned objects still share some information.

To visualize that, consider the Employee class that was introduced in Chapter 4. Figure 6.2 shows what happens when you use the clone method of the Object class to clone such an Employee object. As you can see, the default cloning operation is "shallow"—it doesn't clone objects that are referenced inside other objects. (The figure shows a shared Date object. For reasons that will become clear shortly, this example uses a version of the Employee class in which the hire day is represented as a Date.)

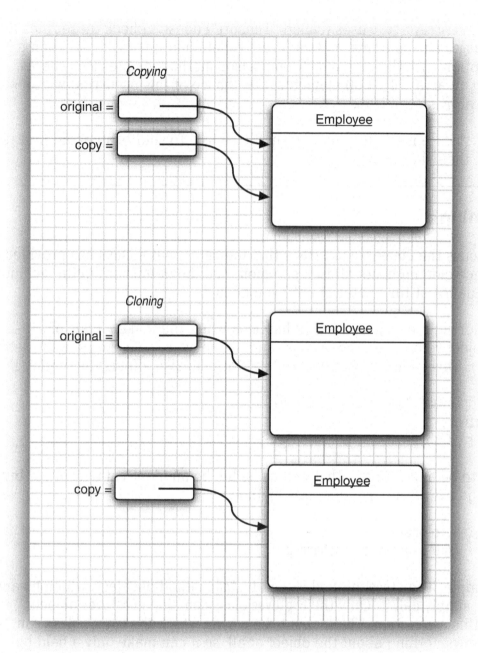

Figure 6.1: Copying and cloning

Does it matter if the copy is shallow? It depends. If the subobject shared between the original and the shallow clone is *immutable*, then the sharing is safe. This certainly happens if the subobject belongs to an immutable class, such as String. Alternatively, the subobject may simply remain constant throughout the lifetime of the object, with no mutators touching it and no methods yielding a reference to it.

Quite frequently, however, subobjects are mutable, and you must redefine the clone method to make a *deep copy* that clones the subobjects as well. In our example, the hireDay field is

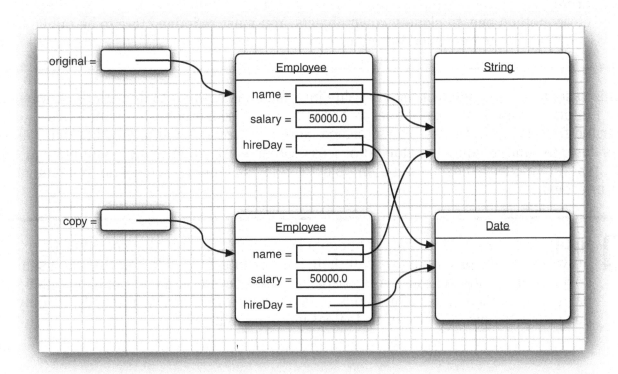

Figure 6.2: A shallow copy

a Date, which is mutable, so it too must be cloned. (For that reason, this example uses a field of type Date, not LocalDate, to demonstrate the cloning process. Had hireDay been an instance of the immutable LocalDate class, no further action would have been required.)

For every class, you need to decide whether

1. The default clone method is good enough;
2. The default clone method can be patched up by calling clone on the mutable subobjects; or
3. clone should not be attempted.

The third option is actually the default. To choose either the first or the second option, a class must

1. Implement the Cloneable interface; and
2. Redefine the clone method with the public access modifier.

 Note: The clone method is declared protected in the Object class, so that your code can't simply call anObject.clone(). But aren't protected methods accessible from any subclass, and isn't every class a subclass of Object? Fortunately, the rules for protected access are more subtle (see Chapter 5). A subclass can call a protected clone method only to clone *its own* objects. You must redefine clone to be public to allow objects to be cloned by any method.

In this case, the appearance of the Cloneable interface has nothing to do with the normal use of interfaces. In particular, it does *not* specify the clone method—that method is inherited from the Object class. The interface merely serves as a tag, indicating that the class designer understands the cloning process. Objects are so paranoid about cloning that they generate a checked exception if an object requests cloning but does not implement that interface.

Note: The Cloneable interface is one of a handful of *tagging interfaces* that Java provides. (Some programmers call them *marker interfaces*.) Recall that the usual purpose of an interface such as Comparable is to ensure that a class implements a particular method or set of methods. A tagging interface has no methods; its only purpose is to allow the use of instanceof in a type inquiry:

```
if (obj instanceof Cloneable) . . .
```

I recommend that you do not use tagging interfaces in your own programs.

Even if the default (shallow copy) implementation of clone is adequate, you still need to implement the Cloneable interface, redefine clone to be public, and call super.clone(). Here is an example:

```
class Employee implements Cloneable
{
   // public access, change return type
   public Employee clone() throws CloneNotSupportedException
   {
      return (Employee) super.clone();
   }
   . . .
}
```

Note: Note that in the Object class, the clone method has return type Object. In a subclass, you can specify the correct return type for your clone methods. This is an example of covariant return types (see Chapter 5).

The clone method that you just saw adds no functionality to the shallow copy provided by Object.clone. It merely makes the method public. To make a deep copy, you have to work harder and clone the mutable instance fields.

Here is an example of a clone method that creates a deep copy:

```
class Employee implements Cloneable
{
   . . .
   public Employee clone() throws CloneNotSupportedException
   {
      // call Object.clone()
      Employee cloned = (Employee) super.clone();

      // clone mutable fields
      cloned.hireDay = (Date) hireDay.clone();

      return cloned;
   }
}
```

The clone method of the Object class threatens to throw a CloneNotSupportedException—it does that whenever clone is invoked on an object whose class does not implement the Cloneable interface. Of course, the Employee and Date classes implement the Cloneable interface, so the exception won't be thrown. However, the compiler does not know that. Therefore, we declared the exception:

```
public Employee clone() throws CloneNotSupportedException
```

 Note: Would it be better to catch the exception instead? (See Chapter 7 for details on catching exceptions.)

```
public Employee clone()
{
   try
   {
      Employee cloned = (Employee) super.clone();
      . . .
   }
   catch (CloneNotSupportedException e) { return null; }
   // this won't happen, since we are Cloneable
}
```

This is appropriate for final classes. Otherwise, it is better to leave the throws specifier in place. That gives subclasses the option of throwing a CloneNotSupportedException if they can't support cloning.

You have to be careful about cloning of subclasses. For example, once you have defined the clone method for the Employee class, anyone can use it to clone Manager objects. Can the

Employee clone method do the job? It depends on the fields of the Manager class. In our case, there is no problem because the bonus field has primitive type. But Manager might have acquired fields that require a deep copy or are not cloneable. There is no guarantee that the implementor of the subclass has fixed clone to do the right thing. For that reason, the clone method is declared as protected in the Object class. But you don't have that luxury if you want the users of your classes to invoke clone.

Should you implement clone in your own classes? If your clients need to make deep copies, then you probably should. Some authors feel that you should avoid clone altogether and instead implement another method for the same purpose. I agree that clone is rather awkward, but you'll run into the same issues if you shift the responsibility to another method. At any rate, cloning is less common than you may think. Less than five percent of the classes in the standard library implement clone.

The program in Listing 6.4 clones an instance of the class Employee (Listing 6.5), then invokes two mutators. The raiseSalary method changes the value of the salary field, whereas the setHireDay method changes the state of the hireDay field. Neither mutation affects the original object because clone has been defined to make a deep copy.

 Note: All array types have a clone method that is public, not protected. You can use it to make a new array that contains copies of all elements. For example:

```
int[] luckyNumbers = { 2, 3, 5, 7, 11, 13 };
int[] cloned = luckyNumbers.clone();
cloned[5] = 12; // doesn't change luckyNumbers[5]
```

Listing 6.4 clone/CloneTest.java

```
 1  package clone;
 2
 3  /**
 4   * This program demonstrates cloning.
 5   * @version 1.11 2018-03-16
 6   * @author Cay Horstmann
 7   */
 8  public class CloneTest
 9  {
10     public static void main(String[] args) throws CloneNotSupportedException
11     {
12        var original = new Employee("John Q. Public", 50000);
13        original.setHireDay(2000, 1, 1);
14        Employee copy = original.clone();
15        copy.raiseSalary(10);
16        copy.setHireDay(2002, 12, 31);
17        System.out.println("original=" + original);
```

```
18          System.out.println("copy=" + copy);
19       }
20 }
```

Listing 6.5 clone/Employee.java

```
1   package clone;
2
3   import java.time.*;
4   import java.util.*;
5
6   public class Employee implements Cloneable
7   {
8      private String name;
9      private double salary;
10     private Date hireDay;
11
12     public Employee(String name, double salary)
13     {
14        this.name = name;
15        this.salary = salary;
16        hireDay = new Date();
17     }
18
19     public Employee clone() throws CloneNotSupportedException
20     {
21        // call Object.clone()
22        Employee cloned = (Employee) super.clone();
23
24        // clone mutable fields
25        cloned.hireDay = (Date) hireDay.clone();
26
27        return cloned;
28     }
29
30     /**
31      * Set the hire day to a given date.
32      * @param year the year of the hire day
33      * @param month the month of the hire day
34      * @param day the day of the hire day
35      */
36     public void setHireDay(int year, int month, int day)
37     {
38        long epochMillis = LocalDate.of(year, month, day)
39              .atStartOfDay(ZoneId.systemDefault())
40              .toEpochSecond() * 1000;
41
42        // example of instance field mutation
43        hireDay.setTime(epochMillis);
44     }
```

```
45
46      public void raiseSalary(double byPercent)
47      {
48         double raise = salary * byPercent / 100;
49         salary += raise;
50      }
51
52      public String toString()
53      {
54         return "Employee[name=" + name + ",salary=" + salary + ",hireDay=" + hireDay + "]";
55      }
56   }
```

6.2. Lambda Expressions

In the following sections, you will learn how to use lambda expressions for defining blocks of code with a concise syntax, and how to write code that consumes lambda expressions.

6.2.1. Why Lambdas?

A lambda expression is a block of code that you can pass around so it can be executed later, once or multiple times. Before getting into the syntax (or even the curious name), let's step back and observe where we have used such code blocks in Java.

In Section 6.1.7, you saw how to do work in timed intervals. Put the work into the actionPerformed method of an ActionListener:

```
class Worker implements ActionListener
{
   public void actionPerformed(ActionEvent event)
   {
      // do some work
   }
}
```

Then, when you want to repeatedly execute this code, you construct an instance of the Worker class. You then submit the instance to a Timer object.

The key point is that the actionPerformed method contains code that you want to execute later.

Or consider sorting with a custom comparator. If you want to sort strings by length instead of the default dictionary order, you can pass a Comparator object to the sort method:

```
class LengthComparator implements Comparator<String>
{
   public int compare(String first, String second)
```

```
    {
        return first.length() - second.length();
    }
}
. . .
Arrays.sort(strings, new LengthComparator());
```

The `compare` method isn't called right away. Instead, the `sort` method keeps calling the `compare` method, rearranging the elements if they are out of order, until the array is sorted. You give the `sort` method a snippet of code needed to compare elements, and that code is integrated into the rest of the sorting logic, which you'd probably not care to reimplement.

Both examples have something in common. A block of code was passed to someone—a timer, or a `sort` method. That code block was called at some later time.

In early versions of Java, giving someone a block of code was not easy. You couldn't just pass code blocks around. Java is an object-oriented language, so you had to construct an object belonging to a class that has a method with the desired code.

In other languages, it is possible to work with blocks of code directly. The Java designers have resisted adding this feature for a long time. After all, a great strength of Java is its simplicity and consistency. A language can become an unmaintainable mess if it includes every feature that yields marginally more concise code. However, in those other languages it isn't just easier to spawn a thread or to register a button click handler; large swaths of their APIs are simpler, more consistent, and more powerful. In Java, one could have written similar APIs taking objects of classes that implement a particular interface, but such APIs would be unpleasant to use.

For some time, the question was not whether to augment Java for functional programming, but how to do it. It took several years of experimentation before a design emerged that is a good fit for Java. In the next section, you will see how you can work with blocks of code in Java.

6.2.2. The Syntax of Lambda Expressions

Consider again the sorting example from the preceding section. We pass code that checks whether one string is shorter than another. We compute

```
first.length() - second.length()
```

What are `first` and `second`? They are both strings. Java is a strongly typed language, and we must specify that as well:

```
(String first, String second) ->
    first.length() - second.length()
```

You have just seen your first *lambda expression*. Such an expression is simply a block of code, together with the specification of any variables that must be passed to the code.

Why the name? Many years ago, before there were any computers, the logician Alonzo Church wanted to formalize what it means for a mathematical function to be effectively computable. (Curiously, there are functions that are known to exist, but nobody knows how to compute their values.) He used the Greek letter lambda (λ) to mark parameters. Had he known about the Java API, he would have written

```
λfirst.λsecond.first.length() - second.length()
```

Note: Why the letter λ? Did Church run out of other letters of the alphabet? Actually, the venerable *Principia Mathematica* used the ^ accent to denote free variables, which inspired Church to use an uppercase lambda Λ for parameters. But in the end, he switched to the lowercase version. Ever since, an expression with parameter variables has been called a lambda expression.

What you have just seen is a simple form of lambda expressions in Java: parameters, the -> arrow, and an expression. If the code carries out a computation that doesn't fit in a single expression, write it exactly like you would have written a method: enclosed in {} and with explicit return statements. For example,

```
(String first, String second) ->
   {
      if (first.length() < second.length()) return -1;
      else if (first.length() > second.length()) return 1;
      else return 0;
   }
```

If a lambda expression has no parameters, you still supply empty parentheses, just as with a parameterless method:

```
() -> { return 1 + (int)(Math.random() * 6); }
```

If the parameter types of a lambda expression can be inferred, you can omit them. For example,

```
Comparator<String> comp =
   (first, second) // same as (String first, String second)
      -> first.length() - second.length();
```

Here, the compiler can deduce that first and second must be strings because the lambda expression is assigned to a string comparator. (We will have a closer look at this assignment in the next section.)

If a method has a single parameter with inferred type, you can even omit the parentheses:

```
ActionListener listener = event ->
   System.out.println("The time is "
      + Instant.ofEpochMilli(event.getWhen()));
      // instead of (event) -> . . . or (ActionEvent event) -> . . .
```

You never specify the result type of a lambda expression. It is always inferred from context. For example, the expression

```
(String first, String second) -> first.length() - second.length()
```

can be used in a context where a result of type int is expected.

Finally, you can use var to denote an inferred type. This isn't common. The syntax was invented for attaching annotations (see Chapter 11):

```
(@NonNull var first, @NonNull var second) -> first.length() - second.length()
```

Note: It is illegal for a lambda expression to return a value in some branches but not in others. For example, (int x) -> { if (x >= 0) return 1; } is invalid.

Preview Note: If a parameter of a lambda expression is never used, you can denote it with an underscore:

```
ActionListener listener = _ ->
   System.out.println("The action occurred at " + Instant.now());
Comparator<String> comp = (_, _) -> 0;
```

This is a preview feature in Java 21.

The program in Listing 6.6 shows how to use lambda expressions for a comparator and an action listener.

Listing 6.6 `lambda/LambdaTest.java`

```
1  package lambda;
2
3  import java.util.*;
4
5  import javax.swing.*;
6  import javax.swing.Timer;
7
```

```
 8   /**
 9    * This program demonstrates the use of lambda expressions.
10    * @version 1.0 2015-05-12
11    * @author Cay Horstmann
12    */
13   public class LambdaTest
14   {
15      public static void main(String[] args)
16      {
17         var planets = new String[] { "Mercury", "Venus", "Earth", "Mars",
18            "Jupiter", "Saturn", "Uranus", "Neptune" };
19         System.out.println(Arrays.toString(planets));
20         System.out.println("Sorted in dictionary order:");
21         Arrays.sort(planets);
22         System.out.println(Arrays.toString(planets));
23         System.out.println("Sorted by length:");
24         Arrays.sort(planets, (first, second) -> first.length() - second.length());
25         System.out.println(Arrays.toString(planets));
26
27         var timer = new Timer(1000, event ->
28            System.out.println("The time is " + new Date()));
29         timer.start();
30
31         // keep program running until user selects "OK"
32         JOptionPane.showMessageDialog(null, "Quit program?");
33         System.exit(0);
34      }
35   }
```

6.2.3. Functional Interfaces

As we discussed, there are many existing interfaces in Java that encapsulate blocks of code, such as ActionListener or Comparator. Lambdas are compatible with these interfaces.

You can supply a lambda expression whenever an object of an interface with a single abstract method is expected. Such an interface is called a *functional interface*.

Note: You may wonder why a functional interface must have a single *abstract* method. Aren't all methods in an interface abstract? Actually, it has always been possible for an interface to redeclare methods from the Object class such as toString or clone, and these declarations do not make the methods abstract. (Some interfaces in the Java API redeclare Object methods in order to attach javadoc comments. Check out the Comparator API for an example.) More importantly, as you saw in Section 6.1.5, interfaces can declare nonabstract methods.

To demonstrate the conversion to a functional interface, consider the `Arrays.sort` method. Its second parameter requires an instance of `Comparator`, an interface with a single method. Simply supply a lambda:

```
Arrays.sort(words,
    (first, second) -> first.length() - second.length());
```

Behind the scenes, the `Arrays.sort` method receives an object of some class that implements `Comparator<String>`. Invoking the `compare` method on that object executes the body of the lambda expression. The management of these objects and classes is completely implementation-dependent, and it can be much more efficient than using traditional inner classes. It is best to think of a lambda expression as a function, not an object, and to accept that it can be passed to a functional interface.

This conversion to interfaces is what makes lambda expressions so compelling. The syntax is short and simple. Here is another example:

```
var timer = new Timer(1000, event ->
    {
        System.out.println("At the tone, the time is "
            + Instant.ofEpochMilli(event.getWhen()));
        Toolkit.getDefaultToolkit().beep();
    });
```

That's a lot easier to read than the alternative with a class that implements the `ActionListener` interface.

In fact, conversion to a functional interface is the *only* thing that you can do with a lambda expression in Java. In other programming languages that support function literals, you can declare function types such as `(String, String) -> int`, declare variables of those types, and use the variables to save function expressions. However, the Java designers decided to stick with the familiar concept of interfaces instead of adding function types to the language.

 Note: You can't even assign a lambda expression to a variable of type `Object`—`Object` is not a functional interface.

6.2.4. Function Types

The Java API defines a number of very generic functional interfaces in the `java.util.function` package. One of the interfaces, `BiFunction<T, U, R>`, describes functions with parameter types T and U and return type R. You can save your string comparison lambda in a variable of that type:

```
BiFunction<String, String, Integer> comp =
    (first, second) -> first.length() - second.length();
```

Note that this interface does not help you with sorting. There is no Arrays.sort method that wants a BiFunction. If you have used a functional programming language before, you may find this curious. But for Java programmers, it's pretty natural. An interface such as Comparator has a specific purpose, not just a method with given parameter and return types. When you want to do something with lambda expressions, you still want to keep the purpose of the expression in mind, and have a specific functional interface for it.

A particularly useful interface in the java.util.function package is Predicate:

```
public interface Predicate<T>
{
    boolean test(T t);
    // additional default and static methods
}
```

The ArrayList class has a removeIf method whose parameter is a Predicate. It is specifically designed to pass a lambda expression. For example, the following statement removes all null values from an array list:

```
list.removeIf(e -> e == null);
```

Another useful functional interface is Supplier<T>:

```
public interface Supplier<T>
{
    T get();
}
```

A supplier has no parameters and yields a value of type T when the get method is called:

```
Supplier<Integer> die = () -> (int)(Math.random() * 6) + 1;
int outcome = die.get();
```

Suppliers are used for *lazy evaluation*. For example, consider the call

```
LocalDate hireDay = Objects.requireNonNullElse(day,
    LocalDate.of(1970, 1, 1));
```

This is not optimal. We expect that day is rarely null, so we only want to construct the default LocalDate when necessary. By using the supplier, we can defer the computation:

```
LocalDate hireDay = Objects.requireNonNullElseGet(day,
    () -> LocalDate.of(1970, 1, 1));
```

The requireNonNullElseGet method only calls the supplier when the value is needed.

Functional interfaces that involve primitive types are a little cumbersone. Consider a function consuming an int and yielding an object of type T. You could use a Function<Integer, T>, but then the argument must be boxed in each call. Instead, there is a functional interface IntFunction<T>. Conversely, if a function has a return value of type int, the ToIntFunction<T> interface is more efficient than Function<T, Integer>. Finally, if both argument and return value are int, there is an IntUnaryOperator interface.

As the user of an API, you don't usually care about this subtlety. Consider the Arrays.setAll method. It sets all values of an array to the result of a function whose argument is the array index. Here, we set all elements to the square of the index:

```
var values = new int[100];
Arrays.setAll(values, i -> i * i); // [0, 1, 4, 9, 16, . . ., 9801]
```

There are overloaded versions of setAll for arrays of type int[], long[], double[], and a generic array T[]. Here, the int[] overload has as second parameter an IntUnaryOperator. But as the user of the method, you don't care. You just supply the lambda expression, which you can do without worrying about the difference between primitive types and their wrapper classes.

Caution: It is nice that a lambda expression can match primitive and wrapper types in a functional interface. But it is an error if both matches could occur. Consider a utility class that provides these methods:

```
public static int[] fill(int n, IntUnaryOperator op)
public static Object[] fill(int n, IntFunction<Object> op)
```

A call fill(n, i -> i * i) will not compile since it is ambiguous.

You can catch such problems in your API by compiling with the -Xlint or -Xlint:overloads flag.

6.2.5. Method References

Sometimes, a lambda expression involves a single method. For example, suppose you simply want to print the event object whenever a timer event occurs. Of course, you could call

```
var timer = new Timer(1000, event -> System.out.println(event));
```

It would be nicer if you could just pass the println method to the Timer constructor. Here is how you do that:

```
var timer = new Timer(1000, System.out::println);
```

The expression System.out::println is a *method reference*. It directs the compiler to produce an instance of a functional interface, overriding the single abstract method of the interface to call the given method. In this example, an ActionListener is produced whose actionPerformed(ActionEvent e) method calls System.out.println(e).

Note: Like a lambda expression, a method reference is not an object. It gives rise to an object when assigned to a variable whose type is a functional interface.

Note: There are ten overloaded println methods in the PrintStream class (of which System.out is an instance). The compiler needs to figure out which one to use, depending on context. In our example, the method reference System.out::println must be turned into an ActionListener instance with a method

```
void actionPerformed(ActionEvent e)
```

The println(Object x) method is selected from the ten overloaded println methods since Object is the best match for ActionEvent. When the actionPerformed method is called, the event object is printed.

Now suppose we assign the same method reference to a different functional interface:

```
Runnable task = System.out::println;
```

The Runnable functional interface has a single abstract method with no parameters

```
void run()
```

In this case, the println() method with no parameters is chosen. Calling task.run() prints a blank line to System.out.

As another example, suppose you want to sort strings regardless of letter case. You can pass this method expression:

```
Arrays.sort(strings, String::compareToIgnoreCase)
```

As you can see from these examples, the :: operator separates the method name from the name of an object or class. There are three variants:

1. *object*::*instanceMethod*
2. *Class*::*instanceMethod*
3. *Class*::*staticMethod*

In the first variant, the method reference is equivalent to a lambda expression whose parameters are passed to the method. In the case of `System.out::println`, the object is `System.out`, and the method expression is equivalent to `x -> System.out.println(x)`.

In the second variant, the first parameter becomes the implicit parameter of the method. For example, `String::compareToIgnoreCase` is the same as `(x, y) -> x.compareToIgnoreCase(y)`.

In the third variant, all parameters are passed to the static method: `Math::pow` is equivalent to `(x, y) -> Math.pow(x, y)`.

Table 6.1 walks you through additional examples.

Note that a lambda expression can only be rewritten as a method reference if the body of the lambda expression calls a single method and doesn't do anything else. Consider the lambda expression

```
s -> s.length() == 0
```

There is a single method call. But there is also a comparison, so you can't use a method reference here.

Table 6.1: Method Reference Examples

Method Reference	Equivalent Lambda Expression	Notes
`separator::equals`	`x -> separator.equals(x)`	This is a method expression with an *object* and an instance method. The lambda parameter is passed as the explicit parameter of the method.
`String::strip`	`x -> x.strip()`	This is a method expression with a *class* and an instance method. The lambda parameter becomes the implicit parameter.
`String::concat`	`(x, y) -> x.concat(y)`	Again, we have an instance method, but this time, with an explicit parameter. As before, the *first* lambda parameter becomes the implicit parameter, and the remaining ones are passed to the method.
`Integer.valueOf`	`x -> Integer.valueOf(x)`	This is a method expression with a *static* method. The lambda parameter is passed to the static method.

Method Reference	Equivalent Lambda Expression	Notes
`Integer.sum`	`(x, y) -> Integer.sum(x, y)`	This is another static method, but this time with two parameters. Both lambda parameters are passed to the static method. The `Integer.sum` method was specifically created to be used as a method reference. As a lambda, you could just write `(x, y) -> x + y`.
`String::new`	`x -> new String(x)`	This is a constructor reference—see Section 6.2.6. The lambda parameters are passed to the constructor.
`String[]::new`	`n -> new String[n]`	This is an array constructor reference—see Section 6.2.6. The lambda parameter is the array length.

Note: When there are multiple overloaded methods with the same name, the compiler will try to find from the context which one you mean. For example, there are two versions of the `Math.max` method, one for integers and one for `double` values. Which one gets picked depends on the method parameters of the functional interface to which `Math::max` is converted. Just like lambda expressions, method references don't live in isolation. They are always turned into instances of functional interfaces.

Note: Sometimes, the API contains methods that are specifically intended to be used as method references. For example, the `Objects` class has a method `isNull` to test whether an object reference is `null`. At first glance, this doesn't seem useful because the test `obj == null` is easier to read than `Objects.isNull(obj)`. But you can pass the method reference to any method with a `Predicate` parameter. For example, to remove all `null` references from a list, you can call

```
list.removeIf(Objects::isNull);
    // A bit easier to read than list.removeIf(e -> e == null);
```

Note: There is a tiny difference between a method reference with an object and its equivalent lambda expression. Consider a method reference such as `separator::equals`. If separator is `null`, forming `separator::equals` immediately throws a

NullPointerException. The lambda expression x -> separator.equals(x) only throws a NullPointerException if it is invoked.

You can capture the this parameter in a method reference. For example, this::equals is the same as x -> this.equals(x). It is also valid to use super. The method expression

    super::*instanceMethod*

uses this as the target and invokes the superclass version of the given method. Here is an artificial example that shows the mechanics:

```java
class Greeter
{
   public void greet(ActionEvent event)
   {
      System.out.println("Hello, the time is "
         + Instant.ofEpochMilli(event.getWhen()));
   }
}

class RepeatedGreeter extends Greeter
{
   public void greet(ActionEvent event)
   {
      var timer = new Timer(1000, super::greet);
      timer.start();
   }
}
```

When the RepeatedGreeter.greet method starts, a Timer is constructed that executes the super::greet method on every timer tick.

6.2.6. Constructor References

Constructor references are just like method references, except that the name of the method is new. For example, Person::new is a reference to a Person constructor. Which constructor? It depends on the context. Suppose you have a list of strings. Then you can turn it into an array of Person objects, by calling the constructor on each of the strings, with the following invocation:

```java
ArrayList<String> names = . . .;
Stream<Person> stream = names.stream().map(Person::new);
List<Person> people = stream.toList();
```

We will discuss the details of the stream, map, and toList methods in Chapter 1 of Volume II. For now, what's important is that the map method calls the Person(String) constructor for each list element. If there are multiple Person constructors, the compiler picks the one with a `String` parameter because it infers from the context that the constructor is called with a string.

You can form constructor references with array types. For example, `int[]::new` is a constructor reference with one parameter: the length of the array. It is equivalent to the lambda expression `n -> new int[n]`.

Array constructor references are useful to overcome a limitation of Java. As you will see in Chapter 8, it is not possible to construct an array of a generic type T. (The expression `new T[n]` is an error since it would be "erased" to `new Object[n]`). That is a problem for library authors. For example, suppose we want to have an array of `Person` objects. The `Stream` interface has a `toArray` method that returns an `Object` array:

```
Object[] people = stream.toArray();
```

But that is unsatisfactory. The user wants an array of references to `Person`, not references to `Object`. The stream library solves that problem with constructor references. Pass `Person[]::new` to the `toArray` method:

```
Person[] people = stream.toArray(Person[]::new);
```

The `toArray` method invokes this constructor to obtain an array of the correct type. Then it fills and returns the array.

Caution: Sometimes, it is surprising which overloaded variant is chosen when passing a method or constructor reference. Consider this code snippet:

```
var dates = new Date[100];
Arrays.setAll(dates, Date::new);
```

At first glance, it looks as if all elements would be set to the current date, by calling the no-argument constructor `new Date()` each time. But actually, the second parameter of `setAll` is an `IntFunction`, which receives the index of the element. Therefore, an entirely different constructor is invoked, `new Date(i)`, where i ranges from 0 to 99. That constructor sets the date to a given number of milliseconds from the "epoch," January 1, 1970.

6.2.7. Variable Scope

Often, you want to be able to access variables from an enclosing method or class in a lambda expression. Consider this example:

```
public static void repeatMessage(String text, int delay)
{
    ActionListener listener = event ->
```

```
        {
            System.out.println(text);
            Toolkit.getDefaultToolkit().beep();
        };
        new Timer(delay, listener).start();
}
```

Consider a call

```
repeatMessage("Hello", 1000); // prints Hello every 1,000 milliseconds
```

Now look at the variable text inside the lambda expression. Note that this variable is *not* defined in the lambda expression. Instead, it is a parameter variable of the repeatMessage method.

If you think about it, something nonobvious is going on here. The code of the lambda expression may run long after the call to repeatMessage has returned and the parameter variables are gone. How does the text variable stay around?

To understand what is happening, we need to refine our understanding of a lambda expression. A lambda expression has three ingredients:

1. A block of code
2. Parameters
3. Values for the *free* variables—that is, the variables that are not parameters and not defined inside the code

In our example, the lambda expression has one free variable, text. The data structure representing the lambda expression must store the values for the free variables—in our case, the string "Hello". We say that such values have been *captured* by the lambda expression. (It's an implementation detail how that is done. For example, one can translate a lambda expression into an object with a single method, so that the values of the free variables are copied into instance variables of that object.)

 Note: The technical term for a block of code together with the values of the free variables is a *closure*. If someone gloats that their language has closures, rest assured that Java has them as well. In Java, lambda expressions are closures.

As you have seen, a lambda expression can capture the value of a variable in the enclosing scope. In Java, to ensure that the captured value is well-defined, there is an important restriction. In a lambda expression, you can only reference variables whose value doesn't change. For example, the following is illegal:

```
public static void countDown(int start, int delay)
{
   ActionListener listener = event ->
      {
         start--; // ERROR: Can't mutate captured variable
         System.out.println(start);
      };
   new Timer(delay, listener).start();
}
```

There is a reason for this restriction. Mutating variables in a lambda expression is not safe when multiple actions are executed concurrently. This won't happen for the kinds of actions that we have seen so far, but in general, it is a serious problem. See Chapter 10 for more information on this important issue.

It is also illegal to refer, in a lambda expression, to a variable that is mutated outside. For example, the following is illegal:

```
public static void repeat(String text, int count)
{
   for (int i = 1; i <= count; i++)
   {
      ActionListener listener = event ->
         {
            System.out.println(i + ": " + text);
               // ERROR: Cannot refer to changing i
         };
      new Timer(1000, listener).start();
   }
}
```

The rule is that any captured variable in a lambda expression must be *effectively final*. An effectively final variable is a variable that is never assigned a new value after it has been initialized. In our case, text always refers to the same String object, and it is OK to capture it. However, the value of i is mutated, and therefore i cannot be captured.

The body of a lambda expression has *the same scope as a nested block*. The same rules for name conflicts and shadowing apply. It is illegal to declare a parameter or a local variable in the lambda that has the same name as a local variable.

```
Path first = Path.of("/usr/bin");
Comparator<String> comp =
   (first, second) -> first.length() - second.length();
   // ERROR: Variable first already defined
```

Inside a method, you can't have two local variables with the same name, and therefore, you can't introduce such variables in a lambda expression either.

When you use the `this` keyword in a lambda expression, you refer to the `this` parameter of the method that creates the lambda. For example, consider

```
public class Application
{
   public void init()
   {
      ActionListener listener = event ->
         {
            System.out.println(this.toString());
            . . .
         }
      . . .
   }
}
```

The expression `this.toString()` calls the `toString` method of the `Application` object, *not* the `ActionListener` instance. There is nothing special about the use of `this` in a lambda expression. The scope of the lambda expression is nested inside the `init` method, and `this` has the same meaning anywhere in that method.

6.2.8. Processing Lambda Expressions

Up to now, you have seen how to produce lambda expressions and pass them to a method that expects a functional interface. Now let us see how to write methods that can consume lambda expressions.

The point of using lambdas is *deferred execution*. After all, if you wanted to execute some code right now, you'd do that, without wrapping it inside a lambda. There are many reasons for executing code later, such as:

- Running the code in a separate thread
- Running the code multiple times
- Running the code at the right point in an algorithm (for example, the comparison operation in sorting)
- Running the code when something happens (a button was clicked, data has arrived, and so on)
- Running the code only when necessary

Let's look at a simple example. Suppose you want to repeat an action n times. The action and the count are passed to a `repeat` method:

```
repeat(10, () -> System.out.println("Hello, World!"));
```

To accept the lambda, we need to pick (or, in rare cases, provide) a functional interface. Table 6.2 lists the most important functional interfaces that are provided in the Java API. In this case, we can use the `Runnable` interface:

```
public static void repeat(int n, Runnable action)
{
   for (int i = 0; i < n; i++) action.run();
}
```

Note that the body of the lambda expression is executed when action.run() is called.

Now let's make this example a bit more sophisticated. We want to tell the action in which iteration it occurs. For that, we need to pick a functional interface that has a method with an int parameter and a void return. The standard interface for processing int values is

```
public interface IntConsumer
{
   void accept(int value);
}
```

Here is the improved version of the repeat method:

```
public static void repeat(int n, IntConsumer action)
{
   for (int i = 0; i < n; i++) action.accept(i);
}
```

And here is how you call it:

```
repeat(10, i -> System.out.println("Countdown: " + (9 - i)));
```

Table 6.2: Common Functional Interfaces

Functional Interface	Parameter Types	Return Type	Abstract Method Name	Description	Other Methods
Runnable	none	void	run	Runs an action without parameters or return value	
Supplier\<T\>	none	T	get	Supplies a value of type T	
Consumer\<T\>	T	void	accept	Consumes a value of type T	andThen

Functional Interface	Parameter Types	Return Type	Abstract Method Name	Description	Other Methods
BiConsumer<T, U>	T, U	void	accept	Consumes values of types T and U	andThen
Function<T, R>	T	R	apply	A function with parameter of type T	compose, andThen, identity
BiFunction<T, U, R>	T, U	R	apply	A function with parameters of types T and U	andThen
UnaryOperator<T>	T	T	apply	A unary operator on the type T	compose, andThen, identity
BinaryOperator<T>	T, T	T	apply	A binary operator on the type T	andThen, maxBy, minBy
Predicate<T>	T	boolean	test	A boolean-valued function	and, or, negate, isEqual, not
BiPredicate<T, U>	T, U	boolean	test	A boolean-valued function with two parameters	and, or, negate

Table 6.3 lists the 34 available specializations for primitive types int, long, and double. As you will see in Chapter 8, it is more efficient to use these specializations than the generic interfaces. For that reason, I used an IntConsumer instead of a Consumer<Integer> in the example of the preceding section.

Table 6.3: Functional Interfaces for Primitive Types
p, q is int, long, double; *P, Q* is Int, Long, Double

Functional Interface	Parameter Types	Return Type	Abstract Method Name
BooleanSupplier	none	boolean	getAsBoolean
*P*Supplier	none	*p*	getAs*P*
*P*Consumer	*p*	void	accept
Obj*P*Consumer\<T>	T, *p*	void	accept
*P*Function\<T>	*p*	T	apply
*P*To*Q*Function	*p*	*q*	applyAs*Q*
To*P*Function\<T>	T	*p*	applyAs*P*
To*P*BiFunction\<T, U>	T, U	*p*	applyAs*P*
*P*UnaryOperator	*p*	*p*	applyAs*P*
*P*BinaryOperator	*p, p*	*p*	applyAs*P*
*P*Predicate	*p*	boolean	test

Tip: Use the standard interfaces for function types whenever you can. For example, suppose you write a method to process files that match a certain criterion. There is a legacy interface java.io.FileFilter. But if you use the standard Predicate\<File> interface, you can take advantage of methods for creating, adapting, and combining predicates. The only reason not to do so would be if you already have many useful methods producing FileFilter instances.

Note: Most of the standard functional interfaces have nonabstract methods for producing or combining functions. For example, Predicate.isEqual(a) is the same as a::equals, but it also works if a is null. There are default methods and, or, negate for combining predicates. For example, Predicate.isEqual(a).or(Predicate.isEqual(b)) is the same as x -> a.equals(x) || b.equals(x).

Note: If you design your own interface with a single abstract method, you can tag it with the @FunctionalInterface annotation. This has two advantages. The compiler gives an error message if you accidentally add another abstract method. And the javadoc page includes a statement that your interface is a functional interface.

It is not required to use the annotation. Any interface with a single abstract method is, by definition, a functional interface. But using the @FunctionalInterface annotation is a good idea.

Note: Some programmers love chains of method calls, such as

```
String input = " 6189700196426901374449562111 ";
boolean isPrime = input.strip().transform(BigInteger::new).isProbablePrime(20);
```

The transform method of the String class (added in Java 12) applies a Function to the string and yields the result. You could have equally well written

```
boolean prime = new BigInteger(input.strip()).isProbablePrime(20);
```

But then your eyes jump inside-out and left-to-right to find out what happens first and what happens next: Calling strip, then constructing the BigInteger, and finally testing if it is a probable prime.

I am not sure that the eyes-jumping-inside-out-and-left-to-right is a huge problem. But if you prefer the orderly left-to-right sequence of chained method calls, then transform is your friend.

Sadly, it only works for strings. Why isn't there a transform(java.util.function.Function) method in the Object class?

The Java API designers weren't fast enough. They had one chance to do this right—in Java 8, when the java.util.function.Function interface was added to the API. Up to that point, nobody could have added a transform(java.util.function.Function) method to their own classes. But in Java 12, it was too late. Someone somewhere could have defined transform(java.util.function.Function) in their class, with a different meaning. Admittedly, it is unlikely that this ever happened, but there is no way to know.

That is how Java works. It takes its commitments seriously, and won't renege on them for convenience.

6.2.9. Creating Comparators

The Comparator interface has a number of convenient static methods for creating comparators. These methods are intended to be used with lambda expressions or method references.

The static comparing method takes a "key extractor" function that maps a type T to a comparable type (such as String). The function is applied to the objects to be compared, and the comparison is then made on the returned keys. For example, suppose you have an array of Person objects. Here is how you can sort them by name:

```
Arrays.sort(people, Comparator.comparing(Person::getName));
```

This is certainly much easier than implementing a Comparator by hand. Moreover, the code is clearer since it is obvious that we want to compare people by name.

You can chain comparators with the thenComparing method for breaking ties. For example,

```
Arrays.sort(people,
    Comparator.comparing(Person::getLastName)
        .thenComparing(Person::getFirstName));
```

If two people have the same last name, then the second comparator is used.

There are a few variations of these methods. You can specify a comparator to be used for the keys that the comparing and thenComparing methods extract. For example, here we sort people by the length of their names:

```
Arrays.sort(people, Comparator.comparing(Person::getName,
    (s, t) -> Integer.compare(s.length(), t.length())));
```

Moreover, both the comparing and thenComparing methods have variants that avoid boxing of int, long, or double values:

```
Arrays.sort(people, Comparator.comparing(Person::getName,
    Comparator.comparingInt(String::length)))
```

A shorter but perhaps less elegant way of producing the preceding operation would be:

```
Arrays.sort(people, Comparator.comparingInt(p -> p.getName().length()));
```

If your key function can return null, you will like the nullsFirst and nullsLast adapters. These static methods take an existing comparator and modify it so that it doesn't throw an exception when encountering null values but ranks them as smaller or larger than regular values. For example, suppose getMiddleName returns a null when a person has no middle name. Then you can use Comparator.comparing(Person::getMiddleName, Comparator.nullsFirst(. . .)).

The nullsFirst method needs a comparator—in this case, one that compares two strings. The naturalOrder method makes a comparator for any class implementing Comparable. A Comparator.<String>naturalOrder() is what we need. (See Chapter 8 for an explanation of this syntax. Fortunately, the generic type can usually be inferred.) Here is the complete call for sorting by potentially null middle names. I use a static import of `java.util.Comparator.*`, to make the expression more legible.

```
Arrays.sort(people, comparing(Person::getMiddleName, nullsFirst(naturalOrder())));
```

The static `reverseOrder` method gives the reverse of the natural order. To reverse any comparator, use the `reversed` instance method. For example, `naturalOrder().reversed()` is the same as `reverseOrder()`.

6.3. Inner Classes

An *inner class* is a class that is defined inside another class. Why would you want to do that? There are two reasons:

- Inner classes can be hidden from other classes in the same package.
- Inner class methods can access the data from the scope in which they are defined—including the data that would otherwise be private.

Inner classes used to be very important for concisely implementing callbacks, but nowadays lambda expressions do a much better job. Still, inner classes can be very useful for structuring your code. The following sections walk you through all the details.

 C++ Note: C++ has *nested classes*. A nested class is contained inside the scope of the enclosing class. Here is a typical example: A linked list class defines a nested class to hold the nodes.

```
template<typename T>
class LinkedList
{
public:
    class Node // a nested class
    {
    public:
        . . .
    private:
        T data;
        Node* next;
    };
    . . .
private:
    Node* head;
    Node* tail;
};
```

Nested classes are similar to inner classes in Java. However, the Java inner classes have an additional feature that makes them richer and more useful than nested classes in C++. An object that comes from an inner class has an implicit reference to the outer class object that instantiated it. Through this pointer, it gains access to the total state of the outer object. For example, in Java, the Iterator class would not need an explicit pointer to the LinkedList into which it points.

In Java, nested classes that are declared as static do not have this added pointer. They are the Java analog to nested classes in C++.

6.3.1. Use of an Inner Class to Access Object State

The syntax for inner classes is rather complex. For that reason, I present a simple but somewhat artificial example to demonstrate the use of inner classes. Let's refactor the TimerTest example and extract a TalkingClock class. The constructor for a talking clock has two parameters: the interval between announcements and a flag to turn beeps on or off.

```java
public class TalkingClock
{
    private int interval;
    private boolean beep;

    public TalkingClock(int interval, boolean beep) { . . . }
    public void start() { . . . }

    public class TimePrinter implements ActionListener
        // an inner class
    {
        . . .
    }
}
```

Note that the TimePrinter class is now located inside the TalkingClock class. This does *not* mean that every TalkingClock has a TimePrinter instance field. As you will see, the TimePrinter objects are constructed by methods of the TalkingClock class.

Here is the TimePrinter class in greater detail. Note that the actionPerformed method checks the beep flag before emitting a beep.

```java
public class TimePrinter implements ActionListener
{
    public void actionPerformed(ActionEvent event)
    {
        System.out.println("At the tone, the time is "
            + Instant.ofEpochMilli(event.getWhen()));
```

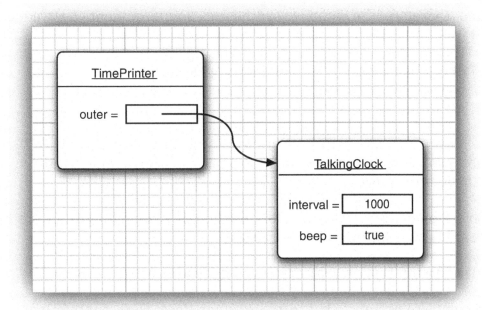

Figure 6.3: An inner class object has a reference to an outer class object.

```
        if (beep) Toolkit.getDefaultToolkit().beep();
    }
}
```

Something surprising is going on. The TimePrinter class has no instance field or variable named beep. Instead, beep refers to the field of the TalkingClock object that created this TimePrinter. As you can see, an inner class method gets to access both its own instance fields *and* those of the outer object creating it.

For this to work, an object of an inner class always gets an implicit reference to the object that created it (see Figure 6.3).

This reference is invisible in the definition of the inner class. However, to illuminate the concept, let us call the reference to the outer object *outer*. Then the actionPerformed method is equivalent to the following:

```
public void actionPerformed(ActionEvent event)
{
    System.out.println("At the tone, the time is "
        + Instant.ofEpochMilli(event.getWhen())));
    if (outer.beep) Toolkit.getDefaultToolkit().beep();
}
```

The outer class reference is set in the constructor. The compiler modifies all inner class constructors, adding a parameter for the outer class reference. The TimePrinter class defines no constructors; therefore, the compiler synthesizes a no-argument constructor, generating code like this:

```
public TimePrinter(TalkingClock clock) // automatically generated code
{
    outer = clock;
}
```

Again, please note that *outer* is not a Java keyword. We just use it to illustrate the mechanism involved in an inner class.

When a TimePrinter object is constructed in the start method, the compiler passes the this reference to the current talking clock into the constructor:

```
var listener = new TimePrinter(this); // parameter automatically added
```

Listing 6.7 shows the complete program that tests the inner class. Have another look at the access control. Had the TimePrinter class been a regular class, it would have needed to access the beep flag through a public method of the TalkingClock class. Using an inner class is an improvement. There is no need to provide accessors that are of interest only to one other class.

 Note: We could have declared the TimePrinter class as private. Then only TalkingClock methods would be able to construct TimePrinter objects. Only inner classes can be private. Regular classes always have either package or public access.

Listing 6.7 innerClass/InnerClassTest.java

```
 1  package innerClass;
 2
 3  import java.awt.*;
 4  import java.awt.event.*;
 5  import java.time.*;
 6
 7  import javax.swing.*;
 8
 9  /**
10   * This program demonstrates the use of inner classes.
11   * @version 1.11 2017-12-14
12   * @author Cay Horstmann
13   */
14  public class InnerClassTest
15  {
16     public static void main(String[] args)
17     {
```

```java
18          var clock = new TalkingClock(1000, true);
19          clock.start();
20
21          // keep program running until the user selects "OK"
22          JOptionPane.showMessageDialog(null, "Quit program?");
23          System.exit(0);
24      }
25  }
26
27  /**
28   * A clock that prints the time in regular intervals.
29   */
30  class TalkingClock
31  {
32      private int interval;
33      private boolean beep;
34
35      /**
36       * Constructs a talking clock.
37       * @param interval the interval between messages (in milliseconds)
38       * @param beep true if the clock should beep
39       */
40      public TalkingClock(int interval, boolean beep)
41      {
42          this.interval = interval;
43          this.beep = beep;
44      }
45
46      /**
47       * Starts the clock.
48       */
49      public void start()
50      {
51          var listener = new TimePrinter();
52          var timer = new Timer(interval, listener);
53          timer.start();
54      }
55
56      public class TimePrinter implements ActionListener
57      {
58          public void actionPerformed(ActionEvent event)
59          {
60              System.out.println("At the tone, the time is "
61                  + Instant.ofEpochMilli(event.getWhen()));
62              if (beep) Toolkit.getDefaultToolkit().beep();
63          }
64      }
65  }
```

6.3.2. Special Syntax Rules for Inner Classes

In the preceding section, we explained the outer class reference of an inner class by calling it *outer*. Actually, the proper syntax for the outer reference is a bit more complex. The expression

OuterClass.this

denotes the outer class reference. For example, you can write the actionPerformed method of the TimePrinter inner class as

```java
public void actionPerformed(ActionEvent event)
{
   . . .
   if (TalkingClock.this.beep) Toolkit.getDefaultToolkit().beep();
}
```

Conversely, you can write the inner object constructor more explicitly, using the syntax

outerObject.new *InnerClass*(*construction arguments*)

For example:

```java
ActionListener listener = this.new TimePrinter();
```

Here, the outer class reference of the newly constructed TimePrinter object is set to the this reference of the method that creates the inner class object. This is the most common case. As always, the this. qualifier is redundant. However, it is also possible to set the outer class reference to another object by explicitly naming it. For example, since TimePrinter is a public inner class, you can construct a TimePrinter for any talking clock:

```java
var jabberer = new TalkingClock(1000, true);
TalkingClock.TimePrinter listener = jabberer.new TimePrinter();
```

Note that you refer to an inner class as

OuterClass.*InnerClass*

when it occurs outside the scope of the outer class.

 Note: As of Java 16, inner classes can have static members. Previously, static methods in inner classes were disallowed, and static fields declared in an inner class had to be final and initialized with a compile-time constant.

Static methods of an inner class can access static fields and methods from the inner class or enclosing classes.

6.3.3. Are Inner Classes Useful? Actually Necessary? Secure?

When inner classes were added to the Java language in Java 1.1, many programmers considered them a major new feature that was out of character with the Java philosophy of being simpler than C++. The inner class syntax is undeniably complex. (It gets more complex as we study anonymous inner classes later in this chapter.) It is not obvious how inner classes interact with other features of the language, such as access control and security.

Inner classes are translated into regular class files with $ (dollar signs) separating the outer and inner class names. For example, the TimePrinter class inside the TalkingClock class is translated to a class file TalkingClock$TimePrinter.class. To see this at work, try the following experiment: run the ReflectionTest program of Chapter 5, and give it the class TalkingClock$TimePrinter to reflect upon. Alternatively, simply use the javap utility:

```
javap -private ClassName
```

 Note: If you use UNIX, remember to escape the $ character when you supply the class name on the command line. That is, run the ReflectionTest or javap program as

```
java --classpath .:../v1ch05 reflection.ReflectionTest \
    innerClass.TalkingClock\$TimePrinter
```

or

```
javap -private innerClass.TalkingClock\$TimePrinter
```

You will get the following printout:

```
public class innerClass.TalkingClock$TimePrinter
    implements java.awt.event.ActionListener
{
    final innerClass.TalkingClock this$0;
    public innerClass.TalkingClock$TimePrinter(innerClass.TalkingClock);
    public void actionPerformed(java.awt.event.ActionEvent);
}
```

You can plainly see that the compiler has generated an additional instance field, this$0, for the reference to the outer class. (The name this$0 is synthesized by the compiler—you cannot refer to it in your code.) You can also see the TalkingClock parameter for the constructor.

Note: Since Java 18, the this$0 field is only provided when it is actually needed. It is dropped if no methods of the inner class access the outer class.

If the compiler can automatically do this transformation, couldn't you simply program the same mechanism by hand? Let's try it. We would make TimePrinter a regular class, outside the TalkingClock class. When constructing a TimePrinter object, we pass it the this reference of the object that is creating it.

```
class TalkingClock
{
   . . .
   public void start()
   {
      var listener = new TimePrinter(this);
      var timer = new Timer(interval, listener);
      timer.start();
   }
}

class TimePrinter implements ActionListener
{
   private TalkingClock outer;
   . . .
   public TimePrinter(TalkingClock clock)
   {
      outer = clock;
   }
}
```

Now let us look at the actionPerformed method. It needs to access outer.beep.

```
if (outer.beep) . . . // ERROR
```

Here we run into a problem. The inner class can access the private data of the outer class, but our external TimePrinter class cannot.

Thus, inner classes are genuinely more powerful than regular classes because they have more access privileges.

6.3.4. Local Inner Classes

If you look carefully at the code of the TalkingClock example, you will find that you need the name of the type TimePrinter only once: when you create an object of that type in the start method.

In a situation like this, you can define the class *locally in a single method*.

```
public void start()
{
   class TimePrinter implements ActionListener
   {
      public void actionPerformed(ActionEvent event)
      {
         System.out.println("At the tone, the time is "
            + Instant.ofEpochMilli(event.getWhen()));
         if (beep) Toolkit.getDefaultToolkit().beep();
      }
   }

   var listener = new TimePrinter();
   var timer = new Timer(interval, listener);
   timer.start();
}
```

Local classes are never declared with an access specifier (that is, public or private). Their scope is always restricted to the block in which they are declared.

Local classes have one great advantage: They are completely hidden from the outside world—not even other code in the TalkingClock class can access them. No method except start has any knowledge of the TimePrinter class.

6.3.5. Accessing Variables from Outer Methods

Local classes have another advantage over other inner classes. Not only can they access the fields of their outer classes; they can even access local variables! However, those local variables must be *effectively* final. That means, they may never change once they have been assigned.

Here is a typical example. Let's move the interval and beep parameters from the TalkingClock constructor to the start method.

```
public void start(int interval, boolean beep)
{
   class TimePrinter implements ActionListener
   {
      public void actionPerformed(ActionEvent event)
      {
         System.out.println("At the tone, the time is "
            + Instant.ofEpochMilli(event.getWhen()));
         if (beep) Toolkit.getDefaultToolkit().beep();
      }
   }
```

```
    var listener = new TimePrinter();
    var timer = new Timer(interval, listener);
    timer.start();
}
```

Note that the TalkingClock class no longer needs to store a beep instance field. It simply refers to the beep parameter variable of the start method.

Maybe this should not be so surprising. The line

```
if (beep) . . .
```

is, after all, ultimately inside the start method, so why shouldn't it have access to the value of the beep variable?

To see why there is a subtle issue here, let's consider the flow of control more closely.

1. The start method is called.
2. The object variable listener is initialized by a call to the constructor of the inner class TimePrinter.
3. The listener reference is passed to the Timer constructor, the timer is started, and the start method exits. At this point, the beep parameter variable of the start method no longer exists.
4. A second later, the actionPerformed method executes if (beep) . . .

For the code in the actionPerformed method to work, the TimePrinter class must have copied the beep field as a local variable of the start method, before the beep parameter value went away. That is indeed exactly what happens. In our example, the compiler synthesizes the name TalkingClock$1TimePrinter for the local inner class. If you use the ReflectionTest program or the javap utility again to spy on the TalkingClock$1TimePrinter class, you will get the following output:

```
class TalkingClock$1TimePrinter
{
    TalkingClock$1TimePrinter();

    public void actionPerformed(java.awt.event.ActionEvent);

    final boolean val$beep;
    final TalkingClock this$0;
}
```

When an object is created, the current value of the beep variable is stored in the val$beep field. As of Java 11, this happens with "nest mate" access. Previously, the inner class constructor had an additional parameter to set the field. Either way, the inner class field persists even if the local variable goes out of scope.

6.3.6. Anonymous Inner Classes

When using local inner classes, you can often go a step further. If you want to make only a single object of this class, you don't even need to give the class a name. Such a class is called an *anonymous inner class*.

```
public void start(int interval, boolean beep)
{
   var listener = new ActionListener()
      {
         public void actionPerformed(ActionEvent event)
         {
            System.out.println("At the tone, the time is "
               + Instant.ofEpochMilli(event.getWhen()));
            if (beep) Toolkit.getDefaultToolkit().beep();
         }
      };
   var timer = new Timer(interval, listener);
   timer.start();
}
```

This syntax is very cryptic indeed. What it means is this: Create a new object of a class that implements the ActionListener interface, where the required method actionPerformed is the one defined inside the braces { }.

In general, the syntax is

```
new SuperType(construction arguments)
   {
      inner class methods and data
   }
```

Here, *SuperType* can be an interface, such as ActionListener; then, the inner class implements that interface. *SuperType* can also be a class; then, the inner class extends that class.

An anonymous inner class cannot have constructors because the name of a constructor must be the same as the name of a class, and the class has no name. Instead, the construction arguments are given to the *superclass* constructor. In particular, whenever an inner class implements an interface, it cannot have any construction arguments. Nevertheless, you must supply a set of parentheses as in

```
new InterfaceType()
   {
      methods and data
   }
```

You have to look carefully to see the difference between the construction of a new object of a class and the construction of an object of an anonymous inner class extending that class.

```
var queen = new Person("Mary");
    // a Person object
var count = new Person("Dracula") { . . . };
    // an object of an inner class extending Person
```

If the closing parenthesis of the construction argument list is followed by an opening brace, then an anonymous inner class is being defined.

Note: Even though an anonymous class cannot have constructors, you can provide an object initialization block:

```
var count = new Person("Dracula")
   {
       { initialization }
       . . .
   };
```

Listing 6.8 contains the complete source code for the talking clock program with an anonymous inner class. If you compare this program with Listing 6.7, you will see that in this case, the solution with the anonymous inner class is quite a bit shorter and, hopefully, with some practice, as easy to comprehend.

For many years, Java programmers routinely used anonymous inner classes for event listeners and other callbacks. Nowadays, you are better off using a lambda expression. For example, the start method from the beginning of this section can be written much more concisely with a lambda expression like this:

```
public void start(int interval, boolean beep)
{
   var timer = new Timer(interval, event ->
      {
          System.out.println( "At the tone, the time is "
             + Instant.ofEpochMilli(event.getWhen()));
          if (beep) Toolkit.getDefaultToolkit().beep();
      });
   timer.start();
}
```

Note: If you store an anonymous class instance in a variable defined with var, the variable knows about added methods or fields:

```
var bob = new Object() { String name = "Bob"; }
System.out.println(bob.name);
```

If you declare bob as having type Object, then bob.name does not compile.

The object constructed with new Object() { String name = "Bob"; } has type "Object with a Sting name field." This is a *nondenotable* type—a type that you cannot express with Java syntax. Nevertheless, the compiler understands the type, and it can set it as the type for the bob variable.

Note: The following trick, called *double brace initialization*, takes advantage of the inner class syntax. Suppose you want to construct an array list and pass it to a method:

```
var friends = new ArrayList<String>();
friends.add("Harry");
friends.add("Tony");
invite(friends);
```

If you don't need the array list again, it would be nice to make it anonymous. But then how can you add the elements? Here is how:

```
invite(new ArrayList<String>() {{ add("Harry"); add("Tony"); }});
```

Note the double braces. The outer braces make an anonymous subclass of ArrayList. The inner braces are an object initialization block (see Chapter 4).

In practice, this trick is rarely useful. More likely than not, the invite method is willing to accept any List<String>, and you can simply pass List.of("Harry", "Tony").

Caution: It is often convenient to make an anonymous subclass that is almost, but not quite, like its superclass. But you need to be careful with the equals method. In Chapter 5, I recommended that your equals methods use a test

```
if (getClass() != other.getClass()) return false;
```

An anonymous subclass will fail this test.

Tip: When you produce logging or debugging messages, you often want to include the name of the current class, such as

```
System.err.println("Something awful happened in " + getClass());
```

But that fails in a static method. After all, the call to getClass calls this.getClass(), and a static method has no this. Use the following expression instead:

```
new Object(){}.getClass().getEnclosingClass() // gets class of static method
```

Here, new Object(){} makes an anonymous object of an anonymous subclass of Object, and getEnclosingClass gets its enclosing class—that is, the class containing the static method.

Listing 6.8 anonymousInnerClass/AnonymousInnerClassTest.java

```java
 1  package anonymousInnerClass;
 2
 3  import java.awt.*;
 4  import java.awt.event.*;
 5  import java.time.*;
 6
 7  import javax.swing.*;
 8
 9  /**
10   * This program demonstrates anonymous inner classes.
11   * @version 1.12 2017-12-14
12   * @author Cay Horstmann
13   */
14  public class AnonymousInnerClassTest
15  {
16     public static void main(String[] args)
17     {
18        var clock = new TalkingClock();
19        clock.start(1000, true);
20
21        // keep program running until the user selects "OK"
22        JOptionPane.showMessageDialog(null, "Quit program?");
23        System.exit(0);
24     }
25  }
26
27  /**
28   * A clock that prints the time in regular intervals.
29   */
30  class TalkingClock
31  {
32     /**
33      * Starts the clock.
34      * @param interval the interval between messages (in milliseconds)
35      * @param beep true if the clock should beep
36      */
37     public void start(int interval, boolean beep)
```

```
38      {
39          var listener = new ActionListener()
40             {
41                 public void actionPerformed(ActionEvent event)
42                 {
43                     System.out.println("At the tone, the time is "
44                         + Instant.ofEpochMilli(event.getWhen()));
45                     if (beep) Toolkit.getDefaultToolkit().beep();
46                 }
47             };
48          var timer = new Timer(interval, listener);
49          timer.start();
50      }
51  }
```

6.3.7. Static Classes

Occasionally, you may want to nest one class inside another, but you don't need the nested class to have a reference to the outer class object. You can suppress the generation of that reference by declaring the nested class static.

The Java Language Specification uses the term "nested class" for any class that is declared inside another class or interface, "static class" for a (necessarily nested) static class, and "inner class" for a nested class that is not static.

Here is a typical example of where you would want to do this. In an ArrayAlg class, we have a task that finds a range of elements of an array. Then you need to return the start and the end of the range. We can achieve that by defining a class Range that holds two values:

```
class Range
{
    private int from;
    private int to;

    public Range(int from) { . . . }
    public void extend() { . . . }
    . . .
}
```

Of course, Range is an exceedingly common name, and in a large project, it is quite possible that some other programmer had the same bright idea and defined another Range class in the same package. We can solve this potential name clash by making Range a public inner class inside ArrayAlg. Then the class will be known to the public as ArrayAlg.Range:

ArrayAlg.Range r = ArrayAlg.longestRun(numbers);

However, unlike the inner classes used in previous examples, we do not want to have a reference to any other object inside a Range object. That reference can be suppressed by declaring the nested class static:

```
class ArrayAlg
{
    public static class Range
    {
        . . .
    }
    . . .
}
```

A static class is exactly like an inner class, except that an object of a static class does not have a reference to the outer class object that generated it. In our example, we must use a static class because the nested class instance is constructed inside a static method:

```
public static Pair longestRun(double[] values)
{
    . . .
    Range current = new Range(. . .);
    . . .
    if (. . .) longest = current;
    . . .
    return longest;
}
```

Had the Range class not been declared as static, the compiler would have flagged the constructor call as an error. After all, there is no implicit object of type ArrayAlg available to initialize the inner class instance.

You should use a static class whenever a nested class does not need to access an outer class object.

Here, I purposefully made the Range class mutable. It might be better to make the Range class immutable, and to declare it as a record. A record is automatically static.

 Note: Just like records, interfaces and enumerations that are declared inside a class or interface are automatically static.

In fact,

Note: Classes that are declared inside an interface are automatically static and public.

 Note: Prior to Java 16, it was not possible to declare a static class inside an inner class. This restriction has now been removed.

Listing 6.9 contains the complete source code of the ArrayAlg class and the nested Pair class.

Listing 6.9 `staticInnerClass/StaticInnerClassTest.java`

```java
package staticInnerClass;

/**
 * This program demonstrates the use of static inner classes.
 * @version 1.1 2023-12-19
 * @author Cay Horstmann
 */
public class StaticInnerClassTest
{
   public static void main(String[] args)
   {
      double[] numbers = { 1, 2, 2, 3, 3, 3, 4, 4, 4, 4, 5, 5, 5, 5, 5, 6, 6, 6, 6 };
      ArrayAlg.Range r = ArrayAlg.longestRun(numbers);
      System.out.println("from = " + r.getFrom());
      System.out.println("to = " + r.getTo());
   }
}

class ArrayAlg
{
   /**
    * A range of index values.
    */
   public static class Range
   {
      private int from;
      private int to;

      /**
       * Constructs a range of length 1.
       * @param from the initial index value of this range
       */
      public Range(int from)
      {
         this.from = from;
```

```
36             this.to = from + 1;
37         }
38
39         /**
40          * Extends this range by one element.
41          */
42         public void extend()
43         {
44             this.to++;
45         }
46
47         /**
48          * Gets the starting index value of this range.
49          * @return the starting index
50          */
51         public int getFrom()
52         {
53             return from;
54         }
55
56         /**
57          * Gets the first index past the end of this range.
58          * @return the past-the-end index
59          */
60         public int getTo()
61         {
62             return to;
63         }
64
65         /**
66          * Returns the number of elements in this range.
67          * @return the number of elements
68          */
69         public int length()
70         {
71             return to - from;
72         }
73     }
74
75     /**
76      * A "run" is a sequence of repeating adjacent elements. For example, in the array
77      * 1 2 3 3 3 4 4, the runs are (trivially) 1 and 2, and 3 3 3 and 4 4.
78      * Returns the range of the longest run.
79      * @param values an array of length at least 1
80      * @return the range of the longest run
81      */
82     public static Range longestRun(double[] values)
83     {
84         Range longest = new Range(0);
85         Range current = new Range(0);
86         for (int i = 1; i < values.length; i++)
87         {
```

```
88              if (values[i] == values[i - 1]) current.extend();
89              else
90              {
91                 if (longest.length() < current.length()) longest = current;
92                 current = new Range(i);
93              }
94           }
95           if (longest.length() < current.length()) longest = current;
96           return longest;
97       }
98    }
```

6.4. Service Loaders

Sometimes, you develop an application with a service architecture. There are platforms that encourage this approach, such as OSGi (https://osgi.org), which are used in development environments, application servers, and other complex applications. Such platforms go well beyond the scope of this book, but the JDK also offers a simple mechanism for loading services, described here. This mechanism is well supported by the Java Platform Module System—see Chapter 12.

Often, when providing a service, a program wants to give the service designer some freedom of how to implement the service's features. It can also be desirable to have multiple implementations to choose from. The ServiceLoader class makes it easy to load services that conform to a common interface.

Define an interface (or, if you prefer, a superclass) with the methods that each instance of the service should provide. For example, suppose your service provides encryption.

```
package serviceLoader;

public interface Cipher
{
   byte[] encrypt(byte[] source, byte[] key);
   byte[] decrypt(byte[] source, byte[] key);
   int strength();
}
```

The service provider supplies one or more classes that implement this service, for example

```
package serviceLoader.impl;

public class CaesarCipher implements Cipher
{
   public byte[] encrypt(byte[] source, byte[] key)
   {
      var result = new byte[source.length];
```

```
        for (int i = 0; i < source.length; i++)
            result[i] = (byte)(source[i] + key[0]);
        return result;
    }

    public byte[] decrypt(byte[] source, byte[] key)
    {
        return encrypt(source, new byte[] { (byte) -key[0] });
    }

    public int strength() { return 1; }
}
```

The implementing classes can be in any package, not necessarily the same package as the service interface. Each of them must have a no-argument constructor.

Now add the names of the classes to a UTF-8 encoded text file in the META-INF/services directory whose name matches the fully qualified interface name. In our example, the file META-INF/services/serviceLoader.Cipher would contain the line

```
    serviceLoader.impl.CaesarCipher
```

In this example, we provide a single implementing class. You could also provide multiple classes and later pick among them.

With this preparation done, the program initializes a service loader as follows:

```
    public static ServiceLoader<Cipher> cipherLoader = ServiceLoader.load(Cipher.class);
```

This should be done just once in the program.

The iterator method of the service loader returns an iterator through all provided implementations of the service. (See Chapter 9 for more information about iterators.) It is easiest to use an enhanced for loop to traverse them. In the loop, pick an appropriate object to carry out the service.

```
    public static Cipher getCipher(int minStrength)
    {
        for (Cipher cipher : cipherLoader) // implicitly calls cipherLoader.iterator()
        {
            if (cipher.strength() >= minStrength) return cipher;
        }
        return null;
    }
```

Alternatively, you can use streams (see Chapter 1 of Volume II) to locate the desired service. The stream method yields a stream of ServiceLoader.Provider instances. That interface has methods type and get for getting the provider class and the provider instance. If you select a provider by type, then you just call type and no service instances are unnecessarily instantiated.

```
public static Optional<Cipher> getCipher2(int minStrength)
{
   return cipherLoader.stream()
      .filter(descr -> descr.type() == serviceLoader.impl.CaesarCipher.class)
      .findFirst()
      .map(ServiceLoader.Provider::get);
}
```

Finally, if you are willing to take any service instance, simply call findFirst:

```
Optional<Cipher> cipher = cipherLoader.findFirst();
```

The Optional class is explained in Chapter 1 of Volume II.

---

java.util.ServiceLoader<S>   1.6

- static <S> ServiceLoader<S> load(Class<S> service)
  creates a service loader for loading the classes that implement the given service interface.
- Iterator<S> iterator()
  yields an iterator that lazily loads the service classes. That is, a class is loaded whenever the iterator advances.
- Stream<ServiceLoader.Provider<S>> stream()   9
  returns a stream of provider descriptors, so that a provider of a desired class can be loaded lazily.
- Optional<S> findFirst()   9
  finds the first available service provider, if any.

---

java.util.ServiceLoader.Provider<S>   9

- Class<? extends S> type()
  gets the type of this provider.
- S get()
  gets an instance of this provider.

6.5. Proxies

In the final section of this chapter, we discuss *proxies*. You can use a proxy to create, at runtime, new classes that implement a given set of interfaces. Proxies are only necessary when you don't yet know at compile time which interfaces you need to implement. This is not a common situation for application programmers, so feel free to skip this section if you are not interested in advanced wizardry. However, for certain systems programming applications, the flexibility that proxies offer can be very important.

6.5.1. When to Use Proxies

Suppose you want to construct an object of a class that implements one or more interfaces whose exact nature you may not know at compile time. This is a difficult problem. To construct an actual class, you can simply use the newInstance method or use reflection to find a constructor. But you can't instantiate an interface. You need to define a new class in a running program.

To overcome this problem, some programs generate code, place it into a file, invoke the compiler, and then load the resulting class file. Naturally, this is slow, and it also requires deployment of the compiler together with the program. The *proxy* mechanism is a better solution. The proxy class can create brand-new classes at runtime. Such a proxy class implements the interfaces that you specify. In particular, the proxy class has the following methods:

- All methods required by the specified interfaces; and
- All methods defined in the Object class (toString, equals, and so on).

However, you cannot define new code for these methods at runtime. Instead, you must supply an *invocation handler*. An invocation handler is an object of any class that implements the InvocationHandler interface. That interface has a single method:

```
Object invoke(Object proxy, Method method, Object[] args)
```

Whenever a method is called on the proxy object, the invoke method of the invocation handler gets called, with the Method object and arguments of the original call. The invocation handler must then figure out how to handle the call.

6.5.2. Creating Proxy Objects

To create a proxy object, use the newProxyInstance method of the Proxy class. The method has three parameters:

- A *class loader*. As part of the Java security model, different class loaders can be used for platform and application classes, classes that are downloaded from the Internet, and so on. We will discuss class loaders in Chapter 9 of Volume II. In this example, we specify the "system class loader" that loads platform and application classes.
- An array of Class objects, one for each interface to be implemented.
- An invocation handler.

There are two remaining questions. How do we define the handler? And what can we do with the resulting proxy object? The answers depend, of course, on the problem that we want to solve with the proxy mechanism. Proxies can be used for many purposes, such as

- Routing method calls to remote servers
- Associating user interface events with actions in a running program
- Tracing method calls for debugging purposes

In our example program, we use proxies and invocation handlers to trace method calls. We define a TraceHandler wrapper class that stores a wrapped object. Its invoke method simply prints the name and arguments of the method to be called and then calls the method with the wrapped object as the implicit argument.

```
class TraceHandler implements InvocationHandler
{
    private Object target;

    public TraceHandler(Object t)
    {
        target = t;
    }

    public Object invoke(Object proxy, Method m, Object[] args)
            throws Throwable
    {
        // print method name and arguments
        . . .
        // invoke actual method
        return m.invoke(target, args);
    }
}
```

Here is how you construct a proxy object that causes the tracing behavior whenever one of its methods is called:

```
Object value = . . .;
// construct wrapper
var handler = new TraceHandler(value);
// construct proxy for one or more interfaces
var interfaces = new Class[] { Comparable.class };
Object proxy = Proxy.newProxyInstance(
    ClassLoader.getSystemClassLoader(),
    new Class[] { Comparable.class }, handler);
```

Now, whenever a method from one of the interfaces is called on proxy, the method name and arguments are printed out and the method is then invoked on value.

In the program shown in Listing 6.10, we use proxy objects to trace a binary search. We fill an array with proxies to the integers 1 . . . 1000. Then we invoke the binarySearch method of the Arrays class to search for a random integer in the array. Finally, we print the matching element.

```
var elements = new Object[1000];
// fill elements with proxies for the integers 1 . . . 1000
for (int i = 0; i < elements.length; i++)
{
   Integer value = i + 1;
   elements[i] = Proxy.newProxyInstance(. . .); // proxy for value;
}

// construct a random integer
Integer key = (int) (Math.random() * elements.length) + 1;

// search for the key
int result = Arrays.binarySearch(elements, key);

// print match if found
if (result >= 0) System.out.println(elements[result]);
```

The Integer class implements the Comparable interface. The proxy objects belong to a class that is defined at runtime. (It has a name such as $Proxy0.) That class also implements the Comparable interface. However, its compareTo method calls the invoke method of the proxy object's handler.

 Note: As you saw earlier in this chapter, the Integer class actually implements Comparable<Integer>. However, at runtime, all generic types are erased and the proxy is constructed with the class object for the raw Comparable class.

The binarySearch method makes calls like this:

```
if (elements[i].compareTo(key) < 0) . . .
```

Since we filled the array with proxy objects, the compareTo calls the invoke method of the TraceHandler class. That method prints the method name and arguments and then invokes compareTo on the wrapped Integer object.

Finally, at the end of the sample program, we call

```
System.out.println(elements[result]);
```

The println method calls toString on the proxy object, and that call is also redirected to the invocation handler.

Here is the complete trace of a program run:

```
500.compareTo(288)
250.compareTo(288)
375.compareTo(288)
312.compareTo(288)
281.compareTo(288)
296.compareTo(288)
288.compareTo(288)
288.toString()
```

You can see how the binary search algorithm homes in on the key by cutting the search interval in half in every step. Note that the toString method is proxied even though it does not belong to the Comparable interface—as you will see in the next section, certain Object methods are always proxied.

Listing 6.10 proxy/ProxyTest.java

```java
 1  package proxy;
 2
 3  import java.lang.reflect.*;
 4  import java.util.*;
 5
 6  /**
 7   * This program demonstrates the use of proxies.
 8   * @version 1.02 2021-06-16
 9   * @author Cay Horstmann
10   */
11  public class ProxyTest
12  {
13     public static void main(String[] args)
14     {
15        var elements = new Object[1000];
16
17        // fill elements with proxies for the integers 1 . . . 1000
18        for (int i = 0; i < elements.length; i++)
19        {
20           Integer value = i + 1;
21           var handler = new TraceHandler(value);
22           Object proxy = Proxy.newProxyInstance(
23              ClassLoader.getSystemClassLoader(),
24              new Class[] { Comparable.class }, handler);
25           elements[i] = proxy;
26        }
27
28        // construct a random integer
29        Integer key = (int) (Math.random() * elements.length) + 1;
30
```

```
31          // search for the key
32          int result = Arrays.binarySearch(elements, key);
33
34          // print match if found
35          if (result >= 0) System.out.println(elements[result]);
36      }
37   }
38
39   /**
40    * An invocation handler that prints out the method name and parameters, then
41    * invokes the original method.
42    */
43   class TraceHandler implements InvocationHandler
44   {
45      private Object target;
46
47      /**
48       * Constructs a TraceHandler.
49       * @param t the implicit parameter of the method call
50       */
51      public TraceHandler(Object t)
52      {
53         target = t;
54      }
55
56      public Object invoke(Object proxy, Method m, Object[] args) throws Throwable
57      {
58         // print implicit argument
59         System.out.print(target);
60         // print method name
61         System.out.print("." + m.getName() + "(");
62         // print explicit arguments
63         if (args != null)
64         {
65            for (int i = 0; i < args.length; i++)
66            {
67               System.out.print(args[i]);
68               if (i < args.length - 1) System.out.print(", ");
69            }
70         }
71         System.out.println(")");
72
73         // invoke actual method
74         return m.invoke(target, args);
75      }
76   }
```

6.5.3. Properties of Proxy Classes

Now that you have seen proxy classes in action, let's go over some of their properties.
Remember that proxy classes are created on the fly in a running program. However, once

they are created, they are regular classes, just like any other classes in the virtual machine.

All proxy classes extend the class Proxy. A proxy class has only one instance field—the invocation handler, which is defined in the Proxy superclass. Any additional data required to carry out the proxy objects' tasks must be stored in the invocation handler. For example, when we proxied Comparable objects in the program shown in Listing 6.10, the TraceHandler wrapped the actual objects.

All proxy classes override the toString, equals, and hashCode methods of the Object class. Like all proxy methods, these methods simply call invoke on the invocation handler. The other methods of the Object class (such as clone and getClass) are not redefined.

The names of proxy classes are not defined. The Proxy class in Oracle's virtual machine generates class names that begin with the string $Proxy.

There is only one proxy class for a particular class loader and ordered set of interfaces. That is, if you call the newProxyInstance method twice with the same class loader and interface array, you get two objects of the same class. You can also obtain that class with the getProxyClass method:

```
Class proxyClass = Proxy.getProxyClass(null, interfaces);
```

A proxy class is always public and final. If all interfaces that the proxy class implements are public, the proxy class does not belong to any particular package. Otherwise, all non-public interfaces must belong to the same package, and the proxy class will also belong to that package.

You can test whether a particular Class object represents a proxy class by calling the isProxyClass method of the Proxy class.

 Note: Calling a default method of a proxy triggers the invocation handler. To actually invoke the method, use the static invokeDefault method of the InvocationHandler interface. For example, here is an invocation handler that calls the default methods and passes the abstract methods to another target:

```
InvocationHandler handler = (proxy, method, args) ->
    {
        if (method.isDefault())
            return InvocationHandler.invokeDefault(proxy, method, args)
        else
            return method.invoke(target, args);
    }
```

`java.lang.reflect.InvocationHandler` **1.3**

- `Object invoke(Object proxy, Method method, Object[] args)`
  define this method to contain the action that you want carried out whenever a method was invoked on the proxy object.
- `static Object invokeDefault(Object proxy, Method method, Object... args)` **16**
  invokes a default method of the proxy instance with the given arguments, bypassing the invocation handler.

`java.lang.reflect.Proxy` **1.3**

- `static Class<?> getProxyClass(ClassLoader loader, Class<?>... interfaces)`
  returns the proxy class that implements the given interfaces.
- `static Object newProxyInstance(ClassLoader loader, Class<?>[] interfaces, InvocationHandler handler)`
  constructs a new instance of the proxy class that implements the given interfaces. All methods call the invoke method of the given handler object.
- `static boolean isProxyClass(Class<?> cl)`
  returns `true` if `cl` is a proxy class.

This ends the final chapter on the object-oriented features of the Java programming language. Interfaces, lambda expressions, and inner classes are concepts that you will encounter frequently, whereas cloning, service loaders, and proxies are advanced techniques that are of interest mainly to library designers and tool builders, not application programmers. You are now ready to learn how to deal with exceptional situations in your programs in Chapter 7.

CHAPTER 7

Exceptions, Assertions, and Logging

In a perfect world, users would never enter data in the wrong form, files they choose to open would always exist, and code would never have bugs. So far, I've mostly presented code as if we all lived in this kind of perfect world. It is now time to turn to the mechanisms the Java programming language has for dealing with the real world of bad data and buggy code.

Encountering errors is unpleasant. If a user loses all the work he or she did during a program session because of a programming mistake or some external circumstance, that user may forever turn away from your program. At the very least, you must:

- Notify the user of an error;
- Save all work; and
- Allow users to gracefully exit the program.

For exceptional situations, such as bad input data with the potential to bomb the program, Java uses a form of error trapping called, naturally enough, *exception handling*. Exception handling in Java is similar to that in C++ or Delphi. The first part of this chapter covers Java's exceptions.

During testing, you need to run lots of checks to make sure your program does the right thing. But those checks can be time-consuming and unnecessary after testing has completed. You could just remove the checks and stick them back in when additional testing is required—but that is tedious. The second part of this chapter shows you how to use the assertion facility for selectively activating checks.

When your program does the wrong thing, you can't always communicate with the user or terminate. Instead, you may want to record the problem for later analysis. The third part of this chapter discusses the standard Java logging framework.

7.1. Dealing with Errors

Suppose an error occurs while a Java program is running. The error might be caused by a file containing wrong information, a flaky network connection, or (I hate to mention it) use of an invalid array index or an object reference that hasn't yet been assigned to an object. Users expect that programs will act sensibly when errors happen. If an operation cannot be completed because of an error, the program ought to either

- Return to a safe state and enable the user to execute other commands; or
- Allow the user to save all work and terminate the program gracefully.

This may not be easy to do, because the code that detects the error condition is usually far away from the code that can roll back the data to a safe state or save the user's work and exit cheerfully. The mission of exception handling is to transfer control from where the error occurred to an error handler that can deal with the situation. To handle exceptional situations in your program, you must take into account the errors and problems that may occur. What sorts of problems do you need to consider?

- *User input errors.* In addition to the inevitable typos, some users like to blaze their own trail instead of following directions. Suppose, for example, that a user asks to connect to a URL that is syntactically wrong. Your code should check the syntax, but suppose it does not. Then the network layer will complain.
- *Device errors.* Hardware does not always do what you want it to. The printer may be turned off. A web page may be temporarily unavailable. Devices will often fail in the middle of a task. For example, a printer may run out of paper during printing.
- *Physical limitations.* Disks can fill up; you can run out of available memory.
- *Code errors.* A method may not perform correctly. For example, it could deliver wrong answers or use other methods incorrectly. Computing an invalid array index, trying to find a nonexistent entry in a hash table, or trying to pop an empty stack are all examples of a code error.

The traditional reaction to an error in a method is to return a special error code that the calling method analyzes. For example, methods that read information back from files often return a -1 end-of-file value marker rather than a standard character. Another common return value to denote an error condition is the null reference.

However, it is not always possible to return an error code. There may be no obvious way of distinguishing valid and invalid data. A method returning an integer cannot simply return -1 to denote the error; the value -1 might be a perfectly valid result.

Returning null to indicate failure is particularly problematic. Consider the listFiles method of the legacy java.io.File class. It returns a File[] array, or null in case of failure. If the programmer did not check for null, a NullPointerException occurs when the return value is first used, masking the original problem.

Java allows every method an alternative exit path if it is unable to complete its task in the normal way. In this situation, the method does not return a value. Instead, it *throws* an object that encapsulates the error information. Note that the method exits immediately; it does not return its normal (or any) value. Moreover, execution does not resume at the code that called the method; instead, the exception-handling mechanism begins its search for an *exception handler* that can deal with this particular error condition.

Exceptions have their own syntax and are part of a special inheritance hierarchy. I'll take up the syntax first and then give a few hints on how to use this language feature effectively.

Tip: Favor methods that use exceptions over those that return error codes. It is easy to forget checking error codes, but exceptions cannot be overlooked. Exceptions can also carry more information. For example, the `delete` method of the legacy `java.io.File` class returns `false` if the deletion was unsuccessful. The `delete` method in the `java.nio.file.Files` class is more useful. In case of failure it throws an exception of a type that clearly indicates the nature of the problem.

7.1.1. The Classification of Exceptions

In the Java programming language, an exception object is always an instance of a class derived from `Throwable`. As you will soon see, you can create your own exception classes if those built into Java do not suit your needs.

Figure 7.1 is a simplified diagram of the exception hierarchy in Java.

Notice that all exceptions descend from `Throwable`, but the hierarchy immediately splits into two branches: `Error` and `Exception`.

The `Error` hierarchy describes internal errors and resource exhaustion situations inside the Java runtime system. You should not throw an object of this type. There is little you can do if such an internal error occurs, beyond notifying the user and trying to terminate the program gracefully. These situations are quite rare.

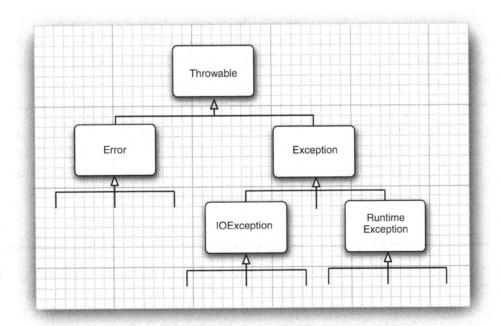

Figure 7.1: Exception hierarchy in Java

When doing Java programming, focus on the Exception hierarchy. The Exception hierarchy also splits into two branches: exceptions that derive from RuntimeException and those that do not. The general rule is this: A RuntimeException happens because you made a programming error. Any other exception occurs because a bad thing, such as an I/O error, happened to your otherwise good program.

Exceptions that inherit from RuntimeException include such problems as

- A bad cast
- An out-of-bounds array access
- A null pointer access

Exceptions that do not inherit from RuntimeException include

- Trying to read past the end of a file
- Trying to open a file that doesn't exist
- Trying to find a Class object for a string that does not denote an existing class

The rule "If it is a RuntimeException, it was your fault" works pretty well. You could have avoided that ArrayIndexOutOfBoundsException by testing the array index against the array bounds. The NullPointerException would not have happened had you checked whether the variable was null before using it.

How about a file that doesn't exist? Can't you first check whether the file exists, and then open it? Well, the file might be deleted right after you checked for its existence. Thus, the notion of "existence" depends on the environment, not just on your code.

The Java Language Specification calls any exception that derives from the class Error or the class RuntimeException an *unchecked* exception. All other exceptions are called *checked* exceptions. This is useful terminology that I also adopt in this book. The compiler checks that you provide exception handlers for all checked exceptions.

Note: The name RuntimeException is somewhat confusing. Of course, all of the errors we are discussing occur at runtime. The name originated in prehistoric times, when the "runtime" of Oak, the predecessor of Java, generated out-of-bounds exceptions and null pointer exceptions. Presumably I/O exceptions were produced by some other component.

C++ Note: If you are familiar with the (much more limited) exception hierarchy of the standard C++ library, you may be really confused at this point. C++ has two fundamental exception classes, runtime_error and logic_error. The logic_error class is the equivalent of Java's RuntimeException and also denotes logical errors in the program. The runtime_error class is the base class for exceptions caused by unpredictable problems. It is equivalent to those exceptions in Java that are *not* of type RuntimeException.

7.1.2. Declaring Checked Exceptions

A Java method can throw an exception if it encounters a situation it cannot handle. The idea is simple: A method will not only tell the Java compiler what values it can return, *it is also going to tell the compiler what can go wrong.* For example, code that attempts to read from a file knows that the file might not exist or that it might be empty. The code that tries to process the information in a file therefore will need to notify the compiler that it can throw some sort of IOException.

The place in which you advertise that your method can throw an exception is the header of the method; the header changes to reflect the checked exceptions the method can throw. For example, here is the declaration of one of the constructors of the FileInputStream class from the standard library. (See Chapter 2 of Volume II for more on input and output.)

```
public FileInputStream(String name) throws FileNotFoundException
```

The declaration says that this constructor produces a FileInputStream object from a String parameter but that it *also* can go wrong in a special way—by throwing a FileNotFoundException. If this sad state should come to pass, the constructor call will not initialize a new FileInputStream object but instead will throw an object of the FileNotFoundException class. If it does, the runtime system will begin to search for an exception handler that knows how to deal with FileNotFoundException objects.

When you write your own methods, you don't have to advertise every possible throwable object that your method might actually throw. To understand when (and what) you have to advertise in the throws clause of the methods you write, keep in mind that an exception is thrown in any of the following four situations:

- You call a method that throws a checked exception—for example, the FileInputStream constructor.
- You detect an error and throw a checked exception with the throw statement (the throw statement is covered in the next section).
- You make a programming error, such as a[-1] = 0 that gives rise to an unchecked exception (in this case, an ArrayIndexOutOfBoundsException).
- An internal error occurs in the virtual machine or runtime library.

If either of the first two scenarios occurs, you must tell the programmers who will use your method about the possibility of an exception. Why? Any method that throws an exception is a potential death trap. If no handler catches the exception, the current thread of execution terminates.

As with Java methods that are part of the supplied classes, you declare that your method may throw an exception with an *exception specification* in the method header.

```
class MyAnimation
{
   . . .
   public Image loadImage(String s) throws IOException
   {
      . . .
   }
}
```

If a method might throw more than one checked exception type, you must list all exception classes in the header. Separate them by commas, as in the following example:

```
class MyAnimation
{
   . . .
   public Image loadImage(String s) throws FileNotFoundException, EOFException
   {
      . . .
   }
}
```

However, you do not need to advertise internal Java errors—that is, exceptions inheriting from Error. Any code could potentially throw those exceptions, and they are entirely beyond your control.

Similarly, you should not advertise unchecked exceptions inheriting from RuntimeException.

```
class MyAnimation
{
   . . .
   void drawImage(int i) throws ArrayIndexOutOfBoundsException // bad style
   {
      . . .
   }
}
```

These runtime errors are completely under your control. If you are so concerned about array index errors, you should spend your time fixing them instead of advertising the possibility that they can happen.

In summary, a method must declare all the *checked* exceptions that it might throw. Unchecked exceptions are either beyond your control (Error) or result from conditions that you should not have allowed in the first place (RuntimeException). If your method fails to faithfully declare all checked exceptions, the compiler will issue an error message.

Of course, as you have already seen in quite a few examples, instead of declaring the exception, you can also catch it. Then the exception won't be thrown out of the method, and no throws specification is necessary. You will see later in this chapter how to decide whether to catch an exception or to enable someone else to catch it.

Caution: If you override a method from a superclass, the checked exceptions that the subclass method declares cannot be more general than those of the superclass method. (It is OK to throw more specific exceptions, or not to throw any exceptions in the subclass method.) In particular, if the superclass method throws no checked exception at all, neither can the subclass. For example, if you override JComponent.paintComponent, your paintComponent method must not throw any checked exceptions, because the superclass method doesn't throw any.

When a method in a class declares that it throws an exception that is an instance of a particular class, it may throw an exception of that class or of any of its subclasses. For example, the FileInputStream constructor could have declared that it throws an IOException. In that case, you would not have known what kind of IOException it is; it could be a plain IOException or an object of one of the various subclasses, such as FileNotFoundException.

C++ Note: The throws specifier is the same as the throw specifier in C++, with one important difference. In C++, throw specifiers are enforced at runtime, not at compile time. That is, the C++ compiler pays no attention to exception specifications. But if an exception is thrown in a function that is not part of the throw list, the unexpected function is called, and, by default, the program terminates.

Also, in C++, a function may throw any exception if no throw specification is given. In Java, a method without a throws specifier may not throw any checked exceptions at all.

7.1.3. How to Throw an Exception

Now, suppose something terrible has happened in your code. You have a method, readData, that is reading in a file whose header promised

```
Content-length: 1024
```

but you got an end of file after 733 characters. You may decide this situation is so abnormal that you want to throw an exception.

You need to decide what exception type to throw. Some kind of IOException would be a good choice. Perusing the Java API documentation, you find an EOFException with the description "Signals that an EOF has been reached unexpectedly during input." Perfect. Here is how you throw it:

```
throw new EOFException();
```

or, if you prefer,

```
var e = new EOFException();
throw e;
```

Here is how it all fits together:

```
String readData(Scanner in) throws EOFException
{
   . . .
   while (. . .)
   {
      if (!in.hasNext()) // EOF encountered
      {
         if (n < len)
            throw new EOFException();
      }
      . . .
   }
   return s;
}
```

The EOFException has a second constructor that takes a string argument. You can put this to good use by describing the exceptional condition more carefully.

```
String gripe = "Content-length: " + len + ", Received: " + n;
throw new EOFException(gripe);
```

As you can see, throwing an exception is easy if one of the existing exception classes works for you. In this case:

1. Find an appropriate exception class.
2. Make an object of that class.
3. Throw it.

Once a method throws an exception, it does not return to its caller. This means you do not have to worry about cooking up a default return value or an error code.

 C++ Note: Throwing an exception is the same in C++ and in Java, with one small difference. In Java, you can throw only objects of subclasses of Throwable. In C++, you can throw values of any type.

7.1.4. Creating Exception Classes

Your code may run into a problem which is not adequately described by any of the standard exception classes. In this case, it is easy enough to create your own exception class. Just derive it from Exception, or from a child class of Exception such as IOException. It is customary to give both a default constructor and a constructor that contains a detailed message. (The toString method of the Throwable superclass returns a string containing that detailed message, which is handy for debugging.)

```
class FileFormatException extends IOException
{
   public FileFormatException() {}
   public FileFormatException(String gripe)
   {
      super(gripe);
   }
}
```

Now you are ready to throw your very own exception type.

```
String readData(Scanner in) throws FileFormatException
{
   . . .
   while (. . .)
   {
      if (ch == -1) // EOF encountered
      {
         if (n < len)
            throw new FileFormatException();
      }
      . . .
   }
   return s;
}
```

---

java.lang.Throwable 1.0

■ Throwable()
  constructs a new Throwable object with no detailed message.
■ Throwable(String message)
  constructs a new Throwable object with the specified detailed message. By convention, all derived exception classes support both a default constructor and a constructor with a detailed message.
■ String getMessage()
  gets the detailed message of the Throwable object.

7.2. Catching Exceptions

You now know how to throw an exception. It is pretty easy: You throw it and you forget it. Of course, some code has to catch the exception. Catching exceptions requires more planning. That's what the next sections will cover.

7.2.1. Catching an Exception

If an exception occurs that is not caught anywhere, the program will terminate and print a message to the console, giving the type of the exception and a stack trace. However, GUI programs may catch exceptions, print stack trace messages, and then go back to the user interface processing loop. (When you are debugging a GUI program, it is a good idea to keep the console on the screen and not minimized.)

To catch an exception, set up a try/catch block. The simplest form of the try block is as follows:

```
try
{
    code
    more code
    more code
}
catch (ExceptionType e)
{
    handler for this type
}
```

Suppose any code inside the try block throws an exception of the class specified in the catch clause, or its subclass. In that case:

1. The program skips the remainder of the code in the try block.
2. The program executes the handler code inside the catch clause.

If none of the code inside the try block throws an exception, then the program skips the catch clause.

If any of the code in a method throws an exception of a type other than the one named in the catch clause, this method exits immediately. (Hopefully, one of its callers has already provided a catch clause for that type.)

To show this at work, here's some fairly typical code for reading in data:

```
public void read(String filename)
{
    try
```

```
   {
      var in = new FileInputStream(filename);
      int b;
      while ((b = in.read()) != -1)
      {
         process input
      }
   }
   catch (IOException exception)
   {
      exception.printStackTrace();
   }
}
```

Notice that most of the code in the try clause is straightforward: It reads and processes bytes until it encounters the end of the file. As you can see by looking at the Java API, there is the possibility that the read method will throw an IOException. In that case, we skip out of the entire while loop, enter the catch clause, and generate a stack trace. For a toy program, that seems like a reasonable way to deal with this exception. What other choice do you have?

Often, the best choice is to do nothing at all and simply pass the exception on to the caller. If an error occurs in the read method, let the caller of the read method worry about it! If we take that approach, then we have to advertise the fact that the method may throw an IOException.

```
public void read(String filename) throws IOException
{
   var in = new FileInputStream(filename);
   int b;
   while ((b = in.read()) != -1)
   {
      process input
   }
}
```

Remember, the compiler strictly enforces the throws specifiers. If you call a method that throws a checked exception, you must either handle it or pass it on.

Which of the two is better? As a general rule, you should catch those exceptions that you know how to handle and propagate those that you do not know how to handle.

When you propagate an exception, you must add a throws specifier to alert the caller that an exception may be thrown.

Look at the Java API documentation to see what methods throw which exceptions. Then decide whether you should handle them or add them to the throws list. There is nothing embarrassing about the latter choice. It is better to direct an exception to a competent handler than to squelch it.

However, when overriding a method, you are not allowed to add more throws specifiers to a subclass method than are present in the superclass method. Then you *must* catch the undeclared checked exceptions. In particular, if you override a method which throws no exceptions (such as compareTo in Comparable), then you have no choice but to catch each checked exception.

 C++ Note: Catching exceptions is almost the same in Java and in C++. Strictly speaking, the analog of

```
catch (Exception e) // Java
```

is

```
catch (Exception& e) // C++
```

There is no analog to the C++ catch (...). This is not needed in Java because all exceptions derive from a common superclass.

 Preview Note: Sometimes, you do not need the exception object in a catch clause. Starting in Java 21, as a preview feature, you can use an underscore as an unnamed variable:

```
catch (FileNotFoundException _)
{
   System.exit(0);
}
```

7.2.2. Catching Multiple Exceptions

You can catch multiple exception types in a try block and handle each type differently. Use a separate catch clause for each type, as in the following example:

```
try
{
   code that might throw exceptions
}
catch (FileNotFoundException e)
{
   emergency action for missing files
}
```

```
catch (UnknownHostException e)
{
    emergency action for unknown hosts
}
catch (IOException e)
{
    emergency action for all other I/O problems
}
```

You need to order the catch clauses so that the more specific exception types come before the more general ones.

The exception object may contain information about the nature of the exception. To find out more about the object, try

```
e.getMessage()
```

to get the detailed error message (if there is one), or

```
e.getClass().getName()
```

to get the actual type of the exception object.

You can catch multiple exception types in the same catch clause. For example, suppose that the action for missing files and unknown hosts is the same. Then you can combine the catch clauses:

```
try
{
    code that might throw exceptions
}
catch (FileNotFoundException | UnknownHostException e)
{
    emergency action for missing files and unknown hosts
}
catch (IOException e)
{
    emergency action for all other I/O problems
}
```

This feature is only needed when catching exception types that are not subclasses of one another.

When you catch multiple exceptions, the exception variable is implicitly final. For example, you cannot assign a different value to e in the body of the clause

```
catch (FileNotFoundException | UnknownHostException e) { . . . }
```

Catching multiple exceptions doesn't just make your code look simpler but also more efficient. The generated bytecodes contain a single block for the shared catch clause.

 Caution: The type of the variable e is *not* the "union type" FileNotFoundException | UnknownHostException, even if your IDE reports it as such. Java variables cannot have such union types. The actual type of e is the least upper bound of those types; in this case, IOException.

In most cases, you don't care. But it matters if you analyze e with a switch. The obvious switch has a problem—it is not exhaustive:

```
catch (FileNotFoundException | UnknownHostException e)
{
    switch (e) // ERROR: not exhaustive
    {
        case FileNotFoundException fe -> . . .;
        case UnknownHostException ue -> . . .;
    }
    . . .
}
```

You can fix the problem by adding a default clause. However, it might be clearer to reorganize the code and use separate catch clauses.

 Caution: Catch clauses do not pay attention to sealed exception hierarchies. Suppose you provide

```
sealed abstract class DomainException extends Exception
        permits FatalDomainException, SurvivableDomainException {}
```

Then the catch clauses

```
try
{
    domainMethod(); // throws DomainException
}
catch (FatalDomainException e) { . . . }
catch (SurvivableDomainException e) { . . . }
```

are not sufficient, even though there can be no other checked exception instances.

7.2.3. Rethrowing and Chaining Exceptions

You can throw an exception in a catch clause. Typically, you do this when you want to change the exception type. If you build a subsystem that other programmers use, it makes a lot of sense to use an exception type that indicates a failure of the subsystem. An example of such an exception type is the ServletException. The code that executes a servlet may not want to know in minute detail what went wrong, but it definitely wants to know that the servlet was at fault.

Here is how you can catch an exception and rethrow it:

```
try
{
    access the database
}
catch (SQLException e)
{
    throw new ServletException("database error: " + e.getMessage());
}
```

Here, the ServletException is constructed with the message text of the exception.

However, it is a better idea to set the original exception as the "cause" of the new exception:

```
try
{
    access the database
}
catch (SQLException original)
{
    var e = new ServletException("database error", original);
    throw e;
}
```

The ServletException class has a constructor to which you can pass the cause. If you use an exception type for which that is not the case, you can instead call

```
e.initCause(original);
```

When the exception is caught, the original exception can be retrieved:

```
Throwable original = caughtException.getCause();
```

This wrapping technique is highly recommended. It allows you to throw high-level exceptions in subsystems without losing the details of the original failure.

Tip: The wrapping technique is also useful if a checked exception occurs in a method that is not allowed to throw a checked exception. You can catch the checked exception and wrap it into a runtime exception.

As this situation often arises with input/output, the Java API provides an UncheckedIOException that you can use as a wrapper for the checked IOException.

Sometimes, you just want to log an exception and rethrow it without any change:

```
try
{
    access the database
}
catch (Exception e)
{
    logger.log(level, message, e);
    throw e;
}
```

There is a subtle point here. Suppose the code is inside a method

```
public void updateRecord() throws SQLException
```

The Java compiler tracks the fact that e originates from the try block. Provided that the only checked exceptions in that block are SQLException instances, and provided that e is not changed in the catch block, it is valid to declare the enclosing method as throws SQLException.

7.2.4. The finally Clause

When your code throws an exception, it stops processing the remaining code in your method and exits the method. This is a problem if the method has acquired some local resource, which only this method knows about, and that resource must be cleaned up. One solution is to catch all exceptions, carry out the cleanup, and rethrow the exceptions. But this solution is tedious because you need to clean up the resource allocation in two places—in the normal code and in the exception code. The finally clause can solve this problem.

 Note: There is a more elegant solution, the try-with-resources statement that you will see in the following section. We discuss the finally mechanism in detail because it is the conceptual foundation. But in practice, you will use try-with-resources statements far more often than finally clauses.

The code in the finally clause executes whether or not an exception was caught. In the following example, the program will close the input stream *under all circumstances*:

```
var in = new FileInputStream(. . .);
try
{
   // 1
   code that might throw exceptions
   // 2
}
catch (IOException e)
{
   // 3
   show error message
   // 4
}
finally
{
   // 5
   in.close();
}
// 6
```

Let us look at the three possible situations in which the program will execute the finally clause.

1. The code throws no exceptions. In this case, the program first executes all the code in the try block. Then, it executes the code in the finally clause. Afterwards, execution continues with the first statement after the finally clause. In other words, execution passes through points 1, 2, 5, and 6.

2. The code throws an exception that is caught in a catch clause—in our case, an IOException. For this, the program executes all code in the try block, up to the point at which the exception was thrown. The remaining code in the try block is skipped. The program then executes the code in the matching catch clause, and then the code in the finally clause.
   If the catch clause does not throw an exception, the program executes the first line after the finally clause. In this scenario, execution passes through points 1, 3, 4, 5, and 6.
   If the catch clause throws an exception, then the exception is thrown back to the caller of this method, and execution passes through points 1, 3, and 5 only.

3. The code throws an exception that is not caught in any catch clause. Here, the program executes all code in the try block until the exception is thrown. The remaining code in the try block is skipped. Then, the code in the finally clause is executed, and the exception is thrown back to the caller of this method. Execution passes through points 1 and 5 only.

You can use the finally clause without a catch clause. For example, consider the following try statement:

```
InputStream in = . . .;
try
{
    code that might throw exceptions
}
finally
{
    in.close();
}
```

The in.close() statement in the finally clause is executed whether or not an exception is encountered in the try block. Of course, if an exception is encountered, it is rethrown and must be caught in another catch clause.

```
InputStream in = . . .;
try
{
    try
    {
        code that might throw exceptions
    }
    finally
    {
        in.close();
    }
}
catch (IOException e)
{
    show error message
}
```

The inner try block has a single responsibility: to make sure that the input stream is closed. The outer try block has a single responsibility: to ensure that errors are reported. Not only is this solution clearer, it is also more functional: Errors in the finally clause are reported.

Caution: A finally clause can yield unexpected results when it contains return statements. Suppose you exit the middle of a try block with a return statement. Before the method returns, the finally block is executed. If the finally block also contains a return statement, then it masks the original return value. Consider this example:

```
public static int parseInt(String s)
{
   try
   {
      return Integer.parseInt(s);
   }
   finally
   {
      return 0; // ERROR
   }
}
```

It looks as if in the call parseInt("42"), the body of the try block returns the integer 42. However, the finally clause is executed before the method actually returns and causes the method to return 0, ignoring the original return value.

And it gets worse. Consider the call parseInt("zero"). The Integer.parseInt method throws a NumberFormatException. Then the finally clause is executed, and the return statement swallows the exception!

The body of the finally clause is intended for cleaning up resources. Don't put statements that change the control flow (return, throw, break, continue) inside a finally clause.

7.2.5. The try-with-Resources Statement

There is a useful shortcut to the code pattern

```
open a resource
try
{
   work with the resource
}
finally
{
   close the resource
}
```

provided the resource belongs to a class that implements the AutoCloseable interface. That interface has a single method

```
void close() throws Exception
```

Note: There is also a Closeable interface. It is a subinterface of AutoCloseable, also with a single close method. However, that method is declared to throw an IOException.

In its simplest variant, the try-with-resources statement has the form

```
try (Resource res = . . .)
{
   work with res
}
```

When the try block exits, then res.close() is called automatically. Here is a typical example—reading all words of a file:

```
try (var in = new Scanner(Path.of("in.txt")))
{
   while (in.hasNext())
      System.out.println(in.next());
}
```

When the block exits normally, or when there was an exception, the in.close() method is called, exactly as if you had used a finally block.

You can specify multiple resources. For example,

```
try (var in = new Scanner(Path.of("in.txt"));
     var out = new PrintWriter("out.txt"))
{
   while (in.hasNext())
      out.println(in.next().toUpperCase());
}
```

No matter how the block exits, both in and out are closed. If you programmed this by hand, you would have needed two nested try/finally statements.

You can provide previously declared effectively final variables in the try header:

```
public static void printAll(String[] lines, PrintWriter out)
{
   try (out) // effectively final variable
   {
      for (String line : lines)
         out.println(line);
   } // out.close() called here
}
```

This is not common, since one generally prefers to invoke close in the same scope in which the object was constructed.

A difficulty arises when the try block throws an exception and the close method also throws an exception. The try-with-resources statement handles this situation quite elegantly. The original exception is rethrown, and any exceptions thrown by close methods are considered "suppressed." They are automatically caught and added to the original exception with the addSuppressed method. If you are interested in them, call the getSuppressed method which yields an array of the suppressed expressions from close methods.

You don't want to program this by hand. Use the try-with-resources statement whenever you need to close a resource.

 Note: A try-with-resources statement can itself have catch clauses and even a finally clause. These are executed after closing the resources.

7.2.6. Analyzing Stack Trace Elements

A *stack trace* is a listing of all pending method calls at a particular point in the execution of a program. You have almost certainly seen stack trace listings—they are displayed whenever a Java program terminates with an uncaught exception.

You can access the text description of a stack trace by calling the printStackTrace method of the Throwable class.

```
var t = new Throwable();
var out = new StringWriter();
t.printStackTrace(new PrintWriter(out));
String description = out.toString();
```

A more flexible approach is the StackWalker class that yields a stream of StackWalker.StackFrame instances, each describing one stack frame. You can iterate over the stack frames with this call:

```
StackWalker walker = StackWalker.getInstance();
walker.forEach(frame -> analyze frame)
```

If you want to process the Stream<StackWalker.StackFrame> lazily, call

```
walker.walk(stream -> process stream)
```

Stream processing is described in detail in Chapter 1 of Volume II.

The StackWalker.StackFrame class has methods to obtain the file name and line number, as well as the class object and method name, of the executing line of code. The toString method yields a formatted string containing all of this information.

 Note: The Throwable.getStackTrace method yields a StackTraceElement[] array with similar information as the stream of StackWalker.StackFrame instances. However, that call is less efficient since it captures the entire stack even though the caller may only need a few frames, and it only provides access to the class names, but not the class objects, of the pending methods.

Listing 7.1 prints the stack trace of a recursive factorial function. For example, if you compute factorial(3), the printout is

```
factorial(3):
stackTrace.StackTraceTest.factorial(StackTraceTest.java:20)
stackTrace.StackTraceTest.main(StackTraceTest.java:36)
factorial(2):
stackTrace.StackTraceTest.factorial(StackTraceTest.java:20)
stackTrace.StackTraceTest.factorial(StackTraceTest.java:26)
stackTrace.StackTraceTest.main(StackTraceTest.java:36)
factorial(1):
stackTrace.StackTraceTest.factorial(StackTraceTest.java:20)
stackTrace.StackTraceTest.factorial(StackTraceTest.java:26)
stackTrace.StackTraceTest.factorial(StackTraceTest.java:26)
stackTrace.StackTraceTest.main(StackTraceTest.java:36)
return 1
return 2
return 6
```

Listing 7.1 stackTrace/StackTraceTest.java

```
 1   package stackTrace;
 2
 3   import java.util.*;
 4
 5   /**
 6    * A program that displays a trace feature of a recursive method call.
 7    * @version 1.10 2017-12-14
 8    * @author Cay Horstmann
 9    */
10   public class StackTraceTest
11   {
12      /**
13       * Computes the factorial of a number
14       * @param n a non-negative integer
```

```
15      * @return n! = 1 * 2 * . . . * n
16      */
17     public static int factorial(int n)
18     {
19        System.out.println("factorial(" + n + "):");
20        var walker = StackWalker.getInstance();
21        walker.forEach(System.out::println);
22        int r;
23        if (n <= 1) r = 1;
24        else r = n * factorial(n - 1);
25        System.out.println("return " + r);
26        return r;
27     }
28
29     public static void main(String[] args)
30     {
31        try (var in = new Scanner(System.in))
32        {
33           System.out.print("Enter n: ");
34           int n = in.nextInt();
35           factorial(n);
36        }
37     }
38 }
```

java.lang.Throwable 1.0

- Throwable(Throwable cause) **1.4**
- Throwable(String message, Throwable cause) **1.4**
  construct a Throwable with a given cause.
- Throwable initCause(Throwable cause) **1.4**
  sets the cause for this object or throws an exception if this object already has a cause. Returns this.
- Throwable getCause() **1.4**
  gets the exception object that was set as the cause for this object, or null if no cause was set.
- StackTraceElement[] getStackTrace() **1.4**
  gets the trace of the call stack at the time this object was constructed.
- void addSuppressed(Throwable t) **7**
  adds a "suppressed" exception to this exception. This happens in a try-with-resources statement where t is an exception thrown by a close method.
- Throwable[] getSuppressed() **7**
  gets all "suppressed" exceptions of this exception. Typically, these are exceptions thrown by a close method in a try-with-resources statement.

---

java.lang.Exception 1.0

- Exception(Throwable cause) **1.4**
- Exception(String message, Throwable cause)
  construct an Exception with a given cause.

---

java.lang.RuntimeException 1.0

- RuntimeException(Throwable cause) **1.4**
- RuntimeException(String message, Throwable cause) **1.4**
  construct a RuntimeException with a given cause.

---

java.lang.StackWalker 9

- static StackWalker getInstance()
- static StackWalker getInstance(StackWalker.Option option)
- static StackWalker getInstance(Set<StackWalker.Option> options)
  get a StackWalker instance. The options include RETAIN_CLASS_REFERENCE,
  SHOW_HIDDEN_FRAMES, and SHOW_REFLECT_FRAMES from the StackWalker.Option enumeration.
- forEach(Consumer<? super StackWalker.StackFrame> action)
  carries out the given action on each stack frame, starting with the most recently
  called method.
- walk(Function<? super Stream<StackWalker.StackFrame>,? extends T> function)
  applies the given function to the stream of stack frames and returns the result of the
  function.

---

java.lang.StackWalker.StackFrame 9

- String getFileName()
  gets the name of the source file containing the execution point of this element, or null
  if the information is not available.
- int getLineNumber()
  gets the line number of the source file containing the execution point of this element,
  or -1 if the information is not available.
- String getClassName()
  gets the fully qualified name of the class whose method contains the execution point
  of this element.
- Class<?> getDeclaringClass()
  gets the Class object of the method containing the execution point of this element. An
  exception is thrown if the stack walker was not constructed with the
  RETAIN_CLASS_REFERENCE option.

- `String getMethodName()`
  gets the name of the method containing the execution point of this element. The name of a constructor is <init>. The name of a static initializer is <clinit>. You can't distinguish between overloaded methods with the same name.
- `boolean isNativeMethod()`
  returns true if the execution point of this element is inside a native method.
- `String toString()`
  returns a formatted string containing the class and method name and the file name and line number, if available.

---

java.lang.StackTraceElement 1.4

- `String getFileName()`
  gets the name of the source file containing the execution point of this element, or null if the information is not available.
- `int getLineNumber()`
  gets the line number of the source file containing the execution point of this element, or -1 if the information is not available.
- `String getClassName()`
  gets the fully qualified name of the class containing the execution point of this element.
- `String getMethodName()`
  gets the name of the method containing the execution point of this element. The name of a constructor is <init>. The name of a static initializer is <clinit>. You can't distinguish between overloaded methods with the same name.
- `boolean isNativeMethod()`
  returns true if the execution point of this element is inside a native method.
- `String toString()`
  returns a formatted string containing the class and method name and the file name and line number, if available.

7.3. Tips for Using Exceptions

There is a certain amount of controversy about the proper use of exceptions. Some programmers believe that all checked exceptions are a nuisance, others can't seem to throw enough of them. I think that exceptions (even checked exceptions) have their place, so I offer you these tips for their proper use.

1. *Exception handling is not supposed to replace a simple test.*
   As an example of this, here's code that tries 10,000,000 times to pop an empty stack. It first does this by finding out whether the stack is empty.

   ```
   if (!s.empty()) s.pop();
   ```

Next, we force it to pop the stack no matter what and catch the EmptyStackException that tells us we should not have done that.

```
try
{
    s.pop();
}
catch (EmptyStackException e)
{
}
```

On my test machine, the version that calls isEmpty ran in 0.167 seconds. The version that catches the EmptyStackException ran in 3.629 seconds.

As you can see, it took far longer to catch an exception than to perform a simple test. The moral is: Use exceptions for exceptional circumstances only.

2. *Do not micromanage exceptions.*

   Some programmers wrap every statement in a separate try block.

```
PrintStream out;
Stack s;

for (i = 0; i < 100; i++)
{
    try
    {
        n = s.pop();
    }
    catch (EmptyStackException e)
    {
        // stack was empty
    }
    try
    {
        out.writeInt(n);
    }
    catch (IOException e)
    {
        // problem writing to file
    }
}
```

This approach blows up your code dramatically. Think about the task that you want the code to accomplish. Here, we want to pop 100 numbers off a stack and save them to a file. (Never mind why—it is just a toy example.) There is nothing we can do if a problem rears its ugly head. If the stack is empty, it will not become occupied. If the file contains an error, the error will not magically go away. It therefore makes sense to wrap the *entire task* in a try block. If any one operation fails, you can then abandon the task.

```
try
{
   for (i = 0; i < 100; i++)
   {
      n = s.pop();
      out.writeInt(n);
   }
}
catch (IOException e)
{
   // problem writing to file
}
catch (EmptyStackException e)
{
   // stack was empty
}
```

This code looks much cleaner. It fulfills one of the promises of exception handling: to *separate* normal processing from error handling.

3. *Make good use of the exception hierarchy.*
   Don't just throw an Exception or RuntimeException. Find an appropriate subclass or create your own.
   Don't just catch Exception. It makes your code hard to read and maintain. Catch only those exception classes that you expect. And don't catch Throwable. You might hide an OutOfMemoryError.
   Respect the difference between checked and unchecked exceptions. Checked exceptions are inherently burdensome—don't throw them for logic errors. (For example, the reflection library gets this wrong. Callers often need to catch exceptions that they know can never happen.)
   Do not hesitate to turn an exception into another exception that is more appropriate. For example, when you parse an integer in a file, catch the NumberFormatException and set it as the cause of a subclass of IOException or MySubsystemException.

4. *Do not squelch exceptions.*
   In Java, there is a tremendous temptation to shut up exceptions. If you're writing a method that calls a method that might throw an exception once a century, the compiler whines because you have not declared the exception in the throws list of your method. You do not want to put it in the throws list because then the compiler will whine about all the methods that call your method. So you just shut it up:

```
public Image loadImage(String s)
{
   try
   {
      code that threatens to throw checked exceptions
   }
   catch (Exception e)
   {} // so there
}
```

Now your code will compile without a hitch. It will run fine, except when an exception occurs. Then, the exception will be silently ignored. If you believe that exceptions are at all important, you should make some effort to handle them right.

5. *When you detect an error, "tough love" works better than indulgence.*
    Some programmers worry about throwing exceptions when they detect errors. Maybe it would be better to return a dummy value rather than throw an exception when a method is called with invalid arguments? For example, should Stack.pop return null, or throw an exception when a stack is empty? I think it is better to throw an EmptyStackException at the point of failure than to have a NullPointerException occur at later time.

6. *Propagating exceptions is not a sign of shame.*
    Some programmers feel compelled to catch all exceptions that are thrown. If they call a method that throws an exception, such as the FileInputStream constructor or the readLine method, they instinctively catch the exception that may be generated. In many situations, it is actually better to *propagate* the exception instead of catching it:

    ```
    public void readStuff(String filename) throws IOException // not a sign of shame!
    {
       var in = new FileInputStream(filename);
       . . .
    }
    ```

    Higher-level methods are often better equipped to inform the user of errors or to abandon unsuccessful commands.

7. *Use standard methods for reporting null-pointer and out-of-bounds exceptions.*
    The Objects class has methods

    ```
    requireNonNull
    checkIndex
    checkFromToIndex
    checkFromIndexSize
    ```

    for these common checks. Use them for parameter validation:

```
public void putData(int position, Object newValue)
{
   Objects.checkIndex(position, data.length);
   Objects.requireNonNull(newValue);
   . . .
}
```

If the method is called with an invalid index or a null argument, an exception is thrown, using the familiar message that the Java library uses.

8. *Don't show stack traces to end users.*
   If your program encounters an unexpected exception, it may seem a good idea to display the stack trace so the users can report it, making it easier for you to pinpoint the issue. However, stack traces can contain implementation details that you do not want to reveal to potential attackers, such as the versions of libraries that you are using.
   Log the stack trace so that you can retrieve it, but only display a summary message to your users.

 Note: Rules 5 and 6 can be summarized as "throw early, catch late."

7.4. Using Assertions

Assertions are a commonly used idiom of defensive programming. In the following sections, you will learn how to use them effectively.

7.4.1. The Assertion Concept

Suppose you are convinced that a particular property is fulfilled, and you rely on that property in your code. For example, you may be computing

```
double y = Math.sqrt(x);
```

You are certain that x is not negative. Perhaps it is the result of another computation that can't have a negative result, or it is a parameter of a method that requires its callers to supply only positive inputs. Still, you want to double-check rather than allow confusing "not a number" floating-point values creep into your computation. You could, of course, throw an exception:

```
if (x < 0) throw new IllegalArgumentException("x < 0");
```

But this code stays in the program, even after testing is complete. If you have lots of checks of this kind, the program may run quite a bit slower than it should.

The assertion mechanism allows you to put in checks during testing and to have them automatically removed in the production code.

The Java language has a keyword `assert`. There are two forms:

```
assert condition;
```

and

```
assert condition : expression;
```

Both statements evaluate the condition and throw an `AssertionError` if it is `false`. In the second statement, the expression is passed to the constructor of the `AssertionError` object and turned into a message string.

 Note: The sole purpose of the *expression* part is to produce a message string. The `AssertionError` object does not store the actual expression value, so you can't query it later. As the JDK documentation states, doing so "would encourage programmers to attempt to recover from assertion failure, which defeats the purpose of the facility."

To assert that x is non-negative, you can simply use the statement

```
assert x >= 0;
```

Or you can pass the actual value of x into the `AssertionError` object, so that it gets displayed later.

```
assert x >= 0 : x;
```

 C++ Note: The assert macro of the C language turns the assertion condition into a string that is printed if the assertion fails. For example, if `assert(x >= 0)` fails, it prints that `"x >= 0"` is the failing condition. In Java, the condition is not automatically part of the error report. If you want to see it, you have to pass it as a string into the `AssertionError` object: `assert x >= 0 : "x >= 0"`.

7.4.2. Assertion Enabling and Disabling

By default, assertions are disabled. Enable them by running the program with the `-enableassertions` or `-ea` option:

```
java -enableassertions MyApp
```

Note that you do not have to recompile your program to enable or disable assertions. Enabling or disabling assertions is a function of the *class loader*. When assertions are disabled, the class loader strips out the assertion code so that it won't slow execution.

You can even turn on assertions in specific classes or in entire packages. For example:

```
java -ea:MyClass -ea:com.mycompany.mylib... MyApp
```

This command turns on assertions for the class MyClass and all classes in the com.mycompany.mylib package *and its subpackages*. The option -ea:... turns on assertions in all classes of the unnamed package.

You can also disable assertions in certain classes and packages with the -disableassertions or -da option:

```
java -ea:... -da:MyClass MyApp
```

Some classes are not loaded by a class loader but directly by the virtual machine. You can use these switches to selectively enable or disable assertions in those classes.

However, the -ea and -da switches that enable or disable all assertions do not apply to the "system classes" without class loaders. Use the -enablesystemassertions/-esa switch to enable assertions in system classes.

It is also possible to programmatically control the assertion status of class loaders. See the API notes at the end of this section.

 Caution: When assertions are turned off, the assertion condition does not execute. Therefore, it is important that the condition does not have a side effect. Here is an example of something that you should not do:

```
File file = new File(filename);
. . .
assert file.delete(); // BAD
```

The intent was to make sure that the delete method returns true, which means the file was properly deleted. But when assertions are turned off, the deletion won't happen!

The remedy is to move the side effect outside the assert statement:

```
boolean deletionSuccessful = file.delete();
assert deletionSuccessful;
```

Note: The source code for the Java library has over four hundred assertions that are commented out. Some programmers comment out assertions after testing because otherwise they take up space in the class files. If you are concerned about that, you can conditionally include them as follows:

```
public static final boolean ASSERTS = true; // Recompile with false for production
. . .
if (ASSERTS) assert x >= 0;
```

7.4.3. Using Assertions for Parameter Checking

The Java language gives you three mechanisms to deal with system failures:

- Throwing an exception
- Logging
- Using assertions

When should you choose assertions? Keep these points in mind:

- Assertion failures are intended to be fatal, unrecoverable errors.
- Assertion checks are turned on only during development and testing. (This is sometimes jokingly described as "wearing a life jacket when you are close to shore, and throwing it overboard once you are in the middle of the ocean.")

Therefore, you would not use assertions for signaling recoverable conditions to another part of the program or for communicating problems to the program user. Assertions should only be used to locate internal program errors during testing.

Let's look at a common scenario—the checking of method parameters. Should you use assertions to check for illegal index values or null references? To answer that question, you have to look at the documentation of the method. Suppose you implement a sorting method.

```
/**
    Sorts the specified range of the specified array in ascending numerical order.
    The range to be sorted extends from fromIndex, inclusive, to toIndex, exclusive.
    @param a the array to be sorted
    @param fromIndex the index of the first element (inclusive) to be sorted
    @param toIndex the index of the last element (exclusive) to be sorted
    @throws IllegalArgumentException if fromIndex > toIndex
    @throws ArrayIndexOutOfBoundsException if fromIndex < 0 or toIndex > a.length
*/
static void sort(int[] a, int fromIndex, int toIndex)
```

The documentation states that the method throws an exception if the index values are incorrect. That behavior is part of the contract that the method makes with its callers. If you implement the method, you have to respect that contract and throw the indicated exceptions. It would not be appropriate to use assertions instead.

Should you assert that a is not null? That is not appropriate either. The method documentation is silent on the behavior of the method when a is null. The callers have the right to assume that the method will return successfully in that case and not throw an assertion error.

However, suppose the method contract had been slightly different:

```
@param a the array to be sorted (must not be null)
```

Now the callers of the method have been put on notice that it is illegal to call the method with a null array. Then the method may start with the assertion

```
assert a != null;
```

Computer scientists call this kind of contract a *precondition*. The original method had no preconditions on its parameters—it promised a well-defined behavior in all cases. The revised method has a single precondition: that a is not null. If the caller fails to fulfill the precondition, then all bets are off and the method can do anything it wants. In fact, with the assertion in place, the method does just that. It sometimes throws an assertion error, and sometimes a null pointer exception, depending on how its class loader is configured.

7.4.4. Using Assertions for Documenting Assumptions

Often, programmers use comments to document their underlying assumptions. Consider this example from https://docs.oracle.com/javase/8/docs/technotes/guides/language/assert.html:

```
if (i % 3 == 0)
   . . .
else if (i % 3 == 1)
   . . .
else // (i % 3 == 2)
   . . .
```

In this case, it makes a lot of sense to use an assertion instead.

```
if (i % 3 == 0)
   . . .
else if (i % 3 == 1)
   . . .
else
{
```

```
    assert i % 3 == 2;
    . . .
  }
```

Of course, it would make even more sense to think through the issue thoroughly. What are the possible values of i % 3? If i is positive, the remainders must be 0, 1, or 2. If i is negative, then the remainders can be -1 or -2. Thus, the real assumption is that i is not negative. A better assertion would be

```
  assert i >= 0;
```

before the if statement.

At any rate, this example shows a good use of assertions as a self-check for the programmer. As you can see, assertions are a tactical tool for testing and debugging. In contrast, logging is a strategic tool for the entire lifecycle of a program. We will examine logging in the next section.

---

java.lang.ClassLoader 1.0

- void setDefaultAssertionStatus(boolean b) **1.4**
  enables or disables assertions for all classes loaded by this class loader that don't have an explicit class or package assertion status.
- void setClassAssertionStatus(String className, boolean b) **1.4**
  enables or disables assertions for the given class and its inner classes.
- void setPackageAssertionStatus(String packageName, boolean b) **1.4**
  enables or disables assertions for all classes in the given package and its subpackages.
- void clearAssertionStatus() **1.4**
  removes all explicit class and package assertion status settings and disables assertions for all classes loaded by this class loader.

7.5. Logging

Every Java programmer is familiar with the process of inserting System.out.println calls into troublesome code to gain insight into program behavior. Of course, once you have figured out the cause of trouble, you remove the print statements—only to put them back in when the next problem surfaces. Logging frameworks are designed to overcome this problem.

7.5.1. Should You Use the Java Logging Framework?

Java has a standard logging framework, usually called after its package name java.util.logging and sometimes abbreviated as j.u.l. However, other logging frameworks have more features and are in common use, such as Log4j (https://logging.apache.org/log4j/2.x) and Logback (https://logback.qos.ch).

If you want to give users of your code the choice of logging framework, then you should use a "façade" library that sends log messages to the preferred framework. A commonly used façade with a pleasant API is SLF4J (https://www.slf4j.org). Another façade is the "platform logging API" (also known as JEP 264). It is very basic but a part of the JDK. The façade is sometimes called the *frontend*. It provides the API that programmers use to log messages. The *backend* is in charge of filtering and formatting the messages, and putting them somewhere. The backend needs to be configurable by deployers, usually by editing configuration files.

In the following sections, I will show you how to use the platform logging API as frontend and java.util.logging as a backend. This can be a reasonable choice if you find the frontend API sufficient, since you can always swap out the backend.

The java.util.logging backend has fewer features than its more popular alternatives, but it suffices for many use cases. Because of its simplicity, it is less susceptible to attacks. In contrast, obscure features of Log4j allowed hackers to craft program inputs that, when logged, caused malicious code execution.

Whether or not you end up using them, studying the platform logging API and java.util.logging backend gives you a good foundation of the capabilities of logging frameworks.

 Note: The API and backend that the following sections describe is for *application logging*. You can also turn on logging for the virtual machine, for example to log garbage collection. Use the -Xlog command-line option when starting the VM. For example,

```
java -Xlog:gc=trace:file=gc.log:uptime,tid MyApp
```

See https://docs.oracle.com/en/java/javase/21/docs/specs/man/java.html#enable-logging-with-the-jvm-unified-logging-framework for details.

7.5.2. Logging 101

Platform loggers implement the System.Logger interface. Each logger has a name. The name can be arbitrary, but it is often the package name of the class whose methods generate logging messages. You get a platform logger like this:

```
System.Logger logger = System.getLogger("com.mycompany.myapp");
```

When you request a logger with a given name for the first time, it is created. Subsequent calls to the same name yield the same logger object.

Now you are ready to log:

```
logger.log(System.Logger.Level.INFO, "Opening file " + filename);
```

The record is printed like this:

```
Aug 04, 2022 09:53:34 AM com.mycompany.myapp.Main read
INFO: Opening file data.txt
```

Note that the time and the names of the calling class and method are automatically included.

To turn off these informational messages when your program is deployed, you can configure the backend. In the case of the java.util.logging backend, prepare a file logging.properties with the following contents:

```
handlers=java.util.logging.ConsoleHandler
com.mycompany.myapp.level=WARNING
```

Then start the application like this:

```
java -Djava.util.logging.config.file=logging.properties com.mycompany.myapp.Main
```

Since the INFO level is below the WARNING level, the message no longer shows up.

The API for getting the logger and logging a message is part of the frontend—in this case, the platform logging API. If you use a different frontend, the API will be different.

The message destination, formatting, and filtering, as well as the mechanisms for the configuration are part of the backend—here, java.util.logging. If you use a different backend, follow its instructions for configuration.

7.5.3. The Platform Logging API

As you saw in the preceding section, each logged message has a level. The enumeration System.Logger.Level has the following values, in decreasing severity: ERROR, WARNING, INFO, DEBUG, and TRACE.

 Tip: With the import statement

```
import static java.lang.System.Logger.Level.*;
```

you can shorten the levels:

```
logger.log(INFO, "Opening file " + filename);
    // Instead of System.Logger.Level.INFO
```

In the above example, the message "Opening file " + filename is created even if the message is suppressed. If you are concerned with the cost of creating the message string, you can use a lambda expression instead:

```
logger.log(INFO, () -> "Opening file " + filename);
```

Then the message is only computed when it is actually logged.

It is common to log an exception. The log includes the stack trace.

```
catch (IOException ex)
{
    logger.log(WARNING, "Cannot open file " + filename, ex);
}
```

You can format the message using a pattern:

```
logger.log(WARNING, "Cannot open file {0}", filename);
```

 Caution: This is *not* a printf style pattern. The pattern is processed by the MessageFormat class that is used for localization of program messages (see Volume II for details). Here, you just need to know that string placeholders are {0}, {1}, and so on. Braces must be escaped with single quotes: '{', '}'. Use two single quotes '' to include a literal single quote in the message.

Log messages can be localized to different languages, using the resource bundle mechanism that is introduced in Volume II.

Supply the bundle and the key for the formatting string:

```
logger.log(WARNING, bundle, "file.bad", filename);
    // Looks up file.bad in the bundle
```

Alternatively, get the logger as

```
System.Logger logger = System.getLogger("com.mycompany.myapp", bundle);
```

When calling one of the logger methods with a String parameter for the message or format, the argument is interpreted as a key in the bundle. The methods with Object or Supplier<String> parameters are unaffected.

Some, but not all combinations of these features (deferred message computation, adding a throwable, formatting, using a bundle) are supported. See the API notes for details.

7.5.4. Logging Configuration

Let us now turn to the logging backend. As already mentioned, the default backend of the platform logging API is `java.util.logging`. The information in the following sections is specific to that backend.

You can change various properties of the backend by editing a configuration file. The default configuration file is located at `conf/logging.properties` in the JDK. To use another file, set the `java.util.logging.config.file` property to the file location by starting your application with

```
java -Djava.util.logging.config.file=configFile MainClass
```

Caution: Calling `System.setProperty("java.util.logging.config.file", configFile)` in `main` has no effect because the log manager is initialized during VM startup, before `main` executes.

You can specify the logging levels for your own loggers by adding lines such as

```
com.mycompany.myapp.level=WARNING
```

That is, append the `.level` suffix to the logger name.

Note: Properties in the logging configuration are not system properties. You cannot set them with the `-D` command-line option. Instead, place the logging properties into a file that you specify with `-Djava.util.logging.config.file=configFile`.

You can also specify the root level:

```
.level=WARNING
```

Caution: For historical reasons, some of the levels have different names in the platform logging API and the `java.util.logging` framework. You need to use the latter in the configuration file. Table 7.1 shows the correspondences.

Table 7.1: Corresponding Levels for Platform Logging and the Java Logging Framework

Platform Logging	java.util.logging
ERROR	SEVERE

WARNING	WARNING
INFO	INFO
DEBUG	FINE
TRACE	FINER

Similar to package names, logger names are hierarchical. In fact, they are more hierarchical than packages. There is no semantic relationship between a package and its parent, but logger parents and children share certain properties. For example, if you turn off messages to the logger "com.mycompany", then its child loggers are also deactivated.

As you will see in the next section, loggers don't actually send the messages to the console—that is the job of the handlers. Handlers also have levels. To see DEBUG/FINE messages on the console, you also need to set

```
java.util.logging.ConsoleHandler.level=FINE
```

 Caution: The settings in the log manager configuration are not system properties. Starting a program with -Dcom.mycompany.myapp.level=FINE does not have any effect on the logger.

It is also possible to change logging levels in a running program by using the jconsole program. For details, see https://www.oracle.com/technical-resources/articles/java/jconsole.html#LoggingControl.

 Note: As of Java 21, the system logger with name java.lang.Runtime logs calls to the Runtime.exit method (which System.exit calls to terminate the virtual machine). The log contains the stack trace, so you can tell how termination was requested. To receive the log message, set

```
java.lang.Runtime.level=FINE
```

in the log configuration.

7.5.5. Log Handlers

The backend of the java.util.logging API is based on *handlers*. The simplest handler is the ConsoleHandler that prints log records to the System.err stream.

Each handler has a parent. By default, the handler simply sends each record to the parent handler. The standard logging configuration uses a `ConsoleHandler` by default. Its default logging level is `INFO`.

To send log records elsewhere, add another handler. The `java.util.logging` API provides two handlers for this purpose: a `FileHandler` and a `SocketHandler`. The `SocketHandler` sends records to a specified host and port. Of greater interest is the `FileHandler` that collects records in a file.

To add a file handler, provide this entry in the logging properties:

```
handlers=java.util.logging.ConsoleHandler,java.util.logging.FileHandler
```

The records are sent to a file java*n*.log in the user's home directory, where *n* is a number to make the file unique. By default, the records are formatted in XML. A typical log record has the form

```
<record>
    <date>2014-08-04T09:53:34</date>
    <millis>1407146014072</millis>
    <sequence>1</sequence>
    <logger>com.mycompany.myapp</logger>
    <level>INFO</level>
    <class>com.horstmann.corejava.Employee</class>
    <method>read</method>
    <thread>10</thread>
    <message>Opening file staff.txt</message>
</record>
```

You can modify the default behavior of the file handler by setting various parameters in the logging properties (see Table 7.2).

You probably don't want to use the default log file name. Use a pattern such as `%h/myapp%u.log` (see Table 7.3 for an explanation of the pattern variables.) The `%u` in the file name pattern yields a unique copy of the log for each application run.

For long-running programs, it is a good idea to turn file rotation on. Log files are kept in a rotation sequence, such as `myapp.log.0`, `myapp.log.1`, `myapp.log.2`, and so on. Whenever a file exceeds the size limit, the oldest log is deleted, the other files are renamed, and a new file with generation number 0 is created.

Table 7.2: File Handler Configuration Parameters

Configuration Property	Description	Default
`java.util.logging.FileHandler.level`	The handler level.	`Level.ALL`

`java.util.logging.FileHandler.append`	When true, log records are appended to an existing file; otherwise, a new file is opened for each program run.	false
`java.util.logging.FileHandler.limit`	The approximate maximum number of bytes to write in a file before opening another (0 = no limit).	0 in the FileHandler class, 50000 in the default log manager configuration
`java.util.logging.FileHandler.pattern`	The file name pattern (see Table 7.3).	%h/java%u.log
`java.util.logging.FileHandler.count`	The number of logs in a rotation sequence.	1 (no rotation)
`java.util.logging.FileHandler.filter`	The filter for filtering log records (see Section 7.5.6).	No filtering
`java.util.logging.FileHandler.encoding`	The character encoding.	The platform character encoding

`java.util.logging.FileHandler.formatter`	The formatter for each log record.	`java.util.logging.XMLFormatter`

Table 7.3: Log File Pattern Variables

Variable	Description
%h	The user's home directory (the `user.home` property).
%t	The system's temporary directory.
%u	A unique number.
%g	The generation number for rotated logs. A .%g suffix is used if rotation is specified and the pattern doesn't contain %g.
%%	The percent character.

 Caution: When `java.util.logging.FileHandler.append` is `true`, and the log format is XML, then a new XML header is emitted when appending to an existing log file. The result is not valid XML.

7.5.6. Filters and Formatters

Besides filtering by logging levels, each handler can have an additional filter that implements the `Filter` interface, a functional interface with a method

```
boolean isLoggable(LogRecord record)
```

To install a filter into a handler, add an entry such as the following into the logging configuration:

```
java.util.logging.ConsoleHandler.filter=com.mycompany.myapp.MyFilter
```

The `ConsoleHandler` and `FileHandler` classes emit the log records in text and XML formats. However, you can define your own formats as well. Extend the `java.util.logging.Formatter` class and override the method

```
String format(LogRecord record)
```

Format the record in any way you like and return the resulting string. In your format method, you can get information about the LogRecord by calling one of the methods in the API notes.

In your format method, you may want to call the method

```
String formatMessage(LogRecord record)
```

That method formats the message part of the record, looking up the message key in a resource bundle and substituting message format parameters.

Many file formats (such as XML) require head and tail parts that surround the formatted records. To achieve this, override the methods

```
String getHead(Handler h)
String getTail(Handler h)
```

Finally, set the formatter in the logging configuration:

```
java.util.logging.FileHandler.formatter=com.mycompany.myapp.MyFormatter
```

7.5.7. A Logging Recipe

With so many options for logging, it is easy to lose track of the fundamentals. The following recipe summarizes the most common operations.

1. For a simple application, choose a single logger. It is a good idea to give the logger the same name as your main application package, such as com.mycompany.myprog. You can always get the logger by calling

   ```
   System.Logger logger = System.getLogger("com.mycompany.myprog");
   ```

   For convenience, you may want to add static fields

   ```
   private static final System.Logger logger
       = System.getLogger("com.mycompany.myprog");
   ```

   to classes with a lot of logging activity.
2. The default logging configuration of the java.util.logging backend logs all messages of level INFO or higher to the console. To customize, prepare a file logging.properties with entries such as the following:

   ```
   handlers=java.util.logging.ConsoleHandler,java.util.logging.FileHandler
   com.mycompany.myapp.level=FINER
   java.util.logging.ConsoleHandler.level=FINE
   ```

   Then start your app with

```
java -Djava.util.logging.config.file=logging.properties com.mycompany.myapp.Main
```

3. Now you are ready to log to your heart's content. Whenever you are tempted to call System.out.println, emit a log message instead:

```
logger.log(System.Logger.Level.TRACE, "File open dialog canceled");
```

It is also a good idea to log unexpected exceptions. For example:

```
try
{
    . . .
}
catch (SomeException e)
{
    logger.log(System.Logger.Level.WARNING, string describing context, e);
}
```

Listing 7.2 puts this recipe to use with an added twist: Logging messages are also displayed in a log window, thanks to a handler whose code is in Listing 7.3.

Run the program as

```
java -Djava.util.logging.config.file=logging.properties logging.LoggingImageViewer
```

Listing 7.2 `logging/LoggingImageViewer.java`

```
 1   package logging;
 2
 3   import java.awt.*;
 4   import java.awt.event.*;
 5   import java.io.*;
 6   import javax.swing.*;
 7
 8   import static java.lang.System.Logger.Level.*;
 9
10
11   /**
12    * A modification of the image viewer program that logs various events. Run as
13    * java -Djava.util.logging.config.file=logging.properties logging.LoggingImageViewer
14    * @version 1.1 2023-09-26
15    * @author Cay Horstmann
16    */
17   public class LoggingImageViewer
18   {
19
20
21       public static void main(String[] args)
```

```
22       {
23          EventQueue.invokeLater(() ->
24             {
25                var frame = new ImageViewerFrame();
26                frame.setTitle("LoggingImageViewer");
27                frame.setDefaultCloseOperation(JFrame.EXIT_ON_CLOSE);
28                System.Logger logger = System.getLogger("com.horstmann.corejava");
29                logger.log(INFO, "Showing frame");
30                frame.setVisible(true);
31             });
32       }
33    }
34
35    /**
36     * The frame that shows the image.
37     */
38    class ImageViewerFrame extends JFrame
39    {
40       private static final int DEFAULT_WIDTH = 300;
41       private static final int DEFAULT_HEIGHT = 400;
42
43       private JLabel label;
44       private static System.Logger logger = System.getLogger("com.horstmann.corejava");
45
46       public ImageViewerFrame()
47       {
48          logger.log(TRACE, "Entering ImageViewerFrame()");
49          setSize(DEFAULT_WIDTH, DEFAULT_HEIGHT);
50
51          // set up menu bar
52          var menuBar = new JMenuBar();
53          setJMenuBar(menuBar);
54
55          var menu = new JMenu("File");
56          menuBar.add(menu);
57
58          var openItem = new JMenuItem("Open");
59          menu.add(openItem);
60          openItem.addActionListener(new FileOpenListener());
61
62          var exitItem = new JMenuItem("Exit");
63          menu.add(exitItem);
64          exitItem.addActionListener(new ActionListener()
65             {
66                public void actionPerformed(ActionEvent event)
67                {
68                   logger.log(INFO, "Exiting.");
69                   System.exit(0);
70                }
71             });
72
73          // use a label to display the images
```

```
 74        label = new JLabel();
 75        add(label);
 76        logger.log(TRACE, "Exiting ImageViewerFrame()");
 77     }
 78
 79     private class FileOpenListener implements ActionListener
 80     {
 81        public void actionPerformed(ActionEvent event)
 82        {
 83           logger.log(TRACE, "Entering ImageViewerFrame.FileOpenListener.actionPerformed(%s)",
 84                 event);
 85
 86           // set up file chooser
 87           var chooser = new JFileChooser();
 88           chooser.setCurrentDirectory(new File("."));
 89
 90           // accept all files ending with .gif
 91           chooser.setFileFilter(new javax.swing.filechooser.FileFilter()
 92              {
 93                 public boolean accept(File f)
 94                 {
 95                    return f.getName().toLowerCase().endsWith(".gif") || f.isDirectory();
 96                 }
 97
 98                 public String getDescription()
 99                 {
100                    return "GIF Images";
101                 }
102              });
103
104           // show file chooser dialog
105           int r = chooser.showOpenDialog(ImageViewerFrame.this);
106
107           // if image file accepted, set it as icon of the label
108           if (r == JFileChooser.APPROVE_OPTION)
109           {
110              String name = chooser.getSelectedFile().getPath();
111              logger.log(DEBUG, "Reading file %s", name);
112              label.setIcon(new ImageIcon(name));
113           }
114           else logger.log(DEBUG, "File open dialog canceled.");
115           logger.log(TRACE, "Exiting ImageViewerFrame.FileOpenListener.actionPerformed");
116        }
117     }
118 }
```

Listing 7.3 `logging/WindowHandler.java`

```java
1   package logging;
2
3   import java.awt.*;
4   import java.awt.event.*;
5   import java.io.*;
6   import java.util.logging.*;
7   import javax.swing.*;
8
9   /**
10   * A handler for displaying log records in a window.
11   */
12  public class WindowHandler extends StreamHandler
13  {
14     private JFrame frame;
15
16     public WindowHandler()
17     {
18        frame = new JFrame();
19        var output = new JTextArea();
20        output.setEditable(false);
21        frame.setSize(200, 200);
22        frame.add(new JScrollPane(output));
23        frame.setFocusableWindowState(false);
24        frame.setVisible(true);
25        setOutputStream(new OutputStream()
26           {
27              public void write(int b)
28              {
29              } // not called
30
31              public void write(byte[] b, int off, int len)
32              {
33                 output.append(new String(b, off, len));
34              }
35           });
36     }
37
38     public void publish(LogRecord record)
39     {
40        if (!frame.isVisible()) return;
41        super.publish(record);
42        flush();
43     }
44  }
```

---

java.lang.System.Logger 9

- `String getName()`
  returns the name of this logger.
- `boolean isLoggable(System.Logger.Level level)`
  returns true if this logger processes logs at the given level.
- `void log(System.Logger.Level level, String msg)`
- `void log(System.Logger.Level level, String msg, Throwable thrown)`
- `void log(System.Logger.Level level, Object obj)`
  log the given message and any provided Throwable, or obj.toString.
- `void log(System.Logger.Level level, Supplier<String> msgSupplier)`
- `void log(System.Logger.Level level, Supplier<String> msgSupplier, Throwable thrown)`
  If this logger processes logs at the given level, invokes the supplier and logs the result and any provided Throwable.
- `void log(System.Logger.Level level, String format, Object... params)`
  logs the formatted message with the given parameters.
- `void log(System.Logger.Level level, ResourceBundle bundle, String format, Object... params)`
  If bundle is null, uses the format string directly, otherwise looks it up using format as key in the bundle. Then uses the format string as a MessageFormat with the given parameters and logs the result.
- `void log(System.Logger.Level level, ResourceBundle bundle, String msg, Throwable thrown)`
  If bundle is null, logs msg, otherwise the string with msg as key in the bundle. Then logs thrown if not null.

---

java.util.logging.Handler 1.4

- `abstract void publish(LogRecord record)`
  sends the record to the intended destination.
- `abstract void flush()`
  flushes any buffered data.
- `abstract void close()`
  flushes any buffered data and releases all associated resources.
- `Filter getFilter()`
- `void setFilter(Filter f)`
  get and set the filter of this handler.
- `Formatter getFormatter()`
- `void setFormatter(Formatter f)`
  get and set the formatter of this handler.
- `Level getLevel()`
- `void setLevel(Level l)`
  get and set the level of this handler.

---

java.util.logging.ConsoleHandler 1.4

■ ConsoleHandler()
constructs a new console handler.

---

java.util.logging.FileHandler 1.4

■ FileHandler(String pattern)
■ FileHandler(String pattern, boolean append)
■ FileHandler(String pattern, int limit, int count)
■ FileHandler(String pattern, int limit, int count, boolean append)
■ FileHandler(String pattern, long limit, int count, boolean append) 9
construct a file handler. See Table 7.3 for the pattern format. limit is the approximate maximum number of bytes before a new log file is opened. count is the number of files in a rotation sequence. If append is true, records should be appended to an existing log file.

---

java.util.logging.LogRecord 1.4

■ Level getLevel()
gets the logging level of this record.
■ String getLoggerName()
gets the name of the logger that is logging this record.
■ ResourceBundle getResourceBundle()
■ String getResourceBundleName()
get the resource bundle, or its name, to be used for localizing the message, or null if none is provided.
■ String getMessage()
gets the "raw" message before localization or formatting.
■ Object[] getParameters()
gets the parameter objects, or null if none is provided.
■ Throwable getThrown()
gets the thrown object, or null if none is provided.
■ String getSourceClassName()
■ String getSourceMethodName()
get the location of the code that logged this record. This information may be supplied by the logging code or automatically inferred from the runtime stack. It might be inaccurate if the logging code supplied the wrong value or if the running code was optimized so that the exact location cannot be inferred.
■ long getMillis()
gets the creation time, in milliseconds since 1970.
■ Instant getInstant() 9
gets the creation time as a java.time.Instant (see Chapter 6 of Volume II).

- `long getSequenceNumber()`
  gets the unique sequence number of this record.
- `long getLongThreadID()` **16**
  gets the unique ID for the thread in which this record was created. (The `getThreadID` method returns int IDs. It is now deprecated because a long-running program might generate more than `Integer.MAX_VALUE` thread IDs.)

`java.util.logging.Filter` 1.4

- `boolean isLoggable(LogRecord record)`
  returns `true` if the given log record should be logged.

`java.util.logging.Formatter` 1.4

- `abstract String format(LogRecord record)`
  returns the string that results from formatting the given log record.
- `String getHead(Handler h)`
- `String getTail(Handler h)`
  return the strings that should appear at the head and tail of the document containing the log records. The `Formatter` superclass defines these methods to return the empty string; override them if necessary.
- `String formatMessage(LogRecord record)`
  returns the localized and formatted message part of the log record.

7.6. Debugging Tips

Suppose you wrote your program and made it bulletproof by catching and properly handling all exceptions. Then you run it, and it does not work right. Now what? (If you never have this problem, you can skip the remainder of this chapter.)

Of course, it is best if you have a convenient and powerful debugger. Debuggers are available as a part of professional development environments such as Eclipse, IntelliJ, and NetBeans. In this section, I offer a number of tips that may be worth trying before you launch the debugger.

1. You can print or log the value of any variable with code like this:

   ```
   System.out.println("x=" + x);
   ```

   or

   ```
   logger.log(DEBUG, "x=" + x);
   ```

If x is a number, it is converted to its string equivalent. If x is an object, Java calls its toString method. It can also be useful to log the state of the this object.

```
logger.log(DEBUG, "this=" + this);
```

Most of the classes in the Java library are very conscientious about overriding the toString method to give you useful information about the class. This is a real boon for debugging. You should make the same effort in your classes.

2. You can put a separate main method in each class. Inside it, put code that demonstrates how the class should be used.

```
public class MyClass
{
    methods and fields
    . . .
    public static void main(String[] args)
    {
        demo code
    }
}
```

Make a few objects, call methods, and show that each of them does the right thing.

3. For more professional unit testing, you should check out JUnit from https://junit.org. JUnit is a very popular unit testing framework that makes it easy to organize suites of test cases. Run the tests whenever you make changes to a class, and add another test case whenever you find a bug.

4. A *logging proxy* is an object of a subclass that intercepts method calls, logs them, and then calls the original method. For example, if you have trouble with the nextDouble method of the Random class, you can create a proxy object as an instance of an anonymous subclass:

```
var generator = new Random()
    {
        public double nextDouble()
        {
            double result = super.nextDouble();
            logger.log(DEBUG, "nextDouble: " + result);
            return result;
        }
    };
```

Whenever the nextDouble method is called, a log message is generated. Note that this only works if the class is not final. With interfaces, one can implement a proxy that logs all methods, as shown in Chapter 6.

5. You can get a stack trace from any exception object with the `printStackTrace` method in the `Throwable` class. The following code catches any exception, prints the exception object and the stack trace, and rethrows the exception so it can find its intended handler.

```
try
{
    . . .
}
catch (Throwable t)
{
    t.printStackTrace();
    throw t;
}
```

You don't even need to catch an exception to generate a stack trace. Simply insert the statement

```
Thread.dumpStack();
```

anywhere into your code to get a stack trace.

6. Normally, the stack trace is displayed on `System.err`. If you want to log or display the stack trace, here is how you can capture it into a string:

```
var out = new StringWriter();
new Throwable().printStackTrace(new PrintWriter(out));
String description = out.toString();
```

7. It is often handy to trap program errors in a file. However, errors are sent to `System.err`, not `System.out`. Therefore, you cannot simply trap them by running

```
java MyProgram > errors.txt
```

Instead, capture the error stream as

```
java MyProgram 2> errors.txt
```

To capture both `System.err` and `System.out` in the same file, use

```
java MyProgram 1> errors.txt 2>&1
```

This works in bash and the Windows shell.

8. Having the stack traces of uncaught exceptions show up in `System.err` is not ideal. These messages are confusing to end users if they happen to see them, and they are not available for diagnostic purposes when you need them. A better approach is to

log them. You can change the handler for uncaught exceptions with the static
`Thread.setDefaultUncaughtExceptionHandler` method:

```
Thread.setDefaultUncaughtExceptionHandler((Thread t, Throwable e) ->
    logger.log(TRACE, "Uncaught exception in " + t, e));
```

9. To watch class loading, launch the Java virtual machine with the `-verbose` flag. You
will get a printout such as the following:

```
[0.012s][info][class,load] opened: /opt/jdk-21.0.1/lib/modules
[0.034s][info][class,load] java.lang.Object source: jrt:/java.base
[0.035s][info][class,load] java.io.Serializable source: jrt:/java.base
[0.035s][info][class,load] java.lang.Comparable source: jrt:/java.base
[0.035s][info][class,load] java.lang.CharSequence source: jrt:/java.base
[0.035s][info][class,load] java.lang.String source: jrt:/java.base
[0.036s][info][class,load] java.lang.reflect.AnnotatedElement source: jrt:/java.base
[0.036s][info][class,load] java.lang.reflect.GenericDeclaration source: jrt:/java.base
[0.036s][info][class,load] java.lang.reflect.Type source: jrt:/java.base
[0.036s][info][class,load] java.lang.Class source: jrt:/java.base
[0.036s][info][class,load] java.lang.Cloneable source: jrt:/java.base
[0.037s][info][class,load] java.lang.ClassLoader source: jrt:/java.base
[0.037s][info][class,load] java.lang.System source: jrt:/java.base
[0.037s][info][class,load] java.lang.Throwable source: jrt:/java.base
[0.037s][info][class,load] java.lang.Error source: jrt:/java.base
[0.037s][info][class,load] java.lang.ThreadDeath source: jrt:/java.base
[0.037s][info][class,load] java.lang.Exception source: jrt:/java.base
[0.037s][info][class,load] java.lang.RuntimeException source: jrt:/java.base
[0.038s][info][class,load] java.lang.SecurityManager source: jrt:/java.base
. . .
```

This can occasionally be helpful to diagnose class path problems.

10. The `-Xlint` option tells the compiler to spot common code problems. For example, if
you compile with the command

```
javac -Xlint sourceFiles
```

the compiler will report missing `break` statements in `switch` statements. (The term
"lint" originally described a tool for locating potential problems in C programs, but
is now generically applied to any tools that flag constructs that are questionable but
not illegal.)
You will get messages such as

```
warning: [fallthrough] possible fall-through into case
```

The string in square brackets identifies the warning category. You can enable and
disable each category. Since most of them are quite useful, it seems best to leave
them all in place and disable only those that you don't care about, like this:

```
javac -Xlint:all,-fallthrough,-serial sourceFiles
```

You get a list of all warnings from the command

```
javac --help -X
```

11. The Java VM has support for *monitoring and management* of Java applications, allowing the installation of agents in the virtual machine that track memory consumption, thread usage, class loading, and so on. This feature is particularly important for large and long-running Java programs. As a demonstration of these capabilities, the JDK ships with a graphical tool called jconsole that displays statistics about the performance of a virtual machine (see Figure 7.2). Start your program, then start jconsole and pick your program from the list of running Java programs.

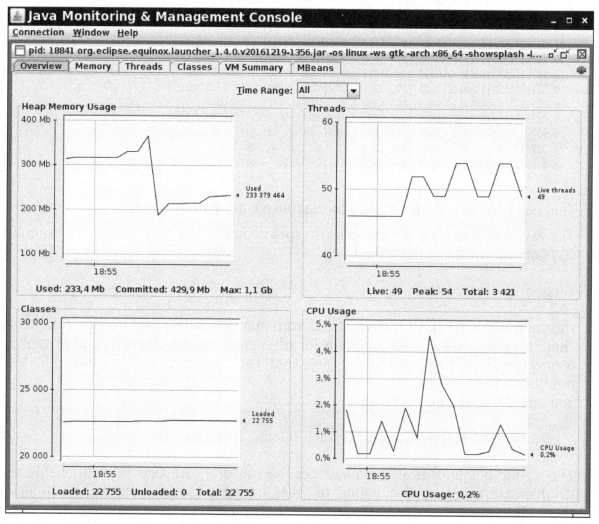

Figure 7.2: The jconsole program

This program gives you a wealth of information about your running program. See
`https://www.oracle.com/technical-resources/articles/java/jconsole.html` for more
information.

12. Java Flight Recorder is an instrumentation technology of the OpenJDK virtual
machine that collects diagnostic and profiling data. You can use the open-source
VisualVM (`https://visualvm.github.io`) and Java Mission Control
(`https://adoptium.net/jmc`) to collect and view flight recording data. These tools also
do everything that you can do with `jconsole`. See `https://github.com/thegreystone/jmc-tutorial` for a comprehensive tutorial for the latter.

13. The JDK comes with a number of command-line tools with overlapping use cases for
monitoring the virtual machine (`jcmd`, `jhsdb`, `jinfo`, `jmap`, `jps`, `jstat`). The `jcmd` tool is a
good starting point since it covers several of those use cases. Run

```
jcmd
```

to get a list of all Java processes on your computer, with process ID and the name of
the main class.
To list system properties or VM flags, run

```
jcmd pidOrMainClass VM.system_properties
jcmd pidOrMainClass VM.flags
```

You can configure the virtual machine log:

```
jcmd pidOrMainClass VM.log output=gc.log what=gc=trace decorators=uptime,tid
```

To get a thread dump, run

```
jcmd pidOrMainClass Thread.print
```

or

```
jcmd pidOrMainClass Thread.dump_to_file -overwrite -format=json dump.json
```

To start Java Flight Recorder, run

```
jcmd pidOrMainClass JFR.start filename=filename
```

To stop recording, run

```
jcmd pidOrMainClass JFR.stop name=1
```

To get a list of all available commands, run

```
jcmd pidOrMainClass
```

To get help for a particular command, run

```
jcmd pidOrMainClass help commandName
```

This chapter introduced you to exception handling and logging. You also saw useful hints for testing and debugging. The next two chapters cover generic programming and its most important application: the Java collections framework.

CHAPTER 8

Generic Programming

Generic classes and methods have type parameters. This allows them to describe precisely how the types should be used in the implementation. Prior to generic classes, programmers had to use the Object class for writing code that works with multiple types. This was both cumbersome and unsafe.

With the introduction of generics, Java has an expressive type system that allows designers to describe in detail how types of variables and methods should vary. In straightforward situations, you will find it simple to implement generic code. In more advanced cases, it can get quite complex—for implemetors. The goal is to provide classes and methods that other programmers can use without surprises.

The introduction of generics in Java 5 was a significant change in the Java programming language. A major design goal was to be backward compatible with earlier releases. As a result, Java generics have some uncomfortable limitations. You will learn about the benefits and challenges of generic programming in this chapter.

8.1. Why Generic Programming?

Generic programming means writing code that can be reused for objects of many different types. For example, you don't want to program separate classes to collect String and File objects. And you don't have to—the single class ArrayList collects objects of any class. This is one example of generic programming.

Actually, Java had an ArrayList class before it had generic classes. Let us investigate how the mechanism for generic programming has evolved, and what that means for users and implementors.

8.1.1. The Advantage of Type Parameters

Before generic classes were added to Java, generic programming was achieved with *inheritance*. The ArrayList class simply maintained an array of Object references:

```
public class ArrayList // before generic classes
{
   private Object[] elementData;
   . . .
```

```
    public Object get(int i) { . . . }
    public void add(Object o) { . . . }
}
```

This approach has two problems. A cast is necessary whenever you retrieve a value:

```
ArrayList files = new ArrayList();
 . . .
String filename = (String) files.get(0);
```

Moreover, there is no error checking. You can add values of any class:

```
files.add(new File(". . ."));
```

This call compiles and runs without error. Elsewhere, casting the result of get to a String will cause an error.

Generics offer a better solution: *type parameters*. The ArrayList class now has a type parameter that indicates the element type:

```
var files = new ArrayList<String>();
```

This makes your code easier to read. You can tell right away that this particular array list contains String objects.

 Note: If you declare a variable with an explicit type instead of var, you can omit the type parameter in the constructor by using the "diamond" syntax:

```
    ArrayList<String> files = new ArrayList<>();
```

The omitted type is inferred from the type of the variable.

You can use diamonds with anonymous subclasses:

```
    ArrayList<String> passwords = new ArrayList<>()
        {
            public String get(int n) { return super.get(n).replaceAll(".", "*"); }
        };
```

The compiler can make good use of the type information too. No cast is required for calling get. The compiler knows that the return type is String, not Object:

```
String filename = files.get(0);
```

The compiler also knows that the add method of an ArrayList<String> has a parameter of type String. That is a lot safer than having an Object parameter. Now the compiler can check that you don't insert objects of the wrong type. For example, the statement

```
files.add(new File(". . .")); // can only add String objects to an ArrayList<String>
```

will not compile. A compiler error is much better than a class cast exception at runtime.

This is the appeal of type parameters: They make your programs easier to read and safer.

8.1.2. Who Wants to Be a Generic Programmer?

It is easy to use a generic class such as ArrayList. Most Java programmers will simply use types such as ArrayList<String> as if they had been built into the language, just like String[] arrays. (Of course, array lists are better than arrays because they can expand automatically.)

However, it is not so easy to implement a generic class. The programmers who use your code will want to plug in all sorts of classes for your type parameters. They will expect everything to work without onerous restrictions and confusing error messages. Your job as a generic programmer, therefore, is to anticipate all the potential future uses of your class.

How hard can this get? Here is a typical issue that the designers of the standard class library had to grapple with. The ArrayList class has a method addAll to add all elements of another collection. A programmer may want to add all elements from an ArrayList<Manager> to an ArrayList<Employee>. But, of course, doing it the other way round should not be legal. How do you allow one call and disallow the other? The Java language designers invented an ingenious new concept, the *wildcard type*, to solve this problem. Wildcard types are rather abstract, but they allow a library builder to make methods as flexible as possible.

Generic programming falls into three skill levels. At a basic level, you just use generic classes—typically, collections such as ArrayList—without thinking how and why they work. Most application programmers will want to stay at that level until something goes wrong. You may, however, encounter a confusing error message when mixing different generic classes, or when interfacing with legacy code that knows nothing about type parameters; at that point, you'll need to learn enough about Java generics to solve problems systematically rather than through random tinkering. Finally, of course, you may want to implement your own generic classes and methods.

Application programmers probably won't write lots of generic code. The JDK developers have already done the heavy lifting and supplied type parameters for all the collection classes. As a rule of thumb, only code that traditionally involved lots of casts from very general types (such as Object or the Comparable interface) will benefit from using type parameters.

In this chapter, I will show you everything you need to know to implement your own generic code. However, I expect that most readers will use this knowledge primarily for help with troubleshooting and to satisfy their curiosity about the inner workings of the parameterized collection classes.

8.2. Defining a Simple Generic Class

A *generic class* is a class with one or more type variables. In this chapter, a simple Pair class is used as an example. This class allows us to focus on generics without being distracted by data storage details. Here is the code for the generic Pair class:

```
public class Pair<T>
{
   private T first;
   private T second;

   public Pair() { first = null; second = null; }
   public Pair(T first, T second) { this.first = first; this.second = second; }

   public T getFirst() { return first; }
   public T getSecond() { return second; }

   public void setFirst(T newValue) { first = newValue; }
   public void setSecond(T newValue) { second = newValue; }
}
```

The Pair class introduces a type variable T, enclosed in angle brackets < >, after the class name. A generic class can have more than one type variable. For example, we could have defined the Pair class with separate types for the first and second field:

```
public class Pair<T, U> { . . . }
```

The type variables are used throughout the class definition to specify method return types and the types of fields and local variables. For example:

```
private T first; // uses the type variable
```

 Note: It is common practice to use uppercase letters for type variables, and to keep them short. The Java library uses the variable E for the element type of a collection, K and V for key and value types of a table, and T (and the neighboring letters U and S, if necessary) for "any type at all."

You *instantiate* the generic type by substituting types for the type variables, such as

```
Pair<String>
```

You can think of the result as an ordinary class with constructors

```
Pair<String>()
Pair<String>(String, String)
```

and methods

```
String getFirst()
String getSecond()
void setFirst(String)
void setSecond(String)
```

In other words, the generic class acts as a factory for ordinary classes.

The program in Listing 8.1 puts the Pair class to work. The static minmax method traverses an array and simultaneously computes the minimum and maximum values. It uses a Pair object to return both results. Recall that the compareTo method compares two strings, returning 0 if the strings are identical, a negative integer if the first string comes before the second in dictionary order, and a positive integer otherwise.

 C++ Note: Superficially, generic classes in Java are similar to template classes in C++. The only obvious difference is that Java has no special template keyword. However, as you will see throughout this chapter, there are substantial differences between these two mechanisms.

Listing 8.1 `pair1/PairTest1.java`

```java
1   package pair1;
2
3   /**
4    * @version 1.01 2012-01-26
5    * @author Cay Horstmann
6    */
7   public class PairTest1
8   {
9      public static void main(String[] args)
10     {
11        String[] words = { "Mary", "had", "a", "little", "lamb" };
12        Pair<String> mm = ArrayAlg.minmax(words);
13        System.out.println("min = " + mm.getFirst());
14        System.out.println("max = " + mm.getSecond());
15     }
16  }
17
18  class ArrayAlg
```

```
19  {
20      /**
21       * Gets the minimum and maximum of an array of strings.
22       * @param a an array of strings
23       * @return a pair with the min and max values, or null if a is null or empty
24       */
25      public static Pair<String> minmax(String[] a)
26      {
27         if (a == null || a.length == 0) return null;
28         String min = a[0];
29         String max = a[0];
30         for (int i = 1; i < a.length; i++)
31         {
32            if (min.compareTo(a[i]) > 0) min = a[i];
33            if (max.compareTo(a[i]) < 0) max = a[i];
34         }
35         return new Pair<>(min, max);
36      }
37  }
```

8.3. Generic Methods

In the preceding section, you have seen how to define a generic class. You can also define a single method with type parameters.

```
class ArrayAlg
{
   public static <T> T getMiddle(T... a)
   {
      return a[a.length / 2];
   }
}
```

This method is defined inside an ordinary class, not inside a generic class. However, it is a generic method, as you can see from the angle brackets and the type variable. Note that the type variables are inserted after the modifiers (public static, in our case) and before the return type.

You can define generic methods both inside ordinary classes and inside generic classes.

When you call a generic method, you can place the actual types, enclosed in angle brackets, before the method name:

```
String middle = ArrayAlg.<String>getMiddle("John", "Q.", "Public");
```

In this case (and indeed in most cases), you can omit the <String> type parameter from the method call. The compiler has enough information to infer the method that you want. It matches the type of the arguments against the generic type T... and deduces that T must be String. That is, you can simply call

```
String middle = ArrayAlg.getMiddle("John", "Q.", "Public");
```

In almost all cases, type inference for generic methods works smoothly. Occasionally, the compiler gets it wrong, and you'll need to decipher an error report. Consider this example:

```
double middle = ArrayAlg.getMiddle(3.14, 1729, 0);
```

The error message complains, in cryptic terms that vary from one compiler version to another, that there are two ways of interpreting this code, both equally valid. In a nutshell, the compiler autoboxed the arguments into a Double and two Integer objects, and then it tried to find a common supertype of these classes. It actually found two: Number and the Comparable interface, which is itself a generic type. In this case, the remedy is to write all arguments as double values.

Tip: Peter von der Ahé recommends this trick if you want to see which type the compiler infers for a generic method call: Purposefully introduce an error and study the resulting error message. For example, consider the call ArrayAlg.getMiddle("Hello", 0, null). Assign the result to a JButton, which can't possibly be right. You will get an error report:

```
found:
java.lang.Object&java.io.Serializable&java.lang.Comparable<? extends
java.lang.Object&java.io.Serializable&java.lang.Comparable<?>>
```

In plain English, you can assign the result to Object, Serializable, or Comparable.

C++ Note: In C++, you place the type parameters after the method name. That can lead to nasty parsing ambiguities. For example, g(f<a,b>(c)) can mean "call g with the result of f<a,b>(c)," or "call g with the two boolean values f<a and b>(c)."

8.4. Bounds for Type Variables

Sometimes, a class or a method needs to place restrictions on type variables. Here is a typical example. We want to compute the smallest element of an array:

```
class ArrayAlg
{
    public static <T> T min(T[] a) // almost correct
    {
        if (a == null || a.length == 0) return null;
```

```
        T smallest = a[0];
        for (int i = 1; i < a.length; i++)
            if (smallest.compareTo(a[i]) > 0) smallest = a[i];
        return smallest;
    }
}
```

But there is a problem. Look inside the code of the min method. The variable smallest has type T, which means it could be an object of an arbitrary class. How do we know that the class to which T belongs has a compareTo method?

The solution is to restrict T to a class that implements the Comparable interface—a standard interface with a single method, compareTo. You can achieve this by giving a *bound* for the type variable T:

```
public static <T extends Comparable> T min(T[] a) . . .
```

Actually, the Comparable interface is itself a generic type. For now, ignore that complexity and the warnings that the compiler generates. Section 8.7 discusses how to properly use type parameters with the Comparable interface.

Now, the generic min method can only be called with arrays of classes that implement the Comparable interface, such as String, LocalDate, and so on. Calling min with a Rectangle array is a compile-time error because the Rectangle class does not implement Comparable.

 C++ Note: In C++, you cannot restrict the types of template parameters. If a programmer instantiates a template with an inappropriate type, an (often obscure) error message is reported inside the template code.

You may wonder why I use the extends keyword rather than the implements keyword in this situation—after all, Comparable is an interface. The notation

```
<T extends BoundingType>
```

expresses that T should be a *subtype* of the bounding type. Both T and the bounding type can be either a class or an interface. The extends keyword was chosen because it is a reasonable approximation of the subtype concept, and the Java designers did not want to add a new keyword (such as sub) to the language.

A type variable can have multiple bounds. For example:

```
T extends Comparable & Serializable
```

The bounding types are separated by ampersands (&) because commas are used to separate type variables.

As with Java inheritance, you can have as many interface supertypes as you like, but at most one of the bounds can be a class. If you have a class as a bound, it must be the first one in the bounds list.

In the next sample program (Listing 8.2), we rewrite the minmax method to be generic. The method computes the minimum and maximum of a generic array, returning a Pair<T>.

Listing 8.2 pair2/PairTest2.java

```java
1   package pair2;
2
3   import java.time.*;
4
5   /**
6    * @version 1.02 2015-06-21
7    * @author Cay Horstmann
8    */
9   public class PairTest2
10  {
11     public static void main(String[] args)
12     {
13        LocalDate[] birthdays =
14           {
15              LocalDate.of(1906, 12, 9), // G. Hopper
16              LocalDate.of(1815, 12, 10), // A. Lovelace
17              LocalDate.of(1903, 12, 3), // J. von Neumann
18              LocalDate.of(1910, 6, 22), // K. Zuse
19           };
20        Pair<LocalDate> mm = ArrayAlg.minmax(birthdays);
21        System.out.println("min = " + mm.getFirst());
22        System.out.println("max = " + mm.getSecond());
23     }
24  }
25
26  class ArrayAlg
27  {
28     /**
29        Gets the minimum and maximum of an array of objects of type T.
30        @param a an array of objects of type T
31        @return a pair with the min and max values, or null if a is null or empty
32     */
33     public static <T extends Comparable> Pair<T> minmax(T[] a)
34     {
35        if (a == null || a.length == 0) return null;
36        T min = a[0];
37        T max = a[0];
38        for (int i = 1; i < a.length; i++)
39        {
40           if (min.compareTo(a[i]) > 0) min = a[i];
```

```
41          if (max.compareTo(a[i]) < 0) max = a[i];
42       }
43       return new Pair<>(min, max);
44    }
45 }
```

8.5. Generic Code and the Virtual Machine

The virtual machine does not have objects of generic types—all objects belong to ordinary classes. An earlier version of the generics implementation was even able to compile a program that used generics into class files that executed on 1.0 virtual machines! In the following sections, you will see how the compiler "erases" type parameters, and what implication that process has for Java programmers.

8.5.1. Type Erasure

Whenever you define a generic type, a corresponding *raw* type is automatically provided. The name of the raw type is simply the name of the generic type, with the type parameters removed. The type variables are *erased* and replaced by their bounding types (or Object for variables without bounds).

For example, the raw type for Pair<T> looks like this:

```
public class Pair
{
   private Object first;
   private Object second;

   public Pair(Object first, Object second)
   {
      this.first = first;
      this.second = second;
   }

   public Object getFirst() { return first; }
   public Object getSecond() { return second; }

   public void setFirst(Object newValue) { first = newValue; }
   public void setSecond(Object newValue) { second = newValue; }
}
```

Since T is an unbounded type variable, it is simply replaced by Object.

The result is an ordinary class, just as you might have implemented it before generics were added to Java.

Your programs may contain different kinds of Pair, such as Pair<String> or Pair<LocalDate>, but erasure turns them all into raw Pair types.

C++ Note: In this regard, Java generics are very different from C++ templates. C++ produces different types for each template instantiation—a phenomenon called "template code bloat." Java does not suffer from this problem.

The raw type replaces type variables with the first bound, or Object if no bounds are given. For example, the type variable in the class Pair<T> has no explicit bounds, hence the raw type replaces T with Object. Suppose we declare a slightly different type:

```java
public class Interval<T extends Comparable & Serializable> implements Serializable
{
    private T lower;
    private T upper;
    . . .
    public Interval(T first, T second)
    {
        if (first.compareTo(second) <= 0) { lower = first; upper = second; }
        else { lower = second; upper = first; }
    }
}
```

The raw type Interval looks like this:

```java
public class Interval implements Serializable
{
    private Comparable lower;
    private Comparable upper;
    . . .
    public Interval(Comparable first, Comparable second) { . . . }
}
```

Note: You may wonder what happens if you switch the bounds: class Interval<T extends Serializable & Comparable>. In that case, the raw type replaces T with Serializable, and the compiler inserts casts to Comparable when necessary. For efficiency, you should therefore put tagging interfaces (that is, interfaces without methods) at the end of the bounds list.

8.5.2. Translating Generic Expressions

When you program a call to a generic method, the compiler inserts casts when the return type has been erased. For example, consider the sequence of statements

```
Pair<Employee> buddies = . . .;
Employee buddy = buddies.getFirst();
```

The erasure of getFirst has return type Object. The compiler automatically inserts the cast to Employee. That is, the compiler translates the method call into two virtual machine instructions:

- A call to the raw method Pair.getFirst
- A cast of the returned Object to the type Employee

Casts are also inserted when you access a generic field. Suppose the first and second fields of the Pair class were public. (Not a good programming style, perhaps, but it is legal Java.) Then the expression

```
Employee buddy = buddies.first;
```

also has a cast inserted in the resulting bytecodes.

8.5.3. Translating Generic Methods

Type erasure also happens for generic methods. Programmers usually think of a generic method such as

```
public static <T extends Comparable> T min(T[] a)
```

as a whole family of methods, but after erasure, only a single method is left:

```
public static Comparable min(Comparable[] a)
```

Note that the type parameter T has been erased, leaving only its bounding type Comparable.

Erasure of methods brings up a couple of complexities. Consider this example:

```
class DateInterval extends Pair<LocalDate>
{
   public void setSecond(LocalDate second)
   {
      if (second.compareTo(getFirst()) >= 0)
         super.setSecond(second);
   }
   . . .
}
```

A date interval is a pair of LocalDate objects, and we'll want to override the methods to ensure that the second value is never smaller than the first. This class is erased to

```
class DateInterval extends Pair // after erasure
{
    public void setSecond(LocalDate second) { . . . }
    . . .
}
```

Perhaps surprisingly, there is another setSecond method, inherited from Pair, namely

```
public void setSecond(Object second)
```

This is clearly a different method because it has a parameter of a different type—Object instead of LocalDate. But it *shouldn't* be different. Consider this sequence of statements:

```
var interval = new DateInterval(. . .);
Pair<LocalDate> pair = interval; // OK--assignment to superclass
pair.setSecond(aDate);
```

Our expectation is that the call to setSecond is polymorphic and that the appropriate method is called. Since pair refers to a DateInterval object, that should be DateInterval.setSecond. The problem is that the type erasure interferes with polymorphism. To fix this problem, the compiler generates a *bridge method* in the DateInterval class:

```
public void setSecond(Object second) { setSecond((LocalDate) second); }
```

To see why this works, let us carefully follow the execution of the statement

```
pair.setSecond(aDate)
```

The variable pair has declared type Pair<LocalDate>, and that type only has a single method called setSecond, namely setSecond(Object). The virtual machine calls that method on the object to which pair refers. That object is of type DateInterval. Therefore, the method DateInterval.setSecond(Object) is called. That method is the synthesized bridge method. It calls DateInterval.setSecond(LocalDate), which is what we want.

Bridge methods can get even stranger. Suppose the DateInterval class also overrides the getSecond method:

```
class DateInterval extends Pair<LocalDate>
{
    public LocalDate getSecond() { return (LocalDate) super.getSecond(); }
    . . .
}
```

In the DateInterval class, there are two getSecond methods:

```
LocalDate getSecond() // defined in DateInterval
Object getSecond() // overrides the method defined in Pair to call the first method
```

You could not write Java code like that; it would be illegal to have two methods with the same parameter types—here, with no parameters. However, in the virtual machine, the parameter types *and the return type* specify a method. Therefore, the compiler can produce bytecodes for two methods that differ only in their return type, and the virtual machine will handle this situation correctly.

 Note: Bridge methods are not limited to generic types. You already saw in Chapter 5 that it is legal for a method to specify a more restrictive return type when overriding another method. For example:

```
public class Employee implements Cloneable
{
    public Employee clone() throws CloneNotSupportedException { . . . }
}
```

The `Object.clone` and `Employee.clone` methods are said to have *covariant return types*.

Actually, the `Employee` class has *two* clone methods:

```
Employee clone() // defined above
Object clone() // synthesized bridge method, overrides Object.clone
```

The synthesized bridge method calls the newly defined method.

In summary, you need to remember these facts about translation of Java generics:

■ There are no generics in the virtual machine, only ordinary classes and methods.
■ All type parameters are replaced by their bounds.
■ Bridge methods are synthesized to preserve polymorphism.
■ Casts are inserted as necessary to preserve type safety.

8.5.4. Calling Legacy Code

When Java generics were designed, a major goal was to allow interoperability between generics and legacy code. Let us look at a concrete example of such legacy. The Swing user interface toolkit provides a `JSlider` class whose "ticks" can be customized with labels that contain text or images. The labels are set with the call

```
void setLabelTable(Dictionary table)
```

The `Dictionary` class maps integers to labels. Before Java 5, that class was implemented as a map of `Object` instances. Java 5 made `Dictionary` into a generic class, but `JSlider` was never updated. At this point, `Dictionary` without type parameters is a raw type. This is where compatibility comes in.

When you populate the dictionary, you can use the generic type.

```
Dictionary<Integer, Component> labelTable = new Hashtable<>();
labelTable.put(0, new JLabel(new ImageIcon("nine.png")));
labelTable.put(20, new JLabel(new ImageIcon("ten.png")));
. . .
```

When you pass the `Dictionary<Integer, Component>` object to `setLabelTable`, the compiler issues a warning.

```
slider.setLabelTable(labelTable); // warning
```

After all, the compiler has no assurance about what the `setLabelTable` might do to the `Dictionary` object. That method might replace all the keys with strings. That breaks the guarantee that the keys have type `Integer`, and future operations may cause class cast exceptions.

You should ponder it and ask what the `JSlider` is actually going to do with this `Dictionary` object. In our case, it is pretty clear that the `JSlider` only reads the information, so you can ignore the warning.

Now consider the opposite case, in which you get an object of a raw type from a legacy class. You can assign it to a variable whose type uses generics, but of course you will get a warning. For example:

```
Dictionary<Integer, Components> labelTable = slider.getLabelTable(); // warning
```

That's OK—review the warning and make sure that the label table really contains `Integer` and `Component` objects. Of course, there never is an absolute guarantee. A malicious coder might have installed a different `Dictionary` in the slider. But again, the situation is no worse than it was before generics. In the worst case, your program will throw an exception.

After you are done pondering the warning, you can use an *annotation* to make it disappear. You can annotate a local variable:

```
@SuppressWarnings("unchecked")
Dictionary<Integer, Components> labelTable = slider.getLabelTable(); // no warning
```

Or you can annotate an entire method, like this:

```
@SuppressWarnings("unchecked")
public void configureSlider() { . . . }
```

This annotation turns off checking for all code inside the method.

8.5.5. Generic Record Patterns

Let us make our Pair class into a record:

```
record Pair<T>(T first, T second) {}
```

Now you can form a record pattern with the generic record:

```
var p = new Pair<String>("Hello", "World");
if (p instanceof Pair(var a, var b)) System.out.println(a + " " + b.toUpperCase());
```

In the pattern, the type argument is inferred—here, as Pair<String>. You can also specify it explicitly:

```
p instanceof Pair<String>(var a, var b)
```

or

```
p instanceof Pair<String>(String a, String b)
```

In this example, the generic record pattern is used in an instanceof expression. You can also use them inside switch. See Section 8.8.12 for an example.

8.6. Inheritance Rules for Generic Types

When you work with generic classes, you need to learn a few rules about inheritance and subtypes. Let's start with a situation which many programmers find unintuitive. Consider a class and a subclass, such as Employee and Manager. Is Pair<Manager> a subtype of Pair<Employee>? Perhaps surprisingly, the answer is "no." For example, the following code will not compile:

```
Pair<Employee> buddies = new Pair<Manager>(ceo, cfo); // illegal
```

In general, there is *no* relationship between Pair<S> and Pair<T>, no matter how S and T are related (see Figure 8.1).

This seems like a cruel restriction, but it is necessary for type safety. Suppose we were allowed to convert a Pair<Manager> to a Pair<Employee>. Consider this code:

```
var managerBuddies = new Pair<Manager>(ceo, cfo);
Pair<Employee> employeeBuddies = managerBuddies; // illegal, but suppose it wasn't
employeeBuddies.setFirst(lowlyEmployee);
```

Clearly, the last statement is legal. But employeeBuddies and managerBuddies refer to the *same object*. We now managed to pair up the CFO with a lowly employee, which should not be possible for a Pair<Manager>.

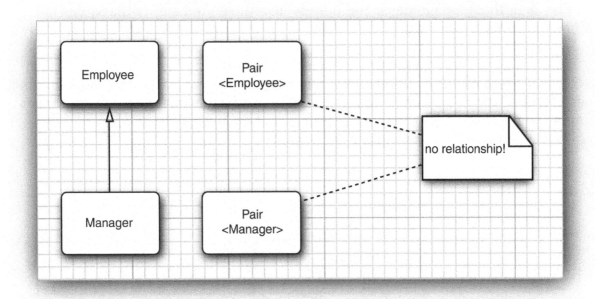

Figure 8.1: No inheritance relationship between Pair classes

  Note: You just saw an important difference between generic types and Java arrays. You can assign a Manager[] array to a variable of type Employee[]:

```
Manager[] managerBuddies = { ceo, cfo };
Employee[] employeeBuddies = managerBuddies; // OK
```

However, arrays come with special protection. If you try to store a lowly employee into employeeBuddies[0], the virtual machine throws an ArrayStoreException.

You can always convert a parameterized type to a raw type. For example, Pair<Employee> is a subtype of the raw type Pair. This conversion is necessary for interfacing with legacy code.

Can you convert to the raw type and then cause a type error? Unfortunately, you can. Consider this example:

```
var managerBuddies = new Pair<Manager>(ceo, cfo);
Pair rawBuddies = managerBuddies; // OK
rawBuddies.setFirst(new File(". . .")); // only a compile-time warning
```

This sounds scary. However, keep in mind that you are no worse off than you were with older versions of Java. The security of the virtual machine is not at stake. When the foreign object is retrieved with getFirst and assigned to a Manager variable, a ClassCastException is thrown, just as in the good old days. You merely lose the added safety that generic programming normally provides.

Finally, generic classes can extend or implement other generic classes. In this regard, they are no different from ordinary classes. For example, the class ArrayList<T> implements the interface List<T>. That means an ArrayList<Manager> can be converted to a List<Manager>. However, as you just saw, an ArrayList<Manager> is *not* an ArrayList<Employee> or List<Employee>. Figure 8.2 shows these relationships.

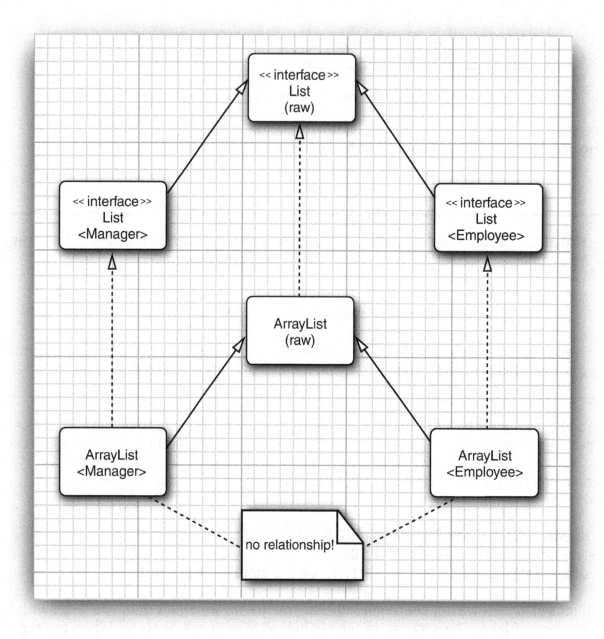

Figure 8.2: Subtype relationships among generic list types

8.7. Wildcard Types

It was known for some time among researchers of type systems that a rigid system of generic types is quite unpleasant to use. The Java designers invented an ingenious (but nevertheless safe) "escape hatch": the *wildcard type*. The following sections show you how to work with wildcards.

8.7.1. The Wildcard Concept

In a wildcard type, a type parameter is allowed to vary. For example, the wildcard type

```
Pair<? extends Employee>
```

denotes any generic Pair type whose type parameter is a subclass of Employee, such as Pair<Manager>, but not Pair<String>.

Let's say you want to write a method that prints out pairs of employees, like this:

```
public static void printBuddies(Pair<Employee> p)
{
   Employee first = p.getFirst();
   Employee second = p.getSecond();
   System.out.println(first.getName() + " and " + second.getName() + " are buddies.");
}
```

As you saw in the preceding section, you cannot pass a Pair<Manager> to that method, which is rather limiting. But the solution is simple—use a wildcard type:

```
public static void printBuddies(Pair<? extends Employee> p)
```

The type Pair<Manager> is a subtype of Pair<? extends Employee> (see Figure 8.3).

Can we use wildcards to corrupt a Pair<Manager> through a Pair<? extends Employee> reference?

```
var managerBuddies = new Pair<Manager>(ceo, cfo);
Pair<? extends Employee> wildcardBuddies = managerBuddies; // OK
wildcardBuddies.setFirst(lowlyEmployee); // compile-time error
```

No corruption is possible. The call to setFirst is a type error. To see why, let us have a closer look at the type Pair<? extends Employee>. Its methods look like this:

```
? extends Employee getFirst()
void setFirst(? extends Employee)
```

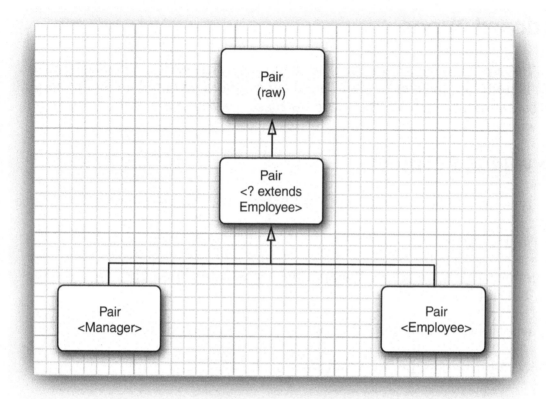

Figure 8.3: Subtype relationships with wildcards

It is impossible to call the setFirst method! Consider the call
wildcardBuddies.setFirst(lowlyEmployee) The compiler knows that the parameter of setFirst
has some specific type, which extends Employee. Is that specific type Employee? Is it Manager,
or some other subclass? There is no way for the compiler to know. Therefore, the compiler
cannot accept lowlyEmployee. For the same reason, the call wildcardBuddies.setFirst(cio),
where cio is a Manager instance, also fails. The compiler must reject all arguments to
setFirst other than null.

The getFirst method continues to work. The return value of getFirst is an instance of some
specific type, which is a subtype of Employee. The compiler doesn't know what that specific
type is, but it can guarantee that the assignment to an Employee reference is safe.

This is the key idea behind bounded wildcards. We now have a way of distinguishing
between the safe accessor methods and the unsafe mutator methods.

8.7.2. Supertype Bounds for Wildcards

Wildcard bounds are similar to type variable bounds, but they have an added
capability—you can specify a *supertype bound*, like this:

```
? super Manager
```

This wildcard is restricted to all supertypes of Manager. (It was a stroke of good luck that the existing super keyword describes the relationship so accurately.)

Why would you want to do this? A wildcard with a supertype bound gives you a behavior that is opposite to that of the wildcards described in Section 8.7.1. You can supply arguments to methods, but you can't use the return values. For example, Pair<? super Manager> has methods that can be described as follows:

```
void setFirst(? super Manager)
? super Manager getFirst()
```

This is not the actual Java syntax, but it shows what the compiler knows. The setFirst parameter type, denoted as ? super Manager, is some specific type T, and Manager is a subtype of T. There are exactly three choices for T: Object, Employee, or Manager. (There would have been more choices if Manager or Employee had implemented interfaces.) However, the compiler cannot know which of these choices applies. Therefore, the compiler cannot accept a call with an argument of type Employee or Object. After all, T might have been Manager. It is only possible to pass an object of type Manager or a subtype such as Executive.

Conversely, if you call getFirst, there is no guarantee about the type of the returned object. You can only assign it to an Object.

Here is a typical example. We have an array of managers and want to put the manager with the lowest and highest bonus into a Pair object. What kind of Pair? A Pair<Manager> is the obvious choice, but there are other possibilities. A Pair<Employee> should be fair game or, for that matter, a Pair<Object> (see Figure 8.4). The following method will accept any appropriate Pair:

```
public static void minmaxBonus(Manager[] a, Pair<? super Manager> result)
{
   if (a.length == 0) return;
   Manager min = a[0];
   Manager max = a[0];
   for (int i = 1; i < a.length; i++)
   {
      if (min.getBonus() > a[i].getBonus()) min = a[i];
      if (max.getBonus() < a[i].getBonus()) max = a[i];
   }
   result.setFirst(min);
   result.setSecond(max);
}
```

Intuitively speaking, wildcards with supertype bounds let you write to a generic object, while wildcards with subtype bounds let you read from a generic object.

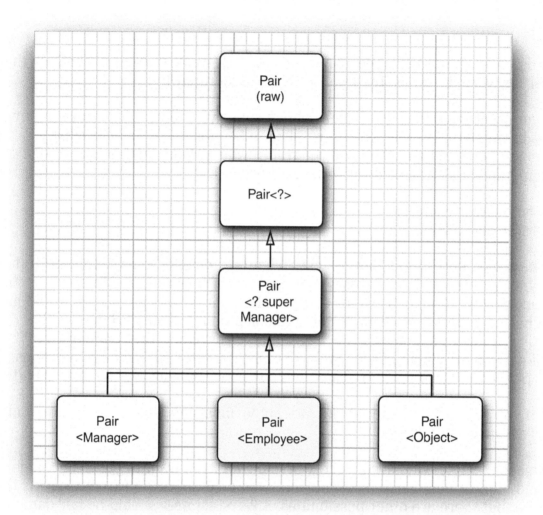

Figure 8.4: A wildcard with a supertype bound

Here is another use for supertype bounds. The Comparable interface is itself a generic type. It is declared as follows:

```
public interface Comparable<T>
{
    public int compareTo(T other);
}
```

Here, the type variable indicates the type of the other parameter. For example, the String class implements Comparable<String>, and its compareTo method is declared as

```
public int compareTo(String other)
```

This is nice—the explicit parameter has the correct type. Before the interface was generic, other was an Object, and a cast was necessary in the implementation of the method.

Now that Comparable is a generic type, perhaps we should have done a better job with the minmax method of the ArrayAlg class? We could have declared it as

```
public static <T extends Comparable<T>> Pair<T> minmax(T[] a)
```

This looks more thorough than just using T extends Comparable, and it would work fine for many classes. For example, if you compute the minimum of a String array, then T is the type String, and String is a subtype of Comparable<String>. But we run into a problem when processing an array of LocalDate objects. As it happens, LocalDate implements ChronoLocalDate, and ChronoLocalDate extends Comparable<ChronoLocalDate>. Thus, LocalDate implements Comparable<ChronoLocalDate> but *not* Comparable<LocalDate>.

In a situation such as this one, supertypes come to the rescue:

```
public static <T extends Comparable<? super T>> Pair<T> minmax(T[] a)
```

Now the compareTo method has the form

```
int compareTo(? super T)
```

Maybe it is declared to take an object of type T, or—for example, when T is LocalDate—a supertype of T. At any rate, it is safe to pass an object of type T to the compareTo method.

To the uninitiated, a declaration such as <T extends Comparable<? super T>> is bound to look intimidating. This is unfortunate, because the intent of this declaration is to help application programmers by removing unnecessary restrictions on the call arguments. Application programmers with no interest in generics will probably learn quickly to gloss over these declarations and just take for granted that library programmers will do the right thing. If you are a library programmer, you'll need to get used to wildcards, or your users will curse you and throw random casts at their code until it compiles.

 Note: Another common use for supertype bounds is a parameter type of a functional interface. For example, the Collection interface has a method

```
default boolean removeIf(Predicate<? super E> filter)
```

The method removes all elements that fulfill the given predicate. For example, if you hate employees with odd hash codes, you can remove them like this:

```
ArrayList<Employee> staff = . . .;
Predicate<Object> oddHashCode = obj -> obj.hashCode() %2 != 0;
staff.removeIf(oddHashCode);
```

You want to be able to pass a Predicate<Object>, not just a Predicate<Employee>. The super wildcard makes that possible.

8.7.3. Unbounded Wildcards

You can even use wildcards with no bounds at all—for example, Pair<?>. At first glance, this looks identical to the raw Pair type. Actually, the types are very different. The type Pair<?> has methods such as

```
? getFirst()
void setFirst(?)
```

The return value of getFirst can only be assigned to an Object. The setFirst method can never be called, *not even with an* Object. That's the essential difference between Pair<?> and Pair: you can call the setFirst method of the raw Pair class with *any* Object.

 Note: You can call setFirst(null).

Why would you ever want such a wimpy type? It is useful for very simple operations. For example, the following method tests whether a pair contains a null reference. It never needs the actual type.

```
public static boolean hasNulls(Pair<?> p)
{
    return p.getFirst() == null || p.getSecond() == null;
}
```

You could have avoided the wildcard type by turning hasNulls into a generic method:

```
public static <T> boolean hasNulls(Pair<T> p)
```

However, the version with the wildcard type seems easier to read.

8.7.4. Wildcard Capture

Let us write a method that swaps the elements of a pair:

```
public static void swap(Pair<?> p)
```

A wildcard is not a type variable, so we can't write code that uses ? as a type. In other words, the following would be illegal:

```
? t = p.getFirst(); // ERROR
p.setFirst(p.getSecond());
p.setSecond(t);
```

That's a problem because we need to temporarily hold the first element when we do the swapping. Fortunately, there is an interesting solution to this problem. We can write a helper method, swapHelper, like this:

```
public static <T> void swapHelper(Pair<T> p)
{
    T t = p.getFirst();
    p.setFirst(p.getSecond());
    p.setSecond(t);
}
```

Note that swapHelper is a generic method, whereas swap is not—it has a fixed parameter of type Pair<?>.

Now we can call swapHelper from swap:

```
public static void swap(Pair<?> p) { swapHelper(p); }
```

In this case, the parameter T of the swapHelper method *captures the wildcard*. It isn't known what type the wildcard denotes, but it is a definite type, and the definition of <T>swapHelper makes perfect sense when T denotes that type.

Of course, in this case, we were not compelled to use a wildcard. We could have directly implemented <T> void swap(Pair<T> p) as a generic method without wildcards. However, consider this example in which a wildcard type occurs naturally in the middle of a computation:

```
public static void maxminBonus(Manager[] a, Pair<? super Manager> result)
{
    minmaxBonus(a, result);
    PairAlg.swapHelper(result); // OK—swapHelper captures wildcard type
}
```

Here, the wildcard capture mechanism cannot be avoided.

Wildcard capture is only legal in very limited circumstances. The compiler must be able to guarantee that the wildcard represents a single definite type. For example, the T in ArrayList<Pair<T>> can never capture the wildcard in ArrayList<Pair<?>>. The array list might hold two Pair<?>, each of which has a different type for ?.

The test program in Listing 8.3 gathers up the various methods discussed in the preceding sections so you can see them in context.

Listing 8.3 pair3/PairTest3.java

```
1   package pair3;
2
3   /**
4    * @version 1.01 2012-01-26
5    * @author Cay Horstmann
6    */
7   public class PairTest3
8   {
9      public static void main(String[] args)
10     {
11        var ceo = new Manager("Gus Greedy", 800000, 2003, 12, 15);
12        var cfo = new Manager("Sid Sneaky", 600000, 2003, 12, 15);
13        var buddies = new Pair<Manager>(ceo, cfo);
14        printBuddies(buddies);
15
16        ceo.setBonus(1000000);
17        cfo.setBonus(500000);
18        Manager[] managers = { ceo, cfo };
19
20        var result = new Pair<Employee>();
21        minmaxBonus(managers, result);
22        System.out.println("first: " + result.getFirst().getName()
23           + ", second: " + result.getSecond().getName());
24        maxminBonus(managers, result);
25        System.out.println("first: " + result.getFirst().getName()
26           + ", second: " + result.getSecond().getName());
27     }
28
29     public static void printBuddies(Pair<? extends Employee> p)
30     {
31        Employee first = p.getFirst();
32        Employee second = p.getSecond();
33        System.out.println(first.getName() + " and " + second.getName() + " are buddies.");
34     }
35
36     public static void minmaxBonus(Manager[] a, Pair<? super Manager> result)
37     {
38        if (a.length == 0) return;
39        Manager min = a[0];
40        Manager max = a[0];
41        for (int i = 1; i < a.length; i++)
42        {
43           if (min.getBonus() > a[i].getBonus()) min = a[i];
44           if (max.getBonus() < a[i].getBonus()) max = a[i];
45        }
46        result.setFirst(min);
47        result.setSecond(max);
48     }
```

```
49
50    public static void maxminBonus(Manager[] a, Pair<? super Manager> result)
51    {
52       minmaxBonus(a, result);
53       PairAlg.swapHelper(result); // OK--swapHelper captures wildcard type
54    }
55    // can't write public static <T super manager> . . .
56 }
57
58 class PairAlg
59 {
60    public static boolean hasNulls(Pair<?> p)
61    {
62       return p.getFirst() == null || p.getSecond() == null;
63    }
64
65    public static void swap(Pair<?> p) { swapHelper(p); }
66
67    public static <T> void swapHelper(Pair<T> p)
68    {
69       T t = p.getFirst();
70       p.setFirst(p.getSecond());
71       p.setSecond(t);
72    }
73 }
```

8.8. Restrictions and Limitations

In the following sections, I discuss a number of restrictions that you need to consider when working with Java generics. Most of these restrictions are a consequence of type erasure.

8.8.1. Type Parameters Cannot Be Instantiated with Primitive Types

You cannot substitute a primitive type for a type parameter. Thus, there is no Pair<double>, only Pair<Double>. The reason is, of course, type erasure. After erasure, the Pair class has fields of type Object, and you can't use them to store double values.

This is an annoyance, to be sure, but it is consistent with the separate status of primitive types in the Java language. It is not a fatal flaw—there are only eight primitive types, and you can always handle them with separate classes and methods when wrapper types are not an acceptable substitute.

8.8.2. Runtime Type Inquiry Only Works with Raw Types

Objects in the virtual machine always have a specific nongeneric type. Therefore, all type inquiries yield only the raw type. For example,

```
if (a instanceof Pair<String>) // ERROR
```

could only test whether a is a Pair of any type. The same is true for the test

```
if (a instanceof Pair<T>) // ERROR
```

or the cast

```
Pair<String> p = (Pair<String>) a; // warning--can only test that a is a Pair
```

To remind you of the risk, you will get a compiler error (with instanceof) or warning (with casts) when you try to inquire whether an object belongs to a generic type.

In the same spirit, the getClass method always returns the raw type. For example:

```
Pair<String> stringPair = . . .;
Pair<Employee> employeePair = . . .;
if (stringPair.getClass() == employeePair.getClass()) // they are equal
```

The comparison yields true because both calls to getClass return Pair.class.

8.8.3. You Cannot Create Arrays of Parameterized Types

You cannot instantiate arrays of parameterized types, such as

```
var table = new Pair<String>[10]; // ERROR
```

What's wrong with that? After erasure, the type of table is Pair[]. You can convert it to Object[]:

```
Object[] objarray = table;
```

An array remembers its component type and throws an ArrayStoreException if you try to store an element of the wrong type:

```
objarray[0] = "Hello"; // ERROR--component type is Pair
```

But erasure renders this mechanism ineffective for generic types. The assignment

```
objarray[0] = new Pair<Employee>();
```

would pass the array store check but still result in a type error. For this reason, arrays of parameterized types are outlawed.

Note that only the creation of these arrays is outlawed. You can declare a variable of type Pair<String>[]. But you can't initialize it with a new Pair<String>[10].

Note: You can declare arrays of wildcard types and then cast them:

```
var table = (Pair<String>[]) new Pair<?>[10];
```

The result is not safe. If you store a Pair<Employee> in table[0] and then call a String method on table[0].getFirst(), you get a ClassCastException.

 Tip: If you need to collect parameterized type objects, simply use an ArrayList: ArrayList<Pair<String>> is safe and effective.

8.8.4. Varargs Warnings

In the preceding section, you saw that Java doesn't support arrays of generic types. In this section, I discuss a related issue: passing instances of a generic type to a method with a variable number of arguments.

Consider this simple method with variable arguments:

```
public static <E> void addAll(Collection<E> coll, E... elements)
{
    for (E element : elements) coll.add(element);
}
```

Recall that the parameter elements is actually an array that holds all supplied arguments.

Now consider this call:

```
Collection<Pair<String>> table = . . .;
Pair<String> pair1 = . . .;
Pair<String> pair2 = . . .;
addAll(table, pair1, pair2);
```

In order to call this method, the Java virtual machine must make an array of Pair<String>, which is against the rules. However, the rules have been relaxed for this situation, and you only get a warning at the call site, not an error. You can suppress that warning by adding the annotation @SuppressWarnings("unchecked") to the method containing the call to addAll. However, this is an annoying burden for the callers of the addAll method. For that reason, there is another warning about "possible heap pollution" at the declaration site.

To avoid both warnings, annotate the addAll method itself with @SafeVarargs:

```
@SafeVarargs
public static <E> void addAll(Collection<E> coll, E... elements)
```

This method can now be called with generic types. By using the annotation, you promise that your method doesn't write to the parameter array, and doesn't pass the array to others who might do that. See the note below for an example of abuse.

The @SafeVarargs annotation can only be used with constructors and methods that are static, final, or private. Any other method could be overridden, making the annotation meaningless.

 Caution: You can use the @SafeVarargs annotation to defeat the restriction against generic array creation, using this method:

```
@SafeVarargs static <E> E[] array(E... array) { return array; }
```

Now you can call

```
Pair<String>[] table = array(pair1, pair2);
```

This seems convenient, but there is a hidden danger. The code

```
Object[] objarray = table;
objarray[0] = new Pair<Employee>();
```

will run without an ArrayStoreException because the array store only checks the erased type. You'll get an exception elsewhere when you work with table[0].

8.8.5. Generic Varargs Do Not Spread Primitive Arrays

Recall that you can pass an array to a varargs parameter. For example, consider the addAll method of the preceding section. When the items to be added happen to be in an array, you just pass the array. The call behaves as if the elements had been "spread out":

```
Collection<String> strings = . . .;
String[] moreStrings = new String[] { "Mary", "had", "a", "little", "lamb" };
addAll(strings, moreStrings);
    // OK, same as addAll(strings, "Mary", "had", "a", "little", "lamb")
```

Of course, the elements are not actually spread out. In fact, the converse is true. If the arguments had been individually specified, they would be gathered in an array, which would then be passed to the method. If you supply an array, it is passed directly.

Now consider a collection of numbers:

```
Collection<Integer> numbers = . . .;
int[] moreNumbers = new int[] { 11, 12, 13, 14, 15 };
addAll(numbers, moreNumbers); // ERROR
```

This does not work. There is no valid match for the type variable E. An int[] cannot be converted to an Integer[].

Here is a more insidious example. The List interface has a static of method:

```
public static <E> List<E> of(E... elements)
```

The call

```
List.of(moreStrings) // ["Mary", "had", "a", "little", "lamb"]
```

yields a list of 5 elements. But

```
List.of(moreNumbers)
```

yields a List<int[]> of a single element, the array of five int values. The type parameter E cannot match the primitive type int, so the moreNumbers elements are not spread. Instead, the type parameter E machtes the array type int[].

8.8.6. You Cannot Instantiate Type Variables

You cannot use type variables in an expression such as new T(. . .). For example, the following Pair<T> constructor is illegal:

```
public Pair() { first = new T(); second = new T(); } // ERROR
```

Type erasure would change T to Object, and surely you don't want to call new Object().

The best workaround is to make the caller provide a constructor expression. For example:

```
Pair<String> p = Pair.makePair(String::new);
```

The makePair method receives a Supplier<T>, the functional interface for a function with no parameters and a result of type T:

```
public static <T> Pair<T> makePair(Supplier<T> constr)
{
    return new Pair<>(constr.get(), constr.get());
}
```

A more traditional workaround is to construct generic objects through reflection, by calling the Constructor.newInstance method.

Unfortunately, the details are a bit complex. You cannot call

```
first = T.class.getConstructor().newInstance(); // ERROR
```

The expression T.class is not legal because it would erase to Object.class. Instead, you must design the API so that you are handed a Class object, like this:

```
public static <T> Pair<T> makePair(Class<T> cl) throws ReflectiveOperationException
{
    Constructor<T> constr = cl.getConstructor();
    return new Pair<>(constr.newInstance(), constr.newInstance());
}
```

The method is declared to throw a ReflectiveOperationException because the class might not have a no-argument constructor.

When calling the method, provide a class literal as follows:

```
Pair<String> p = Pair.makePair(String.class);
```

Note that the Class class is itself generic. For example, String.class is an instance (indeed, the sole instance) of Class<String>. Therefore, the makePair method can infer the type of the pair that it is making.

8.8.7. You Cannot Construct a Generic Array

Just as you cannot instantiate a single generic instance, you cannot instantiate an array. The reasons are different—an array is, after all, filled with null values, which would seem safe to construct. But an array also carries a type, which is used to monitor array stores in the virtual machine. That type is erased. For example, consider

```
public static <T extends Comparable> T[] minmax(T... a)
{
    T[] mm = new T[2]; // ERROR
    . . .
}
```

Type erasure would cause this method to always construct an array Comparable[2].

If the array is only used as a private instance field of a class, you can declare the element type of the array to be the erased type and use casts. For example, the ArrayList class can be implemented as follows:

```
public class ArrayList<E>
{
    private Object[] elements;
    . . .
    @SuppressWarnings("unchecked") public E get(int n) { return (E) elements[n]; }
    public void set(int n, E e) { elements[n] = e; } // no cast needed
}
```

This technique does not work for our `minmax` method since we are returning a `T[]` array, and a runtime error results if we lie about its type. Suppose we implement

```
public static <T extends Comparable> T[] minmax(T... a)
{
   var result = new Comparable[2]; // array of erased type
   . . .
   return (T[]) result; // compiles with warning
}
```

The call

```
String[] names = ArrayAlg.minmax("Tom", "Dick", "Harry");
```

compiles without any warning. A `ClassCastException` occurs when the `Comparable[]` reference is cast to `String[]` after the method returns.

In this situation, it is best to ask the user to provide an array constructor expression:

```
String[] names = ArrayAlg.minmax(String[]::new, "Tom", "Dick", "Harry");
```

The constructor expression `String[]::new` denotes a function that, given the desired length, constructs a `String` array of that length.

The method uses that parameter to produce an array of the correct type:

```
public static <T extends Comparable> T[] minmax(IntFunction<T[]> constr, T... a)
{
   T[] result = constr.apply(2);
   . . .
}
```

A more old-fashioned approach is to use reflection and call `Array.newInstance`:

```
public static <T extends Comparable> T[] minmax(T... a)
{
   var result = (T[]) Array.newInstance(a.getClass().getComponentType(), 2);
   . . .
}
```

The `toArray` method of the `ArrayList` class is not so lucky. It needs to produce a `T[]` array, but it doesn't have the component type. Therefore, there are two variants:

```
Object[] toArray()
T[] toArray(T[] result)
```

The second method receives an array argument. If the array is large enough, it is used. Otherwise, a new array of sufficient size is created, using the component type of result.

8.8.8. Type Variables Are Not Valid in Static Contexts of Generic Classes

You cannot reference type variables in static fields or methods. For example, the following clever idea won't work:

```
public class Singleton<T>
{
   private static T singleInstance; // ERROR

   public static T getSingleInstance() // ERROR
   {
      if (singleInstance == null) construct new instance of T
      return singleInstance;
   }
}
```

If this could be done, then a program could declare a Singleton<Random> to share a random number generator and a Singleton<JFileChooser> to share a file chooser dialog. But it can't work. After type erasure there is only one Singleton class, and only one singleInstance field. For that reason, static fields and methods with type variables are simply outlawed.

8.8.9. You Cannot Throw or Catch Instances of a Generic Class

You can neither throw nor catch objects of a generic class. In fact, it is not even legal for a generic class to extend Throwable. For example, the following definition will not compile:

```
public class Problem<T> extends Exception { /* . . . */ }
   // ERROR--can't extend Throwable
```

However, it is OK to use type variables in exception specifications. The following is legal:

```
interface CheckedConsumer<T, E extends Exception>
{
   void accept(T t) throws E;
}
```

You cannot use a type variable in a catch clause. For example, the following method will not compile:

```
public static <T, E extends Exception> void doWork(CheckedConsumer<T, E> c, T t)
{
   try
   {
      c.accept(t);
   }
   catch (E e) // ERROR--can't catch type variable
   {
      logger.log(ERROR, ". . .", e);
   }
}
```

8.8.10. You Can Defeat Checked Exception Checking

A bedrock principle of Java exception handling is that you must provide a handler for all checked exceptions. You can use generics to defeat this scheme. The key ingredient is this method:

```
@SuppressWarnings("unchecked")
static <T extends Throwable> void throwAs(Throwable t) throws T
{
   throw (T) t;
}
```

Suppose this method is contained in an interface Task. When you have a checked exception e and call

```
Task.<RuntimeException>throwAs(e);
```

then the compiler will believe that e becomes an unchecked exception. The following turns all exceptions into those that the compiler believes to be unchecked:

```
try
{
   do work
}
catch (Throwable t)
{
   Task.<RuntimeException>throwAs(t);
}
```

Let's use this to solve a vexing problem. To run code in a thread, you have to place it into the run method of a class that implements the Runnable interface. But that method is not allowed to throw checked exceptions. We will provide an adaptor from a Task, whose run method is allowed to throw arbitrary exceptions, to a Runnable:

```
interface Task
{
   void run() throws Exception;

   @SuppressWarnings("unchecked")
   static <T extends Throwable> void throwAs(Throwable t) throws T
   {
      throw (T) t;
   }

   static Runnable asRunnable(Task task)
   {
      return () ->
         {
            try
            {
               task.run();
            }
            catch (Exception e)
            {
               Task.<RuntimeException>throwAs(e);
            }
         };
   }
}
```

For example, this program runs a thread that will throw a checked exception:

```
public class Test
{
   public static void main(String[] args)
   {
      var thread = new Thread(Task.asRunnable(() ->
         {
            Thread.sleep(1000);
            System.out.println("Hello, World!");
            throw new Exception("Check this out!");
         }));
      thread.start();
   }
}
```

The Thread.sleep method is declared to throw an InterruptedException, and we no longer have to catch it. Since we don't interrupt the thread, that exception won't be thrown. However, the program throws a checked exception. When you run the program, you will get a stack trace.

What's so remarkable about that? Normally, you have to catch all checked exceptions inside the run method of a Runnable and *wrap them* into unchecked exceptions—the run method is declared to throw no checked exceptions.

But here, we don't wrap. We simply throw the exception, tricking the compiler into believing that it is not a checked exception.

Using generic classes, erasure, and the @SuppressWarnings annotation, we were able to defeat an essential part of the Java type system.

8.8.11. Beware of Clashes after Erasure

It is illegal to create conditions that cause clashes when generic types are erased. Here is an example. Suppose we add an equals method to the Pair class, like this:

```
public class Pair<T>
{
    public boolean equals(T value) { return first.equals(value) && second.equals(value); }
    . . .
}
```

Consider a Pair<String>. Conceptually, it has two equals methods:

```
boolean equals(String) // defined in Pair<T>
boolean equals(Object) // inherited from Object
```

But the intuition leads us astray. The erasure of the method

```
boolean equals(T)
```

is

```
boolean equals(Object)
```

which clashes with the Object.equals method.

The remedy is, of course, to rename the offending method.

The generics specification cites another rule: "To support translation by erasure, we impose the restriction that a class or type variable may not at the same time be a subtype of two interface types which are different parameterizations of the same interface." For example, the following is illegal:

```
class Employee implements Comparable<Employee> { . . . }
class Manager extends Employee implements Comparable<Manager> { . . . } // ERROR
```

Manager would then implement both Comparable<Employee> and Comparable<Manager>, which are different parameterizations of the same interface.

It is not obvious what this restriction has to do with type erasure. After all, the nongeneric version

```
class Employee implements Comparable { . . . }
class Manager extends Employee implements Comparable { . . . }
```

is legal. The reason is far more subtle. There would be a conflict with the synthesized bridge methods. A class that implements Comparable<X> gets a bridge method

```
public int compareTo(Object other) { return compareTo((X) other); }
```

You cannot have two such methods for different types X.

8.8.12. Type Inference in Generic Record Patterns is Limited

When generic types are involved, the compiler may need to work pretty hard to verify exhaustiveness. Consider this incomplete hierarchy of JSON types:

```
sealed interface JSONPrimitive<T> {}
record JSONNumber(double value) implements JSONPrimitive<Double> {}
record JSONBoolean(boolean value) implements JSONPrimitive<Boolean> {}
record JSONString(String value) implements JSONPrimitive<String> {}
```

The switch in the following method is exhaustive:

```
public static <T> double toNumber(JSONPrimitive<T> v)
{
   return switch (v)
      {
         case JSONNumber(var n) -> n;
         case JSONBoolean(var b) -> b ? 1 : 0;
         case JSONString(var s) -> {
            try
            {
               yield Double.parseDouble(s);
            }
            catch (NumberFormatException ex)
            {
               yield Double.NaN;
            }
         }
      };
}
```

At first glance, it appears as if there might be an unbounded number of classes implementing JSONPrimitive<T>, but the compiler can track that there are only three of them.

Now we want to form the sum of two JSON primitives:

```
record Pair<T>(T first, T second)
{
    public static <U> Pair<U> of(U first, U second) { return new Pair<U>(first, second); }
}

public static Object sum(Pair<? extends JSONPrimitive<?>> pair)
{
    return switch (pair)
      {
         case Pair(JSONNumber(var left), JSONNumber(var right)) -> left + right;
         case Pair(JSONBoolean(var left), JSONBoolean(var right)) -> left | right;
         case Pair(JSONString(var left), JSONString(var right)) -> left.concat(right);
         // ERROR--not exhaustive
      };
}
```

This switch is not exhaustive. After all, it would be possible to call sum1 as

```
sum(Pair.of(new JSONNumber(42), new JSONString("Fred")))
```

You can make the switch exhaustive by adding the other six combinations of JSON primitives and throwing an exception in each case. But that is a runtime check. It would be nicer to reject mixed pairs at compile time.

Here is how to only accept homogeneous pairs:

```
public static <T extends JSONPrimitive<U>, U> Object sum(Pair<T> pair)
{
    return switch (pair)
      {
         case Pair(JSONNumber(var left), JSONNumber(var right)) -> left + right;
         case Pair(JSONBoolean(var left), JSONBoolean(var right)) -> left | right;
         case Pair(JSONString(var left), JSONString(var right)) -> left.concat(right);
         default -> throw new AssertionError(); // Sadly Java can't tell this won't happen
      };
}
```

Now the call

```
sum(Pair.of(new JSONNumber(42), new JSONString("Fred")))
```

no longer compiles, since there are no matching types for T and U.

Unfortunately, the default clause is necessary to make the switch exhaustive. In theory, there is enough information to determine that the pair components must be instances of the same type, but the Java type system can't prove it.

 Caution: Trying to use explicit type arguments does not work:

```
public static <T extends JSONPrimitive<U>, U> Object sum(Pair<T> pair)
{
    return switch (pair)
        {
            // ERROR—unsafe casts
            case Pair<JSONNumber>(JSONNumber(var left), JSONNumber(var right))
                -> left + right;
            case Pair<JSONBoolean>(JSONBoolean(var left), JSONBoolean(var right))
                -> left | right;
            case Pair<JSONString>(JSONString(var left), JSONString(var right))
                -> left.concat(right);
        };
}
```

The Java compiler does not know how to prove that the cast from Pair<T> to Pair<JSONNumber> is safe when the components have type JSONNumber.

8.9. Reflection and Generics

Reflection lets you analyze arbitrary objects at runtime. If the objects are instances of generic classes, you don't get much information about the generic type parameters because they have been erased. In the following sections, you will learn what you can nevertheless find out about generic classes with reflection.

8.9.1. The Generic Class Class

The Class class has a type parameter. For example, String.class is actually an object (in fact, the sole object) of the class Class<String>.

The type parameter is useful because it allows the methods of Class<T> to be more specific about their return types. The following methods of Class<T> take advantage of the type parameter:

```
T cast(Object obj)
T[] getEnumConstants()
Class<? super T> getSuperclass()
Constructor<T> getConstructor(Class<?>... parameterTypes)
Constructor<T> getDeclaredConstructor(Class<?>... parameterTypes)
```

The getConstructor method returns an instance of Constructor<T>, so that no cast is required in

```
Class<T> cl = . . .;
T noArgInstance = cl.getConstructor().newInstance();
```

The cast method returns the given object, now declared as type T if its type is indeed a subtype of T. Otherwise, it throws a ClassCastException.

The getEnumConstants method returns null if this class is not an enum class or an array of the enumeration values which are known to be of type T.

---

java.lang.Class<T> 1.0

- T cast(Object obj)
  returns obj if it is null or can be converted to the type T, or throws a ClassCastException otherwise.
- T[] getEnumConstants() **5.0**
  returns an array of all values if T is an enumerated type, null otherwise.
- Class<? super T> getSuperclass()
  returns the superclass of this class, or null if T is not a class or the class Object.
- Constructor<T> getConstructor(Class... parameterTypes) **1.1**
- Constructor<T> getDeclaredConstructor(Class... parameterTypes) **1.1**
  get the public constructor, or the constructor with the given parameter types.

8.9.2. Using Class<T> Parameters for Type Matching

It is sometimes useful to match the type variable of a Class<T> parameter in a generic method. Here is the canonical example:

```
public static <T> Pair<T> makePair(Class<T> c) throws ReflectiveOperationException
{
    Constructor<T> constr = c.getConstructor();
    return new Pair<>(constr.newInstance(), constr.newInstance());
}
```

If you call

```
makePair(String.class)
```

then `String.class` is an object of type `Class<String>`. The type parameter `T` of the `makePair` method matches `String`, and the compiler can infer that the method returns a `Pair<String>`.

8.9.3. Generic Type Information in the Virtual Machine

One of the notable features of Java generics is the erasure of generic types in the virtual machine. Perhaps surprisingly, the erased classes still retain some faint memory of their generic origin. For example, the raw `Pair` class knows that it originated from the generic class `Pair<T>`, even though an object of type `Pair` can't tell whether it was constructed as a `Pair<String>` or `Pair<Employee>`.

Similarly, consider a method

```
public static Comparable min(Comparable[] a)
```

that is the erasure of a generic method

```
public static <T extends Comparable<? super T>> T min(T[] a)
```

You can use the reflection API to determine that

- The generic method has a type parameter called `T`;
- The type parameter has a subtype bound that is itself a generic type;
- The bounding type has a wildcard parameter;
- The wildcard parameter has a supertype bound; and
- The generic method has a generic array parameter.

In other words, you can reconstruct everything about generic classes and methods that their implementors declared. However, you won't know how the type parameters were resolved for specific objects or method calls.

In order to express generic type declarations, use the interface `Type` in the `java.lang.reflect` package. The interface has the following subtypes:

- The `Class` class, describing concrete types
- The `TypeVariable` interface, describing type variables (such as `T extends Comparable<? super T>`)
- The `WildcardType` interface, describing wildcards (such as `? super T`)
- The `ParameterizedType` interface, describing generic class or interface types (such as `Comparable<? super T>`)
- The `GenericArrayType` interface, describing generic arrays (such as `T[]`)

Figure 8.5 shows the inheritance hierarchy. Note that the last four subtypes are interfaces—the virtual machine instantiates suitable classes that implement these interfaces.

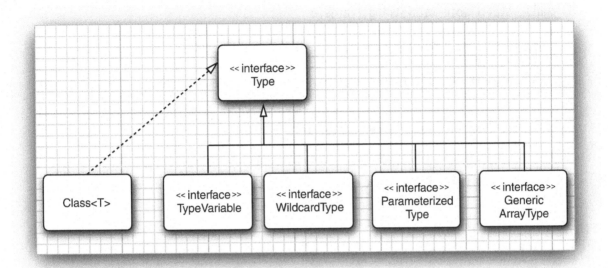

Figure 8.5: The Type interface and its descendants

Listing 8.4 uses the generic reflection API to print out what it discovers about a given class. If you run it with the Pair class, you get this report:

```
class Pair<T> extends java.lang.Object
public T getFirst()
public T getSecond()
public void setFirst(T)
public void setSecond(T)
```

If you run it with ArrayAlg in the PairTest2 directory, the report displays the following method:

```
public static <T extends java.lang.Comparable> Pair<T> minmax(T[])
```

Listing 8.4 genericReflection/GenericReflectionTest.java

```
 1  package genericReflection;
 2
 3  import java.lang.reflect.*;
 4  import java.util.*;
 5
 6  /**
 7   * @version 1.13 2023-12-20
 8   * @author Cay Horstmann
 9   */
10  public class GenericReflectionTest
11  {
```

```
12      public static void main(String[] args)
13      {
14         // read class name from command line args or user input
15         String name;
16         if (args.length > 0) name = args[0];
17         else
18         {
19            try (var in = new Scanner(System.in))
20            {
21               System.out.println("Enter class name (e.g., java.util.Collections): ");
22               name = in.next();
23            }
24         }
25
26         try
27         {
28            // print generic info for class and public methods
29            Class<?> cl = Class.forName(name);
30            printClass(cl);
31            for (Method m : cl.getDeclaredMethods())
32               printMethod(m);
33         }
34         catch (ClassNotFoundException e)
35         {
36            e.printStackTrace();
37         }
38      }
39
40      public static void printClass(Class<?> cl)
41      {
42         System.out.print(cl);
43         printTypes(cl.getTypeParameters(), "<", ", ", ">", true);
44         Type sc = cl.getGenericSuperclass();
45         if (sc != null)
46         {
47            System.out.print(" extends ");
48            printType(sc, false);
49         }
50         printTypes(cl.getGenericInterfaces(), " implements ", ", ", "", false);
51         System.out.println();
52      }
53
54      public static void printMethod(Method m)
55      {
56         String name = m.getName();
57         System.out.print(Modifier.toString(m.getModifiers()));
58         System.out.print(" ");
59         printTypes(m.getTypeParameters(), "<", ", ", "> ", true);
60
61         printType(m.getGenericReturnType(), false);
62         System.out.print(" ");
63         System.out.print(name);
```

```
64          System.out.print("(");
65          printTypes(m.getGenericParameterTypes(), "", ", ", "", false);
66          System.out.println(")");
67       }
68
69       public static void printTypes(Type[] types, String prefix, String separator,
70             String suffix, boolean isDefinition)
71       {
72          if (prefix.equals(" extends ")
73                && Arrays.equals(types, new Type[] { Object.class })) return;
74          if (types.length > 0) System.out.print(prefix);
75          for (int i = 0; i < types.length; i++)
76          {
77             if (i > 0) System.out.print(separator);
78             printType(types[i], isDefinition);
79          }
80          if (types.length > 0) System.out.print(suffix);
81       }
82
83       public static void printType(Type type, boolean isDefinition)
84       {
85          if (type instanceof Class<?> t)
86          {
87             System.out.print(t.getName());
88          }
89          else if (type instanceof TypeVariable<?> t)
90          {
91             System.out.print(t.getName());
92             if (isDefinition)
93                printTypes(t.getBounds(), " extends ", " & ", "", false);
94          }
95          else if (type instanceof WildcardType t)
96          {
97             System.out.print("?");
98             printTypes(t.getUpperBounds(), " extends ", " & ", "", false);
99             printTypes(t.getLowerBounds(), " super ", " & ", "", false);
100         }
101         else if (type instanceof ParameterizedType t)
102         {
103            Type owner = t.getOwnerType();
104            if (owner != null)
105            {
106               printType(owner, false);
107               System.out.print(".");
108            }
109            printType(t.getRawType(), false);
110            printTypes(t.getActualTypeArguments(), "<", ", ", ">", false);
111         }
112         else if (type instanceof GenericArrayType t)
113         {
114            System.out.print("");
115            printType(t.getGenericComponentType(), isDefinition);
```

```
116            System.out.print("[]");
117        }
118    }
119 }
```

8.9.4. Type Literals

Sometimes, you want to drive program behavior by the type of a value. For example, in a persistence mechanism, you may want the user to specify a way of saving an object of a particular class. This is typically implemented by associating the Class object with an action.

However, with generic classes, erasure poses a problem. How can you have different actions for, say, ArrayList<Integer> and ArrayList<String> when both erase to the same raw ArrayList type?

There is a trick that can offer relief in some situations. You can capture an instance of the Type interface that you encountered in the preceding section. Construct an anonymous subclass like this:

```
var type = new TypeLiteral<ArrayList<Integer>>(){} // note the {}
```

The TypeLiteral constructor captures the generic supertype:

```
class TypeLiteral<T>
{
    public TypeLiteral()
    {
        Type parentType = getClass().getGenericSuperclass();
        if (parentType instanceof ParameterizedType paramType)
            type = paramType.getActualTypeArguments()[0];
        else
            throw new UnsupportedOperationException(
                "Construct as new TypeLiteral<. . .>(){}");
    }
    . . .
}
```

If we have a generic type available at runtime, we can match it against the TypeLiteral. We can't get a generic type from an object—it is erased. But, as you have seen in the preceding section, generic types of fields and method parameters survive in the virtual machine.

Injection frameworks such as CDI and Guice use type literals to control injection of generic types. The example program in the book's companion code shows a simpler example. Given an object, we enumerate its fields, whose generic types are available, and look up associated formatting actions.

We format an ArrayList<Integer> by separating the values with spaces, an
ArrayList<Character> by joining the characters to a string. Any other array lists are
formatted by ArrayList.toString.

Listing 8.5 `genericReflection/TypeLiterals.java`

```
 1   package genericReflection;
 2
 3   /**
 4      @version 1.03 2023-12-20
 5      @author Cay Horstmann
 6   */
 7
 8   import java.lang.reflect.*;
 9   import java.util.*;
10   import java.util.function.*;
11
12   /**
13    * A type literal describes a type that can be generic, such as
14    * ArrayList<String>.
15    */
16   class TypeLiteral<T>
17   {
18      private Type type;
19
20      /**
21       * This constructor must be invoked from an anonymous subclass
22       * as new TypeLiteral<. . .>(){}.
23       */
24      public TypeLiteral()
25      {
26         Type parentType = getClass().getGenericSuperclass();
27         if (parentType instanceof ParameterizedType paramType)
28            type = paramType.getActualTypeArguments()[0];
29         else
30            throw new UnsupportedOperationException(
31               "Construct as new TypeLiteral<. . .>(){}");
32      }
33
34      private TypeLiteral(Type type)
35      {
36         this.type = type;
37      }
38
39      /**
40       * Yields a type literal that describes the given type.
41       */
42      public static TypeLiteral<?> of(Type type)
43      {
44         return new TypeLiteral<>(type);
```

```
45        }
46
47        public String toString()
48        {
49            if (type instanceof Class<?> cl) return cl.getName();
50            else return type.toString();
51        }
52
53        public boolean equals(Object otherObject)
54        {
55            return otherObject instanceof TypeLiteral<?> otherLiteral
56                && type.equals(otherLiteral.type);
57        }
58
59        public int hashCode()
60        {
61            return type.hashCode();
62        }
63    }
64
65    /**
66     * Formats objects, using rules that associate types with formatting functions.
67     */
68    class Formatter
69    {
70        private Map<TypeLiteral<?>, Function<?, String>> rules = new HashMap<>();
71
72        /**
73         * Add a formatting rule to this formatter.
74         * @param type the type to which this rule applies
75         * @param formatterForType the function that formats objects of this type
76         */
77        public <T> void forType(TypeLiteral<T> type, Function<T, String> formatterForType)
78        {
79            rules.put(type,  formatterForType);
80        }
81
82        /**
83         * Formats all fields of an object using the rules of this formatter.
84         * @param obj an object
85         * @return a string with all field names and formatted values
86         */
87        public String formatFields(Object obj)
88                throws IllegalArgumentException, IllegalAccessException
89        {
90            var result = new StringBuilder();
91            for (Field f : obj.getClass().getDeclaredFields())
92            {
93                result.append(f.getName());
94                result.append("=");
95                f.setAccessible(true);
96                Function<?, String> formatterForType = rules.get(TypeLiteral.of(f.getGenericType()));
```

```
 97              if (formatterForType != null)
 98              {
 99                 // formatterForType has parameter type ?. Nothing can be passed to its apply
100                 // method. Cast makes the parameter type to Object so we can invoke it.
101                 @SuppressWarnings("unchecked")
102                 Function<Object, String> objectFormatter
103                    = (Function<Object, String>) formatterForType;
104                 result.append(objectFormatter.apply(f.get(obj)));
105              }
106              else
107                 result.append(f.get(obj).toString());
108              result.append("\n");
109           }
110           return result.toString();
111        }
112  }
113
114  public class TypeLiterals
115  {
116     public static class Sample
117     {
118        ArrayList<Integer> nums;
119        ArrayList<Character> chars;
120        ArrayList<String> strings;
121        public Sample()
122        {
123           nums = new ArrayList<>();
124           nums.add(42); nums.add(1729);
125           chars = new ArrayList<>();
126           chars.add('H'); chars.add('i');
127           strings = new ArrayList<>();
128           strings.add("Hello"); strings.add("World");
129        }
130     }
131
132     private static <T> String join(String separator, ArrayList<T> elements)
133     {
134        var result = new StringBuilder();
135        for (T e : elements)
136        {
137           if (result.length() > 0) result.append(separator);
138           result.append(e.toString());
139        }
140        return result.toString();
141     }
142
143     public static void main(String[] args) throws Exception
144     {
145        var formatter = new Formatter();
146        formatter.forType(new TypeLiteral<ArrayList<Integer>>(){},
147           lst -> join(" ", lst));
148        formatter.forType(new TypeLiteral<ArrayList<Character>>(){},
```

```
149            lst -> "\"" + join("", lst) + "\"");
150        System.out.println(formatter.formatFields(new Sample()));
151    }
152 }
```

---

java.lang.Class<T> 1.0

- TypeVariable[] getTypeParameters() **5.0**
  gets the generic type variables if this type was declared as a generic type, or an array of length 0 otherwise.
- Type getGenericSuperclass() **5.0**
  gets the generic type of the superclass that was declared for this type, or null if this type is Object or not a class type.
- Type[] getGenericInterfaces() **5.0**
  gets the generic types of the interfaces that were declared for this type, in declaration order, or an array of length 0 if this type doesn't implement interfaces.

---

java.lang.reflect.Method 1.1

- TypeVariable[] getTypeParameters() **5.0**
  gets the generic type variables if this method was declared as a generic method, or an array of length 0 otherwise.
- Type getGenericReturnType() **5.0**
  gets the generic return type with which this method was declared.
- Type[] getGenericParameterTypes() **5.0**
  gets the generic parameter types with which this method was declared. If the method has no parameters, an array of length 0 is returned.

---

java.lang.reflect.TypeVariable 5.0

- String getName()
  gets the name of this type variable.
- Type[] getBounds()
  gets the subclass bounds of this type variable, or an array of length 0 if the variable is unbounded.

---

java.lang.reflect.WildcardType 5.0

- Type[] getUpperBounds()
  gets the subclass (extends) bounds of this type variable, or an array of length 0 if the variable has no subclass bounds.

■ `Type[] getLowerBounds()`
gets the superclass (`super`) bounds of this type variable, or an array of length 0 if the variable has no superclass bounds.

`java.lang.reflect.ParameterizedType` **5.0**

■ `Type getRawType()`
gets the raw type of this parameterized type.
■ `Type[] getActualTypeArguments()`
gets the type parameters with which this parameterized type was declared.
■ `Type getOwnerType()`
gets the outer class type if this is an inner type, or `null` if this is a top-level type.

`java.lang.reflect.GenericArrayType` **5.0**

■ `Type getGenericComponentType()`
gets the generic component type with which this array type was declared.

You now know how to use generic classes and how to program your own generic classes and methods if the need arises. Just as importantly, you know how to decipher the generic type declarations that you may encounter in the API documentation and in error messages. For an exhaustive discussion of everything there is to know about Java generics, turn to Angelika Langer's excellent list of frequently (and not so frequently) asked questions at `http://angelikalanger.com/GenericsFAQ/JavaGenericsFAQ.html`.

In the next chapter, you will see how the Java collections framework puts generics to work.

CHAPTER 9

Collections

The data structures that you choose can make a big difference when you try to implement methods in a natural style or are concerned with performance. Do you need to search quickly through thousands (or even millions) of sorted items? Do you need to rapidly insert and remove elements in the middle of an ordered sequence? Do you need to establish associations between keys and values?

This chapter shows how the Java Collections Framework can help you accomplish the traditional data structuring needed for serious programming. In college computer science programs, a course called *Data Structures* usually takes a semester to complete, and there are many, many books devoted to this important topic. Our coverage differs from that of a college course; we will skip the theory and just look at how to use the collection classes in the Java API.

9.1. The Java Collections Framework

The initial release of Java supplied only a small set of classes for the most useful data structures: `Vector`, `Stack`, `Hashtable`, `BitSet`, and the `Enumeration` interface that provides an abstract mechanism for visiting elements in an arbitrary container. That was certainly a wise choice—it takes time and skill to come up with a comprehensive collection class library.

With the advent of Java 1.2, the designers felt that the time had come to roll out a full-fledged framework for data structures. They faced a number of conflicting design challenges. They wanted the library to be small and easy to learn. They did not want the complexity of the Standard Template Library (or STL) of C++, but they wanted the benefit of "generic algorithms" that STL pioneered. They wanted the legacy classes to fit into the new framework. As all designers of collections libraries do, they had to make some hard choices, and they came up with a number of idiosyncratic design decisions along the way. In this section, we will explore the basic design of the Java Collections Framework, demonstrate how to put it to work, and explain the reasoning behind some of the more controversial features.

9.1.1. Separating Collection Interfaces and Implementation

As is common with modern data structure libraries, the Java Collections Framework separates *interfaces* and *implementations*. Let us look at that separation with a familiar data structure, the *queue*.

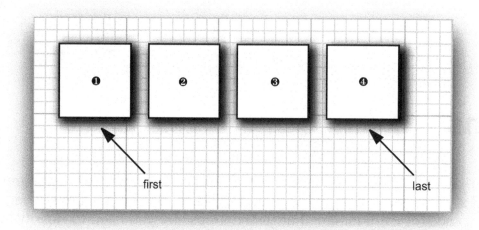

Figure 9.1: A queue

A *queue interface* specifies that you can add elements at the tail end of the queue, remove them at the head, and find out how many elements are in the queue. You use a queue when you need to collect objects and retrieve them in a "first in, first out" fashion (see Figure 9.1).

A minimal form of a queue interface might look like this:

```
public interface Queue<E> // a simplified form of the interface in the Java API
{
   void add(E e);
   E remove();
   int size();
}
```

The interface tells you nothing about how the queue is implemented. Of the two common implementations of a queue, one uses a "circular array" and one uses a linked list (see Figure 9.2).

Each implementation can be expressed by a class that implements the Queue interface. In the Java API, these classes are called ArrayDeque and LinkedList.

```
public class ArrayDeque<E> implements Queue<E> // simplified from the Java API
{
   private int first;
   private int last;
   private E[] elements;

   public ArrayDeque(int numElements) { . . . }
   public void add(E e) { . . . }
```

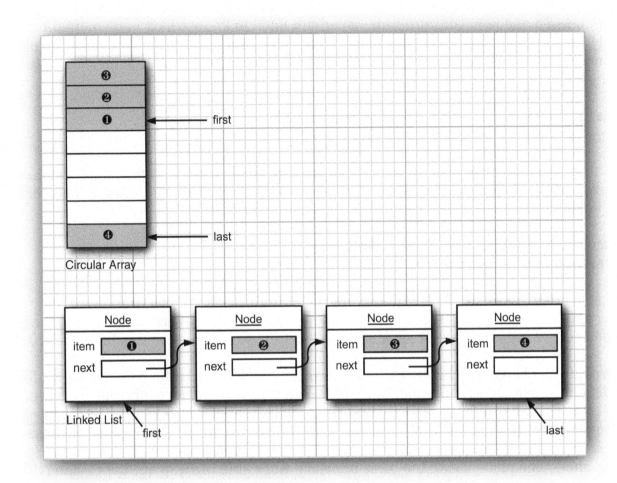

Figure 9.2: Queue implementations

```
    public E remove() { . . . }
    public int size() { . . . }
    . . .
}

public class LinkedList<E> implements Queue<E> // simplified from the Java API
{
    private Node<E> first;
    private Node<E> last;

    public LinkedList() { . . . }
    public void add(E e) { . . . }
    public E remove() { . . . }
    public int size() { . . . }
    . . .
}
```

When you use a queue in your program, you don't need to know which implementation is actually used once the collection has been constructed. Therefore, it makes sense to use the concrete class *only* when you construct the collection object. Use the *interface type* to hold the collection reference.

```
Queue<Customer> expressLane = new ArrayDeque<>(100);
expressLane.add(new Customer("Harry"));
```

With this approach, if you change your mind, you can easily use a different implementation. You only need to change your program in one place—in the constructor call. If you decide that a linked list is a better choice after all, your code becomes

```
Queue<Customer> expressLane = new LinkedList<>();
expressLane.add(new Customer("Harry"));
```

There is another reason to stick with the interface. Both the ArrayDeque and LinkedList classes have methods that are unrelated to queueing. Accidentally using one of them will be reported as a compile-time error, since you can't invoke them on a variable of type Queue.

Why would you choose one implementation over another? The interface says nothing about the efficiency of an implementation. A circular array is more memory-efficient. However, the circular array has a finite capacity and needs to be reallocated whenever it fills up. In fact, measurements show that an ArrayDeque generally outperforms a LinkedList because it has less impact on the garbage collector. When the ArrayDeque appeared in Java 6, the programmers who made use of the Queue interface were able to swap out the LinkedList by changing a single line of code.

9.1.2. The Collection Interface

The fundamental interface for collection classes in the Java Collections Framework is the Collection interface. The interface has two fundamental methods:

```
public interface Collection<E>
{
   boolean add(E element);
   Iterator<E> iterator();
   . . .
}
```

There are several methods in addition to these two; we will discuss them later.

The add method adds an element to the collection. The add method returns true if adding the element actually changes the collection, and false if the collection is unchanged. For example, if you try to add an object to a set and the object is already present, the add request has no effect because sets reject duplicates.

The iterator method returns an object that implements the Iterator interface. With that object, you can visit the elements in the collection one by one. We discuss iterators in the next section.

9.1.3. Iterators

The Iterator interface has four methods:

```
public interface Iterator<E>
{
    boolean hasNext();
    E next();
    default void remove();
    default void forEachRemaining(Consumer<? super E> action);
}
```

By repeatedly calling the next method, you can visit the elements from the collection one by one. However, if you reach the end of the collection, the next method throws a NoSuchElementException. Therefore, you need to call the hasNext method before calling next. That method returns true if the iterator has not yet reached the end, and there is at least one more element to visit. If you want to inspect all elements in a collection, request an iterator and then keep calling the next method while hasNext returns true. For example:

```
Collection<String> coll = . . .;
Iterator<String> iter = coll.iterator();
while (iter.hasNext())
{
    String element = iter.next();
    do something with element
}
```

You can write such a loop more concisely as the "for each" loop:

```
for (String element : coll)
{
    do something with element
}
```

The compiler simply translates the "for each" loop into a loop with an iterator.

The "for each" loop works with any object that implements the Iterable interface, an interface with an abstract method:

```
public interface Iterable<E>
{
   Iterator<E> iterator();
   . . .
}
```

The Collection interface extends the Iterable interface. Therefore, you can use the "for each" loop with any collection in the Java Collections Framework.

Instead of writing a loop, you can call the Collection.forEach or Iterator.forEachRemaining methods with a lambda expression that consumes an element. The lambda expression is invoked on all elements of the collection, or the remaining elements that the iterator can visit.

```
coll.forEach(element -> do something with element);
iter.forEachRemaining(element -> do something with element);
```

The order in which the elements are visited depends on the collection type. If you iterate over an ArrayList, the iterator starts at index 0 and increments the index in each step. However, if you visit the elements in a HashSet, you will get them in an essentially random order. You can be assured that you will encounter all elements of the collection during the course of the iteration, but you cannot make any assumptions about their ordering. This is usually not a problem because the ordering does not matter for computations such as computing totals or counting matches.

 Note: Old-timers will notice that the next and hasNext methods of the Iterator interface serve the same purpose as the nextElement and hasMoreElements methods of an Enumeration. The designers of the Java Collections Framework could have chosen to make use of the Enumeration interface. But they disliked the cumbersome method names and instead introduced a new interface with shorter method names.

There is an important conceptual difference between iterators in the Java collections library and iterators in other libraries. In traditional collections libraries, such as the Standard Template Library of C++, iterators are modeled after array indexes. Given such an iterator, you can look up the element that is stored at that position, much like you can look up an array element a[i] if you have an array index i. Independently of the lookup, you can advance the iterator to the next position. This is the same operation as advancing an array index by calling i++, without performing a lookup. However, the Java iterators do not work like that. The lookup and position change are tightly coupled. The only way to look up an element is to call next, and that lookup advances the position.

Instead, think of Java iterators as being *between elements*. When you call next, the iterator *jumps over* the next element, and it returns a reference to the element that it just passed (see Figure 9.3).

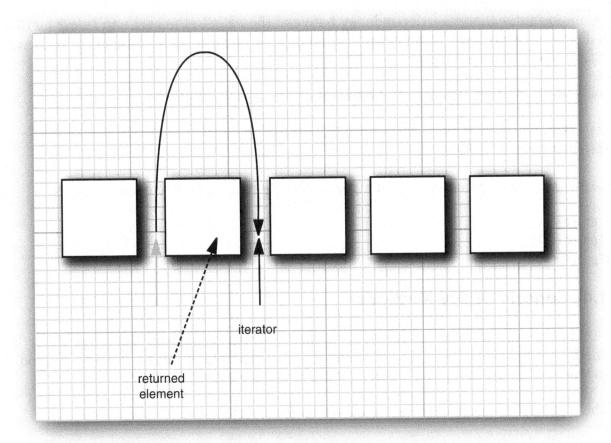

Figure 9.3: Advancing an iterator

 Note: Here is another useful analogy. You can think of Iterator.next as the equivalent of InputStream.read. Reading a byte from a stream automatically "consumes" the byte. The next call to read consumes and returns the next byte from the input. Similarly, repeated calls to next let you read all elements in a collection.

The remove method of the Iterator interface removes the element that was returned by the last call to next. In many situations, that makes sense—you need to see the element before you can decide that it is the one that should be removed. But if you want to remove an element in a particular position, you still need to skip past the element. For example, here is how you remove the first element in a collection of strings:

```
Iterator<String> iter = coll.iterator();
iter.next(); // skip over the first element
iter.remove(); // now remove it
```

More importantly, there is a dependency between the calls to the next and remove methods. It is illegal to call remove if it wasn't preceded by a call to next. If you try, an IllegalStateException is thrown.

If you want to remove two adjacent elements, you cannot simply call

```
iter.remove();
iter.remove(); // ERROR
```

Instead, you must first call next to jump over the element to be removed.

```
iter.remove();
iter.next();
iter.remove(); // OK
```

9.1.4. Generic Utility Methods

The Collection and Iterator interfaces are generic, which means you can write utility methods that operate on any kind of collection. For example, here is a generic method that tests whether an arbitrary collection contains a given element:

```
public static <E> boolean contains(Collection<E> c, Object obj)
{
   for (E element : c)
      if (element.equals(obj))
         return true;
   return false;
}
```

The designers of the Java Collections Framework decided that some of these utility methods are so useful that the framework should make them available. That way, API users don't have to keep reinventing the wheel. The contains method is one such method.

In fact, the Collection<E> interface declares quite a few useful methods that all implementing classes must supply:

```
int size()
boolean isEmpty()
boolean contains(Object obj)
boolean containsAll(Collection<?> c)
boolean add(E obj)
boolean addAll(Collection<? extends E> from)
boolean remove(Object obj)
boolean removeAll(Collection<?> c)
boolean retainAll(Collection<?> c)
```

```
void clear()
Object[] toArray()
T[] toArray(T[] a)
```

 Note: The Collection interface declares the equals and hashCode methods that are inherited from Object. There is no technical need to include these declarations. It merely provides a good place for adding collection-specific API documentation. The Set and List subinterfaces mandate specific behavior for equals. Other collections can inherit Object.equals, or override it and compare the elements in some way. In the latter case, the hashCode method also needs to be overridden.

Many of these methods are self-explanatory; you will find full documentation in the API notes at the end of this section.

 Caution: The Java Collections Framework was designed before generic types were added to Java. For backwards compatibility, the contains and remove methods have a parameter of type Object and not E. The containsAll, removeAll, and retainAll methods have a parameter of type Collection<?> and not Collection<? extends E>.

This means that type errors may not be detected at compile time. As an example, consider this code snippet where accidentally a String is removed from a collection of Path objects:

```
Collection<Path> paths = . . .;
paths.remove("/tmp"); // Compiles, but can have no effect
```

Of course, it is a bother if every class that implements the Collection interface has to supply so many routine methods. To make life easier for implementors, the framework supplies a class AbstractCollection that leaves the fundamental methods size and iterator abstract but implements the routine methods in terms of them. For example:

```
public abstract class AbstractCollection<E>
      implements Collection<E>
{
   . . .
   public abstract Iterator<E> iterator();
   public abstract int size();

   public boolean isEmpty()
   {
      return size() == 0;
   }

   public boolean contains(Object obj)
```

```
    {
        Iterator<E> it = iterator();
        if (o == null)
        {
            while (it.hasNext()) if (it.next() == null) return true;
        }
        else
        {
            while (it.hasNext()) if (o.equals(it.next())) return true;
        }
        return false;
    }
    . . .
}
```

A concrete collection class can now extend the AbstractCollection class. It is up to the concrete collection class to supply iterator and size methods. Mutable collections also need an add method. The other methods have been taken care of by the AbstractCollection superclass. However, if the subclass has a more efficient way of implementing contains, it is free to do so.

This approach is a bit outdated. It would be nicer if the methods were default methods of the Collection interface, but default methods didn't exist when the Java Collections Framework was designed. However, several default methods have been added. Three of them deal with streams (discussed in Volume II). See Section 9.6.6 for the toArray method. In addition, there is a useful method

```
default boolean removeIf(Predicate<? super E> filter)
```

for removing elements that fulfill a condition.

---

java.util.Collection<E> 1.2

- Iterator<E> iterator()
  returns an iterator that can be used to visit the elements in the collection.
- int size()
  returns the number of elements currently stored in the collection.
- boolean isEmpty()
  returns true if this collection contains no elements.
- boolean contains(Object obj)
  returns true if this collection contains an object equal to obj.
- boolean containsAll(Collection<?> other)
  returns true if this collection contains all elements in the other collection.
- boolean add(E element)
  attempts to add an element to the collection. Returns true if the collection changed as a result of this call.

- `boolean addAll(Collection<? extends E> other)`
  adds all elements from the other collection to this collection. Returns `true` if the collection changed as a result of this call.
- `boolean remove(Object obj)`
  attempts to remove an object equal to `obj` from this collection. Returns `true` if a matching object was removed.
- `boolean removeAll(Collection<?> other)`
  removes from this collection all elements from the other collection. Returns `true` if the collection changed as a result of this call.
- `default boolean removeIf(Predicate<? super E> filter)` **8**
  removes all elements for which `filter` returns true. Returns `true` if the collection changed as a result of this call.
- `void clear()`
  removes all elements from this collection.
- `boolean retainAll(Collection<?> other)`
  removes all elements from this collection that do not equal one of the elements in the other collection. Returns `true` if the collection changed as a result of this call.
- `Object[] toArray()`
  returns an array of the objects in the collection.
- `<T> T[] toArray(IntFunction<T[]> generator)` **11**
  returns an array of the objects in the collection. The array is constructed with the generator, which is typically a constructor expression `T[]::new`.

`java.util.Iterator<E>` 1.2

- `boolean hasNext()`
  returns `true` if there is another element to visit.
- `E next()`
  returns the next object to visit. Throws a `NoSuchElementException` if the end of the collection has been reached.
- `void remove()`
  removes the last visited object. This method must immediately follow an element visit. If the collection has been modified since the last element visit, this method throws an `IllegalStateException`. Iterators are not required to support this operation. The default implementation throws an `UnsupportedOperationException`.
- `default void forEachRemaining(Consumer<? super E> action)` **8**
  visits elements and passes them to the given action until no elements remain or the action throws an exception.

9.2. Interfaces in the Collections Framework

The Java Collections Framework defines a number of interfaces for different types of collections. These are shown in Figure 9.4, except for interfaces for concurrent programming, which are covered in Chapter 10.

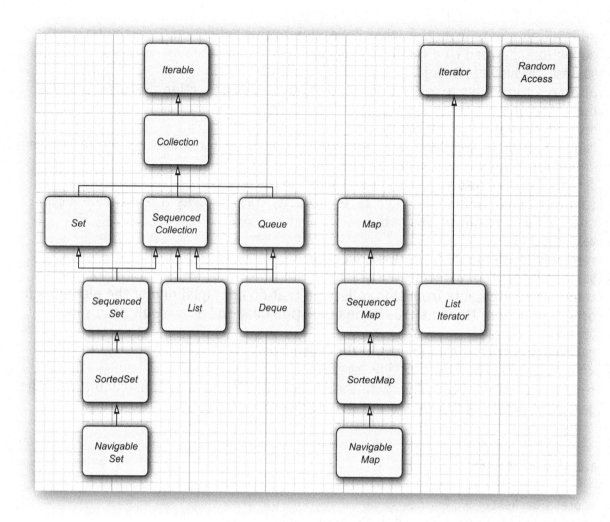

Figure 9.4: The interfaces of the Java Collections Framework

There are two fundamental interfaces for collections: `Collection` and `Map`. As you already saw, you insert elements into a collection with a method

```
boolean add(E element)
```

However, maps hold key/value pairs, and you use the put method to insert them:

```
V put(K key, V value)
```

To read elements from a collection, visit them with an iterator. However, you can read values from a map with the get method:

```
V get(Object key)
```

A List is an *ordered collection*. Elements are added into a particular position in the container. An element can be accessed in two ways: by an iterator or by an integer index. The latter is called *random access* because elements can be visited in any order. In contrast, when using an iterator, one must visit them sequentially.

The List interface defines several methods for random access:

```
void add(int index, E element)
E remove(int index)
E get(int index)
E set(int index, E element)
```

Caution: With a List<Integer, there are two remove methods:

```
boolean remove(int index) // Removes the element with the given index
boolean remove(Integer o) // Removes the element equal to o
```

When calling remove with a parameter of type int, the first method is chosen. No boxing is considered, and there is no warning. This may not be what you want:

```
List<Integer> ids = . . .;
int id = . . .;
if (id == 0) ids.remove(id); // Removes index 0, not the element with value 0
```

Note: The API documentation for the List interface defines the behavior of the equals method for lists. For a list to be equal to another object, the other object must also be a list of some kind. Both lists must have the same size. When iterating over each list, corresponding elements must be equal.

Frankly, there is a problem with the List interface in the Java Collections Framework. There are two kinds of ordered collections, with very different performance tradeoffs. An ordered collection that is backed by an array has fast random access, and it makes sense to use the List methods with an integer index. In contrast, a linked list, while also ordered, has slow random access, and it is best traversed sequentially with an iterator. It would have been better to provide two interfaces.

Note: To avoid carrying out random access operations for linked lists, Java 1.4 introduced a tagging interface, RandomAccess. That interface has no methods, but you can use it to test whether a particular collection supports efficient random access:

```
if (c instanceof RandomAccess)
{
   random traversal
}
else
{
   sequential traversal
}
```

The Set interface has the same instance methods as the Collection interface, but the behavior of the methods is more tightly defined. The add method of a set should reject duplicates. The equals method of a set should be defined so that two sets are identical if they have the same elements, but not necessarily in the same order. The hashCode method should be defined so that two sets with the same elements yield the same hash code.

Why make a separate interface if the method signatures are the same? Conceptually, not all collections are sets. Making a Set interface enables programmers to write methods that accept only sets.

To see why this distinction matters, consider equality testing. Two lists are equal if they have the same elements in the same order. Two sets are equal if they have the same elements in some order. The equals method for a class implementing the Set interface needs to ensure that the argument is also a Set and not just any Collection.

The SortedSet and SortedMap interfaces expose the comparator object used for sorting, and they define methods to obtain views of subsets of the collections. We discuss these in Section 9.5.3.

The interfaces NavigableSet and NavigableMap contain additional methods for finding the next or previous element in sorted sets and maps. The TreeSet and TreeMap classes implement these interfaces. The navigation operations can be efficiently implemented in tree-based data structures.

Java 21 introduces the SequencedCollection<E> interface that provides uniform access to the first and last element of a collection and reverse traversal.

```
E getFirst()
E getLast()
void addFirst(E e)
void addLast(E e)
E removeFirst()
E removeLast()
SequencedCollection<E> reversed()
```

Previously, these operations were carried out by different methods in lists, sets, and deques. The SequencedSet subinterface sharpens the return type of the reversed method to SequencedSet. The SequencedMap interface has analogous methods for maps.

9.3. Concrete Collections

Table 9.1 shows the collections in the Java Collections Framework and briefly describes the purpose of each collection class. (For simplicity, I omit the thread-safe collections that will be discussed in Chapter 10.)

All classes in Table 9.1 implement the Collection interface, with the exception of the classes with names ending in Map. Those classes implement the Map interface instead. We will discuss maps in Section 9.4.

Table 9.1: Concrete Collections in the Java Collections Framework

Collection Type	Description	See
ArrayList	An indexed sequence that grows and shrinks dynamically	Section 9.3.2
LinkedList	An ordered sequence that allows efficient insertion and removal at any location	Section 9.3.1
ArrayDeque	A double-ended queue that is implemented as a circular array	Section 9.3.5
HashSet	An unordered collection that rejects duplicates	Section 9.3.3
TreeSet	A sorted set	Section 9.4.5
EnumSet	A set of enumerated type values	Section 9.4.6
LinkedHashSet	A set that remembers the order in which elements were inserted	Section 9.4.5
PriorityQueue	A collection that allows efficient removal of the smallest element	Section 9.3.6
HashMap	A data structure that stores key/value associations	Section 9.4.1

Collection Type	Description	See
TreeMap	A map in which the keys are sorted	Section 9.4.1
EnumMap	A map in which the keys belong to an enumerated type	Section 9.4.6
LinkedHashMap	A map that remembers the order in which entries were added	Section 9.4.5
WeakHashMap	A map with values that can be reclaimed by the garbage collector if they are not used elsewhere	Section 9.4.4
IdentityHashMap	A map with keys that are compared by ==, not equals	Section 9.4.7

Figure 9.5 shows the relationships between these classes.

9.3.1. Linked Lists

We already used arrays and their dynamic cousin, the ArrayList class, for many examples in this book. However, arrays and array lists suffer from a major drawback. Removing an element from the middle of an array is expensive since all array elements beyond the removed one must be moved toward the beginning of the array (see Figure 9.6). The same is true for inserting elements in the middle.

Another well-known data structure, the *linked list*, solves this problem. Where an array stores object references in consecutive memory locations, a linked list stores each object in a separate *link*. Each link also stores a reference to the next link in the sequence. In the Java Collections Framework, all linked lists are actually *doubly linked*; that is, each link also stores a reference to its predecessor (see Figure 9.7).

Removing an element from the middle of a linked list is an inexpensive operation—only the links around the element to be removed need to be updated (see Figure 9.8).

Perhaps you once took a data structures course in which you learned how to implement linked lists. You may have bad memories of tangling up the links when removing or adding elements in the linked list. If so, you will be pleased to learn that the Java Collections Framework supplies a class LinkedList ready for you to use.

The following code example adds three elements and then removes the second one:

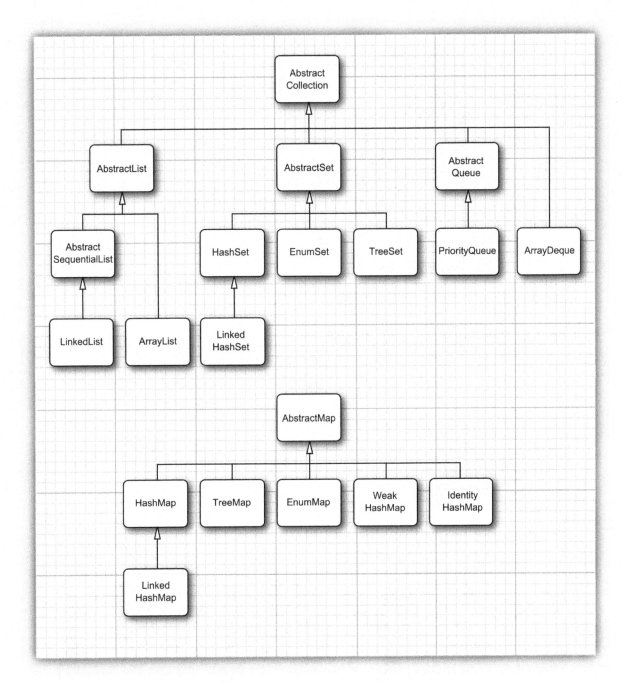

Figure 9.5: Classes in the Java Collections Framework

```
var staff = new LinkedList<String>();
staff.add("Amy");
staff.add("Bob");
staff.add("Carl");
Iterator<String> iter = staff.iterator();
```

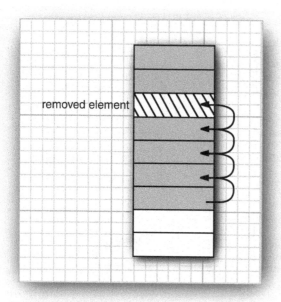

Figure 9.6: Removing an element from an array

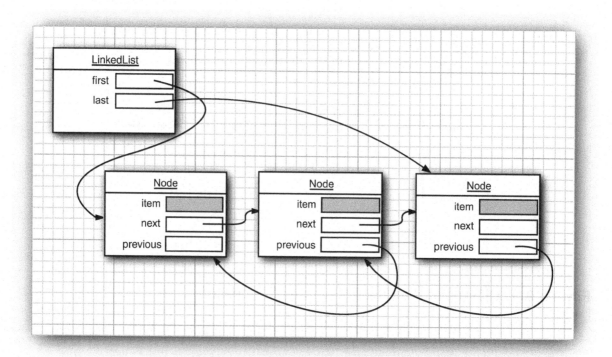

Figure 9.7: A doubly linked list

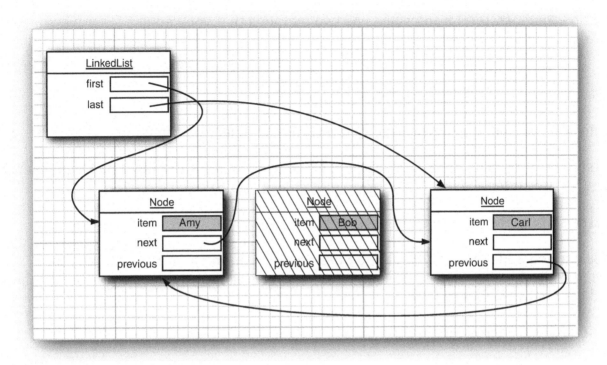

Figure 9.8: Removing an element from a linked list

```
String first = iter.next(); // visit first element (Amy)
String second = iter.next(); // visit second element (Bob)
iter.remove(); // remove last visited element (Bob)
```

There is, however, an important difference between linked lists and generic collections. A linked list is an *ordered collection* in which the position of the objects matters. The LinkedList.add method adds the object to the end of the list. But you will often want to add objects somewhere in the middle of a list. This position-dependent add method is the responsibility of an iterator, since iterators describe positions in collections. Using iterators to add elements makes sense only for collections that have a natural ordering. For example, the *set* data type that we discuss in the next section does not impose any ordering on its elements. Therefore, there is no add method in the Iterator interface. Instead, the Java Collections Framework supplies a subinterface ListIterator that contains an add method:

```
interface ListIterator<E> extends Iterator<E>
{
   void add(E element);
   . . .
}
```

Unlike Collection.add, this method does not return a boolean—it is assumed that the add operation always modifies the list.

In addition, the ListIterator interface has two methods that you can use for traversing a list backwards.

```
boolean hasPrevious()
E previous()
```

Like the next method, the previous method returns the object that it skipped over.

The listIterator method of the LinkedList class returns an iterator object that implements the ListIterator interface.

```
ListIterator<String> iter = staff.listIterator();
```

The add method adds the new element *before* the iterator position. For example, the following code skips past the first element in the linked list and adds "Juliet" before the second element (see Figure 9.9):

```
var staff = new LinkedList<String>();
staff.add("Amy");
staff.add("Bob");
staff.add("Carl");
ListIterator<String> iter = staff.listIterator();
iter.next(); // skip past first element
iter.add("Juliet");
```

If you call the add method multiple times, the elements are simply added in the order in which you supplied them. They are all added in turn before the current iterator position.

When you use the add operation with an iterator that was freshly returned from the listIterator method and that points to the first element of the list, the newly added element becomes the first element. When the iterator has passed the last element of the list (that is, when hasNext returns false), the added element becomes the new tail of the list. If the linked list has n elements, there are $n + 1$ spots for adding a new element. These spots correspond to the $n + 1$ possible positions of the iterator. For example, if a linked list contains three elements, A, B, and C, there are four possible positions (marked as |) for inserting a new element:

```
|ABC
A|BC
AB|C
ABC|
```

 Note: Be careful with the "cursor" analogy. The remove operation does not work exactly like the Backspace key. Immediately after a call to next, the remove method indeed removes the element to the left of the iterator, just like the Backspace key

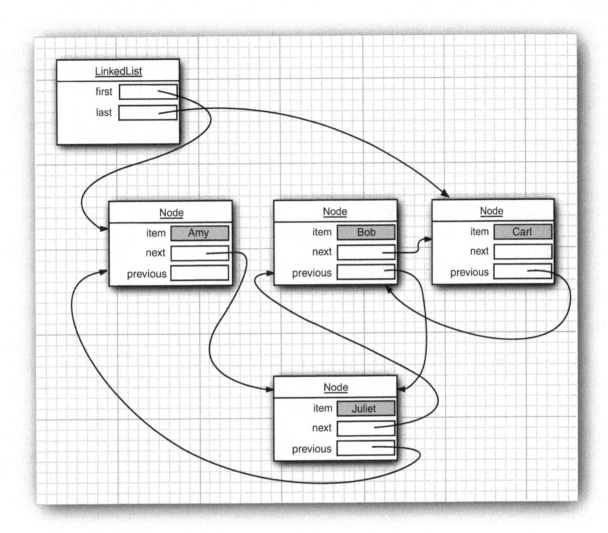

Figure 9.9: Adding an element to a linked list

would. However, if you have just called previous, the element to the right will be removed. And you can't call remove twice in a row.

Unlike the add method, which depends only on the iterator position, the remove method depends on the iterator state.

Finally, a set method replaces the last element, returned by a call to next or previous, with a new element. For example, the following code replaces the first element of a list with a new value:

```
ListIterator<String> iter = list.listIterator();
String oldValue = iter.next(); // returns first element
iter.set(newValue); // sets first element to newValue
```

As you might imagine, if an iterator traverses a collection while another iterator is modifying it, confusing situations can occur. For example, suppose an iterator points before an element that another iterator has just removed. The iterator is now invalid and should no longer be used. The linked list iterators have been designed to detect such modifications. If an iterator finds that its collection has been modified by another iterator or by a method of the collection itself, it throws a ConcurrentModificationException. For example, consider the following code:

```
List<String> list = . . .;
ListIterator<String> iter1 = list.listIterator();
ListIterator<String> iter2 = list.listIterator();
iter1.next();
iter1.remove();
iter2.next(); // throws ConcurrentModificationException
```

The call to iter2.next throws a ConcurrentModificationException since iter2 detects that the list was modified externally.

To avoid concurrent modification exceptions, follow this simple rule: You can attach as many iterators to a collection as you like, provided that all of them are only readers. Alternatively, you can attach a single iterator that can both read and write.

Concurrent modification detection is done in a simple way. The collection keeps track of the number of mutating operations (such as adding and removing elements). Each iterator keeps a separate count of the number of mutating operations that *it* was responsible for. At the beginning of each iterator method, the iterator simply checks whether its own mutation count equals that of the collection. If not, it throws a ConcurrentModificationException.

 Note: There is, however, a curious exception to the detection of concurrent modifications. The linked list only keeps track of *structural* modifications to the list, such as adding and removing links. The set method does *not* count as a structural modification. You can attach multiple iterators to a linked list, all of which call set to change the contents of existing links. This capability is required for a number of algorithms in the Collections class that we discuss later in this chapter.

Now you have seen the fundamental methods of the LinkedList class. Use a ListIterator to traverse the elements of the linked list in either direction and to add and remove elements.

As you saw in Section 9.2, many other useful methods for operating on linked lists are declared in the Collection interface. These are, for the most part, implemented in the AbstractCollection superclass of the LinkedList class. For example, the toString method invokes toString on all elements and produces one long string of the format [A, B, C]. This is handy for debugging. Use the contains method to check whether an element is present in a linked list. For example, the call staff.contains("Harry") returns true if the linked list already contains a string equal to the string "Harry".

The Java Collections Framework also supplies a number of methods that are, from a theoretical perspective, somewhat dubious. Linked lists do not support fast random access. If you want to see the nth element of a linked list, you have to start at the beginning and skip past the first n – 1 elements. There is no shortcut. For that reason, programmers don't usually use linked lists in situations where elements need to be accessed by an integer index.

Nevertheless, the LinkedList class supplies a get method that lets you access a particular element:

```
LinkedList<String> list = . . .;
String obj = list.get(n);
```

Of course, this method is not very efficient. If you find yourself using it, you are probably using a wrong data structure for your problem.

You should *never* use this illusory random access method to step through a linked list. The code

```
for (int i = 0; i < list.size(); i++)
    do something with list.get(i);
```

is staggeringly inefficient. Each time you look up another element, the search starts again from the beginning of the list. The LinkedList object makes no effort to cache the position information.

Note: The get method has one slight optimization: If the index is at least size() / 2, the search for the element starts at the end of the list.

The list iterator interface also has a method to tell you the index of the current position. In fact, since Java iterators conceptually point between elements, it has two of them: The nextIndex method returns the integer index of the element that would be returned by the next call to next; the previousIndex method returns the index of the element that would be returned by the next call to previous. Of course, that is simply one less than nextIndex. These methods are efficient for LinkedList iterators—each iterator keeps a count of its current position. Finally, if you have an integer index n, then list.listIterator(n) returns an iterator that points just before the element with index n. That is, calling next yields the same element as list.get(n); obtaining that iterator is inefficient.

If you have a linked list with only a handful of elements, you don't have to be overly paranoid about the cost of the get and set methods. But then, why use a linked list in the first place? The only reason to use a linked list is to minimize the cost of insertion and removal in the middle of the list. If you have only a few elements, you can just use an ArrayList.

I recommend that you simply stay away from all methods that use an integer index to denote a position in a linked list. If you want random access into a collection, use an array or ArrayList, not a linked list.

The program in Listing 9.1 puts linked lists to work. It simply creates two lists, merges them, then removes every second element from the second list, and finally tests the removeAll method. I recommend that you trace the program flow and pay special attention to the iterators. You may find it helpful to draw diagrams of the iterator positions, like this:

```
|ACE  |BDFG
A|CE  |BDFG
AB|CE B|DFG
. . .
```

Note that the call

```
System.out.println(a);
```

prints all elements in the linked list a by invoking the toString method in AbstractCollection.

Listing 9.1 `linkedList/LinkedListTest.java`

```java
1   package linkedList;
2
3   import java.util.*;
4
5   /**
6    * This program demonstrates operations on linked lists.
7    * @version 1.13 2023-12-05
8    * @author Cay Horstmann
9    */
10  public class LinkedListTest
11  {
12     public static void main(String[] args)
13     {
14        var a = new LinkedList<String>();
15        a.add("Amy");
16        a.add("Carl");
17        a.add("Erica");
18
19        var b = new LinkedList<String>();
20        b.add("Bob");
21        b.add("Doug");
22        b.add("Frances");
23        b.add("Gloria");
24
25        // merge the elements from b into a
26
```

```
27        ListIterator<String> aIter = a.listIterator();
28        Iterator<String> bIter = b.iterator();
29
30        while (bIter.hasNext())
31        {
32           if (aIter.hasNext()) aIter.next();
33           aIter.add(bIter.next());
34        }
35
36        System.out.println(a);
37
38        // remove every second element from b
39
40        bIter = b.iterator();
41        while (bIter.hasNext())
42        {
43           bIter.next(); // skip one element
44           if (bIter.hasNext())
45           {
46              bIter.next(); // skip next element
47              bIter.remove(); // remove that element
48           }
49        }
50
51        System.out.println(b);
52
53        // bulk operation: remove all elements in b from a
54
55        a.removeAll(b);
56
57        System.out.println(a);
58     }
59 }
```

---

java.util.List<E> 1.2

- ■ ListIterator<E> listIterator()
  returns a list iterator for visiting the elements of the list.
- ■ ListIterator<E> listIterator(int index)
  returns a list iterator for visiting the elements of the list whose first call to next will
  return the element with the given index.
- ■ void add(int i, E element)
  adds an element at the specified position.
- ■ boolean addAll(int i, Collection<? extends E> elements)
  adds all elements from a collection to the specified position.
- ■ E remove(int i)
  removes and returns the element at the specified position.
- ■ E get(int i)
  gets the element at the specified position.

- `E set(int i, E element)`
  replaces the element at the specified position with a new element and returns the old element.
- `int indexOf(Object element)`
  returns the position of the first occurrence of an element equal to the specified element, or -1 if no matching element is found.
- `int lastIndexOf(Object element)`
  returns the position of the last occurrence of an element equal to the specified element, or -1 if no matching element is found.

---

java.util.ListIterator<E> 1.2

- `void add(E newElement)`
  adds an element before the current position.
- `void set(E newElement)`
  replaces the last element visited by next or previous with a new element. Throws an `IllegalStateException` if the list structure was modified since the last call to next or previous.
- `boolean hasPrevious()`
  returns true if there is another element to visit when iterating backwards through the list.
- `E previous()`
  returns the previous object. Throws a `NoSuchElementException` if the beginning of the list has been reached.
- `int nextIndex()`
  returns the index of the element that would be returned by the next call to next, or the size of the list if the iterator is past the last element..
- `int previousIndex()`
  returns the index of the element that would be returned by the next call to previous, or -1 if the iterator is before the first element.

---

java.util.LinkedList<E> 1.2

- `LinkedList()`
  constructs an empty linked list.
- `LinkedList(Collection<? extends E> elements)`
  constructs a linked list and adds all elements from a collection.
- `void addFirst(E element)`
- `void addLast(E element)`
  add an element to the beginning or the end of the list.
- `E getFirst()`
- `E getLast()`
  return the element at the beginning or the end of the list.

- ■ E removeFirst()
- ■ E removeLast()

    remove and return the element at the beginning or the end of the list.

9.3.2. Array Lists

In the preceding section, you saw the List interface and the LinkedList class that implements it. The List interface describes an ordered collection in which the position of elements matters. There are two protocols for visiting the elements: through an iterator and by random access with methods get and set. The latter is not appropriate for linked lists, but of course get and set make a lot of sense for arrays. The Java Collections Framework supplies the familiar ArrayList class that also implements the List interface. An ArrayList encapsulates a dynamically reallocated array of objects.

 Note: Java 1.0 came with a different array-based collection, the Vector class. All methods of the Vector class are *synchronized*. It is safe to access a Vector object from two threads. But if you access a vector from only a single thread—by far the more common case—the synchronization is wasteful. In contrast, the ArrayList methods are not synchronized. As you will see in Chapter 10, there are now better threadsafe choices as well. There is no reason to use Vector nowadays unless you need to interface with an ancient API.

9.3.3. Hash Sets

Linked lists and arrays let you specify the order in which you want to arrange the elements. However, if you are looking for a particular element and don't remember its position, you need to visit all elements until you find a match. That can be time consuming if the collection contains many elements. If you don't care about the ordering of the elements, there are data structures that let you find elements much faster. The drawback is that those data structures give you no control over the order in which the elements appear. These data structures organize the elements in an order that is convenient for their own purposes.

A well-known data structure for finding objects quickly is the *hash table*. A hash table computes an integer, called the *hash code*, for each object. A hash code is somehow derived from the instance fields of an object, preferably in such a way that objects with different data yield different codes. Table 9.2 lists a few examples of hash codes that result from the hashCode method of the String class.

Table 9.2: Hash Codes Resulting from the hashCode Method

String	Hash Code
"Lee"	76268

String	Hash Code
"lee"	107020
"eel"	100300

If you define your own classes, you are responsible for implementing your own `hashCode` method—see Chapter 5 for more information. Your implementation needs to be compatible with the `equals` method: If `a.equals(b)`, then `a` and `b` must have the same hash code.

What's important for now is that hash codes can be computed quickly and that the computation depends only on the state of the object that needs to be hashed, not on the other objects in the hash table.

In Java, hash tables are implemented as arrays of linked lists. Each list is called a *bucket* (see Figure 9.10). To find the place of an object in the table, compute its hash code and reduce it modulo the total number of buckets. The resulting number is the index of the bucket that holds the element. For example, if an object has hash code 76268 and there are 128 buckets, then the object is placed in bucket 108 (because the remainder 76268 % 128 is 108). Perhaps you are lucky and there is no other element in that bucket. Then, you simply insert the element into that bucket. Of course, sometimes you will hit a nonempty bucket. This is called a *hash collision*. Then, compare the new object with all objects in that bucket to see if it is already present. If the hash codes are reasonably randomly distributed and the number of buckets is large enough, only a few comparisons should be necessary.

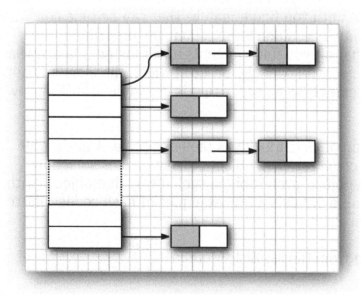

Figure 9.10: A hash table

Note: In the HashMap implementation, a bucket changes from a linked list into a balanced binary tree when its size exceeds a threshold. This improves performance if a hash function was poorly chosen and yields many collisions, or if malicious code tries to flood a hash table with many values that have identical hash codes.

 Tip: If at all possible, the keys of a hash table should belong to a class that implements the Comparable interface. Then you are guaranteed not to suffer poor performance due to poorly distributed hash codes.

If the hash table gets too full, it needs to be *rehashed*. To rehash the table, a table with more buckets is created, all elements are inserted into the new table, and the original table is discarded. The *load factor* determines when a hash table is rehashed. For example, if the load factor is 0.75 (which is the default) and the table is more than 75% full, it is automatically rehashed with twice as many buckets. For most applications, it is reasonable to leave the load factor at 0.75.

If you want more control over the performance of the hash table, you can specify the initial bucket count. You should set it to the expected element count, divided by the load factor. Or, as of Java 19, you can use the static newHashSet convenience method that does this computation for you:

```
HashSet<String> strings = HashSet.newHashSet(expectedElementCount);
```

 Note: Some researchers believe that it is a good idea to make the bucket count a prime number to prevent a clustering of keys. The evidence for this isn't conclusive, however. The Java Collections Framework uses bucket counts that are powers of 2, with a default of 16. (Any value you supply for the bucket count is automatically rounded to the next power of 2.)

Hash tables can be used to implement several important data structures. The simplest among them is the *set* type. A set is a collection of elements without duplicates. The add method of a set first tries to find the object to be added, and adds it only if it is not yet present.

The Java Collections Framework supplies a HashSet class that implements a set based on a hash table. You add elements with the add method. The contains method is redefined to make a fast lookup to see if an element is already present in the set. It checks only the elements in one bucket and not all elements in the collection.

The hash set iterator visits all buckets in turn. Since hashing scatters the elements around in the table, they are visited in a seemingly random order. You would only use a HashSet if you don't care about the ordering of the elements in the collection.

The sample program at the end of this section (Listing 9.2) reads words from a file, adds them to a set, and prints out the first twenty words in the set. For example, you can feed the program the text from *Alice in Wonderland* by launching it from a command shell as

```
java set.SetTest ../gutenberg/alice30.txt
```

Alice in Wonderland has 28,195 words, of which 5,909 are unique, including the copyright notice at the beginning. The words appear in random order. The same words are then inserted into a tree set, which, as you will see in the following section, keeps the elements in sorted order.

Caution: Be careful when you mutate set elements. If the hash code of an element were to change, the element would no longer be in the correct position in the data structure.

```
var rects = new HashSet<Rectangle>();
var rect = new Rectangle(5, 10, 20, 30);
rects.add(rect);
rect.setLocation(0, 0);
    // rects is now [java.awt.Rectangle[x=0,y=0,width=20,height=30]]
rects.remove(new Rectangle(0, 0, 20, 30)); // Returns false, doesn't remove
```

Listing 9.2 set/SetTest.java

```
 1  package set;
 2
 3  import java.io.IOException;
 4  import java.nio.file.Path;
 5  import java.util.*;
 6
 7  /**
 8   * This program compares insertion into a hash set and a tree set.
 9   * Run the program as
10   * java set.SetTest ../gutenberg/alice30.txt
11   * java set.SetTest ../gutenberg/crsto10.txt 100
12   * @version 1.2 2023-12-07
13   * @author Cay Horstmann
14   */
15  public class SetTest
16  {
17     public static void time(Set<String> wordSet, List<String> wordList, int repetitions)
18     {
19        long totalTime = 0;
20        for (int i = 1; i <= repetitions; i++)
21        {
22           for (String word : wordList)
```

```
23          {
24              long start = System.nanoTime();
25              wordSet.add(word);
26              long end = System.nanoTime();
27              totalTime += end - start;
28          }
29      }
30      Iterator<String> iter = wordSet.iterator();
31      for (int i = 1; i <= 20 && iter.hasNext(); i++)
32          System.out.print(iter.next() + " ");
33      System.out.println("...");
34      System.out.printf("%s: %d words, %d distinct, %.3f seconds.%n",
35          wordSet.getClass().getSimpleName(), wordList.size(), wordSet.size(),
36          totalTime * 1E-9);
37   }
38
39   public static void main(String[] args) throws IOException
40   {
41      List<String> words = new ArrayList<>();
42      String filename = args.length > 0 ? args[0] : "../gutenberg/crsto10.txt";
43      int repetitions = args.length > 1 ? Integer.parseInt(args[1]) : 1;
44      try (var in = new Scanner(Path.of(filename))) {
45          while (in.hasNext()) {
46              String word = in.next();
47              words.add(word);
48          }
49      }
50      time(new HashSet<>(), words, repetitions);
51      time(new TreeSet<>(), words, repetitions);
52   }
53 }
```

`java.util.HashSet<E>` 1.2

- `HashSet()`
  constructs an empty hash set.
- `HashSet(Collection<? extends E> elements)`
  constructs a hash set and adds all elements from a collection.
- `HashSet(int initialCapacity)`
  `HashSet(int initialCapacity, float loadFactor)`
  constructs an empty hash set with the specified capacity and load factor, or a load factor of 0.75. If the ratio size/capacity exceeds the load factor, the hash table will be rehashed into a larger one.
- `static <E> HashSet<E> newHashSet(int numMappings)` **19**
  constructs an empty hash set with sufficient initial capacity to hold the expected number of elements (`numMappings`) without rehashing.

---

java.lang.Object **1.0**

- int hashCode()
  returns a hash code for this object. A hash code can be any integer, positive or negative. The definitions of equals and hashCode must be compatible: If x.equals(y) is true, then x.hashCode() must be the same value as y.hashCode().

9.3.4. Tree Sets

The TreeSet class is similar to the hash set, with one added improvement. A tree set is a *sorted collection*. You insert elements into the collection in any order. When you iterate through the collection, the values are automatically presented in sorted order. For example, suppose you insert three strings and then visit all elements that you added.

```
var sorter = new TreeSet<String>();
sorter.add("Bob");
sorter.add("Amy");
sorter.add("Carl");
for (String s : sorter) System.out.println(s);
```

Then, the values are printed in sorted order: Amy Bob Carl. As the name of the class suggests, the sorting is accomplished by a tree data structure. (The current implementation uses a *red-black tree*. For a detailed description of red-black trees see, for example, *Introduction to Algorithms* by Thomas Cormen, Charles Leiserson, Ronald Rivest, and Clifford Stein, The MIT Press, 2022.) Every time an element is added to a tree, it is placed into its proper sorting position. Therefore, the iterator always visits the elements in sorted order.

Adding an element to a tree is slower than adding it to a hash table. But it is still much faster than checking for duplicates in an array or linked list. If the tree contains n elements, then an average of $\log_2 n$ comparisons are required to find the correct position for the new element. For example, if the tree already contains 1,000 elements, adding a new element requires about 10 comparisons.

 Note: In order to use a tree set, you must be able to compare the elements. The elements must implement the Comparable interface, or you must supply a Comparator when constructing the set. (The Comparable and Comparator interfaces were introduced in Chapter 6.)

How much slower is a tree set? Run the program in Listing 9.2 as

```
java set.SetTest ../gutenberg/crsto10.txt 100
```

The Count of Monte Cristo has 466.300 words, each of which is inserted 100 times. On my test machine, the TreeSet is almost 4 times slower. If you don't need the data sorted, there is no reason to pay for the sorting overhead. More important, with some data it is much more difficult to come up with a sort order than a hash function. A hash function only needs to do a reasonably good job of scrambling the objects, whereas a comparison function must tell objects apart with complete precision.

To make this distinction more concrete, consider the task of collecting a set of rectangles. If you use a TreeSet, you need to supply a Comparator<Rectangle>. How do you compare two rectangles? By area? That doesn't work. You can have two different rectangles with different coordinates but the same area, and you want to keep both. The comparator must be compatible with equals; that is, the comparison can only be zero if the elements are equal. There is such a sort order for rectangles (the lexicographic ordering on its coordinates), but it is cumbersome to compute. In contrast, a hash function is already defined for the Rectangle class. It simply hashes the coordinates.

Caution: If the comparator is not compatible with the equals method of the element type, set equality can give inconsistent results. Here is a typical example:

```
var words = new TreeSet<String>(String.CASE_INSENSITIVE_ORDER);
```

The intent is not to collect elements that only differ in letter case:

```
commands.add("QUIT");
commands.add("quit"); // Not added
```

However, now equals is no longer symmetric:

```
commands.equals(Set.of("quit")) // true
Set.of("quit").equals(commands) // false
```

The TreeSet considers two elements equal when the comparator returns zero. But the other set uses String.equals.

A better approach is to use the String.compare ordering and only insert lowercase strings into the set.

Note: The TreeSet class implements the NavigableSet interface. That interface adds several convenient methods for locating adjacent elements. See the API notes for details.

The program in Listing 9.3 builds two tree sets of Item objects. The first one is sorted by part number, the default sort order of Item objects. The second set is sorted by description, using a custom comparator.

Listing 9.3 treeSet/TreeSetTest.java

```
 1  package treeSet;
 2
 3  import java.util.*;
 4
 5  /**
 6   * This program sorts a set of Item objects by comparing their descriptions.
 7   * @version 1.2 2024-12-05
 8   * @author Cay Horstmann
 9   */
10  public class TreeSetTest
11  {
12     public static void main(String[] args)
13     {
14        var parts = new TreeSet<Item>();
15        parts.add(new Item("Toaster", 1234));
16        parts.add(new Item("Widget", 4562));
17        parts.add(new Item("Router", 9912));
18        System.out.println(parts);
19
20        var sortByDescription = new TreeSet<Item>(Comparator.comparing(Item::description));
21
22        sortByDescription.addAll(parts);
23        System.out.println(sortByDescription);
24     }
25  }
```

Listing 9.4 treeSet/Item.java

```
 1  package treeSet;
 2
 3  /**
 4   * An item with a description and a part number.
 5   */
 6  public record Item(String description, int partNumber) implements Comparable<Item>
 7  {
 8     public int compareTo(Item other)
 9     {
10        int diff = Integer.compare(partNumber, other.partNumber);
11        return diff != 0 ? diff : description.compareTo(other.description);
12     }
13  }
```

---

java.util.TreeSet<E> 1.2

- TreeSet()
- TreeSet(Comparator<? super E> comparator)
  construct an empty tree set.
- TreeSet(Collection<? extends E> elements)
- TreeSet(SortedSet<E> s)
  construct a tree set and add all elements from a collection or sorted set (in the latter case, using the same ordering).

---

java.util.SortedSet<E> 1.2

- Comparator<? super E> comparator()
  returns the comparator used for sorting the elements, or null if the elements are compared with the compareTo method of the Comparable interface.
- E first()
- E last()
  return the smallest or largest element in the sorted set.

---

java.util.NavigableSet<E> 6

- E higher(E value)
- E lower(E value)
  return the least element > value or the largest element < value, or null if there is no such element.
- E ceiling(E value)
- E floor(E value)
  return the least element >= value or the largest element <= value, or null if there is no such element.
- E pollFirst()
- E pollLast()
  remove and return the smallest or largest element in this set, or null if the set is empty.

9.3.5. Queues and Deques

As we already discussed, a queue lets you efficiently add an element after the last and remove the first element. A double-ended queue, or *deque*, lets you efficiently add or remove elements at both ends. Adding elements in the middle is not supported. The Deque interface is implemented by the ArrayDeque and LinkedList classes, both of which provide deques whose size grows as needed. In Chapter 10, you will see bounded queues and deques.

In Java 21, the methods

```
E getFirst()
E getLast()
void addFirst(E e)
void addLast(E e)
E removeFirst()
E removeLast()
```

were moved from the Deque interface to the SequencedCollection interface, which the List and Set interfaces also extend. This provides uniform methods for accessing the first and last element of a collection.

---

java.util.Queue<E> 5.0

- boolean add(E e)
- boolean offer(E e)

  add the given element after the last element of this queue and return true, provided the queue is not full. If the queue is full, the first method throws an IllegalStateException, whereas the second method returns false.
- E remove()
- E poll()

  remove and return the first element of this queue, provided the queue is not empty. If the queue is empty, the first method throws a NoSuchElementException, whereas the second method returns null.
- E element()
- E peek()

  return the element at the head of this queue without removing it, provided the queue is not empty. If the queue is empty, the first method throws a NoSuchElementException, whereas the second method returns null.

---

java.util.SequencedCollection<E> 21

- void addFirst(E element)
- void addLast(E element)

  add the given element before the first or after the last elemet of this collection. If the collection is full, throw an IllegalStateException.
- E removeFirst()
- E removeLast()

  remove and return the first or last element of this collection, provided the collection is not empty. If the collection is empty, throw a NoSuchElementException.
- E getFirst()
- E getLast()

  return the first or last element of this collection without removing it, provided the collection is not empty. If the collection is empty, throw a NoSuchElementException.

---

java.util.Deque<E> 6

- `boolean offerFirst(E element)`
- `boolean offerLast(E element)`
  add the given element before the first or after the last element of this deque. If the deque is full, return `false`.
- `E pollFirst()`
- `E pollLast()`
  remove and return the element before the first or after the last element of this deque, provided the deque is not empty. If the deque is empty, return `null`.
- `E peekFirst()`
- `E peekLast()`
  return the first or last element element of this deque without removing it, provided the deque is not empty. If the deque is empty, return `null`.

---

java.util.ArrayDeque<E> 6

- `ArrayDeque()`
- `ArrayDeque(int initialCapacity)`
  construct an unbounded deque with an initial capacity of 16 or the given initial capacity.

9.3.6. Priority Queues

A priority queue retrieves elements in sorted order after they were inserted in arbitrary order. That is, whenever you call the `remove` method, you get the smallest element currently in the priority queue. However, the priority queue does not sort all its elements. If you iterate over the elements, they are not necessarily sorted. The priority queue makes use of an elegant and efficient data structure called a *heap*. A heap is a self-organizing binary tree in which the `add` and `remove` operations cause the smallest element to gravitate to the root, without wasting time on sorting all elements.

Just like a `TreeSet`, a priority queue can either hold elements of a class that implements the `Comparable` interface or a `Comparator` object you supply in the constructor.

A typical use for a priority queue is job scheduling. Each job has a priority. Jobs are added in random order. Whenever a new job can be started, the highest priority job is removed from the queue. (Since it is traditional for priority 1 to be the "highest" priority, the `remove` operation yields the minimum element.)

Listing 9.5 shows a priority queue in action. Unlike iteration in a `TreeSet`, the iteration here does not visit the elements in sorted order. However, removal always yields the smallest remaining element.

Listing 9.5 priorityQueue/PriorityQueueTest.java

```java
1   package priorityQueue;
2
3   import java.util.*;
4   import java.time.*;
5
6   /**
7    * This program demonstrates the use of a priority queue.
8    * @version 1.02 2015-06-20
9    * @author Cay Horstmann
10   */
11  public class PriorityQueueTest
12  {
13     public static void main(String[] args)
14     {
15        var pq = new PriorityQueue<LocalDate>();
16        pq.add(LocalDate.of(1906, 12, 9)); // G. Hopper
17        pq.add(LocalDate.of(1815, 12, 10)); // A. Lovelace
18        pq.add(LocalDate.of(1903, 12, 3)); // J. von Neumann
19        pq.add(LocalDate.of(1910, 6, 22)); // K. Zuse
20
21        System.out.println("Iterating over elements . . .");
22        for (LocalDate date : pq)
23           System.out.println(date);
24        System.out.println("Removing elements . . .");
25        while (!pq.isEmpty())
26           System.out.println(pq.remove());
27     }
28  }
```

---

java.util.PriorityQueue 5.0

- PriorityQueue()
- PriorityQueue(int initialCapacity)
  construct a priority queue for storing Comparable objects.
- PriorityQueue(int initialCapacity, Comparator<? super E> c)
  constructs a priority queue and uses the specified comparator for sorting its elements.

9.4. Maps

A set is a collection that lets you quickly find an existing element. However, to look up an element, you need to have an exact copy of the element to find. That isn't a very common lookup—usually, you have some key information, and you want to look up the associated element. The *map* data structure serves that purpose. A map stores key/value pairs. You can find a value if you provide the key. For example, you may store a table of employee records, where the keys are the employee IDs and the values are Employee objects. In the following sections, you will learn how to work with maps.

9.4.1. Basic Map Operations

The Java Collections Framework supplies two general-purpose implementations for maps: HashMap and TreeMap. Both classes implement the Map interface.

A hash map hashes the keys, and a tree map uses an ordering on the keys to organize them in a search tree. The hash or comparison function is applied *only to the keys*. The values associated with the keys are not hashed or compared.

Should you choose a hash map or a tree map? As with sets, hashing is usually a bit faster, and it is the preferred choice if you don't need to visit the keys in sorted order.

Here is how you set up a hash map for storing employees:

```
var staff = new HashMap<String, Employee>(); // HashMap implements Map
var harry = new Employee("Harry Hacker");
staff.put("987-98-9996", harry);
. . .
```

Whenever you add an object to a map, you must supply a key as well. In our case, the key is a string, and the corresponding value is an Employee object.

To retrieve an object, you must use (and, therefore, remember) the key.

```
var id = "987-98-9996";
Employee e = staff.get(id); // gets harry
```

Caution: For historical reasons, the get method is declared with a parameter of type Object, and not the key type. For example, the following code compiles:

```
long numericId = . . .
Employee e = staff.get(numericId); // Compiles but never gets a value
```

If no information is stored in the map with the particular key specified, get returns null.

The null return value can be inconvenient. Sometimes, you have a good default that can be used for keys that are not present in the map. Then use the getOrDefault method.

```
Map<String, Integer> scores = . . .;
int score = scores.getOrDefault(id, 0); // gets 0 if the id is not present
```

Keys must be unique. You cannot store two values with the same key. If you call the put method twice with the same key, the second value replaces the first one. In fact, put returns the previous value associated with its key argument.

The remove method removes an element with a given key from the map. The size method returns the number of entries in the map.

The easiest way of iterating over the keys and values of a map is the forEach method. Provide a lambda expression that receives a key and a value. That expression is invoked for each map entry in turn.

```
scores.forEach((k, v) ->
    System.out.println("key=" + k + ", value=" + v));
```

Listing 9.6 illustrates a map at work. We first add key/value pairs to a map. Then, we remove one key from the map, which removes its associated value as well. Next, we change the value that is associated with a key and call the get method to look up a value. Finally, we iterate through the entry set.

Listing 9.6 `map/MapTest.java`

```java
1  package map;
2
3  import java.util.*;
4
5  /**
6   * This program demonstrates the use of a map with key type String and value type Employee.
7   * @version 1.12 2015-06-21
8   * @author Cay Horstmann
9   */
10 public class MapTest
11 {
12    public static void main(String[] args)
13    {
14       var staff = new HashMap<String, Employee>();
15       staff.put("144-25-5464", new Employee("Amy Lee"));
16       staff.put("567-24-2546", new Employee("Harry Hacker"));
17       staff.put("157-62-7935", new Employee("Gary Cooper"));
18       staff.put("456-62-5527", new Employee("Francesca Cruz"));
19
20       // print all entries
21
22       System.out.println(staff);
23
24       // remove an entry
25
26       staff.remove("567-24-2546");
27
```

```
28          // replace an entry
29
30          staff.put("456-62-5527", new Employee("Francesca Miller"));
31
32          // look up a value
33
34          System.out.println(staff.get("157-62-7935"));
35
36          // iterate through all entries
37
38          staff.forEach((k, v) ->
39             System.out.println("key=" + k + ", value=" + v));
40      }
41 }
```

---

java.util.Map<K, V> 1.2

- V get(Object key)

  gets the value associated with the key; returns the object associated with the key, or null if the key is not found in the map. Implementing classes may forbid null keys.
- default V getOrDefault(Object key, V defaultValue)

  gets the value associated with the key; returns the object associated with the key, or defaultValue if the key is not found in the map.
- V put(K key, V value)

  puts the association of a key and a value into the map. If the key is already present, the new object replaces the old one previously associated with the key. This method returns the old value of the key, or null if the key was not previously present. Implementing classes may forbid null keys or values.
- void putAll(Map<? extends K, ? extends V> entries)

  adds all entries from the specified map to this map.
- boolean containsKey(Object key)

  returns true if the key is present in the map.
- boolean containsValue(Object value)

  returns true if the value is present in the map.
- default void forEach(BiConsumer<? super K,? super V> action) 8

  applies the action to all key/value pairs of this map.

---

java.util.HashMap<K, V> 1.2

- HashMap()
- HashMap(int initialCapacity)
- HashMap(int initialCapacity, float loadFactor)

  constructs an empty hash map with the specified capacity and load factor (a number between 0.0 and 1.0 that determines at what percentage of fullness the hash table will be rehashed into a larger one). The default load factor is 0.75.

- `static <K, V> HashMap<K, V> newHashMap(int numMappings)` **19**
  constructs an empty hash map with sufficient initial capacity to hold the expected number of entries (numMappings) without rehashing.

---

java.util.TreeMap<K,V> **1.2**

- `TreeMap()`
  constructs an empty tree map for keys that implement the Comparable interface.
- `TreeMap(Comparator<? super K> c)`
  constructs a tree map and uses the specified comparator for sorting its keys.
- `TreeMap(Map<? extends K, ? extends V> entries)`
  constructs a tree map and adds all entries from a map.
- `TreeMap(SortedMap<? extends K, ? extends V> entries)`
  constructs a tree map, adds all entries from a sorted map, and uses the same element comparator as the given sorted map.

---

java.util.SortedMap<K, V> **1.2**

- `Comparator<? super K> comparator()`
  returns the comparator used for sorting the keys, or null if the keys are compared with the compareTo method of the Comparable interface.
- `K firstKey()`
- `K lastKey()`
  returns the smallest or largest key in the map.

9.4.2. Updating Map Entries

A tricky part of dealing with maps is updating an entry. Normally, you get the old value associated with a key, update it, and put back the updated value. But you have to worry about the special case of the first occurrence of a key. Consider using a map for counting how often a word occurs in a file. When we see a word, we'd like to increment a counter like this:

```
counts.put(word, counts.get(word) + 1);
```

That works, except in the case when word is encountered for the first time. Then get returns null, and a NullPointerException occurs.

A simple remedy is to use the getOrDefault method:

```
counts.put(word, counts.getOrDefault(word, 0) + 1);
```

Another approach is to first call the putIfAbsent method. It only puts a value if the key was previously absent (or mapped to null).

```
counts.putIfAbsent(word, 0);
counts.put(word, counts.get(word) + 1); // now we know that get will succeed
```

But you can do better than that. The merge method simplifies this common operation. The call

```
counts.merge(word, 1, Integer::sum);
```

associates word with 1 if the key wasn't previously present, and otherwise combines the previous value and 1, using the Integer::sum function.

Now consider another common situation. We want to associate a set with each key. For example, in a book index, each term has a set of page numbers where the term occurs. Here is how to update the map:

```
var index = new TreeMap<String, TreeSet<Integer>>();
. . .
index.computeIfAbsent(term, k -> new TreeSet<>()).add(pageNumber);
```

Here, it is better to use computeIfAbsent because the TreeSet is only constructed when there was no prior set associated with the term. Conveniently, computeIfAbsent returns the new value, so that we can chain the call to add. In contrast, putIfAbsent returns the previous key or null, which is not useful for chaining.

 Caution: It is tempting to try changing k -> new TreeSet<>() into TreeSet::new, but that does not work. The function has a parameter k for the given key, which would be passed on to the constructor. Fortunately, there is no TreeSet constructor with a String parameter, and the code does not compile.

It could have been worse. Suppose you have a Map<Integer, ArrayList<String>> and call

```
map.computeIfAbsent(n, ArrayList::new)
```

There *is* an ArrayList constructor that takes an integer capacity. For large values of n, large array lists would be allocated, which was surely not intended.

 Caution: The map methods are not very consistent about null values. Some methods treat null as a valid value, but others consider it in the same way as a missing key.

The getOrDefault method falls in the former camp, and putIfAbsent in the latter:

```
counts.put("C++", null);
counts.getOrDefault("C++", -1) // Yields null without using the default
counts.putIfAbsent("C++", 1) // Puts 1, interpreting null as absent
```

The API notes describe other methods for updating map entries that are less commonly used.

---

java.util.Map<K, V> **1.2**

- default V merge(K key, V value, BiFunction<? super V,? super V,? extends V> remappingFunction) **8**
  If key is associated with a non-null value v, applies the function to v and value and either associates key with the result or, if the result is null, removes the key. Otherwise, associates key with value. Returns get(key).
- default V compute(K key, BiFunction<? super K,? super V,? extends V> remappingFunction) **8**
  Applies the function to key and get(key). Either associates key with the result or, if the result is null, removes the key. Returns get(key).
- default V computeIfPresent(K key, BiFunction<? super K,? super V,? extends V> remappingFunction) **8**
  If key is associated with a non-null value v, applies the function to key and v and either associates key with the result or, if the result is null, removes the key. Returns get(key).
- default V computeIfAbsent(K key, Function<? super K,? extends V> mappingFunction) **8**
  Applies the function to key unless key is associated with a non-null value. Either associates key with the result or, if the result is null, removes the key. Returns get(key).
- default void replaceAll(BiFunction<? super K,? super V,? extends V> function) **8**
  Calls the function on all entries. Associates keys with non-null results and removes keys with null results.
- default V putIfAbsent(K key, V value) **8**
  If key is absent or associated with null, associates it with value and returns null. Otherwise returns the associated value.

9.4.3. Map Views

The Java Collections Framework does not consider a map itself as a collection. (Other frameworks for data structures consider a map as a collection of key/value pairs, or as a collection of values indexed by the keys.) However, you can obtain *views* of the map—objects that implement the Collection interface or one of its subinterfaces.

There are three views: the set of keys, the collection of values (which is not a set), and the set of key/value pairs. The keys and key/value pairs form a set because there can be only one copy of a key in a map. The methods

```
Set<K> keySet()
Collection<V> values()
Set<Map.Entry<K, V>> entrySet()
```

return these three views. (The elements of the entry set are objects of a class implementing the Map.Entry interface.)

Note that the keySet is *not* a HashSet or TreeSet, but an object of some other class that implements the Set interface. The Set interface extends the Collection interface. Therefore, you can use a keySet as you would use any collection.

For example, you can enumerate all keys of a map:

```
Set<String> keys = map.keySet();
for (String key : keys)
{
    do something with key
}
```

If you want to look at both keys and values, you can avoid value lookups by enumerating the *entries*. Use the following code skeleton:

```
for (Map.Entry<String, Integer> entry : counts.entrySet())
{
    String k = entry.getKey();
    Integer v = entry.getValue();
    do something with k, v
}
```

The Map.Entry instances are connected to the map. You can use an entry object to update a value in the underlying map.

```
for (Map.Entry<String, Integer> entry : counts.entrySet())
{
    String k = entry.getKey();
    Integer v = entry.getValue();
    entry.setValue(v + 1); // same as counts.put(k, v + 1);
}
```

Conversely, if you update a value through other means (for example, by calling the map's put method), then the entry is also updated.

If you want to pass entries to some other method, you should disassociate them from the map by calling Map.Entry.copyOf(entry). You can also create unassociated Map.Entry instances by calling Map.entry(key, value). This is handy whenever you need a pair of values.

Tip: You can avoid the cumbersome `Map.Entry` by using a `var` declaration.

```
for (var entry : map.entrySet())
{
    do something with entry.getKey(), entry.getValue()
}
```

Or simply use the `forEach` method:

```
map.forEach((k, v) ->
    {
        do something with k, v
    });
```

If you invoke the `remove` method of the iterator on the key set view, you actually remove the key *and its associated value* from the map. However, you cannot *add* an element to the key set view. It makes no sense to add a key without also adding a value. If you try to invoke the `add` method, it throws an `UnsupportedOperationException`. The entry set view has the same restriction, even though it would make conceptual sense to add a new key/value pair.

`java.util.Map<K, V>`   **1.2**

- `Set<Map.Entry<K, V>> entrySet()`
  returns a set view of `Map.Entry` objects, the key/value pairs in the map. You can remove elements from this set and they are removed from the map, but you cannot add any elements.
- `Set<K> keySet()`
  returns a set view of all keys in the map. You can remove elements from this set and the keys and associated values are removed from the map, but you cannot add any elements.
- `Collection<V> values()`
  returns a collection view of all values in the map. You can remove elements from this collection and the removed value and its key are removed from the map, but you cannot add any elements.

`java.util.Map.Entry<K, V>`   **1.2**

- `K getKey()`
- `V getValue()`
  return the key or value of this entry.
- `V setValue(V newValue)`
  changes the value *in the associated map* to the new value and returns the old value.

■ static <K, V> Map.Entry<K,V> copyOf(Map.Entry<? extends K,? extends V> map) **17**
  yields a copy of the given map entry. Unlike the elements of a map's entry set, the
  copy is not "live." Calling setValue does not update any map.

9.4.4. Weak Hash Maps

The Java Collections Framework has several map classes for specialized needs that we
briefly discuss in this and the following sections.

The WeakHashMap class was designed to solve an interesting problem. What happens with a
value whose key is no longer used anywhere in your program? Suppose the last reference
to a key has gone away. Then, there is no longer any way to refer to the value object. But,
as no part of the program has the key any more, the key/value pair cannot be removed
from the map. Why can't the garbage collector remove it? Isn't it the job of the garbage
collector to remove unused objects?

Unfortunately, it isn't quite so simple. The garbage collector traces *live* objects. As long as
the map object is live, *all* buckets in it are live and won't be reclaimed. Thus, your program
should take care to remove unused values from long-lived maps. Or, you can use a
WeakHashMap instead. This data structure cooperates with the garbage collector to remove
key/value pairs when the only reference to the key is the one from the hash table entry.

Here are the inner workings of this mechanism. The WeakHashMap uses *weak references* to
hold keys. A WeakReference object holds a reference to another object—in our case, a hash
table key. Objects of this type are treated in a special way by the garbage collector.
Normally, if the garbage collector finds that a particular object has no references to it, it
simply reclaims the object. However, if the object is reachable *only* by a WeakReference, the
garbage collector still reclaims the object, but places the weak reference that led to it into
a queue. The operations of the WeakHashMap periodically check that queue for newly arrived
weak references. The arrival of a weak reference in the queue signifies that the key was no
longer used by anyone and has been collected. The WeakHashMap then removes the associated
entry.

9.4.5. Linked Hash Sets and Maps

The LinkedHashSet and LinkedHashMap classes remember in which order you inserted items.
That way, you can avoid the seemingly random order of items in a hash table. As entries
are inserted into the table, they are joined in a doubly linked list (see Figure 9.11).

For example, consider the following map insertions from Listing 9.6:

```
var staff = new LinkedHashMap<String, Employee>();
staff.put("144-25-5464", new Employee("Amy Lee"));
staff.put("567-24-2546", new Employee("Harry Hacker"));
staff.put("157-62-7935", new Employee("Gary Cooper"));
staff.put("456-62-5527", new Employee("Francesca Cruz"));
```

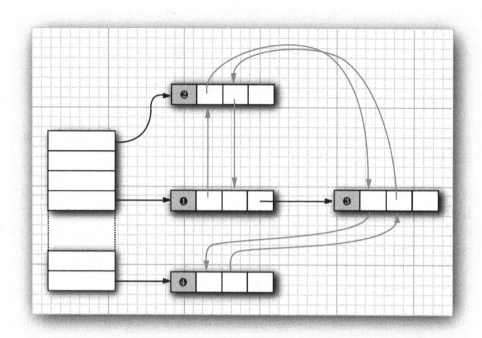

Figure 9.11: A linked hash table

Then, `staff.keySet().iterator()` enumerates the keys in this order:

```
144-25-5464
567-24-2546
157-62-7935
456-62-5527
```

and `staff.values().iterator()` enumerates the values in this order:

```
Amy Lee
Harry Hacker
Gary Cooper
Francesca Cruz
```

A linked hash map can alternatively use *access order*, not insertion order, to iterate through the map entries. Every time you call `get` or `put`, the affected entry is removed from its current position and placed at the *end* of the linked list of entries. (Only the position in the linked list of entries is affected, not the hash table bucket. An entry always stays in the bucket that corresponds to the hash code of the key.) To construct such a hash map, call

```
LinkedHashMap<K, V>(initialCapacity, loadFactor, true)
```

Access order is useful for implementing a "least recently used" discipline for a cache. For example, you may want to keep frequently accessed entries in memory and read less frequently accessed objects from a database. When you don't find an entry in the table, and the table is already pretty full, you can get an iterator into the table and remove the first few elements that it enumerates. Those entries were the least recently used ones.

You can even automate that process. Form a subclass of LinkedHashMap and override the method

```
protected boolean removeEldestEntry(Map.Entry<K, V> eldest)
```

This method is caled after adding a new entry. If the method returns true, the eldest entry is removed. For example, the following cache is kept at a size of at most 100 elements:

```
var cache = new LinkedHashMap<K, V>(128, 0.75F, true)
   {
      protected boolean removeEldestEntry(Map.Entry<K, V> eldest)
      {
         return size() > 100;
      }
   };
```

You can inspect the eldest entry to decide whether to remove it. For example, you may want to check a time stamp stored with eldest and only ask for removal if it is sufficiently old. This will not automatically remove all old elements since the removeEldestEntry method is only called once for each new entry. You are allowed to modify the map in the removeEldestEntry method, for example by removing the initial elements that are sufficiently old. In that case, you *must* return false.

If you need a set of least recently used elements instead of a map, see Section 9.5.4.

9.4.6. Enumeration Sets and Maps

The EnumSet is an efficient set implementation with elements that belong to an enumerated type. Since an enumerated type has a finite number of instances, the EnumSet is internally implemented simply as a sequence of bits. A bit is turned on if the corresponding value is present in the set.

The EnumSet class has no public constructors. Use a static factory method to construct the set:

```
enum Weekday { MONDAY, TUESDAY, WEDNESDAY, THURSDAY, FRIDAY, SATURDAY, SUNDAY };
EnumSet<Weekday> always = EnumSet.allOf(Weekday.class);
EnumSet<Weekday> never = EnumSet.noneOf(Weekday.class);
EnumSet<Weekday> workday = EnumSet.range(Weekday.MONDAY, Weekday.FRIDAY);
EnumSet<Weekday> mwf = EnumSet.of(Weekday.MONDAY, Weekday.WEDNESDAY, Weekday.FRIDAY);
```

You can use the usual methods of the Set interface to modify an EnumSet.

An EnumMap is a map with keys that belong to an enumerated type. It is simply and efficiently implemented as an array of values. You need to specify the key type in the constructor:

```
var personInCharge = new EnumMap<Weekday, Employee>(Weekday.class);
```

 Note: In the API documentation for EnumSet and EnumMap, you will see odd-looking type parameters of the form E extends Enum<E>. This simply means "E is an enumerated type." All enumerated types extend the generic Enum class. For example, Weekday extends Enum<Weekday>.

9.4.7. Identity Hash Maps

The IdentityHashMap has a quite specialized purpose. Here, the hash values for the keys should not be computed by the hashCode method but by the System.identityHashCode method. That's the method that Object.hashCode uses to compute a hash code from the object's memory address. Also, for comparison of objects, the IdentityHashMap uses ==, not equals.

In other words, different key objects are considered distinct even if they have equal contents. This class is useful for implementing object traversal algorithms, such as object serialization, in which you want to keep track of which objects have already been traversed.

 Caution: Java 20 fixed a subtle bug with IdentityHashMap that was introduced in Java 8 (https://bugs.openjdk.org/browse/JDK-8284901). Two uncommon methods falsely used equals instead of ==:

```
void remove(Object key, Object value)
void replace(K key, V oldValue, V newValue)
```

These methods are sometimes used in concurrent algorithms, where a map should only be updated if it hasn't been modified by another thread. One can only imagine the frustration of the first programmer who ran into this bug.

No software system as complex as the Java platform can be completely free from bugs. That is why it is important to regularly update to the latest version.

---

java.util.WeakHashMap<K, V> 1.2

- WeakHashMap()
- WeakHashMap(int initialCapacity)
- WeakHashMap(int initialCapacity, float loadFactor)
  construct an empty hash map with the specified capacity and load factor.

---

java.util.LinkedHashSet<E> 1.4

- LinkedHashSet()
- LinkedHashSet(int initialCapacity)
- LinkedHashSet(int initialCapacity, float loadFactor)
  construct an empty linked hash set with the specified capacity and load factor.

---

java.util.LinkedHashMap<K, V> 1.4

- LinkedHashMap()
- LinkedHashMap(int initialCapacity)
- LinkedHashMap(int initialCapacity, float loadFactor)
- LinkedHashMap(int initialCapacity, float loadFactor, boolean accessOrder)
  construct an empty linked hash map with the specified capacity, load factor, and ordering. The accessOrder parameter is true for access order, false for insertion order.
- protected boolean removeEldestEntry(Map.Entry<K, V> eldest)
  should be overridden to return true if you want the eldest entry to be removed. The eldest parameter is the entry whose removal is being contemplated. This method is called after an entry has been added to the map. The default implementation returns false—old elements are not removed by default. However, you can redefine this method to selectively return true—for example, if the eldest entry fits a certain condition or if the map exceeds a certain size.

---

java.util.EnumSet<E extends Enum<E>> 5.0

- static <E extends Enum<E>> EnumSet<E> allOf(Class<E> enumType)
  returns a mutable set that contains all values of the given enumerated type.
- static <E extends Enum<E>> EnumSet<E> noneOf(Class<E> enumType)
  returns a mutable set that is initially empty.
- static <E extends Enum<E>> EnumSet<E> range(E from, E to)
  returns a mutable set that contains all values between from and to (inclusive).
- static <E extends Enum<E>> EnumSet<E> of(E e)

  . . .
- static <E extends Enum<E>> EnumSet<E> of(E e1, E e2, E e3, E e4, E e5)
- static <E extends Enum<E>> EnumSet<E> of(E first, E... rest)
  return a mutable set containing the given elements which must not be null.
- public static <E extends Enum<E>> EnumSet<E> copyOf(EnumSet<E> s)
- public static <E extends Enum<E>> EnumSet<E> copyOf(Collection<E> c)
  create a mutable set initially containing the given elements. In the second method, c must either be an EnumSet or be nonempty (in order to determine the element type).

---

java.util.EnumMap<K extends Enum<K>, V> 5.0

- EnumMap(Class<K> keyType)
  constructs an empty mutable map whose keys have the given type.

---

java.util.IdentityHashMap<K, V> 1.4

- IdentityHashMap()
- IdentityHashMap(int expectedMaxSize)
  construct an empty identity hash map whose capacity is the smallest power of 2 exceeding 1.5 × expectedMaxSize. (The default for expectedMaxSize is 21.)

---

java.lang.System 1.0

- static int identityHashCode(Object obj) **1.1**
  returns the same hash code (derived from the object's memory address) that Object.hashCode computes, even if the class to which obj belongs has redefined the hashCode method.

9.5. Copies and Views

You might think it is overkill to have lots of interfaces (Figure 9.4) and abstract classes (Figure 9.5) to implement a modest number of concrete collection classes. However, these figures don't tell the whole story. By using *views*, you can obtain other objects that implement the Collection or Map interfaces. You saw one example of this with the keySet method of the map classes. At first glance, it appears as if the method creates a new set, fills it with all the keys of the map, and returns it. However, that is not the case. Instead, the keySet method returns an object of a class that implements the Set interface and whose methods manipulate the original map. Such a collection is called a *view*.

The technique of views has a number of useful applications in the Java Collections Framework. We will discuss these applications in the following sections.

9.5.1. Small Collections

There are static methods yielding a set or list with given elements, and a map with given key/value pairs.

For example,

```
List<String> names = List.of("Peter", "Paul", "Mary");
Set<Integer> numbers = Set.of(2, 3, 5);
```

yield a list and a set with three elements.

You can also provide an array of objects:

```
String[] namesArray = { "Peter", "Paul", "Mary" };
List<String> names = List.of(namesArray); // A list containing three objects
```

 Caution: if you provide an array of primitive type values, the result is a list with a single element, namely the array:

```
int[] numbersArray = { 2, 3, 5 };
List<int[]> arrays = List.of(numbersArray);
    // A list containing a single object, an int[] array
```

There is no convenience method for turning a primitive type array into a list of its wrapped elements.

For a map, you specify the keys and values, like this:

```
Map<String, Integer> scores = Map.of("Peter", 2, "Paul", 3, "Mary", 5);
```

The elements, keys, or values may not be null. Set and map keys may not be duplicated:

```
numbers = Set.of(13, null); // Error--null element
scores = Map.of("Peter", 4, "Peter", 2); // Error--duplicate key
```

 Caution: No guarantee is made about the iteration order of these sets and maps. In fact, the order is deliberately scrambled with a seed that is randomized at each virtual machine startup. Look at these two jshell runs:

```
$ jshell -q
jshell> Set.of("Peter", "Paul", "Mary")
$1 ==> [Peter, Mary, Paul]
jshell> /exit
$ jshell -q
jshell> Set.of("Peter", "Paul", "Mary")
$1 ==> [Paul, Mary, Peter]
```

Some Java programmers write programs whose correctness depends on the assumption that implementation details will never change. That can make it very difficult for the framework implementors to make useful implementation changes. In this case, the message is clear—don't write programs that assume anything about the element order.

The List and Set interfaces have eleven of methods with zero to ten arguments, and an of method with a variable number of arguments. The specializations are provided for efficiency.

For the Map interface, it is not possible to provide a version with variable arguments since the argument types alternate between the key and value types. There is a static method ofEntries that accepts an arbitrary number of Map.Entry<K, V> objects, which you can create with the static entry method. For example,

```
import static java.util.Map.*;
. . .
Map<String, Integer> scores = ofEntries(
    entry("Peter", 2),
    entry("Paul", 3),
    entry("Mary", 5));
```

The of and ofEntries methods produce objects of classes that have an instance variable for each element, or that are backed by an array.

These collection objects are *unmodifiable*. Any attempt to change their contents results in an UnsupportedOperationException.

If you want a mutable collection, you can pass the unmodifiable collection to the constructor:

```
var names = new ArrayList<>(List.of("Peter", "Paul", "Mary")); // A mutable list of names
```

The method call

```
Collections.nCopies(n, anObject)
```

returns an immutable object that implements the List interface and gives the illusion of having n elements, each of which appears as anObject.

For example, the following call creates a List containing 100 strings, all set to "DEFAULT":

```
List<String> settings = Collections.nCopies(100, "DEFAULT");
```

There is very little storage cost—the object is stored only once.

Note: The Collections class contains a number of utility methods with parameters or return values that are collections. Do not confuse it with the Collection interface.

Tip: Java doesn't have a Pair class, and some programmers use a Map.Entry as a poor man's pair.

9.5.2. Unmodifiable Copies and Views

To make an *unmodifiable copy* of a collection, use the copyOf method of the collection type:

```
ArrayList<String> names = . . .;
Set<String> nameSet = Set.copyOf(names); // The names as an unmodifiable set
List<String> nameList = List.copyOf(names); // The names as an unmodifiable list
```

As with the of methods, thecopyOf methods refuse to create collections containing null elements, instead throwing a NullPointerException.

Each copyOf method makes a copy of the collection. If the original collection is modified, the copy is not affected.

If the original collection happens to be unmodifiable and of the correct type, then copyOf simply returns it:

```
Set<String> names = Set.of("Peter", "Paul", "Mary");
Set<String> nameSet = Set.copyOf(names); // No need to make a copy: names == nameSet
```

The Collections class has methods that produce *unmodifiable views* of collections. These views add a runtime check to an existing collection. If an attempt to modify the unmodifiable collection is detected, an exception is thrown.

However, if the original collection changes, the view reflects those changes. That is what makes views different from copies.

You obtain unmodifiable views by eight methods:

```
Collections.unmodifiableCollection
Collections.unmodifiableList
Collections.unmodifiableSet
Collections.unmodifiableSortedSet
Collections.unmodifiableNavigableSet
Collections.unmodifiableMap
Collections.unmodifiableSortedMap
Collections.unmodifiableNavigableMap
```

Each method is defined to work on an interface. For example, Collections.unmodifiableList works with an ArrayList, a LinkedList, or any other class that implements the List interface.

For example, suppose you want to let some part of your code look at, but not touch, the contents of a collection. Here is what you could do:

```
var staff = new LinkedList<String>();
. . .
lookAt(Collections.unmodifiableList(staff));
```

The Collections.unmodifiableList method returns an object of a class implementing the List interface. Its accessor methods retrieve values from the staff collection. Of course, the lookAt method can call all methods of the List interface, not just the accessors. But all mutator methods (such as add) have been redefined to throw an UnsupportedOperationException instead of forwarding the call to the underlying collection.

The unmodifiable view does not make the collection itself immutable. You can still modify the collection through its original reference (staff, in our case). And you can still call mutator methods on the elements of the collection.

The views wrap the *interface* and not the actual collection object, so you only have access to those methods that are defined in the interface. For example, the LinkedList class has convenience methods, addFirst and addLast, that are not part of the List interface. These methods are not accessible through the unmodifiable view.

 Caution: The unmodifiableCollection method (as well as the synchronizedCollection and checkedCollection methods discussed later in this section) returns a collection whose equals method does *not* invoke the equals method of the underlying collection. Instead, it inherits the equals method of the Object class, which just tests whether the objects are identical. If you turn a set or list into just a collection, you can no longer test for equal contents. The view acts in this way because equality testing is not well defined at this level of the hierarchy. The views treat the hashCode method in the same way.

Prefer the unmodifiableSet and unmodifiableList wrappers whose equals and hashCode methods are appropriate for sets and lists.

For example:

```
var names = Set.of("Peter", "Paul", "Mary");
Collections.unmodifiableCollection(names).equals(names) // false
Collections.unmodifiableSet(names).equals(names) // true
```

9.5.3. Subranges

You can form subrange views for a number of collections. For example, suppose you have a list staff and want to extract elements 10 to 19. Use the subList method to obtain a view into the subrange of the list:

```
List<Employee> group2 = staff.subList(10, 20);
```

The first index is inclusive, the second exclusive—just like the parameters for the substring operation of the String class.

You can apply any operations to the subrange, and they automatically reflect the entire list. For example, you can erase the entire subrange:

```
group2.clear(); // staff reduction
```

The elements get automatically cleared from the staff list, and group2 becomes empty.

For sorted sets and maps, you use the sort order, not the element position, to form subranges. The SortedSet interface declares three methods:

```
SortedSet<E> subSet(E from, E to)
SortedSet<E> headSet(E to)
SortedSet<E> tailSet(E from)
```

These return the subsets of all elements that are larger than or equal to from and strictly smaller than to. For sorted maps, the similar methods

```
SortedMap<K, V> subMap(K from, K to)
SortedMap<K, V> headMap(K to)
SortedMap<K, V> tailMap(K from)
```

return views into the maps consisting of all entries in which the *keys* fall into the specified ranges.

The NavigableSet interface gives more control over these subrange operations. You can specify whether the bounds are included:

```
NavigableSet<E> subSet(E from, boolean fromInclusive, E to, boolean toInclusive)
NavigableSet<E> headSet(E to, boolean toInclusive)
NavigableSet<E> tailSet(E from, boolean fromInclusive)
```

9.5.4. Sets From Boolean-Valued Maps

Sometimes, an API provides maps with useful features that you would like in a set. In Section 9.4.5, you saw how you can use a LinkedHashMap to build a cache that discards older elements. The LinkedHashSet class does not have this capability.

If you want to have a set of the 100 least recently inserted strings, make a LinkedHashMap<String, Boolean>, and then call the Collections.newSetFromMap method:

```
Set<String> cache = Collections.newSetFromMap(new LinkedHashMap<String, Boolean>()
   {
      protected boolean removeEldestEntry(Map.Entry<String, Boolean> eldest)
      {
         return size() > 100;
      }
   });
```

The set view is backed by the map. When you add an element e, the view puts an entry with key e and value Boolean.TRUE into the map. If that causes the map to have more than 100 entries, the oldest one is removed.

You should call newSetFromMap with an empty map. Afterwards, do not modify the map, but let all modifications occur through methods of the set view. This is best achieved by passing the map to the newSetFromMap method without retaining a reference to it, as in the preceding example.

The newSetFromMap method is also useful with WeakHashMap (see Section 9.4.4). With a ConcurrentHashMap, use the newKeySet method instead (see Chapter 10).

9.5.5. Reversed Views

The reversed methods of the SequencedCollection and SequencedSet interfaces yield views that view the elements in reverse order. For example, here is how to traverse a list or tree set of strings in reverse:

```
for (String element : collection.reversed())
{
   do something with element
}
```

With SequencedMap, the reversed method views the map with the keys in reverse order.

9.5.6. Checked Views

Checked views are intended as debugging support for a problem that can occur with generic types. As explained in Chapter 8, it is actually possible to smuggle elements of the wrong type into a generic collection. For example:

```
var strings = new ArrayList<String>();
ArrayList rawList = strings; // warning only, not an error,
                             // for compatibility with legacy code
rawList.add(new Date()); // now strings contains a Date object!
```

The erroneous add command is not detected at runtime. Instead, a class cast exception will happen later when another part of the code calls get and casts the result to a String.

A checked view can detect this problem. Define a safe list as follows:

```
List<String> safeStrings = Collections.checkedList(strings, String.class);
```

The view's add method checks that the inserted object belongs to the given class and immediately throws a ClassCastException if it does not. The advantage is that the error is reported at the correct location:

```
ArrayList rawList = safeStrings;
rawList.add(new Date()); // checked list throws a ClassCastException
```

 Caution: The checked views are limited by the runtime checks that the virtual machine can carry out. For example, if you have an ArrayList<Pair<String>>, you cannot protect it from inserting a Pair<Date> since the virtual machine has a single "raw" Pair class.

9.5.7. Synchronized Views

If you access a collection from multiple threads, you need to ensure that the collection is not accidentally damaged. For example, it would be disastrous if one thread tried to add to a hash table while another thread was rehashing the elements.

Instead of implementing thread-safe collection classes, the framework designers used the view mechanism to make regular collections thread-safe. For example, the static synchronizedMap method in the Collections class can turn any map into a Map with synchronized access methods:

```
var map = Collections.synchronizedMap(new HashMap<String, Employee>());
```

You can now access the map object from multiple threads. The methods such as get and put are synchronized—each method call must be finished completely before another thread can call another method. We discuss the issue of synchronized access to data structures in greater detail in Chapter 10.

9.5.8. A Note on Optional Operations

A view usually has some restriction—it may be read-only, it may not be able to change the size, or it may support removal but not insertion (as is the case for the key view of a map). A restricted view throws an UnsupportedOperationException if you attempt an inappropriate operation.

In the API documentation for the collection and iterator interfaces, many methods are described as "optional operations." This seems to be in conflict with the notion of an interface. After all, isn't the purpose of an interface to lay out the methods that a class *must* implement? Indeed, this arrangement is unsatisfactory from a theoretical perspective.

A better solution might have been to design separate interfaces for read-only views and views that can't change the size of a collection. However, that would have tripled the number of interfaces, which the designers of the framework found unacceptable.

Should you extend the technique of "optional" methods to your own designs? I think not. Even though collections are used frequently, the coding style for implementing them is not typical for other problem domains. The designers of a collection class library have to resolve a particularly brutal set of conflicting requirements. Users want the library to be easy to learn, convenient to use, completely generic, idiot-proof, and at the same time as efficient as hand-coded algorithms. It is plainly impossible to achieve all these goals simultaneously, or even to come close. But in your own programming problems, you will rarely encounter such an extreme set of constraints. You should be able to find solutions that do not rely on the drastic measure of "optional" interface operations.

---

java.util.List 1.2

- static <E> List<E> of() **9**
- static <E> List<E> of(E e1) **9**

  . . .

- static <E> List<E> of(E e1, E e2, E e3, E e4, E e5, E e6, E e7, E e8, E e9, E e10) **9**
- static <E> List<E> of(E... elements) **9**
  yield an unmodifiable list of the given elements, which must not be null.
- static <E> List<E> copyOf(Collection<? extends E> coll) **10**
  yields an unmodifiable copy of the given collection.

---

java.util.Set 1.2

- static <E> Set<E> of() **9**
- static <E> Set<E> of(E e1) **9**

  . . .

- static <E> Set<E> of(E e1, E e2, E e3, E e4, E e5, E e6, E e7, E e8, E e9, E e10) **9**
- static <E> Set<E> of(E... elements) **9**
  yield an unmodifiable set of the given elements, which must not be null.
- static <E> Set<E> copyOf(Collection<? extends E> coll) **10**
  yields an unmodifiable copy of the given collection.

---

java.util.Map 1.2

- static <K, V> Map<K, V> of() **9**
- static <K, V> Map<K, V> of(K k1, V v1) **9**

  . . .

- `static <K,V> Map<K,V> of(K k1, V v1, K k2, V v2, K k3, V v3, K k4, V v4, K k5, V v5, K k6, V v6, K k7, V v7, K k8, V v8, K k9, V v9, K k10, V v10)` **9**
  yield an unmodifiable map of the given keys and values, which must not be null.
- `static <K,V> Map.Entry<K,V> entry(K k, V v)` **9**
  yields an unmodifiable map entry of the given key and value, which must not be null.
- `static <K,V> Map<K,V> ofEntries(Map.Entry<? extends K,? extends V>... entries)` **9**
  yields an unmodifiable map of the given entries.
- `static <K, V> Map<K,V> copyOf(Map<? extends K,? extends V> map)` **10**
  yields an unmodifiable copy of the given map.

java.util.Collections 1.2

- `static <E> Set<E> newSetFromMap(Map<E, Boolean> map)` **6**
  yields a set backed by the given map, which should initially be empty and afterwards only accessed through the returned view.
- `static <E> Collection<E> unmodifiableCollection(Collection<E> c)`
- `static <E> SequencedCollection<E> unmodifiableSequencedCollection(SequencedCollection<E> c)` **21**
- `static <E> List<E> unmodifiableList(List<E> c)`
- `static <E> Set<E> unmodifiableSet(Set<E> c)`
- `static <E> SequencedSet<E> unmodifiableSequencedSet(SequencedCollection<E> c)` **21**
- `static <E> SortedSet<E> unmodifiableSortedSet(SortedSet<E> c)`
- `static <E> SortedSet<E> unmodifiableNavigableSet(NavigableSet<E> c)` **8**
- `static <K, V> Map<K, V> unmodifiableMap(Map<K, V> c)`
- `static <K, V> SortedMap<K, V> unmodifiableSortedMap(SortedMap<K, V> c)`
- `static <K, V> SequencedMap<K, V> unmodifiableSequencedMap(SequencedMap<K, V> c)` **21**
- `static <K, V> SortedMap unmodifiableNavigableMap(NavigableMap<K, V> c)` **8**
  construct a view of the collection; the view's mutator methods throw an `UnsupportedOperationException`.
- `static <E> Collection<E> synchronizedCollection(Collection<E> c)`
- `static <E> List synchronizedList(List<E> c)`
- `static <E> Set synchronizedSet(Set<E> c)`
- `static <E> SortedSet synchronizedSortedSet(SortedSet<E> c)`
- `static <E> NavigableSet synchronizedNavigableSet(NavigableSet<E> c)` **8**
- `static <K, V> Map<K, V> synchronizedMap(Map<K, V> c)`
- `static <K, V> SortedMap<K, V> synchronizedSortedMap(SortedMap<K, V> c)`
- `static <K, V> NavigableMap<K, V> synchronizedNavigableMap(NavigableMap<K, V> c)` **8**
  construct a view of the collection; the view's methods are synchronized.

- `static <E> Collection checkedCollection(Collection<E> c, Class<E> elementType)`
- `static <E> List checkedList(List<E> c, Class<E> elementType)`
- `static <E> Set checkedSet(Set<E> c, Class<E> elementType)`
- `static <E> SortedSet checkedSortedSet(SortedSet<E> c, Class<E> elementType)`
- `static <E> NavigableSet checkedNavigableSet(NavigableSet<E> c, Class<E> elementType)` **8**
- `static <K, V> Map checkedMap(Map<K, V> c, Class<K> keyType, Class<V> valueType)`
- `static <K, V> SortedMap checkedSortedMap(SortedMap<K, V> c, Class<K> keyType, Class<V> valueType)`
- `static <K, V> NavigableMap checkedNavigableMap(NavigableMap<K, V> c, Class<K> keyType, Class<V> valueType)` **8**
- `static <E> Queue<E> checkedQueue(Queue<E> queue, Class<E> elementType)` **8**
  construct a view of the collection; the view's methods throw a `ClassCastException` if an element of the wrong type is inserted.
- `static <E> List<E> nCopies(int n, E value)`
  yields an unmodifiable list with n identical values.
- `static <E> List<E> singletonList(E value)`
- `static <E> Set<E> singleton(E value)`
- `static <E> List<E> emptyList()`
- `static <T> Set<T> emptySet()`
- `static <E> SortedSet<E> emptySortedSet()`
- `static NavigableSet<E> emptyNavigableSet()`
- `static <K,V> Map<K,V> emptyMap()`
- `static <K,V> SortedMap<K,V> emptySortedMap()`
- `static <K,V> NavigableMap<K,V> emptyNavigableMap()`
- `static <T> Enumeration<T> emptyEnumeration()`
- `static <T> Iterator<T> emptyIterator()`
- `static <T> ListIterator<T> emptyListIterator()`
  yield an empty collection, map, or iterator.

java.util.Arrays 1.2

- `static <E> List<E> asList(E... array)`
  returns a list view of the elements in an array that is modifiable but not resizable.

java.util.List<E> 1.2

- `List<E> subList(int firstIncluded, int firstExcluded)`
  returns a list view of the elements within a range of positions.

---

java.util.SortedSet<E> 1.2

- `SortedSet<E> subSet(E firstIncluded, E firstExcluded)`
- `SortedSet<E> headSet(E firstExcluded)`
- `SortedSet<E> tailSet(E firstIncluded)`
  return a view of the elements within a range.

---

java.util.NavigableSet<E> 6

- `NavigableSet<E> subSet(E from, boolean fromIncluded, E to, boolean toIncluded)`
- `NavigableSet<E> headSet(E to, boolean toIncluded)`
- `NavigableSet<E> tailSet(E from, boolean fromIncluded)`
  return a view of the elements within a range. The boolean flags determine whether the bounds are included in the view.

---

java.util.SortedMap<K, V> 1.2

- `SortedMap<K, V> subMap(K firstIncluded, K firstExcluded)`
- `SortedMap<K, V> headMap(K firstExcluded)`
- `SortedMap<K, V> tailMap(K firstIncluded)`
  return a map view of the entries whose keys are within a range.

---

java.util.NavigableMap<K, V> 6

- `NavigableMap<K, V> subMap(K from, boolean fromIncluded, K to, boolean toIncluded)`
- `NavigableMap<K, V> headMap(K from, boolean fromIncluded)`
- `NavigableMap<K, V> tailMap(K to, boolean toIncluded)`
  return a map view of the entries whose keys are within a range. The boolean flags determine whether the bounds are included in the view.

---

java.util.SequencedCollection<E> 21

- `SequencedCollection<E> reversed()`
  yields a view of this sequenced collection with the elements in reverse order

---

java.util.SequencedSet<E> 21

- `SequencedSet<E> reversed()`
  yields a view of this sequenced set with the elements in reverse order

---

java.util.SequencedMap<E> 21

■ SequencedMap<E> reversed()
yields a view of this sequenced map with the keys in reverse order

9.6. Algorithms

In addition to implementing collection classes, the Java Collections Framework also provides a number of useful algorithms. In the following sections, you will see how to use these algorithms and how to write your own algorithms that work well with the framework.

9.6.1. Why Generic Algorithms?

Generic collection interfaces have a great advantage—you only need to implement your algorithms once. For example, consider a simple algorithm to compute the maximum element in a collection. Traditionally, programmers would implement such an algorithm as a loop. Here is how you can find the largest element of an array:

```
if (a.length == 0) throw new NoSuchElementException();
T largest = a[0];
for (int i = 1; i < a.length; i++)
   if (largest.compareTo(a[i]) < 0)
      largest = a[i];
```

Of course, to find the maximum of an array list, you would write the code slightly differently.

```
if (v.size() == 0) throw new NoSuchElementException();
T largest = v.get(0);
for (int i = 1; i < v.size(); i++)
   if (largest.compareTo(v.get(i)) < 0)
      largest = v.get(i);
```

What about a linked list? You don't have efficient random access in a linked list, but you can use an iterator.

```
if (l.isEmpty()) throw new NoSuchElementException();
Iterator<T> iter = l.iterator();
T largest = iter.next();
while (iter.hasNext())
{
   T next = iter.next();
   if (largest.compareTo(next) < 0)
      largest = next;
}
```

These loops are tedious to write, and just a bit error-prone. Is there an off-by-one error? Do the loops work correctly for empty containers? For containers with only one element? You don't want to test and debug this code every time, but you also don't want to implement a whole slew of methods, such as these:

```
static <T extends Comparable> T max(ArrayList<T> v)
static <T extends Comparable> T max(LinkedList<T> l)
```

That's where the collection interfaces come in. Think of the *minimal* collection interface that you need to efficiently carry out the algorithm. Random access with get and set comes higher in the food chain than simple iteration. As you have seen in the computation of the maximum element in a linked list, random access is not required for this task. Computing the maximum can be done simply by iterating through the elements. Therefore, you can implement the max method to take *any* object that implements the Collection interface.

```
public static <T extends Comparable> T max(Collection<T> elements)
{
    if (elements.isEmpty()) throw new NoSuchElementException();
    Iterator<T> iter = elements.iterator();
    T largest = iter.next();
    while (iter.hasNext())
    {
        T next = iter.next();
        if (largest.compareTo(next) < 0)
            largest = next;
    }
    return largest;
}
```

Of course, since arrays are not collections, you need to write a separate method for arrays:

```
static <T extends Comparable> T max(T[] a)
```

Generic algorithms are a powerful concept. In fact, the standard C++ library has dozens of useful algorithms, each operating on a generic collection. The Java Collections Framework is not quite so rich, but the Collections and Arrays classes provide the basics: sorting, binary search, and some simple utility algorithms.

 Note: Some useful algorithms are missing from the Java Collections Framework, but you can find them in the streams library that is covered in Volume II. For example, to find the maximum or minimum, turn a collection or array into a stream:

```
largest = coll.stream().max(Comparator.naturalOrder()).get();
```

9.6.2. Sorting and Shuffling

Computer old-timers will sometimes reminisce about how they had to use punched cards and to actually program, by hand, algorithms for sorting. Nowadays, of course, sorting algorithms are part of the standard library for most programming languages, and the Java programming language is no exception.

The sort method in the Collections class sorts a collection that implements the List interface.

```
var staff = new ArrayList<String>();
fill collection
Collections.sort(staff);
```

This method assumes that the list elements implement the Comparable interface. If you want to sort the list in some other way, you can use the sort method of the List interface and pass a Comparator object. Here is how you can sort a list of employees by salary:

```
Collections.sort(staff, Comparator.comparingDouble(Employee::getSalary));
```

If you want to sort a list in *descending* order, use the static convenience method Comparator.reverseOrder(). It returns a comparator that returns b.compareTo(a). For example,

```
Collections.sort(staff, Comparator.reverseOrder());
```

sorts the elements in the list staff in reverse order, according to the ordering given by the compareTo method of the element type. Similarly,

```
Collections.sort(staff, Comparator.comparingDouble(Employee::getSalary).reversed());
```

sorts by descending salary.

You may wonder how the sort method sorts a list. Typically, when you look at a sorting algorithm in a book on algorithms, it is presented for arrays and uses random element access. However, random access in a linked list is inefficient. You can actually sort linked lists efficiently by using a form of merge sort. However, the implementation in the Java programming language does not do that. It simply dumps all elements into an array, sorts the array, and then copies the sorted sequence back into the list.

The sort algorithm used in the Java Collections Framework is a bit slower than QuickSort, the traditional choice for a general-purpose sorting algorithm. However, it has one major advantage: It is *stable*, that is, it doesn't switch equal elements. Why do you care about the order of equal elements? Here is a common scenario. Suppose you have an employee list that you already sorted by name. Now you sort by salary. What happens to employees with equal salary? With a stable sort, the ordering by name is preserved. In other words, the outcome is a list that is sorted first by salary, then by name.

Collections need not implement all of their "optional" methods, so all methods with collection parameters must describe when it is safe to pass a collection to an algorithm. For example, you clearly cannot pass an unmodifiableList list to the sort algorithm. What kind of list *can* you pass? According to the documentation, the list must be modifiable but need not be resizable.

The terms are defined as follows:

- A list is *modifiable* if it supports the set method.
- A list is *resizable* if it supports the add and remove operations.

 Note: In Chapter 6, you have seen the Arrays.sort method. There are two versions, one for sorting an array of Comparable instances, and another with a comparator:

```
String[] staff = . . .;
Arrays.sort(staff);
Arrays.sort(staff, Comparator.comparingDouble(Employee::getSalary));
```

The Collections class has an algorithm shuffle that does the opposite of sorting—it randomly permutes the order of the elements in a list. For example:

```
ArrayList<Card> cards = . . .;
Collections.shuffle(cards, RandomGenerator.getDefault());
```

If you supply a list that does not implement the RandomAccess interface, the shuffle method copies the elements into an array, shuffles the array, and copies the shuffled elements back into the list.

The program in Listing 9.7 fills an array list with 49 Integer objects containing the numbers 1 through 49. It then randomly shuffles the list and selects the first six values from the shuffled list. Finally, it sorts the selected values and prints them.

Listing 9.7 `shuffle/ShuffleTest.java`

```
 1  package shuffle;
 2
 3  import java.util.*;
 4  import java.util.random.*;
 5
 6  /**
 7   * This program demonstrates the random shuffle and sort algorithms.
 8   * @version 1.13 2023-09-30
 9   * @author Cay Horstmann
10   */
11  public class ShuffleTest
```

```
12  {
13      public static void main(String[] args)
14      {
15          var numbers = new ArrayList<Integer>();
16          for (int i = 1; i <= 49; i++)
17              numbers.add(i);
18          Collections.shuffle(numbers, RandomGenerator.getDefault());
19          List<Integer> winningCombination = numbers.subList(0, 6);
20          Collections.sort(winningCombination);
21          System.out.println(winningCombination);
22      }
23  }
```

---

java.util.Collections   1.2

- static <T extends Comparable<? super T>> void sort(List<T> elements)
  sorts the elements in the list, using a stable sort algorithm. The algorithm is guaranteed to run in O($n \log n$) time, where n is the length of the list.
- static void shuffle(List<?> elements)
- static void shuffle(List<?> elements, Random r)
- static void shuffle(List<?> elements, RandomGenerator r)   **21**
  randomly shuffle the elements in the list. This algorithm runs in O($n\, a(n)$) time, where n is the length of the list and $a(n)$ is the average time to access an element.

---

java.util.List<E>   1.2

- default void sort(Comparator<? super T> comparator)   **8**
  sorts this list, using the given comparator.

---

java.util.Comparator<T>   1.2

- static <T extends Comparable<? super T>> Comparator<T> reverseOrder()   **8**
  yields a comparator that reverses the ordering provided by the Comparable interface.
- default Comparator<T> reversed()   **8**
  yields a comparator that reverses the ordering provided by this comparator.

9.6.3. Binary Search

To find an object in an array, you normally visit all elements until you find a match. However, if the array is sorted, you can look at the middle element and check whether it is larger than the element that you are trying to find. If so, keep looking in the first half of the array; otherwise, look in the second half. That cuts the problem in half, and you keep going in the same way. For example, if the array has 1024 elements, you will locate the match (or confirm that there is none) after 10 steps, whereas a linear search would have taken you an average of 512 steps if the element is present, and 1024 steps to confirm that it is not.

The binarySearch of the Collections class implements this algorithm. Note that the collection must already be sorted, or the algorithm will return the wrong answer. Supply the collection (which must implement the List interface) and the target to be located. If the collection is not sorted by the compareTo element of the Comparable interface, supply a comparator object as well.

```
i = Collections.binarySearch(elements, target);
i = Collections.binarySearch(elements, target, comparator);
```

A non-negative return value from the binarySearch method denotes the index of the matching object. That is, elements.get(i) is equal to target under the comparison order. If the value is negative, then there is no matching element. However, you can use the return value to compute the location where you *should* insert target into the collection to keep it sorted. The insertion location is

```
insertionPoint = -i - 1;
```

It isn't simply -i because then the value of 0 would be ambiguous. In other words, the operation

```
if (i < 0)
    elements.add(-i - 1, target);
```

adds the target in the correct place.

To be worthwhile, binary search requires random access. If you have to iterate one by one through half of a linked list to find the middle element, you have lost the advantage of the binary search. The binarySearch algorithm reverts to an iterative algorithm of the same efficiency as linear search if you give it a list that does not implement the RandomAccess interface.

The Arrays class has binary search implementations for arrays of primitive types and objects.

---

java.util.Collections 1.2

- static <T extends Comparable<? super T>> int binarySearch(List<T> elements, T key)
- static <T> int binarySearch(List<T> elements, T key, Comparator<? super T> c)
  search for a key in a sorted list, using a binary search if the element type implements the RandomAccess interface, and a linear search in all other cases. The methods are guaranteed to run in O($a(n)$ log n) time, where n is the length of the list and $a(n)$ is the average time to access an element. The methods return either the index of the key in

the list, or a negative value i if the key is not present in the list. In that case, the key should be inserted at index -i - 1 for the list to stay sorted.

---

java.util.Arrays 1.2

- static int binarySearch(T[] a, T key)
- static int binarySearch(T[] a, int start, int end, T key) **6**
- use the binary search algorithm to search for the key in the sorted array a. If the key is found, its index is returned. Otherwise, a negative value r is returned; −r − 1 is the spot at which key should be inserted to keep a sorted. The component type T of the array can be Object, int, long, short, char, byte, boolean, float, or double.
- static <T> T binarySearch(T[] a, T key, Comparator<? super T> c)
- static <T> T binarySearch(T[] a, int start, int end, T key, Comparator<? super T> c) **6**
  use the binary search algorithm to search for the key in the array a that has been sorted with the given comparator.

9.6.4. Simple Algorithms

The Collections class contains several simple but useful algorithms. Among them is the example from the beginning of this section—finding the maximum value of a collection. Others include copying elements from one list to another, filling a container with a constant value, and reversing a list.

Why supply such simple algorithms in the framework? Surely most programmers could easily implement them with simple loops. I like the algorithms because they make life easier for the programmer *reading* the code. When you read a loop that was implemented by someone else, you have to decipher the original programmer's intentions. For example, look at this loop:

```
for (int i = 0; i < words.size(); i++)
    if (words.get(i).equals("C++")) words.set(i, "Java");
```

Now compare the loop with the call

```
Collections.replaceAll(words, "C++", "Java");
```

When you see the method call, you know right away what the code does.

The API notes at the end of this section describe the simple algorithms in the Collections class.

The default methods Collection.removeIf and List.replaceAll are just a bit more complex. You provide a lambda expression to test or transform elements. For example, here we remove all short words and change the remaining ones to lowercase:

```
words.removeIf(w -> w.length() <= 3);
words.replaceAll(String::toLowerCase);
```

 Caution: The predicate of `removeIf` should only look at the element whose removal is being decided, and not at the collection. If you do the latter, the behavior is implementation-dependent.

The `ArrayList` version of `removeIf` method makes two passes over the elements. It first finds the elements that should be removed, and then it removes all of them. With other collections, matching elements are removed as soon as they are found.

This makes a difference if the predicate reads the collection. Consider this example, where `words` is an `ArrayList` of length 3:

```
var words = new ArrayList<String>(List.of("Ada", "C++", "Java"))
words.removeIf(w -> w.length() == words.size()); // Now words is ["Java"]
```

In the first pass, all words of length 3 are marked for removal, and in the second pass, they are removed.

However, if `words` is a `LinkedList` or a `HashSet`, then the same call to `removeIf` only removes one of the three-letter words. After the first removal, the predicate tests whether the collection has size 2.

Why the difference? A naïve one-pass implementation would have been inefficient for array-backed collections. It didn't immediately occur to the developers that there is an efficient one-pass algorithm. By the time they thought of it, they decided not to use it for compatibility's sake—see `https://bugs.openjdk.org/browse/JDK-8143577`.

---

java.util.Collections 1.2

- `static <T extends Comparable<? super T>> T min(Collection<T> elements)`
- `static <T extends Comparable<? super T>> T max(Collection<T> elements)`
- `static <T> min(Collection<T> elements, Comparator<? super T> c)`
- `static <T> max(Collection<T> elements, Comparator<? super T> c)`
  return the smallest or largest element in the collection. (The parameter bounds are simplified for clarity.)
- `static <T> void copy(List<? super T> to, List<T> from)`
  copies all elements from a source list to the same positions in the target list. The target list must be at least as long as the source list.
- `static <T> void fill(List<? super T> l, T value)`
  sets all positions of a list to the same value.

- `static <T> boolean addAll(Collection<? super T> c, T... values)` **5.0**
  adds all values to the given collection and returns true if the collection changed as a result.
- `static <T> boolean replaceAll(List<T> l, T oldValue, T newValue)` **1.4**
  replaces all elements equal to oldValue with newValue.
- `static int indexOfSubList(List<?> l, List<?> s)` **1.4**
- `static int lastIndexOfSubList(List<?> l, List<?> s)` **1.4**
  return the index of the first or last sublist of l equaling s, or -1 if no sublist of l equals s. For example, if l is [s, t, a, r] and s is [t, a, r], then both methods return the index 1.
- `static void swap(List<?> l, int i, int j)` **1.4**
  swaps the elements at the given offsets.
- `static void reverse(List<?> l)`
  reverses the order of the elements in a list. For example, reversing the list [t, a, r] yields the list [r, a, t]. This method runs in $O(n)$ time, where n is the length of the list.
- `static void rotate(List<?> l, int d)` **1.4**
  rotates the elements in the list, moving the entry with index i to position (i + d) % l.size(). For example, rotating the list [t, a, r] by 2 yields the list [a, r, t]. This method runs in $O(n)$ time, where n is the length of the list.
- `static int frequency(Collection<?> c, Object o)` **5.0**
  returns the count of elements in c that equal the object o.
- `boolean disjoint(Collection<?> c1, Collection<?> c2)` **5.0**
  returns true if the collections have no elements in common.

`java.util.Collection<T>` **1.2**

- `default boolean removeIf(Predicate<? super E> filter)` **8**
  removes all matching elements.

`java.util.List<E>` **1.2**

- `default void replaceAll(UnaryOperator<E> op)` **8**
  applies the operation to all elements of this list.

9.6.5. Bulk Operations

There are several operations that copy or remove elements "in bulk." The call

```
coll1.removeAll(coll2);
```

removes all elements from coll1 that are present in coll2. Conversely,

```
coll1.retainAll(coll2);
```

removes all elements from coll1 that are *not* present in coll2. Here is a typical application.

Suppose you want to find the *intersection* of two sets—the elements that two sets have in common. First, make a new set to hold the result.

```
var result = new HashSet<String>(firstSet);
```

Here, we use the fact that every collection has a constructor whose parameter is another collection that holds the initialization values.

Now, use the retainAll method:

```
result.retainAll(secondSet);
```

It retains all elements that occur in both sets. You have formed the intersection without programming a loop.

You can carry this idea further and apply a bulk operation to a *view*. For example, suppose you have a map that maps employee IDs to employee objects, and you have a set of the IDs of all employees that are to be terminated.

```
Map<String, Employee> staffMap = . . .;
Set<String> terminatedIDs = . . .;
```

Simply form the key set and remove all IDs of terminated employees.

```
staffMap.keySet().removeAll(terminatedIDs);
```

Since the key set is a view into the map, the keys and associated employee names are automatically removed from the map.

By using a subrange view, you can restrict bulk operations to sublists and subsets. For example, suppose you want to add the first ten elements of a list to another container. Form a sublist to pick out the first ten:

```
relocated.addAll(staff.subList(0, 10));
```

The subrange can also be a target of a mutating operation.

```
staff.subList(0, 10).clear();
```

9.6.6. Converting between Collections and Arrays

Large portions of the Java API were designed before the Java Collections Framework was created. As a result, you will occasionally need to translate between traditional arrays and the more modern collections.

If you have an array that you need to turn into a collection, the List.of method serves this purpose. For example:

```
String[] names = . . .;
List<String> staff = List.of(names);
```

Obtaining an array from a collection is a bit trickier. You can use the toArray method:

```
Object[] names = staff.toArray();
```

But the result is an array of *objects*. Even if you know that your collection contained objects of a specific type, you cannot use a cast:

```
String[] names = (String[]) staff.toArray(); // ERROR
```

The array returned by the toArray method was created as an Object[] array, and you cannot change its type. Instead, pass an array constructor expression to the toArray method. The constructor is used to create an array of the correct type:

```
String[] values = staff.toArray(String[]::new);
```

 Note: Prior to JDK 11, you had to use another form of the toArray method, passing an array of the correct type:

```
String[] values = staff.toArray(new String[0]);
```

This toArray method constructs another array of the same type. Or, if the array has sufficient length, it is reused:

```
staff.toArray(new String[staff.size()]);
```

In this case, no new array is created.

9.6.7. Writing Your Own Algorithms

If you write your own algorithm (or, in fact, any method that has a collection as a parameter), you should work with *interfaces*, not concrete implementations, whenever possible. For example, suppose you want to process items. Of course, you can implement a method like this:

```
public void processItems(ArrayList<Item> items)
{
   for (Item item : items)
      do something with item
}
```

However, you now constrained the caller of your method—the caller must supply the items in an ArrayList. If the items happen to be in another collection, they first need to be repackaged. It is much better to accept a more general collection.

You should ask yourself this: What is the most general collection interface that can do the job? Do you care about the order? Then you should accept a List. But if the order doesn't matter, you can accept collections of any kind:

```
public void processItems(Collection<Item> items)
{
    for (Item item : items)
        do something with item
}
```

Now, anyone can call this method with an ArrayList or a LinkedList, or even with an array wrapped in a call to the List.of method.

Tip: In this case, you can do even better by accepting an Iterable<Item>. The Iterable interface has a single abstract method iterator which the enhanced for loop uses behind the scenes. The Collection interface extends Iterable.

Conversely, if your method returns multiple elements, you don't want to constrain yourself against future improvements. For example, consider

```
public ArrayList<Item> lookupItems(. . .)
{
    var result = new ArrayList<Item>();
    . . .
    return result;
}
```

This method promises to return an ArrayList, even though the caller almost certainly doesn't care what kind of lists it is. If instead you return a List, you can at any time add a branch that returns an empty or singleton list by calling List.of.

Note: If it is such a good idea to use collection interfaces as parameter and return type, why doesn't the Java API follow this rule consistently? For example, the JComboBox class has two constructors:

```
JComboBox(Object[] items)
JComboBox(Vector<?> items)
```

The reason is simply timing. The Swing API was created before the Java Collections Framework.

9.7. Legacy Collections

A number of "legacy" container classes have been present since the first release of Java, before there was a collections framework.

They have been integrated into the Java Collections Framework—see Figure 9.12. I will briefly introduce them in the following sections.

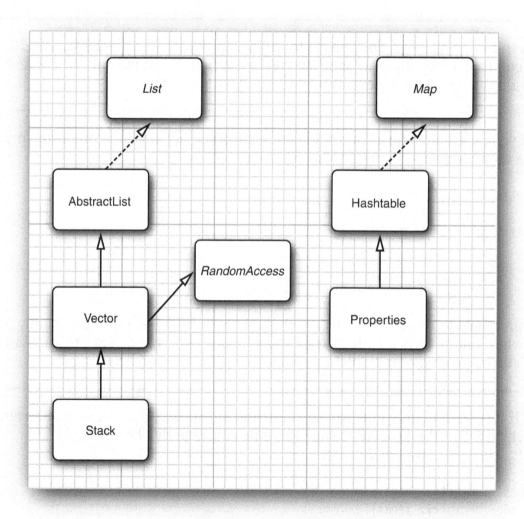

Figure 9.12: Legacy classes in the Java Collections Framework

9.7.1. The Hashtable Class

The classic Hashtable class serves the same purpose as the HashMap class and has essentially the same interface. Just like methods of the Vector class, the Hashtable methods are synchronized. If you do not require compatibility with legacy code, you should use a HashMap instead. If you need concurrent access, use a ConcurrentHashMap—see Chapter 10.

9.7.2. Enumerations

The legacy collections use the Enumeration interface for traversing sequences of elements. The Enumeration interface has two methods, hasMoreElements and nextElement. These are entirely analogous to the hasNext and next methods of the Iterator interface.

If you find this interface with legacy classes, you can use Collections.list to collect the elements in an ArrayList. For example, the LogManager class is only willing to reveal logger names as an Enumeration. Here is how you can get them all:

```
ArrayList<String> loggerNames = Collections.list(LogManager.getLoggerNames());
```

Alternatively, you can turn an enumeration into an iterator:

```
LogManager.getLoggerNames().asIterator().forEachRemaining(n -> { . . . });
```

You will occasionally encounter a legacy method with an enumeration parameter. The static method Collections.enumeration yields an enumeration object that enumerates the elements in the collection. For example:

```
List<InputStream> streams = . . .;
var in = new SequenceInputStream(Collections.enumeration(streams));
    // the SequenceInputStream constructor expects an enumeration
```

 Note: In C++, it is quite common to use iterators as parameters. Fortunately, on the Java platform, very few programmers use this idiom. It is much smarter to pass around the collection than to pass an iterator. The collection object is more useful. The recipients can always obtain the iterator from the collection when they need to do so, plus they have all the collection methods at their disposal. However, you may find enumerations in some legacy code because they were the only available mechanism for generic collections until the Java Collections Framework appeared in Java 1.2.

---

java.util.Enumeration<E> 1.0

- boolean hasMoreElements()
  returns true if there are more elements yet to be inspected.

- `E nextElement()`
  returns the next element to be inspected. Do not call this method if `hasMoreElements()` returned false.
- `default Iterator<E> asIterator()` **9**
  yields an iterator that iterates over the enumerated elements.

---

java.util.Collections 1.2

- `static <T> Enumeration<T> enumeration(Collection<T> c)`
  returns an enumeration that enumerates the elements of c.
- `public static <T> ArrayList<T> list(Enumeration<T> e)`
  returns an array list containing the elements enumerated by e.

9.7.3. Property Maps

A *property map* is a map structure of a special type. It has three particular characteristics:

- The keys and values are strings.
- The map can easily be saved to a file and loaded from a file.
- There is a secondary table for default values.

The Java platform class that implements a property map is called `Properties`. Property maps are useful in specifying configuration options for programs. For example:

```
var settings = new Properties();
settings.setProperty("width", "600.0");
settings.setProperty("filename", "/home/cay/books/corejava/code/v1ch09/raven.html");
```

Use the `getProperty` method to look up the value for a key:

```
String filename = settings.getProperty("filename");
```

 Caution: For historical reasons, the `Properties` class implements `Map<Object, Object>`. Therefore, you can use the `get` and `put` methods of the `Map` interface. But the `get` method returns the type `Object`, and the `put` method allows you to insert any object. It is best to stick with the `getProperty` and `setProperty` methods that work with strings, not objects.

Use the `store` method to save the properties to a file. The second argument is a comment that is included in the file.

```
var out = new FileWriter("program.properties");
settings.store(out, "Program Properties");
```

The sample set gives the following output:

```
#Program Properties
#Sun Dec 31 12:54:19 PST 2023
top=227.0
left=1286.0
width=423.0
height=547.0
filename=/home/cay/books/corejava/code/v1ch09/raven.html
```

To load the properties from a file, use

```
var in = new FileReader("program.properties");
settings.load(in);
```

 Caution: If you use the `load` and `store` methods with input/output streams, then the archaic ISO 8859-1 character encoding is used, and characters > U+00FF are saved as Unicode escapes. For UTF-8, use readers/writers, as in the code snippets above. Prior to Java 18, set the character encoding explicitly to `StandardCharsets.UTF_8`.

The `Properties` class has two mechanisms for providing defaults. First, whenever you look up the value of a string, you can specify a default that should be used automatically when the key is not present.

```
String filename = settings.getProperty("filename", "");
```

If there is a `"filename"` property in the property map, `filename` is set to that string. Otherwise, `filename` is set to the empty string.

If you find it too tedious to specify the default in every call to `getProperty`, you can pack all the defaults into a secondary property map and supply that map in the constructor of your primary property map.

```
var defaultSettings = new Properties();
defaultSettings.setProperty("width", "600");
defaultSettings.setProperty("height", "400");
defaultSettings.setProperty("filename", "");
. . .
var settings = new Properties(defaultSettings);
```

Yes, you can even specify defaults to defaults if you give another property map argument to the `defaultSettings` constructor, but it is not something one would normally do.

The companion code has a sample program that shows how you can use properties for storing and loading program state. The program uses the `ImageViewer` program from

Chapter 2 and remembers the frame position, size, and last loaded file. Run the program, load a file, and move and resize the window. Then close the program and reopen it to see that it remembers your file and your favorite window placement. You can also manually edit the file .corejava/ImageViewer.properties in your home directory.

Properties are simple tables without a hierarchical structure. It is common to introduce a fake hierarchy with key names such as window.main.color, window.main.title, and so on. But the Properties class has no methods that help organize such a hierarchy. If you store complex configuration information, you should use the Preferences class instead—see Chapter 10 of Volume II.

---

java.util.Properties   1.0

- Properties()
  creates an empty property map.
- Properties(Properties defaults)
  creates an empty property map with a map of defaults.
- String getProperty(String key)
  gets a property. Returns the string associated with the key, or the string associated with the key in the default table if it wasn't present in the table, or null if the key wasn't present in the default table either.
- String getProperty(String key, String defaultValue)
  gets a property with a default value if the key is not found. Returns the string associated with the key, or the default string if it wasn't present in the table.
- Object setProperty(String key, String value)
  sets a property. Returns the previously set value of the given key.
- Set<String> stringPropertyNames()   6
  returns a set of all keys, including the keys from the default map.
- void load(Reader in) throws IOException   6
  loads a property map from a reader.
- void store(Writer out, String header)   6
  saves a property map to a writer. The header is in the first line of the stored file.

9.7.4. System Properties

The System.getProperties method yields a Properties object to describe system information. For example, the home directory has the key "user.home".

You can read it with the getProperty method that yields the key as a string:

```
String userDir = System.getProperty("user.home");
```

To get the Java version of the virtual machine, look up the "java.version" property. You get a string such as "21.0.1" (but "1.8.0" up to Java 8.)

Tip: As you can see, the version numbering changed in Java 9. This seemingly small change broke a good number of tools that had relied on the old format. If you parse the version string, be sure to read JEP 322 at https://openjdk.org/jeps/322 to see how version strings will be formatted in the future—or at least, until the numbering scheme changes again.

 Tip: To print out all system properties, run:

```
java -XshowSettings:properties
```

The java.version system property is set by the virtual machine and should not be changed. Other system properties can be set with the -D command line option:

```
java -Duser.language=fr -Duser.country=CA MyProg
```

To make properties available in jshell, use the -R option like this:

```
jshell -R-Duser.language=fr -R-Duser.country=CA
```

To get a numeric or Boolean system property value, use the static methods Boolean.getBoolean(), Integer.getInteger, and Long.getLong:

```
Integer version = Integer.getInteger("java.specification.version");
```

---

java.lang.System 1.0

- Properties getProperties()
  retrieves all system properties. The application must have permission to retrieve all properties, or a security exception is thrown.
- String getProperty(String key)
  retrieves the system property with the given key name. The following properties are always present:

  ```
  java.version
  java.version.date
  java.vendor
  java.vendor.url
  java.home
  java.class.path
  java.library.path
  java.class.version
  java.specification.version
  ```

```
java.specification.vendor
java.specification.name
java.vm.specification.version
java.vm.specification.vendor
java.vm.specification.name
java.vm.version
java.vm.vendor
java.vm.name
os.name
os.version
os.arch
file.separator
path.separator
line.separator
java.io.tmpdir
user.name
user.home
user.dir
native.encoding
stdout.encoding
stderr.encoding
```

---

java.lang.Boolean   **1.0**

- `static boolean getBoolean(String name)`
  Returns true if the system property with the given name has value "true" (ignoring letter case), false otherwise

---

java.lang.Integer   **1.0**

- `static Integer getInteger(String nm)`
- `static Integer getInteger(String nm, int val)`
- `static Integer getInteger(String nm, Integer val)`
  Returns the result of calling Integer.decode on the system property with the given name. If there is no system property with the given name, or its value cannot be decoded, this method returns the default value or, if none provided, null.

---

java.lang.Long 1.0

- static Long getLong(String nm)
- static Long getLong(String nm, int val)
- static Long getLong(String nm, Long val)
  Returns the result of calling Long.decode on the system property with the given name. If there is no system property with the given name, or its value cannot be decoded, this method returns the default value or, if none provided, null.

9.7.5. Stacks

Since version 1.0, the Java API had a Stack class with the familiar push and pop methods. However, the Stack class extends the Vector class, which is not satisfactory from a theoretical perspective—you can apply such un-stack-like operations as insert and remove to insert and remove values anywhere, not just at the top of the stack.

---

java.util.Stack<E> 1.0

- E push(E item)
  pushes item onto the stack and returns item.
- E pop()
  pops and returns the top item of the stack. Don't call this method if the stack is empty.
- E peek()
  returns the top of the stack without popping it. Don't call this method if the stack is empty.

9.7.6. Bit Sets

The Java platform's BitSet class stores a sequence of bits, packed into implementation-specific "words", which are currently long values. That is much more efficient than using an array of boolean values.

The BitSet class gives you a convenient interface for reading, setting, and resetting individual bits. Using this interface avoids the masking and other bit-fiddling operations that are necessary if you store bits in int or long variables.

For example, for a BitSet named bucketOfBits,

    bucketOfBits.get(i)

returns true if the ith bit is on, and false otherwise. Similarly,

    bucketOfBits.set(i)

turns the ith bit on. Finally,

```
bucketOfBits.clear(i)
```

turns the ith bit off.

You can use a BitSet to represent a set of nonnegative integers with an upper bound. Set the ith bit to indicate that the integer i is in the set. This is more efficient than using a Set<Integer> if the upper bound is not too large and the set has many elements.

 C++ Note: The C++ bitset template has the same functionality as the Java platform BitSet.

---

java.util.BitSet 1.0

- BitSet(int initialCapacity)
  constructs a bit set.
- int cardinality() **1.4**
  returns the number of bits that are set, or, when considered as a set of integers, the number of elements.
- int length() **1.2**
  returns the "logical length" (1 plus the index of the highest set bit). This is useful for iterating over the elements.
- int size()
  returns the number of bits currently available in the internal data structure, *not* the number of set elements.
- boolean get(int bit)
  gets a bit.
- void set(int bit)
  sets a bit.
- void clear(int bit)
  clears a bit.
- void and(BitSet set)
  logically ANDs this bit set with another.
- void or(BitSet set)
  logically ORs this bit set with another.
- void xor(BitSet set)
  logically XORs this bit set with another.
- void andNot(BitSet set)
  clears all bits in this bit set that are set in the other bit set.
- IntStream stream() **8**
  yields a stream of the index values of the bits that are set, or, when considered as a set of integers, a stream of the elements.

As an example of using bit sets, I want to show you an implementation of the "sieve of Eratosthenes" algorithm for finding prime numbers. (A prime number is a number like 2, 3, or 5 that is divisible only by itself and 1, and the sieve of Eratosthenes was one of the first methods discovered to enumerate these fundamental building blocks.) This isn't a terribly good algorithm for finding the primes, but for some reason it has become a popular benchmark for compiler performance. (It isn't a good benchmark either, because it mainly tests bit operations.)

Oh well, I bow to tradition and present an implementation. This program counts all prime numbers between 2 and 2,000,000. (There are 148,933 primes in this interval, so you probably don't want to print them all out.)

Without going into too many details of this program, the idea is to march through a bit set with 2 million bits. First, we turn on all the bits. After that, we turn off the bits that are multiples of numbers known to be prime. The positions of the bits that remain after this process are themselves prime numbers. Listing 9.8 lists this program in the Java programming language, and Listing 9.9 is the C++ code.

 Note: Even though the sieve isn't a good benchmark, I couldn't resist timing the two implementations of the algorithm. Here are the timing results with an Intel i7-1165G7 processor and 32 GB of RAM, running Ubuntu 22.04:

- C++ (g++ 11.4.0): 70 milliseconds
- Java (Java 21): 20 milliseconds

I have run this test for thirteen editions of *Core Java*, and in the last nine editions, Java easily beat C++. In all fairness, if one cranks up the optimization level in the C++ compiler, it beats Java with a time of 16 milliseconds. Java could only match that if the program ran long enough to trigger the Hotspot just-in-time compiler.

Listing 9.8 `sieve/Sieve.java`

```
 1  package sieve;
 2
 3  import java.util.*;
 4
 5  /**
 6   * This program runs the Sieve of Erathostenes benchmark. It computes all primes
 7   * up to 2,000,000.
 8   * @version 1.22 2021-06-17
 9   * @author Cay Horstmann
10   */
11  public class Sieve
12  {
13     public static void main(String[] s)
14     {
15        int n = 2000000;
```

```
16        long start = System.nanoTime();
17        var bitSet = new BitSet(n + 1);
18        int i;
19        for (i = 2; i <= n; i++)
20           bitSet.set(i);
21        i = 2;
22        while (i * i <= n)
23        {
24           if (bitSet.get(i))
25           {
26              int k = i * i;
27              while (k <= n)
28              {
29                 bitSet.clear(k);
30                 k += i;
31              }
32           }
33           i++;
34        }
35        long end = System.nanoTime();
36        System.out.println(bitSet.cardinality() + " primes");
37        System.out.println((end - start) / 1000 + " milliseconds");
38     }
39 }
```

Listing 9.9 sieve/sieve.cpp

```
1  /**
2   * @version 1.22 2021-06-17
3   * @author Cay Horstmann
4   */
5
6  #include <bitset>
7  #include <iostream>
8  #include <ctime>
9
10 using namespace std;
11
12 int main()
13 {
14    const int N = 2000000;
15    clock_t cstart = clock();
16
17    bitset<N + 1> b;
18    int i;
19    for (i = 2; i <= N; i++)
20       b.set(i);
21    i = 2;
22    while (i * i <= N)
23    {
```

```
24        if (b.test(i))
25        {
26           int k = i * i;
27           while (k <= N)
28           {
29              b.reset(k);
30              k += i;
31           }
32        }
33        i++;
34     }
35
36     clock_t cend = clock();
37     double millis = 1000.0 * (cend - cstart) / CLOCKS_PER_SEC;
38
39     cout << b.count() << " primes\n" << millis << " milliseconds\n";
40
41     return 0;
42 }
```

This completes our tour through the Java Collections Framework. As you have seen, the framework offers a wide variety of collection classes for your programming needs.

CHAPTER 10

Concurrency

You are probably familiar with *multitasking*—your operating system's ability to have more than one program working at what seems like the same time. For example, you can print while editing or downloading your email. Nowadays, you are likely to have a computer with more than one CPU, but the number of concurrently executing processes is not limited by the number of CPUs. The operating system assigns CPU time slices to each process, giving the impression of parallel activity.

Multithreaded programs extend the idea of multitasking by taking it one level lower: Individual programs will appear to do multiple tasks at the same time. Each task is executed in a *thread*, which is short for thread of control. Programs that can run more than one thread at once are said to be *multithreaded*.

So, what is the difference between multiple *processes* and multiple *threads*? The essential difference is that while each process has a complete set of its own variables, threads share the same data. This sounds somewhat risky, and indeed it can be, as you will see later in this chapter. However, shared variables make communication between threads more efficient and easier to program than interprocess communication. Moreover, on some operating systems, threads are more "lightweight" than processes—it takes less overhead to create and destroy individual threads than it does to launch new processes.

Multithreading is extremely useful in practice. For example, a browser should be able to simultaneously download multiple images. A web server needs to be able to serve concurrent requests. Graphical user interface (GUI) programs have a separate thread for gathering user-interface events from the host operating environment. This chapter shows you how to add multithreading capability to your Java applications.

Fair warning: Concurrent programming can get very complex. In this chapter, I cover all the tools that an application programmer is likely to need. However, for more intricate system-level programming, I suggest that you turn to a more advanced reference, such as *Java Concurrency in Practice* by Brian Goetz et al. (Addison-Wesley Professional, 2006).

10.1. Running Threads

Here is a simple procedure for running a task in a separate thread:

1. Place the code for the task into the run method of a class that implements the Runnable interface. That interface is very simple, with a single method:

```
public interface Runnable
{
   void run();
}
```

Since Runnable is a functional interface, you can make an instance with a lambda expression:

```
Runnable r = () ->
   {
      task code
   };
```

2. Construct a Thread object from the Runnable:

```
var t = new Thread(r);
```

3. Start the thread:

```
t.start();
```

Let us look at a simple program that uses threads to move money between bank accounts. We make use of a Bank class that stores the balances of a given number of accounts. The transfer method transfers an amount from one account to another. See Listing 10.2 for the implementation.

In the first thread, we will move money from account 0 to account 1:

```
Runnable r = () ->
   {
      try
      {
         for (int i = 0; i < STEPS; i++)
         {
            double amount = MAX_AMOUNT * Math.random();
            bank.transfer(0, 1, amount);
            Thread.sleep((int) (DELAY * Math.random()));
         }
      }
      catch (InterruptedException e)
      {
      }
   };
var t = new Thread(r);
t.start();
```

For a given number of steps, this thread transfers a random amount, and then sleeps for a random delay.

We need to catch an InterruptedException that the sleep method threatens to throw. We will discuss this exception in Section 10.3.2. Typically, interruption is used to request that a thread terminates. Accordingly, our run method exits when an InterruptedException occurs.

Note: Calling Math.random() from a large number of different threads is slightly inefficient. For this and the following demonstration programs, we do not care. But see Section 10.5.14 for a more performant approach.

Our program starts a second thread as well that moves money from account 2 to account 3. When you run this program, you get a printout like this:

```
Thread[Thread-1,5,main]    606.77 from 2 to 3 Total Balance:   400000.00
Thread[Thread-0,5,main]     98.99 from 0 to 1 Total Balance:   400000.00
Thread[Thread-1,5,main]    476.78 from 2 to 3 Total Balance:   400000.00
Thread[Thread-0,5,main]    653.64 from 0 to 1 Total Balance:   400000.00
Thread[Thread-1,5,main]    807.14 from 2 to 3 Total Balance:   400000.00
Thread[Thread-0,5,main]    481.49 from 0 to 1 Total Balance:   400000.00
Thread[Thread-0,5,main]    203.73 from 0 to 1 Total Balance:   400000.00
Thread[Thread-1,5,main]    111.76 from 2 to 3 Total Balance:   400000.00
Thread[Thread-1,5,main]    794.88 from 2 to 3 Total Balance:   400000.00
. . .
```

As you can see, the output of the two threads is interleaved, showing that they run concurrently. In fact, sometimes the output is a little messier when two output lines are interleaved.

That's all there is to it! You now know how to run tasks concurrently. The remainder of this chapter tells you how to control the interaction between threads.

The complete code is shown in Listing 10.1.

Caution: Do *not* call the run method of the Thread class or the Runnable object. Calling the run method directly merely executes the task in the *same* thread—no new thread is started. Instead, call the Thread.start method. It creates a new thread that executes the run method.

Note: You can also define a thread by forming a subclass of the Thread class, like this:

```
class MyThread extends Thread
{
    public void run()
    {
        task code
    }
}
```

Then you construct an object of the subclass and call its start method. However, this approach is no longer recommended. You should decouple the *task* that is to be run in parallel from the *mechanism* of running it. As you will see throughout this chapter, there are many ways of scheduling the execution of a task.

Listing 10.1 `threads/ThreadTest.java`

```
 1  package threads;
 2
 3  /**
 4   * @version 1.30 2004-08-01
 5   * @author Cay Horstmann
 6   */
 7  public class ThreadTest
 8  {
 9     public static final int DELAY = 10;
10     public static final int STEPS = 100;
11     public static final double MAX_AMOUNT = 1000;
12
13     public static void main(String[] args)
14     {
15        var bank = new Bank(4, 100000);
16        Runnable task1 = () ->
17           {
18              try
19              {
20                 for (int i = 0; i < STEPS; i++)
21                 {
22                    double amount = MAX_AMOUNT * Math.random();
23                    bank.transfer(0, 1, amount);
24                    Thread.sleep((int) (DELAY * Math.random()));
25                 }
26              }
27              catch (InterruptedException e)
28              {
29              }
30           };
31
32        Runnable task2 = () ->
33           {
```

```
34            try
35            {
36               for (int i = 0; i < STEPS; i++)
37               {
38                  double amount = MAX_AMOUNT * Math.random();
39                  bank.transfer(2, 3, amount);
40                  Thread.sleep((int) (DELAY * Math.random()));
41               }
42            }
43            catch (InterruptedException e)
44            {
45            }
46         };
47
48      new Thread(task1).start();
49      new Thread(task2).start();
50   }
51 }
```

Listing 10.2 threads/Bank.java

```
1  package threads;
2
3  import java.util.*;
4
5  /**
6   * A bank with a number of bank accounts.
7   */
8  public class Bank
9  {
10    private final double[] accounts;
11
12    /**
13     * Constructs the bank.
14     * @param n the number of accounts
15     * @param initialBalance the initial balance for each account
16     */
17    public Bank(int n, double initialBalance)
18    {
19       accounts = new double[n];
20       Arrays.fill(accounts, initialBalance);
21    }
22
23    /**
24     * Transfers money from one account to another.
25     * @param from the account to transfer from
26     * @param to the account to transfer to
27     * @param amount the amount to transfer
28     */
29    public void transfer(int from, int to, double amount)
```

```
30      {
31         if (accounts[from] < amount) return;
32         System.out.print(Thread.currentThread());
33         accounts[from] -= amount;
34         System.out.printf(" %10.2f from %d to %d", amount, from, to);
35         accounts[to] += amount;
36         System.out.printf(" Total Balance: %10.2f%n", getTotalBalance());
37      }
38
39      /**
40       * Gets the sum of all account balances.
41       * @return the total balance
42       */
43      public double getTotalBalance()
44      {
45         double sum = 0;
46
47         for (double a : accounts)
48            sum += a;
49
50         return sum;
51      }
52
53      /**
54       * Gets the number of accounts in the bank.
55       * @return the number of accounts
56       */
57      public int size()
58      {
59         return accounts.length;
60      }
61   }
```

---

java.lang.Thread 1.0

- Thread(Runnable target)

  constructs a new thread that calls the run() method of the specified target.
- void start()

  starts this thread, causing the run() method to be called. This method will return immediately. The new thread runs concurrently.
- void run()

  calls the run method of the associated Runnable.
- static void sleep(long millis)
- static void sleep(Duration duration) **19**

  sleeps for the given number of milliseconds.

---

java.lang.Runnable 1.0

- void run()
  must be overridden and supplied with instructions for the task that you want to have executed.

10.2. Thread States

Threads can be in one of six states:

- New
- Runnable
- Blocked
- Waiting
- Timed waiting
- Terminated

Each of these states is explained in the sections that follow.

To determine the current state of a thread, simply call the getState method.

10.2.1. New Threads

When you create a thread with the new operator—for example, new Thread(r)—the thread is not yet running. This means that it is in the *new* state. When a thread is in the new state, the program has not started executing code inside of it. A certain amount of bookkeeping needs to be done before a thread can run.

10.2.2. Runnable Threads

Once you invoke the start method, the thread is in the *runnable* state. A runnable thread may or may not actually be running. It is up to the thread scheduler to give the thread time to run. (The Java specification does not call this a separate state, though. A running thread is still in the runnable state.)

Once a thread is running, it doesn't necessarily keep running. In fact, it is desirable that running threads occasionally pause so that other threads have a chance to run. The details of thread scheduling depend on the services that the operating system provides, and on the nature of the thread.

As of Java 21, there are two kinds of threads: *platform threads* and *virtual threads*. A Java platform thread corresponds to a thread provided by the operating system, which schedules its execution. Virtual threads run on platform threads and are scheduled by the Java runtime. As you will see in Section 10.3.1, virtual threads are used in applications with many more concurrent tasks than available platform threads.

Each processor can run one platform thread at a time. On a machine with multiple processors, you can have multiple threads run in parallel. If there are more runnable threads than available processors, some of them are not actually running. They need to be scheduled for execution.

Platform threads use *preemptive scheduling*. Each running thread is given a slice of time to perform its task. When that slice of time is exhausted, the operating system *preempts* the thread and gives another thread an opportunity to work. When selecting the next platform thread, the operating system takes into account the thread *priorities*—see Section 10.3.6 for more information.

Virtual threads use *cooperative scheduling*. A virtual thread loses control only when it calls the yield method, or when it is blocked.

---

java.lang.Thread 1.0

- static void yield()

  signals to the scheduler that this thread is willing to yield execution to another thread. Note that this is a static method.

10.2.3. Blocked and Waiting Threads

When a thread is blocked or waiting, it is temporarily inactive. It doesn't execute any code and consumes minimal resources. It is up to the thread scheduler to reactivate it. The details depend on how the inactive state was reached.

- When the thread tries to acquire an intrinsic object lock (but not a Lock in the java.util.concurrent library) that is currently held by another thread, it becomes *blocked*. (We discuss java.util.concurrent locks in Section 10.5.3 and intrinsic object locks in Section 10.5.6.) The thread becomes unblocked when all other threads have relinquished the lock and the thread scheduler has allowed this thread to hold it.
- When the thread waits for another thread to notify the scheduler of a condition, it enters the *waiting* state. We discuss conditions in Section 10.5.4. This happens by calling the Object.wait or Thread.join methods, or by waiting for a Lock or Condition in the java.util.concurrent library.
- Several methods have a timeout parameter. Calling them causes the thread to enter the *timed waiting* state. This state persists either until the timeout expires or the appropriate notification has been received. Methods with timeout include Thread.sleep and the timed versions of Object.wait, Thread.join, Lock.tryLock, and Condition.await.

Figure 10.1 shows the states that a thread can have and the possible transitions from one state to another.

In practice, the difference between the blocked and waiting states is not usually significant. We will often say that a thread is blocked when it is in the blocked, waiting, or timed waiting state. When a thread is blocked or waiting (or, of course, when it terminates), another thread will be scheduled to run.

When a thread is reactivated (for example, because its timeout has expired or it has succeeded in acquiring a lock), it becomes runnable and is eligible for being scheduled.

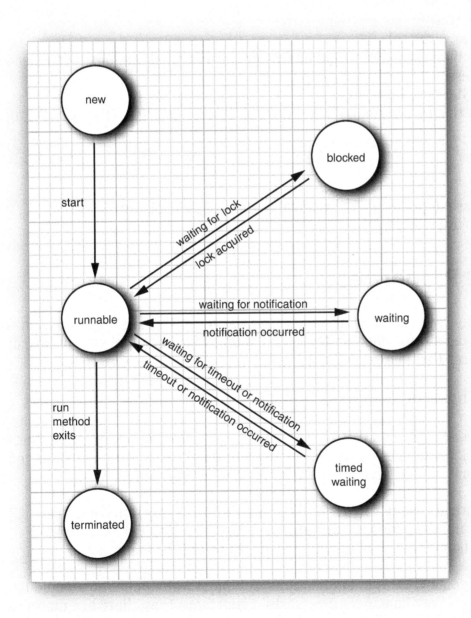

Figure 10.1: Thread states

10.2.4. Terminated Threads

A thread is terminated for one of two reasons:

- It dies a natural death because the run method exits normally.
- It dies abruptly because an uncaught exception terminates the run method.

---

java.lang.Thread 1.0

- `void join()`
  waits for the specified thread to terminate.
- `void join(long millis)`
- `void join(Duration duration)` **19**
  wait for the specified thread to terminate or for the specified number of milliseconds or duration to pass.
- `Thread.State getState()` **5.0**
  gets the state of this thread: one of NEW, RUNNABLE, BLOCKED, WAITING, TIMED_WAITING, or TERMINATED.
- `void stop()`
- `void suspend()`
- `void resume()`
  These methods are deprecated for removal and, as of Java 21, throw an UnsupportedOperationException.

10.3. Thread Properties

In the following sections, we discuss the various properties of threads: platform and virtual threads, the interrupted status, daemon threads, handlers for uncaught exceptions, as well as some legacy features that you should not use.

10.3.1. Virtual Threads

By default, a Java thread runs on a *platform thread* provided by the operating system in which the Java virtual machine executes. For many workloads, this is a good arrangement since operating systems have evolved to do a good job of thread scheduling.

However, platform threads are not lightweight. They require a few thousand CPU instructions to start, and they consume (or at least reserve) a significant amount of memory. This limits the number of platform threads that the CPU can handle.

This is a problem for some classes of applications. A typical web application would like to serve a very large number of concurrent requests, many more than there are platform threads. The application can handle the workload because the tasks don't do CPU-intensive work. Each task spends most of its time blocking on database queries or other external requests.

One solution is to use a non-blocking API for the requests. Instead of a synchronous call

```
response = service.request(parameters);
process(response);
```

pass the processing code as a callback:

```
service.request(parameters, response -> process(response));
```

Then the call to request returns immediately without blocking, freeing its thread to serve additional requests. The callback is invoked when the response is available.

Non-blocking APIs provide high throughput, but at a steep cost for the programmer. Instead of using familiar programming constructs for sequences, branches, loops, and exception handling, all program logic must be placed into callback code.

Virtual threads, available in Java 21, are an attractive alternative. A virtual thread is *mounted* on a platform thread and *unmounted* when it encounters a blocking operation. When the result of the operation becomes available, the virtual thread can again be scheduled, and it is remounted when a platform thread becomes available.

The term "virtual thread" is meant to be analogous to virtual memory. Just like virtual memory is mapped to a smaller amount of actual RAM, virtual threads are mounted on a smaller number of platform threads. These platform threads are called the *carrier threads*. By default, the scheduler uses one carrier thread per processor. This can be tuned with the `jdk.virtualThreadScheduler.parallelism` VM option.

Virtual threads have the same API as platform threads. A simple way to create and start a virtual thread is:

```
Thread t = Thread.startVirtualThread(myRunnable);
```

The `isVirtual` method of the `Thread` class returns `true` when a thread is virtual.

---

java.lang.Thread 1.0

- `boolean isVirtual()` **21**
  returns `true` when this thread is virtual.
- `static Thread startVirtualThread(Runnable task)` **21**
  starts and returns a virtual thread running the given task.

10.3.2. Thread Interruption

A thread terminates when its run method returns—by executing a return statement, after executing the last statement in the method body, or if an exception occurs that is not caught in the method.

Caution: In the initial release of Java, there also was a `stop` method that another thread could call to terminate a thread. However, that method was soon recognized to be unsafe and now throws an `UnsupportedOperationException` instead of stopping the thread.

There is no way to *force* a thread to terminate. However, the `interrupt` method can be used to *request* termination of a thread.

When the `interrupt` method is called on a thread, the *interrupted status* of the thread is set. This is a `boolean` flag that is present in every thread. Each thread should occasionally check whether it has been interrupted.

To find out whether the interrupted status was set, first call the static `Thread.currentThread` method to get the current thread, and then call the `isInterrupted` method:

```
while (!Thread.currentThread().isInterrupted() && more work to do)
{
   do more work
}
```

However, if a thread is blocked, it cannot check the interrupted status. This is where the `InterruptedException` comes in. When the `interrupt` method is called on a thread that blocks on a call such as `sleep` or `wait`, the blocking call is terminated by an `InterruptedException`. There are blocking I/O calls that cannot be interrupted. Then the `InterruptedException` is thrown when the I/O operation has completed.

There is no language requirement that a thread which is interrupted should terminate. Interrupting a thread simply grabs its attention. The interrupted thread can decide how to react to the interruption. Some threads are so important that they should handle the exception and continue. But far more often, a thread will simply want to interpret an interruption as a request for termination. The run method of such a thread has the following form:

```
Runnable r = () ->
   {
      try
      {
         . . .
         while (!Thread.currentThread().isInterrupted() && more work to do)
         {
            do more work
         }
      }
      catch (InterruptedException e)
      {
```

```
         // thread was interrupted
      }
      finally
      {
         cleanup, if required
      }
      // exiting the run method terminates the thread
   };
```

The isInterrupted check is neither necessary nor useful if you call the sleep method (or another interruptible method) after every work iteration. If you call the sleep method when the interrupted status is set, it doesn't sleep. Instead, it clears the status (!) and throws an InterruptedException. Therefore, if your loop calls sleep, don't check the interrupted status. Instead, catch the InterruptedException, like this:

```
Runnable r = () ->
   {
      try
      {
         . . .
         while (more work to do)
         {
            do more work
            Thread.sleep(delay);
         }
      }
      catch (InterruptedException e)
      {
         // thread was interrupted during sleep
      }
      finally
      {
         cleanup, if required
      }
      // exiting the run method terminates the thread
   };
```

 Note: There are two very similar methods, interrupted and isInterrupted. The interrupted method is a static method that checks whether the *current* thread has been interrupted. Furthermore, calling the interrupted method *clears* the interrupted status of the thread. On the other hand, the isInterrupted method is an instance method that you can use to check whether any thread has been interrupted. Calling it does not change the interrupted status.

You'll find lots of published code in which the InterruptedException is squelched at a subtask level, like this:

```
void mySubTask()
{
   . . .
   try
   {
      sleep(delay);
   }
   catch (InterruptedException e)
   {
      // Nothing here--BAD
   }
   . . .
}
```

Don't do that! If you do, the task cannot be interrupted while it is sleeping. You have two reasonable choices:

- Tag your method with throws InterruptedException and drop the try block. Then the caller (or, ultimately, the run method) can catch it.

  ```
  void mySubTask() throws InterruptedException
  {
     . . .
     sleep(delay);
     . . .
  }
  ```

- If you cannot do that, set the interrupted status in the catch clause. Then the caller can test it.

  ```
  void mySubTask()
  {
     . . .
     try
     {
        sleep(delay);
     }
     catch (InterruptedException e)
     {
        Thread.currentThread().interrupt();
     }
     . . .
  }
  ```

---

java.lang.Thread 1.0

- `void interrupt()`
  sends an interrupt request to a thread. The interrupted status of the thread is set to true. If the thread is currently blocked, then an `InterruptedException` is thrown.
- `static boolean interrupted()`
  tests whether the *current* thread (that is, the thread that is executing this instruction) has been interrupted. Note that this is a static method. The call has a side effect—it resets the interrupted status of the current thread to `false`.
- `boolean isInterrupted()`
  tests whether a thread has been interrupted. Unlike the `static interrupted` method, this call does not change the interrupted status of the thread.
- `static Thread currentThread()`
  returns the `Thread` object representing the currently executing thread.

10.3.3. Daemon Threads

You can turn a thread into a *daemon thread* by calling

```
t.setDaemon(true);
```

There is nothing demonic about such a thread. A daemon is simply a thread that has no other role in life than to serve others. Examples are timer threads that send regular "timer ticks" to other threads or threads that clean up stale cache entries. When only daemon threads remain, the virtual machine exits. There is no point in keeping the program running if all remaining threads are daemons.

All virtual threads are daemon threads. Calling `setDaemon(false)` has no effect on a virtual thread.

---

java.lang.Thread 1.0

- `void setDaemon(boolean isDaemon)`
  marks this thread as a daemon thread or a user thread. This method must be called before the thread is started.

10.3.4. Thread Names and Ids

By default, threads have catchy names such as `Thread-2`. You can set any name with the `setName` method:

```
var t = new Thread(runnable);
t.setName("Web crawler");
```

That can be useful in thread dumps.

Each thread also has a positive ID number that you can retrieve as

```
long id = t.threadId();
```

 Caution: There is also a getId method. It is deprecated because it was not defined as final. Someone might override it to return something other than the thread ID. Call the final threadId method instead.

---

java.lang.Thread 1.0

- void setName(String name)
- String getName()
  sets or gets the name of this thread.
- long threadId() 19
  returns the unique ID of this thread.

10.3.5. Handlers for Uncaught Exceptions

The run method of a thread cannot throw any checked exceptions, but it can be terminated by an unchecked exception. In that case, the thread terminates.

However, there is no catch clause to which the exception can be propagated. Instead, just before the thread dies, the exception is passed to a handler for uncaught exceptions.

The handler must belong to a class that implements the Thread.UncaughtExceptionHandler interface. That interface has a single method,

```
void uncaughtException(Thread t, Throwable e)
```

You can install a handler into any thread with the setUncaughtExceptionHandler method. You can also install a default handler for all threads with the static method setDefaultUncaughtExceptionHandler of the Thread class. A replacement handler might use the logging API to send reports of uncaught exceptions into a log file. If you don't install a default handler, the default handler is null.

If you don't install an uncaught exception handler for a thread, it uses a handler that takes the following actions:

1. If the thread's thread group has a parent, then the uncaughtException method of the parent group is called. (This is not common.)
2. Otherwise, if the Thread.getDefaultUncaughtExceptionHandler method returns a non-null handler, it is called.
3. Otherwise, if the Throwable is an instance of the deprecated ThreadDeath class (which was once used to stop a thread), nothing happens.

4. Otherwise, the name of the thread and the stack trace of the Throwable are printed on System.err.

That is the stack trace that you have undoubtedly seen many times in your programs.

 Note: Technically, the uncaught exception handler is defined by a thread's *thread group*. A thread group is a collection of threads that can be managed together. By default, all threads that you create belong to the same thread group, but it is possible to establish other groupings. Since there are now better features for operating on collections of threads, I recommend that you do not use thread groups in your programs.

---

java.lang.Thread 1.0

- static void setDefaultUncaughtExceptionHandler(Thread.UncaughtExceptionHandler handler) **5.0**
- static Thread.UncaughtExceptionHandler getDefaultUncaughtExceptionHandler() **5.0**
  set or get the default handler for uncaught exceptions.
- void setUncaughtExceptionHandler(Thread.UncaughtExceptionHandler handler) **5.0**
- Thread.UncaughtExceptionHandler getUncaughtExceptionHandler() **5.0**
  set or get the handler for uncaught exceptions. If no handler is installed, the thread group object is the handler.

---

java.lang.Thread.UncaughtExceptionHandler 5.0

- void uncaughtException(Thread t, Throwable e)
  defined to log a custom report when a thread is terminated with an uncaught exception.

---

java.lang.ThreadGroup 1.0

- void uncaughtException(Thread t, Throwable e)
  calls this method of the parent thread group if there is a parent, or calls the default handler of the Thread class if there is a default handler, or otherwise prints a stack trace to the standard error stream.

10.3.6. Thread Priorities

Every thread has a *priority*. By default, a thread inherits the priority of the thread that constructed it. You can increase or decrease the priority of any platform thread with the setPriority method. You can set the priority to any value between MIN_PRIORITY (defined as 1 in the Thread class) and MAX_PRIORITY (defined as 10). NORM_PRIORITY is defined as 5.

Whenever the platform thread scheduler has a chance to pick a new thread, it prefers threads with higher priority. However, thread priorities are *highly system-dependent*. Since the Java virtual machine relies on the thread implementation of the host platform, the Java thread priorities are mapped to the priority levels of the host platform, which may have more or fewer thread priority levels.

For example, Windows has seven priority levels. Some of the Java priorities will map to the same operating system level. In the OpenJDK VM for Linux, thread priorities are ignored altogether—all threads have the same priority.

Thread priorities may have been useful in early versions of Java that didn't use operating systems threads. You should not use them nowadays.

For backwards compatibility, all virtual threads have priority NORM_PRIORITY. Attempting to change the priority has no effect.

---

java.lang.Thread 1.0

- void setPriority(int newPriority)
  sets the priority of this thread. The priority must be between Thread.MIN_PRIORITY and Thread.MAX_PRIORITY. Use Thread.NORM_PRIORITY for normal priority.
- static int MIN_PRIORITY
  is the minimum priority that a Thread can have. The minimum priority value is 1.
- static int NORM_PRIORITY
  is the default priority of a Thread. The default priority is 5.
- static int MAX_PRIORITY
  is the maximum priority that a Thread can have. The maximum priority value is 10.

10.3.7. Thread Factories and Builders

You often want to produce multiple threads with the same properties. The ThreadFactory interface has a single method

```
Thread newThread(Runnable r)
```

that produces a new thread instance which, when started, will execute the given Runnable.

You can provide your own class that implements this interface, or, since Java 21, use a convenient builder syntax.

The static methods Thread.ofPlatform() and Thread.ofVirtual() yield builders for platform or virtual threads. You can customize the threads to be built:

```
Thread.Builder builder = Thread.ofVirtual().name("request-", 1);
```

See the API notes for additional customization methods.

Then call either unstarted or start to get a single thread, or factory to get a thread factory:

```
Thread t = builder.unstarted(myRunnable);
builder.start(myRunnable);

ThreadFactory factory = builder.factory();
t = factory.newThread(myRunnable);
```

---

java.util.concurrent.ThreadFactory 5.0

- Thread newThread(Runnable r)
  creates a thread that, when started, calls the run method of the given Runnable.

---

java.lang.Thread 1.0

- Thread.Builder.OfPlatform ofPlatform() **21**
- Thread.Builder.OfVirtual ofVirtual() **21**
  create a builder for platform or virtual threads.

---

java.lang.Thread.Builder 21

- Thread.Builder name(String prefix, long start)
- Thread.Builder name(String name)
  cause the built threads to be named with the given prefix and a counter with the given start value, or with the given name.
- ThreadFactory factory()
  yields a factory for building threads with the configuration of this builder.
- Thread unstarted(Runnable task)
- Thread start(Runnable task)
  construct a thread executing the given task. The second method starts the thread.
- Thread.Builder uncaughtExceptionHandler(Thread.UncaughtExceptionHandler ueh)
  causes the built threads to use the given uncaught exception handler.

---

java.lang.Thread.Builder.OfPlatform 21

- Thread.Builder.OfPlatform daemon()
- Thread.Builder.OfPlatform daemon(boolean on)
  cause the built threads to be daemon threads unless on is false.

- `Thread.Builder.OfPlatform stackSize(long stackSize)`
- `Thread.Builder.OfPlatform group(ThreadGroup group)`
- `Thread.Builder.OfPlatform priority(int priority)`
  cause the built threads to have the given stack size hint, group, or priority (not recommended).

10.4. Coordinating Tasks

It is common to break tasks into subtasks whose results are combined when they are available. In the following sections, you will see the tools that the Java concurrency framework provides for coordinating concurrent tasks.

10.4.1. Callables and Futures

A `Runnable` encapsulates a task that runs asynchronously; you can think of it as an asynchronous method with no parameters and no return value. A `Callable` is similar to a `Runnable`, but it returns a value. The `Callable` interface is a parameterized type, with a single method `call`.

```
public interface Callable<V>
{
    V call() throws Exception;
}
```

The type parameter is the type of the returned value. For example, a `Callable<Integer>` represents an asynchronous task that eventually returns an `Integer` object.

A `Future` holds the *result* of an asynchronous task. When you schedule a task for execution, you receive a `Future` object. Using the `Future` object, you can obtain the result when it is ready.

The `Future<V>` interface has the following methods:

```
V get()
V get(long timeout, TimeUnit unit)
V resultNow()
Throwable exceptionNow()
void cancel(boolean mayInterrupt)
boolean isCancelled()
boolean isDone()
Future.State state()
```

A call to the first get method blocks until the task is finished. The second get method also blocks, but it throws a `TimeoutException` if the call timed out before the task finished. If the thread running the task is interrupted, both methods throw an `InterruptedException`. If the task was terminated with an exception, the get methods throw an ExecutionException whose cause is the terminating exception.

If the task has already finished, get returns immediately.

The resultNow method is a non-blocking version of get that you should only call if you know that the task has completed successfully. If you know that the task has failed, you can retrieve the terminating exception with the exceptionNow method.

You can attempt to cancel the task with the cancel method. If the task has not yet started, it is canceled and will never start. If the task is currently in progress, it is interrupted if the mayInterrupt parameter is true, and otherwise runs to completion.

Caution: Task cancelation in Java always requires cooperation from the task implementor. As described in Section 10.3.2, the task needs to monitor the interrupted status of the thread.

The isDone method returns true if the task has completed (successfully or unsuccessfully), or it has been canceled.

The state method returns the task state as a value of the Task.State enumeration with four values:

- RUNNING: The task has not completed and was not cancelled
- SUCCESS: The task has completed successfully
- FAILED: The task has completed with an exception
- CANCELLED: The task was cancelled

You should call the state method before calling resultNow or exceptionNow.

One way to execute a Callable is to use a FutureTask, which implements both the Future and Runnable interfaces, so that you can construct a thread for running it:

```
Callable<Integer> task = . . .;
var futureTask = new FutureTask<Integer>(task);
var t = new Thread(futureTask); // futureTask is a Runnable
t.start();
. . .
Integer result = futureTask.get(); // futureTask is a Future
```

More commonly, you will pass a Callable to an executor. That is the topic of the next section.

To get a Future for a Runnable, you can call:

```
var futureTask = new FutureTask<Void>(myRunnable, null);
```

---

java.util.concurrent.Callable<V> 5.0

- `V call()`
  runs a task that yields a result.

---

java.util.concurrent.Future<V> 5.0

- `V get()`
- `V get(long time, TimeUnit unit)`
  get the result, blocking until it is available or the given time has elapsed. Throw a `CancellationException` if the task was canceled, an `ExecutionException` whose cause is the terminating exception if the task completed unsuccessfully, and an `InterruptedException` if the current thread was interrupted. The second method throws a `TimeoutException` if the task was not done within the given timeout.
- `V resultNow()` **19**
  gets the result if the task completed successfully, throws an `IllegalStateException` otherwise.
- `Throwable exceptionNow()` **19**
  gets the terminating exception if the task completed unsuccessfully, throws an `IllegalStateException` otherwise.
- `boolean cancel(boolean mayInterrupt)`
  attempts to cancel the execution of this task. If the task has already started and the `mayInterrupt` parameter is `true`, it is interrupted. Returns `true` if the cancellation was successful.
- `boolean isCancelled()`
  returns `true` if the task was canceled before it completed.
- `boolean isDone()`
  returns `true` if the task completed, successfully or unsuccessfully, or was canceled.
- `Future.State state()` **19**
  returns the state of this task, as `RUNNING`, `SUCCESS`, `FAILED`, or `CANCELLED`.

---

java.util.concurrent.FutureTask<V> 5.0

- `FutureTask(Callable<V> task)`
  constructs an object that is both a `Future<V>` and a `Runnable`.
- `FutureTask(Runnable task, V result)`
  constructs an object that, as a `Runnable`, executes the task, and as a `Future<V>`, yields the result upon completion.

10.4.2. Executors

Constructing a new platform thread is somewhat expensive because it involves interaction with the operating system. If your program creates a large number of short-lived platform threads, you should not run each task on a separate thread, but use a *thread pool* instead. A thread pool contains a number of threads that are ready to execute your tasks. You submit Runnable or Callable tasks to the pool, and one of the threads calls the run or call method. When the method exits, the thread doesn't die but stays around to serve the next request.

An *executor* is an object to which you submit tasks. For platform threads, that is a thread pool. Virtual threads are inexpensive to create and should never be pooled. An executor for virtual threads will simply start a new virtual thread for each submitted task.

The Executors class has a number of static factory methods for constructing executors. Table 10.1 lists the most useful ones.

Table 10.1: Common Executors Factory Methods

Method	Description
newCachedThreadPool	New threads are created as needed; idle threads are kept for 60 seconds.
newFixedThreadPool	The pool contains a fixed set of threads; idle threads are kept indefinitely.
newSingleThreadExecutor	A "pool" with a single thread that executes the submitted tasks sequentially.
newVirtualThreadPerTaskExecutor	An executor that runs each task on a new virtual thread.

The newCachedThreadPool method constructs a thread pool that executes each task immediately, using an existing idle thread when available and creating a new thread otherwise. The newFixedThreadPool method constructs a thread pool with a fixed size. If more tasks are submitted than there are idle threads, the unserved tasks are placed on a queue. They are run when other tasks have completed. The newSingleThreadExecutor is a degenerate pool of size 1 where a single thread executes the submitted tasks, one after another.

Use a cached thread pool when you have platform threads that are short-lived or spend a lot of time blocking. However, if you have threads that are working hard without blocking, you don't want to run a large number of them together. For optimum speed, the number of concurrent threads is the number of processor cores. In such a situation, you should use a fixed thread pool that bounds the total number of concurrent platform threads.

Another reason for using a fixed thread pool is to throttle the number of concurrent tasks. If many of the tasks access a service that can only handle a limited number of concurrent clients, then you can use the pool size to enforce that limit. This is a rather crude way of tuning an application, but it is surprisingly common because it is easy to do.

 Caution: If your application uses virtual threads, you need to come up with alternative mechanisms for throttling concurrent requests, such as a counting semaphore or bounded queue.

For example, this code snippet limits the number of concurrent web requests:

```
private static final int CONCURRENT_REQUESTS = 200;
private static final Semaphore SEMAPHORE = new Semaphore(CONCURRENT_REQUESTS);
...
public static String get(URI uri) throws InterruptedException, IOException {
    var request = HttpRequest.newBuilder().uri(uri).GET().build();
    SEMAPHORE.acquire();
    try {
        return client.send(request, HttpResponse.BodyHandlers.ofString()).body();
    } finally {
        SEMAPHORE.release();
    }
}
```

With a high number of concurrent requests, the acquire method blocks. For virtual threads, that is not a problem. For effective scaling, it is better to move the blocking to the point of pressure instead of the thread pool.

The single-thread executor is potentially useful for performance analysis. If you temporarily replace a cached or fixed thread pool with a single-thread pool, you can measure how much slower your application runs without the benefit of concurrency.

Most of the Executors factory methods have a version with a ThreadFactory parameter, allowing you to customize the threads that execute the submitted tasks. If you provide your own factory for a thread pool, it should produce platform threads, not virtual threads, since pooling virtual threads is never useful. If you want to customize virtual threads, pass a factory for virtual threads to the newThreadPerTaskExecutor method.

All of the Executors factory methods return objects of classes that implement the ExecutorService interface. Submit a Runnable or Callable to an ExecutorService with one of the following methods:

```
Future<T> submit(Callable<T> task)
Future<?> submit(Runnable task)
Future<T> submit(Runnable task, T result)
```

When you call submit, the executor will schedule the submitted task. You get back a Future object that you can use to get the result or cancel the task.

The second submit method returns a Future<?>. The get method blocks until completion and then returns null.

 Note: Other methods in the java.util.concurrent API return a Future<Void> instead of a Future<?>. For all practical purposes these types have the same function. You can use instances to query the task state and to block until the task completes, but there is no result value.

The third version of submit yields a Future whose get method returns the given result object upon completion.

When you are done with an executor, call the close method. An executor that is closed down accepts no new tasks. The close method blocks until all submitted tasks are finished. (If the thread calling close is interrupted, then the submitted tasks are canceled.) A convenient way to invoke close is to use a try-with-resources statement:

```
try (ExecutorService executor = Executors.newVirtualThreadPerTaskExecutor()) {
    . . .
    Future<V> f = submit(myCallable);
    . . .
} // executor.close() called here
```

 Note: Some programmers view an executor as a global resource. There are situations where a global executor makes sense, but you should not hesitate to have local executors, submit a few tasks, and then close them. This is particularly useful with virtual threads, where the blocking call to close is not a concern.

There are other methods to shut down an executor: shutdown, shutdownNow, and awaitTermination. These give you some finer-grained control, and they are needed in legacy code since the close method was only added in Java 19. If you need to run the demo program in this section with an older version of Java, replace the call executor.close() with:

```
executor.shutdown();
executor.awaitTermination(10, TimeUnit.MINUTES);
```

Here, in summary, is what you do to use an executor:

1. Call one of the static methods of the Executors class, most commonly newCachedThreadPool, newFixedThreadPool, or newVirtualThreadPerTaskExecutor.
2. Call submit to submit Callable or Runnable objects.

3. Hang on to the returned Future objects so that you can query task states, get the results, or cancel the tasks.
4. Shut down the executor when you no longer want to submit any tasks.

 Caution: When an executor uses threads from a thread factory, setting the factory's uncaught exception handler has no effect. Thread pools need to install their own handler for catching task exceptions.

---

java.util.concurrent.Executors 5.0

- static ExecutorService newCachedThreadPool()
- static ExecutorService newCachedThreadPool(ThreadFactory threadFactory)
  returns a cached thread pool that creates threads as needed and terminates threads that have been idle for 60 seconds.
- static ExecutorService newFixedThreadPool(int threads)
- static ExecutorService newFixedThreadPool(int threads, ThreadFactory threadFactory)
  returns a thread pool that uses the given number of threads to execute tasks.
- static ExecutorService newSingleThreadExecutor()
- static ExecutorService newSingleThreadExecutor(ThreadFactory threadFactory)
  returns an executor that executes tasks sequentially in a single thread.
- static ExecutorService newVirtualThreadPerTaskExecutor() **21**
- static ExecutorService newThreadPerTaskExecutor(ThreadFactory threadFactory) **21**
  returns an executor that executes each task in a new virtual thread, or a thread produced by the given factory.

---

java.util.concurrent.ExecutorService 5.0

- Future<T> submit(Callable<T> task)
- Future<T> submit(Runnable task, T result)
- Future<?> submit(Runnable task)
  submit the given task for execution.
- void close() **19**
  sets this executor into shutdown mode where it no longer accepts new submissions, and blocks until the already submitted tasks have completed. If interrupted while blocking, running tasks are interrupted.
- void shutdown()
  sets this executor into shutdown mode where it no longer accepts new submissions. This method does not block for completion of submitted tasks.
- List<Runnable> shutdownNow()
  sets this executor into shutdown mode, interrupts tasks that have started, and removes tasks that have not yet started. Returns a list of the removed tasks. This method does not block for completion of submitted tasks.

■ boolean awaitTermination(long timeout, TimeUnit unit)
blocks until all submitted tasks have completed, the timeout has elapsed, or the blocking is interrupted. Returns true if all tasks have completed.

10.4.3. Invoking a Group of Tasks

Often, you want to launch multiple concurrent tasks and get the result of the first successful one, or combine the results of all completed ones.

The invokeAny method submits all tasks in a collection of Callable objects and blocks until one of them has completed successfully, returning its result. Any tasks that have not completed are canceled. You don't know which task succeeded—presumably, it is the one that finished most quickly. If no task succeeded, an ExecutionException is thrown.

Use this method for a search problem in which you are willing to accept any solution. For example, suppose that you need to find a factor of a large integer—a computation that is required for breaking the RSA cipher. You could submit a number of tasks, each attempting a factorization with numbers in a different range. As soon as one of these tasks has an answer, your computation can stop.

The invokeAll method submits all tasks in a collection of Callable objects, blocks until all of them complete, and returns a list of Future objects that represent the solutions to all tasks, in the same order as the submitted tasks. You can process the results of the computation like this:

```
List<Callable<T>> tasks = . . .;
List<Future<T>> results = executor.invokeAll(tasks);
for (Future<T> result : results) {
    if (result.state() == Future.State.SUCCESS)
        process result.resultNow();
    else
        handle result.exceptionNow();
}
```

The call to invokeAll blocks until all tasks have completed. If you want to obtain the results in the order in which they are available, use an ExecutorCompletionService.

Start with an executor, obtained in the usual way. Then construct an ExecutorCompletionService. Submit tasks to the completion service. The service manages a blocking queue of Future objects, containing the results of the submitted tasks as they become available:

```
var service = new ExecutorCompletionService<T>(executor);
for (Callable<T> task : tasks) service.submit(task);
for (int i = 0; i < tasks.size(); i++) {
    Future<T> result = service.take();
}
```

The program in Listing 10.3 shows how to use callables and executors. In the first computation, we count how many files in a directory tree contain a given word. We make a separate task for each file:

```
Set<Path> files = descendants(Path.of(start));
var tasks = new ArrayList<Callable<Long>>();
for (Path file : files)
{
   Callable<Long> task = () -> occurrences(word, file);
   tasks.add(task);
}
```

Then we pass the tasks to an executor service:

```
ExecutorService executor = Executors.newCachedThreadPool();
List<Future<Long>> results = executor.invokeAll(tasks);
```

To get the combined count, we add all results, blocking until they are available:

```
long total = 0;
for (Future<Long> result : results)
   total += result.get();
```

The program also displays the time spent during the search. Unzip the source code for the JDK somewhere and run the search. Then replace the executor service with a single-thread executor and try again to see whether the concurrent computation was faster. Also try with virtual threads.

In the second part of the program, we search for the first file that contains the given word. We use invokeAny to parallelize the search. Here, we have to be more careful about formulating the tasks. The invokeAny method terminates as soon as any task *returns*. So we cannot have the search tasks return a boolean to indicate success or failure. We don't want to stop searching when a task failed. Instead, a failing task throws a NoSuchElementException. Also, when one task has succeeded, the others are canceled. Therefore, we monitor the interrupted status. If the underlying thread is interrupted, the search task prints a message before terminating, so that you can see that the cancellation is effective.

```
public static Callable<Path> searchForTask(String word, Path path)
{
   return () ->
      {
         try (var in = new Scanner(path))
         {
            while (in.hasNext())
            {
               if (in.next().equals(word)) return path;
               if (Thread.currentThread().isInterrupted())
```

```
        {
            System.out.println("Search in " + path + " canceled.");
            return null;
        }
    }
    throw new NoSuchElementException();
    }
  };
}
```

 Preview Note: Just like structured programming replaced "goto" statements with branches, loops, and functions, *structured concurrency* is an effort to find programming constructs that make it easier to reason about concurrent programs.

Java 21 contains a preview of a structured concurrency API. Tasks are submitted to a StructuredTaskScope. Then the join method blocks until the scope is *shut down*, according to the scope's shutdown policy. The API provides two simple policies ShutdownOnFailure and ShutdownOnSuccess. Here is a usage example:

```
// Java 21 preview API
try (var scope = new StructuredTaskScope.ShutdownOnFailure()) {
    Supplier<T1> f1 = scope.fork(callable1);
    Supplier<T2> f2 = scope.fork(callable2);
    scope.join();
    scope.throwIfFailed();
    result = combine(f1.get(), f2.get());
}
```

When the try block ends, we can be sure that all subtasks have completed.

If either subtask fails, the scope shuts down, canceling the other task, and the first exception is rethrown.

If the current thread is interrupted, the scope is closed and both tasks are canceled.

You could have achieved almost the same effect with ExecutorService.invokeAll, except that invokeAll waits for completion of all tasks even if one of them fails. If you prefer that policy, it is easy to implement a scope subclass.

The structured programming API is flexible and convenient, and it provides runtime checks and observability features for the nesting of scopes.

Listing 10.3 executors/ExecutorDemo.java

```java
 1  package executors;
 2
 3  import java.io.*;
 4  import java.nio.file.*;
 5  import java.time.*;
 6  import java.util.*;
 7  import java.util.concurrent.*;
 8  import java.util.stream.*;
 9
10  /**
11   * This program demonstrates the Callable interface and executors.
12   * @version 1.02 2023-07-27
13   * @author Cay Horstmann
14   */
15  public class ExecutorDemo
16  {
17     /**
18      * Counts occurrences of a given word in a file.
19      * @return the number of times the word occurs in the given word
20      */
21     public static long occurrences(String word, Path path)
22     {
23        try (var in = new Scanner(path))
24        {
25           int count = 0;
26           while (in.hasNext())
27              if (in.next().equals(word)) count++;
28           return count;
29        }
30        catch (IOException ex)
31        {
32           return 0;
33        }
34     }
35
36     /**
37      * Returns all descendants of a given directory--see Chapters 1 and 2 of Volume II.
38      * @param rootDir the root directory
39      * @return a set of all descendants of the root directory
40      */
41     public static Set<Path> descendants(Path rootDir) throws IOException
42     {
43        try (Stream<Path> entries = Files.walk(rootDir))
44        {
45           return entries.filter(Files::isRegularFile)
46              .collect(Collectors.toSet());
47        }
48     }
```

```
49
50    /**
51     * Yields a task that searches for a word in a file.
52     * @param word the word to search
53     * @param path the file in which to search
54     * @return the search task that yields the path upon success
55     */
56    public static Callable<Path> searchForTask(String word, Path path)
57    {
58        return () ->
59            {
60                try (var in = new Scanner(path))
61                {
62                    while (in.hasNext())
63                    {
64                        if (in.next().equals(word)) return path;
65                        if (Thread.currentThread().isInterrupted())
66                        {
67                            System.out.println("Search in " + path + " canceled.");
68                            return null;
69                        }
70                    }
71                    throw new NoSuchElementException();
72                }
73            };
74    }
75
76    public static void main(String[] args)
77            throws InterruptedException, ExecutionException, IOException
78    {
79        try (var in = new Scanner(System.in))
80        {
81            System.out.print("Enter base directory (e.g. /opt/jdk-21-src): ");
82            String start = in.nextLine();
83            System.out.print("Enter keyword (e.g. volatile): ");
84            String word = in.nextLine();
85
86            Set<Path> files = descendants(Path.of(start));
87            var tasks = new ArrayList<Callable<Long>>();
88            for (Path file : files)
89            {
90                Callable<Long> task = () -> occurrences(word, file);
91                tasks.add(task);
92            }
93            ExecutorService executor = Executors.newCachedThreadPool();
94            // use a single thread executor instead to see if multiple threads
95            // speed up the search
96            // ExecutorService executor = Executors.newSingleThreadExecutor();
97            // Or try virtual threads
98            // ExecutorService executor = Executors.newVirtualThreadPerTaskExecutor();
99            Instant startTime = Instant.now();
100           List<Future<Long>> results = executor.invokeAll(tasks);
```

```
101          Instant endTime = Instant.now();
102          long total = 0;
103          for (Future<Long> result : results)
104             total += result.get();
105          System.out.println("Occurrences of " + word + ": " + total);
106          System.out.println("Time elapsed: "
107             + Duration.between(startTime, endTime).toMillis() + " ms");
108
109          var searchTasks = new ArrayList<Callable<Path>>();
110          for (Path file : files)
111             searchTasks.add(searchForTask(word, file));
112          startTime = Instant.now();
113          Path found = executor.invokeAny(searchTasks);
114          endTime = Instant.now();
115          System.out.println(word + " occurs in: " + found);
116          System.out.println("Time elapsed: "
117             + Duration.between(startTime, endTime).toMillis() + " ms");
118
119          executor.close();
120       }
121    }
122 }
```

---

java.util.concurrent.ExecutorService   5.0

- ▪ T invokeAny(Collection<Callable<T>> tasks)
- ▪ T invokeAny(Collection<Callable<T>> tasks, long timeout, TimeUnit unit)
  execute the given tasks and return the result of one that completed successfully, canceling the remaining tasks. The second method throws a TimeoutException if a timeout occurs.
- ▪ List<Future<T>> invokeAll(Collection<Callable<T>> tasks)
- ▪ List<Future<T>> invokeAll(Collection<Callable<T>> tasks, long timeout, TimeUnit unit)
  execute the given tasks and return the results when all tasks have completed. The second method throws a TimeoutException if a timeout occurs.

---

java.util.concurrent.ExecutorCompletionService<V>   5.0

- ▪ ExecutorCompletionService(Executor e)
  constructs an executor completion service that collects the results of the given executor.
- ▪ Future<V> submit(Callable<V> task)
- ▪ Future<V> submit(Runnable task, V result)
  submit a task to the underlying executor.
- ▪ Future<V> take()
  removes the next completed result, blocking if no completed results are available.

- `Future<V> poll()`
- `Future<V> poll(long time, TimeUnit unit)`
  remove and return the next completed result, or returns `null` if no completed results are available. The second method waits for the given time.

10.4.4. Thread-Local Variables

Sometimes you want to make a task-specific object available to all methods that collaborate on the task, without having to pass the object as a parameter of each method call. You can use a *thread-local variable* for this purpose. This is not an actual variable, but an object whose get and set methods access a value that depends on the current thread.

Suppose, for example, that you want to share a database connection. Declare a variable

```
public static final ThreadLocal<Connection> CONNECTION = new ThreadLocal<>();
```

When the task starts, initialize the connection for this thread:

```
CONNECTION.set(connect(uri, username, password));
```

The task calls some methods, all within the same thread, and eventually one of them needs the connection:

```
Connection connection = CONNECTION.get();
var result = connection.executeQuery(query);
```

Note that the same call may happen on multiple threads. Each of them gets its own connection object.

 Caution: When executing tasks with a thread pool, you don't want to make thread-local data available to the other tasks that are scheduled on the same thread. You also want to make sure they get garbage collected when your task is done. It is essential that you call

```
CONNECTION.remove();
```

upon task completion (successfully or with an exception).

An `InheritableThreadLocal` is a subclass of `ThreadLocal`, used to propagate thread-local data to subtasks. When a new thread is started, it receives a copy of the parent's inheritable thread locals. (The copy is necessary because the child thread might mutate the thread-local values.)

Tip: Sharing resource-intensive objects as thread locals can be a problem when migrating to virtual threads. There will likely be far more of them than threads in a thread pool, and now you have many more instances. In such a situation, you should rethink your sharing strategy.

To identify the use of thread-local variables, run with the VM flag `jdk.traceVirtualThreadLocals`. You will get a stack trace when a virtual thread mutates a thread-local variable.

 Preview Note: Scoped values are a preview feature of Java 21 that provide a more performant version of inheritable thread-local variables. Scoped values have per-thread instances, but they are immutable and have a bounded lifetime. Scoped values are inherited in virtual threads created by a `StructuredTaskScope`. This code snippet shows how to use them:

```
public static final ScopedValue<Connection> CONNECTION = ScopedValue.newInstance();
. . .
ScopedValue.where(CONNECTION, connect(uri, username, password)).run(() -> doWork());
. . .
public void doWork() {
    . . .
    Connection connection = CONNECTION.get();
    var result = connection.executeQuery(query);
    . . .
}
```

When using virtual threads, prefer scoped values over thread-local variables.

`java.lang.ThreadLocal<T>` 1.2

- `T get()`
  gets the current value of this thread. If get is called for the first time and set was never called, the value is obtained by calling `initialize`.
- `void set(T t)`
  sets a new value for this thread.
- `void remove()`
  removes the value for this thread.

10.4.5. The Fork-Join Framework

Some applications use a large number of threads that are mostly idle. An example would be a web server that uses one thread per connection. Other applications use one thread per processor core, in order to carry out computationally intensive tasks, such as image or video processing. The fork-join framework is designed to support the latter. Suppose you have a processing task that naturally decomposes into subtasks, like this:

```
if (problemSize < threshold)
{
    solve problem directly
}
else
{
    break problem into subproblems
    recursively solve each subproblem
    combine the results
}
```

One example is image processing. To enhance an image, you can transform the top half and the bottom half. If you have enough idle processors, those operations can run in parallel. (You will need to do a bit of extra work along the strip that separates the two halves, but that's a technical detail.)

Here, we discuss a simpler example. Suppose we want to count how many elements of an array fulfill a particular property. We cut the array in half, compute the counts of each half, and add them up.

To put the recursive computation in a form that is usable by the framework, supply a class that extends RecursiveTask<T> (if the computation produces a result of type T) or RecursiveAction (if it doesn't produce a result). Override the compute method to generate and invoke subtasks and to combine their results.

```
class Counter extends RecursiveTask<Integer>
{
    . . .
    protected Integer compute()
    {
        if (to - from < THRESHOLD)
        {
            solve problem directly
        }
        else
        {
            int mid = from + (to - from) / 2;
            var first = new Counter(values, from, mid, filter);
            var second = new Counter(values, mid, to, filter);
            invokeAll(first, second);
            return first.join() + second.join();
        }
    }
}
```

The invokeAll method receives a number of tasks and blocks until all of them have completed. The join method yields the result. Here, we apply join to each subtask and return the sum.

 Note: There is also a get method for getting the current result, but it is less attractive since it can throw checked exceptions that we are not allowed to throw in the compute method.

Listing 10.4 shows the complete example.

Behind the scenes, the fork-join framework uses an effective heuristic, called *work stealing*, for balancing the workload among available threads. Each worker thread has a deque (double-ended queue) for tasks. A worker thread pushes smaller subtasks onto the head of its own deque. (Only one thread accesses the head, so no locking is required.) When a worker thread is idle, it "steals" a task from the tail of another deque (which requires locking). By stealing larger subtasks, which are at the tail, more time elapses until the next "theft", reducing contention at the tails.

 Caution: Fork-join pools are optimized for nonblocking workloads. If you add many blocking tasks into a fork-join pool, you can starve it. It is possible to overcome this by having tasks implement the ForkJoinPool.ManagedBlocker interface, but this is an advanced technique that we won't discuss.

Listing 10.4 forkJoin/ForkJoinTest.java

```java
package forkJoin;

import java.util.concurrent.*;
import java.util.function.*;

/**
 * This program demonstrates the fork-join framework.
 * @version 1.02 2021-06-17
 * @author Cay Horstmann
 */
public class ForkJoinTest
{
    public static void main(String[] args)
    {
        final int SIZE = 10000000;
        var numbers = new double[SIZE];
        for (int i = 0; i < SIZE; i++) numbers[i] = Math.random();
        var counter = new Counter(numbers, 0, numbers.length, x -> x > 0.5);
```

```
19          var pool = new ForkJoinPool();
20          pool.invoke(counter);
21          System.out.println(counter.join());
22      }
23  }
24
25  class Counter extends RecursiveTask<Integer>
26  {
27      public static final int THRESHOLD = 1000;
28      private double[] values;
29      private int from;
30      private int to;
31      private DoublePredicate filter;
32
33      public Counter(double[] values, int from, int to, DoublePredicate filter)
34      {
35          this.values = values;
36          this.from = from;
37          this.to = to;
38          this.filter = filter;
39      }
40
41      protected Integer compute()
42      {
43          if (to - from < THRESHOLD)
44          {
45              int count = 0;
46              for (int i = from; i < to; i++)
47              {
48                  if (filter.test(values[i])) count++;
49              }
50              return count;
51          }
52          else
53          {
54              int mid = from + (to - from) / 2;
55              var first = new Counter(values, from, mid, filter);
56              var second = new Counter(values, mid, to, filter);
57              invokeAll(first, second);
58              return first.join() + second.join();
59          }
60      }
61  }
```

10.5. Synchronization

In most practical multithreaded applications, two or more threads need to share access to the same data. What happens if two threads have access to the same object and each calls a method that modifies the state of the object? As you might imagine, the threads can step on each other's toes. Depending on the order in which the data were accessed, corrupted objects can result. Such a situation is often called a *race condition*.

10.5.1. An Example of a Race Condition

To avoid corruption of shared data by multiple threads, you must learn how to *synchronize the access*. In this section, you'll see what happens if you do not use synchronization. In the next section, you'll see how to synchronize data access.

In the next test program, we continue working with our simulated bank. Unlike the example in Section 10.1, we randomly select the source and destination of the transfer. Since this will cause problems, let us look more carefully at the code for the transfer method of the Bank class.

```
public void transfer(int from, int to, double amount)
   // CAUTION: unsafe when called from multiple threads
{
   System.out.print(Thread.currentThread());
   accounts[from] -= amount;
   System.out.printf(" %10.2f from %d to %d", amount, from, to);
   accounts[to] += amount;
   System.out.printf(" Total Balance: %10.2f%n", getTotalBalance());
}
```

Here is the code for the Runnable instances. The run method keeps moving money out of a given bank account. In each iteration, the run method picks a random target account and a random amount, calls transfer on the bank object, and then sleeps.

```
Runnable r = () ->
   {
      try
      {
         while (true)
         {
            int toAccount = (int) (bank.size() * Math.random());
            double amount = MAX_AMOUNT * Math.random();
            bank.transfer(fromAccount, toAccount, amount);
            Thread.sleep((int) (DELAY * Math.random()));
         }
      }
      catch (InterruptedException e)
      {
      }
   };
```

When this simulation runs, we do not know how much money is in any one bank account at any time. But we do know that the total amount of money in all the accounts should remain unchanged because all we do is move money from one account to another.

At the end of each transaction, the `transfer` method recomputes the total and prints it.

This program never finishes. Just press Ctrl+C to kill the program.

Here is a typical printout:

```
. . .
Thread[Thread-11,5,main]     588.48 from 11 to 44 Total Balance:  100000.00
Thread[Thread-12,5,main]     976.11 from 12 to 22 Total Balance:  100000.00
Thread[Thread-14,5,main]     521.51 from 14 to 22 Total Balance:  100000.00
Thread[Thread-13,5,main]     359.89 from 13 to 81 Total Balance:  100000.00

. . .
Thread[Thread-36,5,main]     401.71 from 36 to 73 Total Balance:   99291.06
Thread[Thread-35,5,main]     691.46 from 35 to 77 Total Balance:   99291.06
Thread[Thread-37,5,main]      78.64 from 37 to 3 Total Balance:    99291.06
Thread[Thread-34,5,main]     197.11 from 34 to 69 Total Balance:   99291.06
Thread[Thread-36,5,main]      85.96 from 36 to 4 Total Balance:    99291.06

. . .
Thread[Thread-4,5,main]Thread[Thread-33,5,main]        7.31 from 31 to 32 Total Balance:
99979.24
        627.50 from 4 to 5 Total Balance:   99979.24

. . .
```

As you can see, something is very wrong. For a few transactions, the bank balance remains at $100,000, which is the correct total for 100 accounts of $1,000 each. But after some time, the balance changes slightly. When you run this program, errors may happen quickly, or it may take a very long time for the balance to become corrupted. This situation does not inspire confidence, and you would probably not want to deposit your hard-earned money in such a bank.

See if you can spot the problems with the code in Listing 10.5 and the Bank class in Listing 10.2. We will unravel the mystery in the next section.

Listing 10.5 unsynch/UnsynchBankTest.java

```
1  package unsynch;
2
3  /**
4   * This program shows data corruption when multiple threads access a data structure.
5   * @version 1.33 2023-07-30
6   * @author Cay Horstmann
7   */
```

```
 8   public class UnsynchBankTest
 9   {
10      public static final int NACCOUNTS = 100;
11      public static final double INITIAL_BALANCE = 1000;
12      public static final double MAX_AMOUNT = 1000;
13      public static final int DELAY = 10;
14
15      public static void main(String[] args)
16      {
17         var bank = new Bank(NACCOUNTS, INITIAL_BALANCE);
18         for (int i = 0; i < NACCOUNTS; i++)
19         {
20            int fromAccount = i;
21            Runnable r = () ->
22               {
23                  try
24                  {
25                     while (true)
26                     {
27                        int toAccount = (int) (bank.size() * Math.random());
28                        double amount = MAX_AMOUNT * Math.random();
29                        bank.transfer(fromAccount, toAccount, amount);
30                        Thread.sleep((int) (DELAY * Math.random()));
31                     }
32                  }
33                  catch (InterruptedException e)
34                  {
35                  }
36               };
37            Thread.ofPlatform().start(r);
38         }
39      }
40   }
```

10.5.2. The Race Condition Explained

In the previous section, we ran a program in which several threads updated bank account balances. After a while, errors crept in and some amount of money was either lost or spontaneously created. This problem occurs when two threads are simultaneously trying to update an account. Suppose two threads simultaneously carry out the instruction

```
accounts[to] += amount;
```

The problem is that these are not *atomic* operations. The instruction might be processed as follows:

1. Load accounts[to] into a register.
2. Add amount.
3. Move the result back to accounts[to].

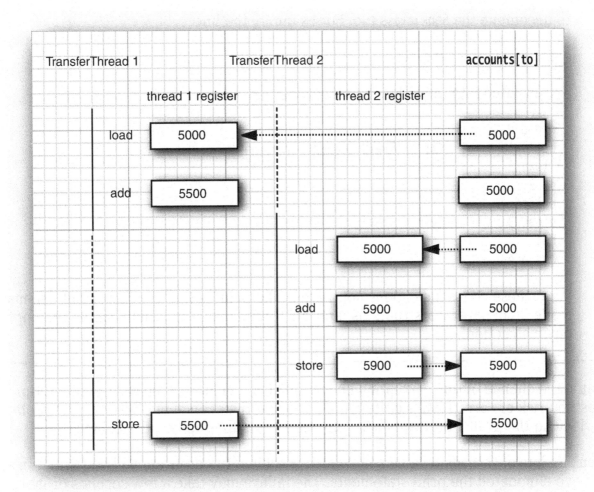

Figure 10.2: Simultaneous access by two threads

Now, suppose the first thread executes Steps 1 and 2, and then it is preempted. Suppose the second thread awakens and updates the same entry in the account array. Then, the first thread awakens and completes its Step 3.

That action wipes out the modification of the other thread. As a result, the total is no longer correct (see Figure 10.2).

The UnsyncBankTest program demonstrates this corruption. (There is also a slight chance of false alarms during the computation of getTotalBalance.)

 Note: You can actually peek at the virtual machine bytecodes that execute each statement in our class. Run the command

```
javap -c -v Bank
```

to decompile the Bank.class file. For example, the line

```
accounts[to] += amount;
```

is translated into the following bytecodes:

```
aload_0
getfield        #2; // Field accounts:[D
iload_2
dup2
daload
dload_3
dadd
dastore
```

What these codes mean does not matter. The point is that the increment command is made up of several instructions, and the thread executing them can be preempted at any instruction.

What is the chance of this corruption occurring? On a modern processor with multiple cores, the risk of corruption is quite high. I boosted the chance of observing the problem by interleaving the print statements with the statements that update the balance.

If you run lots of threads on a heavily loaded machine, the program will still fail even after you have eliminated the print statements. The failure may take a few seconds or many hours or to occur. Frankly, there are few things worse in the life of a programmer than an error that only manifests itself irregularly.

The real problem is that the work of the transfer method can be preempted in the middle. If we could ensure that the method runs to completion before the thread loses control, the state of the bank account object would never be corrupted.

10.5.3. Lock Objects

There are two mechanisms for protecting a code block from concurrent access. The Java language provides a synchronized keyword for this purpose, and the java.util.concurrent package provides explicit classes for locking. The synchronized keyword automatically provides a lock as well as an associated "condition," which makes it powerful and convenient for many cases that require explicit locking. However, I believe that it is easier to understand the synchronized keyword after you have seen locks and conditions in isolation. I explain the explicit classes here and in Section 10.5.4. Once you have understood these building blocks, you can read about the synchronized keyword in Section 10.5.6.

The basic outline for protecting a code block with a ReentrantLock is:

```
myLock.lock(); // a ReentrantLock object
try
{
    critical section
}
finally
{
    myLock.unlock(); // make sure the lock is unlocked even if an exception is thrown
}
```

This construct guarantees that only one thread at a time can enter the critical section. As soon as one thread locks the lock object, no other thread can get past the `lock` statement. When other threads call `lock`, they are deactivated until the first thread unlocks the lock object.

Caution: It is critically important that the `unlock` operation is enclosed in a `finally` clause. If the code in the critical section throws an exception, the lock must be unlocked. Otherwise, the other threads will be blocked forever.

Note: When you use locks, you cannot use the try-with-resources statement. The `unlock` method isn't called `close`. Some programmers proposed to make `Lock` extend `AutoCloseable`, with `close` calling `lock`. But Java designers felt that lock usage is fairly uncommon and deserves to be noticeable.

Let us use a lock to protect the `transfer` method of the Bank class.

```
public class Bank
{
    private final Lock bankLock = new ReentrantLock();
    . . .
    public void transfer(int from, int to, int amount)
    {
        bankLock.lock();
        try
        {
            System.out.print(Thread.currentThread());
            accounts[from] -= amount;
            System.out.printf(" %10.2f from %d to %d", amount, from, to);
            accounts[to] += amount;
            System.out.printf(" Total Balance: %10.2f%n", getTotalBalance());
        }
        finally
        {
```

```
            bankLock.unlock();
        }
    }
}
```

Suppose one thread calls transfer and gets preempted before it is done. Suppose a second thread also calls transfer. The second thread cannot acquire the lock and is blocked in the call to the lock method. It is deactivated and must wait for the first thread to finish executing the transfer method. When the first thread unlocks the lock, then the second thread can proceed (see Figure 10.3).

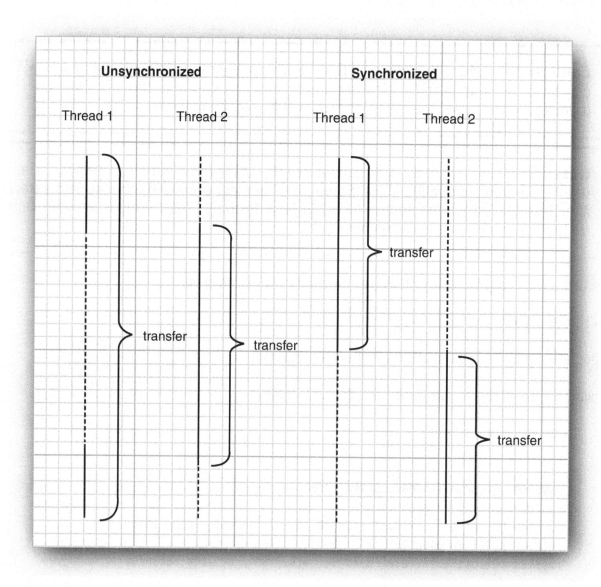

Figure 10.3: Comparison of unsynchronized and synchronized threads

Try it out. Add the locking code to the transfer method and run the program again. You can run it forever, and the bank balance will not become corrupted.

Note that each Bank object has its own ReentrantLock object. If two threads try to access the same Bank object, then the lock serves to serialize the access. However, if two threads access different Bank objects, each thread acquires a different lock and neither thread is blocked. This is as it should be, because the threads cannot interfere with one another when they manipulate different Bank instances.

The lock is called *reentrant* because a thread can repeatedly acquire a lock that it already owns. The lock has a *hold count* that keeps track of the nested calls to the lock method. The thread has to call unlock for every call to lock in order to relinquish the lock. Because of this feature, code protected by a lock can call another method that uses the same lock.

For example, the transfer method calls the getTotalBalance method, which also locks the bankLock object, which now has a hold count of 2. When the getTotalBalance method exits, the hold count is back to 1. When the transfer method exits, the hold count is 0, and the thread relinquishes the lock.

In general, you will want to use a lock around any block of code that updates or inspects a shared object, so you can be assured that these operations run to completion before another thread can use the same object.

 Caution: Be careful to ensure that the code in a critical section is not bypassed by throwing an exception. If an exception is thrown before the end of the section, the finally clause will relinquish the lock, but the object may be in a damaged state.

---

java.util.concurrent.locks.Lock 5.0

- void lock()
  acquires this lock; blocks if the lock is currently owned by another thread.
- void unlock()
  releases this lock.

---

java.util.concurrent.locks.ReentrantLock 5.0

- ReentrantLock()
  constructs a reentrant lock that can be used to protect a critical section.
- ReentrantLock(boolean fair)
  constructs a lock with the given fairness policy. A fair lock favors the thread that has been waiting for the longest time. However, this fairness guarantee can be a significant drag on performance. Therefore, by default, locks are not required to be fair.

Caution: It sounds nice to be fair, but fair locks can be *a lot slower* than regular locks. You should only enable fair locking if you truly know what you are doing and have a specific reason to consider fairness essential for your program. Even if you use a fair lock, you have no guarantee that the thread scheduler is fair. If the thread scheduler chooses to neglect a thread that has been waiting a long time for the lock, it doesn't get the chance to be treated fairly by the lock.

10.5.4. Condition Objects

Often, a thread enters a critical section only to discover that it can't proceed until a condition is fulfilled. Use a *condition object* to manage threads that have acquired a lock but cannot do useful work. In this section, I introduce the implementation of condition objects in the Java library. (For historical reasons, condition objects are often called *condition variables*.)

Let us refine our simulation of the bank. We do not want to transfer money out of an account that does not have the funds to cover the transfer. Note that we cannot use code like

```
if (bank.getBalance(from) >= amount)
   bank.transfer(from, to, amount);
```

It is entirely possible that the current thread will be deactivated between the successful outcome of the test and the call to transfer.

```
if (bank.getBalance(from) >= amount)
      // thread might be deactivated at this point
   bank.transfer(from, to, amount);
```

By the time the thread is running again, the account balance may have fallen below the withdrawal amount. You must make sure that no other thread can modify the balance between the test and the transfer action. You do so by protecting both the test and the transfer action with a lock:

```
public void transfer(int from, int to, int amount)
{
   bankLock.lock();
   try
   {
      while (accounts[from] < amount)
      {
         // wait
         . . .
      }
      // transfer funds
```

```
      . . .
    }
    finally
    {
        bankLock.unlock();
    }
}
```

Now, what do we do when there is not enough money in the account? We wait until some other thread has added funds. But this thread has just gained exclusive access to the bankLock, so no other thread has a chance to make a deposit. This is where condition objects come in.

A lock object can have one or more associated condition objects. You obtain a condition object with the newCondition method. It is customary to give each condition object a name that evokes the condition that it represents. For example, here we set up a condition object to represent the "sufficient funds" condition.

```
class Bank
{
    . . .
    private final Condition sufficientFunds = bankLock.newCondition();
    . . .
}
```

If the transfer method finds that sufficient funds are not available, it calls

```
sufficientFunds.await();
```

The current thread is now deactivated and gives up the lock. This lets in another thread that can, we hope, increase the account balance.

There is an essential difference between a thread that is waiting to acquire a lock and a thread that has called await. Once a thread calls the await method, it enters a *wait set* for that condition. The thread is *not* made runnable when the lock is available. Instead, it stays deactivated until another thread has called the signalAll method on the same condition.

When another thread has transferred money, it should call

```
sufficientFunds.signalAll();
```

This call reactivates all threads waiting for the condition. When the threads are removed from the wait set, they are again runnable and the scheduler will eventually activate them again. At that time, they will attempt to reenter the object. As soon as the lock is available, one of them will acquire the lock *and continue where it left off*, returning from the call to await.

At this time, the thread should test the condition again. There is no guarantee that the condition is now fulfilled—the signalAll method merely signals to the waiting threads that it *may be* fulfilled at this time and that it is worth checking for the condition again.

 Note: In general, a call to await should be inside a loop of the form

```
while (!(OK to proceed))
    condition.await();
```

It is crucially important that *some* other thread calls the signalAll method eventually. When a thread calls await, it has no way of reactivating itself. It puts its faith in the other threads. If none of them bother to reactivate the waiting thread, it will never run again. This can lead to unpleasant *deadlock* situations. If all other threads are blocked and the last active thread calls await without unblocking one of the others, it also blocks. No thread is left to unblock the others, and the program hangs.

When should you call signalAll? The rule of thumb is to call signalAll whenever the state of an object changes in a way that might be advantageous to waiting threads. For example, whenever an account balance changes, the waiting threads should be given another chance to inspect the balance. In our example, we call signalAll when we have finished the funds transfer.

```
public void transfer(int from, int to, int amount)
{
    bankLock.lock();
    try
    {
        while (accounts[from] < amount)
            sufficientFunds.await();
        // transfer funds
        . . .
        sufficientFunds.signalAll();
    }
    finally
    {
        bankLock.unlock();
    }
}
```

Note that the call to signalAll does not immediately activate a waiting thread. It only unblocks the waiting threads so that they can compete for entry into the object after the current thread has relinquished the lock.

Another method, signal, unblocks only a single thread from the wait set, chosen at random. That is more efficient than unblocking all threads, but there is a danger. If the randomly chosen thread finds that it still cannot proceed, it becomes blocked again. If no other thread calls signal again, the system deadlocks.

 Caution: A thread can only call await, signalAll, or signal on a condition if it owns the lock of the condition.

The sample program in the synch package has the same main method as the unsynch version in Listing 10.5, but the Bank class (Listing 10.6) uses locks. You will notice that nothing ever goes wrong. The total balance stays at $100,000 forever. No account ever has a negative balance. (Again, press Ctrl+C to terminate the program.) You may also notice that the program runs a bit slower—that is the price you pay for the added bookkeeping involved in the synchronization mechanism.

When reading through the source code, notice that the transfer and getTotalBalance methods are protected by a lock, but the size method is not. In this simulation, the number of accounts never changes after construction, so there is no need for granting exclusive access to the size method.

Listing 10.6 synch/Bank.java

```
1   package synch;
2
3   import java.util.*;
4   import java.util.concurrent.locks.*;
5
6   /**
7    * A bank with a number of bank accounts that uses locks for serializing access.
8    */
9   public class Bank
10  {
11     private final double[] accounts;
12     private final Lock bankLock = new ReentrantLock();
13     private final Condition sufficientFunds = bankLock.newCondition();
14
15     /**
16      * Constructs the bank.
17      * @param n the number of accounts
18      * @param initialBalance the initial balance for each account
19      */
20     public Bank(int n, double initialBalance)
21     {
22        accounts = new double[n];
23        Arrays.fill(accounts, initialBalance);
24     }
25
26     /**
```

```
27    * Transfers money from one account to another.
28    * @param from the account to transfer from
29    * @param to the account to transfer to
30    * @param amount the amount to transfer
31    */
32   public void transfer(int from, int to, double amount) throws InterruptedException
33   {
34      bankLock.lock();
35      try
36      {
37         while (accounts[from] < amount)
38            sufficientFunds.await();
39         System.out.print(Thread.currentThread());
40         accounts[from] -= amount;
41         System.out.printf(" %10.2f from %d to %d", amount, from, to);
42         accounts[to] += amount;
43         System.out.printf(" Total Balance: %10.2f%n", getTotalBalance());
44         sufficientFunds.signalAll();
45      }
46      finally
47      {
48         bankLock.unlock();
49      }
50   }
51
52   /**
53    * Gets the sum of all account balances.
54    * @return the total balance
55    */
56   public double getTotalBalance()
57   {
58      bankLock.lock();
59      try
60      {
61         double sum = 0;
62
63         for (double a : accounts)
64            sum += a;
65
66         return sum;
67      }
68      finally
69      {
70         bankLock.unlock();
71      }
72   }
73
74   /**
75    * Gets the number of accounts in the bank.
76    * @return the number of accounts
77    */
78   public int size()
```

```
79     {
80         return accounts.length;
81     }
82  }
```

java.util.concurrent.locks.Lock 5.0

■ Condition newCondition()
  returns a condition object associated with this lock.

java.util.concurrent.locks.Condition 5.0

■ void await()
  puts this thread on the wait set for this condition.
■ void signalAll()
  unblocks all threads in the wait set for this condition.
■ void signal()
  unblocks one randomly selected thread in the wait set for this condition.

10.5.5. Deadlocks

Locks and conditions cannot solve all problems that might arise in multithreading. Consider the following situation:

1. Account 1: $200
2. Account 2: $300
3. Thread 1: Transfer $300 from Account 1 to Account 2
4. Thread 2: Transfer $400 from Account 2 to Account 1

As Figure 10.4 indicates, Threads 1 and 2 are clearly blocked. Neither can proceed because the balances in Accounts 1 and 2 are insufficient.

It is possible that all threads get blocked because each is waiting for more money. Such a situation is called a *deadlock*.

In our program, a deadlock cannot occur for a simple reason. Each transfer amount is for, at most, $1,000. Since there are 100 accounts and a total of $100,000 in them, at least one of the accounts must have at least $1,000 at any time. The thread moving money out of that account can therefore proceed.

But if you change the run method of the threads to remove the $1,000 transaction limit, deadlocks will occur quickly. Try it out. Set NACCOUNTS to 10. Construct each transfer runnable with a max value of 2 * INITIAL_BALANCE and run the program. The program will run for a while and then hang.

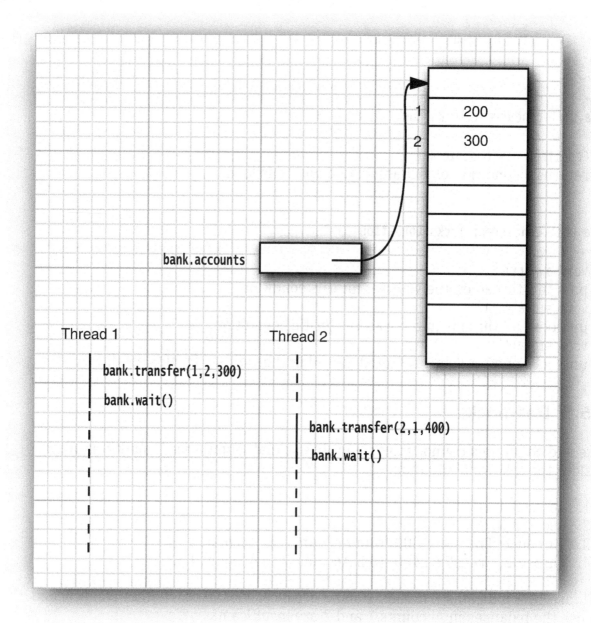

Figure 10.4: A deadlock situation

 Tip: When the program hangs, press Ctrl+\. You will get a thread dump that lists all threads. Each thread has a stack trace, telling you where it is currently blocked. Alternatively, run jconsole, as described in Chapter 7, and consult the Threads panel (see Figure 10.5).

Another way to create a deadlock is to make the ith thread responsible for putting money into the ith account, rather than for taking it out of the ith account. In this case, there is a

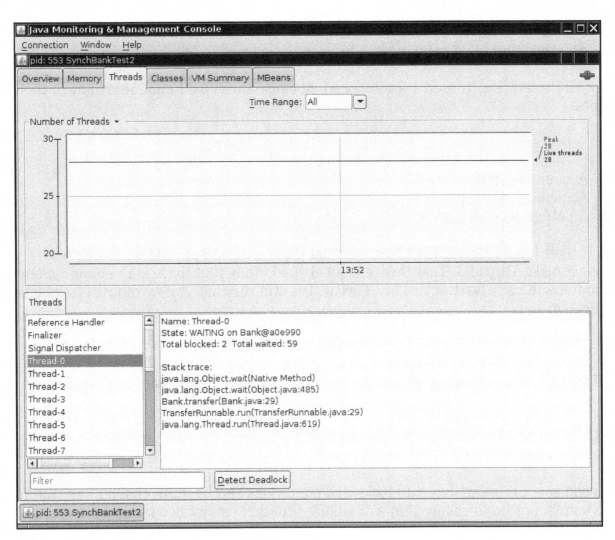

Figure 10.5: The Threads panel in jconsole

chance that all threads will simultaneously try to overdraw the same account, leaving no thread that can replenish it. Try it out. In the SynchBankTest program, turn to the run method of the TransferRunnable class. In the call to transfer, flip fromAccount and toAccount. Run the program and see how it deadlocks almost immediately.

Here is another situation in which a deadlock can occur easily. Change the signalAll method to signal in the SynchBankTest program. You will find that the program eventually hangs. (Again, set NACCOUNTS to 10 to observe the effect more quickly.) Unlike signalAll, which notifies all threads that are waiting for added funds, the signal method unblocks only one thread. If that thread can't proceed, all threads can be blocked. Consider the following sample scenario of a developing deadlock:

1. Account 1: $1,990
2. All other accounts: $990 each

3. Thread 1: Transfer $995 from Account 1 to Account 2
4. All other threads: Transfer $995 from their account to another account

Clearly, all threads but Thread 1 are blocked, because there isn't enough money in their accounts.

Thread 1 proceeds. Afterward, we have the following situation:

1. Account 1: $995
2. Account 2: $1,985
3. All other accounts: $990 each

Then, Thread 1 calls signal. The signal method picks a thread at random to unblock. Suppose it picks Thread 3. That thread is awakened, finds that there isn't enough money in its account, and calls await again. But Thread 1 is still running. A new random transaction is generated, say,

1. Thread 1: Transfer $997 from Account 1 to Account 2

Now, Thread 1 also calls await, and *all* threads are blocked. The system has deadlocked.

The culprit here is the call to signal. It only unblocks one thread, and it may not pick the thread that is essential to make progress. (In our scenario, Thread 2 must proceed to take money out of Account 2.)

As you can see, programming with locks and conditions can be quite challenging. You must design your program to ensure that a deadlock situation cannot occur.

10.5.6. The synchronized Keyword

In the preceding sections, you saw how to use Lock and Condition objects. Before going any further, let us summarize the key points about locks and conditions:

- A lock protects sections of code, allowing only one thread to execute the code at a time.
- A lock manages threads that are trying to enter a critical section.
- A lock can have one or more associated condition objects.
- Each condition object manages threads that have entered a critical section but that cannot proceed.

The Lock and Condition interfaces give programmers a high degree of control over locking. However, in most situations, you don't need that control—you can use a mechanism that is built into the Java language. Ever since version 1.0, *every object* in Java has an intrinsic lock. If a method is declared with the synchronized keyword, the object's lock protects the entire method. That is, to call the method, a thread must acquire the intrinsic object lock.

In other words,

```
public synchronized void method()
{
    method body
}
```

is the equivalent of

```
public void method()
{
    this.intrinsicLock.lock();
    try
    {
        method body
    }
    finally
    {
        this.intrinsicLock.unlock();
    }
}
```

For example, instead of using an explicit lock, we can simply declare the transfer method of the Bank class as synchronized.

The intrinsic object lock has a single associated condition. The wait method adds a thread to the wait set, and the notifyAll/notify methods unblock waiting threads. In other words, calling wait or notifyAll is the equivalent of

```
intrinsicCondition.await();
intrinsicCondition.signalAll();
```

 Note: The wait, notifyAll, and notify methods are final methods of the Object class. The Condition methods had to be named await, signalAll, and signal so that they don't conflict with those methods.

For example, you can implement the Bank class in Java like this:

```
class Bank
{
    private double[] accounts;

    public synchronized void transfer(int from, int to, int amount)
            throws InterruptedException
    {
        while (accounts[from] < amount)
            wait(); // wait on intrinsic object lock's single condition
```

```
      accounts[from] -= amount;
      accounts[to] += amount;
      notifyAll(); // notify all threads waiting on the condition
   }

   public synchronized double getTotalBalance()
   {
      . . .
   }
}
```

As you can see, using the synchronized keyword yields code that is much more concise. Of course, to understand this code, you have to know that each object has an intrinsic lock, and that the lock has an intrinsic condition. The lock manages the threads that try to enter a synchronized method. The condition manages the threads that have called wait.

It is also legal to declare static methods as synchronized. If such a method is called, it acquires the intrinsic lock of the associated class object. For example, if the Bank class has a static synchronized method, then the lock of the Bank.class object is locked when it is called. As a result, no other thread can call this or any other synchronized static method of the same class.

The intrinsic locks and conditions have some limitations. Among them:

- Virtual threads are *pinned* when acquiring an intrinsic lock. They cannot be unmounted from their carrier thread until the lock is relinquished. Pinning is not a problem if the critical section is immediately exited. But if the virtual thread blocks while pinned, this can seriously degrade throughput and even cause starvation of the carrier thread pool.
- You cannot interrupt a thread that is trying to acquire an intrinsic lock. With a ReentrantLock, you can call lockInterruptibly.
- You cannot specify a timeout when trying to acquire an intrinsic lock.
- Having a single condition per lock can be inefficient.

What should you use in your code—Lock and Condition objects or synchronized methods? Here is my recommendation:

- It is best to use neither Lock/Condition nor the synchronized keyword. In many situations, you can use one of the mechanisms of the java.util.concurrent package that do all the locking for you. For example, in Section 10.6.1, you will see how to use a blocking queue to synchronize threads that work on a common task.
- If the synchronized keyword works for your situation, by all means, use it. You'll write less code and have less room for error. Listing 10.7 shows the bank example, implemented with synchronized methods. However, consider the fact that the lock is public—see the next section.
- Use Lock/Condition if you use virtual threads, or if you really need the additional power that these constructs give you.

Tip: To find out whether pinned threads are blocked, start the JVM with one of the options

```
-Djdk.tracePinnedThreads=short
-Djdk.tracePinnedThreads=full
```

You get a stack trace that shows when a pinned thread blocks:

```
. . .
org.apache.tomcat.util.net.SocketProcessorBase.run(SocketProcessorBase.java:49)
   <== monitors:1
. . .
```

Note that you get only one warning per pinning location!

Alternatively, record with Java Flight Recorder, view with your favorite mission control viewer, and look for VirtualThreadPinned and VirtualThreadSubmitFailed events.

Listing 10.7 synch2/Bank.java

```java
1   package synch2;
2
3   import java.util.*;
4
5   /**
6    * A bank with a number of bank accounts that uses synchronization primitives.
7    */
8   public class Bank
9   {
10     private final double[] accounts;
11
12     /**
13      * Constructs the bank.
14      * @param n the number of accounts
15      * @param initialBalance the initial balance for each account
16      */
17     public Bank(int n, double initialBalance)
18     {
19        accounts = new double[n];
20        Arrays.fill(accounts, initialBalance);
21     }
22
23     /**
24      * Transfers money from one account to another.
25      * @param from the account to transfer from
26      * @param to the account to transfer to
27      * @param amount the amount to transfer
```

```
28        */
29       public synchronized void transfer(int from, int to, double amount)
30              throws InterruptedException
31       {
32          while (accounts[from] < amount)
33             wait();
34          System.out.print(Thread.currentThread());
35          accounts[from] -= amount;
36          System.out.printf(" %10.2f from %d to %d", amount, from, to);
37          accounts[to] += amount;
38          System.out.printf(" Total Balance: %10.2f%n", getTotalBalance());
39          notifyAll();
40       }
41
42       /**
43        * Gets the sum of all account balances.
44        * @return the total balance
45        */
46       public synchronized double getTotalBalance()
47       {
48          double sum = 0;
49
50          for (double a : accounts)
51             sum += a;
52
53          return sum;
54       }
55
56       /**
57        * Gets the number of accounts in the bank.
58        * @return the number of accounts
59        */
60       public int size()
61       {
62          return accounts.length;
63       }
64    }
```

---

java.lang.Object 1.0

- void notifyAll()

  unblocks the threads that called wait on this object. This method can only be called from within a synchronized method or block. The method throws an IllegalMonitorStateException if the current thread is not the owner of the object's lock.

- void notify()

  unblocks one randomly selected thread among the threads that called wait on this object. This method can only be called from within a synchronized method or block. The method throws an IllegalMonitorStateException if the current thread is not the owner of the object's lock.

- `void wait()`
  causes a thread to wait until it is notified. This method can only be called from within a synchronized method or block. It throws an `IllegalMonitorStateException` if the current thread is not the owner of the object's lock.
- `void wait(long millis)`
- `void wait(long millis, int nanos)`
  cause a thread to wait until it is notified or until the specified amount of time has passed. These methods can only be called from within a synchronized method or block. They throw an `IllegalMonitorStateException` if the current thread is not the owner of the object's lock. The number of nanoseconds may not exceed 1,000,000.

10.5.7. Synchronized Blocks

As we just discussed, every Java object has a lock. A thread can acquire the lock by calling a synchronized method. There is a second mechanism for acquiring the lock: by entering a *synchronized block*. When a thread enters a block of the form

```java
synchronized (obj) // this is the syntax for a synchronized block
{
    critical section
}
```

then it acquires the lock for `obj`.

You will sometimes find "ad hoc" locks, such as

```java
public class Bank
{
    private double[] accounts;
    private final Object lock = new Object();
    . . .
    public void transfer(int from, int to, int amount)
    {
        synchronized (lock) // an ad-hoc lock
        {
            accounts[from] -= amount;
            accounts[to] += amount;
        }
        System.out.println(. . .);
    }
}
```

Here, the `lock` object is created only to use the lock that every Java object possesses.

Caution: With synchronized blocks, be careful about the lock object. For example, this will not work:

```
private final String lock = "LOCK";
. . .
synchronized (lock) { . . . } // Don't lock on string literal!
```

If this occurs twice in the same program, the locks are *the same object* since string literals are shared. This can lead to a deadlock.

Also, stay away from using primitive type wrappers as locks:

```
private final Integer lock = new Integer(42); // Don't lock on wrappers
```

The constructor call new Integer(42) is deprecated, and you don't want a maintenance programmer to change the call to Integer.valueOf(42). If done twice with the same magic number, the lock will be accidentally shared.

If you need to modify a static field, lock on the specific class, not on the value returned by getClass():

```
synchronized (MyClass.class) { staticCounter++; } // OK
synchronized (getClass()) { staticCounter++; } // Don't
```

If the method containing this code is called from a subclass, then getClass() returns a different Class object! You are no longer guaranteed mutual exclusion!

In general, if you must use synchronized blocks, *know your lock object*! You must use the same lock for all critical sections, and nobody else must use your lock.

Sometimes, programmers use the lock of an object to implement additional atomic operations—a practice known as *client-side locking*. Consider, for example, the Vector class, which is a list whose methods are synchronized. Now suppose we stored our bank balances in a Vector<Double>. Here is a naive implementation of a transfer method:

```
public void transfer(Vector<Double> accounts, int from, int to, int amount) // ERROR
{
    accounts.set(from, accounts.get(from) - amount);
    accounts.set(to, accounts.get(to) + amount);
    System.out.println(. . .);
}
```

The get and set methods of the Vector class are synchronized, but that doesn't help us. It is entirely possible for a thread to be preempted in the transfer method after the first call to get has been completed. Another thread may then store a different value into the same position. However, we can hijack the lock:

```
public void transfer(Vector<Double> accounts, int from, int to, int amount)
{
   synchronized (accounts)
   {
      accounts.set(from, accounts.get(from) - amount);
      accounts.set(to, accounts.get(to) + amount);
   }
   System.out.println(. . .);
}
```

This approach works, but it is entirely dependent on the fact that the Vector class uses the intrinsic lock for all of its mutator methods. However, is this really a fact? The documentation of the Vector class makes no such promise. You have to carefully study the source code and hope that future versions do not introduce unsynchronized mutators. As you can see, client-side locking is very fragile and not generally recommended.

 Note: The Java virtual machine has built-in support for synchronized methods. However, synchronized blocks are compiled into a lengthy sequence of bytecodes to manage the intrinsic lock.

10.5.8. The Monitor Concept

Locks and conditions are powerful tools for thread synchronization, but they are not very object-oriented. For many years, researchers have looked for ways to make multithreading safe without forcing programmers to think about explicit locks. One of the most successful solutions is the *monitor* concept that was pioneered by Per Brinch Hansen and Tony Hoare in the 1970s. In the terminology of Java, a monitor has these properties:

- A monitor is a class with only private fields.
- Each object of that class has an associated lock.
- All methods are locked by that lock. In other words, if a client calls obj.method(), then the lock for obj is automatically acquired at the beginning of the method call and relinquished when the method returns. Since all fields are private, this arrangement ensures that no thread can access the fields while another thread manipulates them.
- The lock can have any number of associated conditions.

Earlier versions of monitors had a single condition, with a rather elegant syntax. You can simply call await accounts[from] >= amount without using an explicit condition variable. However, research showed that indiscriminate retesting of conditions can be inefficient. This problem is solved with explicit condition variables, each managing a separate set of threads.

The Java designers loosely adapted the monitor concept. *Every object* in Java has an intrinsic lock and an intrinsic condition. If a method is declared with the synchronized keyword, it acts like a monitor method. The condition variable is accessed by calling `wait/notifyAll/notify`.

However, a Java object differs from a monitor in three important ways, compromising thread safety:

■ Fields are not required to be `private`.
■ Methods are not required to be `synchronized`.
■ The intrinsic lock is available to clients.

This disrespect for security enraged Per Brinch Hansen. In a scathing review of the multithreading primitives in Java, he wrote: "It is astounding to me that Java's insecure parallelism is taken seriously by the programming community, a quarter of a century after the invention of monitors and Concurrent Pascal. It has no merit" (Java's Insecure Parallelism, *ACM SIGPLAN Notices* 34:38–45, April 1999).

10.5.9. Volatile Fields

Sometimes, it seems excessive to pay the cost of synchronization just to read or write an instance field or two. After all, what can go wrong? Unfortunately, with modern processors and compilers, there is plenty of room for error.

■ Computers with multiple processors can temporarily hold memory values in registers or local memory caches. As a consequence, threads running in different processors may see different values for the same memory location!
■ Compilers can reorder instructions for maximum throughput. Compilers won't choose an ordering that changes the meaning of the code, but they make the assumption that memory values are only changed when there are explicit instructions in the code. However, a memory value can be changed by another thread!

If you use locks to protect code that can be accessed by multiple threads, you won't have these problems. Compilers are required to respect locks by flushing or re-fetching register values, not reordering instructions inappropriately, and issuing memory fence instructions. The details are explained in the Java Memory Model Specification (section 17.4 of the Java Language Specification). Much of the specification is highly complex and technical, but the section also contains a number of clearly explained examples.

 Note: Brian Goetz coined the following "synchronization motto": "If you write a variable which may next be read by another thread, or you read a variable which may have last been written by another thread, you must use synchronization."

The `volatile` keyword offers a lock-free mechanism for synchronizing access to an instance field. If you declare a field as `volatile`, then the compiler and the virtual machine take into account that the field may be concurrently updated by another thread.

For example, suppose an object has a `boolean` flag done that is set by one thread and queried by another thread. As we already discussed, you can use a lock:

```
private boolean done;
public synchronized boolean isDone() { return done; }
public synchronized void setDone() { done = true; }
```

Perhaps it is not a good idea to use the intrinsic object lock. The `isDone` and `setDone` methods can block if another thread has locked the object. If that is a concern, one can use a separate lock just for this variable. But this is getting to be a lot of trouble.

In this case, it is reasonable to declare the field as `volatile`:

```
private volatile boolean done;
public boolean isDone() { return done; }
public void setDone() { done = true; }
```

The compiler will insert the appropriate code to ensure that a change to the done variable in one thread is visible from any other thread that reads the variable.

 Caution: Volatile variables do not provide any atomicity. For example, the method

```
public void flipDone() { done = !done; } // not atomic
```

is not guaranteed to flip the value of the field. There is no guarantee that the reading, flipping, and writing is uninterrupted.

10.5.10. Final Fields

As you saw in the preceding section, you cannot safely read a field from multiple threads unless you use locks or the `volatile` modifier.

There is one other situation in which it is safe to access a shared field—when it is declared final. Once the constructor has completed, any thread with a reference to the object will see the final fields with their initialized values.

Consider

```
public class Bank
{
    final HashMap<String, Double> accounts;

    public Bank()
    {
```

```
        accounts = new HashMap<>();
    }
}
```

Other threads get to see the initialized `accounts` variable after the constructor has finished.

Without using `final`, there would be no guarantee that other threads would see the updated value of `accounts`—they might all see `null`, not the constructed `HashMap`.

Of course, the operations on the map are not thread-safe. If multiple threads mutate and read the map, you still need synchronization.

 Caution: The guarantee has an important caveat: the reference to `this` must not have *escaped* during construction. The reference escapes if the constructor assigns `this` to a field of another object or passes `this` to another method.

An object is *properly constructed* if the `this` reference does not escape during construction. If an object was properly constructed and all fields are `final`, it can be safely shared without synchronization.

10.5.11. Atomics

You can declare shared variables as `volatile` provided you perform no operations other than assignment.

There are a number of classes in the `java.util.concurrent.atomic` package that use efficient machine-level instructions to guarantee atomicity of other operations without using locks. For example, the `AtomicInteger` class has methods `incrementAndGet` and `decrementAndGet` that atomically increment or decrement an integer. For example, you can safely generate a sequence of numbers like this:

```
public static final AtomicLong nextNumber = new AtomicLong();
// in some thread. . .
long id = nextNumber.incrementAndGet();
```

The `incrementAndGet` method atomically increments the `AtomicLong` and returns the post-increment value. That is, the operations of getting the value, adding 1, setting it, and producing the new value cannot be preempted. It is guaranteed that the correct value is computed and returned, even if multiple threads access the same instance concurrently.

There are methods for atomically setting, adding, and subtracting values, but if you want to make a more complex update, you have to use the `compareAndSet` method. For example, suppose you want to keep track of the largest value that is observed by different threads. The following won't work:

```
public static final AtomicLong largest = new AtomicLong();
// in some thread. . .
largest.set(Math.max(largest.get(), observed)); // ERROR--race condition!
```

This update is not atomic. Instead, provide a lambda expression for updating the variable, and the update is done for you. In our example, we can call

```
largest.updateAndGet(x -> Math.max(x, observed));
```

or

```
largest.accumulateAndGet(observed, Math::max);
```

The accumulateAndGet method takes a binary operator that is used to combine the atomic value and the supplied argument.

There are also methods getAndUpdate and getAndAccumulate that return the old value.

 Note: These methods are also provided for the classes AtomicInteger, AtomicIntegerArray, AtomicIntegerFieldUpdater, AtomicLongArray, AtomicLongFieldUpdater, AtomicReference, AtomicReferenceArray, and AtomicReferenceFieldUpdater.

When you have a very large number of threads accessing the same atomic values, performance suffers because the optimistic updates require too many retries. The LongAdder and LongAccumulator classes solve this problem. A LongAdder is composed of multiple variables whose collective sum is the current value. Multiple threads can update different summands, and new summands are automatically provided when the number of threads increases. This is efficient in the common situation where the value of the sum is not needed until after all work has been done. The performance improvement can be substantial.

If you anticipate high contention, you should simply use a LongAdder instead of an AtomicLong. The method names are slightly different. Call increment to increment a counter or add to add a quantity, and sum to retrieve the total.

```
final var adder = new LongAdder();
for (. . .)
   executor.submit(() ->
      {
         while (. . .)
         {
            . . .
            if (. . .) adder.increment();
         }
```

```
    });
    . . .
long total = adder.sum();
```

 Note: Of course, the increment method does *not* return the old value. Doing that would undo the efficiency gain of splitting the sum into multiple summands.

The LongAccumulator generalizes this idea to an arbitrary accumulation operation. In the constructor, you provide the operation, as well as its neutral element. To incorporate new values, call accumulate. Call get to obtain the current value. The following has the same effect as a LongAdder:

```
final var adder = new LongAccumulator(Long::sum, 0);
// in some thread. . .
adder.accumulate(value);
```

Internally, the accumulator has variables $a_1, a_2, \ldots, a_n$. Each variable is initialized with the neutral element (0 in our example).

When accumulate is called with value v, then one of them is atomically updated as $a_i = a_i\ op\ v$, where *op* is the accumulation operation written in infix form. In our example, a call to accumulate computes $a_i = a_i + v$ for some i.

The result of get is $a_1\ op\ a_2\ op \ldots op\ a_n$. In our example, that is the sum of the accumulators, $a_1 + a_2 + \ldots + a_n$.

To compute maximum or minimum, use Math.max or Math.min for the operation. In general, the operation must be associative and commutative. That means that the final result must be independent of the order in which the intermediate values were combined.

There are also DoubleAdder and DoubleAccumulator that work in the same way, except with double values.

10.5.12. On-Demand Initialization

Sometimes, you have a data structure that you only want to initialize when it is first needed. And you want to ensure that initialization happens exactly once. Instead of designing your own mechanism, make use of the fact that the virtual machine executes a static initializer exactly once when the class is first used. The virtual machine ensures this with a lock, so you don't have to program your own.

```
public class OnDemandData
{
    // private constructor to ensure only one object is constructed
```

```
    private OnDemandData()
    {
        . . .
    }

    public static OnDemandData getInstance()
    {
        return Holder.INSTANCE;
    }

    // only initialized on first use, i.e. in the first call to getInstance
    private static class Holder
    {
        // VM guarantees that this happens lazily and at most once
        static final OnDemandData INSTANCE = new OnDemandData();
    }
}
```

 Caution: To use this idiom, you must ensure that the constructor doesn't throw any exceptions. The virtual machine will not make a second attempt to initialize the holder class.

10.5.13. Safe Publication

As you saw in Section 10.5.10, the final fields of a properly constructed object will be seen by all threads with their initialized values. What about the non-final fields?

The Java language makes no guarantee in general. For example, consider:

```
public class BankAccount
{
    private double balance;

    public BankAccount(double initialBalance) { balance = initialBalance; }
    public double getBalance() { return balance; }
    . . .
}
```

If you construct a new BankAccount(1000) object in one thread, and another thread has a reference to the object, it might see getBalance() return zero.

Of course, a mutable BankAccount class should have thread-safe methods getBalance, deposit, withdraw that protect the balance field with a lock. Then getBalance will report the correct balance.

Now consider the hopefully uncommon case where you share an object that is neither thread-safe nor immutable. Then you need to ensure that the object is *safely published*—that is, all fields are visible with the values that were set in the constructor. This is ensured when the object reference is stored:

- In a static initializer (as in the preceding section)
- In a `volatile` field or `AtomicReference`
- In any field when the assignment is protected by a lock
- In a `final` field of a properly constructed object

The third condition is fulfilled when a `Runnable` or `Callable` is an inner class or lambda expression that captures a variable from the enclosing scope. The captured variable is stored in a `final` field of the inner class.

The last condition is fulfilled when you store the object reference in a thread-safe data structure, for example a `BlockingQueue` or `ConcurrentHashMap`. The retrieving thread will see the object in its published state.

As you can see, in most reasonable circumstances, nothing evil will happen. If you find yourself in a situation where these details matter, you are on thin ice and may want to rethink your sharing strategy.

10.5.14. Sharing with Thread-Local Variables

In the preceding sections, we discussed the risks of sharing variables between threads. Sometimes, you can avoid sharing by giving each thread its own instance, using the thread-local variables (see Section 10.4.4). For example, the `SimpleDateFormat` class is not thread-safe. Suppose we have a static variable

```
public static final SimpleDateFormat DATEFORMAT = new SimpleDateFormat("yyyy-MM-dd");
```

If two threads execute an operation such as

```
String DATEFORMAT = dateFormat.format(new Date());
```

then the result can be garbage since the internal data structures used by the `dateFormat` can be corrupted by concurrent access. You could use synchronization, which is expensive, or you could construct a local `SimpleDateFormat` object whenever you need it, but that is also wasteful.

To construct one instance per thread, use the following code:

```
public static final ThreadLocal<SimpleDateFormat> DATEFORMAT =
    ThreadLocal.withInitial(() -> new SimpleDateFormat("yyyy-MM-dd"));
```

To access the actual formatter, call

```
String dateStamp = DATEFORMAT.get().format(new Date());
```

The first time you call get in a given thread, the lambda in the constructor is called. From then on, the get method returns the instance belonging to the current thread.

 Preview Note: As pointed out in Section 10.4.4, thread-local variables may not be appropriate for large numbers of virtual threads. Extent locals, a preview feature in Java 21, provide a more performant alternative.

A related problem is the generation of random numbers in multiple threads. The java.util.Random class is thread-safe. However, the computation that yields a new random value and updates the state of the generator can be inefficient if multiple threads use a single shared generator.

You could use the ThreadLocal helper to give each thread a separate generator. But there is a convenience class that is optimized for this situation:

```
int random = ThreadLocalRandom.current().nextInt(upperBound);
```

The call ThreadLocalRandom.current() returns a random number generator with a per-thread state. In its current implementation, it stores the generator state in instance variables of the Thread object.

---

java.lang.ThreadLocal<T> 1.2

- static <S> ThreadLocal<S> withInitial(Supplier<? extends S> supplier) **8**
  creates a thread-local variable whose initial value is produced by invoking the given supplier.

---

java.util.concurrent.ThreadLocalRandom 7

- static ThreadLocalRandom current()
  returns a random generator class whose state is local to the current thread.

10.6. Thread-Safe Collections

If multiple threads concurrently modify a data structure, such as a hash table, it is easy to damage that data structure. (See Chapter 9 for more information on hash tables.) For example, one thread may begin to insert a new element. Suppose it is preempted in the middle of rerouting the links between the hash table's buckets. If another thread starts traversing the same list, it may follow invalid links and create havoc, perhaps throwing exceptions or getting trapped in an infinite loop.

You can protect a shared data structure by supplying a lock, but it is usually easier to choose a thread-safe implementation instead. In the following sections, we discuss the thread-safe collections that the Java library provides.

10.6.1. Blocking Queues

Many threading problems can be formulated elegantly and safely by using one or more queues. Producer threads insert items into the queue, and consumer threads retrieve them. The queue lets you safely hand over data from one thread to another. For example, consider our bank transfer program. Instead of accessing the bank object directly, the transfer threads insert transfer instruction objects into a queue. Another thread removes the instructions from the queue and carries out the transfers. Only that thread has access to the internals of the bank object. No synchronization is necessary. (Of course, the implementors of the thread-safe queue classes had to worry about locks and conditions, but that was their problem, not yours.)

A *blocking queue* causes a thread to block when you try to add an element when the queue is currently full or to remove an element when the queue is empty. Blocking queues are a useful tool for coordinating the work of multiple threads. Worker threads can periodically deposit intermediate results into a blocking queue. Other worker threads remove the intermediate results and modify them further. The queue automatically balances the workload. If the first set of threads runs slower than the second, the second set blocks while waiting for the results. If the first set of threads runs faster, the queue fills up until the second set catches up. Table 10.2 shows the methods for blocking queues.

Table 10.2: Blocking Queue Methods

Method	Normal Action	Action in Special Circumstances
add	Adds an element	Throws an IllegalStateException if the queue is full
element	Returns the head element	Throws a NoSuchElementException if the queue is empty
offer	Adds an element and returns true	Returns false if the queue is full
peek	Returns the head element	Returns null if the queue is empty
poll	Removes and returns the head element	Returns null if the queue is empty
put	Adds an element	Blocks if the queue is full
remove	Removes and returns the head element	Throws a NoSuchElementException if the queue is empty

Method	Normal Action	Action in Special Circumstances
take	Removes and returns the head element	Blocks if the queue is empty

The blocking queue methods fall into three categories that differ by the action they perform when the queue is full or empty. If you use the queue as a thread management tool, use the put and take methods. The add, remove, and element operations throw an exception when you try to add to a full queue or get the head of an empty queue. Of course, in a multithreaded program, the queue might become full or empty at any time, so you will instead want to use the offer, poll, and peek methods. These methods simply return with a failure indicator instead of throwing an exception if they cannot carry out their tasks.

 Note: The poll and peek methods return null to indicate failure. Therefore, it is illegal to insert null values into these queues.

There are also variants of the offer and poll methods with a timeout. For example, the call

```
boolean success = q.offer(x, 100, TimeUnit.MILLISECONDS);
```

tries for 100 milliseconds to insert an element to the tail of the queue. If it succeeds, it returns true; otherwise, it returns false when it times out. Similarly, the call

```
Object head = q.poll(100, TimeUnit.MILLISECONDS);
```

tries for 100 milliseconds to remove the head of the queue. If it succeeds, it returns the head; otherwise, it returns null when it times out.

The put method blocks if the queue is full, and the take method blocks if the queue is empty. These are the equivalents of offer and poll with no timeout.

The java.util.concurrent package supplies several variations of blocking queues. By default, the LinkedBlockingQueue has no upper bound on its capacity, but a maximum capacity can be optionally specified. The LinkedBlockingDeque is a double-ended version. The ArrayBlockingQueue is constructed with a given capacity and an optional parameter to require fairness. If fairness is specified, then the longest-waiting threads are given preferential treatment. As always, fairness exacts a significant performance penalty, and you should only use it if your problem specifically requires it.

The PriorityBlockingQueue is a priority queue, not a first-in/first-out queue. Elements are removed in order of their priority. The queue has unbounded capacity, but retrieval will block if the queue is empty. (See Chapter 9 for more information on priority queues.)

The TransferQueue interface allows a producer thread to wait until a consumer is ready to take on an item. When a producer calls

```
q.transfer(item);
```

the call blocks until another thread removes it. The LinkedTransferQueue class implements this interface.

The program in Listing 10.8 shows how to use a blocking queue to control a set of threads. The program searches through all files in a directory and its subdirectories, printing lines that contain a given keyword.

A producer thread enumerates all files in all subdirectories and places them in a blocking queue. This operation is fast, and the queue would quickly fill up with all files in the file system if it was not bounded.

We also start a large number of search threads. Each search thread takes a file from the queue, opens it, prints all lines containing the keyword, and then takes the next file. We use a trick to terminate the application when no further work is required. In order to signal completion, the enumeration thread places a special termination object into the queue. (This is similar to a dummy suitcase with a label "last bag" in a baggage claim belt.) When a search thread takes the special object, it terminates, after putting the object back for other consumers to see.

Note: Some programmers use the term "poison pill" for an object that signals termination to the consumers.

Note that no explicit thread synchronization is required. In this application, we use the queue data structure as a synchronization mechanism.

Listing 10.8 blockingQueue/BlockingQueueTest.java

```java
1   package blockingQueue;
2
3   import java.io.*;
4   import java.nio.file.*;
5   import java.util.*;
6   import java.util.concurrent.*;
7   import java.util.stream.*;
8
9   /**
10   * @version 1.04 2023-07-30
11   * @author Cay Horstmann
12   */
13   public class BlockingQueueTest
```

```
14  {
15      private static final int FILE_QUEUE_SIZE = 10;
16      private static final int SEARCH_THREADS = 100;
17      private static final Path TERMINATION = Path.of("");
18      private static BlockingQueue<Path> queue = new ArrayBlockingQueue<>(FILE_QUEUE_SIZE);
19
20      public static void main(String[] args)
21      {
22          try (var in = new Scanner(System.in))
23          {
24              System.out.print("Enter base directory (e.g. /tmp/jdk-21-src): ");
25              String directory = in.nextLine();
26              System.out.print("Enter keyword (e.g. volatile): ");
27              String keyword = in.nextLine();
28
29              Runnable enumerator = () ->
30                  {
31                      try
32                      {
33                          enumerate(Path.of(directory));
34                          queue.put(TERMINATION);
35                      }
36                      catch (IOException e)
37                      {
38                          e.printStackTrace();
39                      }
40                      catch (InterruptedException e)
41                      {
42                      }
43                  };
44
45              Thread.ofPlatform().start(enumerator);
46              for (int i = 1; i <= SEARCH_THREADS; i++)
47              {
48                  Runnable searcher = () ->
49                      {
50                          try
51                          {
52                              boolean done = false;
53                              while (!done)
54                              {
55                                  Path file = queue.take();
56                                  if (file == TERMINATION)
57                                  {
58                                      queue.put(file);
59                                      done = true;
60                                  }
61                                  else search(file, keyword);
62                              }
63                          }
64                          catch (IOException e)
65                          {
```

```
 66                          e.printStackTrace();
 67                     }
 68                 catch (InterruptedException e)
 69                     {
 70                     }
 71             };
 72             Thread.ofPlatform().start(searcher);
 73         }
 74     }
 75 }
 76
 77     /**
 78      * Recursively enumerates all files in a given directory and its subdirectories.
 79      * See Chapters 1 and 2 of Volume II for the stream and file operations.
 80      * @param directory the directory in which to start
 81      */
 82     public static void enumerate(Path directory) throws IOException, InterruptedException
 83     {
 84         try (Stream<Path> children = Files.list(directory))
 85         {
 86             for (Path child : children.toList())
 87             {
 88                 if (Files.isDirectory(child))
 89                     enumerate(child);
 90                 else
 91                     queue.put(child);
 92             }
 93         }
 94     }
 95
 96     /**
 97      * Searches a file for a given keyword and prints all matching lines.
 98      * @param file the file to search
 99      * @param keyword the keyword to search for
100      */
101     public static void search(Path file, String keyword) throws IOException
102     {
103         try (var in = new Scanner(file))
104         {
105             int lineNumber = 0;
106             while (in.hasNextLine())
107             {
108                 lineNumber++;
109                 String line = in.nextLine();
110                 if (line.contains(keyword))
111                     System.out.printf("%s:%d:%s%n", file, lineNumber, line);
112             }
113         }
114     }
115 }
```

---

java.util.concurrent.ArrayBlockingQueue<E> 5.0

- ArrayBlockingQueue(int capacity)
- ArrayBlockingQueue(int capacity, boolean fair)
  construct a blocking queue with the given capacity and fairness settings. The queue is implemented as a circular array.

---

java.util.concurrent.LinkedBlockingQueue<E> 5.0

---

java.util.concurrent.LinkedBlockingDeque<E> 6

- LinkedBlockingQueue()
- LinkedBlockingDeque()
  construct an unbounded blocking queue or deque, implemented as a linked list.
- LinkedBlockingQueue(int capacity)
- LinkedBlockingDeque(int capacity)
  construct a bounded blocking queue or deque with the given capacity, implemented as a linked list.

---

java.util.concurrent.PriorityBlockingQueue<E> 5.0

- PriorityBlockingQueue()
- PriorityBlockingQueue(int initialCapacity)
- PriorityBlockingQueue(int initialCapacity, Comparator<? super E> comparator)
  construct an unbounded blocking priority queue implemented as a heap. The default for the initial capacity is 11. If the comparator is not specified, the elements must implement the Comparable interface.

---

java.util.concurrent.BlockingQueue<E> 5.0

- void put(E element)
  adds the element, blocking if necessary.
- E take()
  removes and returns the head element, blocking if necessary.
- boolean offer(E element, long time, TimeUnit unit)
  adds the given element and returns true if successful, blocking if necessary until the element has been added or the time has elapsed.
- E poll(long time, TimeUnit unit)
  removes and returns the head element, blocking if necessary until an element is available or the time has elapsed. Returns null upon failure.

`java.util.concurrent.BlockingDeque<E>` 6

- void putFirst(E element)
- void putLast(E element)
  add the element, blocking if necessary.
- E takeFirst()
- E takeLast()
  remove and return the head or tail element, blocking if necessary.
- boolean offerFirst(E element, long time, TimeUnit unit)
- boolean offerLast(E element, long time, TimeUnit unit)
  add the given element and return true if successful, blocking if necessary until the element has been added or the time has elapsed.
- E pollFirst(long time, TimeUnit unit)
- E pollLast(long time, TimeUnit unit)
  remove and return the head or tail element, blocking if necessary until an element is available or the time has elapsed. Returns null upon failure.

`java.util.concurrent.TransferQueue<E>` 7

- void transfer(E element)
- boolean tryTransfer(E element, long time, TimeUnit unit)
  transfer a value, or try transferring it with a given timeout, blocking until another thread has removed the item. The second method returns true if successful.

10.6.2. Efficient Maps, Sets, and Queues

The java.util.concurrent package supplies efficient implementations for maps, sorted sets, and queues: ConcurrentHashMap, ConcurrentSkipListMap, ConcurrentSkipListSet, and ConcurrentLinkedQueue.

These collections use sophisticated algorithms that minimize contention by allowing concurrent access to different parts of the data structure.

Unlike most collections, the size method of these classes does not necessarily operate in constant time. Determining the current size of one of these collections usually requires traversal.

 Note: Some applications use humongous concurrent hash maps, so large that the size method is insufficient because it returns an int. What is one to do with a map that has over two billion entries? The mappingCount method returns the size as a long.

The collections return *weakly consistent* iterators. That means that the iterators may or may not reflect all modifications that are made after they were constructed, but they will not return a value twice and they will not throw a ConcurrentModificationException.

Note: In contrast, an iterator of a collection in the java.util package throws a ConcurrentModificationException when the collection has been modified after construction of the iterator.

The concurrent hash map can efficiently support a large number of readers and a bounded number of writers.

Note: A hash map keeps all entries with the same hash code in the same "bucket." Some applications use poor hash functions, and as a result all entries end up in a small number of buckets, severely degrading performance. Even generally reasonable hash functions, such as that of the String class, can be problematic. For example, an attacker can slow down a program by crafting a large number of strings that hash to the same value. In recent Java versions, the concurrent hash map organizes the buckets as trees, not lists, when the key type implements Comparable, guaranteeing $O(\log n)$ performance.

---

java.util.concurrent.ConcurrentLinkedQueue<E> 5.0

- ConcurrentLinkedQueue<E>()
  constructs an unbounded, nonblocking queue that can be safely accessed by multiple threads.

---

java.util.concurrent.ConcurrentHashMap<K, V> 5.0

- ConcurrentHashMap<K, V>()
- ConcurrentHashMap<K, V>(int initialCapacity)
- ConcurrentHashMap<K, V>(int initialCapacity, float loadFactor, int concurrencyLevel)
  construct a hash map that can be safely accessed by multiple threads. The default for the initial capacity is 16. If the average load per bucket exceeds the load factor, the table is resized. The default is 0.75. The concurrency level is the estimated number of concurrent writer threads.

---

java.util.concurrent.ConcurrentSkipListSet<E> 6

- ■ ConcurrentSkipListSet<E>()
- ■ ConcurrentSkipListSet<E>(Comparator<? super E> comp)
  construct a sorted set that can be safely accessed by multiple threads. The first constructor requires that the elements implement the Comparable interface.

---

java.util.concurrent.ConcurrentSkipListMap<K, V> 6

- ■ ConcurrentSkipListMap<K, V>()
- ■ ConcurrentSkipListMap<K, V>(Comparator<? super K> comp)
  construct a sorted map that can be safely accessed by multiple threads. The first constructor requires that the keys implement the Comparable interface.

10.6.3. Atomic Update of Map Entries

The original version of ConcurrentHashMap only had a few methods for atomic updates, which made for somewhat awkward programming. Suppose we want to count how often certain features are observed. As a simple example, suppose multiple threads encounter words, and we want to count their frequencies.

Can we use a ConcurrentHashMap<String, Long>? Consider the code for incrementing a count. Obviously, the following is not thread-safe:

```
Long oldValue = map.get(word);
Long newValue = oldValue == null ? 1 : oldValue + 1;
map.put(word, newValue); // ERROR--might not replace oldValue
```

Another thread might be updating the exact same count at the same time.

 Note: Some programmers are surprised that a supposedly thread-safe data structure permits operations that are not thread-safe. But there are two entirely different considerations. If multiple threads modify a plain HashMap, they can destroy the internal structure (an array of linked lists). Some of the links may go missing, or even go in circles, rendering the data structure unusable. That will never happen with a ConcurrentHashMap. In the example above, the code for get and put will never corrupt the data structure. But, since the sequence of operations is not atomic, the result is not predictable.

In old versions of Java, it was necessary to use the replace method, which atomically replaces an old value with a new one, provided that no other thread has come before and replaced the old value with something else. You had to keep doing it until the attempt succeeded:

```
do
{
   oldValue = map.get(word);
   newValue = oldValue == null ? 1 : oldValue + 1;
}
while (!map.replace(word, oldValue, newValue));
```

An alternative was to use a ConcurrentHashMap<String, AtomicLong> and the following update code:

```
map.putIfAbsent(word, new AtomicLong());
map.get(word).incrementAndGet();
```

Unfortunately, in the first line, a new AtomicLong is constructed for each increment, and it will be discarded when it is not needed.

Nowadays, the Java API provides methods that make atomic updates more convenient and performant. The compute method is called with a key and a function to compute the new value. That function receives the key and the associated value, or null if there is none, and it computes the new value. For example, here is how we can update a map of integer counters:

```
map.compute(word, (k, v) -> v == null ? 1 : v + 1);
```

 Note: You cannot have null values in a ConcurrentHashMap. There are many methods that use a null value as an indication that a given key is not present in the map.

There are also variants computeIfPresent and computeIfAbsent that only compute a new value when there is already an old one, or when there isn't yet one. A map of LongAdder counters can be updated with

```
map.computeIfAbsent(word, k -> new LongAdder()).increment();
```

That is almost like the call to putIfAbsent that you saw before, but the LongAdder constructor is only called when a new counter is actually needed.

You often need to do something special when a key is added for the first time. The merge method makes this particularly convenient. It has a parameter for the initial value that is used when the key is not yet present. Otherwise, the function that you supplied is called, combining the existing value and the initial value. (Unlike compute, the function does *not* process the key.)

```
map.merge(word, 1L, (existingValue, newValue) -> existingValue + newValue);
```

or simply

```
map.merge(word, 1L, Long::sum);
```

It doesn't get more concise than that.

 Note: If the function that is passed to compute or merge returns null, the existing entry is removed from the map.

 Caution: When you use compute or merge, keep in mind that the function that you supply should not do a lot of work. While that function runs, some other updates to the map may be blocked. Of course, that function should also not update other parts of the map.

The program in Listing 10.9 uses a concurrent hash map to count all words in the Java files of a directory tree.

Listing 10.9 `concurrentHashMap/CHMDemo.java`

```java
1  package concurrentHashMap;
2
3  import java.io.*;
4  import java.nio.file.*;
5  import java.util.*;
6  import java.util.concurrent.*;
7  import java.util.stream.*;
8
9  /**
10  * This program demonstrates concurrent hash maps.
11  * @version 1.01 2023-07-30
12  * @author Cay Horstmann
13  */
14  public class CHMDemo
15  {
16     public static ConcurrentHashMap<String, Long> map = new ConcurrentHashMap<>();
17
18     /**
19      * Adds all words in the given file to the concurrent hash map.
20      * @param file a file
21      */
22     public static void process(Path file)
23     {
24        try (var in = new Scanner(file))
25        {
26           while (in.hasNext())
27           {
28              String word = in.next();
```

```
29              map.merge(word, 1L, Long::sum);
30           }
31        }
32        catch (IOException e)
33        {
34           e.printStackTrace();
35        }
36     }
37
38     /**
39      * Returns all descendants of a given directory--see Chapters 1 and 2 of Volume II
40      * @param rootDir the root directory
41      * @return a set of all descendants of the root directory
42      */
43     public static Set<Path> descendants(Path rootDir) throws IOException
44     {
45        try (Stream<Path> entries = Files.walk(rootDir))
46        {
47           return entries.collect(Collectors.toSet());
48        }
49     }
50
51     public static void main(String[] args)
52           throws InterruptedException, ExecutionException, IOException
53     {
54        ExecutorService executor = Executors.newVirtualThreadPerTaskExecutor();
55        Path pathToRoot = Path.of(".");
56        for (Path p : descendants(pathToRoot))
57        {
58           if (p.getFileName().toString().endsWith(".java"))
59              executor.execute(() -> process(p));
60        }
61        executor.close();
62        map.forEach((k, v) ->
63           {
64              if (v >= 10)
65                 System.out.println(k + " occurs " + v + " times");
66           });
67     }
68 }
```

10.6.4. Bulk Operations on Concurrent Hash Maps

The Java API provides bulk operations on concurrent hash maps that can safely execute even while other threads operate on the map. The bulk operations traverse the map and operate on the elements they find as they go along. No effort is made to freeze a snapshot of the map in time. Unless you happen to know that the map is not being modified while a bulk operation runs, you should treat its result as an approximation of the map's state.

There are three kinds of operations:

- search applies a function to each key and/or value, until the function yields a non-null result. Then the search terminates and the function's result is returned.
- reduce combines all keys and/or values, using a provided accumulation function.
- forEach applies a function to all keys and/or values.

Each operation has four versions:

- *operation*Keys: operates on keys.
- *operation*Values: operates on values.
- *operation*: operates on keys and values.
- *operation*Entries: operates on Map.Entry objects.

With each of the operations, you need to specify a *parallelism threshold*. If the map contains more elements than the threshold, the bulk operation is parallelized. If you want the bulk operation to run in a single thread, use a threshold of Long.MAX_VALUE. If you want the maximum number of threads to be made available for the bulk operation, use a threshold of 1.

Let's look at the search methods first. Here are the versions:

```
U searchKeys(long threshold, Function<? super K, ? extends U> f)
U searchValues(long threshold, Function<? super V, ? extends U> f)
U search(long threshold, BiFunction<? super K, ? super V,? extends U> f)
U searchEntries(long threshold, Function<Map.Entry<K, V>, ? extends U> f)
```

For example, suppose we want to find the first word that occurs more than 1,000 times. We need to search keys and values:

```
String result = map.search(threshold, (k, v) -> v > 1000 ? k : null);
```

Then result is set to the first match, or to null if the search function returns null for all inputs.

The forEach methods have two variants. The first one simply applies a *consumer* function for each map entry, for example

```
map.forEach(threshold,
    (k, v) -> System.out.println(k + " -> " + v));
```

The second variant takes an additional *transformer* function, which is applied first, and its result is passed to the consumer:

```
map.forEach(threshold,
    (k, v) -> k + " -> " + v, // transformer
    System.out::println); // consumer
```

The transformer can be used as a filter. Whenever the transformer returns `null`, the value is silently skipped. For example, here we only print the entries with large values:

```
map.forEach(threshold,
    (k, v) -> v > 1000 ? k + " -> " + v : null, // filter and transformer
    System.out::println); // the nulls are not passed to the consumer
```

The reduce operations combine their inputs with an accumulation function. For example, here is how you can compute the sum of all values:

```
Long sum = map.reduceValues(threshold, Long::sum);
```

As with `forEach`, you can also supply a transformer function. Here we compute the length of the longest key:

```
Integer maxlength = map.reduceKeys(threshold,
    String::length, // transformer
    Integer::max); // accumulator
```

The transformer can act as a filter, by returning `null` to exclude unwanted inputs. Here, we count how many entries have value > 1000:

```
Long count = map.reduceValues(threshold,
    v -> v > 1000 ? 1L : null,
    Long::sum);
```

Note: If the map is empty, or all entries have been filtered out, the reduce operation returns `null`. If there is only one element, its transformation is returned, and the accumulator is not applied.

There are specializations for `int`, `long`, and `double` outputs with suffixes `ToInt`, `ToLong`, and `ToDouble`. You need to transform the input to a primitive value and specify a default value and an accumulator function. The default value is returned when the map is empty.

```
long sum = map.reduceValuesToLong(threshold,
    Long::longValue, // transformer to primitive type
    0, // default value for empty map
    Long::sum); // primitive type accumulator
```

Caution: These specializations act differently from the object versions where there is only one element to be considered. Instead of returning the transformed element, it is accumulated with the default. Therefore, the default must be the neutral element of the accumulator.

10.6.5. Concurrent Set Views

Suppose you want a large, thread-safe set instead of a map. There is no `ConcurrentHashSet` class, and you know better than trying to create your own. Of course, you can use a `ConcurrentHashMap` with bogus values, but then you get a map, not a set, and you can't apply operations of the Set interface.

The static `newKeySet` method yields a `Set<K>` that is actually a wrapper around a `ConcurrentHashMap<K, Boolean>`. (All map values are `Boolean.TRUE`, but you don't actually care since you just use it as a set.)

```
Set<String> words = ConcurrentHashMap.<String>newKeySet();
```

Of course, if you have an existing map, the `keySet` method yields the set of keys. That set is mutable. If you remove the set's elements, the keys (and their values) are removed from the map. But it doesn't make sense to add elements to the key set, because there would be no corresponding values to add. There is a second `keySet` method to `ConcurrentHashMap`, with a default value, to be used when adding elements to the set:

```
Set<String> words = map.keySet(1L);
words.add("Java");
```

If "Java" wasn't already present in `words`, it now has a value of one.

 Note: You could also use the `Collections.newSetFromMap` method, but `newKeySet` is simpler and a bit more efficient.

10.6.6. Copy on Write Arrays

The `CopyOnWriteArrayList` and `CopyOnWriteArraySet` are thread-safe collections in which all mutators make a copy of the underlying array. This arrangement is useful if the threads that iterate over the collection greatly outnumber the threads that mutate it. When you construct an iterator, it contains a reference to the current array. If the array is later mutated, the iterator still has the old array, but the collection's array is replaced. As a consequence, the older iterator has a consistent (but potentially outdated) view that it can access without any synchronization expense.

10.6.7. Parallel Array Algorithms

The Arrays class has a number of parallelized operations. The static `Arrays.parallelSort` method can sort an array of primitive values or objects. For example,

```
var contents = Files.readString(Path.of("alice.txt"));
String[] words = contents.split("\\PL+"); // split along nonletters
Arrays.parallelSort(words);
```

When you sort objects, you can supply a Comparator.

```
Arrays.parallelSort(words, Comparator.comparing(String::length));
```

With all methods, you can supply the bounds of a range, such as

```
Arrays.parallelSort(words, words.length / 2, words.length); // sort the upper half
```

 Note: At first glance, it seems a bit odd that these methods have parallel in their name, since the user shouldn't care how the sorting happens. However, the API designers wanted to make it clear that the sorting is parallelized. That way, users are on notice to avoid comparators with side effects.

The parallelSetAll method fills an array with values that are computed from a function. The function receives the element index and computes the value at that location.

```
Arrays.parallelSetAll(values, i -> i % 10);
    // fills values with 0 1 2 3 4 5 6 7 8 9 0 1 2 . . .
```

Clearly, this operation benefits from being parallelized. There are versions for all primitive type arrays and for object arrays.

Finally, there is a parallelPrefix method that replaces each array element with the accumulation of the prefix for a given associative operation. Huh? Here is an example. Consider the array [1, 2, 3, 4, . . .] and the × operation. After executing Arrays.parallelPrefix(values, (x, y) -> x * y), the array contains

[1, 1 × 2, 1 × 2 × 3, 1 × 2 × 3 × 4, . . .]

Perhaps surprisingly, this computation can be parallelized. First, join neighboring elements, as indicated here:

[1, 1 × 2, 3, 3 × 4, 5, 5 × 6, 7, × 8]

The gray values are left alone. Clearly, one can make this computation in parallel in separate regions of the array. In the next step, update the indicated elements by multiplying them with elements that are one or two positions below:

[1, 1 × 2, 1 × 2 × 3, 1 × 2 × 3 × 4, 5, 5 × 6, 5 × 6 × 7, 5 × 6 × 7 × 8]

This, again, can be done in parallel. After log *n* steps, the process is complete. This is a win over the straightforward linear computation if sufficient processors are available. On special-purpose hardware, this algorithm is commonly used, and users of such hardware are quite ingenious in adapting it to a variety of problems.

10.6.8. Older Thread-Safe Collections

Ever since the initial release of Java, the Vector and Hashtable classes provided thread-safe implementations of a dynamic array and a hash table. These classes are now considered obsolete, having been replaced by the ArrayList and HashMap classes. Those classes are not thread-safe. Instead, a different mechanism is supplied in the collections library. Any collection class can be made thread-safe by means of a *synchronization wrapper*:

```
List<E> synchArrayList = Collections.synchronizedList(new ArrayList<>());
Map<K, V> synchHashMap = Collections.synchronizedMap(new HashMap<>());
```

The methods of the resulting collections use locking to provide thread-safe access.

You should make sure that no thread accesses the data structure through the original unsynchronized methods. The easiest way to ensure this is not to save any reference to the original object. Simply construct a collection and immediately pass it to the wrapper, as we did in our examples.

You still need to use "client-side" locking if you want to *iterate* over the collection while another thread has the opportunity to mutate it:

```
synchronized (synchHashMap)
{
    Iterator<K> iter = synchHashMap.keySet().iterator();
    while (iter.hasNext()) . . .;
}
```

You must use the same code if you use a "for each" loop because the loop uses an iterator. Note that the iterator actually fails with a ConcurrentModificationException if another thread mutates the collection while the iteration is in progress. The synchronization is still required so that the concurrent modification can be reliably detected.

You are usually better off using the collections defined in the java.util.concurrent package instead of the synchronization wrappers. In particular, the ConcurrentHashMap has been carefully implemented so that multiple threads can access it without blocking each other, provided they access different buckets. One exception is an array list that is frequently mutated. In that case, a synchronized ArrayList can outperform a CopyOnWriteArrayList.

```
java.util.Collections  1.2
```

- static <E> Collection<E> synchronizedCollection(Collection<E> c)
- static <E> List synchronizedList(List<E> c)
- static <E> Set synchronizedSet(Set<E> c)
- static <E> SortedSet synchronizedSortedSet(SortedSet<E> c)
- static <K, V> Map<K, V> synchronizedMap(Map<K, V> c)
- static <K, V> SortedMap<K, V> synchronizedSortedMap(SortedMap<K, V> c)
  construct a view of the collection whose methods are synchronized.

10.7. Asynchronous Computations

So far, our approach to concurrent computation has been to break up a task, and then wait until all pieces have completed. Waiting works well with virtual threads, but with platform threads, a wait-free, or *asynchronous*, programming style provides higher throughput. The following sections are devoted to asynchronous computations.

10.7.1. Completable Futures

When you have a Future object, you need to call get to obtain the value, blocking until the value is available. The CompletableFuture class implements the Future interface, and it provides a second mechanism for obtaining the result. You register a *callback* that will be invoked (in some thread) with the result once it is available.

```
CompletableFuture<String> f = . . .;
f.thenAccept(s -> Process the result string s);
```

In this way, you can process the result without blocking once it is available.

There are a few API methods that return CompletableFuture objects. For example, you can fetch a web page asynchronously with the HttpClient class that you will encounter in Chapter 4 of Volume II:

```
HttpClient client = HttpClient.newHttpClient();
HttpRequest request = HttpRequest.newBuilder(URI.create(urlString)).GET().build();
CompletableFuture<HttpResponse<String>> f = client.sendAsync(
    request, BodyHandlers.ofString());
```

It is nice if there is a method that produces a ready-made CompletableFuture, but most of the time, you need to make your own. To run a task asynchronously and obtain a CompletableFuture, you don't submit it directly to an executor service. Instead, you call the static method CompletableFuture.supplyAsync. Here is how to read the web page without the benefit of the HttpClient class:

```
public CompletableFuture<String> readPage(URI uri)
{
    return CompletableFuture.supplyAsync(() ->
        {
            try
            {
                return new String(uri.toURL().openStream().readAllBytes());
            }
            catch (IOException e)
            {
                throw new UncheckedIOException(e);
            }
        }, executor);
}
```

If you omit the executor, the task is run on a default executor (namely the executor returned by ForkJoinPool.commonPool()). You usually don't want to do that.

 Caution: Note that the first parameter of the supplyAsync method is a Supplier<T>, not a Callable<T>. Both interfaces describe functions with no parameters and return type T, but a Supplier function cannot throw a checked exception. As you can see from the code above, that was not an inspired choice.

A CompletableFuture can complete in two ways: either with a result, or with an uncaught exception. In order to handle both cases, use the whenComplete method. The supplied function is called with the result (or null if none) and the exception (or null if none).

```
f.whenComplete((s, t) ->
    {
        if (t == null)
        {
            Process the result s;
        }
        else
        {
            Process the Throwable t;
        }
    });
```

The CompletableFuture is called completable because one can set a completion value. (In other concurrency libraries, such an entity is called a *promise*, and the act of completion is called "fulfilling the promise".) As a consumer of the Future, you don't care how the value is set. That is the job of the producer of the promise. The supplyAsync method produces a CompletableFuture, and it sets the completion value when the task has finished. Other producers can use a more complex approach. For example, this example produces a future where two tasks work simultaneously on completing it:

```
var f = new CompletableFuture<Integer>();
executor.execute(() ->
   {
      int n = workHard(arg);
      f.complete(n);
   });
executor.execute(() ->
   {
      int n = workSmart(arg);
      f.complete(n);
   });
executor.execute(() ->
   {
      try
      {
         Thread.sleep(timeout);
         f.completeExceptionally(new TimeoutException());
      }
      catch (InterruptedException e)
      {
         f.completeExceptionally(e);
      }
   });
```

It is safe to call complete or completeExceptionally on the same instance in multiple threads. If the future is already completed, these calls have no effect.

Caution: Unlike a plain Future, the computation of a CompletableFuture is not interrupted when you invoke its cancel method. Canceling simply completes the future exceptionally, with a CancellationException. In general, this makes sense since a CompletableFuture may not have a single thread that is responsible for its completion. However, this restriction also applies to CompletableFuture instances returned by methods such as supplyAsync, which could in principle be interrupted.

10.7.2. Composing Completable Futures

Nonblocking calls are implemented through callbacks. The programmer registers a callback for the action that should occur after a task completes. Of course, if the next action is also asynchronous, the next action after that is in a different callback. Even though the programmer thinks in terms of "first do step 1, then step 2, then step 3," the program logic can become dispersed in "callback hell." It gets even worse when one has to add error handling. Suppose step 2 is "the user logs in." You may need to repeat that step since the user can mistype the credentials. Trying to implement such a control flow in a set of callbacks, or to understand it once it has been implemented, can be quite challenging.

The CompletableFuture class addresses this problem by providing a mechanism for *composing* asynchronous tasks into a processing pipeline.

For example, suppose we want to extract all images from a web page. Let's say we have a method

```
public CompletableFuture<String> readPage(URI uri)
```

that yields the text of a web page when it becomes available. If the method

```
public List<URI> getImageLinks(String page)
```

yields the links of images in an HTML page, you can schedule it to be called when the page is available:

```
CompletableFuture<String> contents = readPage(uri);
CompletableFuture<List<URI>> imageLinks = contents.thenApply(this::getImageLinks);
```

The thenApply method doesn't block either. It returns another future. When the first future has completed, its result is fed to the getImageLinks method, and the return value of that method becomes the final result.

With completable futures, you just specify what you want to have done and in which order. It won't all happen right away, of course, but what is important is that all the code is in one place.

Conceptually, CompletableFuture is a simple API, but there are many variants of methods for composing completable futures. Let us first look at those that add an action to a single future (see Table 10.3). In the table, I use a shorthand notation for the ponderous functional interfaces, writing T -> U instead of Function<? super T, ? extends U>. These aren't actual Java types, of course.

You have already seen the thenApply method. Suppose f is a T -> U function. The call

```
CompletableFuture<U> future.thenApply(f);
```

returns a future that applies the function f to the result of future when it is available.

The thenCompose method, instead of taking a T -> U function, receives a function mapping T to CompletableFuture<U>. That sounds rather abstract, but it can be quite natural. It is a function that eventually yields a U.

The call

```
CompletableFuture<U> future.thenCompose(f);
```

works exactly like thenApply, applying f to the result of future. However, the result of f is not immediately available. When it arrives, the composition completes.

In the preceding section, you saw the whenComplete method for handling exceptions. There is also a handle method that requires a function processing the result or exception and computing a new result. In many cases, it is simpler to call the exceptionally method instead. That method computes a dummy value when an exception occurs:

```
CompletableFuture<List<URI>> imageLinks = readPage(uri)
    .exceptionally(ex -> "<html></html>")
    .thenApply(this::getImageLinks);
```

You can handle a timeout in the same way:

```
CompletableFuture<List<URI>> imageLinks = readPage(uri)
    .completeOnTimeout("<html></html>", 30, TimeUnit.SECONDS)
    .thenApply(this::getImageLinks);
```

Alternatively, you can throw an exception on timeout:

```
CompletableFuture<String> = readPage(uri).orTimeout(30, TimeUnit.SECONDS);
```

The methods in Table 10.3 with void result are normally used at the end of a processing pipeline.

Table 10.3: Adding an Action to a CompletableFuture<T> Object

Method	Parameter	Description
thenApply	T -> U	Apply a function to the result.
thenAccept	T -> void	Like thenApply, but with void result.
thenCompose	T -> CompletableFuture<U>	Invoke the function on the result and execute the returned future.
thenRun	Runnable	Execute the Runnable with void result.
handle	(T, Throwable) -> U	Process the result or error and yield a new result.
whenComplete	(T, Throwable) -> void	Like handle, but with void result.

Method	Parameter	Description
exceptionally	Throwable -> U	Compute a result from the error.
exceptionallyCompose	Throwable -> CompletableFuture<U>	Invoke the function on the exception and execute the returned future.
completeOnTimeout	T, long, TimeUnit	Yield the given value as the result in case of timeout.
orTimeout	long, TimeUnit	Yield a TimeoutException in case of timeout.

Now let us turn to methods that combine multiple futures (see Table 10.4).

The first three methods run a CompletableFuture<T> and a CompletableFuture<U> action concurrently and combine the results.

The next three methods run two CompletableFuture<T> actions concurrently. As soon as one of them finishes, its result is passed on, and the other result is ignored.

Finally, the static allOf and anyOf methods shown in Table 10.5 take a variable number of completable futures and yield a CompletableFuture<Void> that completes when all of them, or any one of them, completes. The allOf method does not yield a result. The anyOf method does *not* terminate the remaining tasks.

 Caution: The anyOf may yield a future that completed exceptionally even if others completed successfully.

Table 10.4: Combining Another Future with a CompletableFuture<T>

Method	Parameters	Description
thenCombine	CompletableFuture<U>, (T, U) -> V	Execute both and combine the results with the given function.
thenAcceptBoth	CompletableFuture<U>, (T, U) -> void	Like thenCombine, but with void result.
runAfterBoth	CompletableFuture<?>, Runnable	Execute the runnable after both complete.
applyToEither	CompletableFuture<T>, T -> V	When a result is available from one or the other, pass it to the given function.

Method	Parameters	Description
acceptEither	CompletableFuture<T>, T -> void	Like applyToEither, but with void result.
runAfterEither	CompletableFuture<?>, Runnable	Execute the runnable after one or the other completes.

Table 10.5: Combining Multiple Futures

Method	Parameter	Description
static allOf	CompletableFuture<?>...	Complete with void result after all given futures complete (some perhaps with an exception).
static anyOf	CompletableFuture<?>...	Complete after any of the given futures completes, yielding its result or exception.

Note: For each method shown, there are also two Async variants for specifying the executor of the "dependent completion" (that is, the action to be executed upon completion of the future) executor. One of the variants uses a default executor (not recommended), and the other has an Executor parameter.

For a pipeline of actions, start off with an Async variant to set the desired executor, and then use the non-Async methods to continue with the same executor.

Note: Technically speaking, the methods in this section have parameters of type CompletionStage, not CompletableFuture. The CompletionStage interface describes how to compose asynchronous computations, whereas the Future interface focuses on the result of a computation. A CompletableFuture is both a CompletionStage and a Future.

Listing 10.10 shows a complete program that reads a web page, scans it for images, loads the images and saves them locally. Note how all asynchronous methods return a CompletableFuture. To kick off the computation, we use a little trick. Rather than calling the readPage method in a lambda expression passed to supplyAsync, a completed future provides the URI argument, which is then composed with this::readPage. That way, the pipeline has a very uniform appearance:

```
CompletableFuture.completedFuture(uri)
   .thenComposeAsync(this::readPage, executor)
   .thenApply(this::getImageLinks)
   .thenCompose(this::getImages)
   .thenAccept(this::saveImages);
```

Tip: This example shows the ideal form of an asynchronous pipeline. Each step is a function of one of the following three types:

- An asynchronous function T -> CompletableFuture<U> that yields a result in the future, passed to thenCompose
- A synchronous function T -> U that returns a result immediately, passed to thenApply
- A final consumer that returns no result, passed to thenAccept

The initial completedFuture provides the argument for the first function.

The first asynchronous step uses composeAsync to supply an executor.

Listing 10.10 completableFutures/CompletableFutureDemo.java

```
 1   package completableFutures;
 2
 3   import java.awt.image.*;
 4   import java.io.*;
 5   import java.net.*;
 6   import java.util.*;
 7   import java.util.concurrent.*;
 8   import java.util.regex.*;
 9
10   import javax.imageio.*;
11
12   /**
13    * @version 1.02 2023-07-30
14    * @author Cay Horstmann
15    */
16   public class CompletableFutureDemo
17   {
18      private static final Pattern IMG_PATTERN = Pattern.compile(
19          "[<]\\s*[iI][mM][gG]\\s*[^>]*[sS][rR][cC]\\s*[=]\\s*['\"]([^'\"]*)['\"][^>]*[>]");
20      private ExecutorService executor = Executors.newCachedThreadPool();
21      private URI uriToProcess;
22
23      public CompletableFuture<String> readPage(URI uri)
24      {
25         return CompletableFuture.supplyAsync(() -> {
```

```java
26          try
27          {
28             var contents = new String(uri.toURL().openStream().readAllBytes());
29             System.out.println("Read page from " + uri);
30             return contents;
31          }
32          catch (IOException e)
33          {
34             throw new UncheckedIOException(e);
35          }
36       }, executor);
37    }
38
39    public List<URI> getImageLinks(String webpage) // not blocking
40    {
41       var result = new ArrayList<URI>();
42       Matcher matcher = IMG_PATTERN.matcher(webpage);
43       while (matcher.find())
44       {
45          URI uri = URI.create(uriToProcess + "/" + matcher.group(1));
46          result.add(uri);
47       }
48       System.out.println("Found links: " + result);
49       return result;
50    }
51
52    public CompletableFuture<List<BufferedImage>> getImages(List<URI> uris)
53    {
54       return CompletableFuture.supplyAsync(() -> {
55          try
56          {
57             var result = new ArrayList<BufferedImage>();
58             for (URI uri : uris)
59             {
60                result.add(ImageIO.read(uri.toURL()));
61                System.out.println("Loaded " + uri);
62             }
63             return result;
64          }
65          catch (IOException e)
66          {
67             throw new UncheckedIOException(e);
68          }
69       }, executor);
70    }
71
72    public void saveImages(List<BufferedImage> images)
73    {
74       System.out.println("Saving " + images.size() + " images");
75       try
76       {
77          for (int i = 0; i < images.size(); i++)
```

```
78          {
79              String filename = "/tmp/image" + (i + 1) + ".png";
80              ImageIO.write(images.get(i), "PNG", new File(filename));
81          }
82      }
83      catch (IOException e)
84      {
85          throw new UncheckedIOException(e);
86      }
87      executor.shutdown();
88  }
89
90  public CompletableFutureDemo(URI uri)
91  {
92      uriToProcess = uri;
93  }
94
95  public void run() throws IOException, InterruptedException
96  {
97      CompletableFuture.completedFuture(uriToProcess)
98          .thenComposeAsync(this::readPage, executor)
99          .thenApply(this::getImageLinks)
100         .thenCompose(this::getImages)
101         .thenAccept(this::saveImages);
102
103     // or use the HTTP client:
104     /*
105     HttpClient client = HttpClient.newBuilder().build();
106     HttpRequest request = HttpRequest.newBuilder(uriToProcess).GET().build();
107     client.sendAsync(request, BodyHandlers.ofString())
108         .thenApply(HttpResponse::body)
109         .thenApply(this::getImageLinks)
110         .thenCompose(this::getImages)
111         .thenAccept(this::saveImages);
112     */
113 }
114
115 public static void main(String[] args)
116         throws IOException, InterruptedException
117 {
118     new CompletableFutureDemo(URI.create("http://horstmann.com/index.html")).run();
119 }
120 }
```

10.7.3. Long-Running Tasks in User-Interface Callbacks

One of the reasons to use threads is to make your programs more responsive. This is particularly important in an application with a user interface. With Swing, JavaFX, and Android, user-interface components are not thread-safe, and all user-interface actions run in a single thread. When your program needs to do something time-consuming, you cannot do the work in the user-interface thread, or the user interface will be frozen. Instead, fire up another worker thread.

For example, if you want to read a file when the user clicks a button, don't do this:

```
var open = new JButton("Open");
open.addActionListener(event ->
   { // BAD--long-running action is executed on UI thread
      var in = new Scanner(file);
      while (in.hasNextLine())
      {
         String line = in.nextLine();
         . . .
      }
   });
```

Instead, do the work in a separate thread.

```
open.addActionListener(event ->
   { // GOOD--long-running action in separate thread
      Runnable task = () ->
         {
            var in = new Scanner(file);
            while (in.hasNextLine())
            {
               String line = in.nextLine();
               . . .
            }
         };
      executor.execute(task);
   });
```

However, you cannot directly update the user interface from the worker thread that executes the long-running task. Since Swing, JavaFX, and Android are not thread-safe, you cannot manipulate user-interface elements from multiple threads, or they risk becoming corrupted. In fact, JavaFX and Android check for this, and throw an exception if you try to access the user interface from a thread other than the UI thread.

Therefore, you need to schedule any UI updates to happen on the UI thread. Each user-interface library provides some mechanism to schedule a Runnable for execution on the UI thread. For example, in Swing, you call

```
EventQueue.invokeLater(() -> label.setText(percentage + "% complete"));
```

It is tedious to implement user feedback in a worker thread, so each user-interface library provides some kind of helper class for managing the details, such as SwingWorker in Swing, Task in JavaFX, and AsyncTask in Android. You specify actions for the long-running task

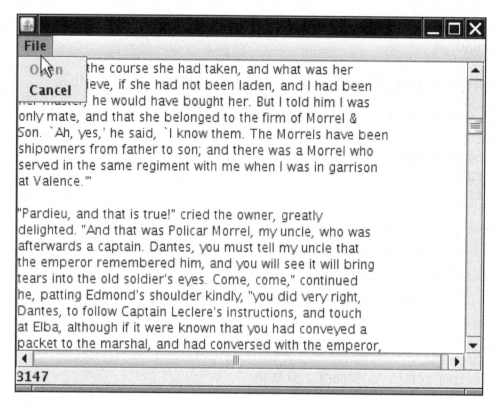

Figure 10.6: Loading a file in a separate thread

(which is run on a separate thread) as well as progress updates and the final disposition (which are run on the UI thread).

The program in Listing 10.11 has commands for loading a text file and for canceling the file loading process. You should try the program with a long file, such as the full text of *The Count of Monte Cristo*, supplied in the gutenberg directory of the book's companion code. The file is loaded in a separate thread. While the file is being read, the Open menu item is disabled and the Cancel item is enabled (see Figure 10.6). After each line is read, a line counter in the status bar is updated. After the reading process is complete, the Open menu item is reenabled, the Cancel item is disabled, and the status line text is set to Done.

This example shows the typical UI activities of a background task:

- After each work unit, update the UI to show progress.
- After the work is finished, make a final change to the UI.

The SwingWorker class makes it easy to implement such a task. Override the doInBackground method to do the time-consuming work and occasionally call publish to communicate work progress. This method is executed in a worker thread. The publish method causes a process method to execute in the event dispatch thread to deal with the progress data. When the work is complete, the done method is called in the event dispatch thread so that you can finish updating the UI.

Whenever you want to do some work in the worker thread, construct a new worker. (Each worker object is meant to be used only once.) Then call the execute method. You will typically call execute on the event dispatch thread, but that is not a requirement.

It is assumed that a worker produces a result of some kind; therefore, SwingWorker<T, V> implements Future<T>. This result can be obtained by the get method of the Future interface. Since the get method blocks until the result is available, you don't want to call it immediately after calling execute. It is a good idea to call it only when you know that the work has been completed. Typically, you call get from the done method. (There is no requirement to call get. Sometimes, processing the progress data is all you need.)

Both the intermediate progress data and the final result can have arbitrary types. The SwingWorker class has these types as type parameters. A SwingWorker<T, V> produces a result of type T and progress data of type V.

To cancel the work in progress, use the cancel method of the Future interface. When the work is canceled, the get method throws a CancellationException.

As already mentioned, the worker thread's call to publish will cause calls to process on the event dispatch thread. For efficiency, the results of several calls to publish may be batched up in a single call to process. The process method receives a List<V> containing all intermediate results.

Let us put this mechanism to work for reading in a text file. As it turns out, a JTextArea is quite slow. Appending lines from a long text file (such as all lines in *The Count of Monte Cristo*) takes considerable time.

To show the user that progress is being made, we want to display the number of lines read in a status line. Thus, the progress data consist of the current line number and the current line of text. We package these into a record:

```
private record ProgressData(int number, String line) {}
```

The final result is the text that has been read into a StringBuilder. Thus, we need a SwingWorker<StringBuilder, ProgressData>.

In the doInBackground method, we read a file, a line at a time. After each line, we call publish to publish the line number and the text of the current line.

```
@Override public StringBuilder doInBackground() throws IOException, InterruptedException
{
    int lineNumber = 0;
    var in = new Scanner(new FileInputStream(file));
    while (in.hasNextLine())
```

```
        {
            String line = in.nextLine();
            lineNumber++;
            text.append(line).append("\n");
            var data = new ProgressData(lineNumber, line);
            publish(data);
            Thread.sleep(1); // to test cancellation; no need to do this in your programs
        }
        return text;
    }
```

We also sleep for a millisecond after every line so that you can test cancellation without getting stressed out, but you wouldn't want to slow down your own programs by sleeping. If you comment out this line, you will find that *The Count of Monte Cristo* loads quite quickly, with only a few batched user-interface updates.

In the process method, we ignore all line numbers but the last one, and we concatenate all lines for a single update of the text area.

```
    @Override public void process(List<ProgressData> data)
    {
        if (isCancelled()) return;
        var b = new StringBuilder();
        statusLine.setText("" + data.getLast().number());
        for (ProgressData d : data) b.append(d.line()).append("\n");
        textArea.append(b.toString());
    }
```

In the done method, the text area is updated with the complete text, and the Cancel menu item is disabled.

Note how the worker is started in the event listener for the Open menu item.

This simple technique allows you to execute time-consuming tasks while keeping the user interface responsive.

Listing 10.11 swingWorker/SwingWorkerTest.java

```
1   package swingWorker;
2
3   import java.awt.*;
4   import java.io.*;
5   import java.util.*;
6   import java.util.List;
7   import java.util.concurrent.*;
8
```

```java
 9  import javax.swing.*;
10
11  /**
12   * This program demonstrates a worker thread that runs a potentially time-consuming task.
13   * @version 1.13 2023-10-11
14   * @author Cay Horstmann
15   */
16  public class SwingWorkerTest
17  {
18      public static void main(String[] args) throws Exception
19      {
20          EventQueue.invokeLater(() ->
21              {
22                  var frame = new SwingWorkerFrame();
23                  frame.setDefaultCloseOperation(JFrame.EXIT_ON_CLOSE);
24                  frame.setVisible(true);
25              });
26      }
27  }
28
29  /**
30   * This frame has a text area to show the contents of a text file, a menu to open a file and
31   * cancel the opening process, and a status line to show the file loading progress.
32   */
33  class SwingWorkerFrame extends JFrame
34  {
35      private JFileChooser chooser;
36      private JTextArea textArea;
37      private JLabel statusLine;
38      private JMenuItem openItem;
39      private JMenuItem cancelItem;
40      private SwingWorker<StringBuilder, ProgressData> textReader;
41      public static final int TEXT_ROWS = 20;
42      public static final int TEXT_COLUMNS = 60;
43
44      public SwingWorkerFrame()
45      {
46          chooser = new JFileChooser();
47          chooser.setCurrentDirectory(new File("."));
48
49          textArea = new JTextArea(TEXT_ROWS, TEXT_COLUMNS);
50          add(new JScrollPane(textArea));
51
52          statusLine = new JLabel(" ");
53          add(statusLine, BorderLayout.SOUTH);
54
55          var menuBar = new JMenuBar();
56          setJMenuBar(menuBar);
57
58          var menu = new JMenu("File");
59          menuBar.add(menu);
60
```

```
61          openItem = new JMenuItem("Open");
62          menu.add(openItem);
63          openItem.addActionListener(event ->
64             {
65                // show file chooser dialog
66                int result = chooser.showOpenDialog(null);
67
68                // if file selected, set it as icon of the label
69                if (result == JFileChooser.APPROVE_OPTION)
70                {
71                   textArea.setText("");
72                   openItem.setEnabled(false);
73                   textReader = new TextReader(chooser.getSelectedFile());
74                   textReader.execute();
75                   cancelItem.setEnabled(true);
76                }
77             });
78
79          cancelItem = new JMenuItem("Cancel");
80          menu.add(cancelItem);
81          cancelItem.setEnabled(false);
82          cancelItem.addActionListener(event -> textReader.cancel(true));
83          pack();
84       }
85
86       private record ProgressData(int number, String line) {}
87
88       private class TextReader extends SwingWorker<StringBuilder, ProgressData>
89       {
90          private File file;
91          private StringBuilder text = new StringBuilder();
92
93          public TextReader(File file)
94          {
95             this.file = file;
96          }
97
98          // the following method executes in the worker thread; it doesn't touch Swing components
99
100         public StringBuilder doInBackground() throws IOException, InterruptedException
101         {
102            int lineNumber = 0;
103            try (var in = new Scanner(new FileInputStream(file)))
104            {
105               while (in.hasNextLine())
106               {
107                  String line = in.nextLine();
108                  lineNumber++;
109                  text.append(line).append("\n");
110                  var data = new ProgressData(lineNumber, line);
111                  publish(data);
112                  Thread.sleep(1); // to test cancellation; no need to do this in your programs
```

```
113                }
114            }
115            return text;
116         }
117
118         // the following methods execute in the event dispatch thread
119
120         public void process(List<ProgressData> data)
121         {
122            if (isCancelled()) return;
123            var builder = new StringBuilder();
124            statusLine.setText("" + data.getLast().number());
125            for (ProgressData d : data) builder.append(d.line()).append("\n");
126            textArea.append(builder.toString());
127         }
128
129         public void done()
130         {
131            try
132            {
133               StringBuilder result = get();
134               textArea.setText(result.toString());
135               statusLine.setText("Done");
136            }
137            catch (InterruptedException ex)
138            {
139            }
140            catch (CancellationException ex)
141            {
142               textArea.setText("");
143               statusLine.setText("Cancelled");
144            }
145            catch (ExecutionException ex)
146            {
147               statusLine.setText("" + ex.getCause());
148            }
149
150            cancelItem.setEnabled(false);
151            openItem.setEnabled(true);
152         }
153      }
154 }
```

`javax.swing.SwingWorker<T, V>` 6

- `abstract T doInBackground()`
  is the method to override to carry out the background task and to return the result of the work.

- void process(List<V> data)

  is the method to override to process intermediate progress data in the event dispatch thread.
- void publish(V... data)

  forwards intermediate progress data to the event dispatch thread. Call this method from doInBackground.
- void execute()

  schedules this worker for execution on a worker thread.
- SwingWorker.StateValue getState()

  gets the state of this worker—one of PENDING, STARTED, or DONE.

10.8. Processes

Up to now, you have seen how to execute Java code in separate threads within the same program. Sometimes, you need to execute another program. For this, use the ProcessBuilder and Process classes. The Process class executes a command in a separate operating system process and lets you interact with its standard input, output, and error streams. The ProcessBuilder class lets you configure a Process object.

 Note: The ProcessBuilder class is a more flexible replacement for the Runtime.exec calls.

10.8.1. Building a Process

Start by specifying the command that you want to execute. You can supply a List<String> or simply the strings that make up the command.

```
var builder = new ProcessBuilder("gcc", "myapp.c");
```

 Caution: The first string must be an executable command, not a shell builtin. For example, to run the dir command in Windows, you need to build a process with strings "cmd.exe", "/C", and "dir".

Each process has a *working directory*, which is used to resolve relative directory names. By default, a process has the same working directory as the virtual machine, which is typically the directory from which you launched the java program. You can change it with the directory method:

```
builder = builder.directory(path.toFile());
```

Note: Each of the methods for configuring a `ProcessBuilder` returns itself, so that you can chain commands. Ultimately, you will call

```
Process p = new ProcessBuilder(command).directory(file)....start();
```

Next, you will want to specify what should happen to the standard input, output, and error streams of the process. By default, each of them is a pipe that you can access with

```
OutputStream processIn = p.getOutputStream();
InputStream processOut = p.getInputStream();
InputStream processErr = p.getErrorStream();
```

or, for text input and output

```
BufferedWriter processIn = p.outputWriter();
BufferedReader processOut = p.inputReader();
BufferedReader processErr = p.errorReader();
```

Note that the input stream of the process is an output stream in the JVM! You write to that stream, and whatever you write becomes the input of the process. Conversely, you read what the process writes to the output and error streams. For you, they are input streams. The same holds for readers and writers.

You can specify that the input, output, and error streams of the new process should be the same as the JVM. If the user runs the JVM in a console, any user input is forwarded to the process, and the process output shows up in the console. Call

```
builder.inheritIO();
```

to make this setting for all three streams. If you only want to inherit some of the streams, pass the value

```
ProcessBuilder.Redirect.INHERIT
```

to the `redirectInput`, `redirectOutput`, or `redirectError` methods. For example,

```
builder.redirectOutput(ProcessBuilder.Redirect.INHERIT);
```

You can redirect the process streams to files by supplying `File` objects:

```
builder.redirectInput(inputFile)
   .redirectOutput(outputFile)
   .redirectError(errorFile)

;
```

The files for output and error are created or truncated when the process starts. To append to existing files, use

```
builder.redirectOutput(ProcessBuilder.Redirect.appendTo(outputFile));
```

It is often useful to merge the output and error streams, so you can see the outputs and error messages in the sequence in which the process generates them. Call

```
builder.redirectErrorStream(true);
```

to activate the merging. If you do that, you can no longer call redirectError on the ProcessBuilder or getErrorStream on the Process.

You may also want to modify the environment variables of the process. Here, the builder chain syntax breaks down. You need to get the builder's environment (which is initialized by the environment variables of the process running the JVM), then put or remove entries.

```
Map<String, String> env = builder.environment();
env.put("LANG", "fr_FR");
env.remove("JAVA_HOME");
Process p = builder.start();
```

If you want to pipe the output of one process into the input of another (as with the | operator in a shell), use the startPipeline method. Pass a list of process builders and read the result from the last process. Here is an example, enumerating the unique extensions in a directory tree:

```
List<Process> processes = ProcessBuilder.startPipeline(List.of(
    new ProcessBuilder("find", "/opt/jdk-21"),
    new ProcessBuilder("grep", "-o", "\\.[^./]*$"),
    new ProcessBuilder("sort"),
    new ProcessBuilder("uniq")
));
Process last = processes.getLast();
var result = new String(last.getInputStream().readAllBytes());
```

Of course, this particular task would be more efficiently solved by making the directory walk in Java instead of running four processes. Chapter 2 of Volume II will show you how to do that.

10.8.2. Running a Process

After you have configured the builder, invoke its start method to start the process. If you configured the input, output, and error streams as pipes, you can now write to the input stream and read the output and error streams. For example,

```
Process process = new ProcessBuilder("/bin/ls", "-l")
   .directory(Path.of("/tmp").toFile())
   .start();
try (var in = new Scanner(process.getInputStream()))
{
   while (in.hasNextLine())
      System.out.println(in.nextLine());
}
```

 Caution: There is limited buffer space for the process streams. You should not flood the input, and you should read the output promptly. If there is a lot of input and output, you may need to produce and consume it in separate threads.

To wait for the process to finish, call

```
int result = process.waitFor();
```

or, if you don't want to wait indefinitely,

```
long delay = . . .;
if (process.waitFor(delay, TimeUnit.SECONDS))
{
   int result = process.exitValue();
   . . .
}
else
{
   process.destroyForcibly();
}
```

The first call to waitFor returns the exit value of the process (by convention, 0 for success or a nonzero error code). The second call returns true if the process didn't time out. Then you need to retrieve the exit value by calling the exitValue method.

Instead of waiting for the process to finish, you can just leave it running and occasionally call isAlive to see whether it is still alive. To kill the process, call destroy or destroyForcibly. The difference between these calls is platform-dependent. On UNIX, the former terminates the process with SIGTERM, the latter with SIGKILL. (The supportsNormalTermination method returns true if the destroy method can terminate the process normally.)

Finally, you can receive an asynchronous notification when the process has completed. The call process.onExit() yields a CompletableFuture<Process> that you can use to schedule any action.

```
process.onExit().thenAccept(
   p -> System.out.println("Exit value: " + p.exitValue()));
```

 Note: Since Java 21, the logger with name java.lang.ProcessBuilder logs processes executed by Runtime.exec and ProcessBuilder at the logging levels DEBUG and TRACE. The command arguments are only included at the TRACE level. Both levels log the process id, directory, command, and stack trace.

10.8.3. Process Handles

To get more information about a process that your program started, or any other process that is currently running on your machine, use the ProcessHandle interface. You can obtain a ProcessHandle in four ways:

1. Given a Process object p, p.toHandle() yields its ProcessHandle.
2. Given a long operating system process ID, ProcessHandle.of(id) yields the handle of that process.
3. ProcessHandle.current() is the handle of the process that runs this Java virtual machine.
4. ProcessHandle.allProcesses() yields a Stream<ProcessHandle> of all operating system processes that are visible to the current process.

Given a process handle, you can get its process ID, its parent process, its children, and its descendants:

```
long pid = handle.pid();
Optional<ProcessHandle> parent = handle.parent();
Stream<ProcessHandle> children = handle.children();
Stream<ProcessHandle> descendants = handle.descendants();
```

 Note: The Stream<ProcessHandle> instances that are returned by the allProcesses, children, and descendants methods are just snapshots in time. Any of the processes in the stream might be terminated by the time you get around to seeing them, and other processes may have started that are not in the stream.

The info method yields a ProcessHandle.Info object with methods for obtaining information about the process.

```
Optional<String[]> arguments()
Optional<String> command()
Optional<String> commandLine()
```

```
Optional<Instant> startInstant()
Optional<Duration> totalCpuDuration()
Optional<String> user()
```

All of these methods return `Optional` values since it is possible that a particular operating system may not be able to report the information.

For monitoring or forcing process termination, the `ProcessHandle` interface has the same `isAlive`, `supportsNormalTermination`, `destroy`, `destroyForcibly`, and `onExit` methods as the `Process` class. However, there is no equivalent to the `waitFor` method.

Listing 10.12 shows how to start a process and read its output, and how to list all Java processes.

Listing 10.12 process/ProcessDemo.java

```
 1   package process;
 2
 3   import java.io.IOException;
 4   import java.nio.file.Path;
 5   import java.util.Scanner;
 6
 7   /**
 8    * This program demonstrates running a process and reading its output, and listing all Java
 9    * processes
10    * @version 1.1 2023-10-11
11    * @author Cay Horstmann
12    */
13   public class ProcessDemo
14   {
15      public static void main(String[] args) throws IOException, InterruptedException
16      {
17         Process p = new ProcessBuilder("/bin/ls", "-l")
18            .directory(Path.of("/tmp").toFile())
19            .start();
20         try (var in = new Scanner(p.getInputStream()))
21         {
22            while (in.hasNextLine())
23               System.out.println(in.nextLine());
24         }
25         System.out.println("pid: " + p.toHandle().pid());
26         int result = p.waitFor();
27         System.out.println("Exit value: " + result);
28
29         ProcessHandle.allProcesses()
30            .map(ProcessHandle::info)
31            .filter(info -> info.command().filter(s -> s.contains("java")).isPresent())
```

```
32            .forEach(info -> info.commandLine().ifPresent(System.out::println));
33      }
34  }
```

---

java.lang.ProcessBuilder 5.0

- ProcessBuilder(String... command)
- ProcessBuilder(List<String> command)

  construct a process builder with the given command and arguments.

- ProcessBuilder directory(File directory)

  sets the working directory for the process.

- ProcessBuilder inheritIO() **9**

  makes the process use the standard input, output, and error of the virtual machine.

- ProcessBuilder redirectErrorStream(boolean redirectErrorStream)

  If redirectErrorStream is true, the standard error of the process is merged into the standard output.

- ProcessBuilder redirectInput(File file) **7**
- ProcessBuilder redirectOutput(File file) **7**
- ProcessBuilder redirectError(File file) **7**

  redirect the standard input, output, or error of the process to the given file.

- ProcessBuilder redirectInput(ProcessBuilder.Redirect source) **7**
- ProcessBuilder redirectOutput(ProcessBuilder.Redirect destination) **7**
- ProcessBuilder redirectError(ProcessBuilder.Redirect destination) **7**

  redirect the standard input, output, or error of the process, where destination is one of:

  - Redirect.PIPE—the default behavior, access via the Process object
  - Redirect.INHERIT—the stream from the virtual machine
  - Redirect.DISCARD
  - Redirect.from(file)
  - Redirect.to(file)
  - Redirect.appendTo(file)

- Map<String, String> environment()

  yields a mutable map for setting environment variables for the process.

- Process start()

  starts the process and yields its Process object.

- static List<Process> startPipeline(List<ProcessBuilder> builders) **9**

  starts a pipeline of processes, connecting the standard output of each process to the standard input of the next one.

---

java.lang.Process 1.0

- abstract OutputStream getOutputStream()

  gets a stream for writing to the input stream of the process.

- `abstract InputStream getInputStream()`
- `abstract InputStream getErrorStream()`

get an input stream for reading the output or error stream of the process.

- `abstract int waitFor()`

waits for the process to finish and yields the exit value.

- `boolean waitFor(long timeout, TimeUnit unit)` **8**

waits for the process to finish, but no longer than the given timeout. Returns `true` if the process exited.

- `abstract int exitValue()`

returns the exit value of the process. By convention, a nonzero exit value indicates an error.

- `boolean isAlive()` **8**

checks whether this process is still alive.

- `abstract void destroy()`
- `Process destroyForcibly()` **8**

terminate this process, either normally or forcefully.

- `boolean supportsNormalTermination()` **9**

checks whether this process can be terminated normally or must be destroyed forcefully.

- `ProcessHandle toHandle()` **9**

yields the `ProcessHandle` describing this process.

- `CompletableFuture<Process> onExit()` **9**

yields a `CompletableFuture` that is executed when this process exits.

---

java.lang.ProcessHandle **9**

- `static Optional<ProcessHandle> of(long pid)`
- `static Stream<ProcessHandle> allProcesses()`
- `static ProcessHandle current()`

yield the process handle(s) of the process with the given PID, of all processes, or the process of the virtual machine.

- `Stream<ProcessHandle> children()`
- `Stream<ProcessHandle> descendants()`

yield the process handles of the children or descendants of this process.

- `long pid()`

yields the PID of this process.

- `ProcessHandle.Info info()`

yields detail information about this process.

java.lang.ProcessHandle.Info 9

- `Optional<String[]> arguments()`
- `Optional<String> command()`
- `Optional<String> commandLine()`
- `Optional<Instant> startInstant()`
- `Optional<Duration> totalCpuDuration()`
- `Optional<String> user()`
  yield the given detail information if available.

CHAPTER 11

Annotations

Annotations are tags that you insert into your source code so that some tool can process them. The tools can operate on the source level, or they can process class files into which the compiler has placed annotations.

Annotations do not change the way your programs are compiled. The Java compiler generates the same virtual machine instructions with or without the annotations.

To benefit from annotations, you need to select a processing tool and use annotations that your processing tool understands, before you can apply that tool to your code.

There is a wide range of uses for annotations. For example, JUnit (available at https://junit.org) uses annotations to mark methods that execute tests and to specify how the tests should be run. Jakarta Persistence (https://jakarta.ee/specifications/persistence/) uses annotations to define mappings between classes and database tables, so that objects can be persisted automatically without the developer having to write SQL queries.

In this chapter, you will learn the details of the annotation syntax, how to define your own annotations, and how to write annotation processors.

Note: For a compelling use of annotations, check out JCommander (https://jcommander.org) and picocli (https://picocli.info). These libraries use annotations for the processing of command-line arguments.

11.1. Using Annotations

Here is an example of a simple annotation:

```
class CacheTest
{
   . . .
   @Test void checkRandomInsertions()
}
```

The annotation @Test annotates the checkRandomInsertions method. In Java, an annotation is used like a modifier (such as public or static). The name of each annotation is preceded by an @ symbol.

By itself, the @Test annotation does not do anything. It needs a tool to be useful. When running JUnit, it finds the methods that are annotated with @Test and calls them.

11.1.1. Annotation Elements

Annotations can have key/value pairs called *elements,* such as

```
@RepeatedTest(value=10, failureThreshold=3)
```

The names and types of the permissible elements are defined by each annotation (see Section 11.2). The elements can be processed by the tools that read the annotations.

An annotation element is one of the following:

- A primitive type value
- A String
- A Class object
- An instance of an enum
- An annotation
- An array of the preceding (but not an array of arrays)

To illustrate these possibilities, here is a @BugReport annotation, not from an actual library:

```
@BugReport(showStopper=true,
    assignedTo="Harry",
    testCase=CacheTest.class,
    status=BugReport.Status.CONFIRMED,
    ref=@Reference(id=11235811),
    reportedBy={"Harry", "Fred"})
```

Note: Since annotations are processed by the compiler, all element values must be compile-time constants.

Caution: An annotation element can never have the value null.

If an element value is an array with a single element, you can omit the braces:

```
@BugReport(reportedBy="Harry") // Same as reportedBy={"Harry"}
```

Elements can have default values. For example, the `failureThreshold` element of the JUnit `@RepeatedTest` annotation has default `Integer.MAX_VALUE`. Therefore, the annotation `@RepeatedTest(value=10)` is equivalent to `@RepeatedTest(value=10, failureThreshold=Integer.MAX_VALUE)`. When running this test, it is repeated ten times, no matter how often it failed.

If the element name is `value`, and that is the only element you specify, you can omit `value=`. For example, `@RepeatedTest(10)` is the same as `@RepeatedTest(value=10)`.

11.1.2. Multiple and Repeated Annotations

An item can have multiple annotations:

```
@Test
@Tag("localized")
void testHello()
```

If the author of an annotation declared it to be repeatable, you can repeat the same annotation multiple times:

```
@Tag("localized")
@Tag("showstopper")
void testHello()
```

11.1.3. Annotating Declarations

So far, you have seen annotations applied to method declarations. There are many other places where annotations can occur. They fall into two categories: *declarations* and *type uses*. Declaration annotations can appear at the declarations of

- Classes (including `enum`) and interfaces (including annotation interfaces)
- Methods
- Constructors
- Fields (including `enum` constants and record components)
- Local variables (including those declared in `for` and try-with-resources statements)
- Parameter variables and `catch` clause parameters
- Type parameters
- Packages and modules

For classes, interfaces, and modules, put the annotations before the `class`, `interface`, or `module` keyword and any modifiers:

```
@Entity public class User { . . . }
```

For variables, put them before the type:

```
@SuppressWarnings("unchecked") List<User> users = . . .;
public User getUser(@Param("id") String userId)
```

This also holds for record components:

```
public record Rectangle(@ToString(includeName=false) Point topLeft,
    int width, int height) {}
```

A type parameter in a generic class or method can be annotated like this:

```
public class Cache<@NonNull V> { . . . }
```

A package is annotated in a file `package-info.java` that contains only the package statement preceded by annotations.

```
/**
    Package-level documentation
*/
@Generated("com.horstmann.generator")
package com.horstmann.corejava.generated;
import javax.annotation.processing.Generated;
```

Note that the `import` statement for the annotation comes *after* the package declaration.

 Note: Annotations for local variables and packages are discarded when a class is compiled. Therefore, they can only be processed at the source level.

11.1.4. Annotating Type Uses

A declaration annotation provides some information about the item being declared. For example, in the declaration

```
public User getUser(@NonNull String userId)
```

it is asserted that the `userId` parameter is not `null`.

 Note: The `@NonNull` and `@Localized` annotations are a part of the Checker Framework (`https://types.cs.washington.edu/checker-framework`). With that framework, you can include assertions in your program, such that a parameter is non-null or that a `String` has been localized—that is, adapted to the user's local language and usage. A static analysis tool then checks whether the assertions are valid in a given body of source code.

Now, suppose we have a parameter of type List<String>, and we want to express that all of the strings are non-null. That is where type use annotations come in. Place the annotation before the type argument: List<@NonNull String>

Type use annotations can appear in the following places:

- With generic type arguments: List<@NonNull String>, Comparator.<@NonNull String> reverseOrder().
- In any position of an array: @NonNull String[][] words (words[i][j] is not null), String @NonNull [][] words (words is not null), String[] @NonNull [] words (words[i] is not null).
- With superclasses and implemented interfaces: class Warning extends @Localized Message.
- With constructor invocations: new @Localized String(. . .).
- With nested types: Map.@Localized Entry.
- With casts and instanceof checks: (@Localized String) text, if (text instanceof @Localized String). (The annotations are only for use by external tools. They have no effect on the behavior of a cast or an instanceof check.)
- With exception specifications: public String read() throws @Localized IOException.
- With wildcard types and type bounds: List<@Localized ? extends Message>, List<? extends @Localized Message>.
- With method and constructor references: @Localized Message::getText.

There are a few type positions that cannot be annotated:

```
@NonNull String.class // Error--cannot annotate class literal
import java.lang.@NonNull String; // Error--cannot annotate import
```

You can place annotations before or after other modifiers such as private and static. It is customary (but not required) to put type use annotations after other modifiers, and declaration annotations before other modifiers. For example,

```
private @NonNull String text; // Annotates the type use
@Id private String userId; // Annotates the variable
```

 Note: As you will see in Section 11.2, an annotation author needs to specify where a particular annotation can appear. If an annotation is permissible both for a variable and a type use, and it is used in a variable declaration, then both the variable and the type use are annotated. For example, consider

```
public User getUser(@NonNull String userId)
```

if @NonNull can apply both to parameters and to type uses, the userId parameter is annotated, and the parameter type is @NonNull String.

11.1.5. Making Receivers Explicit

Suppose you want to annotate parameters that are not being mutated by a method.

```
public class Point
{
    public boolean equals(@Nullable Object other) { . . . }
}
```

Then a tool that processes this annotation would, upon seeing a call

```
p.equals(q)
```

reason that q has not been changed.

But what about p?

When the method is called, the receiver variable this is bound to p, but this is never declared, so you cannot annotate it.

Actually, you can declare it, with a rarely used syntax variant, just so that you can add an annotation:

```
public class Point
{
    public boolean equals(@NonNull Point this, @Nullable Object other) { . . . }
}
```

The first parameter is called the *receiver parameter*. It must be named this. Its type is the class that is being constructed.

 Note: You can provide a receiver parameter only for methods, not for constructors. Conceptually, the this reference in a constructor is not an object of the given type until the constructor has completed. Instead, an annotation placed on the constructor describes a property of the constructed object.

A different hidden parameter is passed to the constructor of an inner class, namely the reference to the enclosing class object. You can make this parameter explicit as well:

```
static class Sequence
{
    private int from;
    private int to;

    class Iterator implements java.util.Iterator<Integer>
```

```
{
    private int current;

    public Iterator(@NonNull Sequence Sequence.this)
    {
        this.current = Sequence.this.from;
    }
    . . .
}
. . .
}
```

The parameter must be named just like when you refer to it, *EnclosingClass*.this, and its type is the enclosing class.

11.2. Defining Annotations

Each annotation must be declared by an *annotation interface*, with the @interface syntax. The methods of the interface correspond to the elements of the annotation. For example, the JUnit Test annotation is defined by the following interface:

```
@Target(ElementType.METHOD)
@Retention(RetentionPolicy.RUNTIME)
public @interface RepeatedTest
{
    int failureThreshold();
    . . .
}
```

The @interface declaration creates an actual Java interface. Tools that process annotations receive objects that implement the annotation interface. When the JUnit test runner tool gets an object that implements RepeatedTest, it simply invokes the failureThreshold method to retrieve the failure threshold of a particular RepeatedTest annotation.

The element declarations in the annotation interface are actually method declarations. The methods of an annotation interface can have no parameters and no throws clauses, and they cannot be generic.

The @Target and @Retention annotations are *meta-annotations*. They annotate the @RepeatedTest annotation, indicating the places where the annotation can occur and where it can be accessed.

The value of the @Target meta-annotation is an array of ElementType objects, specifying the items to which the annotation can apply. You can specify any number of element types, enclosed in braces. For example,

```
@Target({ElementType.FIELD, ElementType.RECORD_COMPONENT, ElementType.TYPE})
public @interface ToString
```

Table 11.1 shows all possible targets. The compiler checks that you use an annotation only where permitted. For example, if you apply @ToString to a method, a compile-time error results.

 Note: An annotation without an @Target restriction can be used with any declarations but not with type parameters and type uses. (These were the only possible targets in the first Java release that supported annotations.)

Table 11.1: Element Types for the @Target Annotation

Element Type	Annotation Applies To
ANNOTATION_TYPE	Annotation type declarations
MODULE	Modules
PACKAGE	Packages
TYPE	Classes (including enum) and interfaces (including annotation types)
METHOD	Methods
CONSTRUCTOR	Constructors
FIELD	Fields (including enum constants)
PARAMETER	Method or constructor parameters
RECORD_COMPONENT	Record components
LOCAL_VARIABLE	Local variables
TYPE_PARAMETER	Type parameters
TYPE_USE	Uses of a type

When you annotate a record component, the annotation is applied to the fields and methods to which the component gives rise, provided the annotation is permitted on fields or methods. For example, in the annotation

```
public record Rectangle(@ToString(includeName=false) Point topLeft,
    int width, int height) {}
```

the topLeft field receives the annotation if its target types include ElementType.FIELD.

The @Retention meta-annotation specifies where the annotation can be accessed. There are three choices.

1. RetentionPolicy.SOURCE: The annotation is available to source processors, but it is not included in class files.
2. RetentionPolicy.CLASS: The annotation is included in class files, but the virtual machine does not load them. This is the default.
3. RetentionPolicy.RUNTIME: The annotation is available at runtime and can be accessed through the reflection API.

You will see examples of all three scenarios later in this chapter.

There are several other meta-annotations—see Section 11.3 for a complete list.

To specify a default value for an element, add a default clause after the method defining the element. For example,

```
public @interface RepeatedTest
{
   int failureThreshold() default Integer.MAX_VALUE;
   . . .
}
```

This example shows how to denote a default of an empty array and a default for an annotation:

```
public @interface BugReport
{
   String[] reportedBy() default {};
      // Defaults to empty array
   Reference ref() default @Reference(id=0);
      // Default for an annotation
   . . .
}
```

 Caution: Defaults are not stored with the annotation; instead, they are dynamically computed. If you change a default and recompile the annotation class, all annotated elements will use the new default, even in class files that have been compiled before the default changed.

All annotation interfaces implicitly extend the java.lang.annotation.Annotation interface. That interface is a regular interface, *not* an annotation interface. See the API notes at the end of this section for the methods provided by this interface.

You cannot extend annotation interfaces, and you never supply classes that implement annotation interfaces. Instead, source processing tools and the virtual machine generate proxy classes and objects when needed.

---

java.lang.annotation.Annotation 5.0

- `Class<? extends Annotation> annotationType()`
  returns the `Class` object that represents the annotation interface of this annotation object. Note that calling `getClass` on an annotation object would return the actual class, not the interface.
- `boolean equals(Object other)`
  returns `true` if `other` is an object that implements the same annotation interface as this annotation object and if all elements of this object and `other` are equal.
- `int hashCode()`
  returns a hash code, compatible with the `equals` method, derived from the name of the annotation interface and the element values.
- `String toString()`
  returns a string representation that contains the annotation interface name and the names and values of the elements.

11.3. Annotations in the Java API

The Java API defines a number of annotation interfaces in the `java.lang`, `java.lang.annotation`, and `javax.annotation` packages. Four of them are meta-annotations that describe the behavior of annotation interfaces. The others are regular annotations that you can use to annotate items in your source code. Table 11.2 shows these annotations. I will discuss them in detail in the following two sections.

Table 11.2: Annotations in the Java API

Annotation Interface	Applicable To	Purpose
Override	Methods	Checks that this method overrides a superclass method.
Serial	Methods	Checks that this method is a correct serialization method.
Deprecated	All declarations	Marks item as deprecated.

SuppressWarnings	All declarations except packages	Suppresses warning messages of a given type.
SafeVarargs	Methods and constructors	Asserts that the varargs parameter is safe to use.
FunctionalInterface	Interfaces	Marks an interface as functional (with a single abstract method).
Generated	All declarations	Marks an item as source code that has been generated by a tool.
Target	Annotations	Specifies the locations to which this annotation can be applied.
Retention	Annotations	Specifies where this annotation can be used.
Documented	Annotations	Specifies that this annotation should be included in the documentation of annotated items.
Inherited	Annotations	Specifies that this annotation is inherited by subclasses.
Repeatable	Annotations	Specifies that this annotation can be applied multiple times to the same item.

11.3.1. Annotations for Compilation

The @Deprecated annotation can be attached to any items whose use is no longer encouraged. The compiler will warn when you use a deprecated item. This annotation has the same role as the @deprecated JavaDoc tag. However, the annotation persists until runtime.

 Note: The jdeprscan utility which is part of the JDK can scan a set of JAR files for deprecated elements.

The @Override annotation makes the compiler check that the annotated method really overrides a method from the superclass. For example, if you declare

```
public class Point
{
   @Override public boolean equals(Point other) { . . . }
   . . .
}
```

then the compiler will report an error—this equals method does not override the equals method of the Object class because that method has a parameter of type Object, not Point.

The @Serial annotation checks that methods used for serialization, which are not declared in interfaces, have the correct parameter types.

The @SuppressWarnings annotation tells the compiler to suppress warning messages of a particular category, for example

```
@SuppressWarnings("unchecked") T[] result
    = (T[]) Array.newInstance(cl, n);
```

The @SafeVarargs annotation asserts that a method does not corrupt its varargs parameter (see Chapter 8).

The @Generated annotation is intended for use by code generator tools. Any generated source code can be annotated to differentiate it from programmer-provided code. For example, a code editor can hide the generated code, or a code generator can remove older versions of generated code. Each annotation must contain a unique identifier for the code generator. A date string (in ISO 8601/RFC 3339 format) and a comment string are optional. For example,

```
@Generated(value="com.horstmann.generator",
    date="2015-01-04T12:08:56.235-0700");
```

You have seen the FunctionalInterface annotation in Chapter 6. It is used to annotate conversion targets for lambda expressions, such as

```
@FunctionalInterface
public interface IntFunction<R>
{
   R apply(int value);
}
```

If you later add another abstract method, the compiler will generate an error.

Of course, you should only add this annotation to interfaces that describe functions. There are other interfaces with a single abstract method (such as AutoCloseable) that are not conceptually functions.

11.3 ■ Annotations in the Java API

11.3.2. Meta-Annotations

You have already seen the @Target and @Retention meta-annotations in Section 11.2.

The @Documented meta-annotation gives a hint to documentation tools such as JavaDoc. Documented annotations should be treated just like other modifiers (such as private or static) for documentation purposes. In contrast, other annotations should not be included in the documentation.

For example, the @SuppressWarnings annotation is not documented. If a method or field has that annotation, it is an implementation detail that is of no interest to the JavaDoc reader. On the other hand, the @FunctionalInterface annotation is documented since it is useful for the programmer to know that the interface is intended to describe a function. Figure 11.1 shows the documentation.

The @Inherited meta-annotation applies only to annotations for classes. When a class has an inherited annotation, then all of its subclasses automatically have the same annotation. This makes it easy to create annotations that work similar to marker interfaces (such as the Serializable interface).

Suppose you define an inherited annotation @Persistent to indicate that objects of a class can be saved in a database. Then the subclasses of persistent classes are automatically annotated as persistent.

```
@Inherited @interface Persistent { }

@Persistent class Employee { . . . }
class Manager extends Employee { . . . } // Also @Persistent
```

The @Repeatable meta-annotation makes it possible to apply the same annotation multiple times. For example, the JUnit @Tag annotation is repeatable. It can be used like this:

```
@Tag("localized")
@Tag("showstopper")
void testHello() { . . . }
```

For historical reasons, the implementor of a repeatable annotation needs to provide a *container annotation* that holds the repeated annotations in an array.

Here is how to define the @Tag annotation and its container:

```
@Repeatable(Tag.class)
@interface Tag
{
    String value();
}
```

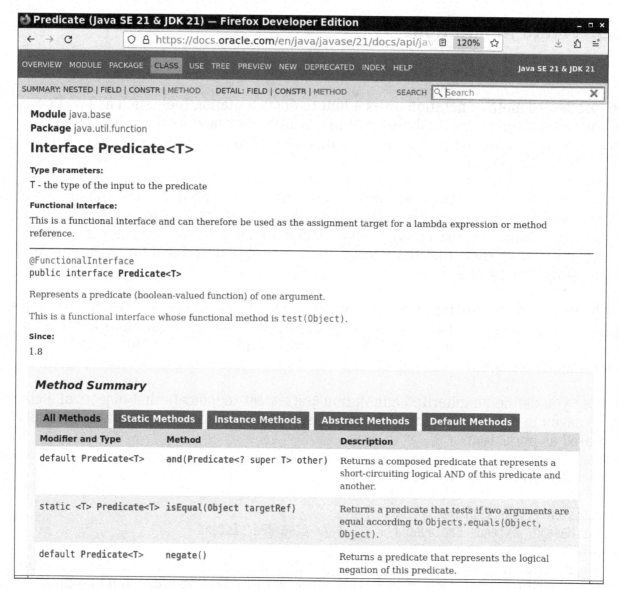

Figure 11.1: A documented annotation

```
@interface Tags
{
   Tag[] value();
}
```

Whenever the user supplies two or more @Tag annotations, they are automatically wrapped into a @Tags annotation. This complicates processing of the annotation, as you will see in the next section.

11.4. Processing Annotations at Runtime

So far, you have seen how to add annotations to source files and how to define annotation types. Now the time has come to see what good can come out of that.

In this section, I show you a simple example of processing an annotation at runtime using the reflection API that you have already seen in Chapter 5. Suppose we want to reduce the tedium of implementing toString methods. Of course, one can write a generic toString method using reflection that simply includes all field names and values. But suppose we want to customize that process. We may not want to include all fields, or we may want to skip class and variable names. For example, for the Point class we may prefer [5,10] instead of Point[x=5,y=10]. Of course, any number of other enhancements would be plausible, but let's keep it simple. The point is to demonstrate what an annotation processor can do.

Annotate all classes that you want to benefit from this service with the @ToString annotation. In addition, all fields that should be included need to be annotated as well. The annotation is defined like this:

```
@Target({ElementType.FIELD, ElementType.RECORD_COMPONENT, ElementType.TYPE})
@Retention(RetentionPolicy.RUNTIME)
public @interface ToString
{
    boolean includeName() default true;
}
```

Here are annotated Point and Rectangle classes:

```
@ToString(includeName=false)
public class Point
{
    @ToString(includeName=false) private int x;
    @ToString(includeName=false) private int y;
    . . .
}

@ToString
public record Rectangle(
    @ToString(includeName=false) Point topLeft,
    @ToString int width,
    @ToString int height)
{}
```

The intent is for a rectangle to be represented as string as Rectangle[[5, 10],width=20,height=30].

At runtime, we cannot modify the implementation of the toString method for a given class. Instead, let us provide a method that can format any object, discovering and using the ToString annotations if they are present.

The key are the methods

```
T getAnnotation(Class<T>)
T getDeclaredAnnotation(Class<T>)
T[] getAnnotationsByType(Class<T>)
T[] getDeclaredAnnotationsByType(Class<T>)
Annotation[] getAnnotations()
Annotation[] getDeclaredAnnotations()
boolean isAnnotationPresent(Class<? extends Annotation> annotationClass)
```

of the AnnotatedElement interface. The reflection classes Class, Field, Parameter, Method, Constructor, and Package implement that interface.

As with other reflection methods, the methods with Declared in their name yield annotations in the class itself, whereas the others include inherited ones. In the context of annotations, this means that the annotation is @Inherited and applied to a superclass.

If an annotation is not repeatable, call getAnnotation to locate it. For example:

```
Class<?> cl = obj.getClass();
ToString ts = cl.getAnnotation(ToString.class);
if (ts != null && ts.includeName()) . . .
```

Note that you pass the class object for the annotation (here, ToString.class) and you get back an object of some proxy class that implements the ToString interface. You can then invoke the interface methods to get the values of the annotation elements. If the annotation is not present, the getAnnotation method returns null.

It gets a bit messy if an annotation is repeatable. If you call getAnnotation to look up a repeatable annotation, and the annotation was actually repeated, then you also get null. That is because the repeated annotations were wrapped inside the container annotation.

In this case, you should call getAnnotationsByType. That call "looks through" the container and gives you an array of the repeated annotations. If there was just one annotation, you get it in an array of length 1. With this method, you don't have to worry about the container annotation.

The getAnnotations method gets all annotations (of any type) with which an item is annotated, with repeated annotations wrapped into containers.

Listing 11.2 shows the implementation of the annotation-aware toString method.

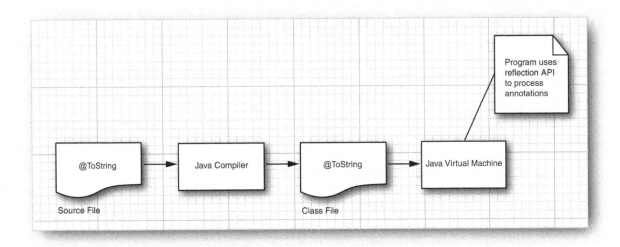

Figure 11.2: Processing annotations at runtime

When a class is annotated with ToString, the method iterates over its fields and prints the ones that are also annotated. If the includeName element is true, then the class or field name is included in the string.

Note that the method calls itself recursively. Whenever an object belongs to a class that isn't annotated, its regular toString method is used and the recursion stops.

Figure 7.1 shows how annotations are handled in this example.

This is a simple but typical use of the runtime annotation API. Look up classes, fields, and so on, using reflection; call getAnnotation or getAnnotationsByType on the potentially annotated elements to retrieve the annotations; then, invoke the methods of the annotation interfaces to obtain the element values.

Listing 11.1 `runtimeAnnotations/RuntimeAnnotationDemo.java`

```
 1  package runtimeAnnotations;
 2
 3  public class RuntimeAnnotationDemo
 4  {
 5     public static void main(String[] args)
 6     {
 7        var rect = new Rectangle(new Point(5, 10), 20, 30);
 8        System.out.println(ToStrings.toString(rect));
 9     }
10  }
```

Listing 11.2 runtimeAnnotations/ToStrings.java

```
1  package runtimeAnnotations;
2
3  import java.lang.reflect.*;
4
5  public class ToStrings
6  {
7     public static String toString(Object obj)
8     {
9        if (obj == null) return "null";
10       Class<?> cl = obj.getClass();
11       ToString ts = cl.getAnnotation(ToString.class);
12       if (ts == null) return obj.toString();
13       var result = new StringBuilder();
14       if (ts.includeName()) result.append(cl.getName());
15       result.append("[");
16       boolean first = true;
17       for (Field f : cl.getDeclaredFields())
18       {
19          ts = f.getAnnotation(ToString.class);
20          if (ts != null) {
21             if (first) first = false; else result.append(",");
22             f.setAccessible(true);
23             if (ts.includeName())
24             {
25                result.append(f.getName());
26                result.append("=");
27             }
28             try
29             {
30                result.append(ToStrings.toString(f.get(obj)));
31             }
32             catch (ReflectiveOperationException ex)
33             {
34                ex.printStackTrace();
35             }
36          }
37       }
38       result.append("]");
39       return result.toString();
40    }
41 }
```

---

java.lang.reflect.AnnotatedElement **5.0**

- boolean isAnnotationPresent(Class<? extends Annotation> annotationType)
  returns true if this item has an annotation of the given type.

- `<T extends Annotation> T getAnnotation(Class<T> annotationType)`
  gets the annotation of the given type, or `null` if this item has no such annotation.
- `<T extends Annotation> T[] getAnnotationsByType(Class<T> annotationType)` **8**
  gets all annotations of a repeatable annotation type (see Section 11.3.2). If none are present, an array of length 0 is returned.
- `Annotation[] getAnnotations()`
  gets all annotations present for this item, including inherited annotations. If none are present, an array of length 0 is returned.
- `Annotation[] getDeclaredAnnotations()`
  gets all annotations declared for this item, excluding inherited annotations. If none are present, an array of length 0 is returned.

11.5. Source-Level Annotation Processing

In the preceding section, you saw how to analyze annotations in a running program. Another use for annotation is the automatic processing of source files to produce more source code, configuration files, scripts, or whatever else one might want to generate.

To show you the mechanics, I will repeat the example of generating `toString` methods. However, this time, let's generate them in Java source. Then the methods will get compiled with the rest of the program, and they will run at full speed instead of using reflection.

11.5.1. Annotation Processors

Annotation processing is integrated into the Java compiler. During compilation, you can *invoke annotation processors* by running

```
javac -processor ProcessorClassName₁,ProcessorClassName₂,. . . sourceFiles
```

The compiler locates the annotations of the source files. Each annotation processor is executed in turn and given the annotations in which it expressed an interest. If an annotation processor creates a new source file, the process is repeated. Once a processing round yields no further source files, all source files are compiled.

 Note: An annotation processor can only generate new source files. It cannot modify an existing source file.

An annotation processor implements the `Processor` interface, generally by extending the `AbstractProcessor` class. You need to specify which annotations your processor supports. In our case:

```
@SupportedAnnotationTypes("annotations.ToString")
@SupportedSourceVersion(SourceVersion.RELEASE_8)
public class ToStringAnnotationProcessor extends AbstractProcessor
```

```
{
    public boolean process(Set<? extends TypeElement> annotations,
            RoundEnvironment currentRound)
    {
        . . .
    }
}
```

A processor can claim specific annotation types, wildcards such as "com.horstmann.*" (all annotations in the com.horstmann package or any subpackage), or even "*" (all annotations).

The process method is called once for each round, with the set of all annotations that were found in any files during this round, and a RoundEnvironment reference that contains information about the current processing round.

11.5.2. The Language Model API

Use the *language model* API for analyzing source-level annotations. Unlike the reflection API, which presents the virtual machine representation of classes and methods, the language model API lets you analyze a Java program according to the rules of the Java language.

The compiler produces a tree whose nodes are instances of classes that implement the javax.lang.model.element.Element interface and its subinterfaces, TypeElement, VariableElement, ExecutableElement, and so on. These are the compile-time analogs to the Class, Field/Parameter, Method/Constructor reflection classes.

I do not want to cover the API in detail, but here are the highlights that you need to know for processing annotations.

- The RoundEnvironment gives you a set of all elements annotated with a particular annotation, by calling the one of the methods

    ```
    Set<? extends Element> getElementsAnnotatedWith(Class<? extends Annotation> a)
    Set<? extends Element> getElementsAnnotatedWithAny(
        Set<Class<? extends Annotation>> annotations)
    ```

    The second method is useful for repeated annotations.
- The source-level equivalent of the AnnotatedElement interface is AnnotatedConstruct. Use the methods

    ```
    A getAnnotation(Class<A> annotationType)
    A[] getAnnotationsByType(Class<A> annotationType)
    ```

    to get the annotation or repeated annotations for a given annotation class.

- A `TypeElement` represents a class or interface. The `getEnclosedElements` method yields a list of its fields and methods.
- Calling `getSimpleName` on an `Element` or `getQualifiedName` on a `TypeElement` yields a `Name` object that can be converted to a string with `toString`.

11.5.3. Using Annotations to Generate Source Code

Let us return to our task of automatically generating `toString` methods. We can't put these methods into the original classes—annotation processors can only produce new classes, not modify existing ones.

Therefore, we'll add all methods into a utility class `ToStrings`:

```
public class ToStrings
{
   public static String toString(Point obj)
   {
      Generated code
   }
   public static String toString(Rectangle obj)
   {
      Generated code
   }
   . . .
   public static String toString(Object obj)
   {
      return Objects.toString(obj);
   }
}
```

Since we don't want to use reflection, we annotate accessor methods, not fields:

```
@ToString
public class Rectangle
{
   . . .
   @ToString(includeName=false) public Point getTopLeft() { return topLeft; }
   @ToString public int getWidth() { return width; }
   @ToString public int getHeight() { return height; }
}
```

The annotation processor should then generate the following source code:

```
public static String toString(Rectangle obj)
{
   var result = new StringBuilder();
   result.append("Rectangle");
```

```
      result.append("[");
      result.append(toString(obj.getTopLeft()));
      result.append(",");
      result.append("width=");
      result.append(toString(obj.getWidth()));
      result.append(",");
      result.append("height=");
      result.append(toString(obj.getHeight()));
      result.append("]");
      return result.toString();
   }
```

The "boilerplate" code is in gray. Here is an outline of the method that produces the
toString method for a class with given TypeElement:

```
   private void writeToStringMethod(PrintWriter out, TypeElement te)
   {
      String className = te.getQualifiedName().toString();
      Print method header and declaration of string builder
      ToString ann = te.getAnnotation(ToString.class);
      if (ann.includeName()) Print code to add class name
      for (Element c : te.getEnclosedElements())
      {
         ann = c.getAnnotation(ToString.class);
         if (ann != null)
         {
            if (ann.includeName()) Print code to add field name
            Print code to append toString(obj.methodName())
         }
      }
      Print code to return string
   }
```

And here is an outline of the process method of the annotation processor. It creates a source
file for the helper class and writes the class header and one method for each annotated
class.

```
   public boolean process(Set<? extends TypeElement> annotations,
         RoundEnvironment currentRound)
   {
      if (annotations.size() == 0) return true;
      try
      {
         JavaFileObject sourceFile = processingEnv.getFiler().createSourceFile(
            "annotations.ToStrings");
         try (var out = new PrintWriter(sourceFile.openWriter()))
         {
```

```
        Print code for package and class
        for (Element e : currentRound.getElementsAnnotatedWith(ToString.class))
            if (e instanceof TypeElement te)
                writeToStringMethod(out, te);
        Print code for toString(Object)
      }
   }
   catch (IOException ex)
   {
      processingEnv.getMessager().printMessage(Kind.ERROR, ex.getMessage());
   }
   return true;
}
```

Note that the process method is called in subsequent rounds with an empty list of annotations. It then returns immediately so it doesn't create the source file twice.

 Tip: To see the rounds, run the javac command with the -XprintRounds flag:

```
Round 1:
  input files: {rect.Point, rect.Rectangle, rect.SourceLevelAnnotationDemo}
  annotations: [sourceAnnotations.ToString]
  last round: false
Round 2:
  input files: {sourceAnnotations.ToStrings}
  annotations: []
  last round: false
Round 3:
  input files: {}
  annotations: []
  last round: true
```

To run the example program, first build the annotation processor, then use it to compile the demo:

```
javac sourceAnnotations/ToStringAnnotationProcessor.java
javac -XprintRounds -processor sourceAnnotations.ToStringAnnotationProcessor rect/*.java
java rect.SourceLevelAnnotationDemo
```

This example demonstrates how tools can harvest source file annotations to produce other files. The generated files don't have to be source files. Annotation processors may choose to generate XML descriptors, property files, shell scripts, HTML documentation, and so on.

Note: Some people have suggested using annotations to remove an even bigger drudgery. Wouldn't it be nice if trivial getters and setters were generated automatically? For example, the annotation

```
@Property private String title;
```

could produce the methods

```
public String getTitle() { return title; }
public void setTitle(String title) { this = title; }
```

However, those methods need to be added to the *same class*. This requires editing a source file, not just generating another file, and is beyond the capabilities of annotation processors. It would be possible to build another tool for this purpose, but such a tool would go beyond the mission of annotations. An annotation is intended as a description *about* a code item, not a directive for adding or changing code.

A popular tool called Project Lombok has found a way around this limitation. By modifying internal compiler data structures during annotation processing, it can produce getter and setter methods. At least for now, it works, but it is not standard Java.

Listing 11.3 `rect/SourceLevelAnnotationDemo.java`

```java
1  package rect;
2
3  import sourceAnnotations.ToStrings;
4
5  public class SourceLevelAnnotationDemo
6  {
7     public static void main(String[] args)
8     {
9        var rect = new Rectangle(new Point(5, 10), 20, 30);
10       System.out.println(ToStrings.toString(rect));
11    }
12 }
```

Listing 11.4 `sourceAnnotations/ToStringAnnotationProcessor.java`

```java
1  package sourceAnnotations;
2
3  import java.beans.*;
4  import java.io.*;
5  import java.util.*;
```

```
 6
 7  import javax.annotation.processing.*;
 8  import javax.lang.model.*;
 9  import javax.lang.model.element.*;
10  import javax.tools.*;
11  import javax.tools.Diagnostic.Kind;
12
13  @SupportedAnnotationTypes("sourceAnnotations.ToString")
14  @SupportedSourceVersion(SourceVersion.RELEASE_21)
15  public class ToStringAnnotationProcessor extends AbstractProcessor
16  {
17     public boolean process(Set<? extends TypeElement> annotations,
18           RoundEnvironment currentRound)
19     {
20        if (annotations.size() == 0) return true;
21        try
22        {
23           JavaFileObject sourceFile
24              = processingEnv.getFiler().createSourceFile("sourceAnnotations.ToStrings");
25           try (var out = new PrintWriter(sourceFile.openWriter()))
26           {
27              out.println("// Automatically generated by"
28                 + " sourceAnnotations.ToStringAnnotationProcessor");
29              out.println("package sourceAnnotations;");
30              out.println("public class ToStrings {");
31
32              for (Element e : currentRound.getElementsAnnotatedWith(ToString.class))
33                 if (e instanceof TypeElement te)
34                    writeToStringMethod(out, te);
35              out.println("   public static String toString(Object obj) {");
36              out.println("      return java.util.Objects.toString(obj);");
37              out.println("   }");
38              out.println("}");
39           }
40        }
41        catch (IOException e)
42        {
43           processingEnv.getMessager().printMessage(Kind.ERROR, e.getMessage());
44        }
45        return true;
46     }
47
48     private void writeToStringMethod(PrintWriter out, TypeElement te)
49     {
50        String className = te.getQualifiedName().toString();
51        out.println("   public static String toString(" + className + " obj) {");
52        ToString ann = te.getAnnotation(ToString.class);
53        out.println("      var result = new StringBuilder();");
54        if (ann.includeName())
55           out.println("      result.append(\"" + className + "\");");
56        out.println("      result.append(\"[\");");
57        boolean first = true;
```

```
58    for (Element c : te.getEnclosedElements())
59    {
60       String methodName = c.getSimpleName().toString();
61       ann = c.getAnnotation(ToString.class);
62       if (ann != null)
63       {
64          if (first) first = false; else out.println("          result.append(\",\");");
65          if (ann.includeName())
66          {
67             String fieldName = Introspector.decapitalize(
68                methodName.replaceAll("^(get|is)", ""));
69                // Turn getWidth into width, isDone into done, getURL into URL
70             out.println("          result.append(\"" + fieldName + "=" + "\");");
71          }
72          out.println("          result.append(toString(obj." + methodName + "()));");
73       }
74    }
75    out.println("          result.append(\"]\");");
76    out.println("          return result.toString();");
77    out.println("    }");
78    }
79 }
```

11.6. Bytecode Engineering

You have seen how annotations can be processed at runtime or at the source code level. There is a third possibility: processing at the bytecode level. Unless annotations are removed at the source level, they are present in the class files. The class file format is documented (see https://docs.oracle.com/javase/specs/jvms/se21/html). The format is rather complex, and it would be challenging to process class files without special libraries. One such library is the ASM library, available at https://asm.ow2.org. Download asm-9.6.jar and asm-commons-9.6.jar and place them in a directory of your choice, called *asm* in the instructions.

11.6.1. Modifying Class Files

In this section, we use ASM to add logging messages to annotated methods. If a method is annotated with

```
@LogEntry(logger=loggerName)
```

then we add the bytecodes for the following statement at the beginning of the method:

```
System.getLogger(loggerName).log(System.Logger.Level.TRACE,
   "Entering {0}.{1}", className, methodName);
```

For example, if you annotate the hashCode method of the Item class as

```
@LogEntry(logger="com.horstmann") public int hashCode()
```

then a message similar to the following is printed whenever the method is called:

```
Dec 03, 2023 5:58:44 PM set.Item hashCode
INFO: Entering set.Item.hashCode
```

To achieve this, we do the following:

1. Load the bytecodes in the class file.
2. Locate all methods.
3. For each method, check whether it has a LogEntry annotation.
4. If it does, add the bytecodes for the following instructions at the beginning of the method:

```
ldc loggerName
invokestatic System.getLogger(String)
getstatic System.Logger.Level.INFO
ldc "Entering {0}.{1}"
iconst_2
anewarray
dup
iconst_0
ldc className
aastore
dup
iconst_1
ldc methodName
aastore
invokeinterface System.Logger.log(System.Logger.Level, String, Object[])
```

Inserting these bytecodes sounds tricky, but the ASM library makes it fairly straightforward. I won't describe the process of analyzing and inserting bytecodes in detail. The important point is that the program in Listing 11.5 edits a class file and inserts a logging call at the beginning of the methods annotated with the LogEntry annotation.

For example, here is how you add the logging instructions to Item.java in Listing 11.6, where *asm* is the directory into which you installed the ASM library:

```
javac set/Item.java
javac -classpath .:asm/\* bytecodeAnnotations/EntryLogger.java
java -classpath .:asm/\* bytecodeAnnotations.EntryLogger set/Item.class
```

As always, with Windows, you use \ instead of / as file separator and ; instead of : as path separator, and you do not escape the *.

Try running

```
javap -c set.Item
```

before and after modifying the Item class file. You can see the inserted instructions at the beginning of the hashCode, equals, and compareTo methods.

```
public int hashCode();
    Code:
       0: ldc #42 // String com.horstmann
       2: invokestatic #48
          // Method java/lang/System.getLogger:(Ljava/lang/String;)Ljava/lang/System$Logger;
       5: getstatic #54
          // Field java/lang/System$Logger$Level.INFO:Ljava/lang/System$Logger$Level;
       8: ldc #56 // String Entering {0}.{1}
      10: iconst_2
      11: anewarray #4 // class java/lang/Object
      14: dup
      15: iconst_0
      16: ldc #58 // String set.Item
      18: aastore
      19: dup
      20: iconst_1
      21: ldc #77 // String hashCode
      23: aastore
      24: invokeinterface #65, 4 // InterfaceMethod java/lang/System$Logger.log:
          // (Ljava/lang/System$Logger$Level;Ljava/lang/String;[Ljava/lang/Object;)V
       . . .
```

The index values into the constant pool may be different when you try this.

The SetTest program in Listing 11.7 inserts Item objects into a hash set. When you run it with the modified class file, you will see the logging messages.

```
Dec 03, 2023 5:58:44 PM set.Item hashCode
INFO: Entering set.Item.hashCode
Dec 03, 2023 5:58:44 PM set.Item hashCode
INFO: Entering set.Item.hashCode
Dec 03, 2023 5:58:44 PM set.Item hashCode
INFO: Entering set.Item.hashCode
Dec 03, 2023 5:58:44 PM set.Item equals
INFO: Entering set.Item.equals
[[description=Microwave, partNumber=4104], [description=Toaster, partNumber=1279]]
```

Note the call to equals when we insert the same item twice.

This example shows the power of bytecode engineering. Annotations are used to add directives to a program, and a bytecode editing tool picks up the directives and modifies the virtual machine instructions.

Listing 11.5 bytecodeAnnotations/EntryLogger.java

```java
 1  package bytecodeAnnotations;
 2
 3  import java.io.*;
 4  import java.nio.file.*;
 5
 6  import org.objectweb.asm.*;
 7  import org.objectweb.asm.commons.*;
 8
 9  /**
10   * Adds "entering" logs to all methods of a class that have the LogEntry annotation.
11   * @version 1.22 2023-12-01
12   * @author Cay Horstmann
13   */
14  public class EntryLogger extends ClassVisitor
15  {
16     private String className;
17
18     /**
19      * Constructs an EntryLogger that inserts logging into annotated methods of a given class.
20      */
21     public EntryLogger(ClassWriter writer, String className)
22     {
23        super(Opcodes.ASM8, writer);
24        this.className = className;
25     }
26
27     public MethodVisitor visitMethod(int access, String methodName, String desc,
28           String signature, String[] exceptions)
29     {
30        MethodVisitor mv = cv.visitMethod(access, methodName, desc, signature, exceptions);
31        return new AdviceAdapter(Opcodes.ASM8, mv, access, methodName, desc)
32           {
33              private String loggerName;
34
35              public AnnotationVisitor visitAnnotation(String desc, boolean visible)
36              {
37                 return new AnnotationVisitor(Opcodes.ASM8)
38                    {
39                       public void visit(String name, Object value)
40                       {
41                          if (desc.equals("LbytecodeAnnotations/LogEntry;")
42                                && name.equals("logger"))
43                             loggerName = value.toString();
44                       }
45                    };
46              }
47
48              public void onMethodEnter()
```

```
 49                    {
 50                        if (loggerName != null)
 51                        {
 52                            /*
 53                            visitLdcInsn(loggerName);
 54                            visitMethodInsn(INVOKESTATIC, "java/util/logging/Logger", "getLogger",
 55                                "(Ljava/lang/String;)Ljava/util/logging/Logger;", false);
 56                            visitLdcInsn(className);
 57                            visitLdcInsn(methodName);
 58                            visitMethodInsn(INVOKEVIRTUAL, "java/util/logging/Logger", "entering",
 59                                "(Ljava/lang/String;Ljava/lang/String;)V", false);
 60                            */
 61                            visitLdcInsn(loggerName);
 62                            visitMethodInsn(INVOKESTATIC, "java/lang/System", "getLogger",
 63                                "(Ljava/lang/String;)Ljava/lang/System$Logger;", false);
 64                            visitFieldInsn(Opcodes.GETSTATIC, "java/lang/System$Logger$Level", "INFO",
 65                                "Ljava/lang/System$Logger$Level;");
 66                            visitLdcInsn("Entering {0}.{1}");
 67
 68                            // Create an array of Objects with a length of 2
 69                            mv.visitInsn(Opcodes.ICONST_2);  // array length
 70                            mv.visitTypeInsn(Opcodes.ANEWARRAY, "java/lang/Object");  // array type
 71
 72                            // Add two objects to the array
 73                            mv.visitInsn(Opcodes.DUP);  // duplicate array reference
 74                            mv.visitInsn(Opcodes.ICONST_0);  // index 0
 75                            visitLdcInsn(className);
 76                            mv.visitInsn(Opcodes.AASTORE);  // store in array
 77
 78                            mv.visitInsn(Opcodes.DUP);  // duplicate array reference
 79                            mv.visitInsn(Opcodes.ICONST_1);  // index 1
 80                            visitLdcInsn(methodName);
 81                            mv.visitInsn(Opcodes.AASTORE);  // store in array
 82
 83                            visitMethodInsn(INVOKEINTERFACE, "java/lang/System$Logger", "log",
 84                                "(Ljava/lang/System$Logger$Level;Ljava/lang/String;[Ljava/lang/Object;)V",
 85                                true);
 86                            loggerName = null;
 87                        }
 88                    }
 89                };
 90    }
 91
 92    /**
 93     * Adds entry logging code to the given class.
 94     * @param args the name of the class file to patch
 95     */
 96    public static void main(String[] args) throws IOException
 97    {
 98        if (args.length == 0)
 99        {
100            System.out.println("USAGE: java bytecodeAnnotations.EntryLogger classfile");
```

```
101          System.exit(1);
102       }
103       Path path = Path.of(args[0]);
104       var reader = new ClassReader(Files.newInputStream(path));
105       var writer = new ClassWriter(
106          ClassWriter.COMPUTE_MAXS | ClassWriter.COMPUTE_FRAMES);
107       var entryLogger = new EntryLogger(writer,
108          path.toString().replace(".class", "").replaceAll("[/\\\\]", "."));
109       reader.accept(entryLogger, ClassReader.EXPAND_FRAMES);
110       Files.write(Path.of(args[0]), writer.toByteArray());
111    }
112 }
```

Listing 11.6 set/Item.java

```
 1 package set;
 2
 3 import java.util.*;
 4 import bytecodeAnnotations.*;
 5
 6 /**
 7  * An item with a description and a part number.
 8  * @version 1.01 2012-01-26
 9  * @author Cay Horstmann
10  */
11 public class Item
12 {
13    private String description;
14    private int partNumber;
15
16    /**
17     * Constructs an item.
18     * @param aDescription the item's description
19     * @param aPartNumber the item's part number
20     */
21    public Item(String aDescription, int aPartNumber)
22    {
23       description = aDescription;
24       partNumber = aPartNumber;
25    }
26
27    /**
28     * Gets the description of this item.
29     * @return the description
30     */
31    public String getDescription()
32    {
33       return description;
34    }
35
```

```
36      public String toString()
37      {
38         return "[description=" + description + ", partNumber=" + partNumber + "]";
39      }
40
41      @LogEntry(logger = "com.horstmann")
42      public boolean equals(Object otherObject)
43      {
44         if (this == otherObject) return true;
45         if (otherObject == null) return false;
46         if (getClass() != otherObject.getClass()) return false;
47         var other = (Item) otherObject;
48         return Objects.equals(description, other.description) && partNumber == other.partNumber;
49      }
50
51      @LogEntry(logger = "com.horstmann")
52      public int hashCode()
53      {
54         return Objects.hash(description, partNumber);
55      }
56   }
```

Listing 11.7 set/SetTest.java

```
1    package set;
2
3    import java.util.*;
4    import java.util.logging.*;
5
6    /**
7     * @version 1.03 2018-05-01
8     * @author Cay Horstmann
9     */
10   public class SetTest
11   {
12      public static void main(String[] args)
13      {
14         Logger.getLogger("com.horstmann").setLevel(Level.FINEST);
15         var handler = new ConsoleHandler();
16         handler.setLevel(Level.FINEST);
17         Logger.getLogger("com.horstmann").addHandler(handler);
18
19         var parts = new HashSet<Item>();
20         parts.add(new Item("Toaster", 1279));
21         parts.add(new Item("Microwave", 4104));
22         parts.add(new Item("Toaster", 1279));
23         System.out.println(parts);
24      }
25   }
```

11.6.2. Modifying Bytecodes at Load Time

In the last section, you saw a tool that edits class files. However, it can be cumbersome to add yet another tool into the build process. An attractive alternative is to defer the bytecode engineering until *load time*, when the class loader loads the class.

The *instrumentation API* has a hook for installing a bytecode transformer. The transformer must be installed before the main method of the program is called. You can meet this requirement by defining an *agent*, a library that is loaded to monitor a program in some way. The agent code can carry out initializations in a premain method.

Here are the steps required to build an agent:

1. Implement a class with a method

   ```
   public static void premain(String arg, Instrumentation instr)
   ```

   This method is called when the agent is loaded. The agent can get a single command-line argument, which is passed in the arg parameter. The instr parameter can be used to install various hooks.
2. Make a manifest file EntryLoggingAgent.mf that sets the Premain-Class attribute, for example:

   ```
   Premain-Class: bytecodeAnnotations.EntryLoggingAgent
   ```

3. Package the agent code and the manifest into a JAR file:

   ```
   javac -classpath .:asm/\* bytecodeAnnotations/EntryLoggingAgent.java
   jar cvfm EntryLoggingAgent.jar bytecodeAnnotations/EntryLoggingAgent.mf \
       bytecodeAnnotations/Entry*.class
   ```

To launch a Java program together with the agent, use the following command-line options:

```
java -javaagent:AgentJARFile=agentArgument . . .
```

For example, to run the SetTest program with the entry logging agent, call

```
javac set/*.java
java -javaagent:EntryLoggingAgent.jar=set.Item -classpath .:asm/\* set.SetTest
```

The Item argument is the name of the class that the agent should modify.

Listing 11.8 shows the agent code. The agent installs a class file transformer. The transformer first checks whether the class name matches the agent argument. If so, it uses the EntryLogger class from the preceding section to modify the bytecodes. However, the modified bytecodes are not saved to a file. Instead, the transformer returns them for

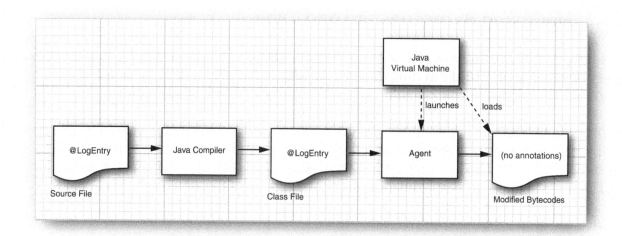

Figure 11.3: Modifying classes at load time

loading into the virtual machine (see Figure 11.3). In other words, this technique carries out "just in time" modification of the bytecodes.

Listing 11.8 `bytecodeAnnotations/EntryLoggingAgent.java`

```
1   package bytecodeAnnotations;
2
3   import java.lang.instrument.*;
4   import java.security.*;
5   import org.objectweb.asm.*;
6
7   /**
8    * @version 1.11 2018-05-01
9    * @author Cay Horstmann
10   */
11  public class EntryLoggingAgent
12  {
13     public static void premain(final String arg, Instrumentation instr)
14     {
15        instr.addTransformer(new ClassFileTransformer() {
16           public byte[] transform(ClassLoader loader, String className, Class<?> cl,
17              ProtectionDomain pd, byte[] data) throws IllegalClassFormatException
18           {
19              if (!className.replace("/", ".").equals(arg)) return null;
20              var reader = new ClassReader(data);
21              var writer = new ClassWriter(
22                 ClassWriter.COMPUTE_MAXS | ClassWriter.COMPUTE_FRAMES);
23              var el = new EntryLogger(writer, className);
24              reader.accept(el, ClassReader.EXPAND_FRAMES);
25              return writer.toByteArray();
```

```
26            }});
27      }
28 }
```

In this chapter, you have learned how to

- Add annotations to Java programs
- Design your own annotation interfaces
- Implement tools that make use of the annotations

You have seen three technologies for processing code: scripting, compiling Java programs, and processing annotations. The first two were quite straightforward. On the other hand, building annotation tools is undeniably complex and not something that most developers will need to tackle. This chapter gave you the background for understanding the inner workings of the annotation tools you will encounter, and perhaps piqued your interest in developing your own tools.

The following chapter discusses the Java Platform Module System, a key feature for insuring the integrity of the Java platform.

CHAPTER 12

The Java Platform Module System

An important characteristic of object-oriented programming is encapsulation. A class declaration consists of a public interface and a private implementation. A class can evolve by changing the implementation without affecting its users. A module system provides the same benefits for programming in the large. A module can make classes and packages selectively available so that its evolution can be controlled.

Several existing Java module systems rely on class loaders to isolate classes. However, Java 9 introduced a new system, called the Java Platform Module System, that is supported by the Java compiler and virtual machine. It was designed to modularize the large code base of the Java platform. You can, if you choose, use this system to modularize your own applications.

Whether or not you use Java platform modules in your own applications, you may be impacted by the modularized Java platform. This chapter shows you how to declare and use Java platform modules. You will also learn how to migrate your applications to work with the modularized Java platform and third-party modules.

12.1. The Module Concept

In object-oriented programming, the fundamental building block is the class. Classes provide encapsulation. Private features can only be accessed by code that has explicit permission—namely, the methods of the class. This makes it possible to reason about access. If a private variable has changed, you can produce a set of all possible culprits. If you need to modify the private representation, you know which methods are affected.

In Java, packages provide the next larger organizational grouping. A package is a collection of classes. Packages also provide a level of encapsulation. Any feature with package access (neither public nor private) is accessible only from methods in the same package.

However, in large systems, this level of access control is not enough. Any public feature (that is, a feature that is accessible outside a package) is accessible everywhere. Suppose you want to modify or drop a rarely used feature. Once it is public, there is no way to reason about the impact of that change.

This is the situation that the Java platform designers faced. Over twenty years, the JDK grew by leaps and bounds, but clearly some features are now essentially obsolete. Everyone's favorite example is CORBA. When was the last time you used it? Yet, the `org.omg.corba` package was shipped with every JDK until Java 10. As of Java 11, those few who still need it must add the required JAR files to their projects.

What about `java.awt`? It shouldn't be required in a server-side application, right? Except that the class `java.awt.DataFlavor` is used in the implementation of SOAP, an XML-based web services protocol.

The Java platform designers, faced with a giant hairball of code, decided that they needed a structuring mechanism that provides more control. They looked at existing module systems (such as OSGi) and found them unsuitable for their problem. Instead, they designed a new system, called the *Java Platform Module System*, that is now a part of the Java language and virtual machine. That system has been used successfully to modularize the Java API, and you can, if you so choose, use it with your own applications.

A Java platform module consists of

- A collection of packages
- Optionally, resource files and other files such as native libraries
- A list of the accessible packages in the module
- A list of all modules on which this module depends

The Java platform enforces encapsulation and dependencies, both at compile time and in the virtual machine.

Why should you consider using the Java Platform Module System for your own programs instead of following the traditional approach of using JAR files on the class path? There are two advantages.

1. Strong encapsulation: You can control which of your packages are accessible, and you don't have to worry about maintaining code that you didn't intend for public consumption.
2. Reliable configuration: You avoid common class path problems such as duplicate or missing classes.

There are some issues that the Java Platform Module System does not address, such as versioning of modules. There is no support for specifying which version of a module is required, or for using multiple versions of a module in the same program. These can be desirable features, but you must use mechanisms other than the Java Platform Module System if you need them.

12.2. Naming Modules

A module is a collection of packages. The package names in the module need not be related. For example, the module `java.sql` contains packages `java.sql`, `javax.sql`, and `javax.transaction.xa`. Also, as you can see from this example, it is perfectly acceptable for the module name to be the same as a package name.

Just like a package name, a module name is made up of letters, digits, underscores, and periods. Also, just as with package names, there is no hierarchical relationship between modules. If you had a module com.horstmann and another module com.horstmann.corejava, they would be unrelated, as far as the module system is concerned.

When creating a module for use by others, it is important to ensure that its name is globally unique. It is expected that most module names will follow the "reverse domain name" convention, just like package names.

The easiest approach is to name a module after the top-level package that the module provides. For example, the SLF4J logging façade has a module org.slf4j with packages org.slf4j, org.slf4j.spi, org.slf4j.event, and org.slf4j.helpers.

This convention prevents package name conflicts in modules. Any given package can only be placed in one module. If your module names are unique and your package names start with the module name, then your package names will also be unique.

You can use shorter module names for modules that are not meant to be used by other programmers, such as a module containing an application program. Just to show that it can be done, I will do the same in this chapter. Modules with what could plausibly be library code will have names such as com.horstmann.util, and modules containing programs (with a class that has a main method) will have catchy names such as v1ch12.hellomod.

 Note: Module names are only used in module declarations. In the source files for your Java classes, you never refer to module names; instead, use package names the way they have always been used.

12.3. The Modular "Hello, World!" Program

Let us put the traditional "Hello, World!" program into a module. First, we need to put the class into a package—the "unnamed package" cannot be contained in a module. Here it is:

```
package com.horstmann.hello;

public class HelloWorld
{
   public static void main(String[] args)
   {
      System.out.println("Hello, Modular World!");
   }
}
```

So far, nothing has changed. To make a module v1ch12.hellomod containing this package, you need to add a module declaration. You place it in a file named module-info.java, located in the base directory (that is, the same directory that contains the com directory). By convention, the name of the base directory is the same as the module name.

```
v1ch12.hellomod/
 └ module-info.java
   com/
    └ horstmann/
      └ hello/
        └ HelloWorld.java
```

The module-info.java file contains the module declaration:

```
module v1ch12.hellomod
{
}
```

This module declaration is empty because the module has nothing to offer to anyone, nor does it need anything.

Now, compile as usual:

```
javac v1ch12.hellomod/module-info.java \
    v1ch12.hellomod/com/horstmann/hello/HelloWorld.java
```

The module-info.java file doesn't look like a Java source file, and of course there can't be a class with the name module-info, since class names cannot contain hyphens. The module keyword, as well as keywords requires, exports, and so on, that you will see in the following sections, are "restricted keywords" that have a special meaning only in module declarations. The file is compiled into a class file module-info.class that contains the module definition in binary form.

To run this program as a modular application, you specify the *module path*, which is similar to the class path but contains modules. You also specify the main class in the format *modulename/classname*:

```
java --module-path v1ch12.hellomod \
    --module v1ch12.hellomod/com.horstmann.hello.HelloWorld
```

Instead of --module-path and --module, you can use the single-letter options -p and -m:

```
java -p v1ch12.hellomod -m v1ch12.hellomod/com.horstmann.hello.HelloWorld
```

Either way, the "Hello, Modular World!" greeting will appear, demonstrating that you have successfully modularized your first application.

Note: When you compile this module, you get a warning:

```
warning: [module] module name component v1ch12 should avoid terminal digits
```

This warning is intended to discourage programmers from adding version numbers to module names. You can ignore the warning, or suppress it with an annotation:

```
@SuppressWarnings("module")
module v1ch12.hellomod
{
}
```

In this one respect, the module declaration is just like a class declaration: You can annotate it. (The annotation type must have target ElementType.MODULE.)

12.4. Requiring Modules

Let us make a new module v1ch12.requiremod in which a program uses a JOptionPane to show the "Hello, Modular World!" message:

```
package com.horstmann.hello;

import javax.swing.JOptionPane;

public class HelloWorld
{
    public static void main(String[] args)
    {
        JOptionPane.showMessageDialog(null, "Hello, Modular World!");
    }
}
```

Now compilation fails with this message:

```
error: package javax.swing is not visible
  (package javax.swing is declared in module java.desktop,
   but module v1ch12.requiremod does not read it)
```

The JDK has been modularized, and the javax.swing package is now contained in the java.desktop module. Our module needs to declare that it relies on that module:

```
module v1ch12.requiremod
{
    requires java.desktop;
}
```

It is a design goal of the module system that modules are explicit about their requirements, so the virtual machine can ensure that all requirements are fulfilled before starting a program.

In the preceding section, the need for explicit requirements did not arise because we only used the java.lang and java.io packages. These packages are included in the java.base module which is required by default.

Note that our v1ch12.requiremod module lists only its own module requirements. It requires the java.desktop module so that it can use the javax.swing package. The java.desktop module itself declares that it requires three other modules, namely java.datatransfer, java.prefs, and java.xml.

Figure 12.1 shows the *module graph* whose nodes are modules. The edges of the graph (that is, the arrows joining nodes) are either declared requirements or, when no requirement is declared, the implied requirement of java.base.

You cannot have cycles in the module graph—that is, a module cannot directly or indirectly require itself.

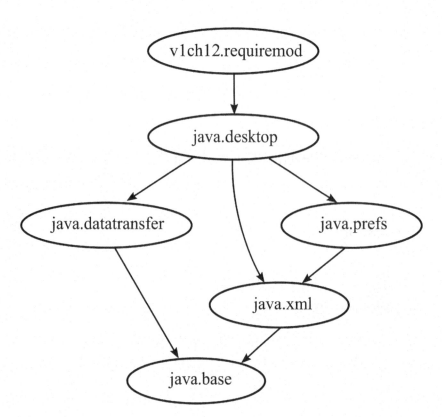

Figure 12.1: The module graph of the Swing "Hello, Modular World" application

A module does not automatically pass on access rights to other modules. In our example, the java.desktop module declares that it requires java.prefs, and the java.prefs module declares that it requires java.xml. That does not give java.desktop the right to use packages from the java.xml module. It needs to explicitly declare that requirement. In mathematical terms, the requires relationship is not "transitive." Generally, this behavior is desirable because it makes requirements explicit, but as you will see in Section 12.11, you can relax it in some cases.

 Note: The error message at the beginning of this section stated that our v1ch12.requiremod module did not "read" the java.desktop module. In the parlance of the Java Platform Module System, module *M reads* module *N* in the following cases:

1. *M* requires *N*.
2. *M* requires a module that transitively requires *N* (see Section 12.11).
3. *N* is *M* or java.base.

12.5. Exporting Packages

In the preceding section, you saw that a module must require another module if it wants to use its packages. However, that does not automatically make all packages in the required module available. A module states which of its packages are accessible, using the exports keyword. For example, here is a part of the module declaration for the java.xml module:

```
module java.xml
{
    exports javax.xml;
    exports javax.xml.catalog;
    exports javax.xml.datatype;
    exports javax.xml.namespace;
    exports javax.xml.parsers;
    . . .
}
```

This module makes many packages available, but hides others (such as jdk.xml.internal) by not exporting them.

When a package is exported, its public and protected classes and interfaces, and their public and protected members, are accessible outside the module. (As always, protected types and members are accessible only in subclasses and the same package.)

However, a package that is not exported is not accessible outside its own module. This is quite different from Java before modules. In the past, you were able to use public classes from any package, even if it was not part of the public API. For example, it was commonly recommended to use classes such as sun.misc.BASE64Encoder or `com.sun.rowset.CachedRowSetImpl` when the public API did not provide the appropriate functionality.

Nowadays, you can no longer access unexported packages from the Java platform API since all of them are contained inside modules. As a result, some programs will no longer run with Java 9. Of course, nobody ever committed to keeping non-public APIs available, so this should not come as a shock.

Let us put exports to use in a simple situation. We will prepare a module `com.horstmann.greet` that exports a package, also called `com.horstmann.greet`, following the convention that a module that provides code for others should be named after the top-level package inside it. There is also a package `com.horstmann.greet.internal` that we don't export.

A public `Greeter` interface is in the first package.

```
package com.horstmann.greet;

public interface Greeter
{
    static Greeter newInstance()
    {
        return new com.horstmann.greet.internal.GreeterImpl();
    }

    String greet(String subject);
}
```

The second package has a class that implements the interface. The class is public since it is accessed in the first package.

```
package com.horstmann.greet.internal;

import com.horstmann.greet.Greeter;

public class GreeterImpl implements Greeter
{
    public String greet(String subject)
    {
        return "Hello, " + subject + "!";
    }
}
```

The `com.horstmann.greet` module contains both packages but only exports the first:

```
module com.horstmann.greet
{
    exports com.horstmann.greet;
}
```

The second package is inaccessible outside the module.

We put our application into a second module, which will require the first module:

```
module v1ch12.exportedpkg
{
    requires com.horstmann.greet;
}
```

 Note: The exports statement is followed by a package name, whereas requires is followed by a module name.

Our application now uses a Greeter to obtain a greeting:

```
package com.horstmann.hello;

import com.horstmann.greet.Greeter;

public class HelloWorld
{
    public static void main(String[] args)
    {
        Greeter greeter = Greeter.newInstance();
        System.out.println(greeter.greet("Modular World"));
    }
}
```

Here is the source file structure for these two modules:

```
com.horstmann.greet
├ module-info.java
└ com
   └ horstmann
      └ greet
         ├ Greeter.java
         └ internal
            └ GreeterImpl.java
v1ch12.exportedpkg
├ module-info.java
└ com
```

```
└ horstmann
  └ hello
    └ HelloWorld.java
```

To build this application, first compile the `com.horstmann.greet` module:

```
javac com.horstmann.greet/module-info.java \
    com.horstmann.greet/com/horstmann/greet/Greeter.java \
    com.horstmann.greet/com/horstmann/greet/internal/GreeterImpl.java
```

Then compile the application module with the first module on the module path:

```
javac -p com.horstmann.greet v1ch12.exportedpkg/module-info.java \
    v1ch12.exportedpkg/com/horstmann/hello/HelloWorld.java
```

Finally, run the program with both modules on the module path:

```
java -p v1ch12.exportedpkg:com.horstmann.greet \
    -m v1ch12.exportedpkg/com.horstmann.hello.HelloWorld
```

This example demonstrates how an implementation can be hidden in a module. The implementing class is inaccessible outside the module. Clients use an interface and a factory method, instead of instantiating the implementing class.

 Note: In the Windows `cmd` shell, you have to enclose `v1ch12.exportedpkg:com.horstmann.greet` in quotation marks because the colon character has a special meaning. You also need to use ^ instead of \ for multiline commands.

 Tip: To build this application with Eclipse, make a separate project for each module. In the `v1ch12.exportedpkg` project, edit the project properties. In the Projects tab, add the `com.horstmann.greet` module to the module path—see Figure 12.2.

You have now seen the `requires` and `exports` statements that form the backbone of the Java Platform Module System. As you can see, the module system is conceptually simple. Modules specify what modules they need, and which packages they offer to other modules. Section 12.12 shows a minor variation of the `exports` statement.

 Caution: A module does not provide a scope. You cannot have two packages with the same name in different modules. This is true even for hidden packages (that is, packages that are not exported.)

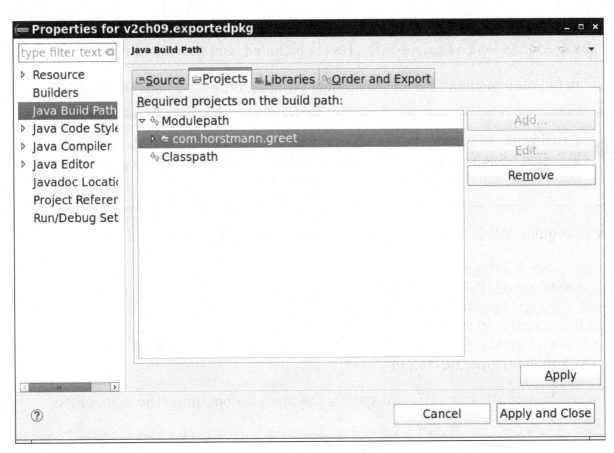

Figure 12.2: Adding a dependent module to an Eclipse project

12.6. Modular JARs

So far, we have simply compiled modules into the directory tree of the source code. Clearly, that is not satisfactory for deployment. Instead, a module can be deployed by placing all its classes in a JAR file, with a `module-info.class` in the root. Such a JAR file is called a *modular JAR*.

To create a modular JAR file, use the `jar` tool in the usual way. If you have multiple packages, it is best to compile with the `-d` option which places class files into a separate directory. The directory is created if it doesn't already exists. Then use the `-C` option of the jar command to change to that directory when collecting files.

```
javac -d modules/com.horstmann.greet \
    com.horstmann.greet/module-info.java \
    com.horstmann.greet/com/horstmann/greet/internal/GreeterImpl.java \
    com.horstmann.greet/com/horstmann/greet/Greeter.java
jar -c -v -f com.horstmann.greet.jar -C modules/com.horstmann.greet .
```

If you use a build tool such as Maven, Ant, or Gradle, just keep building your JAR file as you always do. As long as module-info.class is included, you get a modular JAR.

Then, include the modular JAR in the module path, and the module will be loaded.

 Caution: In the past, classes of a package were sometimes distributed over multiple JAR files. (Such a package is called a "split package".) This was probably never a good idea, and it is not possible with modules.

As with regular JAR files, you can specify a main class in a modular JAR:

```
javac -p com.horstmann.greet.jar \
   -d modules/v1ch12.exportedpkg \
   v1ch12.exportedpkg/module-info.java \
   v1ch12.exportedpkg/com/horstmann/hello/HelloWorld.java
jar -c -v -f v1ch12.exportedpkg.jar -e com.horstmann.hello.HelloWorld \
   -C modules/v1ch12.exportedpkg .
```

When you launch the program, you specify the module containing the main class:

```
java -p com.horstmann.greet.jar:v1ch12.exportedpkg.jar -m v1ch12.exportedpkg
```

When creating a JAR file, you can optionally specify a version number. Use the --module-version argument, and also add the version number to the JAR file name:

```
jar -c -v -f com.horstmann.greet-1.0.jar --module-version 1.0 -C com.horstmann.greet .
```

As already discussed, the version number is not used by the Java Platform Module System for resolving modules, but it can be queried by other tools and frameworks.

 Note: You can find out the version number through the reflection API. In our example:

```
Optional<String> version = Greeter.class.getModule().getDescriptor().rawVersion();
```

yields an Optional containing the version string "1.0".

 Note: The module equivalent to a class loader is a *layer*. The Java Platform Module System loads the JDK modules and application modules into the *boot layer*. A program can load other modules, using the layer API (which is not covered in this book). Such a program may choose to take module versions into account. It is expected that developers of programs such as Java EE application servers will make use of the layer API to provide support for modules.

 Tip: If you want to load a module into JShell, include the JAR on the module path and use the --add-modules option:

```
jshell --module-path com.horstmann.greet-1.0.jar --add-modules com.horstmann.greet
```

12.7. Modules and Reflective Access

In the preceding sections, you saw that the module system enforces encapsulation. A module can only access explicitly exported packages from another module. In the past, it was always possible to overcome pesky access restrictions by using reflection. As you have seen in Chapter 5, reflection can access private members of any class.

However, in the modular world, that is no longer true. If a class is inside a module, reflective access to non-public members will fail. Specifically, recall how we accessed private fields:

```
Field f = obj.getClass().getDeclaredField("salary");
f.setAccessible(true);
double value = f.getDouble(obj);
f.setDouble(obj, value * 1.1);
```

The call f.setAccessible(true) succeeds unless a security manager disallows private field access. However, it is not common to run Java applications with security managers, and there are many libraries that use reflective access. Typical examples are object-relational mappers, such as JPA, that automatically persist objects in databases and libraries that convert between objects and XML or JSON, such as JAXB and JSON-B.

If you use such a library, and you also want to use modules, you have to be careful. To demonstrate this issue, let us place the ObjectAnalyzer class from Chapter 5 into a module com.horstmann.util. That class has a toString method that prints the fields of an object, using reflection.

A separate v1ch12.openpkg module contains a simple Country class:

```
package com.horstmann.places;

public class Country
{
    private String name;
    private double area;

    public Country(String name, double area)
```

```
    {
        this.name = name;
        this.area = area;
    }
    // . . .
}
```

A short program demonstrates how to analyze a `Country` object:

```
package com.horstmann.places;

import com.horstmann.util.*;

public class Demo
{
    public static void main(String[] args) throws ReflectiveOperationException
    {
        var belgium = new Country("Belgium", 30510);
        var analyzer = new ObjectAnalyzer();
        System.out.println(analyzer.toString(belgium));
    }
}
```

Now compile both modules and the `Demo` program:

```
javac com.horstmann.util/module-info.java \
    com.horstmann.util/com/horstmann/util/ObjectAnalyzer.java
javac -p com.horstmann.util v1ch12.openpkg/module-info.java \
    v1ch12.openpkg/com/horstmann/places/*.java
java -p v1ch12.openpkg:com.horstmann.util -m v1ch12.openpkg/com.horstmann.places.Demo
```

The program will fail with an exception:

```
Exception in thread "main" java.lang.reflect.InaccessibleObjectException:
    Unable to make field private java.lang.String com.horstmann.places.Country.name
    accessible: module v1ch12.openpkg does not "opens com.horstmann.places" to module
    com.horstmann.util
```

Of course, in pristine theory, it is wrong to violate encapsulation and poke around in the private members of an object. But mechanisms such as object-relational mapping or XML/JSON binding are so common that the module system must accommodate them.

Using the opens keyword, a module can *open* a package, which enables reflective access to all instances of classes in the given package. Here is what our module has to do:

```
module v1ch12.openpkg
{
    requires com.horstmann.util;
    opens com.horstmann.places;
}
```

With this change, the ObjectAnalyzer will work correctly.

A module can be declared as open, such as

```
open module v1ch12.openpkg
{
    requires com.horstmann.util;
}
```

An open module grants runtime access to all of its packages, as if all packages had been declared with exports and opens. However, only explicitly exported packages are accessible at compile time. Open modules combine the compile-time safety of the module system with the classic permissive runtime behavior.

Recall from Chapter 5 that JAR files can contain, in addition to class files and a manifest, *file resources* which can be loaded with the method Class.getResourceAsStream, and now also with Module.getResourceAsStream. If a resource is stored in a directory that matches a package in a module, then the package must be opened to the caller. Resources in other directories, as well as the class files and manifest, can be read by anyone.

 Note: For a more realistic example, we can convert the Country object to XML or JSON, using the JSON-B specification. To use the Yasson implementation of JSON-B, download the JAR files jakarta.json-api-2.1.2.jar, jakarta.json.bind-api-3.0.0.jar, parsson-1.1.4.jar, and yasson-3.0.3.jar from the Maven Central Repository. Place the JAR files on the module path and run the com.horstmann.places.Demo program in the v1ch12.openpkg2 module. When the com.horstmann.places package is opened, conversion to JSON succeeds.

 Note: It is possible that future libraries will use *variable handles* instead of reflection for reading and writing fields. A VarHandle is similar to a Field. You can use it to read or write a specific field of any instance of a specific class. However, to obtain a VarHandle, the library code needs a Lookup object:

```
public Object getFieldValue(Object obj, String fieldName, Lookup lookup)
        throws NoSuchFieldException, IllegalAccessException
{
    Class<?> cl = obj.getClass();
```

```
      Field field = cl.getDeclaredField(fieldName);
      VarHandle handle = MethodHandles.privateLookupIn(cl, lookup)
         .unreflectVarHandle(field);
      return handle.get(obj);
   }
```

This works provided the Lookup object is generated in the module that has the permission to access the field. Some method in the module simply calls MethodHandles.lookup(), which yields an object encapsulating the access rights of the caller. In this way, one module can give permission for accessing private members to another module. The practical issue is how those permissions can be given with a minimum of hassle.

12.8. Automatic Modules

You now know to put the Java Platform Module System to use. If you start with a brand-new project in which you write all the code yourself, you can design modules, declare module dependencies, and package your application into modular JAR files.

However, that is an extremely uncommon scenario. Almost all projects rely on third-party libraries. Of course, you can wait until the providers of all libraries have turned them into modules, and then modularize your own code.

But what if you don't want to wait? The Java Platform Module System provides two mechanisms for crossing the chasm that separates today's premodular world and fully modular applications: automatic modules and the unnamed module.

For migration purposes, you can turn any JAR file into a module simply by placing it onto a directory in the module path instead of the class path. A JAR without a module-info.class on the module path is called an *automatic module*. An automatic module has the following properties:

1. The module implicitly has a requires clause for all other modules.
2. All of its packages are exported and opened.
3. If there is an entry with key Automatic-Module-Name in the JAR file manifest META-INF/MANIFEST.MF, its value becomes the module name.
4. Otherwise the module name is obtained from the JAR file name, dropping any trailing version number and replacing sequences of non-alphanumeric characters with a dot.

The first two rules imply that the packages in the automatic module act as if they were on the class path. The reason for using the module path is for the benefit of other modules, allowing them to express dependencies on this module.

Suppose, for example, that you are implementing a module that processes CSV files and uses the Apache Commons CSV library. You would like to express in your `module-info.java` file that your module depends on Apache Commons CSV.

If you add `commons-csv-1.9.0.jar` onto the module path, then your modules can reference the module. Its name is `commons.csv` since the trailing version number `-1.9.0` is removed and the non-alphanumeric character `-` is replaced by a dot.

This name might be an acceptable module name because Commons CSV is well known and it is unlikely that someone else will try to use the same name for a different module. But it would be better if the maintainers of this JAR file could use a name that they control, preferably the top-level package name `org.apache.commons.csv`, as the module name. They just need to add a line

```
Automatic-Module-Name: org.apache.commons.csv
```

to the `META-INF/MANIFEST.MF` file inside the JAR. In fact, they did just that with `commons-csv-1.10.0.jar`.

Eventually, hopefully, they will turn the JAR file into a true module by adding `module-info.java` with that module name. Every other module that refers to the CSV module with that name will just continue to work.

 Note: The migration plan to modules is a great social experiment, and nobody knows whether it will end well. Before you put third-party JARs on the module path, check whether they are modular, and if not, whether their manifest has a module name. If not, you can still turn the JAR into an automatic module, but be prepared to update the module name later.

To experiment with automatic JARs, download versions 1.9.0 and 1.10.0 of the Commons CSV library from `https://commons.apache.org/proper/commons-csv`. The `v2ch9.automod` module in the companion code contains a simple program that reads a CSV file with country data:

```java
package com.horstmann.places;

import java.io.*;
import org.apache.commons.csv.*;

public class CSVDemo
{
    public static void main(String[] args) throws IOException
    {
        var in = new FileReader("countries.csv");
        Iterable<CSVRecord> records = CSVFormat.EXCEL.withDelimiter(';')
                .withHeader().parse(in);
```

```
    for (CSVRecord record : records)
    {
       String name = record.get("Name");
       double area = Double.parseDouble(record.get("Area"));
       System.out.println(name + " has area " + area);
    }
  }
}
```

To use `commons-csv-1.9.0.jar` as an automatic module, we need to require it using its file name:

```
@SuppressWarnings("module")
module v1ch12.automod
{
    requires commons.csv;
}
```

For `commons-csv-1.10.0.jar`, use the `Automatic-Module-Name` from the manifest:

```
requires org.apache.commons.csv
```

Here are the commands for compiling and running the program:

```
javac -p v1ch12.automod:commons-csv-1.10.0.jar \
    v1ch12.automod/com/horstmann/places/CSVDemo.java \
    v1ch12.automod/module-info.java
java -p v1ch12.automod:commons-csv-1.10.0.jar \
    -m v1ch12.automod/com.horstmann.places.CSVDemo
```

12.9. The Unnamed Module

Any class that is not on the module path is part of an *unnamed module*. Technically, there may be more than one unnamed module, but all of them together act as if they are a single module which is called *the* unnamed module. As with automatic modules, the unnamed module can access all other modules, and all of its packages are exported and opened.

However, *no explicit module* can access the unnamed module. (An explicit module is a module that is neither automatic nor unnamed—that is, a module with a `module-info.class` on the module path.) In other words, explicit modules are always free from the "class path hell."

Consider, for example, the program of the preceding section. Suppose you put `commons-csv-1.9.0.jar` onto the class path instead of the module path:

```
java --module-path v1ch12.automod \
  --class-path commons-csv-1.10.0.jar \
  -m v1ch12.automod/com.horstmann.places.CSVDemo
```

Now the program won't start:

```
Error occurred during initialization of boot layer
java.lang.module.FindException: Module commons.csv not found, required by v1ch12.automod
```

Therefore, migration to the Java Platform Module System is necessarily a bottom-up process:

1. The Java platform itself is modularized.
2. Next, libraries are modularized, either by using automatic modules or by turning them into explicit modules.
3. Once all libraries used by your application are modularized, you can turn the code of your application into a module.

 Note: Automatic modules *can* read the unnamed module, so their dependencies can go onto the class path.

12.10. Command-Line Flags for Migration

Even if your programs do not use modules, you cannot escape the modular world when using Java 9 and beyond. Your application code may reside on the class path in an unnamed module, so that all packages are exported and opened. Still, the code interacts with the Java platform, which is modularized.

As of Java 11, compile-time encapsulation is strictly enforced. However, before Java 16, runtime access was permitted. The default behavior was to display a warning on the console for the first instance of each offense. As of Java 16, reflective access at runtime is also enforced. In order to give you time to prepare for that change, the java launcher in Java 9 through 16 had an --illegal-access flag with four possible settings:

1. --illegal-access=permit was the Java 9 default behavior, printing a message for the first instance of illegal access.
2. --illegal-access=warn prints a message for each illegal access.
3. --illegal-access=debug prints a message and stack trace for each illegal access.
4. --illegal-access=deny was the Java 16 default behavior, denying all illegal access.

The --illegal-access flag is no longer usable as of Java 17.

The --add-exports and --add-opens flags allow you to tweak legacy applications. Consider an application that uses an internal API which is no longer accessible, such as `com.sun.rowset.CachedRowSetImpl`. The best remedy is to change the implementation. (As of Java 7, you can get a cached row set from a `RowSetProvider`.) But suppose you don't have access to the source code.

In that case, start the application with the `--add-exports` flag. Specify the module and the package that you want to export, and the module to which you want to export the package, which in our case is the unnamed module.

```
java --add-exports java.sql.rowset/com.sun.rowset=ALL_UNNAMED \
    -jar MyApp.jar
```

Now, suppose your application uses reflection to access private fields or methods. Reflection inside the unnamed module is OK, but it is no longer possible to reflectively access non-public members of the Java platform classes. For example, some libraries that dynamically generate Java classes call the protected `ClassLoader.defineClass` method through reflection. If an application uses such a library, add the flag

```
--add-opens java.base/java.lang=ALL-UNNAMED
```

When adding all those command-line options to get a legacy app to work, you may well end up with the command line from hell. To better manage multiple options, you can put them in one or more files specified with an @ prefix. For example,

```
java @options1 @options2 -jar MyProg.java
```

where the files `options1` and `options2` contain options for the `java` command.

There are a few syntax rules for the options files:

- Separate options with spaces, tabs, or newlines.
- Use double quotes around arguments that include spaces, such as `"Program Files"`.
- A line ending in a \ is merged with the next line.
- Backslashes must be escaped, such as `C:\\Users\\Fred`.
- Comment lines start with #.

12.11. Transitive and Static Requirements

In Section 12.4, you have seen the basic form of the `requires` statement. In this section, you will see two variants that are occasionally useful.

In some situations, it can be tedious for a user of a given module to declare all required modules. Consider, for example, the `java.desktop` module. It requires three modules: `java.prefs`, `java.datatransfer` and `java.xml`. The `java.prefs` module is only used internally. However, classes from `java.datatransfer` and `java.xml` appear in the public API, in methods such as

```
java.awt.datatransfer.Clipboard java.awt.Toolkit.getSystemClipboard()
java.beans.XMLDecoder(org.xml.sax.InputSource is)
```

That is not something that a user of the java.desktop module should have to think about.
For that reason, the java.desktop module declares the requirement with the transitive
modifier:

```
module java.desktop
{
    requires java.prefs;
    requires transitive java.datatransfer;
    requires transitive java.xml;

    . . .

}
```

Any module that declares a requirement on java.desktop now automatically requires these
two modules.

Note: Some programmers recommend that you should always use requires
transitive when a package from another module is used in the public API. But that is
not a requirement of the Java language. Consider, for example, the java.sql module:

```
module java.sql
{
    requires transitive java.logging;

    . . .

}
```

There is a single use of a package from the java.logging module in the entire java.sql
API, namely the java.sql.Driver.parentLogger method that returns a
java.util.logging.Logger. It would have been perfectly acceptable to not declare this
module requirement as transitive. Then, those modules—and only those—who
actually use that method would need to declare that they require java.logging.

One compelling use of the requires transitive statement is an *aggregator* module—a
module with no packages and only transitive requirements. One such module is the java.se
module, declared like this:

```
module java.se
{
    requires transitive java.compiler;
    requires transitive java.datatransfer;
    requires transitive java.desktop;

    . . .

    requires transitive java.sql;
```

```
  requires transitive java.sql.rowset;
  requires transitive java.xml;
  requires transitive java.xml.crypto;
}
```

A programmer who isn't interested in fine-grained module dependencies can simply require java.se and get all modules of the Java SE platform.

Finally, there is an uncommon requires static variant that declares that a module must be present at compile time but is optional at runtime. There are two use cases:

1. To access an annotation that is processed at compile time and declared in a different module.
2. To use a class in a different module if it is available, and otherwise do something else, such as:

```
try
{
   new oracle.jdbc.driver.OracleDriver();
   . . .
}
catch (NoClassDefFoundError er)
{
   Do something else
}
```

12.12. Qualified Exporting and Opening

In this section, you will see a variant of the exports and opens statement that narrows their scope to a specified set of modules. For example, the java.base module contains a statement

```
exports sun.net to
   java.net.http,
   jdk.naming.dns;
```

Such a statement is called a *qualified export*. The listed modules can access the exported package, but other modules cannot.

Excessive use of qualified exports can indicate a poor modular structure. Nevertheless, they can arise when modularizing an existing code base. Here, the sun.net package is placed inside the java.base module because that is where it is mostly needed. However, a couple of other modules also use that package. The Java platform designers didn't want to make java.base even bigger, and they didn't want to make the internal sun.net package generally available. In a greenfield project, one can instead design a more modular API.

Similarly, you can restrict the opens statement to specific modules. For example, in Section 12.7 we could have used a qualified opens statement, like this:

```
module v1ch12.openpkg
{
    requires com.horstmann.util;
    opens com.horstmann.places to com.horstmann.util;
}
```

Now the com.horstmann.places package is only opened to the com.horstmann.util module.

12.13. Service Loading

The ServiceLoader class (see Chapter 6) provides a lightweight mechanism for matching up service interfaces with implementations. The Java Platform Module System makes this mechanism easier to use.

Here is a quick reminder of service loading. A service has an interface and one or more possible implementations. Here is a simple example of an interface:

```
public interface GreeterService
{
    String greet(String subject);
    Locale getLocale();
}
```

One or more modules provide implementations, such as

```
public class FrenchGreeter implements GreeterService
{
    public String greet(String subject) { return "Bonjour " + subject; }
    public Locale getLocale() { return Locale.FRENCH; }
}
```

The service consumer must pick an implementation among all offered implementations, based on whatever criteria it deems appropriate.

```
ServiceLoader<GreeterService> greeterLoader = ServiceLoader.load(GreeterService.class);
GreeterService chosenGreeter;
for (GreeterService greeter : greeterLoader)
{
    if (. . .)
    {
        chosenGreeter = greeter;
    }
}
```

In the past, implementations were offered by placing text files into the META-INF/services directory of the JAR file containing the implementation classes. The module system provides a better approach. Instead of text files, you can add statements to the module descriptors.

A module providing an implementation of a service adds a provides statement that lists the service interface (which may be defined in any module) and the implementing classes (which must be a part of this module). Here is an example from the jdk.security.auth module:

```
module jdk.security.auth
{
    . . .
    provides javax.security.auth.spi.LoginModule with
        com.sun.security.auth.module.Krb5LoginModule,
        com.sun.security.auth.module.UnixLoginModule,
        com.sun.security.auth.module.JndiLoginModule,
        com.sun.security.auth.module.KeyStoreLoginModule,
        com.sun.security.auth.module.LdapLoginModule,
        com.sun.security.auth.module.NTLoginModule;
}
```

A consuming module contains a uses statement.

```
module java.base
{
    . . .
    uses javax.security.auth.spi.LoginModule;
}
```

When code in a consuming module calls ServiceLoader.load(*ServiceInterface*.class), the matching provider classes will be loaded, even though they may not be in accessible packages.

In our code example, we provide implementations for a German and French greeter in the package com.horstmann.greetsvc.internal. The service module exports the com.horstmann.greetsvc package, but not the package with the implementations. The provides statement declares the service and its implementing classes in the unexported package:

```
module com.horstmann.greetsvc
{
    exports com.horstmann.greetsvc;

    provides com.horstmann.greetsvc.GreeterService with
        com.horstmann.greetsvc.internal.FrenchGreeter,
        com.horstmann.greetsvc.internal.GermanGreeterFactory;
}
```

The v1ch12.useservice module consumes the service. Using the ServiceLoader facility, we iterate over the provided services and pick the one matching the desired language:

```
package com.horstmann.hello;

import java.util.*;
import com.horstmann.greetsvc.*;

public class HelloWorld
{
   public static void main(String[] args)
   {
      ServiceLoader<GreeterService> greeterLoader
            = ServiceLoader.load(GreeterService.class);
      String desiredLanguage = args.length > 0 ? args[0] : "de";
      GreeterService chosenGreeter = null;
      for (GreeterService greeter : greeterLoader)
      {
         if (greeter.getLocale().getLanguage().equals(desiredLanguage))
            chosenGreeter = greeter;
      }
      if (chosenGreeter == null)
         System.out.println("No suitable greeter.");
      else
         System.out.println(chosenGreeter.greet("Modular World"));
   }
}
```

The module declaration requires the service module and declares that the GreeterService is being used.

```
module v1ch12.useservice
{
   requires com.horstmann.greetsvc;
   uses com.horstmann.greetsvc.GreeterService;
}
```

As a result of the provides and uses declarations, the module that consumes the service is allowed access to the module-private implementation classes.

To build and run the program, first compile the service:

```
javac com.horstmann.greetsvc/module-info.java \
   com.horstmann.greetsvc/com/horstmann/greetsvc/GreeterService.java \
   com.horstmann.greetsvc/com/horstmann/greetsvc/internal/*.java
```

Then compile and run the consuming module:

```
javac -p com.horstmann.greetsvc \
   v1ch12.useservice/com/horstmann/hello/HelloWorld.java \
   v1ch12.useservice/module-info.java
java -p com.horstmann.greetsvc:v1ch12.useservice \
   -m v1ch12.useservice/com.horstmann.hello.HelloWorld
```

12.14. Tools for Working with Modules

This section covers the jdeps, jlink, and jmod tools that are a part of the Java Development Kit.

The jdeps tool analyzes the dependencies of a given set of JAR files. Suppose, for example, that you want to modularize JUnit 4. Run

```
jdeps -s junit-4.12.jar hamcrest-core-1.3.jar
```

The -s flag generates a summary output:

```
hamcrest-core-1.3.jar -> java.base
junit-4.12.jar -> hamcrest-core-1.3.jar
junit-4.12.jar -> java.base
junit-4.12.jar -> java.management
```

That tells you the module graph, as shown in the following figure.

If you omit the -s flag, you get the module summary followed by a mapping from packages to required packages and modules. If you add the -v flag, the listing maps classes to required packages and modules.

The --generate-module-info option produces module-info files for each analyzed module:

```
jdeps --generate-module-info /tmp/junit junit-4.12.jar hamcrest-core-1.3.jar
```

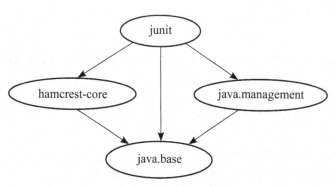

Figure 12.3: The JUnit4 Module Graph

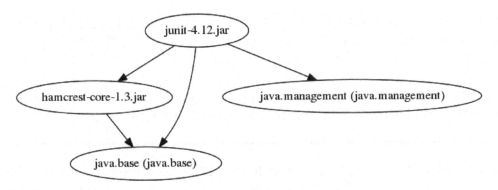

Figure 12.4: The Dot Output of jdeps

 Note: There is also an option to generate graphical output in the "dot" language for describing graphs. Assuming you have the dot tool installed, run these commands:

```
jdeps -s -dotoutput /tmp/junit junit-4.12.jar hamcrest-core-1.3.jar
dot -Tpng /tmp/junit/summary.dot > /tmp/junit/summary.png
```

Then summary.png looks as in the following figure.

Use the jlink tool to produce an application that executes without a separate Java runtime. The resulting image is much smaller than the entire JDK. You specify the modules that you want to have included and an output directory.

```
jlink --module-path com.horstmann.greet.jar:v1ch12.exportedpkg.jar:$JAVA_HOME/jmods \
    --add-modules v1ch12.exportedpkg --output /tmp/hello
```

The output directory has a subdirectory bin with a java executable. If you run

```
bin/java -m v1ch12.exportedpkg
```

the main method of the module's main class is invoked.

The point of jlink is that it bundles up the minimal set of modules required to run the application. You can list them all:

```
bin/java --list-modules
```

In this example, the output is

```
v1ch12.exportedpkg
com.horstmann.greet
java.base@21
```

All modules are included in a *runtime image* file lib/modules. On my computer, that file is 29MB, whereas the runtime image of all JDK modules takes up 133MB. The entire application takes up 55MB, a fraction of the size of the JDK.

This can be the basis of a useful tool for packaging applications. You would still need to produce file sets for multiple platforms and launch scripts for the application.

 Note: You can inspect the runtime image with the jimage command. However, the format is internal to the JVM, and runtime images are not meant to be generated or used by other tools.

Finally, the jmod tool builds and inspects the module files that are included with the JDK. When you look into the jmods directory inside the JDK, you will find a file with extension jmod for each module. There is no longer a rt.jar file.

Like JAR files, these files contain class files. In addition, they can hold native code libraries, commands, header files, configuration files, and legal notices. The JMOD files use the ZIP format. You can inspect their contents with any ZIP tool.

Unlike JAR files, JMOD files are only useful for linking—that is, for producing runtime images. There is no need for you to produce JMOD files unless you also want to bundle binary files such as native code libraries with your modules.

This brings us to the end of the chapter on the Java Platform Module System, and this book. Hopefully you have enjoyed your in-depth tour through the core features of the Java language and platform, and are ready to put your knowledge to work in your projects.

Appendix

This appendix lists all keywords and keyword-like words of the Java language. A "restricted keyword" is a keyword only in a module declaration, and otherwise an identifier. A "restricted identifier" is an identifier unless it is used in certain positions. For example, var is always an identifier unless it is used where a type is expected. The symbols null, false, and true are not keywords but literals.

Table 13.1: Java Keywords

Keyword	Meaning	Type	See Chapter
abstract	An abstract class or method	Keyword	5
assert	Used to locate internal program error	Keyword	7
boolean	The Boolean type	Keyword	3
break	Breaks out of a switch or loop	Keyword	3
byte	The 8-bit integer type	Keyword	3
case	A case of a switch	Keyword	3
catch	The clause of a try block catching an exception	Keyword	7
char	The type for UTF-16 code units	Keyword	3
class	Defines a class type	Keyword	4
const	Not used	Keyword	
continue	Continues at the end of a loop	Keyword	3
default	The default clause of a switch, or a default method in an interface	Keyword	3, 6
do	The top of a do/while loop	Keyword	3
double	The double-precision floating-number type	Keyword	3
else	The else clause of an if statement	Keyword	3
enum	An enumerated type	Keyword	3

Keyword	Meaning	Type	See Chapter
exports	Exports a package of a module	Restricted keyword	12
extends	Defines the parent class of a class, or an upper bound of a wildcard	Keyword	4
false	One of the two Boolean values	Literal	3
final	A constant, or a class or method that cannot be overridden	Keyword	5
finally	The part of a try block that is always executed	Keyword	7
float	The single-precision floating-point type	Keyword	3
for	A loop type	Keyword	3
goto	Not used	Keyword	
if	A conditional statement	Keyword	3
implements	Defines the interface(s) that a class implements	Keyword	6
import	Imports a package	Keyword	4
instanceof	Tests if an object is an instance of a class	Keyword	5
int	The 32-bit integer type	Keyword	3
interface	An abstract type with methods that a class can implement	Keyword	6
long	The 64-bit long integer type	Keyword	3
native	A method implemented by the host system	Keyword	13 (Vol. II)
new	Allocates a new object or array	Keyword	3
non-sealed	A subtype of a sealed type of which arbitrary subtypes may be formed	Keyword	5
null	A null reference	Literal	3

Keyword	Meaning	Type	See Chapter
module	Declares a module	Restricted keyword	12
open	Modifies a module declaration	Restricted keyword	12
opens	Opens a package of a module	Restricted keyword	12
package	A package of classes	Keyword	4
permits	Introduces a list of permitted subtypes of a sealed type	Restricted identifier	3
private	A feature that is accessible only by methods of this class	Keyword	4
protected	A feature that is accessible only by methods of this class, its children, and other classes in the same package	Keyword	5
provides	Indicates that a module uses a service	Restricted keyword	12
public	A feature that is accessible by methods of all classes	Keyword	4
record	Declares a class with a given set of final instance variables	Restricted identifier	4
return	Returns from a method	Keyword	3
sealed	A type with a controlled set of direct subtypes	Restricted identifier	5
short	The 16-bit integer type	Keyword	3
static	A feature that is unique to a class or interface, not to instances of a class	Keyword	3, 6
strictfp	Use strict rules for floating-point computations (obsolete)	Keyword	2

Keyword	Meaning	Type	See Chapter
super	The superclass object or constructor, or a lower bound in a wildcard	Keyword	5
switch	A selection statement or expression	Keyword	3
synchronized	A method or code block that is atomic to a thread	Keyword	12
this	The implicit argument of a method, or a constructor of this class	Keyword	4
throw	Throws an exception	Keyword	7
throws	The exceptions that a method can throw	Keyword	7
to	A part of an exports or opens declaration	Restricted keyword	12
transient	Marks data that should not be persistent	Keyword	2 (Vol. II)
transitive	Modifies a requires declaration	Restricted keyword	12
true	One of the two Boolean values	Literal	3
try	A block of code that traps exceptions	Keyword	7
uses	Indicates that a module uses a service	Restricted keyword	12
var	Declares a variable whose type is inferred	Restricted identifier	3
void	Denotes a method that returns no value	Keyword	3
volatile	Ensures that a field is coherently accessed by multiple threads	Keyword	12
when	Introduces a guard of a pattern	Restricted keyword	5
while	A loop	Keyword	3

Keyword	Meaning	Type	See Chapter
`with`	Defines the service class in a `provides` statement	Restricted keyword	12
`yield`	Yields the value of a `switch` expression	Restricted identifier	3
`_` (underscore)	An unnamed variable or pattern (preview)	Keyword	5

Index

Symbols

! operator   54, 59
!= operator   54, 59, 97
"""...""" (triple quotes, for text blocks)   73
"..." (single quotes, for strings)   35
(number sign)
  in javadoc hyperlinks   211
  printf flag   81
$ (dollar sign)
  delimiter, for inner classes   381
  in variable names   44
  printf flag   81
% (percent sign)
  arithmetic operator   48, 59
  conversion character   80
& (ampersand)
  bitwise operator   57, 59
  in bounding types   466
  in reference parameters (C++)   169
&& operator   54, 59
> (right angle bracket)
  in shell syntax   85, 454
  relational operator   54, 59
>& (shell syntax)   454
>>, >>> operators   57, 59
>= operator   54, 59
< (left angle bracket)
  in shell syntax   85
  printf flag   81
  relational operator   54, 59
<< operator   57, 59
<...> (angle brackets)   258, 462
<= operator   54, 59
', " (single, double quote), escape sequences for   40
((left parenthesis)   81
  printf flag   81
(...) (parentheses)
  empty, in method calls   35
  for casts   52, 59, 234
  for operator hierarchy   58
* (asterisk)
  arithmetic operator   48, 59
  for annotation processors   729
  in class path   198
  in imports   189
+ (plus sign)
  arithmetic operator   48, 52, 59
  for objects and strings   60, 251, 252
  printf flag   81
++ operator   54, 59
, (comma)
  operator (C++)   59
  printf flag   81
- (minus sign)
  arithmetic operator   48, 59

printf flag   81
-> operator
  in lambda expressions   355
  in switch expressions   103
-- operator   54, 59
. (period)   197, 198
... (ellipsis)   270
.class extension   32
.exe extension   203
.java extension   32
/ (slash)   48, 59
/* ... */ comments   35
/** ... */ (Javadoc comment delimiters)   35, 206, 207
// comments   35
0, 0b, 0B, 0x, 0X prefixes (in integers)   37
0, printf flag   81
2> (shell syntax)   454
: (colon)
  in assertions   432
  in class path (UNIX)   197
  inheritance token (C++)   218
:: (C++ operator)   151, 160, 221, 361
; (semicolon)
  in class path (Windows)   197
  in statements   34, 43
= operator   45, 53
== operator   54, 59
  for class objects   298
  for enumerated types   278
  for floating-point numbers   97
  for identity hash maps   560
  for strings   65
  wrappers and   266
? (question mark)
  for wildcard types   477
?: operator   55, 59
  with pattern matching   237
@ (at sign)   207, 208
  in java command-line options   766
[...] (brackets)
  empty, in generics   464
  for arrays   112, 115
\ (backslash)
  escape sequence for   40
  in file names   83
  in text blocks   74
\b (backslash character literal)   40
\f (form feed character literal)   40
\n (newline character literal)   40, 74
\r (carriage return character literal)   40
\s (space character literal)   40, 75
\t (tab character literal)   40
\u (Unicode character literal)   40, 41
^ (caret)   57, 59, 356
_ (underscore)
  as a reserved word   779

L

The #1 language
for today's tech trends

www.oracle.com/java